THE EXPEDITIONS OF
John Charles Frémont

John Charles Frémont as he looked about 1849. From a print in
Walter Colton's *Three Years in California* (New York, 1850).

THE EXPEDITIONS OF
John Charles Frémont

VOLUME 2 SUPPLEMENT
Proceedings of the Court-Martial

EDITED BY

MARY LEE SPENCE AND DONALD JACKSON

UNIVERSITY OF ILLINOIS PRESS

URBANA, CHICAGO, AND LONDON

CONTENTS

INTRODUCTION

The court-martial proceedings in the case of Lieut. Col. John C. Frémont were first printed in 1848 by order of the U.S. Senate. This facsimile edition of that Senate document is intended as a supplement to Vol. 2 of *The Expeditions of John Charles Frémont,* which covers the period from May 1845 to mid-March 1848. Not only are the proceedings a rich source of primary material on the American conquest of California, but they also bring into perspective the roles of what one of the witnesses, Edward F. Beale, liked to call "the three parties"—Frémont, Commodore Robert F. Stockton, and Brig. Gen. Stephen Watts Kearny.[1] Through them, too, is mirrored Frémont's bitterness, as well as the savage invective of his father-in-law, Thomas H. Benton, who was convinced that the military explorer was the victim of military jealousy.

When it began its deliberations on 2 November 1847 at the Washington Arsenal, the military court of justice drew up the curtain on the most dramatic Army hearing since the court-martial of Gen. James Wilkinson nearly forty years before. Frémont's wife was there, as were many veterans of his third expedition. Army officers attended as either witnesses or spectators, congressmen turned out, and the eastern journals sent their reporters.

Frémont was being tried for defiance of his superior officer, Stephen Watts Kearny, in California the previous winter. When Kearny arrived in San Diego in December 1846, having been badly mauled by the Californians at San Pasqual, he found Commodore Robert F. Stockton in control of the town and preparing for the reconquest of Los Angeles. Almost immediately the two officers engaged in some preliminary sparring over the supremacy of command, but despite this, Kearny and his troops aided Stockton in the successful march on the pueblo. When Frémont arrived, having

---

[1] 7 May 1848 letter of Samuel F. DuPont reporting a conversation with Beale at Mazatlán, in DU PONT, 391–92.

accepted the Californians' surrender in the liberal Treaty of Cahuenga, Kearny and Stockton intensified their struggle. Kearny instructed Frémont to make no changes in the organization of the California Battalion, even if ordered by Stockton, without his express approval. In a letter of 17 January 1847 Frémont replied that until Kearny and Stockton resolved the question of rank between themselves, he would continue to report to and receive orders from Stockton, who had been exercising the functions of civil and military governor since the summer of 1846. The issue was clearly joined. Stockton claimed the right to establish a government by virtue of military conquest and orders of the Navy Department to Commodore Sloat; Kearny asserted the same right by virtue of instructions from the War Department.[2] Caught between the aspirations of the two, Frémont chose Stockton, but Washington ultimately confirmed Kearny's supremacy, and the stage was set for the dramatic court-martial.

When he returned to Washington in September 1847, Kearny preferred a single charge of mutiny (with eight specifications) against Frémont.[3] But as eventually drawn by the judge advocate, there were three: mutiny, disobeying the lawful command of his superior officer, and conduct prejudicial to good order and military discipline. The specifications for the second and third charges were primarily restatements of the details of the first. As lawyer-author Kenneth M. Johnson points out in *The Frémont Court Martial,* "It was the old criminal law theory—if we cannot convict him of murder, perhaps a verdict of negligent homicide can be reached." Coached by the able legal counsel of Benton and William C. Jones, Frémont condemned the multiplication of charges built upon the same set of facts and included this as one of seven irregularities in the ordering of the trial. Two other errors to which he particularly pointed were the failure of President James K. Polk to institute a court of inquiry before ordering a general court-martial and the apparent lack of a prosecutor for some of the charges against him.

---

[2] To Kearny, on 3 June 1846, Secretary of War William L. Marcy had written, "Should you conquer and take possession of New Mexico and Upper California, or considerable places in either, you will establish temporary civil government therein." On 18 June, after noting that troops were being sent around Cape Horn to California, he wrote, "These troops and such as may be organized in California will be under your command."

[3] Kearny to R. Jones, 11 Sept. 1847, DNA-94, LR, K-217 1847.

Frémont was especially sensitive on the latter point, since his efforts to be tried on charges contained in certain newspaper stories had been rejected by the Secretary of War for want of a "substantive" prosecutor. Frémont pointed out the irregularities not in order to benefit by objection, he said, but merely to prevent "the evil example becoming a precedent, and to vindicate his own intellect from the suspicion of admitting the correctness of such proceedings." Desiring a hearing on the merits of the case only, he pleaded "not guilty."

In preparing his defense, he had two objectives. One was to show that his trial was basically the trial of the dispute of command between Kearny and Stockton; hence he was entitled to copies of all orders and directives to Kearny as well as to the various naval commanders in California. To this end, he sought to show that California had been conquered and a government established by Stockton before the arrival of Kearny's Army of the West. Thus, he insisted, the general's instructions from the Secretary of War, designed for an unconquered territory, were no longer applicable. His second objective was to discredit Kearny as a prosecuting witness by impeaching his motives in bringing the charges, by showing his vindictive temper, and by exhibiting his defective and equivocating memory. This approach—to show that Kearny bore false witness—permitted the defense a wide latitude of questioning, although the judge advocate frequently objected to the irrelevancy of one subject or another. And while the court tried to avoid passing on collateral issues, it noted on the day it announced its verdict that throughout the trial it had not held the accused to a strict legal defense and, in his final summary, had allowed him to use "indiscriminately" matter which had been rejected and that which had been admitted in evidence.

Kearny early testified that within a week of receiving the key 17 January letter, he had decided to arrest Frémont. Frémont argued, and offered to prove to the court, that while Kearny had kept this intention secret, William H. Emory, a confidential member of the general's staff sent east with dispatches, was using the press to prejudice the public mind and prepare it for the explorer's trial. As an example of a punitive mind, Frémont could cite Kearny's failure to communicate to him the War and Navy department's instructions of November 1846, which clearly indicated that President Polk had decided to give to Kearny control of the administrative functions of government in California. As evidence of ill-will and of a failing memory, Frémont implied to the tribunal that Kearny's testimony on the "business" interview between the two in Monterey in March 1847 was incomplete. The general could remember only that Frémont had made the long ride from Los Angeles to insult him and to offer his resignation from the Army. He further accused Kearny of attempting to keep away important witnesses, particularly Archibald H. Gillespie, who had helped organize the California Battalion and had played a major role in the conquest.

Kearny, of course, was the premier witness for the prosecution, and his testimony cast Frémont in the role of a bargainer for the governorship of California, thus ascribing a base and sordid motive for his mutiny. Frémont showed that he had come to the interview in which the bargaining allegedly took place at Kearny's express invitation, and that he had left his 17 January letter indicating his position in the general's hands at the very time he was supposedly rushing off to ask Stockton to appoint him governor "at once." If Kearny believed him guilty of mutiny in January 1847, countered Frémont, why did he not suppress it then, and why did he not inform Stockton at the time of the explorer's alleged offer to swap control of the California Battalion for the governorship? To be sure, in using this argument, Frémont ignored the fact that Senator Benton was a friend of Kearny's in the political world and was likewise chairman of the Senate Military Affairs Committee—a reality which might well induce even a brash general to deal gently with an erring lieutenant colonel who happened to be married to the senator's attractive young daughter. Throughout his defense Frémont implied vigorously that Kearny had tried to seduce him from his loyalty to Stockton and, that failing, had raised against him the false accusation of bartering for the post of governor.

Frémont also insisted that the California Battalion had been raised and officered exclusively under naval authority and had never been under Kearny's control. His 14 January letter, alleged by Kearny to have been the formal report of the battalion to him as commanding officer, was merely a private note for the general's information, written after he had received four such private notes from Kearny, Frémont maintained.

Kearny was followed on the witness stand by his subordinate, Philip St. George Cooke, who testified that officers of the battalion, acting on a directive of Frémont, had refused to obey orders at San Gabriel to turn over their mountain howitzers and ordnance stores. In cross-examination the defense was able to read into the record not only the "Justice" letter from the *Missouri Republican* (which Cooke had probably authored) but also one of Cooke's official reports, which evinced a deep-seated prejudice against Frémont. In that report Cooke had implied that Kearny's order to muster the California Battalion into federal service had been ignored, when in reality William N. Loker, the adjutant, had polled the members about whether they wanted to be so mustered. The defense also suggested that Cooke might have used the Mormons and dragoons to "crush" Frémont, had he found him rather than Richard Owens at San Gabriel. It went on to imply—and Cooke vehemently denied it—that Cooke had kept memoranda of the conversations between Col. Richard B. Mason and Frémont, and that he had dishonorably revoked the safe-conduct passes issued to Mexican Californians by Frémont. Cooke was forced to admit that "in coming down the Missouri," Kearny had indicated that if Frémont were tried at all, it would be exclusively on documentary evidence. Benton was thus able to add some evidence to his accusation that Frémont had been forced into choosing between a surprise court-martial with few witnesses or allowing ruinous charges supported by a defamatory press campaign to hang over his head for a long time while witnesses were summoned from California.

Henry S. Turner, another of Kearny's staff officers, and Willard P. Hall, a Missouri congressman who had traveled to California with Cooke's Mormon Battalion, were also witnesses for the prosecution. William H. Emory, described by Turner as "beset with one mania, a greediness after immortality,"[4] should have been there but was not. He was finally called by the defense, which in so doing sacrificed the right to cross-examine, for the court would not permit it to impeach its own witness.

Stockton, Gillespie, and William H. Russell, Frémont's secretary of state, were the principal witnesses for the defense. Unfortunately for Frémont, much of Stockton's testimony had little bearing on the charges, and there is some evidence to indicate that Stockton and Kearny had come to a *rapprochement*. On the eve of the com-

---

[4] TURNER, 94.

modore's testimony, Kearny could write his brother-in-law, "Colonel Benton will be very disappointed in the testimony of Commodore S as I think when he hears it. I have been led to believe that it will be much more against the defense than in its favor."[5]

Continuing until 11 January, the court-martial adjourned until 24 January, when Frémont began the reading of the long defense which his father-in-law had prepared. Several days earlier Benton had read parts of it to his friend and fellow Democrat, Francis P. Blair, who viewed it as "the clearest, most logical legal pointed battery of well arranged facts combined with strong thought that he had ever met with." "The style," he wrote former President Martin Van Buren, "is remarkably perspicacious and simple and I am persuaded that as a whole it will make a strong impression on the public, although not on the court, which is understood long since to have decided the case against Frémont by a most embittered majority of *one*." He predicted that "these partizans" of Kearny would "whittle down their sentence to the smallest degree and will probably recommend mercy to get mercy shown to themselves." But he thought they would get none and that Benton would pursue them to their graves with his battle-ax. "I have never known," he continued, "our good friend roused to such a pitch of cool fixed, reflecting, desperate resolution as in the present instance. Sampson when he shook down the temple upon his head, was not more determined to make the operation of his strength fatal than Benton is now and yet his understanding was never fuller of light and more far-seeing than it is now in the context of his passion."[6]

Nonetheless, on 31 January the court found Frémont guilty on all charges and specifications and sentenced him to dismissal from the service. Seven members of the board, as Blair had predicted, recommended him to the clemency of the president, who, after reading the case and consulting with his cabinet, decided to approve the sentence but remit the penalty. Polk was not satisfied that mutiny had been proven, but he did see proof of disobedience of orders and conduct prejudicial to good order and military discipline. Rather than accept the president's decision and admit in any way the justice of the court's findings, Frémont resigned from the Army.

[5] CLARKE, 358.
[6] Blair to Van Buren, Silver Spring, 23 Jan. 1847 [1848] (DLC—Van Buren Papers).

His letters of resignation and their acceptance by the War Department appear on the last page of the Senate document.

Kearny's partisans have condemned the court as being under the influence of Benton—or at least of fearing his influence—a charge which some of Frémont's champions admitted was valid. Others have viewed the same body as essentially hostile; indeed, Benton charged that the explorer had been judged by a professional clique jealous of anyone who had not won his promotions in the regular way. In the face of such divergent opinions of the tribunal, some brief notes on its composition may be pertinent.

Of the original court of thirteen, of which Brig. Gen. George M. Brooke was president, five were West Point graduates, but when Lieut. Col. Thomas F. Hunt replaced Bvt. Maj. Archibald McCall, the number fell to four. The judge advocate or prosecuting attorney for the Army, thirty-four-year-old John Fitzgerald Lee, was likewise a West Point graduate.

Including Hunt (and excluding McCall, who did not serve), eleven members of the court had been commissioned between 1808 and 1817, and thus each had thirty years or more of regular Army service. A twelfth member, Richard Delafield, had twenty-nine. Frémont was slightly acquainted with Brooke, who, after doing his duty on the court, was ordered to the Upper Mississippi to establish military posts in the Sioux country. British Capt. Andrew Cathcart went up the river with Brooke and described him as "a regular trump, not quite our style of general officer; swears audaciously, liquors considerable, chews a gum and smokes like a chimney."[7] More polished than Brooke was Delafield. Scion of a wealthy New York family, he was at the time of Frémont's court-martial in charge of the defenses of New York harbor, but he had been superintendent of the U.S. Military Academy between 1838 and 1845 and would serve in that capacity again from 1856 to 1861. Delafield became brigadier general and chief of engineers in 1864. Another member of the court, René Edward DeRussy, had been director of the academy from 1833 to 1838. He would command the Corps of Engineers in Washington from 1858 to 1861, when he became supervisor of defenses on the Pacific Coast. Like Frémont, Lieut. Col. Stephen H. Long, who was to become Abert's successor as chief of

---

[7] Cathcart to C. J. Colville, Galena, Ill., 29 Aug. 1848 (National Register of Archives, Scotland).

the Bureau of Topographical Engineers in 1861, had achieved distinction as an explorer. In 1820 he headed an expedition to the Rockies and in 1823 to the sources of the Minnesota River.

During the trial Maj. James Duncan Graham, who had been with Long on the expedition to the Rockies, was nominated for the brevet of lieutenant colonel for his services in helping determine the boundary line between the United States and the provinces of Canada and New Brunswick. But after the trial Benton moved in the Senate that the nomination of Graham be rejected "for conduct unbecoming an officer and a gentleman, and unbecoming a judge on a court martial." He specifically charged that Graham felt malice and envy toward Frémont and was actually privy to an attempt on the part of General Kearny to obtain an interview with Commodore Stockton (the leading witness for Frémont) before he was examined. Allegedly Kearny wanted to prevent testimony on the essential point of supremacy of command in California. Benton also charged that Graham, whom he "individualized by the name, style, and description of COLLATERAL GRAHAM," had consented to Kearny's own interrogation. Benton's charges caused Graham to ask the Adjutant General for a general court-martial, which was not granted.[8]

One of the older members of the court, J. P. Taylor, was the brother of Gen. Zachary Taylor. The youngest member, Maj. Edwin Wright Morgan, a graduate of the U.S. Military Academy, had resigned his commission in 1839 but had been reappointed major in 1847. Soon after Frémont's trial ended, he left the Army permanently and pursued a career in railroad engineering and education. Six members—Brooke, Churchill, Delafield, DeRussy, Taylor, and Craig—were to attain the rank of brigadier or major general, either by regular or brevet commission. Churchill's brevet came because of his "gallant and meritorious conduct" in the battle of Buena Vista.

In his censure of the proceedings Benton made clear that he always excepted the judge advocate, Brooke, Taylor, Hunt, and Baker.

---

[8] Graham to R. Jones, 19 Aug. 1848, DNA-94, LR, G-347 1848, f/w M-1339 1848; Graham's correspondence, printed in Washington *Daily Union,* 25 Aug. 1848; Benton's speech opposing the nomination of Kearny for the brevet of major general, *Congressional Globe,* 1847–48, 30th Cong., 1st sess., Appendix, pp. 977–1040.

According to information leaked to him, these four members of the court had been opposed to conviction; since none were West Point graduates, Benton was probably more convinced than ever that Frémont had paid the penalty of not having entered the Army through the gates of the academy. Furthermore, "he had done worse: he had become distinguished." But it was Kearny and his "strikers" and "stickers"—Emory, Cooke, and Mason—rather than members of the court who bore the brunt of Benton's opprobrium.[9]

Rather than tarnishing Frémont's national reputation, the court-martial actually added to it, and the trial wrote indelibly into the public mind the fact—or fiction, as some historians would have it—that he had played a daring role in the acquisition of California. Some officers might hail the outcome as a victory for military discipline,[10] but the populace did not rate his insubordination as a very grave offense and undoubtedly agreed with four members of the court that a more seasoned officer might have agonized over the relative rank and rights of the commodore and the brigadier general. The next year a new administration would seek again his public service by appointing him one of the commissioners to establish the boundary line between the United States and Mexico. To gain public recognition, Frémont accepted, but he soon resigned to take a seat in Congress as senator from the new state of California.[11]

The court-martial did have an effect upon his character. While he was not a man to look back, lose courage, or indulge in post-trial recriminations, the wound still burned, and he became more determined than ever to win laurels as an explorer and to wrest from Congress financial support for new expeditions in 1848 and 1853. In both attempts he was to fail. As a result of the trial he became more aloof; his friendships with Gillespie and Stockton seem to have ceased. He also became sensitive about his own honor and less sensi-

---

[9] BENTON, 2:715–19; Benton's speech, *Congressional Globe,* 1847–48, 30th Cong., 1st sess., Appendix, pp. 977–1040.

[10] See 2 April 1848 letter in DU PONT, 377.

[11] Shortly before his election to the Senate, JCF explained his actions to Jacob R. Snyder: "Respect to the President, together with a full appreciation of the consideration which had induced him to make the appointment, did not, in my judgment, permit me to decline, and I accordingly accepted the commission, with the intention which I *then expressed* to Mr. Beale and others shortly afterwards to resign" (11 Dec. 1849 letter in *Alta California,* 15 Dec. 1849).

tive about the welfare of the men who joined his expeditions.[12] His growing callousness is also revealed in sharp financial dealings in California in the 1850s with respect to his Mariposa estate and government contracts to supply beef to the California Indians. But the trial and the attending publicity were important factors in his selection by the Republican party in 1856 as its candidate for president.

The manuscript record of the court-martial proceedings down to the beginning of Frémont's long defense may be found in EE-575 of the Records of the Judge Advocate General's Office, National Archives. His defense constituted Appendix 4 of the printed Senate document, and consequently may be found on pp. 365–446 of this volume. It was also issued separately in pamphlet form: *Defence of Lt. Col. Frémont before the Court Martial* (Washington, D.C., 1848).

Many persons mentioned in the proceedings are identified in Vol. 2 and not identified here, but persons mentioned for the first time are identified in notes at the end of the volume, keyed to the pertinent page and line of text. Explanatory notes and corrections of typographical and spelling errors in the Senate document are handled in the same manner.

Names of authors in SMALL CAPITALS are citations to sources listed in the bibliography on pp. 459–460. The following symbols are to record groups in the National Archives:

DNA-24   Records of the Bureau of Naval Personnel
DNA-45   Naval Records Collection of the Office of Naval Records and Library
DNA-94   Records of the Adjutant General's Office
DNA-153   Records of the Judge Advocate General's Office

---

[12] For JCF's sensitivity, see his 10 July 1854 letter to William H. Emory requesting that he make a public correction of his statement that a member of Mr. Benton's family had been dismissed from the Army (New York *Times,* 14 July 1854).

MESSAGE

OF THE

PRESIDENT OF THE UNITED STATES,

COMMUNICATING

The proceedings of the court martial in the trial of Lieutenant Colonel Frémont.

April 7, 1848.
Ordered to lie on the table, and be printed.

To the Senate of the United States:

I communicate, herewith, a report of the Secretary of War, transmitting "a copy of the proceedings of the general court martial in the case of Lieutenant Colonel Frémont," called for by a resolution of the Senate of the 29th February, 1848.

JAMES K. POLK.

Washington, *April* 7, 1848.

War Department,
Washington, April 5, 1848.

Sir: I have caused to be prepared, in pursuance of your directions, and have the honor to transmit, herewith, "a copy of the proceedings of the general court martial in the case of Lieutenant Colonel Frémont," which you were requested, by a resolution of the Senate of the 29th of February last, to communicate to that body.

Very respectfully, your obedient servant,

W. L. MARCY,
Secretary of War.

The President
of the United States.

Proceedings of a general court martial, held at Washington arsenal, D. C., by virtue of the following orders:

GENERAL ORDERS, }   WAR DEPARTMENT,
No. 32.   ADJUTANT GENERAL'S OFFICE,
              Washington, September 27, 1847.

A general court martial, to consist of thirteen members, will assemble at Fort Monroe, Virginia, at 11 o'clock, a. m., on the 2d day of November, 1847, or as soon thereafter as practicable, for the trial of Lieutenant Colonel *John C. Frémont*, of the regiment of mounted riflemen.

Detail for the court.

Brevet Brigadier General G. M. Brooke, colonel 5th infantry.
Colonel S. Churchill, inspector general.
Colonel J. B. Crane, 1st artillery.
Brevet Colonel M. M. Payne, 4th artillery.
Brevet Lieutenant Colonel S. H. Long, corps of topographical engineers.
Lieutenant Colonel R. E. De Russey, corps of engineers.
Lieutenant Colonel J. P. Taylor, subsistence department.
Brevet Lieutenant Colonel H. R. Craig, ordnance department.
Major R. L. Baker, ordnance department.
Major J. D. Graham, corps of topographical engineers.
Major R. Delafield, corps of engineers.
Brevet Major G. A. McCall, assistant adjutant general.
Major E. W. Morgan, 11th infantry.
Captain John F. Lee, ordnance department, is appointed the judge advocate of the court.

Should any of the officers named in the detail be prevented from attending at the time and place specified, the court will, nevertheless, proceed to, and continue the business before it, provided the number of the members present be not less than *nine.*

By order of the President.

R. JONES, *Adj't. General.*

SPECIAL ORDERS, }   WAR DEPARTMENT,
No 55.   ADJUTANT GENERAL'S OFFICE,
             Washington, October 28, 1847.

The general court martial directed to assemble at Fort Monroe the 2d day of November next, for the trial of Lieutenant Colonel Frémont, of the mounted rifle regiment, pursuant to general orders No. 32, will meet on the day appointed, at the Washington arsenal, District of Columbia, instead of Fort Monroe. The members of the court, and the witnesses in the case, will, accordingly, give attendance at the Washington arsenal.

By order of the President.

R. JONES, *Adj't. General.*

WASHINGTON ARSENAL, D. C.,
12 o'clock, November 2, 1847.

The court met pursuant to the foregoing orders.

Present:

Brevet Brigadier General G. M. Brooke.
Colonel S. Churchill.
Colonel J. B. Crane.
Brevet Colonel M. M. Payne.
Brevet Lieutenant Colonel S. H. Long.
Lieutenant Colonel R. E. De Russey.
Lieutenant Colonel J. P. Taylor.
Brevet Lieutenant Colonel H. K. Craig.
Major R. L. Baker.
Major J. D. Graham.
Major R. Delafield.
Major E. W. Morgan.
Captain J. F. Lee, judge advocate.
Lieutenant Colonel John C. Frémont, also present in court.

The judge advocate read the orders convening the court, and called the roll of the members, when, Major McCall being absent, the court adjourned, to wait his arrival till to-morrow morning, November 3d, at 10 o'clock.

---

12 o'CLOCK, WEDNESDAY, *Nov.* 3, 1847.

The court met pursuant to adjournment.

Present, all the members except Major McCall, as yesterday. Also present, the judge advocate and Lieutenant Colonel Frémont.

The president presented the following order:

SPECIAL ORDERS, No. 58.	WAR DEPARTMENT, ADJUTANT GENERAL'S OFFICE, *Washington, Nov.* 3, 1847.

In consequence of the inability, from sickness, of Brevet Major *G. A. McCall*, assistant adjutant general, to attend as a member of the general court martial, convened by general orders, No. 32, of September 27th, ultimo, Lieutenant Colonel T. F. Hunt, deputy quartermaster general, is detailed to complete the organization of the court, and will report in person to the president thereof.

By order of the President.

R. JONES, *Adj't. General.*

Lieutenant Colonel Hunt took his seat on the court next below Lieutenant Colonel De Russey.

The proceedings of yesterday were read over by the judge advocate, with the orders assembling and detailing the court, and Lieutenant Colonel Frémont was asked by the judge advocate if he had any objection to any members of the court named in the orders, now present, and he replied in the negative. Then, in the presence of Lieutenant Colonel Frémont, the oath prescribed by law was duly administered by the judge advocate to the president and members, and also, the oath prescribed by law was duly administered to the judge advocate by the president.

Lieutenant Colonel Frémont then presented to the court a paper, in writing, as follows:

MR. PRESIDENT: In preferring the usual request to be allowed counsel in this case, I wish to state that it is no part of my intention or desire to make defence on any legal or technical point, but only to have friendly assistance in bringing out the merits of the case in lucid and proper order, and in obtaining a full trial on the merits, in the shortest time, and with the least amount of trouble to the court. With this view, no objection will be made to the relevancy or legality of any question proposed by the prosecution, the court, or any member of the court; nor to any question which goes to show my motives, either by words or acts, in aggravation of the offences alleged against me; nor to the *authenticity* of nay evidence, written or printed, which I know or believe to be authentic; nor will any question be proposed, or motion made on my part, knowingly, of a nature to give just ground of objection on the part of the prosecution, or to cause delay in the trial, or give trouble to the court. But the waiver of proof to the authencity of papers is made on the express condition, that all the persons brought from California by General Kearny, for witnesses, and listed as such with the charges, and summoned, shall be sworn on the part of the prosecution, so as to save to me my right of cross-examination.

In this way I hope to facilitate the progress of the trial—to get at once into the merits—to spare this court the most unpleasant part of an unpleasant dutý—and enable them the sooner to obey the feelings which call them to a very different service.

I name as the counsel asked to be allowed me the two friends who accompany me, Thomas H. Benton and William Carey Jones, esquires.

Whereupon the court ordered that the gentlemen named by Lieutenant Colonel Frémont be received as his counsel, subject to the customary restrictions imposed on counsel by courts martial.

The following charges were then read by the judge advocate:

Charges against Lieutenant Colonel John C. Frémont, of the regiment of mounted riflemen, United States army, preferred against him by order of the War Department on information of Brigadier General S. W. Kearny.

Charge 1.—Mutiny.

Specification 1.—In this that he, Lieutenant Colonel John C. Frémont, of the regiment of mounted riflemen, United States army, being in command of a battalion of volunteers, organized in California for the United States service, having received the lawful command of his superior officer, Brigadier General S. W. Kearny, in the following words, to wit:

HEAD-QUARTERS ARMY OF THE WEST,
Ciudad de los Angeles, January 16, 1847.

By direction of Brigadier General Kearny I send you a copy of a communication to him from the Secretary of War, dated June 18, 1846, in which is the following: " These troops and such as may be organized in California will be under your command." The general directs that no change will be made in the organization of your battalion of volunteers, or officers appointed in it, without his sanction or approval being first obtained.

Very respectfully,

W. H. EMORY,
Lieutenant and Acting Assistant Adjutant General.

To Lieutenant Colonel J. C. FREMONT,
Mounted riflemen, commanding battalion California volunteers.

And having received with this order a copy of instructions from the War Department to General Kearny, in the following words, to wit:

WAR DEPARTMENT,
Washington, June 18, 1846.

SIR: *   *   *   *   *   *   *   *
I have nothing of importance to add to the despatches which have been already forwarded to you.

Since my last letter it has been determined to send a small force around Cape Horn to California. The arms, cannon and provisions to be sent to the Pacific will be accompanied by one company of artillery of the regular army; arrangements are now on foot to send a regiment of volunteers by sea. These troops and such as may be organized in California will be under your command.

More than common solicitude will be felt here in regard to the expedition committed to you, and it is desired that you should avail yourself of all occasions to inform the government of your progress and prospects.

The President desires your opinion, as early as you are in a situation to give it, of the practicability of your reaching California in the course of this autumn, or in the early part of next winter. I need not repeat the expression of his wishes, that you should take military possession of that country as soon as it can be safely done.

I am, with great respect, your obedient servant,

W. L. MARCY,
Secretary of War.

To Colonel S. W. KEARNY.

—did reply to General Kearny and his order aforesaid, in a written answer, in the following words, to wit:

CIUDAD DE LOS ANGELES,
January 17, 1847.

SIR: I have the honor to be in receipt of your favor of last night, in which I am directed to suspend the execution of orders which, in my capacity of military commandant of this territory, I had received from Commodore Stockton, governor and commander-in-chief in California.

I avail myself of an early hour this morning to make such a reply as the brief time allowed for reflection will enable me.

I found Commodore Stockton in possession of the country, exercising the functions of military commandant and civil governor, as early as July of last year; and shortly thereafter I received from him the commission of military commandant, the duties of which I immediately entered upon, and have continued to exercise to the present moment.

I found also, on my arrival at this place some three or four days since, Commodore Stockton still exercising the functions of civil and military governor, with the same apparent deference to his rank on the part of all officers (including yourself) as he maintained and required when he assumed in July last.

I learned also, in conversation with you, that, on the march from San Diego, recently, to this place, you entered upon and discharged duties implying an acknowledgment on your part of supremacy to Commodore Stockton.

I feel myself, therefore, with great deference to your professional and personal character, constrained to say that, until you and Commodore Stockton adjust between yourselves the question of rank, where I respectfully think the difficulty belongs, I shall have to report and receive orders, as herefore, from the commodore.

With considerations of high regard, I am your obedient servant,

J. C. FRÉMONT, *Lt. Col. U. S. A.,*
and military commandant of the territory of California.
To Brig. Gen. S. W. KEARNY,
United States Army.

—and did thereby refuse to obey the aforesaid lawful commands of his superior officer, General Kearny, or to receive and obey any other order from him; but did declare himself to be the military commandant of the territory of California, thereby resisting and throwing off the authority of his superior officer there present and exercising command by orders from the President of the United States, and placing himself in open mutiny against said superior officer. This at Ciudad de los Angeles, California, on the seventeenth day of January, eighteen hundred and forty-seven, notwithstanding he had, on the thirteenth of January, eighteen hundred and forty-seven, officially reported his battalion to Brigadier General Kearny, by writing, in words the following, to wit:

ON THE MARCH, *January 13, 1847.*

DEAR SIR: I have the honor to report to you my arrival at this place with 400 mounted riflemen and six pieces of artillery, including among the latter two pieces lately in possession of the Californians. Their entire force, under the command of D. Andro Pico, have this day laid down their arms and surrendered to my command.

Very respectfully, your obedient servant,

J. C. FRÉMONT, *Lt. Col. U. S. A.*
and military commandant of the territory of California.

Brigadier General S. W. KEARNY,
Commanding U. S. forces, Puebla de los Angeles.

Specification 2.—In this, that he, Lieutenant Colonel John C. Frémont, of the regiment of mounted riflemen, United States army, being in command of a battalion of volunteers organized in California, which were placed by the aforesaid orders of the Secretary of War, of June eighteenth, eighteen hundred and forty-six, under the command of Brigadier General Kearny, did issue an order to Captain J. K. Wilson, at Angeles, January twenty-fifth, eighteen hundred and forty-seven, in the following words, to wit:

ANGELES, *January* 25, 1847.

SIR: You are hereby authorized and directed to raise a company of men to constitute the second company of artillery in the California service, and for that purpose are detached from your present command.

You will please report the number you may be able to enlist with as little delay as possible.

You are authorized to enlist the men for three months, and to promise them, as compensation, twenty-five dollars per month.

Respectfully,

J. C. FRÉMONT, *Lt. Col.,*
commanding California forces in the U. S. service.

To Capt. J. K. WILSON, *Light Artillery.*

—thereby raising and attempting to raise troops, in violation and contempt of the lawful command aforesaid of his superior officer, Brigadier General Kearny, of date January sixteenth, eighteen hundred and forty-seven, and thereby acting openly in defiance of, and in mutiny against, the authority of his superior officer aforesaid, by raising and attempting to raise troops, and by proclaiming himself to be, and assuming to act as, the commander of the United States forces in California.

Specification 3.—In this, that he, Lieutenant Colonel John C. Frémont, of the regiment of mounted riflemen, United States army, being in command of a battalion of mounted riflemen organized in California for the United States service, which was placed by orders aforesaid from the Secretary of War, of June eighteenth, eighteen hundred and forty-six, under command of Brigadier General Kearny, did, at Ciudad de los Angeles, California, on the fifth day of February, eighteen hundred and forty-seven, issue an order to Louis McLane, a passed midshipman in the United States navy, in the following words, to wit

CIUDAD DE LOS ANGELES, *February* 5, 1847.

SIR: I feel it my duty, as the representative of the United States government in California, to instruct you to proceed forthwith north as far as in your discretion may seem necessary, and exercise your best efforts in, enlisting troops for the term of six months, compensation to be $—— per month, to be employed in the service of the United States, and at such points in the territory of California as in my judgment they are most required. You are furthermore instructed to proceed as far as the town of Yerba Buena, on the San Francisco bay, and examine diligently into the the state of the naval or military defence of that town, and particularly to inquire into the best means of fortifying the mouth of the bay against the ingress of all enemies; and I particularly recommend to you to cause to be commenced the erection of a fort or battery on White island, calculated, when completed, to prevent the entrance of any ship or vessel that may be forbidden to do so by said United States.

To enable you to carry into effect the foregoing instructions, you are hereby authorized and required to call on all officers under my command to extend to you any assistance of money, men, or property that in your judgment may be necessary to accomplish the same.

In witness whereof, I have hereunto set my hand and affixed my seal, at the capital of California, this date before written.

J. C. FREMONT, *Governor of California.*
Attest:
    W. H. RUSSELL, *Secretary of State.*

To Major LOUIS MCLANE,
    U. S. Army, California regiment.

—thereby raising and attempting to raise troops in violation and contempt of the aforesaid lawful command of his superior officer, Brigadier General Kearny, dated January sixteenth, eighteen hundred and forty-seven; and thereby acting in defiance of the authority, and in mutiny against his superior officer aforesaid, in raising and attempting to raise these troops, and in proclaiming himself to be, and in assuming to act as, the governor of California.

Specifiation 4.—In this, that he, Lieutenant Colonel John C. Frémont, of the regiment of mounted riflemen, United States army, being in command of a battalion of mounted riflemen organized in California for the United States service, and placed by orders aforesaid from the Secretary of War, of June eighteenth, eighteen hundred and forty-six, under command of Brigadier General Kearny, did, at Ciudad de los Angeles, California, on the seventh of February, eighteen hundred and forty-seven, write to Commodore

Shubrick, commanding the United States naval forces in the Pacific, a letter in words following, to wit:

CIUDAD DE LOS ANGELES,
February 7, 1847.

SIR: I had the honor, at a late hour of last night, to receive your favor of the 25th ultimo, and, fully coinciding with the opinion that you express, that a co-operation of our respective commands, as a precautionary measure at least, is of primary importance, I hasten to acknowledge its receipt, and signify to you my earnest desire to see you and consult on the measures calculated in our judgments to be the most certain of making our labors conduce to the interest of our government.

Not having had, as you remarked, any communication since your arrival on this coast with Commodore Stockton, you seem not to have been made acquainted with the fact that, by a commission from the commodore, I had been placed in command of the territory as civil governor, which I beg leave herewith to communicate to you.

It is also proper to advise you that General Kearny, who comes to California with instructions from the Secretary of War, dated as early as June last, (designed for a state of affairs which he by no means found, to wit: the country still unconquered, and which, of course, being intended for very different circumstances, cannot have application here,) claims himself to have supreme command in California, which position I felt it my duty to deny him, and, in language respectful, but decisive of my purpose, communicated to him.

The subjoined reasons led me to the conclusion I adopted. The conquest of California was undertaken and completed by the joint effort of Commodore Stockton and myself, in obedience to what we regarded paramount duties from us to our government; that done, the next necessary step in order was the organization of a civil government, designed to maintain the conquest by the exercise of mild and wholesome civil restraints over the people, rather than by the iron rule of military force.

The result of our labors, which were precisely what was contemplated by the instructions of General Kearny, were promptly communicated to the Executive of the Union by an express, which has not yet brought back the approval or disapproval of the government. General Kearny's instructions being, therefore, to the letter fully anticipated by others, I did not feel myself at liberty to yield a position so important to the interests of my country until, after a full understanding of all the grounds, it should be the pleasure of my government that I should do so.

I trust the foregoing explanation will fully satisfy you that the position I take is an incident to the extraordinary circumstances surrounding me, and is borne out by a rigid adherence to the line of duty.

The insurrection which broke out here in September last, and which it required a considerable force and a large expenditure of money to put down, has left me in rather an embarrassed condition for funds to redeem my engagements to my men, and to cancel the necessary obligations created by the quartermaster and commissariat department of the command. If, therefore, you can, at any day, advance me a considerable sum of money it will tend greatly to subserve the interests of the country and relieve an embarrassment which, as an officer of the government, heavily presses me.

I start off, simultaneous with this, a courier to the United States with important despatches; but thinking, perhaps, that you might wish to avail yourself of so good an opportunity of forwarding despatches, I have ordered him to remain on the border of the settlements until the return of my courier from you. The precise point where my courier will remain recruiting his animals being at this time unknown to me, you will please send your despatches by the return courier to me, and I will forward them to the party homeward bound.

With considerations of high respect, I am, sir, your obedient servant,

J. C. FRÉMONT,
Governor of California.

Commodore W. Branford Shubrick,
　　Commanding United States naval forces,
　　　　in the Pacific ocean, Bay of Monterey.

—thereby continuing and re-asserting his resistance of the lawful authority of his superior officer, Brigadier General Kearny, assuming to be governor of California, and endeavoring to persuade the said naval commander to support and countenance him in his mutiny against his said superior and commanding officer.

Specification 5.—In this, that he, Lieutenant Colonel John C. Frémont, of the regiment of mounted riflemen, United States army, being in command of a battalion of volunteers, organized in California for the United States service, and placed under command of Brigadier General Kearny, by aforesaid orders from the War Department, dated June eighteenth, eighteen hundred and forty-six, did, at Angeles, on the eleventh day of February, eighteen hundred and forty-seven, write to W. P. Hall in the following words, to wit:

Government House,
Angeles, February 11, 1847.

Sir: The position I occupy as the chief representative of the United States government in California renders it an imperative duty on me that I should prudently, but with energy, exert all the powers with which I am clothed to retain the conquest we have made, and strengthen it by all means possible.

The executive office of California, which, I understand, centers supreme civil and military command in the territory, was actually assigned me as early as September last, and my entering on the duties of the same was postponed only in consequence of an insurrection that broke out in this portion of the territory, which it took some months to quell; that done, I assumed the office of governor, as had been previous'y arranged.

I learn with surprise and mortification that General Kearny, in obedience to what I cannot but regard as obsolete instructions from the Secretary of War, means to question my right, and, viewing my position and claim clear and indisputable, I cannot, without considering myself derelict to my trust and unworthy the station of an American officer, yield, or to permit myself to be interfered with by any other, until directed to do so by the proper authorities at home, predicated in full and ample despatches that I forwarded to Washington as early as August of last year.

I require the co-operation, with a view to the important object of preserving the peace and tranquility of California, of every American citizen and soldier in the territory, and must expressly inhibit, from all quarters, all arguments and intimations that may tend to weaken my authority, by inducing the belief that my present position is an act of usurpation, unjust, and will not be sanctioned by my government.

Intimations, not perhaps susceptible of positive proof, have reached me that you were using your talents and high character as a member of the American Congress, in your intercourse with citizens of this place and the troops under my immediate command, to raise doubts, if not questioning altogether the legitimacy or validity of my tenure of office.

I feel myself constrained therefore, in obedience to the behests and high interests of my government, as well as the respect I cherish for the position you occupy, to inquire of you, in frankness, whether the intimations alluded to have any foundation in fact or truth.

Cherishing a confident belief that you must on reflection concur with me in thinking that, at this juncture, anything more calculated to weaken me, or embarrass, must be inexpedient and improper, 1 trust a frank negative answer from you will dissipate my doubts, and admonish me that the inquiry I have made was altogether unnecessary.

With considerations of high respect, I am, your obedient servant,

J. C. FRÉMONT,
Governor of California.

To the Hon. WILLARD P. HALL.

—thereby avowing and justifying his resistance and mutiny against his superior officer, Brigadier General Kearny, and endeavoring to persuade and incite the said Hall, a person of influence in California, to aid and abet him therein, and to prevent said Hall from supporting the lawful authority of Brigadier General Kearny.

Specification 6.—In this, that he, Lieutenant Colonel John C. Frémont, of the regiment of mounted riflemen, United States army, did, at Ciudad de los Angeles, on the second of March, eighteen hundred and forty-seven, in contempt of the lawful authority of his superior officer, Brigadier General Kearny, assume to be and to act as, governor of California, in executing a deed or instrument of writing in the following words, to wit:

In consideration of Francis Temple having conveyed to the United States of North America a certain island, commonly called White or Bird island, situated near the mouth of San Francisco bay, I, J. C. Frémont, governor of California, and in virtue of my office as aforesaid, hereby oblige myself as the legal representative of the United States, and my successors in office, to pay the said Francis Temple, his heirs or assigns, the sum of five thousand dollars, ($5,000,) to be paid at as early a day as possible after the receipt of funds from the United States.

In witness whereof, I have hereunto set my hand, and caused the seal of the territory of California to be af-
[SEAL.]   fixed, at the Ciudad de los Angeles, the capital of California, this 2d day of March, A. D. 1847.

J. C. FRÉMONT.

Attest:
WM. H. RUSSELL, *Secretary of State.*

Specification 7.—In this, that he, Lieutenant Colonel John C. Frémont, of the regiment of mounted riflemen, United States army, being in command of a battalion of volunteers organized in California for the United States service, which, by aforesaid orders from the War Department, dated June eighteenth, eighteen hundred and forty-six, were placed under command of Brigadier General Kearny, and having been officially informed by W. Branford Shubrick, as commander-in-chief of the naval forces in the Pacific, in a letter, dated United States ship Independence, Monterey, February twenty-three, eighteen hundred and forty-seven, in the following words, to wit: "General Kearny, I am instructed, is the commanding military officer in California, and invested by the President with the administrative functions of government over the people and territory;" and having received on the eleventh of March, eighteen hundred and forty-seven, from General Kearny, by the hands of Captain H. S. Turner, United States army, a circular proclamation in the following words, to wit:

Circular.

To all whom it may concern, be it known:

That the President of the United States, desirous to give and secure to the people of California a share of the good government and happy civil organization enjoyed by the people of the United States, and to protect them at the same time from the attacks of foreign foes and from internal commotions, has invested the undersigned with separate and distinct powers, civil and military; a cordial co-operation in the exercise of which, it is hoped and believed, will have the happy result desired.

To the commander-in-chief of the naval forces the President has assigned the regulation of the import trade, the conditions on which vessels of all nations, our own as well as foreign, may be admitted in the ports of the territory, and the establishment of all port regulations.

To the commanding military officer the President has assigned the direction of the operations on land, and has invested him with administrative functions of government over the people and territory occupied by the forces of the United States.

Done at Monterey, capital of California, this first day of March, A. D. 1847.

W. BRANFORD SHUBRICK,
Commander-in-chief of the naval forces.
S. W. KEARNY,
Brig. General, U. S. A., and Governor of California.

And having, at the same time, on the eleventh day of March, eighteen hundred and forty-seven, received from Brigadier General Kearny, by the hands of Captain H. S. Turner, the following order, in terms, to wit:

Orders, }   HEAD-QUARTERS, 10TH MILITARY DEPARTMENT,
.\' }   *Monterey, March* 1, 1847.

I. With a view to regulate payment, it is necessary that the battalion of California volunteers, now under the command of Lieutenant Colonel Frémont of the army, and stationed at the Ciudad de los Angeles, if not originally mustered under the law of May thirteenth, and the supplemental law of June 18, 1846, should now be mustered into service under those laws.

II. This muster will be made at once by Lieutenant Colonel Frémont; should any men of that battalion be unwilling to continue in service under the above laws, they will be conducted by Lieutenant Colonel Frémont to Yerba Buena, via Monterey, and be there discharged.

III. Lieutenant Colonel P. St. G. Cooke, now in command of the Mormon battalion, is entrusted with the supervision of the southern military district, for the protection and defence of which he will make the necessary provision; posting his command (to consist of company C, 1st dragoons, the Mormon battalion, and the California volunteers) at such places as he may deem most eligible.

By order of Brigadier General S. W. Kearny.

H. S. TURNER,
Captain A. A. A. General.

—did, at Ciudad de los Angeles, on the fifteenth day of March, eighteen hundred and forty-seven, issue orders to Captain Richard Owens, in the following, to wit:

CIUDAD DE LOS ANGELES, *March* 15, 1847.

SIR: In the performance of a portion of my official duties, it becomes necessary that I should visit in person the northern district of the territory, where I shall probably be detained some 15 or 20 days, and the better to possess you of my views in my absence, and to render your authority in the meantime undoubted, I have considered it proper to issue the following orders:

1st. You will continue with the entire battalion at San Gabriel, observing order, vigilance, and exercising as much discipline as in your discretion can be prudently enforced.

2d. You will make no move whatever from San Gabriel, in my absence, unless to report an actual invasion, or obey the order of any officer that does not emanate from me.

3d. You will take the best possible care of the public arms and munitions belonging to the command, and turn them over to no corps without my special orders.

4th. The general police of the garrison and strict regard to the public interest will, of course, as commandant ad interim, constantly engage your best efforts.

Very respectfully, your obedient servant,

J. C. FREMONT,
Lieutenant Colonel United States Army,
and commandant of California battalion.

Captain RICHARD OWENS,
Acting commandant of California battalion.

—thereby himself resisting the authority and disobeying the orders of Brigadier General Kearny, as conveyed to him in the aforesaid order No. 2, of the 10th military department, by continuing in service the entire California battalion contrary to said orders; and by ordering the battalion to remain at San Gabriel, contrary to the said orders from Brigadier General Kearny to march them to Yerba Buena. Thereby further inciting and ordering said Captain Owens, with the force of this battalion, which he had placed under said Owens's command, to disobey the order and resist the authority of any officer but himself, and specially ordering him not to surrender the arms and munitions of the battalion, in obedience to which order from Lieutenant Colonel J. C. Frémont, said Owens did, at Ciudad de los Angeles, on the twenty-fourth of March, eighteen hundred and forty-seven, refuse to submit to the authority of Lieutenant Colonel P. St. G. Cooke, appointed in aforesaid department orders, by Brigadier General Kearny, to command the district in which his battalion was stationed—did refuse to surrender to said Lieutenant Colonel Cooke, or to permit said Lieutenant Colonel Cooke to take possession of two howitzers brought by the 1st dragoons from Fort Leavenworth, and then at San Gabriel; which said mutiny and resistance of lawful authority, by said Captain Owens, was by the incitement and positive order, as aforesaid of Lieutenant Colonel J. C. Frémont, notwithstanding he, Lieutenant Colonel J. C. Frémont had officially, informed Captain Turner at Pueblo de los Angeles, on the twelfth of March, eighteen hundred and forty-seven, that he would obey and execute the said orders of Brigadier General Kearny, to wit: 10th military department, orders No. 2, of March 1, 1847.

Specification 8.—In this, that he, Lieutenant Colonel John C. Frémont, of the regiment of mounted riflemen, United States army, being in command of a battalion of volunteers, organized in California for the United States service, having, on the eleventh day of March, eighteen hundred and forty-seven, received the lawful order of his superior officer, Brigadier General Kearny, to wit: the aforesaid orders No. 2, dated head-quarters, 10th military department, Monterey, March first, eighteen hundred and forty-seven, whereby he was ordered to march such part of said battalion as refused to be mustered into service, to Yerba Buena, there to be discharged, did refuse to obey said orders, and did make known his refusal to Lieutenant Colonel Cooke, commanding the district in which his battalion was serving, by a written communication in terms, to wit:

CIUDAD DE LOS ANGELES, *March* 16, 1847.

SIR: I am instructed by Governor Frémont to acknowledge, a few moments since, the receipt of your communication of the 14th instant, and to say in reply that the volunteers, consisting of the California battalion, decline, without an individual exception, to be mustered into the United States service, conformable to order No. 2, of the 10th military department, referred to by you.

The governor considers it unsafe, at this time, when rumor is rife with a threatened insurrection, to discharge the battalion, and will decline doing so; and, whilst they remain in service, he regards his force quite sufficient for the protection of the artillery and ordnance stores at the mission of San Gabriel.

I am, with considerations of respect, your obedient servant,
WM. H. RUSSELL,
Secretary of State.

To P. ST. GEORGE COOKE,
Lieutenant Colonel, commanding,
Mission San Luis regiment.

—therein still assuming to be, and to act as, governor of California, retaining in service an armed force contrary to the order of his superior officer, Brigadier General Kearny, and refusing to march them according to his orders.

Specification 9.—In this, that he, Lieutenant Colonel John C. Frémont, of the regiment of mounted riflemen, United States army, being in command of a battalion of volunteers, organized in California for the United States service, and under the lawful command of Brigadier General Kearny, and having received on the eleventh of March, eighteen hundred and forty-seven, at Ciudad de los Angeles, as set out in the seventh specification to this charge, due and official notification from Brigadier General Kearney and Commodore Shubrick, that the President of the United States had invested General Kearny with the military command in California, and with the administrative functions of government over the people and territory occupied by the forces of the United States, did, nevertheless, at Ciudad de los Angeles, on the twenty-first day of

March, eighteen hundred and forty-seven, issue the following order to the collector of the port of San Pedro, in terms, to wit

CIUDAD DE LOS ANGELES,
March 21, 1847

SIR: You are hereby ordered and permitted, in the case of F. Hultman, to receive government payment in payment of his custom-house dues.

Very respectfully,

J. C. FRÉMONT,
Governor of California.
By WM. H. RUSSELL,
Secretary of State.

To DAVID W. ALEXANDER,
Collector of the port of San Pedro.

N. B. Mr. Hultman will be entitled to the usual discount by prompt payment.

WM. H. RUSSELL, for

J. C. FRÉMONT, Governor.

—thereby assuming to be, and to act as, governor of California, in contempt of the authority and in usurpation of the power of his superior officer, whereby the collector of the port aforesaid did receive, in payment of customs, the certificates of the staff officers of his battalion of California volunteers, to the amount of seventeen hundred and thirty-one dollars and forty-one and a half cents, which paper was purchased by the holder, from whom the collector was ordered to receive it at a discount of thirty per cent.

Specification 10.—In this, that he, Lieutenant Colonel John C. Frémont, of the regiment of mounted riflemen, United States army, after he had been duly informed by his superior officer, Brigadier General Kearny, that he, General Kearny, had been invested by the President of the United States with the command of the troops in California, by exhibiting to him, Lieutenant Colonel Frémont, on the sixteenth of January, eighteen hundred and forty-seven, at Ciudad de los Angeles, the aforesaid orders from the War Department, dated June eighteenth, eighteen hundred and forty-six, did, notwithstanding, disregard and set aside the lawful authority of said superior officer, and did himself usurp and exercise the functions of said superior officer, in the following official acts and matters, to wit:

1st. In ordering a general court martial at Ciudad de los Angeles, on the twenty-fourth of January, eighteen hundred and forty-seven, by his own authority; and, in the order, proclaiming himself to be, and assuming to act as, " the military commander-in-chief of California."

2d. In publishing a general order at Ciudad de los Angeles, on the twenty-fifth of January, eighteen hundred and forty-seven, in which he, Lieutenant Colonel Frémont, is styled "the military commander-in-chief of California."

3d. In approving at Ciudad de los Angeles, on the twenty-seventh of January, eighteen hundred and forty-seven, the proceed ings of a general court martial, called as aforesaid, by his order of January twenty-four, eighteen hundred and forty-seven, by which court martial Private George Smith of the California volunteers was sentenced to twenty-two months at hard labor, and Lieutenant Rock sentenced to be cashiered; and in declaring himself to be, and in assuming to act, in his general order aforesaid, approving said proceedings, " the governor of California."

4th. In accepting, by a general order published at Angeles, on the thirteenth of February, eighteen hundred and forty-seven, the resignation of the following commissioned officers of the California battalion of volunteers, to wit: Captains L. H. Ford, Samuel Gibson, and Wm. Findlay, and Lieutenants W. Baldridge, Renshaw, W. Blackburn, J. Scott, J. R. Barton, and J. M. Hudspeth, in contempt and violation of the aforesaid order, dated January sixteenth, eighteen hundred and forty-seven, which he had received from Brigadier General Kearny at Ciudad de los Angeles, on the sixteenth of January, eighteen hundred and forty-seven.

Specification 11.—In this, that he, Lieutenant Colonel John C. Frémont, of the regiment of mounted riflemen, United States army, did fail to obey the order of Brigadier General Kearny to repair to Monterey, as communicated to him verbally by Brigadier General Kearny, on the twenty-sixth of March, eighteen hundred and forty-seven, and repeated to him in writing on the twenty-eighth of March, eighteen hundred and forty-seven, in words following, to wit:

HEAD-QUARTERS, 10TH MILITARY DEPARTMENT,
Monterey, California, March 28, 1847.

SIR: This will be handed to you by Colonel Mason, 1st dragoons, who goes to the southern district, clothed by me with full authority to give such orders and instructions, upon all matters both civil and military, in that section of country, as he may deem proper and necessary. Any instructions he may give to you will be considered as coming from myself.

I deem it proper to suggest to you, that should there be at the Peubla any unsettled accounts or demands against the government, incurred by your orders or approval, which you may not have already authenticated and completed for the action of the disbursing officers, that you at once do so, as it may be necessary for you to proceed from here to Washington city; and should there be any of the party which accompanied you from Missouri still with you, and under pay from the topographical department, you will cause them to come to this place, that they may be returned home and discharged, and be of no further expense to the United States, unless they prefer being discharged at once in this country.

In twelve days after you have embarked the volunteers at San Pedro I desire to see you at this place.

Very respectfully, your obedient servant,

S. W. KEARNY,
, Brig. Gen. and Governor of California.

Lieut. Col. J. C. FREMONT,
Regiment of mounted riflemen, commanding battalion
of California volunteers, Ciudad de los Angeles.

—but did remain at the Ciudad de los Angeles, until after the arrival there of Brigadier General Kearny, on the ninth of May, eighteen hundred and forty-seven, and till the order was then and there verbally repeated to him.

Charge 2.—Disobedience of the lawful command of his superior officer.

Specification 1.—In this, that he, Lieutenant Colonel John C. Frémont, of the regiment of mounted riflemen, United States army, being in command of a battalion of volunteers, organized in California for the United States service, having received the lawful command of his superior officer, Brigadier General S. W. Kearny, in the following words, to wit:

HEAD-QUARTERS, ARMY OF THE WEST,
Ciudad de los Angeles, January 16, 1847.

By direction of Brigadier General Kearny, I send you a copy of a communication to him from the Secretary of War, dated June 18, 1846, in which is the following: "These troops, and such as may be organized in California, will be under your command." The general directs that no change will be made in the organization of your battalion of volunteers or officers appointed in it, without his sanction or approval being first obtained.

Very respectfully,

WM. H. EMORY,
Lieut. and acting Ass't Adjutant General.

To Lieut. Col. J. C. FRÉMONT,
Mounted Riflemen, comm'g batt. California Volunteers.

—and having received with this order a copy of instructions from the War Department to General Kearny, in the following words, to wit:

WAR DEPARTMENT,
Washington, June 18, 1846.

SIR: *   *   ɔ   *   *   *   *   *

I have nothing of importance to add to the despatches which have already been forwarded to you. Since my last letter, it has been determined to send a small force round Cape Horn to California.

The arms, cannon, and provisions, to be sent to the Pacific, will be accompanied by one company of artillery of the regular army. Arrangements are now on foot to send a regiment of volunteers by sea.

These troops, and such as may be organized in California, will be under your command. More than common solicitude will be felt here in regard to the expedition committed to you, and it is desired that you should avail yourself of all occasions to inform the government of your progress and prospects. The President desires your opinion, as early as you are in a situation to give it, of the practicability of your reaching California in the course of this autumn, or in the early part of next winter. I need not repeat the expression of his wishes that you should take military possession of that country, as soon as it can be safely done.

I am, with great respect, your obedient servant,

W. L. MARCY,
Secretary of War.

To Colonel S. W. KEARNY.

—did reply to General Kearny and his order aforesaid, in a written answer, in the following words, to wit:

CIUDAD DE LOS ANGELES,
January 17, 1847.

SIR: I have the honor to be in receipt of your favor of last night, in which I am directed to suspend the execution of orders which, in my capacity of military commandant of this territory, I had received from Commodore Stockton, governor and commander-in-chief in California.

I avail myself of an early hour this morning to make such a reply as the brief time allowed for reflection will enable me.

I found Commodore Stockton in possession of the country, exercising the functions of military commandant and civil governor, as early as July of last year; and shortly thereafter I received from him the commission of military commandant, the duties of which I immediately entered upon, and have continued to exercise to the present moment. I found also, on my arrival at this place, some three or four days since, Commodore Stockton still exercising the functions of civil and military governor, with the same apparent deference to his rank on the part of all officers (including yourself) as he maintained and required when he assumed in July last.

I learned also, in conversation with you, that on the march from San Diego recently to this place, you entered upon and discharged duties, implying an acknowledgment, on your part, of supremacy to Commodore Stockton.

I feel, therefore, with great deference to your professional and personal character, constrained to say, that, until you and Commodore Stockton adjust between yourselves the question of rank, where, I respectfully think, the difficulty belongs, I shall have to report and receive orders, as heretofore, from the commodore.

With considerations of high regard, I am, sir, your obedient servant,

J. C. FRÉMONT,
Lt. Col. U. S. army and mil. com. of the ter. of California.

To Brigadier General S. W. KEARNY,
United States army.

—and did thereby refuse to obey the aforesaid lawful command of his superior officer, Brigadier General Kearny, and did thereby refuse to receive and obey any other order from him. This at Ciudad de los Angeles, on the seventeenth of January, eighteen hundred and forty-seven, notwithstanding he had, on the thirteenth of January, eighteen hundred and forty-seven, officially reported his battalion to Brigadier General Kearny, by writing, in words following to wit:

ON THE MARCH, *January* 13, 1847.

DEAR SIR: I have the honor to report to you my arrival at this place, with 400 mounted riflemen and six pieces of artillery, including among the latter two pieces lately in the possession of the Californians.

Their entire force, under the command of D. Andre Pico, have this day laid down their arms and surrendered to my command.

Very respectfully, your obedient servant,
J. C. FRÉMONT,
Lt. Col. U. S. army and mil. com. of the ter. of California.

Brigadier General S. W. KEARNY,
Commanding U. S. forces, Pueblo de los Angeles.

Specification 2.—In this, that he, Lieutenant Colonel John C. Frémont, of the regiment of mounted riflemen, United States army, being in command of a battalion of volunteers, organized in California, which were placed by the aforesaid orders of the Secretary of War, of June eighteenth, eighteen hundred and forty-six, under the command of Brigadier General Kearny, did issue an order to Captain J. K. Wilson, at Angeles, January twenty-fifth, eighteen hundred and forty-seven, in the following words, to wit:

ANGELES, *January* 25, 1847.

SIR: You are hereby authorized and directed to raise a company of men to constitute the second company of artillery in the California service, and for that purpose are detached from your present command.

You will please report the number you may be able to enlist, with as little delay as possible.

You are authorized to enlist the men for three months, and to promise them as compensation twenty-five dollars per month.

Respectfully,

J. C. FRÉMONT,
Lt. Col. commanding California forces in the U. S. service.

To Captain J. K. WILSON,
Light Artillery.

—and did thereby disobey the aforesaid lawful command of his superior officer, Brigadier General Kearny, dated January sixteenth, eighteen hundred and forty-seven.

Specification 3.—In this, that he, Lieutenant Colonel John C. Frémont, of the regiment of mounted riflemen, United States army, being in command of a battalion of mounted riflemen, organized in California for the United States service, which was placed by orders aforesaid from the Secretary of War, of June eighteenth, eighteen hundred and forty-six, under command of Brigadier General Kearny, did, at Ciudad de los Angeles, California, on the fifth day of February, eighteen hundred and forty-seven, issue an order to Louis McLean, a passed midshipman in the United States navy, in the following words, to wit:

Ciudad de los Angeles,
February 5, 1847.

Sir: I feel it my duty, as the representative of the United States government in California, to instruct you to proceed forthwith north, as far as in your discretion may seem necessary, and exercise your best efforts in enlisting troops, for the term of six months; compensation to be $— per month, to be employed in the service of the United States, and at such points in the territory of California as in my judgment they are most required.

You are furthermore instructed to proceed as far as the town of Yerba Buena, on the San Francisco bay, and examine diligently into the state of the naval or military defences of that town, and particularly to enquire into the best means of fortifying the mouth of the bay against the ingress of all enemies, and I particularly recommend to you to be forthwith commenced the erection of a fort, or battery, on White Island, calculated, when completed, to prevent the entrance of any ship or vessel that may be forbidden to do so by the said United States.

To enable you to carry into effect the foregoing instructions, you are hereby authorized and required to call on all officers under my command to extend to you any assistance of money, men, or property, that in your judgment may be necessary fully to accomplish the same.

In witness whereof, I have hereunto set my hand, and affixed my seal, at the capital of California, this date before written.

J. C. FRÉMONT,
Governor of California.

Attest:
Wm. H. Russell,
 Secretary of State.

To Major Louis McLane,
 United States army, California regiment.

—and did thereby disobey the aforesaid lawful command of his superior officer, Brigadier General Kearny, dated January sixteenth, eighteen hundred and forty-seven.

Specification 4.—In this, that he, Lieutenant Colonel John C. Frémont, of the regiment of mounted riflemen, United States army, being in command of a battalion of volunteers, organized in California for the United States service, which, by aforesaid orders from the War Department, dated June eighteenth, eighteen hundred and forty-six, were placed under command of Brigadier General Kearny, and having been officially informed by W. Branford Shubrick, as commander-in-chief of the naval forces in the Pacific, in a letter, dated U. S. ship Independence, Monterey, February twenty-third, eighteen hundred and forty-seven, in the following words, to wit:

General Kearny, I am instructed, "is the commanding military officer in California, and invested by the President with the administrative functions of government over the people and territory," and having received on the eleventh of March, eighteen hundred and forty-seven, from General Kearny, by the hands of Captain H. S. Turner, U. S. army, a circular proclamation, in the following words, to wit:

Circular.

To all whom it may concern, be it known :

That the President of the United States, desirous to give and secure to the people of California a share of the good and happy civil organization enjoyed by the people of the United States, and to protect them at the same time from the attacks of foreign foes and from internal commotions, has invested the undersigned with separate and distinct powers, civil and military; and a cordial cöoperation in the exercise of which it is hoped and believed, will have the happy results desired.

To the commander-in-chief of the naval forces the President has assigned the regulation of the import trade, the conditions on which vessels of all nations, our own as well as foreign, may be admitted into the ports of the territory, and the establishment of all port regulations.

To the commanding military officer the President has assigned the direction of the operations on land, and has invested him with administration functions of government over the people and territory occupied by the forces of the United States.

Done at Monterey, capital of California, this first day of March, A. D., 1847.

W. BRANFORD SHUBRICK,
Commander-in-chief of the naval forces.
S. W. KEARNY,
Brig. Gen., U. S. A., and Governor of California.

—and having at the same time, on the eleventh of March, 1847, received from Brigadier General Kearny, by the hands of Captain H. S. Turner, the following order, in terms, to wit:

ORDERS, } HEAD-QUARTERS, 10TH MILITARY DEPARTMENT,
No. 2. }   *Monterey, March 1, 1847.*

1. With a view to regular payment, it is necessary that the

battalion of California volunteers, now under the command of
Lieutenant Colonel Frémont, of the army, and stationed at the
Ciudad de los Angeles, if not originally mustered under the law
of May 13, and the supplemental law of June 18, 1846, should
now be mustered into the service under those laws. This muster
will be made at once by Lieutenant Colonel Frémont; should any
of the men of that battalion be unwilling to continue in service
under the above named laws, they will be conducted by Lieutenant
Colonel Frémont to Yerba Buena via Monterey, and be there
discharged.

3. Lieutenant Colonel P. St. G. Cooke, now in command of the
Mormon battalion, is entrusted with the supervision of the southern
military district, for the protection and defence of which he will
make the necessary provision, posting his command (to consist of
company C, 1st dragoons, the Mormon battalion, and the California volunteers) at such places as he may deem most eligible.

By order of Brigadier General S. W. Kearny.
H. S. TURNER,
Captain A. A. A. General.

—did, at Ciudad de los Angeles, on the fifteenth day of March,
1847, issue orders to Captain Richard Owens, in the words following, to wit :

CIUDAD DE LOS ANGELES,
March 15, 1847.

SIR : In the performance of a portion of my official duties, it
becomes necessary that I should visit in person the northern district of the territory, where I shall probably be detained some
fifteen or twenty days, and the better to possess you of my views
in my absence and to render your authority in the meantime
undoubted, I have considered it proper to issue the following
orders :

1st. You will continue with the entire battalion at San Gabriel,
observing order, vigilance, and exercising as much discipline as in
your discretion can be prudently enforced.

2d. You will make no move whatever from San Gabriel in my
absence, unless to repel an actual invasion, or obey the order of
any officer that does not emanate from me.

3d. You will take the best possible care of the public arms and
munitions belonging to the command, and turn them over to no
corps without my special order.

4th. The general police of the garrison, and strict regard to no
public interests, will, of course. as commandant ad interim, constantly engage your best efforts.

Very respectfully, your obedient servant,
J. C. FRÉMONT,
Lieut. Col. U. S. A., and com'd't of California bat.
To Captain RICHARD OWENS,
Act. com'd't of California bat.

—and did, thereby, disobey the lawful command of his superior officer, Brigadier General Kearny, as conveyed by him in the aforesaid order, No. 2, of the 10th military department, by continuing in service the whole California battalion, contrary to said orders, and by ordering the battalion to remain at San Gabriel, contrary to said orders from Brigadier General Kearny to march them to Yerba Buena, notwithstanding he, Lieutenant Colonel John C. Frèmont, had officially informed Captain Turner, at Pueblo de los Angeles, on the 12th of March, 1847, that he would obey and execute the said orders of the 10th military department, dated March 1st, 1847.

Specification 5.—In this, that he, Lieutenant Colonel John C. Frémont, of the regiment of mounted riflemen, United States army, being in command of a battalion of volunteers, organized in California for the United States service, having, on the 11th of March, 1847, received the lawful order of his superior officer, Brigadier General Kearny, to wit: the aforesáid orders, No. 2, dated head-quarters, 10th military department, Monterey, March 1st, 1847, whereby he was ordered to march such part of said battalion as refused to be mustered into service to Yerba Buena, there to be discharged, did refuse to obey said order, and did make known his refusal to Lieutenant Colonel Cooke, commanding the district in which his battalion was serving, by a written communication in terms, to wit:

Ciudad de los Angeles,
March 16, 1847.

Sir: I am instructed by Governor Frémont to acknowledge, a few moments since, the receipt of your communication of the 14th instant, and to say in reply, that the volunteers constituting the California battalion decline, without an individual exception, to be mustered into the United States service, conformable to order, No. 2, of the 10th military department referred to by you.

The governor considers it unsafe at this time, when rumor is rife with a threatened insurrection, to discharge the battalion, and will decline doing so, and, whilst they remain in service, he regards his force quite sufficient for the protection of the artillery and ordnance stores at the mission of San Gabriel.

I am, with consideration of respect, your obedient servant,

WM. H. RUSSELL,
Secretary of State.

To P. St. G. Cooke,
   Lieut. Col. comd'g mission, San Luis regiment.

Specification 6.—In this, that he, Lieutenant Colonel John C. Frémont of the regiment of mounted riflemen, United States army, after he had been duly informed by his superior officer, Brigadier General Kearny, that he, Brigadier General Kearny, had been invested by the President of the United States with the command of the troops in California, by exhibiting to him, Lieutenant

Colonel John C. Frémont, on the 16th of January, 1847, at Ciudad de los Angeles, the aforesaid orders from the War Department, dated June 18th, 1846, and after he had duly received, on the 16th of January, 1847, the aforesaid lawful command of his superior officer, Brigadier General Kearny, on that day to make no changes in the organization of his battalion or officers appointed in it, except with the approval of said Brigadier General Kearny, did, notwithstanding, disobey said lawful command of his superior officer, by accepting, in a general order published at Angeles on the 13th of February, 1847, the resignations of the following commissioned officers of the California battalion of volunteers, to wit: Captains H. L. Ford, Samuel Gibson, and Wm. Findlay, and Lieutenants W. Baldridge, Rhenshaw, W. Blackburn, J. Scott, J. R. Barton, and J. M. Hudspeth.

Specification 7.—In this, that he, Lieutenant Colonel John C. Frémont, of the regiment of mounted riflemen, United States army, did fail to obey the orders of Brigadier General Kearny, to repair to Monterey, as communicated to him verbally by said Brigadier General Kearny, on the 26th of March, 1847, and repeated to him in writing on the 28th of March, 1847, in words following, to wit:

HEAD-QUARTERS, 10TH MILITARY DEPARTMENT,
Monterey, California, March 28, 1847.

SIR : This will be handed to you by Colonel Mason, 1st dragoons, who goes to the southern district, clothed by me with full authority to give such orders and instructions upon all matters, both civil and military, in that section of country, as he may deem proper and necessary. Any instructions he may give to you will be considered as coming from myself.

I deem it proper to suggest to you that should there be at the Puebla any unsettled accounts or demands against the government, incurred by your orders or approval, which you may not have already authenticated and completed for the action of the disbursing officers, that you at once do so, as it may be necessary for you to proceed from here to Washington city; and should there be any of the party which accompanied you from Missouri still with you, and under pay from the topographical department, you will cause them to come to this place, that they may be returned home and discharged, and be of no further expense to the United States, unless they prefer being discharged at once in the country.

In twelve days after you have embarked the volunteers at San Pedro I desire to see you in this place.

Very respectfully, your obedient servant,
S. W. KEARNY,
Brigadier General, and Governor of California.
Lieutenant Colonel J. C. FREMONT,
Regiment of mounted riflemen, com'd'g battalion
California volunteers, Ciudad de los Angeles.

—but did remain at the Ciudad de los Angeles until after the arrival there of Brigadier General Kearny, on the ninth of May, 1847, and till the order was then and there verbally repeated to him.

Charge 3.—Conduct to the prejudice of good order and military discipline.

Specification 1.—In this, that he, Lieutenant Colonel John C. Frémont, of the regiment of mounted riflemen, United States army, being in command of a battalion, organized in California for the United States service, and placed by orders aforesaid from the Secretary of War, of June 18, 1846, under command of Brigadier General Kearny, did, at Ciudad de los Angeles, California, on the 7th of February, 1847, write to Commodore Shubrick, commanding the United States naval forces in the Pacific, a letter, in words as hereinbefore recited in the fourth specification to the first charge, thereby officially informing said naval commander that he had refused to acknowledge the lawful authority of his superior officer, Brigadier General Kearny, and endeavoring to persuade said naval commander to support and countenance him therein. This to the prejudice of good order and military discipline.

Specification 2.—In this, that he, Lieutenant Colonel John C. Frémont, of the regiment of mounted riflemen, United States army, being in command of a battalion of volunteers, organized in California for the United States service, and placed under command of Brigadier General Kearny, by aforesaid orders from the War Department, dated June 18, 1846, did, at Angeles, on the 11th of February, 1847, write to W. P. Hall, in words as hereinbefore recited in the fifth specification to the first charge, thereby avowing his resistance of the authority of his superior officer, Brigadier General Kearny, and endeavoring to prevent said Hall from supporting the lawful authority of Brigadier General Kearny. This to the prejudice of good order and military discipline.

Specification 3.—In this, that he, Lieutanant Colonel John C. Frémont, of the regiment of mounted riflemen, United States army, did, at Ciudad de los Angeles, on the 2d of March, 1847, in contempt of the lawful authority of his superior officer, Brigadier General Kearny, assume to be, and to act as, governor of California, in executing a deed or instrument of writing, in words as hereinbefore recited in the sixth specification to the first charge, thereby assuming and exercising the functions and authority of his superior officer, Brigadier General Kearny, to the prejudice of good order and military discipline.

Specification 4.—In this, that he, Lieutenant Colonel John C. Frémont, of the regiment of mounted riflemen, United States army, being in command of a battalion of volunteers, organized in California for the United States service, which, by aforesaid orders from the War Department, dated June eighteenth, eighteen hundred and forty-six, were placed under command of Brigadier General Kearny, and having been officially informed by W. Branford Shubrick, as commander-in-chief of the naval forces in the Pacific, in a letter, dated United States ship Independence, Monterey, February twenty-third, eighteen hundred and forty-seven, in the following words, to wit:

" General Kearny, I am instructed, is the commanding military officer in California, and invested, by the President, with the administrative functions of government over the people and territory;" and having received, on the eleventh of march, eighteen hundred and forty-seven, from General Kearny, by the hands of Captain H. S. Turner, United States army, a circular proclamation in words as hereinbefore recited in the seventh specification to the first charge, did, notwithstanding, at Ciudad de los Angeles, on the fifteenth day of March, eighteen hundred and forty-seven, issue written orders to Captain Richard Owens, of the California battalion, in words as hereinbefore recited in the seventh specification to the first charge, thereby ordering said Owens not to obey the orders of any officer but himself; this to the prejudice of good order and military discipline.

Specification 5.—In this, that he, Lieutenant Colonel John C. Frémont, of the regiment of mounted riflemen, United States army, after he had been duly informed by his superior officer, Brigadier General Kearny, that he, General Kearny, had been invested, by the President of the United States, with the command of the troops in California, by exhibiting to him, Lieutenant Colonel John C. Frémont, on the sixteenth of January, eighteen hundred and forty-seven, at Ciudad de los Angeles, the aforesaid orders from the War Department, dated June eighteenth, eighteen hundred and forty-six, did, notwithstanding, disregard the lawful authority of said superior officer, and did himself usurp and exercise the functions of said superior officer in the several official acts and matters, to wit: as hereinbefore recited in the tenth specification to the first charge; that is to say, in ordering a general court martial at Ciudad de los Angeles, on the twenty-fourth of January, eighteen hundred and forty-seven; and in approving, at Ciudad de los Angeles, on the twenty-seventh of January, eighteen hundred and forty-seven, the proceedings of the court; and in accepting, at Angeles, on the thirteenth of February, eighteen hundred and forty-seven, the resignations of officers in the California battalion; all this being in usurpation of the functions and authority of his superior officer, Brigadier General Kearny, and to the prejudice of order and military discipline; to which charges and specifications Lieutenant Colonel Frémont pleaded not guilty.

The president of the court then stated that application had been made to admit reporters into the court room to report the daily proceedings of the court for publication, and Lieutenant Colonel Frémont presented to the court a written paper, as follows:

" MR. PRESIDENT: So far as a prohibition to publish the proceedings of the court is intended for the benefit of the accused, I do hereby renounce and waive all such benefit, and agree to the publication of everything."

Whereupon the court was cleared, and, after mature deliberation, the following order was directed to be entered upon the record:

"Application having been made to the court to admit reporters, the court decline (while all their proceedings are open to the public, except when the court is closed for deliberation) to make any order sanctioning or approving the publication of their proceedings."

The court was then opened and this order announced by the judge advocate. The court then, at a quarter before three o'clock, adjourned to meet to-morrow morning at *ten o'clock.*

---

10 o'clock, Thursday, *November* 4, 1847.

The court met pursuant to adjournment.

Present: all the members as yesterday; the judge advocate and Lieutenant Colonel Frémont.

The proceedings of yesterday were read over. The judge advocate gave notice to all persons in court, summoned as witnesses, to retire and wait till called for.

S. W. Kearny, a brigadier general in the army of the United States, called as a witness for the prosecution, being duly sworn according to law, testified as follows:

Examined by the judge advocate.

Question. Under what commission in the army, and what instructions from the government of the United States, were you in California, from and after the 16th of January, 1847?

Answer. I was in California as a brigadier general in the army of the United States, and under instructions from the War Department of June 3d, 1846, a copy of which I now present to the court, a copy furnished me from the War Department, and certified by the chief clerk to be a true copy.

Here General Kearny handed a paper to the judge advocate, which was read in evidence, with consent of Lieutenant Colonel Frémont, as follows:

[Confidential.]

War Department,
Washington, June 3, 1846.

Sir: I herewith send you a copy of my letter to the governor of Missouri for an additional force of one thousand mounted men.

The object of thus adding to the force under your command is not, as you will perceive, fully set forth in that letter, for the reason that it is deemed prudent that it should not, at this time, become a matter of public notoriety; but to you it is proper and necessary that it should be stated.

It has been decided by the President to be of the greatest importance, in the pending War with Mexico, to take the earliest possession of Upper California. An expedition with that view is hereby ordered, and you are designated to command it. To enable you to be in sufficient force to conduct it successfully, this adtional force of a thousand mounted men has been provided, to follow you in the direction of Santa Fé, to be under your orders, or the officer you may leave in command at Santa Fé.

It cannot be determined how far this additional force will be behind that designed for the Santa Fé expedition, but it will not probably be more than a few weeks. When you arrive at Santa Fé with the force already called, and shall have taken possession of it, you may find yourself in a condition to garrison it with a small part of your command, (as the additional force will soon be at that place,) and with the remainder press forward to California. In that case you will make such arrangements, as to being followed by the reinforcements before mentioned, as in your judgment may be deemed safe and prudent. I need not say to you that in case you conquer Santa Fé, (and with it will be included the department or State of New Mexico,) it will be important to provide for retaining safe possession of it. Should you deem it prudent to have still more troops for the accomplishment of the object herein designated, you will lose no time in communicating your opinion on that point, and all others connected with the enterprise, to this department. Indeed, you are hereby authorized to make a direct requisition for it upon the governor of Missouri.

It is known that a large body of Mormon emigrants are *en route* to California, for the purpose of settling in that country. You are desired to use all proper means to have a good understanding with them, to the end that the United States may have their co-operation in taking possession of, and holding that country. It has been suggested here, that many of these Mormons would willingly enter into the service of the United States, and aid us in our expedition against California. You are hereby anthorized to muster into service such as can be induced to volunteer; not, however, to a number exceeding one-third of your entire force. Should they enter the service, they will be paid as other volunteers, and you can allow them to designate, so far as it can be properly done, the persons to act as officers thereof. It is understood that a considerable number of American citizens are now settled on the Sacramento river, near Suter's establishment, called Nueva Helvetica, who are well disposed towards the United States. Should you, on your arrival in the country, find this to be the true state of things there, you are authorized to organize and receive into the service of the United States, such portion of these citizens as you may think useful to aid you to hold the possession of the country. You will in that case allow them, so far as you shall judge proper, to select their own officers. A large discretionary power is invested in you in regard to these matters, as well as to all others in relation to the expeditions confided to your command.

The choice of routes by which you will enter California will be left to your better knowledge and ample means of getting accurate information. We are assured that a southern route (called the caravan route, by which the wild horses are brought from that country into New Mexico) is practicable; and it is suggested as not improbable, that it can be passed over in the winter months, or, at least, late in autumn. It is hoped that this information may prove to be correct.

In regard to the routes, the practicability of procuring needful supplies for men and animals, and transporting baggage, is a point to be well considered. Should the President be disappointed in his cherished hope that you will be able to reach the interior of Upper California before winter, you are then desired to make the best arrangement you can for sustaining your forces during the winter and for an early movement in the spring. Though it is very desirable that the expedition should reach California this season, (and the President does not doubt you will make every possible effort to accomplish this object,) yet if, in your judgment, it cannot be undertaken with a reasonable prospect of success, you will defer it, as above suggested, until spring. You are left unembarrassed by any specific directions in this matter.

It is expected that the naval forces of the United States which are now, or will soon be in the Pacific, will be in possession of all the towns on the sea coast, and will co-operate with you in the conquest of California. Arms, ordnance, munitions of war, and provisions, to be used in that country, will be sent by sea to our squadron in the Pacific for the use of the land forces.

Should you conquer and take possession of New Mexico and Upper California, or considerable places in either, you will establish temporary civil governments therein; abolishing all arbitrary restrictions that may exist, so far as it may be done with safety. In performing this duty, it would be wise and prudent to continue in their employment all such of the existing officers as are known to be friendly to the United States, and will take the oath of allegiance to them. The duties at the custom-houses ought at once to be reduced to such a rate as may be barely sufficient to maintain the necessary officers, without yielding any revenue to the government.

You may assure the people of those provinces that it is the wish and design of the United States to provide for them a free government, with the least possible delay, similar to that which exists in our territories. They will then be called on to exercise the rights of freemen in electing their own representatives to the territorial legislature. It is foreseen that what relates to the civil government will be a difficult and unpleasant part of your duty, and much must necessarily be left to your own discretion.

In your whole conduct you will act in such a manner as best to conciliate the inhabitants, and render them friendly to the United States.

It is desirable that the usual trade between the citizens of the United States and the Mexican provinces should be continued, as far as practicable, under the changed condition of things between the two countries. In consequence of extending your expedition into California, it may be proper that you should increase your supply for goods to be distributed as presents to the Indians. The United States Superintendent of Indian Affairs at St. Louis will aid you in procuring these goods. You will be furnished with a proclamation in the Spanish language, to be issued by you, and circulated among the Mexican people, on your entering into or approaching their country.

You will use your utmost endeavors to have the pledges and promises therein contained carried out to the utmost extent.

I am directed by the President to say, that the rank of Brevet Brigadier General will be conferred on you as soon as you commence your movement towards California, and sent round to you by sea, or over the country, or to the care of the commandant of our squadron in the Pacific. In that way cannon, arms, ammunition and supplies for the land forces will be sent to you.

Very respectfully, your obedient servant,
              W. L. MARCY,
                        Secretary of War.

Colonel S. W. KEARNY,
        Fort Leavenworth, Missouri.

                    WAR DEPARTMENT,
                        November 1, 1847.

I hereby certify that the foregoing is a true copy from the records of the War Department.
              ARCHIBALD CAMPBELL,
                        Chief Clerk.

General Kearny resumed his testimony as follows:

I also present an original paper, being orders to me from the War Department, dated June 18, 1846. The paper was here received by the judge advocate and read in evidence, as follows :

                    WAR DEPARTMENT,
                Washington, June 18, 1846.

SIR: By direction of the President, I have given to the bearer hereof, Colonel James W. Magaffin, a letter of introduction to you, and trust you will derive advantage from his knowledge of the country in which you are to carry on military operations, and the assistance he may afford in securing supplies, &c.

I have nothing of importance to add to the despatches which have been already forwarded to you. Since my last letter it has been determined to send a small force round Cape Horn to California. The arms, cannon, and provisions, to be sent to the Pacific, will be accompanied by one company of artillery of the regular army. Arrangements are now on foot to send a regiment of volunteers by sea. These troops, and such as may be organized in California, will be under your command.

More than common solicitude will be felt here in regard to the expedition committed to you, and it is desired that you should avail yourself of all occasions to inform the government of your progress and prospects. The President desires your opinion, as early as you are in a situation to give it, of the practicability of your reaching California in the course of this autumn, or in the early part of next winter. I need not repeat the expression of his wishes that you should take military possession of that country as soon as it can be safely done.

I am, with great respect, your obedient servant,

WM. L. MARCY,
Secretary of War.

To Colonel S. W. KEARNY.

General Kearny resumed his testimony as follows:

I had a letter of instructions from the general-in-chief. I have it not with me and do not remember its date.

The Judge advocate, by consent, exhibited to General Kearny, a letter in the printed documents of the 2d session of the 29th Congress, signed by General Scott and addressed to Colonel S. W. Kearny, which General Kearny believed to be a true copy of the letter referred to by him. It was accordingly read to the court, but being found to contain nothing material or additional to the orders and instructions hereinbefore recorded, it was ordered by the court that it need not be entered on this record, or offered in evidence—this on the suggestion of the judge advocate, by consent of Lieutenant Colonel Frémont.

General Kearny resumed his testimony as follows:

I recollect no other instruction, besides these mentioned, that I carried with me to California, or that I had with me at the time referred to in your question.

Question. Did you exhibit these instructions, authorizing you to take the chief command in California, or any part of them, to Lieutenant Colonel Frémont?

Answer. The letter of June 3d, from the Secretary of War, was not exhibited by me to Lieutenant Colonel Frémont. But I informed him of the contents of it. An extract from the letter of June 18th, from the Secretary of War, was by my orders furnished to him by Lieutenant Emory.

Question. What orders did you give Lieutenant Colonel Frémont in reference to his coming to Monterey?

Answer. On the 1st of March, 1847, I was at Monterey, and there issued 10th military department orders, No. 2, which I sent to Lieutenant Colonel Frémont, and with it a letter of the same date, of which this is a copy. Colonel Frémont must have the original, unless he has destroyed it. I submit also a copy of the 10th military department orders, No. 2, which were received by Colonel Frémont:

These two papers, offered in evidence by General Kearny, and admitted by Lieutenant Colonel Frémont, were then read as follows:

HEAD-QUARTERS, 10TH MILITARY DEPARTMENT,
Monterey, (U. C.,) March 1, 1847.

SIR: By department orders, No. 2, of this date, (which will be handed to you by Captain Turner, 1st dragoons, A. A. A. G. for my command,) you will see that certain duties are there required of you as commander of the battalion of California volunteers.

In addition to the duties above referred to, I have now to direct that you will bring with you, and with as little delay as possible, all the archives and public documents and papers which may be subject to your control, and which appertain to the government of California, that I may receive them from your hands at this place, the capital of the territory.

I have directions from the general-in-chief not to detain you in this country against your wishes a moment longer than the necessities of the service may require; and you will be at liberty to leave here after you have complied with these instructions, and those in the order referred to.

Very respectfully, your obedient servant,
S. W. KEARNY,
Brig. General, and Governor of California.

Lt. Col. J. C. FRÉMONT, *Regt. of Mt. Riflemen,*
Com'g Bat. of California Vols., Ciudad de los Angeles.

ORDERS, ? HEAD-QUARTERS, 10TH MILITARY DEPARTMENT,
No. 2. $\quad$ *Monterey, March* 1, 1847

1. With a view to regular payment, it is necessary that the battalion of California volunteers, now under the command of Lieut. Colonel Frémont, of the army, and stationed at the Ciudad de los Angeles, if not originally mustered under the law of May 13th, and the supplemental law of June 18, 1846, should now be mustered into service under these laws. This muster will be made at once by Lieutenant Colonel Frémont. Should any men of that battalion be unwilling to continue in service under the above named laws, they will be conducted by Lieutenant Colonel Frémont to Yerba Buena, via Monterey, and be there discharged.

2. Lieutenant Gillespie, of the marines, now serving with the battalion of California volunteers, is relieved from that duty. He will repair to Washington city, and will report himself to the commanding officer of his corps.

3. Lieutenant Colonel P. St. G. Cooke, now in command of the Mormon battalion, is entrusted with the supervision of the southern military district, for the protection and defence of which he will make the necessary provisions, posting his command (to consist of company C, 1st dragoons, the Mormon battalion, and the California volunteers) at such places as he may deem most eligible.

4. Lieutenant Colonel Cooke will designate an officer to receive all public property which the senior naval officer, at San Diego, may be caused to be turned over.

5. Major Swords, quartermaster, and Paymaster Cloud, will repair to head-quarters, at Monterey, and report themselves to the general commanding.

By order of Brigadier General S. W. Kearny.
H. S. TURNER,
Captain, A. A. A. General.

General Kearney resumed his testimony as follows:

About the 26th of March, Lieutenant Colonel Frémont came to Monterey from Los Angeles, and calling upon me in my quarters, I had a conversation with him; the close of the conversation was a reiteration to him of my orders to him of the 1st of March, and for him to come to Monterey with the least practicable delay. Then, on the 28th of March, I addressed him a written communication, which is among the papers furnished you.

A paper was handed by the judge advocate to General Kearny, examined by him, when he resumed his testimony as follows:

It is a copy of my letter of March 28th, 1847, to Lieutenant Colonel Frémont. The original I suppose he has, if he has not destroyed it.

The following was then read as an authentic copy by the judge advocate with the consent of Lieutenant Colonel Frémont:

HEAD-QUARTERS, 10TH MILITARY DEPARTMENT,
Monterey, California, March 28, 1847.

SIR: This will be handed to you by Colonel Mason, 1st dragoons, who goes to the southern district, clothed by me with full authority to give such orders and instructions upon all matters, both civil and military, in that section of country, as he may deem proper and necessary. Any instructions he may give to you will be considered as coming from myself.

I deem it proper to suggest to you that, should there be at the Puebla any unsettled accounts or demands against the government, incurred by your orders or approval, which you may not have already authenticated and completed for the action of the disbursing officers, that you at once do so, as it may be necessary for you to proceed from here to Washington City; and, should there be any of the party which accompanied you from Missouri still with you, and under pay from the topographical department, you will cause them to come to this place, that they may be returned home and discharged, and be of no further expense to the United States, unless they prefer being discharged at once in this country.

In twelve days after you have embarked the volunteers at San Pedro I desire to see you at this place.

Very respectfully, your obedient servant,
         S. W. KEARNY,
       Brig. Gen., and Governor of California.

Lieut. Col. J. C. FREMONT,
    Reg't. of mounted riflemen,
       commanding battal'n Cal. Vols. Ciudad de los Angeles.

The judge advocate called the attention of General Kearny to the use of the word "destroyed," in his testimony, in regard to orders, &c., received by Lieutenant Colonel Frémont.

General Kearny said: I meant by no means to intimate that Colonel Frémont had designedly destroyed, or lost, papers. I meant merely, in presenting copies, to say, that the originals were received by him, and were, of course, not in my hands.

General Kearny resumed his testimony as follows: I waited in Monterey for the arrival of Lieutenant Colonel Frémont, who did not come, and in May I went to los Angeles, and there found him on my arrival at that place, on the ninth of that month. I repeated the order to him, and he left a few days afterwards in obedience to the order.

On reading over to General Kearny the foregoing testimony for correction, if erroneously recorded, he stated:

I did not understand the extent of the first question put to me, in regard to my instructions in California, as I now understand it.

I supposed it to inquire only into the orders I carried with me to California. I answered it fully in that meaning of it; but I now understand it to embrace, and call for, all the orders I received in California. I now state that I received other orders and instructions while I remained in California, besides those I have exhibited.

The judge advocate stated that the question was meant to refer to the instructions from the government, under which General Kearny was exercising command in California during the period of time referred to in the charges against Lieutenant Colonel Frémont, and during which Lieutenant Colonel Frémont is charged to have resisted his authority; and it was meant afterwards to inquire, what portion of these orders had been made known to Lieutenant Colonel Frémont.

General Kearney resumed his testimony.

Question. Have you any further answer to make to the question under that explanation of it?

Answer. No sir, I have not.

At a quarter past 12 o'clock the court took a recess of fifteen minutes.

At half past 12, court in session; all the members present, the judge advocate and Lieutenant Colonel Frémont.

General Kearny a witness—examination in chief continued:

Question. Look at this paper—is it the official order received by you establishing the 10th military department?

Answer. Yes, sir; and I received it about the 13th of February, 1847, from the hands of Colonel Mason, in California.

The following is a copy of the order, proved by the witness, here entered on the record:

GENERAL ORDERS,   HEAD-QUARTERS OF THE ARMY,
No. 49.   ADJUTANT GENERAL'S OFFICE,
          Washington, Nov. 3, 1846.

In addition to the present military geographical departments, the following are created:

Department No. 9.—So much of the Mexican province of New Mexico as has been, or may be, subjected to the arms or the authority of the United States. Head-quarters, Santa Fé.

Department No. 10.—The territory of Oregon, and so much of the Mexican provinces of the Californias as has been, or may be, subjected to the arms or the authority of the United States. Head-quarters, in the field.

By command of Major General Scott.

W. G. FREEMAN,
Assist. Adj. Gen.

Question. Is the paper handed you the original, received by you from Lieutenant Colonel Frémont?

State when and where, and under what circumstances it was presented to you by him.

Answer. It is the original. The paper here shown the witness was read in evidence, as follows:

CIUDAD DE LOS ANGELES,
January 17, 1847.

SIR: I have the honor to be in receipt of your favor of last night, in which I am directed to suspend the execution of orders which, in my capacity of military commandant of this territory, I had received from Commodore Stockton, governor and commander-in-chief in California.

I avail myself of an early hour this morning to make such a reply as the brief time allowed me for reflection will enable me.

I found Commodore Stockton in possession of the country, exercising the functions of military commandant and civil governor, as early as July of last year; and, shortly thereafter, I received from him the commission of military commandant, the duties of which I immediately entered upon, and have continued to exercise to the present moment.

I found, also, on my arrival at this place, some three or four days since, Commodore Stockton still exercising the functions of civil and military governor with the same apparent deference to his rank on the part of all officers (including yourself) as he maintained and required when he assumed in July last.

I learned, also, in conversation with you, that, on the march from San Diego, recently, to this place, you entered upon and discharged duties, implying an acknowledgment on your part, of supremacy to Commodore Stockton.

I feel myself, therefore, with great deference to your professional and personal character, constrained to say, that, until you and Commodore Stockton adjust between yourselves the question of rank, where I respectfully think the difficulty belongs, I shall have to report and receive orders, as heretofore, from the commodore.

With considerations of high regard, I am your obedient servant,

J. C. FRÉMONT,
Lt. Col. U. S. A., and military commandant
of the territory of California.

To Brig. Gen. S. W. KEARNY,
U. S. Army.

General Kearny resumed his testimony.

About the 14th of January, 1847, I received from Lieutenant Colonel Frémont a communication dated the day previous; that is, dated the 13th of January, 1846, being by mistake for 1847, which I furnished, with the charges, to the adjutant general.

A paper was here handed the witness by the judge advocate, which he stated to be the original communication to which he refers.

It was then read in evidence by the judge advocate, as follows:

On the march, *Jan.* 13, 1846.

Dear Sir: I have the honor to report to you my arrival at this place, with 400 mounted riflemen and six pieces of artillery, including, among the latter, two pieces lately in the possession of the Californians.

Their entire force, under the command of D. Andre Pico, have this day laid down their arms and surrendered to my command.

Very respectfully, your obedient servant,
J. C. FRÉMONT,
Lt. Col. U. S. A., and military commandant
of the territory of California.

Brig. Gen. S. W. Kearny,
commanding U. S. forces,
Puebla de los Angeles.

General Kearny resumed his testimony, as follows:

Upon the day of the receipt of this report of the 14th of January, Lieutenant Colonel Frémont, at the head of the battalion of volunteers, entered into the city of Los Angeles. On the 16th of January, an order was sent to him relating to his battalion, by my direction, signed by Lieutenant Emory, a copy of which I have furnished among your papers, and can identify if I see it.

A paper was here shown to the witness: He said, this is a copy of the order which I directed Lieutenant Emory to furnish to Lieutenant Colonel Frémont.

The paper here proved by the witness was then read in evidence as follows, by consent:

Head-quarters Army of the West,
Ciudad de los Angeles, January 16, 1847.

By direction of Brigadier General Kearny, I send you a copy of a communication to him from the Secretary of War, dated June 18, 1846, in which is the following: "these troops, and such as may be organized in California, will be under your command." The general directs that no change will be made in the organization of your battalion of volunteers, or officers appointed in it, without his sanction or approval being first obtained.

Very respectfully,

W. H. EMORY,
Lieut. and A. A. A. General.

To Lieut. Col. J. C. Frémont.
Mounted Riflemen, comd'g bat. California vol.

War Department,
Washington, June 18, 1846.

Sir :

*   *   *   *   *   *   *   *

I have nothing of importance to add to the despatches which have been already forwarded to you.

Since my last letter it has been determined to send a small force round Cape Horn to California.

The arms, cannon, and provisions to be sent to the Pacific, will be accompanied by one company of artillery, of the regular army; arrangements are now on foot to send a regiment of volunteers by sea.

These troops, and such as may be organized in California, will be under your command.

More than common solicitude will be felt in regard to the expedition committed to you, and it is desired that you should avail yourself of all occasions to inform the government of your progress and prospects. The President desires your opinion, as early as you are in a situation to give it, of the practicability of your reaching California in the course of this autumn, or in the early part of next winter. I need not repeat the expression of his wishes that you should take military possession of that country, as soon as it can be safely done.

I am, with great respect, your obedient servant,

W. L. MARCY,
Secretary of War

To Colonel S. W. Kearny.

General Kearny resumed his testimony, as follows :

On the day subsequent, namely, on the 17th of January, Lieutenant Colonel Frémont came to my quarters, and in conversation I asked him if he had received the communication from me of the day previous. He acknowledged the receipt of it, stated that he had written a reply and had left it with his clerk to copy. About this time a person entered the room with a paper in his hand, which Lieutenant Colonel Frémont took, overlooked, and then used a pen on my table to sign it, his clerk having told him that his signature was wanting. Having signed the paper, Colonel Frémont then handed it to me. It was his letter to me of January 17. At my request, he took a seat at my table whilst I read it.

Having finished the reading of it, I told Lieutenant Colonel Frémont, that I was a much older man than himself, that I was a much older soldier than himself, that I had great regard for his wife, and great friendship for his father-in-law, Colonel Benton, from whom I had received many acts of kindness, that these considerations induced me to volunteer advice to him, and the advice was, that he should take that letter back and destroy it, that I was willing to forget it. Lieut. Col. Frémont declined taking it back, and told me that Com. Stockton would support him in the position taken in that letter. I told him that Commodore Stockton could not support him in disobeying the orders of his senior officer, and that, if he persisted in it, he would unquestionably ruin himself. He told me that Commodore Stockton was about organizing a civil government and intended to appoint him as governor of the territory. I told him Commodore Stockton had no such authority, that authority having been conferred on me by the President' of the United States. He asked me if I would appoint him governor. I told him I expected shortly to leave California for Missouri; that I had, previous to leaving Santa Fé, asked for permission to do so, and was in hopes of receiving it; that as soon as the country was quieted I should, most probably, organize a civil government in California, and that I, at that time, knew of no objections to my appointing him as the governor. He then stated to me that he would see Commodore Stockton, and that, unless he appointed him governor at once, he would not obey his orders, and left me.

The judge advocate here finished the direct examination of General Kearny, and notified Lieutenant Colonel Frémont that he was now ready for cross-examination.

Whereupon, Lieutenant Colonel Frémont presented a written address to the court, which was read as follows :

Mr. President : Before putting any questions to the witness. and to enable the judge advocate and the court the better to understand the relevancy of the questions put, I think it best to give some idea of the general scope, or nature of my defence. This can be done, with respect to one main branch of the defence, by reading a paragraph from a paper addressed by my counsel to the War Department, asking for several orders and reports preparatory to the trial, and which paragraph is in these words :

In looking over the charges and specifications, it is seen that the imputed acts of mutiny and disobedience, and disorderly conduct, refer to a period of time when Commodore Stockton and General Kearny were contending for the supreme command in California, and when the decision of that contention was attempted to be devolved upon Lieutenant Colonel Frémont, as commander of the California battalion, by General Kearny giving him orders in contradiction of those of Commodore Stockton, which decision Lieutenant Colonel Frémont declined to make, and determined to remain as he, and the battalion were, under the command of

Commodore Stockton, until his two superiors decided their own contest. Looking upon this to be the correct answer, the undersigned feel it to be their duty to PROTEST, and do hereby PROTEST, against now trying that question in the person of Lieutenant Colonel Frémont, in a charge of mutiny and disobedience of orders, and conduct prejudicial to good order; charges going to his life and character, for not obeying the orders of General Kearny. They make this PROTEST, and reserving to Lieutenant Colonel Frémont all the benefits to be hereafter derived from it, they deem it their duty to prepare for the trial of the charges and specifications as made, (which is, in fact, the trial of Commodore Stockton, of the navy, in the person of Lieutenant Colonel Frémont, of the army,) and for that purpose they claim the benefit of all the defences which Commodore Stockton could himself demand, if personally on trial before a naval court martial.

Under this sense of duty, and with a full conviction that they cannot do justice to Commodore Stockton, (to whom, happily, a decision against him will be legally nugatory, and may be contradicted by the decision of a naval court martial, while, unhappily, it will be fatal to Colonel Frémont,) they ask to be furnished, as early as possible, with official copies of all orders to Commodore Sloat, (under whom Lieutenant Colonel Frémont first served,) also, to Commodore Stockton and Commodore Shubrick, and any other naval officers charging them with military or civil powers in California; also, with copies of all their reports in which Lieutenant Colonel Frémont, or the California battalion is mentioned, or referred to; also, copies of all communications from them, or either of them, which show the nature or extent of powers which they, the said naval commanders, actually exercised in California; also, copies of the joint proclamation of Commodore Shubrick and General Kearny, in settling the boundaries of power in California between themselves; also, a copy of General Kearny's proclamation at the same time; also, a copy of the orders to General Kearny to proceed to California; and a copy of the orders, if any, to proceed from California to Mexico; and a copy of the orders, if any, which relate to Lieutenant Colonel Frémont in or from California; and a copy of the orders, if any, by which General Kearny brought home to the United States the *topographical* party, formerly under the command of Lieutenant Colonel Frémont, when brevet captain of topographical engineers. * * *

Another branch of the defence will go to impeach the motives of the prosecutor, by showing his acts and conduct towards me during a period of six months and twenty-one days of time, and over a distance of about three thousand miles of travelling, and for that purpose to avail myself of all the rights of a cross-examination of the prosecutor and his witnesses, as well as the direct examination of my own.

This is sufficient to give a general idea of the main branches of the defence, and will enable the judge advocate and the court the better to understand the drift and relevancy of questions, and the effect of answers; and, in my opinion, will be a convenience to them.

The plea of not guilty gives no notice of the intended defence; special pleas are discouraged, and this statement is intended to give the notice which the plea of not guilty withholds.

J. C. FRÉMONT,
Lieutenant Colonel, U. S. Army.

General Kearny cross-examined by Lieutenant Colonel Frémont.

Question. At what time did you form the design to arrest Lieutenant Colonel Frémont?

Answer. I formed the design shortly after receiving his letter of January 17. That word shortly would not imply immediately. It may have been a week.

Question. At what time did you communicate that design to him, and where?

Answer. I communicated it to him at Fort Leavenworth, on the 22d of August, when I arrested him.

Question. Did you write from Monterey, in the month of May last, to Colonel Benton, to inform him of your design to arrest Lieutenant Colonel Frémont?

Answer. I did not.

Question. Or at any time?

Answer. I wrote to Colonel Benton, in the month of May, from Los Angeles, telling him that the conduct of Lieutenant Colonel Frémont had been in opposition to my orders, and those of the War Department. Delicacy prevented me from saying further to Colonel Benton on the subject. Colonel Benton must have the letter, I presume.

Question. Was Lieutenant Colonel Frémont then at Los Angeles?

Answer. He was there about that time.

Question. Did you, at the same time, give Lieutenant Colonel Frémont the same information?

Answer. I did not consider it obligatory to do so, and I did not.

Question. Will you state whether, after the commencement of your march from Santa Fé, you met an express from Commodore Stockton and Lieutenant Colonel Frémont bearing despatches for the government, and whether you received any information from that express which induced you to depart from the orders which you had received; and, if so, to what extent did you so depart from your orders?

Answer. I met an express on the Del Norte from California, sent there by Commodore Stockton and Lieutenant Colonel Frémont, on his way with despatches for Washington city. I received no information which induced me to depart from the orders which I had received.

Question. Did you turn back any of your force at that time, and countermand the march of any troops intended to follow you?

Answer. In consequence of the information received by me from the express, I left on the Del Norte, in New Mexico, 200 dragoons.

which I had previously determined to take with me to California. I can state in a few words that I started from Santa Fé for California with 300 dragoons, leaving instructions for the Mormon battalion and a mounted company of volunteers to follow me, the company was to be under the command of Captain Hudson. The battalion, and the whole, as I thought, would be under the command of Captain Allen.

Question. What amount of force did you intend to take with you before you met the express?

Answer. The 300 dragoons, and to be followed by the Mormon battalion, of which I had received no written report as to numbers, but which I presumed would average about 500 men, besides the company of volunteers, under Captain Hudson, which, I presumed, would be about 80 strong.

Question. What proportion did the force you carried on bear to the strength of the Mormon battalion, which was to follow you?

Answer. The force I carried with me was 100 dragoons. The Mormon battalion and Captain Hudson's company, I presume, would be about 550 or 580.

Question. Will you state with what object you proceeded to California after meeting the express, hearing his information, and diminishing your dragoons?

Answer. The object of my proceeding to California was to comply with the instructions which I had received from the War Department.

Question. Did the express remonstrate against being turned back, and did you insist and assert a right to order him back?

Answer. The express was Mr. Carson, who was at first very unwilling to return with me; he being desirous of proceeding to Washington, to convey letters and communications to that place, which he had received from Lieutenant Colonel Frémont and Commodore Stockton. He told me that he had pledged himself that they should be received in Washington. I at last persuaded him to return with me by telling him that I would send in his place, as the bearer of those despatches, Mr. Fitzpatrick, who was an old friend of Lieutenant Colonel Frémont, and had travelled a great deal with him. Mr. Carson, upon that, was perfectly satisfied, and told me so.

Question. Did he not also tell you that he was to carry back despatches from Washington to Commodore Stockton and Lieutenant Colonel Frémont?

Answer. He did not. He told me that they had asked him to return, but he had not consented to do so; and he has since told me that he would not have done so.

Question. At what time did the reply to the despatches, thus taken from Carson, reach California?

Answer. I know not.

Question. Will you state what part of California you were aiming to approach, and when and where you were first met by a detachment from Commodore Stockton, and where was Commodore Stockton at that time?

Answer. I was aiming to approach the lower part of Upper Cali fornia, and I was first met by a detachment from Commodore Stockton not far from what is called Warner's rancho, Agua Calienta; Commodore Stockton was at that time at San Diego.

Question. At what distance from San Diego were you when met by the detachment?

Answer. I presume somewhere about 35 miles.

Question. What was the strength and composition of that detachment, and under what orders, and for what purpose did the officer commanding it say it came?

Answer. It was a detachment of volunteers under Captain Gillespie, I believe about 20 or 30 strong. It came from Commodore Stockton to give me information of the state of affairs in that part of California.

Question. What other officer was with the detachment besides Captain Gillespie?

Answer. Midshipman Beale was with it. I recollect of none other. There was a Mr. Rousseau, whether he belonged to the navy or not I do not remember.

Question. Did the detachment continue with you on your march to San Diego?

Answer. It did.

Question. Did you have an action with the Californians before you got to San Diego?

Answer. I had.

Question. What was the force on each side, and where was the action?

Answer. The action was at San Pasqual. The force of the Californians I could not know, but I afterwards heard it amounted to about 160 men. I subsequently heard it was much larger. Our own force consisted of dragoons and volunteers, numbering, I suppose, about 80. The balance of the command was left under Major Swords to protect the baggage.

Question. Did you loose cannon in that action; and was it afterwards recovered, and by whom?

Objection being made to the question by a member of the court, the judge advocate was directed to ask Lieutenant Colonel Frémont to explain to the court the object and relevancy of the question.

It being near 3 o'clock, and to afford Lieutenant Colonel Frémont time for a written reply and explanations, the court adjourned to meet to-morrow, November 5th, at 10 o'clock.

————

FRIDAY, *November 5*, 1847—10 *o'clock.*

The court met pursuant to adjournment.

Present: All the members as yesterday; the judge advocate and Lieutenant Colonel Frémont.

The proceedings of yesterday were read over. General Kearny stated that he had not fully apprehended a question put to him yesterday in regard to the instructions and orders under which he acted in California. His answer, therefore, was not complete and sufficient. He desired to correct his testimony in that respect by further evidence to-day.

The judge advocate stated, that as the correction would involve a long statement in regard to the instructions which General Kearny had received, he proposed to suspend the cross-examination, to recall General Kearny as a witness for the prosecution and resume his examination in chief, and thus afford the defence the opportunity of cross-examination hereafter, upon this and the other matters on which they are now examining at the same time; which was agreed to.

The judge advocate presented a paper to the court, as follows:

In reply to the paper presented by Lieutenant Colonel Frémont on Wednesday, wherein he waives any defence that he might make on any ground merely legal and technical, and offers to admit the authenticity of any evidence written or printed which he may believe to be authentic, but demands as a condition, that the witnesses summoned for the prosecution shall all be sworn for the prosecution, in order to his cross-examination of them, the judge advocate thinks it in place now to state, that witnesses were summoned for the prosecution whose evidence does not appear to him necessary to support any part of the charges; he does not suppose the demand made of him by the defence, in regard to those witnesses, to be according to practice or the rights of the defence. But he consents and will call witnesses on the part of the prosecution. If the cross-examination may give the defence any advantage as to the range and extent of enquiry, or any other, which the direct examination of the same witnesses, as witnesses for the defence would not, the judge advocate does not deem it his duty to withhold it, especially in view of the spirit and frankness with which Lieutenant Colonel Frémont has waived all defence merely technical and foreign from the merits. The judge advocate considers that in making this consent, he surrenders to the defence no undue advantage in regard to witnesses who are above suspicion, and before a court martial where all fees of witnesses are paid by the United States. At the same time, however, he will not propose to Lieutenant Colonel Frémont to admit any written evidence which he could not otherwise prove, so that the waiver of proof shall operate merely for the despatch of business. Beyond this, in a trial on capital charges, he does not consider it proper that the prosecution should derive any aids from the frankness of the defence. He desires, so far as depends on him, to conduct the prosecution in the same spirit.

As to an inquiry into matters which may be important in the history of California, and would render the record of this court a full report of all the late military operations in that territory, yet would have no connection with these charges, the judge advocate is compelled to say that he has no knowledge on those matters, no evidence to offer in regard to them, and can have no part in any such inquiry. Being not connected with these charges, or with the interests of the prosecution, the conduct of which has been imposed on him, he leaves it to the court to consider and judge how far they will proceed in such investigations.

He will content himself, whenever his duty appears to him to require it, with intimating to the court his opinion that the inquiry is not relevant.

Lieutenant Colonel Frémont presented the following paper to the court:

November 5.

Mr. President: The object of the question put by me and objected to, is to show that General Kearny lost a cannon at San Pasqual, and that it was recovered by me in the capitulation of Cowenga, and that recovery never reported by General Kearny to the government.

I conceive the question to be both relevant and material; relevant, because it refers to a fact supposed to have occurred to General Kearny in the military execution of his orders; and material, because if the answer to the last clause of the interrogatory, and to a succeeding question which I intended to put, should be as supposed by me, it may be a circumstance to be used in the defence, and for the court to judge of, in a future state of the proceedings.

The loss of cannon is a great grief in all armies; the recovery is a subject of exultation. The loss is often without discredit; the recovery is always with honor. They are trophies which one side is proud to take and the other to recover. The loss and recovery of these trophies is a point of honor, independent of the value of the thing, and for which brave men die. The loss is always excused and lamented; the recovery is always reported and celebrated. If, in the case supposed by the question, I recover a cannon which General Kearny lost in action, and that circumstance came to his knowledge and he never reported it to the government, that omission to report a fact so material to me, may go to show the state of his temper towards me, and be used in the defence in the impeachment of the motives and credit of the prosecutor.

The object of the question is certainly not visible to the court as it now stands, and I am willing to modify it so as to show the object, and save the court the trouble of a decision.

My counsel advise me that I have latitude in a cross-examination to bring in circumstances from any distance that bear on the case, elucidate its merits, or aid the defence, and considering, as was shown in the testimony yesterday, that my arrest was resolved on seven months before I knew it, that it was concealed from me during all that time, and only made known in the moment of its execution, on the frontiers of the United States.

That I am here on the coast of the Atlantic, to be tried for imputed offences on the coast of the Pacific, without any warning to enable me to bring a particle of testimony from that far distant theatre, while the prosecutor attends, with a train of witnesses brought by himself above three thousand miles, to testify against me; considering this, my counsel advise me that I am entitled to the widest latitude that is ever granted in a cross-examination; but I will not stretch that latitude, or give trouble to the court; and although advised by counsel that I have a right in this cross-examination either to lead the witness to the object I have in view, or to conceal it from him, yet I will in every case show the object to the court, when desired, and therefore, will at present waive an answer to the question put, and put another in the form following:

Did you lose a cannon at the action at San Pasqual, and was that cannon recovered by Lieutenant Colonel Frémont, and did you know of that recovery, and ever report it to the government?

J. C. FRÉMONT,
Lieutenant Colonel Mounted Riflemen.

Whereupon, the court was cleared for deliberation, and after mature consideration, decided to allow the question. The court also made the following order:

The court were informed in the opening of the cross-examination, that it is the design of the defence to impeach the motives of the leading prosecuting witness, and now that objection has been raised to this particular question, the court find occasion to express the opinion that it is competent for the accused to show the motives of the witness only so far as those motives afford ground to impute perjury to him as a witness, or to raise a reasonable presumption that such witness has colored his testimony against the accused; any inquiry into motives, not for this purpose, and not having an apparent tendency to discredit the witness, is not admissible.

The court would be very unwilling to assign in advance the limits to which the evidence for the defence may be carried. It is clear, however, that no evidence can be useful to the defence, or proper to be received by the court, which does not tend to disprove the charges directly, or to discredit some witness, or go in mitigation.

The court was then opened, Lieutenant Colonel Frémont present.

The judge advocate announced the decision and order made in closed session. General Kearney, a witness, called to answer to the last interrogatory proposed by Lieutenant Colonel Frémont.

The judge advocate said to him: General Kearny, the question appears to me to impute official misconduct to you in omitting, from malice, to do justice in your report, for which you would be answerable before a military court. The court permit the question to be asked; you know your privilege as a witness to object to the question.

You have heard the question; what answer do you make?

Answer. There is no question which the accused can put to me, but what I shall be most willing and most free to answer.

At the battle of San Pasqual, the dragoons, under the command of Captain Moore, had two howitzers, under the charge of a subaltern, with them; near the close of the action, after the Californians had been routed, and when they were retreating, the officer in charge of the howitzers brought them to the front, and before they could be turned round and unlimbered, so as to be fired upon the retreating enemy, the two mules before one of them became alarmed and ran off, following the enemy, and by that means the howitzer was lost to us.

In the latter end of December, an expedition was organized at San Diego, to march to Los Angeles to assist Lieutenant Colonel Frémont, and was organized in consequence, as I believe, of a paper which I addressed to Commodore Stockton, of which I now hand you an authentic copy. The paper presented by the witness was read as follows:

SAN DIEGO, *December* 22, 1846.

DEAR COMMODORE: If you can take from here a sufficient force to oppose the Californians now supposed to be near the Pueblos, and waiting for the approach of Lieutenant Colonel Frémont, I advise that you do so, and that you march with that force as early as possible in the direction of the Pueblos, by which you will either be able to form a junction with Lieutenant Colonel Frémont, or make a diversion very much in his favor.

I do not think that Lieutenant Colonel Frémont should be left unsupported to fight a battle upon which the fate of California may for a long time depend, if there are troops here to act in concert with him. Your force, as it advances, might surprise the enemy at the San Luis mission, and make prisoners of them.

I shall be happy, in such an expedition, to accompany and to give you any aid either of head or hand of which I may be capable.

Yours truly,

S. W. KEARNY, *Brig. Gen.*

Commodore R. F. STOCKTON,
    Commanding U. S. forces, San Diego

General Kearny resumed his testimony as follows:

Commodore Stockton at that time was acting as governor of California, so styling himself. He had at San Diego some two or three ships of the Pacific squadron, which he commanded.

The sailors and marines were on shore, excepting, as I supposed, a sufficient number to take care of the ships. He determined upon this expedition, and on the morning of the 29th of December the troops were paraded for the march. The troops consisted of about 500 sailors and marines, about 60 dragoons, and about 40 or 50 volunteers. Whilst on parade, Commodore Stockton called several officers together, (Captain Turner of the dragoons, and Lieutenant Minor of the navy, I knew were present, and several others.) He then remarked to them to the following purport:

"Gentlemen, General Kearny has kindly consented to take command of the troops on this expedition. You will therefore look upon him as your commander. I shall go along as governor and commander-in-chief in California." We marched towards Los Angeles, and on the 8th and on the 9th of January, Governor

Flores, with his whole California force, came out and fought us. We defeated them each day; and after the defeat of the 9th of January, the California force dispersed; Governor Flores went off to Sonora; and a small party under Don Andres Pico, which party I have never understood exceeded 50 or 60 men, went to Cowenga and entered into a capitulation with Lieutenant Colonel Frémont. The troops under my command marched into Los Angeles on the 10th of January. Lieutenant Colonel Frémont came in there with his battalion on the 14th. In the capitulation entered into by Don Andres Pico, I was officially informed by Lieutenant Colonel Frémont that he had taken two cannon from the Californians. What cannon they were, he never reported to me either by letter or by word; nor do I at this moment know, except from rumor, that one of the cannon taken by Lieutenant Colonel Frémont at the capitulation was the cannon lost at San Pasqual.

It being noticed by a member that the answer was not full in reply to every part of the question, General Kearny continued:

The report alluded to from Lieutenant Colonel Frémont in relation to the cannon is contained in his letter to me of the 13th of January. I received no other report from him on the subject, nor has he ever mentioned it to me since.

The cross-examination here rested for the present, and General Kearney was called to supply the omission made by him in his testimony of yesterday. The direct examination of him as a witness for the prosecution now resumed, by consent.

General Kearney testified as follows:

I would now state, upon hearing the proceedings of yesterday read over this morning by the judge advocate, I find that the question put to me in relation to the orders under which I was acting in California, is more comprehensive than I supposed it to be. I have now to say that I had other orders whilst in California, than those I mentioned yesterday. Among those orders is one from the general-in-chief, dated November 3, 1846, the original of which I now present to you.

The paper here handed to the judge advocate was then read in evidence as follows:

HEAD-QUARTERS OF THE ARMY,
Washington, November 3, 1846.

SIR: We have received from you many official reports, the latest dated September 16. A special acknowledgment of them, by dates, will go herewith, from the adjutant general's office.

Your march upon and conquest of New Mexico, together with the military dispositions made for holding that province, have won for you, I am authorized to say, the emphatic approbation of the Executive, by whom it is not doubted your movement upon and occupation of Upper California, will be executed with like energy, judgment and success.

You will, at Monterey, or the Bay of San Francisco, find an engineer officer (Lieutenant Hallack) and a company of United States artillery, under Captain Tompkins. It is probable that an officer of engineers, or of topographical engineers, has accompanied you from Santa Fé. Those officers, and the company of artillery, aided by other troops under your command, ought promptly to be employed in erecting and garrisoning durable defences for holding the Bays of Monterey and San Francisco, together with such other important points in the same province as you may deem it necessary to occupy. Intrenching tools, ordnance and ordnance stores went out in the ship Lexington with Captain Tompkins. Further ordnance supplies may be soon expected.

It is perceived by despatches received at the Navy Department, from the commander of the United States squadron on the coast of the Pacific, that certain volunteers were taken into service by him, from the settlers about the bays of Monterey and San Francisco, to aid him in seizing and holding that country; with a view to regular payment, it is desirable that these volunteers, if not originally mustered, should be caused by you to be regularly mustered into service, (retrospectively,) under the volunteer act of May 13, 1846, amended by an act of the following month. This may be done with the distinct understanding, that, if not earlier discharged as no longer needed, you will discharge them at any time they may signify a wish to that effect.

You will probably find certain port charges and regulations established for the harbors of the province, by the commanders of the United States squadron upon its coast.

The institution and alteration of such regulations appertain to the naval commander, who is instructed by the proper department to confer on the subject with the commander of the land forces. As established, you will in your sphere, cause those regulations to be duly respected and enforced. On the other hand the appointment of temporary collectors of the several ports appertains to the civil governor of the province, who will be, for the time, senior officer of the land forces in the country. Collectors, however, who have been already appointed by the naval commander, will not be unnecessarily changed.

As a guide to the civil governor of California, in our hands, see the letter of June the 3d, (last,) addressed to you by the Secretary of War. You will not, however, formally declare the province to be annexed. Permanent incorporation of the territory must depend on the government of the United States.

After occupying with our forces all necessary points in Upper California, and establishing a temporary civil government therein, as well as assuring yourself of its internal tranquility and the absence of any danger of re-conquest on the part of Mexico, you may charge Colonel Mason, United States 1st dragoons, the bearer of this open letter, or the land officer next in rank to your own, with your several duties, and return yourself, with a sufficient escort of troops, to St. Louis. Missouri. But the body of the United States dragoons that accompanied you to California will remain there until further orders.

It is not known what portion of the Missouri volunteers, if any, marched with you from Santa Fé for the Pacific. If any, it is necessary to provide for their return to their homes and honorable discharge, and, on the same supposition, they may serve you as a sufficient escort to Missouri.

It is known that Lieutenant Colonel Frémont, of the United States rifle regiment, was, in July last, with a party of men, in the service of the United States topographical engineers, in the neighborhood of San Francisco, on Monterey bay, engaged in joint operations against Mexico with the United States squadron on that coast. Should you find him there, it is desired that you do not detain him, against his wishes, a moment longer than the necessities of the service may require.

I need scarcely enjoin deference, and the utmost cordiality on the part of our land forces, towards those of our navy in the joint service on the distant coast of California—reciprocity may be confidently expected; and towards that end, frequent conferences between commanders of the two arms are recommended. Harmony in co-operation and success cannot but follow.

Measures have been taken to supply the disbursing officers, who have preceded and who may accompany you, with all necessary funds; of those measures you will be informed by Colonel Mason.

I remain, sir, with great respect, your most obedient servant,

WINFIELD SCOTT.

Brigadier General S. W. KEARNY,
U. S. A. Comd'g. U. S. forces, 10*th Mil. Department.*

At 1 o'clock the court adjourned, to meet to-morrow at 10 o'clock.

---

10 O'CLOCK, SATURDAY, *November* 6, 1847.

The court met pursuant to adjournment.

Present: all the members, the judge advocate, and Lieutenant Colonel Frémont.

The court being informed of the death of Captain William H. Churchill, of the army, on duty in Mexico,

Ordered, That in testimony of respect for his memory, and of their sympathy with his father, a member of this court, this court do now adjourn.

And the court adjourned to meet on Monday, the 8th instant, at 10 o'clock.

---

10 O'CLOCK, MONDAY, *November* 8, 1847

The court met pursuant to adjournment.

Present: all the members, the judge advocate, and Lieutenant Colonel Frémont.

The proceedings of Friday and Saturday were read over.

Brigadier General Kearny, a witness for the prosecution, resumed his testimony, in chief, as follows:

With the letter to me, from the general-in-chief, of November 3d, I received at the same time, by the hands of Colonel Mason, a copy of a letter to Commodore Stockton, from the Secretary of the Navy, dated November 5, 1846; a printed copy of the letter referred to by the witness was here offered by him. By consent of Lieutenant Colonel Frémont, it was read in evidence, as an authentic copy, as follows:

[Confidential.]

UNITED STATES NAVY DEPARTMENT,
Washington, November 5, 1846.

COMMODORE: Commodore Sloat has arrived in this city and delivered your letter of the 28th July, ultimo, with the copy of your address to the people of California, which accompanied it. The department is gratified that you joined the squadron before the state of the commodore's health rendered it necessary for him to relinquish his important command.

The difficulties and embarrassments of the command, without a knowledge of the proceedings of Congress on the subject of the war with Mexico, and in the absence of the instructions of the department, which followed those proceedings, are justly appreciated, and it is highly gratifying that so much has been done in anticipation of the orders which have been transmitted.

You will without doubt have received the despatches of the 15th of May last, addressed to Commodore Sloat; and I now send you for your guidance a copy of instructions to Commodore Shubrick, of the 17th of August. He sailed early in September, in the razee Independence, with orders to join the squadron with the least possible delay. On his assuming the command, you may hoist a red pendant. If you prefer you may hoist your pendant on the Savannah, and return with her and the Warren.

The existing war with Mexico has been commenced by her. Every disposition was felt and manifested by the United States government to procure redress for the injuries of which we complained, and to settle all complaints on her part in the spirit of peace and of justice, which has ever characterized our intercourse with foreign nations. That disposition still exists; and whenever the authorities of Mexico shall manifest a willingness to adjust unsettled points of controversy between the two republics, and to restore an honorable peace, they will be met in a corresponding spirit.

This consummation is not to be expected, nor is our national honor to be maintained without a vigorous prosecution of the war on our part. Without being animated by any ambitious spirit of conquest, our naval and military forces must hold the ports and territory of the enemy, of which possession has been obtained by their arms. You will, therefore, under no circumstances, voluntarily lower the flag of the United States, or relinquish the actual possession of Upper California. Of other points of the Mexican territory, which the forces under your command may occupy, you will maintain the possession, or withdraw, as in your judgment may be most advantageous in prosecution of the war.

In regard to your intercourse with the inhabitants of the country, your views are judicious, and you will conform to the instructions heretofore given. You will exercise the rights of a belligerent, and if you find that the liberal policy of our government, in purchasing and paying for required supplies, is misunderstood, and its exercise is injurious to the public interest, you are at liberty to take them from the enemy without compensation, or pay such prices as may be deemed just and reasonable. The best policy in this respect depends on a knowledge of circumstances in which you are placed, and is left to your discretion.

The Secretary of War has ordered Colonel R. B. Mason, first United States dragoons, to proceed to California, via Panama, who will command the troops and conduct the military operations in the Mexican territory bordering on the Pacific, in the absence of Brigadier General Kearny.

The commander of the naval forces will consult and co-operate with him in his command, to the same extent as if he held a higher rank in the army. In all questions of relative rank, he is to be regarded as having only the rank of colonel.

The President has deemed it best for the public interests to invest the military officer commanding with the direction of the operations on land, and with the administrative functions of government over the people and territory occupied by us. You will relinquish to Colonel Mason or to General Kearney, if the latter shall arrive before you have done so, the entire control over these matters, and turn over to him all papers necessary to the performance of his duties.

If officers of the navy are employed in the performance of civil or military duties, you will withdraw or continue them at your discretion, taking care to put them to their appropriate duty in the squadron, if the army officer commanding does not wish their services on land.

The establishment of port regulations is a subject over which it is deemed, by the President, most appropriate that the naval commander shall exercise jurisdiction. You will establish these and communicate them to the military commander, who will carry them into effect, so far as his co-operation may be necessary, suggesting, for your consideration, modifications or alterations.

The regulations of import trade is also confided to you. The conditions under which vessels of our own citizens, and of neutrals, may be admitted into ports of the enemy, in your possession, will be prescribed by you, subject to the instructions heretofore given. To aid you, copies of instructions to the collectors in the United States, from the Treasury Department, on the same subject, are inclosed. On cargoes of neutrals, imported into such ports, you may impose moderate duties, not greater in amount than those collected in the ports of the United States. The collection of these duties will be made by civil officers, to be appointed, and subject to the same rules as other persons charged with civil duties in the country. These appointments will be made by the military officers, on consultation with you.

The President directs me to impress most earnestly on the naval officers, as it is impressed on those of the army, the importance of harmony in the performance of their delicate duties while co-operating. They are arms of one body, and will, I doubt not, vie with each other in showing which can render the most efficient aid to the other in the execution of common orders, and in sustaining the national honor, which is confided to both.

You will make your communications to the department as frequent as possible.

The great distance at which your command is placed, and the impossibility of maintaining a frequent or regular communication with you, necessarily induce the department to leave much of the details of your operations to your discretion.

The confident belief is entertained that, with the general outline given in the instructions, you will pursue a course which will make the enemy sensible of our powers to inflict on them the evils of war, while it will secure to the United States, if a definitive treaty of peace shall give us California, a population impressed with our justice, grateful for our clemency, and prepared to love our institutions and to honor our flag.

On your being relieved in the command of the squadron, you will hand your instructions to the officer relieving you.

I am, very respectfully, your obedient servant,
J. Y. MASON.

Commodore R. F. STOCKTON,
Commanding U. S. naval forces on the west coast of Mexico.

General Kearny.—Continued.

I received, at the same time, an extract from the army regulations, as to the relative rank between army and navy officers; that regulation is in the edition of 1825. Those papers I received from Colonel Morgan, about the 13th of February, 1847.

By consent of Lieutenant Colonel Fremont, a printed copy of the regulation referred to by the witness was here read in evidence, as follows:

Article 6. Relative rank and precedence of land and sea officers: 24. The military officers of the land and sea services of the United States shall rank together as follows: 1st. A lieutenant of the navy with captains of the army; 2d. a master commandant with majors; 3d. a captain of the navy, from the date of his commission, with lieutenant colonels; 4th. five years thereafter, with colonels; 5th. ten years thereafter, with brigadier generals, and 6th. fifteen years after the date of his commission, with major generals. But should there be created in the navy the rank of rear admiral, then such rank only shall be considered equal to that of major general.

25. Nothing in the preceding paragraph shall authorize a land officer to command any United States vessel, or navy yard; nor any sea officer to command any part of the army on land; neither shall

an officer of the one service have a right to *demand* any compliment, on the score of rank, from an officer of the other service.

26. Land troops, *serving* on board of a United States vessel as marines, shall be subject to the orders of the sea officers in command thereof. Other land troops, embarked on board such vessels for transportation merely, will be considered, in respect to the naval commanders, as passengers; subject, nevertheless, to the internal regulations of the vessels.

General Kearny continued his testimony:

Upon the arrival in California of Colonel Stevenson, of the New York regiment, early in March, I received from him a communication to me from the War Department, of September 12, 1846.

A printed copy of the communication, here referred to by the witness, was, by consent of Lieutenant Colonel Frémont, then read in evidence by the judge advocate, as follows:

WAR DEPARTMENT,
Washington, September 12, 1846.

SIR: A volunteer regiment, raised in the State of New York, engaged to serve during the war with Mexico, and to be discharged wherever they may be at its termination, if in a territory of the United States, has been mustered into the service, and is about to embark at the port of New York for California. This force is to be a part of your command; but as it may reach the place of its destination before you are in a condition to subject it to your orders, the colonel of the regiment, J. D. Stevenson, has been furnished with instructions for his conduct in the mean time.

I herewith send you a copy thereof, as well as a copy of the instructions of the Navy Department to the commander of the naval squadron in the Pacific; a copy of a letter to General Taylor, with a circular from the Treasury Department; a copy of a letter from General Scott to Captain Tompkins; and a copy of general regulations, relative to the respective rank of naval and army officers. These, so far as applicable, will be looked upon in the light of instructions to yourself. The department is exceedingly desirous to be furnished by you with full information of your progress and proceedings, together with your opinion and views as to your movements into California, having reference as to time, route, &c., &c.

Beyond the regiment under the command of Colonel S. Price, and the separate battalion called for at the time by the President from the governor of Missouri, a requisition for one regiment of infantry was issued on the 18th of July last, but the information subsequently received here, induced the belief that it would not be needed; and the difficulty of passing it over the route, at so late a period in the season, with the requisite quantity of supplies, &c., was deemed so great that the orders to muster into service have been countermanded. It will not be sent. Your views as to the sufficiency of your force, and the practicability of sustaining a large one, &c., are desired.

I am, with great respect, your obedient servant,
W. L. MARCY,
Secretary of War.

General S. W. KEARNY,
Fort Leavenworth, Missouri.

General Kearny continued:

With that letter I received a copy of the papers alluded to in it; and it will thus be seen that I received duplicate copies of the army regulations of 1825, relating to the rank of army and navy officers. Upon the arrival of Paymaster Rich in California, about the 23d of April, I received from the War Department a letter, dated January eleventh, of which these are copies.

The papers here handed to the judge advocate by the witness, were read in evidence, by consent of Lieutenant Colonel Frémont, as follows:

WAR DEPARTMENT,
Washington, January 11, 1847.

SIR: Your communication from Santa Fé of the 22d of September, accompanied by a copy of the laws prepared for the government of New Mexico, and established in that territory, was received at this department on the 23d of November last. Soon after the meeting of Congress, the President was called on, by a resolution of the House of. Representatives, for the *orders* and instructions, issued to the officers of the army and navy by him, for the civil government of the territories which had been, or might be acquired by our arms. I herewith send you a copy of the President's message, with the documents, sent to Congress in answer to that resolution.

By this you will learn the President's views as to the power and authority to be exercised in the territories conquered and occupied by our forces.

These views are presented more in detail in instructions prepared under his directions by the Secretary of the Navy, bearing date this day, an extract of which is herewith transmitted for your information, and particularly for the guidance of your conduct. This document is so full and clear on all points, in regard to which you may desire the directions of the government, that I do not deem it necessary to enlarge upon it. It is proper to remark that the provisions of the laws which have been established for the government of the territory in New Mexico, are in some few respects beyond the line designated by the President, and propose to confer upon the people of the territory political rights under the constitution of the United States. Such rights can only be acquired by the action of Congress. So far as the code of laws established in New Mexico by your authority, attempts to confer such rights, it is not approved by the President, and he directs me to instruct you not to carry such parts into effect.

Under the law of nations, the power conquering a territory or country has a right to establish a civil government within the same, as a means of securing the conquest, or with a view to protecting the persons and property of the people, and it is not intended to limit you in the full exercise of this authority. Indeed, it is desired you should exercise it in such a manner as to inspire confidence in the people that our power is to be firmly sustained in that country. The territory in our military occupation, acquired from the enemy by our arms, cannot be regarded, the war still continuing, as permanently annexed to the United States, though our authority to exercise civil government over it is not by that circumstance the least restricted.

It is important that the extent and character of our possession in the territories conquered from the enemy should not be open to question or cavil. This remark, though having reference to all our acquisitions, is in an especial manner applicable to the Californias.

As to upper California, it is presumed no doubt can arise, but it may not be so clear as to lower California. It is expected that our flag will be hoisted in that part of the country, and actual possession taken, and continuously held, of some place or places in it, and our civil jurisdiction there asserted and upheld.

A copy of this communication will be sent to the commanding officer at Santa Fé, with instructions to conform his conduct to the views herein presented.

Very respectfully, your obedient servant,
W. L. MARCY,
Secretary of War.

Brigadier General STEPHEN W. KEARNY,
Commanding U. S. army in California, Mexico.

The foregoing is a true copy from the records.
A. CAMPBELL,
Chief Clerk.

WAR DEPARTMENT, *November* 5, 1847.

Extract of a despatch to Commodore Stockton.

NAVY DEPARTMENT, *January* 11, 1847.

SIR: Your communications, dated at Monterey on the 18th and 19th of September, were received at the department on the 26th December, ultimo, by the hands of Mr. Norris, whose activity and intelligence in executing his orders entitle him to my thanks.

You will probably have received, before this can reach you, my despatches, which were entrusted to Lieutenant Watson, of the United States navy, under date of the 5th of November, in which, as commander-in-chief of the United States naval forces in the Pacific, you are informed that the President " has deemed it best for the public interests to invest the military officer commanding with the direction of the operations on land, and with the administrative functions of government, over the people and territory occupied by us."

Accompanying this I send you copies of the President's annual message, transmitted to Congress on the 8th December, ultimo, with the accompanying documents, including the annual reports of the War and Navy Departments. I also send you a printed copy of the document, No. 19, of the House of Representatives.

You will perceive from these papers the view taken by the Executive of the measures which had been adopted by the military and naval commanders in those States of Mexico of which we have acquired possession by military conquest. I see no reason to qualify the opinion which I expressed in my report, that " your measures, in regard to the conquered territory, are believed to be warranted by the laws of war."

And, in answer to your suggestions that "a general approval, by the government of the United States, of your conduct, if they do approve, to be published in the Californian, would have a good effect," I have been directed by the President to communicate a more full statement of his views of the principles which govern the conduct of our officers in the circumstances in which you have been placed, and on which the instructions heretofore given were based.

By the constitution of the United States, the power to declare war is vested in Congress. The war with Mexico exists by her own act, and the declaration of the Congress of the United States.

It is the duty of the executive to carry on the war, with all the rights, and subject to all the duties imposed by the laws of nations; a code binding on both belligerents.

The possession of portions of the enemy's territory, acquired by justifiable acts of war, gives to us the right of government during the continuance of our possession, and imposes on us a duty to the inhabitants who are thus placed under our dominion. This right of possession, however, is temporary, unless made absolute by subsequent events. If, being in possession, a treaty of peace is made and duly ratified, on the principle of " uti possedetis," that is, that each of the belligerent parties shall enjoy the territory of which it shall be in possession at the date of the treaty, or if the surrender of the territory is not stipulated in the treaty so ratified, then the imperfect title, acquired by conquest, is made absolute, and the inhabitants, with the territory, are entitled to all the benefits of the federal constitution of the United States, to the same extent as the citizens of any other part of the Union.

The course of our government, in regard to California or other portions of the territory of Mexico, now or hereafter to be in our possession by conquest, depends on those on whom the constitution imposes the duty of making and carrying treaties into effect. Pending the war, our possession gives only such rights as the laws of nations recognise, and the government is military, performing such civil duties as are necessary to the full enjoyment of the advantages resulting from the conquest, and to the due protection of the rights of persons and of property of the inhabitants.

No political right can be conferred on the inhabitants, thus situated, emanating from the constitution of the United States.

That instrument establishes a form of government for those who are within our limits and owe voluntary allegiance to it. Unless incorporated with the assent of Congress by ratified treaty or by legislative act, as in the case of Texas, our rights over enemy's territory in our possession, are only such as the laws of war confer, and theirs no more than are derived from the same authority.

They are, therefore, entitled to no representation in the Congress of the United States.

Without anticipating what may be the terms of a treaty, which it is hoped will be entered into between the two republics, there will be no revocation of the orders given in my despatch of the 5th of November last. "That, under no circumstances, will you voluntarily lower the flag of the United States, or relinquish the actual possession of California" with all the rights which it confers.

In the discharge of the duty of government in the conquered territory during our military possession, it has not been deemed improper, or unwise, that the inhabitants should be permitted to participate in the selection of agents to make, or execute, the laws to be enforced. Such a privilege cannot fail to produce ameliorations of the despotic character of martial law, and constitute checks voluntarily and appropriately submitted to by officers of the United States, all whose instructions are based on the will of the governed.

I have regarded your measures in authorizing the election of agents, charged with making laws, or, in executing them, as founded on this principle; and, so far as they carry out the rights of temporary government under existing rights of possession, they are approved. But no offices created, or laws or regulations made to protect the rights, or perform the duties resulting from our conquests, can lawfully continue beyond the duration of the state of things which now exists, without authority of future treaty, or act of Congress.

At present it is needless, and might be injurious to the public interests to agitate the question in California as to how long those persons who have been elected, for a prescribed period of time, will have official authority.

If our right of possession become absolute, such an inquiry is needless; and, if by treaty, or otherwise, we lose the possession, those who follow us will govern the country. The President, however, anticipates no such result. On the contrary, he foresees no contingency in which the United States will ever surrender or relinquish the possession of the Californias. The number of official appointments with civil or military duties, other than those devolved on our navy and army by our own laws, should be made as small as possible, and the expenses of the local government should be kept within the limits of the revenues received in the territory, if it can be done without detriment to the public interest.

General Kearny continued:

On the 9th of May, 1847, I received a copy of a communication to me, or the commanding officer at Santa Fé, from the War Department, dated December 10, 1846; that order was not applicable to me in California, and I have not a copy of it.

I believe I have now fully answered the question proposed to me.

Question. The instructions to you from the War Department, dated September 12, 1846, already offered by you to the court, referred to other orders and instructions enclosed therein, some of which have not been placed before the court. Do they contain anything material or additional to those you have already produced, which would make them proper to be offered in this place, and in answer to the question to which your evidence has been given. If so, will you produce them?

Answer. Not to my knowledge. I believe I have stated them all.

Question. Did you receive any official communication of the orders of government to the naval commanders in the Pacific, before the time when you received, by the hands of Colonel Mason, as stated in your testimony, a copy of the instructions to Commodore Stockton, dated November 5, 1846?

Answer. I have no recollection of receiving any; but I saw a communication from the Navy Department to Commodore Sloat, of July 12, 1846, which was brought by Commodore Shubrick to California, where he arrived about the latter end of January, and which he told me he had received from the captain of the Lexington, at Valparaiso, which communication had been sent from the United States by that vessel.

These instructions Commodore Shubrick showed to me about the 10th of February, 1847. In that communication was a paragraph directing that it should be shown to me.

The despatch here referred to by witness was then read in evidence, from a printed copy, by consent of Lieutenant Colonel Frémont, as follows:

UNITED STATES NAVY DEPARTMENT,
Washington, July 12, 1846.

COMMODORE: Previous instructions have informed you of the intention of this government, pending the war with Mexico, to take and hold possession of California; for this end, a company of artillery, with cannon, mortars, and munitions of war, is sent to you in the Lexington, for the purpose of co-operating with you according to the best of your judgment, and of occupying, under your directions, such post or posts as you may deem expedient in the Bay of Monterey, or in the Bay of San Francisco, or in both. In the absence of a military officer higher than captain, the selection of the first American post or posts on the waters of the Pacific, in California, is left to your discretion.

The object of the United States is, under its rights as a belligerent nation, to possess itself entirely of Upper California.

When San Francisco and Monterey are secured, you will, if possible, send a small vessel of war to take and hold possession of the port of San Diego; and it would be well to ascertain the views of the inhabitants of the Puebla de los Angeles, who, according to information received here, may be counted upon as desirous of coming under the jurisdiction of the United States.

If you can take possession of it, you should do so. The object of the United States has reference to ultimate peace with Mexico; and if, at that peace, the basis of the *uti possedetis* shall be established, the government expects, through your forces, to be found in actual possession of Upper California.

This will bring with it the necessity of a civil administration. Such a government should be established, under your protection; and, in selecting persons to hold office, due respect should be had to the wishes of the people of California, as well as to the actual possessors of authority in that province.

It may be proper to require an oath of allegiance to the United States from those who are entrusted with authori

You will also assure the people of California   he protection of the United States.

In reference to commercial regulations in the ports of which you are in actual possession, ships and produce of the United States should come and go free of duty.

For your further instruction, I enclose to you a copy of confidential instructions from the War Department to Brigadier General S. W. Kearny, who is ordered, overland, to California. You will also communicate your instructions to him, and inform him that they have the sanction of the President.

The government relies on the land and naval forces to co-operate with each other in the most friendly and effective manner.

After you shall have secured Upper California, if your force is sufficient, you will take possession and keep the harbors on the Gulf of California, as far down, at least, as Guaymas; but this is not to interfere with the permanent occupation of California.

A regiment of volunteers, from the State of New York, to serve during the war, have been called for by the government, and are expected to sail from the first to the tenth of August. This regiment will, in the first instance, report to the naval commander on your station; but will ultimately be under the command of General Kearny, who is appointed to conduct the expedition by land.

The term of three years having nearly expired since you have been in command of the Pacific squadron, Commodore Shubrick will soon be sent out in the Independence to relieve you.

The department confidently hopes that all Upper California will be in our hands before the relief shall arrive.

Very respectfully,

GEORGE BANCROFT.

Commore JOHN D. SLOAT,
    Commanding U. S. naval forces in the Pacific ocean.

Question. You have referred to the march of the naval forces, with some dragoons and volunteers from San Diego to the Pueblos, under your command, and accompanied by Commodore Stockton. Explain the nature of the command which you held over those troops, and the nature of the authority, if any, which Commodore Stockton exercised on the expedition over the troops, or over yourself?

Answer. By the act of Commodore Stockton, who styled himself governor of California, the sailors and marines were placed under my command, on the 29th of December, 1846, for the march to Los Angeles. I commanded them on the expedition; Commodore Stockton accompanied us; I exercised no command whatever over Commodore Stockton, nor did he exercise any whatever over me. His relative rank with army officers being that of Colonel, I acknowledged his right at any time to resume the command of his sailors and marines; but which he did not resume until about the 17th of January, 1847.

The judge advocate here proposed to suspend the testimony of General Kearny, and offer, in continuation of evidence, the documentary evidence in his hands.

The court took a recess of thirty minutes, to allow the judge advocate a conference with Lieutenant Colonel Frémont; at the expiration of which time, the court met again in session.

Present: all the members; the judge advocate and Lieutenant Colonel Frémont.

The judge advocate announced that Lieutenant Colonel Frémont consents to admit as authentic the following papers:

1. An original from Lieutenant Colonel Frémont to Captain J. K. Wilson, dated Angeles, 25th January, 1847, as recited in the second specification to the first charge.

2. An original from Lieutenant Colonel Frémont, dated Ciudad de los Angeles, February 5, 1847, as recited in this record, in the third specification to the first charge.

3. A letter from Lieutenant Colonel Frémont to Commodore W. Branford Shubrick, dated Ciudad de los Angeles, February 7, 1847, as recited in this record, in the fourth specification to the first charge.

4. An original from Lieutenant Colonel Frémont to W. P. Hall, dated government house, Angeles, February 11, 1847, as recited in this record, in the fifth specification to the first charge.

5. A deed from Lieutenant Colonel Frémont to Francis Temple, dated Ciudad de los Angeles, March 2, 1847, as recited in this record, in the sixth specification to the first charge.

6. A letter from Lieutenant Colonel Frémont to Captain Richard Owens, dated Ciudad de los Angeles, March 15, 1847, as recited in this record, in the seventh specification to the first charge.

7. A letter signed Wm. H. Russell to Lieutenant Colonel P. St. G. Cooke, in the name and by authority of Lieutenant Colonel Frémont, dated Ciudad de los Angeles, March 16, 1847, as recited in this record, in the eighth specification to the first charge.

8. A letter by authority and in the name of Lieutenant Colonel

Frémont, signed Wm. H. Russell, Secretary of State, to David W. Alexander, collector of the port of San Pedro, dated Ciudad de los Angeles, March 21, 1847, as recited in this record, in the ninth specificatin to the first charge. Also,

9. An extract from a letter from Commodore Shubrick to Lieutenant Colonel Frémont, dated Monterey, February 13, as recited in this record, in the seventh specification to the first charge, in the words, "General Kearny, I am instructed, is the commanding military officer in California, and invested by the President with the adminstrative functions of government over the people and territory." And Lieutenant Colonel Frémont consents that the exhibits and recital of these several papers, as made in the second, third, fourth, fifth, sixth, seventh, eighth, and ninth specifications to the first charge, shall be admitted as correct and exact without proof. Lieutenant Colonel Frémont further consents to the following extracts from the order book of his battalion being read in evidence, as follows :

GENERAL ORDERS,   HEAD-QUARTERS, CALIFORNIA BAT.,
No. 11.   *Ciudad de los Angeles, January* 24, 1847.

A general court martial, to consist of thirteen members, will convene at 10 o'clock, a. m., on Monday, the 25th instant for the trial, &c., &c., &c.   *   *   *   *   *   *   *   *

By order of Lieutenant Colonel J. C. Frémont, commanding California battalion, and military commander-in-chief of California.
THEO. TALBOTT,
Adjutant California battalion, U. S. forces.

[2.]
GENERAL ORDERS,   HEAD-QUARTERS, CALIFORNIA BAT.,
No. 12.   *Ciudad de los Angeles, January* 25, 1847.

*   *   *   *   *   *   *   *

By order of Lieutenant Colonel J. C. Frémont, commanding California battalion, and military commander-in-chief of California.
THEO. TALBOTT,
Adjutant California battalion, U. S. forces.

[3.]
GENERAL ORDERS,   HEAD-QUARTERS, CALIFORNIA BAT.,
No. 13.   *Ciudad de los Angeles, January* 27, 1847.

Extract from the proceedings of a general court martial convened by general orders, No. 11.

George Smith, a private in Captain Thompson's company, accused of stabbing Lieutenant Rock with intent to kill, was found guilty, and sentenced unanimously by the court to twenty-two months imprisonment at hard labor.

Lieutenant Rock, charged with drunkenness and unofficer like conduct, by quarrelling and fighting with a private of the name of

George Smith, in his company, was found guilty of both charges, and, in pursuance of the penalty fixed by the rules and articles of war, was cashiered, which is the sentence of the court.

Lieutenant Rock was convicted on the 83d article of the army regulations, which reads as follows: "Any commissioned officer convicted by a general court martial of ungentlemanly or unofficerlike conduct, shall be dismissed the service."

Approved:

J. C. FRÉMONT,
Governor of California.

A true copy.

W. H. RUSSELL,
Judge Advocate.

[4]

HEAD-QUARTERS, ANGELES,
February 13, 1847.

It is the unpleasant duty of the commanding officer to communicate to the battalion that, in the exercise of an undoubted right, but at an inconvenient time of the public service, and for reasons that it is to be regretted should have exerted any influence at all, the following officers, viz: Captain H. L. Ford, Captain Samuel Gibson, Captain Wm. Finlay, and Lieutenants W. Baldridge, Rheusani W. Blackburn, J. Scott, J. R. Barton, and J. M. Hudspeth, have tendered their resignations; and the commanding officer, consulting what he considers the public interest, and impressed with the idea that, to ensure a wholesome police and thereby the efficiency of the command, it is a primary consideration that the officers not only possess zeal, but a love for the service, which he regrets to find does not seem to be felt by the foregoing gentlemen, reluctantly yields his assent to their requests, and permits them to resign, which is hereby ordered.

The vacancies occasioned by the foregoing resignations will be supplied by the commanding officer at the earliest convenience.

By order.

WM. N. LOKE,
Adjutant California Battalion.

Cross-examination of General Kearny—now resumed.

Question. Did you not believe, from the terms of Lieutenant Colonel Frémont's report to you, of the 13th of January, announcing his approach to *Los Angeles*, "*with six pieces of artillery, including two pieces lately in the possession of the Californians*," that one of those pieces *must* be that which you lost at San Pasqual, and that through delicacy to you he would not so describe it?

Answer. I did not.

Question. Did you ever inquire of him to know what cannon these were?

Answer. I did not.

Question. Were not all the cannon which the Californin battalion brought into Los Angeles placed before Lieutenant Colonel Frémont's quarters, and remained there for public examination?

Answer. I never was at Colonel Frémont's quarters; I knew not where his quarters were; and therefore knew not what was in front of them.

Question. In seventh specification, of charge first, you charge Lieutenant Colonel Frémont with refusing to give up two cannon *"brought by the 1st dragoons from Fort Leavenworth, and then at San Gabriel."* Will you state what two cannon you mean those to be, and how they got from Fort Leavenworth to San Gabriel?

Answer. The charges upon which Colonel Frémont is now arraigned are not my charges. I preferred a single charge against Lieutenant Colonel Frémont. These charges, upon which he is now arraigned, have been changed from mine.

The two howitzers, however, referred to, are the howitzers which were brought by the 1st dragoons from Fort Leavenworth. They were carried from Fort Leavenworth to California by the 1st dragoons. One of them, as has been previously stated, was lost at the battle of San Pasqual; the other we took with us from San Diego to Los Angeles, it being then in charge of the sailors. I left it at Los Angeles, and know not how it got from there to San Gabriel.

Question. Do you know that one of those cannon was the one lost by you at San Pasqual?

Answer. I do not.

Question. Did you give any information to the person who drew the seventh specification to the first charge, in relation to the cannon?

Answer. I did not.

Question. Was Captain Turner, of the 1st dragoons, with you on the march from Santa Fe, and at the action at San Pasqual? And in what capacity, if any, in the staff did he act?

Answer. Captain Turner was with me on the march from Santa Fe; he had left Fort Leavenworth with me as acting assistant adjutant general to the army under my command, and continued in that capacity until after the action of San Pasqual, where Captain Moore was killed, when he was assigned to the command of the dragoons.

Question. Did you *"report"* the results of the action of San Pasqual to Commodore Stockton, through Captain Turner?

Answer. I did not. I was badly wounded at that battle, and shortly after my wounds were dressed, and I was lying on the ground, Captain Turner came to me and read to me a letter, and asked permission to send it; which I acceded to. It was addressed to Commodore Stockton.

Question. Could you have got to San Diego after the action of San Pasquel without aid from Commodore Stockton; and, if not, why?

Answer. It is impossible for me to tell. We were surrounded by a much larger body of Californians than our own numbers.

Whether we could have cut our way through them or not, I cannot tell. But I had no doubt but we could have done so.

Question. Did you take post on a hill of rocks?

Answer. The battle of San Pasqual was fought on the sixth of December. We proceeded, on the seventh, on our march towards San Diego—the enemy in sight, and around us. When near San Bernardo, the enemy endeavored to get possession of a hill covered with rocks; we marched towards it to prevent them from getting it; we drove them from it, and occupied it.

Question. How long did you remain on that hill?

Answer. On the morning of the eighth, when we were nearly ready to move, the mules having been placed in front of the rough ambulance upon which we were to carry our wounded, the doctor reported to me that proceeding at that time, and in that way, would endanger the lives of the wounded. I accordingly gave directions that we should remain there. On the 10th of December, I stated to the doctor, and to others, that we would leave the next morning, which we accordingly did, Lieutenant Gray, of the navy, with a gallant command of sailors and marines, having come into our camp the night of the tenth. When we left, on the morning of the eleventh, the enemy was no longer in sight; and I presume they left there in consequence of the arrival of Lieutenant Gray and his command.

Question. Was there wood, grass, or water on that hill?

Answer. There was, I believe, some little brush-wood, little or no grass, and we got plenty of water by digging for it at the foot of the hill.

Question. Did you turn loose your mules from that hill, or a part of them, and if so how many?

Answer. There were several mules lost from us whilst we were on that hill; I know not how many. Captain Turner, of the dragoons, then in command of them, thinking his dragoons were much more efficient on foot than mounted on those tired and broken down animals, which they had ridden from Santa Fé, and, therefore, cared not about being encumbered with them.

Question. Did the mules and horses have sufficient grass and water on the hill?

Answer. I do not believe that they had sufficient grass; they had plenty of water, being watered once or twice a day.

Question. Was there a creek in view with grass and wood upon it?

Answer. There was.

Question. Why did you not go to it to obtain grass and wood and water?

Answer. From the few men which we had, and the much greater number of the enemy, it would have been necessary for us, in going for grass and water, to have taken all our wounded men with us, as it would not have answered for us to have divided our small force.

Question. Was it not a better place to encamp?

Answer. Most unquestionably not for my command.

Question. Did the Californians occupy it?

Answer. They were on a hill not far from it; a portion of them, I believe, were on the creek some distance above our camp.

Question. Did you see Godey and his two companions taken prisoners, and did you make any efforts to relieve them?

The court was here ordered to be cleared. Lieutenant Colonel Frémont desired the judge advocate to say to the court, that if any objection was made to this question, he desired an opportunity to explain it and show its relevancy.

After some discussion in closed session, the court was ordered to be opened, and Lieutenant Colonel Frémont to be informed that the court will receive the explanation which he offers, which was done accordingly; and then Lieutenant Colonel Frémont requested that he might be allowed time to prepare his statement, and to present it at the meeting of the court to-morrow.

The judge advocate suggested that he would read over the evidence of the witness to him, as was necessary, before adjournment, which would bring the court to near the proper hour of adjournment; which was assented to by the court, and done accordingly.

The court then adjourned, before 3 o'clock, to meet to-morrow morning at 10 o'clock.

Tuesday, *November 9, 1847—10 o'clock.*

The court met pursuant to adjournment.

Present: All the members; the judge advocate and Lieutenant Colonel Frémont.

The proceedings of yesterday were read over. Lieutenant Colonel Frémont presented a paper to the court, which was read by him, as follows:

Mr. President: The object of the question objected to, and of those which go to the same point, is to show that General Kearny could not have got to San Diego without aid from Commodore Stockton, then governor of California; and thereby to make it clear that he had not come into California, according to the orders from the War Department, to conquer and take possession of it.

The orders of June 3, 1846, say: " It has been decided by the President to be of the greatest importance in the pending war with Mexico to take the earliest possession of Upper California. An expedition with that view is hereby ordered, and you are designated to command it. To enable you to be in sufficient force to conduct it successfully, this additional force of a thousand mounted men has been provided, to follow you in the direction of Santa Fé, to be under your orders, or the officer you may leave in command in Santa Fé.   *   *   *   *   *   *   *   *
Should you conquer and take possession of New Mexico and Upper California, or considerable places in either, you will establish temporary civil government therein," &c., &c.

From these orders it is clear that General Kearny was intended to go with a body of troops adequate to the conquest of an unconquered and far distant province, and not to go with a body guard of one hundred men to take possession of a conquered country. The right to establish a civil government in California was contingent upon the fact of the conquest. Should the conquest be made and possession taken, then he was to establish a civil government.

Now if there was no conquest to be made—if that work had already been done, and a civil government already established—the case contemplated by the orders could not exist, and thus the orders having nothing to operate upon were null.

The words " conquer and take possession," can only apply to an enemy's country; the authority to establish a civil government could only apply where there was none. If more than this, it so happened that General Kearny took the express of Governor Stockton to make a guide of him to the conquered country, and could not have got there with his escort without the aid of Governor Stockton; it becomes a glaring case of orders suspended by events, and no longer in force.

The first part of this case has already been made out. When General Kearny, at the outset of his march, met the express of Governor Stockton, and learnt that the country was conquered, a civil government established, a governor at the head of it, and despatches to that effect forwarded to the metropolitan government, he felt that his mission of conquest was at an end—that his orders were superseded by events—and immediately acted upon that conviction. He turned back part of his force, reduced his troops to an escort of a hundred dragoons, took Governor Stockton's express for a guide, and went on, not to conquer, but to take possession of a conquest already made, and to dispossess not a Mexican, but an American governor. This has been already shown, and thereby a point gained to be used in the defence. The second part of the same point of defence remains to be shown, namely, that General Kearny could not have got to the conquered country, nor to the presence of the American governor, whom he was going to replace, without the aid of that governor! that, far from conquering the country, he was not even able to get to it. The questions already put were intended to go to the establishment of that position, and a few others intended to follow it were meant for the same purpose.

Direct testimony, to be offered hereafter, was intended to complete that view of the case. The question asked and objected to, namely, if General Kearny, while on the hill of rocks, did not see three of his men taken prisoners, without effort to save them, would go to show his feeble condition; for, certainly, he would not have suffered that capture to have been made in his view if he had been able to prevent it. If, in addition to this, it should be shown by answers to succeeding questions, that one of these men was recovered the same day by exchange; that General Kearny sent to San Diego to Governor Stockton for aid, and received it, in a detachment of above 200 men, and never moved till it came; that he burnt and destroyed public stores: if this should be shown, the case of inability to get to San Diego, without the aid of the governor he was going to replace, will be so far made out as to require but little from other testimony to make it complete.

It is believed that the accused has a right to this defence upon the *words* of the order of 3d June, and still more upon the reason and object of that order. *" Should you conquer and take posses- sion"* are words which apply to an operation against enemies! not against ourselves. The further clause, *" You will establish tempora- ry civil government,"* clearly makes this establishment of gov- ernment contingent upon the conquest, and upon the want of govern- ment which would then exist. Upon the order, then, in itself, from its *words*, reason and object, it is manifest that General Kearny had no warrant for proceeding to California, and claiming the government.

In fact, his turning back part of his troops, and proceeding with a personal guard, was a declaration on his part, that he considered his orders superseded by events unknown to the War Department at the time they were given, and no longer obligatory upon him.

In no other way can he justify his march with an escort only, when he had been ordered to take an army.

The march with the escort was without warrant, as it seems to me; and the same view of the case which induced General Kearny to turn back part of his troops, on meeting Governor Stockton's express, should have induced him to turn back the whole, hurry on the express to Washington, and turn his own steps in the direc- tion that Colonel Doniphan took soon after. If he had done so, his whole conduct would have rested on one and the same reason; that of orders superseded by events. At present it rests upon dif- ferent reasons; turning back his troops on one, namely, that the country was conquered; proceeding with an escort; another, namely, that he wished to be governor of California, in a case not contemplated by his orders.

The various and important orders and instructions from the Sec- retaries of the Navy, (Messrs. Bancroft and Mason,) to Commo- dore Sloat and his successor in California, (Commodore Stockton,) read in evidence yesterday, by the prosecution, all show that this trial is a question between General Kearny and Commodore Stock- ton, as governor of California, and gives to me all the rights of defence which belong to Governor Stockton, if himself regularly on trial.

This view of the case was presented by my counsel to the War Department, on the 25th ultimo, and copies asked of all papers, orders, and instructions in the Navy Department to the naval com- manders on the California station, relating to the conquest and government of that province, in addition to all similar papers in the War Department to General Kearny. These copies have been furnished me, and will be used at the proper time for the defence.

They seem also to have been furnished to the prosecution, (and in my opinion very properly,) and three of these naval orders and instructions given in evidence (very properly I think) on yesterday. This introduction, by the prosecution, of these naval orders and instructions, confirms the view which my counsel had taken of my defence, and gives me a *right*, in their opinion, to pursue it, and in the exercise of that right, to ask any question which Commodore Stocktou could ask if he was on trial before a naval court. With this view it has been already shown that General Kearny turned back Governor Stockton's express, to make a guide of him to California; and I wish to show, that so far from conquering California, and thereby acquiring a right to establish a government in it, all this was done before General Kearny left Santa Fé, and that he could not have gotten to San Diego without the aid of Governor Stockton, nor from San Diego to Los Angeles.

J. C. FRÉMONT,
Lieut. Col. mounted riflemen.

On the reading of the foregoing paper, General Kearny requested the judge advocate to say to the court on his part, that " he requested to say a word to the court in relation to that ' paper.' " The court was then cleared for deliberation. After mature deliberation the court decided that the question shall not be put to the witness. The court decided to enter the paper of Lieutenant Colonel Frémont on the record.

The court decided to hear what the witness wishes to say to them in relation to that paper. The court was then opened. Lieutenant Colonel Frémont appeared in court. The decisions in closed session were announced.

General Kearny called.

I would state to the court that the accused, by the advice of his counsel, has, in the paper presented to the court, charged me with going to California. I perceive that the judge advocate, by shaking his head, objects to my going into this statement. If he has any legal objection, I do not wish to embarrass the court, and will waive the permission the court have given me.

The president asked, is there any objection? No objection was made. The following was presented by Lieutenant Colonel Frémont: " I have no objection to General Kearny making his statement, and will not claim any right of reply."

General Kearny continued.—He has stated that the march with the escort was without warrant, as it seemed to him; he has reflected upon my motives; he says that my going rests upon different reasons; one was, as taken from his own paper, that I wished to be governor of California, not contemplated by my orders. In reply I have to say, that I went to California in compliance with instructions to me from the War Department, of June 3 and June 18, 1846, in which I am told that it is the cherished wish of the Executive, that I should go there, and likewise from a letter from my friend, Colonel Benton, telling me that I was to be the civil and military governor of the territory.

Cross-examination resumed.

Question. Did your assistant adjutant general make a report of the results of the actions of the 8th and 9th of January to Governor Stockton?

Answer. Not by my knowledge or consent, but did communicate to Commodore Stockton, a list of the killed and wounded in those actions.

Question. Is this paper, addressed to "His Excellency R. F. Stockton, Governor of California," &c., &c., a copy of that list of killed and wounded?

Answer. I think it probable that it is. I have never before seen this paper. At Los Angeles, Lieutenant Emory, the acting assistant adjutant general to my command, told me that Commodore Stockton wanted a list of the killed and wounded in the actions of the 8th and 9th of January. I directed him to furnish it. He gave me one copy, which I thought was among my papers here, but which I do not find.

The paper here shown the witness, with the question, was then read, as follows:

CIUDAD DE LOS ANGELES, *January* 11, 1847.

SIR: I have the honor to furnish a statement of the killed and wounded in the actions of the 8th and 9th instant, and also a report from the senior surgeon present, John S. Griffin.

January eighth.

KILLED.

Artillery.—1 private, (a United States seaman.)

WOUNDED.

Artillery.—1 private, volunteer, from the California battalion.
Foot.—7 privates, (United States seamen.)
Marines.—1 private.
Total, 1 killed, 9 wounded.

January ninth.

WOUNDED.

First dragoons.—1 private.
Foot.—1 officer, (Lieutenant Rowan, United States navy.)
          2 privates, (United States seamen.)
California battalion.—1 officer, (Captain Gillespie.)

I am, sir, very respectfully, your obedient servant,
                                        W. H. EMORY,
        Lieut. Topographical Engineers, and A. A. General.

His Excellency R. F. STOCKTON,
        Governor of California, &c., &c., &c.

Statement of killed and wounded in the action of the 8th January,
1847.

KILLED.

Frederick Straus, seaman United States ship Portsmouth, artillery
corps; cannon shot in neck.

WOUNDED.

1. Jacob Hait, volunteer artillery, driver, wounded in left breast;
died on evening of the 9th.
2. Thomas Smith, ordinary seaman, ship Cyanne, company D,
musketeers; shot by accident through the right thigh; died on night
of the 8th.
3. Wm. Cope, seaman, United States ship Savannah, company B,
musketeers; wounded in right thigh and right arm severe.
4. George Bantam, ordinary seaman, United States ship Cyanne,
pikeman, punctured wounds of hand; accident slight.
5. Patrick Campbell, seaman, United States ship Cyanne, company D, musketeers; wounded in thigh, by spent ball, slight.
6. Wm. Scott, private, United States marines, United States ship
Portsmouth; wound in chest; spent ball; slight.
7. James Hendry, seaman, United States ship Congress, company
A, musketeers, wounded over stomach; spent ball; slight.
8. Joseph Wilson, seaman, United States ship Congress, company A, musketeers, wounded in right thigh; spent ball; slight.
9. Ivory Coffin, seaman, United States ship Savannah, company
B, musketeers, contusion of right knee; spent ball; slight.

WOUNDED ON THE NINTH.

1. Mark A. Child, private, company C, 1st regiment United
States dragoons, gun shot, wounded in right heel, penetrating up
wards into the ankle joint; severe.
2. James Campbell, ordinary seaman, United States ship Congress, company D, carbineers, wound in right foot; second toe am-
putated; accidental discharge of his own carbine; severe.
3. George Crawford, B, mate United States ship Cyanne, company D, musketeers; wounded in left thigh severe.
Lieutenant Rowan, United States navy, and Captain Gillespie,
California battalion, slightly contused by spent balls.
I am, sir, most respectfully, your obedient servant,
                                    JOHN S. GRIFFIN,
                              Assistant Surgeon, U. S. Army.
Captain W. H. EMORY,
        Assistant Adjutant General, U. S. forces.

CIUDAD DE LOS ANGELES,
        California, January 11, 1847.

Question. Did you, at Los Angeles, from the 10th to the 13th of

January inclusive, address notes to Lieutenant Colonel Frémont; and if so, how many, and for what object?

Answer. Between those dates I addressed, I think, three communications to Lieutenant Colonel Frémont. An armistice, agreed upon between himself and Don Andreas Pico, was sent to me by Commodore Stockton. From that armistice I was induced to believe that the whole California force, with the exception of their governor, Flores, and a party with him, were near Lieutenant Colonel Frémont. The object of my communications to Lieutenant Colonel Frémont was to inform him of our being in possession of Los Angeles, and having a strong military force there with us. I was apprehensive for his safety, and I volunteered to Commodore Stockton to take 250 or 300 of the sailors and marines and go to Lieutenant Colonel Frémont's rescue. Commodore Stockton told me he did not think Lieutenant Colonel Frémont was in any danger, and I did not go.

Question. Were they official orders or familiar notes of information, in relation to impending military events, and desiring information of Lieutenant Colonel Frémont's movements in return?

Answer. They were what are termed semi-official; written in a familiar manner, of which I have no copies. I keep a copy of all my official communications.

Question. Did either of these notes give information that Governor Stockton was at Los Angeles?

Answer. I have no recollection of it.

Question. Did one of these notes (that of the 12th, at 6 o'clock in the evening) contain these words, "Dear Frémont: I am here in possession of this place, with sailors and marines, &c., &c. Acknowledge the hour of the receipt of this, and when I may expect you. Regards to Russell?"

Answer. I cannot answer, but I think it highly probable it did. As I stated before I kept no copies of those semi-official papers.

Question. Do you know, or believe from information, that the armistice was made at 4 o'clock in the evening of the 12th of January, at San Fernando, distant about twenty-five miles from Los Angeles?

Answer. Los Angeles was about that distance, as we understood, from San Fernando. I do not know at what time the armistice was concluded. It is a subject very easily to be proven by others.

Question. Did you, on the 10th of January, write to Lieutenant Colonel Frémont, as follows:

DEAR FREMONT: We are in possession of this place, with a force of marines and sailors, having marched into it this morning. Join me as soon as you can, or let me know if you want us to march to your assistance; avoid charging the enemy; their force does not exceed 400, perhaps not more than 300. Please acknowledge the receipt of this, and despatch the bearer at once."

The judge advocate objected to this mode of examining a witness on the contents of papers which are in the hands of the examining party and which they do not produce.

The court was cleared to deliberate on the objection. The court sustained the objection.

The Court was then opened. Lieutenant Colonel Frémont in court. The decision in closed session was announced.

Question. Did you address the accompanying letter to Lieutenant Colonel Frémont, at the time of its date ?

Answer. That is my writing and that is my note.

A letter, as follows, was exhibited to the witness with this question:

PUEBLO DE LOS ANGELES,
Sunday, January 10, 1846, 4 *p. m.*

DEAR FREMONT : We are in possession of this place, with a force of marines and sailors, having marched into it this morning. Join us as soon as you can, or let me know, if you want us to march to your assistance; avoid charging the enemy; their force does not exceed 400, perhaps not more than 300. Please acknowledge the receipt of this, and despatch the bearer at once.

Yours,

S. W. KEARNY,
Brigadier General, U. S. Army.

Lieutenant Colonel J. C FREMONT,
Mounted riflemen, commanding, &c., &c.

Question. Did you also address this one to him at the time of its date ?

Answer. That is my writing and that is my note.

A letter, as follows, was exhibited to the witness with this question:

PUEBLO DE LOS ANGELES,
Tuesday, January 12, 1847, 6 *p. m.*

DEAR FREMONT : I am here in possession of this place, with sailors and marines. We met and defeated the whole force of the Californians on the 8th and the 9th; they have not now to exceed 300 men concentrated; avoid charging them, and come to me at this place. Acknowledge the hour of receipt of this, and when I may expect you. Regard to Russell.

Yours,

S. W. KEARNY,
Brigadier General.

Lieutenant Colonel FREMONT.

Question. Did you also address this one to him at the time it bears date ?

Answer. That is my writing, and that is my note.

The paper here handed to witness was read, as follows:

CIUDÀD DE LOS ANGELES,
January 13*th,* 1847—12 (*noon.*)

DEAR FREMONT: We are in force in this place—sailors and marines—join us as *soon as possible.* We are ignorant of your movements, and know nothing of you further than your armistice of yesterday.

Yours,

S. W. KEARNEY,
Brigadier General.

Lieut. Col. FREMONT.

Question. Did you also write this one to him at the time of its date? and were the two first words of the five after the signature, underscored by you as they now appear?

Answer. That is my writing and that is my note; and, though I have no recollection of underscoring those words, I have no doubt but I did so. I will go a little further and explain to the court for the benefit of the accused. We understood that the California battalion, under Lieutenant Colonel Frémont, had no sabres: I was of the opinion at the time I wrote this note—I have been of the opinion since, and I am still of the opinion—that, if he had charged the Californians, with his battalion without sabres, he would have been defeated.

A letter, as follows, was exhibited to the witness with this question:

CIUDAD DE LOS ANGELES,
January 13th, 1847—2 p. m.

DEAR FREMONT: We have been here since the 10th—have plenty of marines and sailors—we know nothing of you except your armistice of yesterday, signed by yourself. I have sent several letters to you, and fear they have been intercepted, as I have received no answer. Come here *at once* with your whole force and join us, or, if you cannot, let me know it, and I will go to you. The enemy cannot *possibly* have near you more than 300, most *probably* not more than 150 men. Acknowledge the *hour* of receiving this, and send back the bearer *at once*, and write but little, as it may get into the hands of the enemy instead of mine.

We defeated the enemy on the 8th and on the 9th, during our march. Since then, they have been much scattered, and several, no doubt, gone home.

I repeat we are ignorant of every thing relating to your command, except what we conjecture from your armistice, signed by yourself.

Yours,

S. W. KEARNEY,
Brigadier General.

Do not charge the enemy.
Lt. Col. J. C. FREMONT,
Mounted Riflemen, &c., &c.

The evidence given to-day was read over to witness, and then, at ten minutes before three o'clock, the court adjourned, to meet to-morrow at 10 o'clock.

WEDNESDAY, *November* 10, 1847—10 *o'clock.*

The court met pursuant to adjournment.

Present: All the members; the judge advocate and Lieutenant Colonel Frémont.

The proceedings of yesterday were read over. General Kearny appeared in court and asked permission to make a statement in explanation of his testimony on Monday—leave was granted. General Kearney stated: In reading over, in the papers this morning, the proceedings of Monday, I find the following question put to me, and my answer.

Question. Do you know that one of those cannon was the one lost by you at San Pasqual?

Answer. I do not.

I have now to explain that I had no personal knowledge of it; but I had a knowledge of it from an official report made to my staff officer by Lieutenant Colonel Cooke. The report I herewith present.

General Kearney presented the report. The judge advocate objected to it, as inadmissible in evidence—being a statement of some matters on which these charges are founded, and not sworn to.

The court was cleared for deliberation, and decided not to receive the paper in evidence. The court was then opened, and took a recess for ten minutes; at the expiration of which time, the court was again in session. Present: all the members; the judge advocate and Lieutenant Colonel Frémont. The decision in closed session was announced.

General Kearney said he had nothing further to say.

The judge advocate stated: I am compelled to give notice to the defence, that I must, hereafter, ask the court to restrict the cross-examination to matters which relate to the case under trial. I have been able to perceive the force and effect of but a very small portion of the testimony elicited by the cross-examination, and of far the greater part, I have not seen the relevancy at all. I was unwilling, however, to raise objections, as it is often difficult to foresee the bearing of testimony, and the effect to which it may be tending. But it does seem to me, that the cross-examination is diverging, as it continues, into subjects more and more remote from the charges. I am perfectly aware that no technical or equivocating defence is intended; that the defence means to go upon the substantial equity and honor of the charges; that they ought to be allowed the utmost latitude proper in cross-examinations; still the evidence must be confined within the limits of law and practice.

The events in California which have no connexion with these charges, the conduct and motives of actors there who are not on trial here, cannot be developed by means of this proceeding. This is a trial on specific charges; a trial upon other charges has been denied, as has been made public by the defence.

It can only be regretted, as regards the wishes of those who seek a more general inquest into the military events of California, that this form of proceeding, this trial before court martial, on specific charges, cannot admit it. I must, therefore, ask that the defence be confined within reasonable limits. My reluctance to restrain the range of the evidence has been manifest, and testimony, too widely irrelevant, has been admitted; my duty leaves me now no alternative. If the same course of cross-examination is continued, I shall be forced to take the sense of the court on every such question as it is offered.

Cross-examination resumed.

Question. You said, in your direct examination, that, on the day subsequent, to wit: On the 17th of January, *Lieutenant Colonel Frémont came to my quarters.* Now, did he come of his own head, as the statement implies; or, was he invited by you to come?

Answer. I have no recollection of having invited him to come.

Question. Is this paper an original?

Answer. Yes, sir, that is my writing, and that is my note.

The paper here shown witness: then read as follows:

January 17.

DEAR COLONEL: I wish to see you on business.
Yours,
S. W. KEARNY,
Brigadier General.

Lieut. Col. FREMONT.

Question. What time of the day was that note written and sent?

Answer. I presume it was written in the morning.

Question. In your direct examination, you speak of the clerk who brought Lieutenant Colonel Frémont's letter, of the 17th. Who was that person?

Answer. I do not know. I had never seen him before; nor do I know that I have ever seen him since.

Question. Was it not Mr. Christopher Carson?

Answer. I think not.

Question. Do you know the composition of the California battalion in which you directed no change to be made?

The judge advocate stated that he did not see the relevancy of the question.

Lieutenant Colonel Frémont stated: It belongs to a class of questions which cannot be waived; and the benefit of which Lieutenant Colonel Frémont will ask for.

The judge advocate withdrew the objection.

Answer. I do not. It was composed partly of artillery, and partly of riflemen, all mounted men. What portion of them were artillery, I do not know. I would state, in continuation of that sentence, that, when the battalion marched in Los Angeles, there were a number of men on foot who I believe and understood had lost their horses.

Question. Were there not naval officers with commands in

Answer. There were.

Question. What naval officers?

Answer. Midshipman McLane and Midshipman Wilson. I have no recollection of others.

Question. Was not Gillespie's company a part of it?

Answer. Captain Gillespie had marched with me from San Diego to Los Angeles, and was serving under me. If his company was with the California battalion, I did not know it.

Question. Were not the land services of these officers at an end with the termination of the expedition?

Answer. I know not.

Question. Do you know whether Gillespie's company was officially reported by Assistant Adjutant General Emory, as a part of the California battalion?

Answer. I do not.

Question. Were not the men of the battalion, in part, composed of emigrants from the Sacramento valley, who had left their families in tents, and joined the battalion for the expedition only?

Answer. I know not. But I think that I understood that they were; I understood that a part of the battalion were engaged for the expedition.

Question. Do you know, whether the officers of the battalion raised it, and marched it, under commissions from Commodore Stockton?

Answer. I do not. I have always understood that Lieutenant Colonel Frémont had raised that battalion under the orders of Commodore Stockton.

Question. With what commission?

Answer. I never heard of Commodore Stockton conferring a commission on Lieutenant Colonel Frémont, farther than having appointed him military commandant.

Question. Did you ever hear or understand that Lieutenant Colonel Frémont raised that battalion, before he knew of his appointment of lieutenant colonel in the United States army?

Answer. I always understood that Lieutenant Colonel Frémont had, in the month of June, 1846, which must have been before he knew of his appointment of lieutenant colonel, raised a part of that battalion. The balance of the battalion, as I have understood, was raised in the summer and fall of 1846. I know not at what time Lieutenant Colonel Frémont received information of his appointment as lieutenant colonel.

Question. Do you know what was the nature of the re-organization which Governor Stockton commanded in the California battalion, and which you forbid?

Answer. I do not. I learned that Commodore Stockton was about re-organizing that battalion, and I then gave my orders to Lieutenant Colonel Frémont against it.

Question. Do you know, or have you reason to believe, that that battalion was raised as part of the forces under the naval officers, by special order of the President, to be used by them in conquering California, and holding it against all enemies for the United States, whether Mexican, British, or Indian?

A member objected. The court was cleared for deliberation.

The judge advocate stated that Lieutenant Colonel Frémont regarded the question as vital. The court decided that the question be put, striking out the word " British."

The court was opened. Lieutenant Colonel Frémont in court. The decision was announced. General Kearny a witness. Question put as amended.

Answer. I do not.

Question. In what character did you forbid the execution of Commodore Stockton's order, relative to the re-organization of the California battalion, as Brigadier General, or as commander-in-chief, by virtue of Governor Stockton's command?

Answer. I did it by virtue of my commission as a Brigadier General in the army of the United States. The Secretary of War, in his instructions to me of the 18th of June, having directed that the troops organized in California would be a part of my command.

Question. In what character did you command Lieutenant Colonel Frémont to desist from re-organizing the battalion, as lieutenant colonel of the mounted rifles, or as commandant of the battalion?

Answer. He was lieutenant colonel of the army, and the commandant of the battalion. I gave him the order accordingly.

Question. At what time did you give the order to forbid the organization?

Answer. On the 16th of January, I gave directions that no change should be made in the organization of the battalion, without my sanction or approval being first obtained.

Question. At what hour of the day?

Answer. To the best of my recollection it was in the morning.

Question. At what time in the morning? before noonday?

Answer. It is impossible for me to remember the hour of the morning; but I should think it was before noonday. The particular time can be proven by others.

Question. Did not Governor Stockton, in writing, suspend you from all command on that day, and sign that order as commander-in-chief?

Answer. On the 16th of January, as I remember, having ad-dressed a communication to Commodore Stockton, objecting to his forming a civil government for California, I received a communication from him in reply, in which he stated that he would do nothing, desist from nothing, or alter anything on my demand. He added that he would report me to the President, and ask for recall; in the meantime, that he suspended me from command; which suspension, I considered, he meant the sailors and marines; and I gave up the command of those sailors and marines accordingly; a right which I always conceded to him. My letter to Lieutenant Colonel Frémont must have been written before my letter to Commodore Stockton, as it is first copied in my letter book.

Question. Had you not " *exhausted the argument*" with Commodore Stockton before you gave that order to Lieutenant Colonel Frémont?

Answer. I had not.

Question. Had you not been in controversy with him about the governorship, both verbally and in writing, from the time you first came to San Diego?

Answer. I arrived at San Diego on the 12th of December, and on the 28th I had a conversation with him relating to the order to me from the War Department respecting the civil government of California. I had no other conversation with him on that subject, to the best of my recollection, at any other time.

Question. Did you have farther controversy about the governorship *after* you gave that order to Lieutenant Colonel Frémont not to re-organize the battalion?

Answer. I had not, no farther than that which has already been stated.

Question. Did you write to Governor Stockton, on the 17th of January, a letter in relation to the point in controversy between you, namely, the governorship of California?

Answer. I did. My letter of the 17th of January to Commodore Stockton, had reference to my letter to him of the day previous, and his reply thereto.

Question. What time of the day? before or after the interview with Lieutenant Colonel Frémont?

Answer. I cannot remember.

Question. In that letter did you use the words "collision," "civil wars," &c., &c., as being "*prevented*," and that you would be silent, &c., &c., &c.?

Answer. I remember the letter well. I have a copy of it here. The letter is as follows:

HEAD-QUARTERS, ARMY OF THE WEST,
Ciudad de los Angelos, January 17, 1847.

SIR: In my communication to you of yesterday's date, I stated that I had learned that you were engaged in organizing a civil government for California. I referred you to the President's instructions to me, (the originals of which you have seen, and copies of which I furnished you,) to perform that duty; and I added that, if you had any authority from the President, or any of his organs, for what you were doing, I would cheerfully acquiesce, and if you have not such authority, I demanded that you cease farther proceedings in the matter. Your reply of the same date refers me to a conversation held at San Diego, and adds that you "cannot do anything, nor desist from anything, or alter anything, on your [my] demand."

As in consequence of the defeat of the enemy on the 8th and 9th instant by the troops under my command, and the capitulation entered into on the 13th instant by Lieutenant Colonel Frémont with the leaders of the Californians, in which the people under arms and in the field agreed to disperse and remain quiet and peaceably, the country may now for the first time be considered as conquered and taken possession of by us, and as I am prepared to carry out the President's instructions to me, which you oppose, I must, for the purpose of preventing collision between us, and, possibly, a civil war in consequence of it, remain silent for the present, leaving with you the great responsibility of doing that for which you have no authority, and preventing me from complying with the President's orders.

Very respectfully, your obedient servant,

S. W. KEARNEY, *Brig. Gen.*

Commodore R. F. STOCKTON,
 U. S. Navy, Acting Gov. of California.

Question. Did you write to the Secretary of War before you left Los Angeles, that "after the arrival of the Mormon battalion and the New York regiment, you would have the *arrangement* of *affairs* in that country"?

Answer. I did. A copy of the letter is in my letter book as follows:

HEAD-QUARTERS ARMY, OF THE WEST,
Ciudad de los Angeles, West California, January 14, 1847.

SIR: This morning Lieutenant Colonel Frémont, of the regiment of mounted riflemen, reached here with 400 volunteers from the Sacramento. The enemy capitulated with him yesterday near San Fernando, and agreed to lay down their arms, and we have now the prospect of having peace and quietness in this country, which I hope may not be interrupted again. I have not yet received any information of the troops which were to come from New York, nor of those to follow me from New Mexico, but presume they will be here before long. On their arrival I will, agreeably to the instructions of the President, have the management of affairs in this country, and will endeavor to carry out his views in relation to it.

Very respectfully, your obedient servant,

S. W. KEARNY, *Brig. Gen.*

Brigadier General R. JONES,
 Adjutant General U. S. A.

The copies of these letters, read by consent, from the order-book of General Kearny.

Question. Did the Mormons and the New York regiment arrive before you attempted to get command of the California battalion, through your order to, and interview with, Lieutenant Colonel Frémont of the 17th January?

Answer. The California battalion was under my command from the time of Lieutenant Colonel Frèmont's reporting it to me on the 13th of January. The Mormon battalion arrived at San Diego about the 29th of January, and the New York regiment arrived at San Francisco early in March.

Question. Was the attempt to get command of the California battalion on the 16th and the 17th of January, in virtue of your authority as commanding them and other forces, or as brigadier general? And was that attempt to get the command of that battalion in opposition to Governor Stockton?

Answer. I was a brigadier general in the army, and the accused a lieutenant colonel in it. I was in the command of the battalion at the time; I made no attempt to get the command—the battalion was already under me.

Question. Was not Commodore Stockton's order suspending you, express in suspending you from all command of the United States *forces* in that place, to wit, Los Angeles?

Answer. I do not remember the exact phraseology; the letter can be produced.

Question. Was not your order to Lieutenant Colonel Frémont, forbidding him to reorganize the battalion, delivered to him by Lieutenant Emory at 8 o'clock in the night of the 16th of January?

Answer. I know not; Lieutenant Emory is here in the city, and can answer that question.

Lieutenant Colonel Frémont stated that he has many more questions to offer, founded on papers; but he will produce the papers to-morrow, and save the court the trouble of examining the witness on their contents.

The evidence given to-day was read over to the witness. General Kearny said, in explanation—In my testimony as to the time of my giving the order, on the 16th of January, to Lieutenant Colonel Frémont, I alluded to the time of writing it.

The court went into close session. After a short time, was again opened.

Lieutenant Colonel Frémont being present; and at 5 minutes before 3 o'clock, adjourned to meet to-morrow at 10 o'clock.

THURSDAY, *Nov.* 11, 1847.—10 *o'clock.*

The court met pursuant to adjournment.

Present: all the members, the judge advocate and Lieutenant Conel Frémont.

The proceedings of yesterday were read over.

Cross-examination resumed.

General Kearny, a witness.

Question. With respect to the governorship, did not Commodore Stockton in his first conversation with you at San Diego, in December let you know that it was not an open question, "that he had pledged it to Lieutenant Colonel Frémont, and sent on his recommendation to the government; that his appointment was before the government, and their approval or disapproval probably on its way to him; and, if you had not interfered with his express, it (the approval of the appointment) would probably be returned from Washington by the middle of January;" and, if not, what did he say?

Answer. I have no recollection, whatever, of having had but one conversation with Commodore Stockton on the subject of the governorship of California; that conversation was at San Diego, on the 28th of December. In that conversation I told Commodore Stockton that he had seen, by my official communications, the instructions of the President to me relating to California; that I had come to California with but a small military force; that, deference and respect for his situation, he being then in command of the Pacific squadron, and having a large force of sailors and marines, prevented me, at that time, from relieving him and taking charge of the civil government of the country; that, as soon as my command was increased, I would take charge of affairs in California, agreeably to my instructions. Commodore Stockton said, in reply, that he had, in the month of August, reported the state of affairs in California to Washington, and that he could not permit himself to be interfered with until he received an answer to that report. I have no recollection, whatever, of his having mentioned the name of Lieutenant Colonel Frémont in that conversation; but he had, previous to that conversation, sent me a copy of a communication of his, I think, directed to the Navy Department, stating that he intended appointing Lieutenant Colonel Frémont the governor of the territory.

Question. What induced Commodore Stockton to send you a copy of that dispatch?

Answer. I reached San Diego on the 12th of December; on the 13th, I put all my official orders and communications from Washington into the hands of Commodore Stockton for his information; he returned them to me on the 16th, with a communication from himself, and with them a copy of several of his public papers. I have previously, in a letter, stated that he returned those papers to me on the 14th, but, on reading his letter to me, I find it was the 16th of December.

Question. Did not Commodore Stockton in that communication, inform you that Captain Frémont was appointed major by him, and Lieutenant Gillespie, of the marines, captain, in the California battalion?

The judge advocate asked if General Kearny had the paper?

General Kearny said: I have not the paper with me—it may be among my papers in this city; I think it is in Missouri. If a copy of it is shewn to me I should remember it.

The judge advocate here explained to the witness that the words "that communication," referred to the copy of the despatch of Commodore Stockton to the Navy Department enclosed to General Kearny.

General Kearny said: I understood it to refer to his letter to me, and not to his dispatch to the Navy Department.

A copy of the dispatch in question was here shown the witness.

General Kearny said: Among the papers sent to me by Commodore Stockton, on the 16th of December, was a copy of his letter to the Navy Department of August 28th, 1846, the second paragraph of which states, that he had organized the California battalion of mounted riflemen, by the appointment of all necessary officers, and received them as volunteers in the service of the United States. Captain Frémont was appointed major, and Lieutenant Gillespie captain of the battalion. That letter as printed in the House documents No. 19, of the last session of Congress, page 106, I believe to be a true copy of the paper he sent me.

A member objected that where a paper is produced and proved, the whole paper must be given to the court, and not a part.

The court was cleared. After mature deliberation, the court decided that the whole dispatch must be read.

The court was then opened. Lieutenant Colonel Frémont appeared. The decision in closed session was announced. The paper was then read as follows:

CIUDAD DE LOS ANGELES,
August 28, 1846.

SIR: You have already been informed of my having, on the 23d of July, assumed the command of the United States forces on the west coast of Mexico. I have now the honor to inform you that the flag of the United States is flying from every commanding position in the territory of California, and that this rich and beautiful country belongs to the United States, and is forever free from Mexican dominion.

On the day after I took this command I organized the California battalion of mounted riflemen, by the appointment of all the necessary officers, and received them as volunteers into the service of the United States; Captain Frémont was appointed major, and Lieutenant Gillespie, captain of the battalion.

The next day they were embarked on board the sloop-of-war Cyane, Commander Dupont, and sailed from Monterey for San Diego, that they might be landed to the southward of the Mexican forces, amounting to 500 men, under General Castro and Governor Pico, and who were well fortified at the "camp of the Mesa," three miles from this city. A few days after the Cyane left, I sailed, in the Congress, for San Pedro, the port of entry for this department, and thirty miles from this place, where I landed with my gallant sailor army, and marched directly for the redoubtable "camp of the Mesa." But when we arrived within twelve miles of the camp, General Castro broke ground and run for the city of Mexico. The governor of the territory and the other principal officers separated in different parties, and ran away in different directions.

Unfortunately the mounted riflemen did not get up in time to head them off. We have since, however, taken most of the principal officers; the rest will be permitted to remain quiet at home, under the restrictions contained in my proclamation of the 17th.

On the 13th of August, having been joined by Major Frémont, with about eighty riflemen, and Mr. Larkin, late American consul we entered this famous "City of the Angels," the capital of the Californias, and took unmolested possession of the government house.

Thus, in less than a month after I assumed the command of the United States force in California, we have chased the Mexican army more than 300 miles along the coast; pursued them 30 miles in the interior of their own country; routed and dispersed them, and secured the territory to the United States; ended the war; restored peace and harmony among the people, and put a civil government into successful operation.

The Warren and Cyane sailed a few days since to blockade the west coast of Mexico, south of San Diego; and, having almost finished my work here, I will sail in the Congress as soon as the store-ship arrives, and I can get supplied with provisions, on a cruise for the protection of our commerce, and dispose of the other vessels as most effectually to attain that object, and, at the same time, to keep the southern coast strictly blockaded.

When I leave the territory, I will appoint Major Frémont to be governor, and Lieutenant Gillespie to be secretary.

I inclose you several papers, marked from 1 to 14 inclusive, including this letter and the first number of the "Californian," by which you will see what sort of a government I have established, and how I am proceeding.

I have no time to specify individual merit, but I cannot omit to say that I do not think that ardent patriotism and indomitable courage have ever been more evident than amongst the officers and men, 360 in number, from the frigate Congress, who accompanied me on this trying and hazardous march; a longer march, perhaps, than has ever been made in the interior of a country, by sailors, after an enemy. I would likewise say that the conduct of the officers and men of the whole squadron has been praiseworthy. I have received your dispatch of the 13th of May, and, at the same time, a Mexican account of the proceedings of Congress, and the President's proclamation, by the United States ship Warren, from Mazatlan.

Faithfully, your obedient servant,

R. F. STOCKTON.

To the Hon. George Bancroft,
  Secretary of the Navy, Washington, D. C.

Question. Did not Commodore Stockton inform you at San Diego that California had been conquered in July and August, in the preceding year; that an insurrection had broken out in the south, at Los Angeles; that he had sent Major Frémont to the north to prevent the insurrection from breaking out there, and to raise troops in the American settlements of the Sacramento, and march them down to Los Angeles, while he would march up to the same place from San Diego; that the two movements were combined; and that he was only waiting to hear of the approach of Frémont to begin his own movement? and if not, what did he say?

Answer. Commodore Stockton did inform me, in the conversation alluded to between us, that California had been conquered in July and August of the same year; this conversation was held in the month of December, 1846; he told me that Major Frémont had gone to the north, to raise men and increase the command of volunteers by raising men near the Sacramento. I did not understand him to say that it was done by his (Commodore Stockton's) orders; but I understood, that is, the impression left on my mind from that. conversation is, that Lieutenant Colonel Frémont had gone back from the neighborhood of Santa Barbara, to raise these men and increase his command by his own volition. I have no recollection whatever of such conversation, as is supposed, in the question from the words "while he would march up," to the end of the question.

Question. Do you know whether Commodore Stockton sent a gun-boat to flank and cover the march of the battalion, as it passed the maritime pass of the Rincon? and that Lieutenant Selden, of the navy, commanded that gun-boat?

Answer. I have always understood that such was the case; I do not know it personally.

Question. Do you know that Commodore Stockton sent, or procured to go with orders, to Lieutenant Colonel Frémont, on his march down, Captain Hamlin, of the whale brig Stonington; and that he overtook the battalion between the Rincon pass and the pass of San Fernando, going through the enemy in the night, and delivered the orders?

Answer. Captain Hamblin, I think, was with us some few days after we left San Diego; on our march to Los Angeles he left us; and I understood that he had been sent by Commodore Stockton to Lieutenant Colonel Frémont, for what purpose, or with what orders, I never understood. I presumed—

The judge advocate requested the witness to answer the questions as clearly and briefly as possible; to speak as to his own knowledge; not deliver as evidence hearsay. He had no wish to prevent the witness from making all needful explanations in his testimony.

General Kearny said: I know nothing about it. Many questions have been put to me in regard to facts of which I have no personal knowledge; but I have given my impressions and opinions, in order to answer the questions of the accused in good faith, and to give all the information in my possession.

A paper was received from Lieutenant Colonel Frémont, and read as follows:

Lieutenant Colonel Frémont proposes to found a series of questions upon the papers produced, but is willing that the papers should be read to the court; that the witness should testify as he deemed right as to any part of their contents, and that, afterwards, he might be interrogated by all who have a right to put questions. Lieutenant Colonel Frémont proposes this for the convenience of the court and witness, and to supersede interrogatories founded on the contents of the papers, before they are read. He is willing that the witness should know the contents of the papers before he is interrogated, and before he answers. The papers Lieutenant Colonel Frémont produces, and on which he would found questions, are neither his own, nor originals, nor in his exclusive possession; but he makes no legal question, and is willing that the papers be read as intimated.

J. C. FRÉMONT,
Lieut. Col., Mounted Riflemen.

The judge advocate said he too was unwilling to make a legal question; but the legality of receiving in evidence one of those papers forces itself on the attention of the court. It is a letter from Commodore Stockton to the Secretary of the Navy. It appears to be his own report and narrative of certain operations in California. The judge advocate thinks it cannot be offered as evidence to prove what is contained in it, for the same reason as the court yesterday refused to admit the reading of Colonel Cook's report. He supposes the writers of both those reports will be here, and will personally be examined before the court.

The other papers are a correspondence between General Kearny and Commodore Stockton; they may, he supposes, go to important points in the equity and law of the defence.

Lieutenant Colonel Frémont said that he would waive and withdraw any paper that was objected to. He wished to cause no embarrassments whatever.

The court was ordered to be cleared. After mature deliberation, the court decided not to receive any papers in advance of testimony, in relation to which they are said to be offered.

When a question is propounded to a witness, on either side, the court will judge of its relevancy to the matter under trial. It will be the best time, when a question is thus admitted, to judge of the propriety of admitting any paper, as evidence, connected with the answer to such question.

The court declined, under this decision, to hear the papers which are now offered read at this time.

The court was then opened. Lieutenant Colonel Frémont present. The decision, in closed session, was announced.

General Kearny, a witness—cross-examination continued.

Question. Did Lieutenant Colonel Frémont send the armistice of the 12th of January to yourself, or to Commodore Stockton?

Answer. He did not send it to me; but I presume he sent it to Commodore Stockton, as Commodore Stockton sent it to me.

Question. Did he send the capitulation of the 13th to yourself, or to Commodore Stockton?

Answer. He did not send it to me; I knew not whether he sent it to Commodore Stockton.

Question. Do you know whether he sent Colonel Russell, on the 13th, to Los Angeles, to ascertain who was in command, and to deliver the capitulation, of which he was the bearer, to the commander-in-chief of the forces?

Answer. I do not. I saw Colonel Russell in Los Angeles before the arrival, as I remember, of Lieutenant Colonel Frémont with his battalion. What his object was in coming in advance of Col. Frémont he never told me; nor have I to this moment understood.

Question. Did Lieutenant Talbott, adjutant of the California battalion, bring you the note of the 13th from Lieutenant Colonel Frémont? And do you know whether he (Lieutenant Talbott is) now in Mexico?

Answer. I do not know Lieutenant Talbott by sight. If I should see him at this moment I would not know him. I know not where he is.

Question. Who brought that note?

Answer. I do not remember.

Question. On his arrival at Los Angeles, with his battalion, did, or did not, Lieutenant Colonel Frémont *report* personally first to Commodore Stockton, and immediately after *call* upon you?

Answer. I know not. He called upon me. At what time he called upon Commodore Stockton, whether before or after calling upon me, I know not.

Question. Did not Lieutenant Colonel Frémont, on the 16th of January, urge you to have a personal interview with Commodore Stockton, and express his hope and belief that everything could be settled between you in such an interview?

Answer. In the conversation with Lieutenant Colonel Frémont, on the 17th of January, he expressed a great desire that I should have an interview with Commodore Stockton. I told him I was willing to have such an interview, but I would not ask for it.

Question. At what time did you leave Los Angeles? the day, and the time of the day?

Answer. I left Los Angeles on the 18th of January, 1847; I presume about 10 o'clock in the morning.

Question. Did you leave any orders for Lieutenant Colonel Frémont, or take leave of him, or give notice to him of your going away, or of where you were going?

Answer. I did not.

Question. Was the order to Lieutenant Colonel Frémont, forbidding him to re-organize the California battalion, intended to detach him from duty with that battalion, or to keep the battalion, as it existed, under your command?

Answer. It was intended, as expressed, that no change should be made in it without my approval being first obtained.

The testimony was read over to the witness. He stated, in explanation: In referring to the copies of his public papers given me by Commodore Stockton, at San Diego, on the 16th of December, 1846, I meant the papers issued by himself. He did not show or send to me any official papers received by him. And then, at five minutes before three, the court adjourned to meet to-morrow at 10 o'clock.

FRIDAY, *November* 12, 1847.—10 *o'clock.*

The court met pursuant to adjournment.

Present: all the members, the judge advocate, and Lieutenant Colonel Frémont.

The proceedings of yesterday were read over.

Cross-examination resumed.

General Kearney, a witness.

Question. In your direct examination, giving an account of the interview with Lieutenant Colonel Frémont, on the 17th January, you omitted to say whether any person was present to hear the conversation; will you now state how it was?

Answer. There was no one present but Lieutenant Colonel Frémont and myself.

Question. In your direct examination, giving an account of that conversation, you said that he (Lieutenant Colonel Frémont) asked you if you would appoint him governor? Now had you not yourself volunteered that appointment to him through Colonel Russell, and with many encomiums upon him, before he arrived at Los Angeles?

Answer. I had not. I may have spoken to Colonel Russell highly of Lieutenant Colonel Frémont.

Question. Did Colonel Russell, by your invitation, sup with you on the evening of the 13th, being the day before the arrival of the California battalion in Los Angeles?

Answer. Captain Turner, of the dragoons, and myself messed together; we occupied, at Los Angeles, but one room. Colonel Russell supped with us, and slept with Captain Turner, the evening and night of his arrival at that place; he supped with us by our mutual invitation; very probably, by my own.

Question. Did he lie in bed with you by your invitation that night, the whole night, or any part of it?

Answer. He did not; he lay with Captain Turner.

Question. Do you recollect of any unusual means used by you to keep him awake, and to keep up conversation with him?

Answer. I do not; but I know I went to sleep before himself and Captain Turner.

Question. Did you, in the night, and while Russell was in bed, say to him: "Russell, you are drowsy," and thereupon send out and get spirits for him to drink, in order to keep him awake for conversation?

Answer. I have no recollection whatever of having done so; and do not believe that I did so.

Question. Was the praise of Lieutenant Colonel Frémont a theme with you in your conversation with Colonel Russell that night?

Answer. I think it highly probable; I may have spoken to Col. Russell that evening very highly of Lieutenant Colonel Frémont.

Question. Was the capitulation of Cowengo a subject of your conversation with Colonel Russell that night?

Answer. I think it was.

Question. Did you applaud that capitulation?

Answer. I did not say any thing against it; I understood that it had been disapproved by others.

Question. Did you not inform Colonel Russell that Stockton was greatly opposed to that capitulation?

Answer. I had understood that Commodore Stockton was opposed to it, and I think I told Colonel Russell so.

Question. Did you not inform Colonel Russell that Captain Emory was the enemy of Lieutenant Colonel Frémont, and warn him, as the friend of Lieutenant Colonel Frémont, of that enmity?

Answer. I do not think that I did so.

Question. Did you not say these words to Colonel Russell: "His (Captain Emory's) quarters are the *hot-bed* of Frémont's enemies?"

Answer. I never said to Colonel Russell any thing of the kind; and I never said so to any one.

Question. Did you say any thing on the subject of Lieutenant Emory's enmity to Lieutenant Colonel Frémont; and if so, what was it?

Answer. I have no recollection whatever of having said to Col. Russell any thing relating to the enmity of Lieutenant Emory to Lieutenant Colonel Frémont.

Question. Did you not, on the 16th of January, in a personal interview with Lieutenant Colonel Frémont, make the offer, of your own head, of governor, and say to him that you should soon return to Missouri, under leave obtained to that effect, and that in "four" or "six" weeks you would appoint him governor?

Answer. I did not. But in the conversation with Lieutenant Colonel Frémont, on the 17th of January, I stated that, before leaving Santa Fé, I had applied for permission to return home, and that previous to my doing so I would most probably organize a civil government in California. He asked me if I would appoint him the governor, and when I told him that, at that time, I considered the state of the country required a military government, but that possibly in a month or six weeks the country might be sufficiently quieted to admit of the establishment of a civil government.

Question. In the same direct examination you said: "that Lieutenant Colonel Frémont informed you that Commodore Stockton was *about* to organize a civil government, and *intended* to appoint him governor of the territory," do you not *now* know that whatever conversation took place on that subject occurred on the 16th, and not on the 17th?

Answer. I do not.

Question. Did you not on the 16th write to Commodore Stockton: "I am informed that you are now engaged in organizing a civil government, and appointing officers for it in this territory"?

The judge advocate said: Have you the letter, or has it been before the court?

Answer. I did. A copy of the letter is here in my letter book.

The court ordered the letter to be read. It was read from the copy by consent, as follows:

HEAD-QUARTERS, ARMY OF THE WEST,
Ciudad de los Angeles, January 16, 1847.

SIR: I am informed that you are now engaged in organizing a civil government, and appointing officers for it in this territory. As this duty has been specially assigned to myself, by orders of the President of the United States, conveyed in letters to me from the Secretary of War, of June 3, and 18, 1846, the originals of which I gave to you on the 12th, and which you returned to me on the 13th, and copies of which I furnished you with, the 26th of December, I have to ask, if you have any authority from the President, from the Secretary of the Navy, or from any other channel of the President's, to form such government, and make such appointments? If you have such authority, and will show it to me, or will furnish me with certified copies of it, I will cheerfully acquiesce in what you are doing. If you have not such authority, I then demand that you cease all further proceedings relating to the formation of a civil government for this territory, as I cannot recognise in you any right in assuming to perform duties confided to me by the President.

Very respectfully,

S. W. KEARNY,
Brigadier General U. S. A.

Commodore R. F. STOCKTON,
U. S. Navy, Acting Governor.

Question. Did you not on the 17th of January write to Commodore Stockton as follows: " In my communication to you of yesterday's date, I stated that I had learned that you were engaged in organizing a civil government for California"? and describing Commodore Stockton in that letter as acting governor?

The judge advocate said: under the decision of the court, produce the letter. The letter, on examination, found in the record of Wednesday, November 10.

Answer. I did.
Question. Was it not Lieutenant Colonel Frémont that informed you, as stated in these two letters, that Governor Stockton was then, to wit, on the 16th, engaged in appointing civil officers for the territory?
Answer. I had learned it from other sources; Lieutenant Colonel Frémont did not inform me of it on the 16th.
Question. Were not the appointments, of which you were informed, mentioned in the plural, namely: " *officers*" for the territory?
Answer. It was.
Question. Were not those appointments subordinate to the governor, and consisting of secretary and councillors?
Answer. The appointments that I understood Commodore Stockton was about to make were those of governor and secretary of

state. I did not at that time learn any thing of the appointment of councillors.

Question. Did you, or did you not, understand from Lieutenant Colonel Frémont, or any person, that Governor Stockton, through deference to his designated successor, (Lieutenant Colonel Frémont,) gave up his own choice (Captain Gillespie) as secretary, (whom he had recommended to the President,) and appointed Colonel W. H. Russell?

Answer. I did not. I understood that Colonel Russell was to be appointed secretary of state.

Question. Did you, or did you not, understand from Lieutenant Colonel Frémont, or some person, on that 16th day of January, that Governor Stockton, through deference to him as his successor, appointed Señor Bandini as a councillor, against his own first intentions?

Answer. I did not.

A member objecting, the court was ordered to be cleared. After mature deliberation the court decided that the court cannot admit heresay evidence, and must insist upon the defence confining itself to the issue.

The court was then opened. Lieutenant Colonel Frémont appeared in court. The decision in closed session was announced.

The court took a recess of fifteen minutes, at the close of which time the court again in session. Present: all the members, the judge advocate, and Lieutenant Colonel Frémont.

General Kearny, a witness—Cross-examination continued.

Question. In your direct examination, you said (in answer to Lieutenant Colonel Frémont's alleged inquiry, if you would appoint him governor) that as soon as the country was quieted, you should most probably organize a civil government; now, was it with you a mere question of probability, on the 17th of January, that you would organize a civil government in California on our getting quiet possession of it?

The judge advocate suggested to Lieutenant Colonel Frémont to explain the object of the present cross-examination; which he did explain to the judge advocate.

The court was ordered to be cleared. After mature deliberation the court decided that the question shall be put to the witness.

The court was then opened; Lieutenant Colonel Frémont appeared in court. The decision in closed session was then announced.

General Kearny, a witness—Cross-examination continued.

The last question on the record was read to the witness.

Answer. My instructions from the President of the United States, through the Secretary of War, were to organize a civil government; and I intended at a proper time to do so. The enemy had been lately defeated, on the 8th and 9th of January; and I did not consider the country sufficiently quiet at that time for a civil government.

Question. You said in your direct examination, in reference to Lieutenant Colonel Frémont's alleged question to you, that, at that time, *to wit*, on the 17th, you saw no objection to appointing him as governor when you returned to Missouri; now, was not that alleged answer, if it was made, made after that letter had been signed in your presence, and refused to be taken back?

Answer. That answer was made after the paper had been signed in my presence, and before the conversation between us was concluded. I intended, as I told Lieutenant Colonel Frémont, that I was willing that he should take the letter back; and I was in hopes he would have done so; when I should have taken no further notice of it.

Question. Was it not after you had told him of his unquestionable ruin if he persisted, and after he had persisted in adhering to that letter?

Answer. I am trying to remember; after a pause, witness said: my memory will not serve me to answer that question.

Question. In your cross-examination yesterday, you stated that " in the conversation with Lieutenant Colonel Frémont, on the 17th of January, he expressed a great desire that I should have an interview with Commodore Stockton; I told him I was willing to have such an interview, but would not ask it;" had you forgotten that circumstance when, on the first day of your direct examination, you gave your full testimony of the interview and conversation with Lieutenant Colonel Frémont on the 17th?

Answer. I endeavored in my testimony to tell what passed between Lieutenant Colonel Frémont and myself. If I have omitted anything, I will with great pleasure answer and explain to the accused anything which may be submitted to me, and which he may remember.

Question. You said, in your cross-examination of yesterday, that he expressed great *desire* for the interview; did he not appear to be distressed at the state of things between you and Commodore Stockton?

Answer. He did.

Question. When you said that you were willing to have such an interview, but would not ask it, did not Lieutenant Colonel Frémont instantly offer to see Governor Stockton, obtain his consent, and arrange the interview?

Answer. Most unquestionably he did not. Lieutenant Colonel Frémont might have effected an interview between Commodore Stockton and myself; perhaps there were but few others at Los Angeles who could have done it.

Question. Did you not leave Los Angeles at or before 10 o'clock the next morning, without notice to Lieutenant Colonel Frémont, or waiting for him to bring an answer from Governor Stockton?

Answer. I left Los Angeles on the morning of the 18th, probably about 10 o'clock, and, as I have previously stated, without giving any notice to Lieutenant Colonel Frémont of my intentions of doing so. I sent no message to Commodore Stockton; and, therefore, could not expect an answer to be brought to me.

Question. Did you do your utmost endeavor to suppress the mu-tiny of which Lieutenant Colonel Frémont is charged to be guilty, and to have committed in your quarters and in your presence?

The judge advocate said the question was improper, but he had no objection to the witness answering it.

Lieutenant Colonel Frémont suggested that the witness had the privilege to answer it or not.

Answer. I repeat, that there is no question that the accused will put to me but I will answer most freely. Nothing further passed between Lieutenant Colonel Frémont and myself, in the interview alluded to, than I have stated.

The testimony was read over to the witness, and then, at five minutes before three, the court adjourned to meet to-morrow at 10 o'clock.

- - -

SATURDAY, *November 13*, 1847.—10 *o'clock.*

The court met pursuant to adjournment.

Present: All the members, the judge advocate, and Lieutenant Colonel Frémont.

The proceedings of yesterday were read. General Kearny being in court said: I would wish to add to the close of my last answer of yesterday these words, " to the best of my recollection."

Lieutenant Colonel Frémont asked a conference with the judge advocate. He placed in the hands of the judge advocate, a corres-pondence with the War Department, respecting the charges which he desired to submit to the court for their decision, whether they will receive those letters at this time and place them on the record?

Lieutenant Colonel Frémont desired the judge advocate also to say to the court, that one of his counsel, who had been invited by the War Department to inspect the records of the adjutant general's office to procure documentary evidence for the defence, had dis-covered there evidence of great importance, which the office could not furnish in time for their use this day before the court. He, therefore, requested the court to adjourn after considering the pa-pers submitted this morning, in order to give the defence time to produce the evidence in question.

The court was cleared for deliberation. The judge advocate stated, the papers now submitted for the consideration of the court, were a letter from the counsel of Lieutenant Colonel Frémont to the adjutant general of the army, informing him of the testimony of General Kearny, stating that these charges now under trial are not his charges, and inquiring of the adjutant general to know from what source the charges came, and the adjutant general's reply thereto by order of the War Department.

The court declined to hear the papers read, and directed them to be returned.

The court further decided, that it will shield no witness from any lawful impeachment of his credibility; but when, in cross-examination, a question on collateral matter is allowed to be answered, the party propounding the interrogatory must abide by that answer, and not undertake to controvert it by opposing evidence.

If these papers are offered to contradict the witness as to the origin of the charges, the court deems that they fall within the above rule. For any other purpose an inquiry into the origin of the charges is equally beyond the province of the court; the court considering it irrelevant to the issue it is ordered to try.

The court was then opened. Lieutenant Colonel Frémont in court. The decision in closed session was announced. The court then adjourned at twelve o'clock, in compliance with the application of Lieutenant Colonel Frémont, till Monday, November 15, at 10 o'clock.

MONDAY, *November* 15, 1847.—10 *o'clock*.

The court met pursuant to adjournment.

Present: All the members, the judge advocate, and Lieutenant Colonel Frémont.

The proceedings of Saturday were read over.

General Kearny, a witness—Cross-examination continued.

Question. Did you write a letter to the Secretary of War on the 17th of January, 1847; and is this a true copy of that letter?

Answer. I did write a letter of this date to the adjutant general, and I believe this to be a true and correct copy.

The letter here shown the witness, was then read in evidence, as follows:

HEAD-QUARTERS, ARMY OF THE WEST,
Ciudad de los Angeles, January 17, 1847.

SIR: I enclose herewith a copy of three communications. No. 1, being instructions from me (of yesterday) to Lieutenant Colonel Frémont, relating to his battalion of volunteers—2, reply of Lieutenant Colonel Frémont of this date, refusing obedience to my orders—3, letter from me of this date, to Commodore R. F. Stockton on his assuming powers not given him, and preventing me from complying with the instructions of the President of the United States, conveyed in letters to me from the Secretary of War.

It will be seen by the President and Secretary of War that I am not recognised in my official capacity, either by Commodore Stockton or Lieutenant Colonel Frémont, both of whom refuse to obey my orders or the instructions of the President; and as I have no troops in the country under my authority, excepting a few dragoons, I have no power of enforcing them.

I have to state that the march of the troops from San Diego to this place was reluctantly consented to by Commodore Stockton on my urgent advice, that he should not leave Lieutenant Colonel Frémont unsupported to fight a battle on which the fate of California might for a long time depend.

The correspondence to prove which is now with my papers at San Diego, and a copy of which will be furnished to you on my return to that place.

Very respectfully, your obedient servant,
S. W. KEARNY,
Brigadier General.

The ADJUTANT GENERAL,
U. S. A., Washington, D. C.

A true copy.

E. D. TOWNSEND,
A. A. General.

Question. Was that letter written after your interview of the same day with Lieutenant Colonel Frémont?

Answer. It must have been, as I remember.

Question. In that letter we find these words, "Both of whom (Commodore Stockton and Lieutenant Colonel Frémont) refuse to obey my orders." Will you please to state what had occurred between the close of the interview with Lieutenant Colonel Frémont and the writing of that letter which induced you to report an absolute refusal on the part of Lieutenant Colonel Frémont to obey you, when, according to your direct testimony, before this court, his last words to you were conditional, to wit: he would go and see Commodore Stockton, and, unless he gave him the governorship at once, he would not obey him?

Answer. The extract, as given in the question from the accused, is but a part of the sentence; and there is an omission of the following words: "or the instructions of the President." I wrote that sentence after the interview, as I remember, with Lieutenant Colonel Frémont, and after he had left me and I had heard nothing further from him.

Question. In that same letter are these words, "And as I have no troops in the country, under my authority, except a few dragoons, I have no power of enforcing them," (the orders under which you went to California.) Now what did you mean by that word "enforcing"?

Answer. I meant that if I had troops under me, I would never permit a junior officer to disobey my orders.

Question. Did you write a letter to the Secretary of War, on the 15th of March, 1847, from Monterey? and is this a true copy from that letter?

Answer. I did write a letter to the Adjutant General of the army, on the 15th of March, 1847; and I believe that to be a true copy, as far as it goes, from the original. This letter is not complete.

The judge advocate asked him for a complete copy, under the rule of this court. The extract of the letter, as furnished Lieutenant Colonel Frémont from the office of the Adjutant General, certified to be a true copy by Assistant Adjutant General Townsend, and which was presented by Lieutenant Colonel Frémont with the question, was here read to the court; then the remainder of the letter, as it appears on the letter book of General Kearny, was also read.

[No. 7.]

HEAD-QUARTERS, 10TH MILITARY DEPARTMENT,
Monterey, California, March 15, 1847.

SIR: As the ship Savannah is getting ready to leave here for New York, I avail myself of the opportunity to write by her.

Accompanied by Captain Turner, 1st dragoons, and Lieutenant Warner, topographical engineers, I left San Diego on the 31st January, as I informed you I should do in my letter of the day previous, and reaching this port on the 8th February, I was much gratified in finding the ship Independence, with Commodore Shubrick, and the ship Lexington, which had brought out Captain Tompkins's company, 3d artilllery.

On my showing to Commodore Shubrick my instructions from the War Department, of June 3 and 18, 1846, he was at once prepared to pay all proper respect to them, and being at that time the commander-in-chief of the naval forces on this station, he acknowledged me as the head and commander of the troops in California, which Commodore Stockton and Lieutenant Colonel Frémont had hitherto refused. He then showed me the instructions to Commodore Sloat, of July 12th, from the Navy Department, received by the Lexington at Valparaiso, on the 2d December, and which he had brought with him from there, and as they contained directions for Commodore Sloat to take charge of the civil affairs in California, I immediately told Commodore Shubrick that I cheerfully acquiesced and was ready to afford him any assistance in my power. We agreed upon our separate duties, and I then went to the bay of San Francisco, taking with me Lieutenant Halleck, of the engineers, besides Captain Turner and Lieutenant Warner, when was made a reconnoissance of the bay with a view to the selection of sites for fortifications for the protection of the shipping in the harbor, and the security of the land forces.

Colonel Mason, 1st dragoons, arrived at the bay February 12, with letters and instructions to me from Washington, as late as November 5, and was accompanied by Lieutenant Watson, of the navy, with instructions to Commodore Shubrick. On my return here, and on my showing to Commodore Shubrick my instructions, and seeing his, we deemed it advisable to inform the people in California at once of the President's instructions to us, and we jointly issued a circular on the 1st March, and I, with his approval, and that of Commodore Biddle, (who arrived on the 2d,) issued a proclamation on the 4th, (dated the 1st,) a copy of which papers in print is enclosed herewith.

Upon Commodore Biddle's arrival, I had a full understanding with him relating to our duties, and I take pleasure here to acknowledge the great courtesy I have received from both these gentlemen, and to add that, so long as either continues in the command of the naval forces on this station, there is no possibility of any other than a cordial and harmonious co-operation between us.

On the 2d instant I sent Captain Turner to the Ciudad de los Angeles, carrying with him department orders, No. 2, and my letter to Lieutenant Colonel Frémont, both of March 1, a copy of which is enclosed. I have not heard of his arrival there.

On the 5th instant Colonel Stevenson, with three companies of his regiment, (the 7th New York volunteers,) arrived at the bay of San Francisco; on leaving which, I issued orders, No. 4, a copy of which is enclosed. The heavy ordnance stores brought out by that regiment will be landed at San Francisco, and be protected by the command to be stationed there. That brought out by the Lexington is still on board of her in this harbor, as at present there is no place on shore where I am willing to trust it

From the large amount of ordnance stores sent to California by the department, I presume the territory will never be restored to Mexico! and it should not be! Should it be restored, Mexico could not possibly hold it three months.

The people in the territory (Californians as well as emigrants) would resist Mexican authority, and there would follow dissensions, quarrels, and fighting between them, until humanity would compel our government to interpose a strong arm to put a stop to such civil war, and to take the country again under her protection.

The Californians are now quiet, and I shall endeavor to keep them so by mild and gentle treatment; had they received such treatment from the time our flag was hoisted here in July last, I believe there would have been but little or no resistance on their part.

They have been most cruelly and shamefully abused by our own people, by the volunteers (American emigrants) raised in this part of the country, and on the Sacramento. Had they not resisted, they would have been unworthy the names of men.

Very respectfully, your most obedient servant,

S. W. KEARNY,
Brigadier General

Brig. Gen. R. Jones,
  Adj't. Gen. United States Army, Washington.

A true copy:

E. D. TOWNSEND,
Assistant Adjutant General.

*   *   *   *   *   *   *   *

If the people remain quiet, and California continues under our flag, it will ere long be a bright star in our Union. The climate is pure and healthy, physicians meeting with no encouragement, as its inhabitants are never sick; the soil is rich, and there is much unsettled land that will admit of a dense population. California, with Oregon, is destined to supplant the Sandwich islands, and will furnish our 600 whaling vessels, and our 20,000 sailors in them, besides our navy and our troops, with their breadstuffs and most of the other articles they are to consume.

At present the population is small, most probably not exceeding 12,000, of which about one-fifth are emigrants. A very few years will add greatly to the latter class. Besides these, there are about 15,000 Indians, nearly one-third being called Christian Indians, who speak the Spanish language; the remainder are the wild Indians, who live in the mountains, and subsist, in a great measure, upon the horses and cattle they steal from the farms.

The Christian Indians are the laborers and servants of the country, and are held, if not in bondage like our own slaves, at least very much like it.

For the preservation of peace and quiet, now so happily existing in California, and to protect the people from the Indians depredating upon them, there should be kept in the territory, for some years to come, about 1,000 soldiers; they should be enlisted expressly to serve here, as I suggested in my letter to you of the 16th September last. We can get no recruits here.

The bay of San Francisco, Monterey, and Diego, afford excellent harbors, and they should be protected by permanent fortifications. I have directed the old Spanish fort, at the entrance of the bay of San Francisco, to be put in good order, and guns to be mounted there. It will be a barbette battery; its position is a highly important one, as no vessel can enter without passing under its guns; the distance from it to the opposite shore being less than one mile; the work will cost but a few thousand dollars.

There are other places in the bay where extensive fortifications should be erected, and which will cost much money. These will not be commenced till an appropriation is made, or orders received for it. The subject will be fully presented to you after the engineer officers have made a careful examination and report upon it. I have not heard of Colonel Price and his Missouri regiment since I left New Mexico, and presume he must have passed the winter there. I, of course, cannot know if he intends this spring to avail himself of the authority to come here, which I gave him on the 2d October last, a copy of which I furnished you. I have to acknowledge the receipt, by Colonel Mason, of the following papers:

Letter from Secretary of War to General Kearny, September 12, with papers referred to.

Letter from Secretary of War to Colonel Stevenson, September 11.

Letter from Secretary of War to Colonel Stevenson, September 15.

Letter from the general-in-chief to General Kearny, November 3.

Letter from the adjutant general to General Kearny, November 4.

Letter from Secretary of Navy to Commodore Shubrick, August 17.

Letter from Secretary of Navy to Commodore Stockton, November 5.

Circular of Secretary of War, October 15; and general orders Nos. 34, 43, 45, 48, 49.

Agreeably to directions in yours, of November 4th, I have numbered this letter 7, of this year; mine to you, of January 12th, would be No. 1; January 14th, No. 2; January 16th, No. 3; January 17th, No. 4; January 23d, No. 5; January 30th, No. 6. I enclose a copy of the rough notes of the journal of our march from New Mexico to California, kept by my late aid-de-camp, Captain Johnston, 1st dragoons. When I receive the journal of the march of the Mormon battalion, I will forward it to you. Lieutenant Emory, of the topographical engineers, having gone to Washington, will there prepare for your office his notes and map of the country passed over by us. I enclose letter of March 14th, from Captain Tompkins, 3d artillery, stating that he had concluded to resign his commission in the army of the United States, and requesting its acceptance at the earliest convenient date, and I recommend that he be gratified, at the close of the war.

Very respectfully, your obedient servant,

S. W. KEARNY,
Brigadier General.

Brigadier General R. JONES,
Adj. Gen. U. S. A., Washington.

Lieutenant Colonel Frémont presented the following paper to the court: "Lieutenant Colonel Frémont would explain to the court, that in all instances where he presents extracts of letters, it is in pursuance of a request from the State, Navy, and War Departments, not to require copies of any matter not applicable to the case. In the present instance, the portion omitted appears to relate to subjects entirely disconnected from the case before the court, and was therefore omitted in the copy furnished from the department."

The court was cleared to consider what part of the letter should be recorded.

The court decided that the whole paper should be recorded; the extract as furnished from the War Department, and the continuation of the letter as furnished from the letter book of General Kearny; both being admitted by consent as authentic copies.

The court was then opened; Lieutenant Colonel Frémont in court. The decision in closed session was announced.

General Kearny, a witness—Cross-examination continued.

Question. You say the circular of yourself and Commodore

Shubrick was drawn up on the 4th of March, and dated on the first of that month; now, when and where was it promulgated?

Answer. I stated no such thing.

Question. You state in your letter of the 15th of March, that you issued a proclamation on the 4th, dated on the 1st of March; now, when and where was that proclamation promulgated?

Answer. It was promulgated throughout California; it was given in manuscript to the printer on the 4th of March; many copies of it were printed and distributed immediately after;. the copies were sent by the printer to me; and Mr. Larkin, at whose house I was staying, took them from me to distribute; the printers, as I understood him, distributed some; I believe they were printed on the 5th. If the object of the accused is to inquire of me whether Captain Turner, when he went below, took a copy of that paper, I will say that he did not.

Question. From what point was the promulgation made?

Answer. It was made from Monterey, where it is dated.

Question. In that same letter you say, "He (Commodore Shubrick) then showed me the instructions to Commodore Sloat, of July 12th, from the Navy Department, received by the Lexington, at Valparaiso, on the 2d December, and which he had brought with him from there; and as they contained directions for Commodore Sloat to take charge of the *civil* affairs in California, I immediate told Commodore Shubrick that I acquiesced, and was ready to afford him any assistance in my power." Now, was not Commodore Stockton (the successor of Commodore Sloat) as fully in exercise of the civil government, when you got to San Diego, as Commodore Shubrick was when you got to Monterey?

Answer. When I reached San Diego, on the 12th of December, 1846, Commodore Stockton was there, and in full exercise of all the orders which he had received from the Navy Department, and of those which he had received frcm Commodore Sloat. When I got to Monterey, early in February, Commodore Shubrick was there, and I know not of his being at that time at the head of the civil government at all.

Question. In that same letter from Monterey, you write as follows: "The Californians are now quiet, and I shall endeavor to keep them so by mild and gentle treatment; had they received such treatment from the time our flag was hoisted here, in July last, I believe there would have been little or no resistance on their part; they have been most cruelly and shamefully abused by our own people, by the volunteers (American emigrants) raised in this part of the country, and on the Sacramento. Had they not resisted they would have been unworthy the names of men." Now did any part of this denunciation of the American settlers apply to Lieutenant Colonel Frémont, or to the men under his command? or did you exempt him from its application?

Answer. It did apply to Lieutenant Colonel Frémont's command of volunteers.

Question. Did you give Lieutenant Colonel Frémont any notice of what you had so written?

Answer. I did not.

Question. By the word " resistance," as used in the last quoted paragraph of your letter, do you mean the insurrection at *Los Angeles*, in September, 1846?

Answer. I meant that there would have been, in my opinion, but little resistance on the part of the Californians at any time.

Lieutenant Colonel Frémont requested that the witness would answer whether he referred to the insurrection at Los Angeles?

Answer. I did not refer particularly to that time.

Question. To what act of the Californians does the word " resistance" refer?

Answer. It refers to many acts of the men belonging to the California battalion, done under the eyes of Lieutenant Colonel Frémont, which acts I will state if requested.

The court was cleared for deliberation. The judge advocate thought the acts of the California battalion, under the eyes of Lieutenant Colonel Frémont, which are referred to as having produced resistance in California, ought not to be brought before the court, as they have no relation to the charges.

The court decided that these acts shall not be brought before it; and, as these are suggested by the witness as the cause of his report, the court decline to inquire further into that report.

The court was then opened; Lieutenant Colonel Frémont in court. The decision in closed session was announced.

General Kearny, a witness.—Cross-examination continued.

Question. What did you mean by words " unquestionable ruin," as alleged to have been addressed by you to Lieutenant Colonel Frémont on the 17th of January? and did you there contemplate his arrest and trial before a court martial?

Answer. I meant as the words imply. I did not then contemplate at that time the arrest of Lieutenant Colonel Frémont, because I was in hopes that a little reflection would convince him of the error of adhering to the course indicated in his letter to me.

Question. Did you make known your intention to arrest him to Commodore Shubrick and Commodore Biddle?

Answer. I did to Commodore Biddle, and I think to Commodore Shubrick.

Question. How did you obtain the letter from Commodore Shubrick set out in specification 4, charge 1?

The question was objected to. The court was cleared for deliberation. The court decided that the question shall not be put.

The court was opened; Lieutenant Colonel Frémont in court. The decision in closed session was announced.

General Kearny offered to the judge advocate to show how he received the letter. The judge advocate said that the court had decided not to inquire into it.

Question. Did you communicate the instructions of the fifth of November, 1846, to Lieutenant Colonel Frémont?

Answer. I did not. I am not in the habit of communicating to my juniors the instructions I receive from my seniors, unless required to do so in those instructions.

Question. Do you know whether the said instructions were communicated to him by Commodore Shubrick or Commodore Biddle?

Answer. I do not believe that they were; but I know not.

Question. Was Lieutenant Colonel Frémont *relieved* of his duties and functions of governor of California, under the appointment of Commodore Stockton, and approval by the President, before the orders of March 1st were given to him?

Answer. I never heard that the appointment of Lieutenant Colonel Frémont, as governor of California, made by Commodore Stockton, has been approved by the President. He was not relieved in his duties as governor until the first of March, when I assumed those duties myself.

Question. Was that the only mode in which he was relieved?

Answer. It was.

Question. Did Commodore Shubrick " *relinquish*" to you, according to the instructions of the 5th of November, 1846, the administration of the civil government of California; and if so, when?

Answer. I am not aware that he assumed at any time the administration of the civil government of California.

Question. Were there any other orders, of March 1st, to Lieutenant Colonel Frémont, besides those already mentioned by you, namely: to bring the government archives from Los Angeles to Monterey, and to muster the California battalion?

Answer. 10th military department orders, No. 2, of March 1st, and my letter of instructions to him of same date, are the only orders, in my recollection, given to him. With those communications, sent by me to Lieutenant Colonel Frémont, was a copy of general orders, No. 49, establishing the 10th military department, and Commodore Shubrick's and my own circular, (the joint circular,) of March 1st. I recollect no other orders.

Question. Did you write an official letter to Lieutenant Colonel Frémont on March 1st; and is this the original?

Answer. This is my writing; and this is my official communication to him.

The letter here shown to witness then read, as follows:

HEAD-QUARTERS, 10TH MILITARY DEPARTMENT,
Monterey, (U. C.,) March 1, 1847.

SIR: By department orders, No. 2, of this date, which will be handed to you by Captain Turner, 1st dragoons, acting assistant adjutant general for my command, you will see that certain duties are there required of you, as commander of the battalion of California volunteers. In addition to the duties above referred to, I have now to direct that you will bring with you, and with as little delay as possible, all the archives and public documents and papers which may be subject to your control, and which appertain to the government of California, that I may receive them from your hands at this place, the capital of the territory. I have directions from the general-in-chief not to detain you in this country against your wishes, a moment longer than the necessities of the service may require, and you will be at liberty to leave here after you have complied with these instructions, and those in the " orders" referred to.

Very respectfully, your obedient servant,
                                    S. W. KEARNY,
          Brigadier General, and Governor of California.

To Lieut. Colonel J. C. Frémont,
          Regiment of Mounted Riflemen, com'd'g bat.
                    of California volunteers, Ciudad de los Angeles.

Question. In that letter you say, " I have directions from the general-in-chief not to detain you in this country, against your wishes, a moment longer than the necessities of the service may require, and you will be at liberty to leave here after you have complied with these instructions, and those in the orders referred to." Now, what were the necessities of the service, on the said first of March, which prevented you from permitting Lieutenant Colonel Frémont to leave California as soon as he pleased?

A member objecting, the court was cleared for deliberation, and decided that the question was irrelevant, and should not be put. The court was opened; Lieutenant Colonel Frémont in court. The decision in closed session was announced.

          General Kearny, a witness.—Cross-examination continued.

Question. Did he not apply to you for leave to go to his regiment in Mexico? Did he not say that he had 120 picked horses and 60 men ready to go, with *pinoli* and dried beef for their support; and with these men and horses could go to Taylor's right, and thence to his regiment? and did he not believe that regiment would be on the way to the city of Mexico? and if not, will you tell all that did pass, if anything, in relation to going to his regiment?

The judge advocate handed the question to the president, with a suggestion that it belonged to the class of questions objected to and ruled out by the court. The president not considering the question materially objectionable, it was put.

Answer. In a conversation with Lieutenant Colonel Frémont, at Los Angeles, about the 10th or 11th of May, 1847, he did apply to me for permission to go to join General Taylor's army. He told me that he had a sufficient number of men, which, with his knowledge of the country, would enable him to get there. I refused to let him go. What his belief was in relation to the movements of his regiment, I do not know.

Question. Did he ask permission to come home, after that refu-
ful, by a direct route from Los Angeles?

Answer. He did make that request of me, which I refused.

Question. Did you order him to turn over the astronomical instruments which he had in his possession from the Topographical
Bureau, and which he had used in his explorations?

Answer. I did. I forget the exact phraseology of the order. It
was made out by the acting assistant adjutant general, Captain
Turner, and I have no copy of it.

Question. In your direct testimony, you gave an account of the
latter part of a conversation had with Lieutenant Colonel Frémont,
at Monterey; will you now give the fore part of that conversation?

Answer. Lieutenant Colonel Frémont came to my quarters at
Monterey about the 26th of March; Colonel Mason, of the 1st dragoons, was present; Lieutenant Colonel Frémont said to me that
he wished to have some conversation with me; I answered him, I
was ready to hold it. He made some remarks about the presence
of Colonel Mason; I told him that Colonel Mason had been sent
out by the War Department to relieve me in my command in California as soon as I thought proper to leave it, and that there was
no conversation which I could hold with him, on public affairs, but
that it was proper Colonel Mason should be present at. He then
told me that perhaps I had Colonel Mason there to take advantage
of some unguarded expressions of his. His reply to me was offensive, and I told him that I could hardly believe that he would
come into my quarters and intentionally insult me. He made no
reply; nor did he state what the object of his remark to me was.

I after that told Lieutenant Colonel Frémont, that I had on the
first of March sent, by Captain Turner, orders to him, and I wanted
to know most distinctly from him, before I had any further conversation with him, whether he intended to obey those orders or
not. He hesitated; I then told him to reflect well upon the answer which he was to make to me, for his answer would be a very
important one; if he wanted an hour for consideration, to take it;
if he wanted a day for consideration, he could take it. Upon that
he left my room, and, I presume, in about an hour he returned, and
said that he would obey my orders. That is the beginning of that
conversation.

Question. Did not Lieutenant Colonel Frémont wait on you the
evening before the day of that interview, (as a call of etiquette
and duty,) and immediately on his arrival at Monterey?

Answer. I have no recollection of it; but I am far from saying
that he did not.

Question. Did not Lieutenant Colonel Frémont, the next morning, (the 26th of March,) through Mr. Larkin, the American consul, ask an interview with you on business; and did not the interview of that day take place in consequence of that request?

Answer. It did. I will now add, that I think Lieutenant Colonel Frémont, with Mr. Larkin, came to see me on the evening previous.

Question. Was not that business to see if you would provide for the payment of arrearages of the government incurred while he was governor of California under Governor Stockton's appointment?

Answer. What Lieutenant Colonel Frémont's object or business with me was, I never knew; and it has frequently been the subject of conversation between myself and others as to what brought Lieutenant Colonel Frémont to Monterey at that time.

The testimony taken to-day was read over to the witness, and then, at five minutes before three, the court adjourned to meet to-morrow at 10 o'clock.

Tuesday, *November* 16, 1847.—10 *o'clock.*

The court met pursuant to adjournment.

Present: all the members, the judge advocate, and Lieutenant Colonel Frémont.

The proceedings of yesterday were read over. Lieutenant Colonel Frémont presented a paper to the court, as follows:

Mr. President: There appears to have been an entire misapprehension of the meaning of the question offered yesterday, and through that misapprehension not answered, to wit: as to the acts of "*resistance*" on the part of the Californian people, and not as to the acts of the California battalion, alleged to have produced that "*resistance.*" The object is to know if the insurrection of September last is intended to be included under that word "*resistance.*"

J. C. FRÉMONT,
Lieutenant Colonel Mounted Riflemen.

The court was cleared for deliberation. After mature deliberation, the court decided that the subject alluded to in Lieutenant Colonel Frémont's paper, last presented, has no relation whatever to the charges and specifications under trial. The court adheres to its decision of yesterday, that it cannot inquire into acts of resistance any more than into the acts of oppression, which are alleged as leading to that resistance.

The court was opened. Lieutenant Colonel Frémont in court. The decision, in closed session, was announced.

General Kearny, a witness.—Cross-examination continued.

Question. Did you not grant the interview, as requested through Mr. Larkin; and did not Lieutenant Colonel Frémont appear accordingly at your quarters, at the expected time?

Answer. I did; and Lieutenant Colonel Frémont appeared at my quarters accordingly.

Question. Did not Lieutenant Colonel Frémont come alone?

Answer. I think Mr. Larkin opened the door of my quarters; Lieutenant Colonel Frémont entered; Mr. Larkin closed the door and retired.

Question. Was not Colonel Mason with you, and by your request; and to be present at your intended interrogation on the point of obedience?

Answer. Colonel Mason was with me, at my request.

Question. Do you not know, or believe, that Lieutenant Colonel Frémont made an extraordinary ride in that visit of his to Monterey, and indicative of extraordinary business?

Answer. I understood that Lieutenant Colonel Frémont had come up from Los Angeles in about four days, perhaps less. It was a very short time for such a ride, the distance being nearly 400 miles.

Question. Does not the following paragraph from the Californian newspaper, of March 27th, correctly describe that ride? "Lieutenant Colonel Frémont arrived here day before yesterday, in three days, ten hours, from Los Angeles, (400 miles,) on business with Governor Kearny, and left again yesterday afternoon for the purpose of embarking his battalion for this port. He expects to be in Monterey again by the 10th or 12th of April. The colonel will have ridden over 800 miles in eight days, including all delays on this trip."

Answer. As I stated before I believe the ride from Los Angeles may have been made in less than four days; whether this account in the Californian newspaper, that he had rode it in three days and ten hours, is correct or not, I cannot tell. He left Monterey on the 26th of March, as I believe, with orders from me to embark such men of the California battalion as would not be mustered into service on board of a ship, which I was to send to San Pedro; the ship to be furnished to me by orders from Commodore Biddle. It was supposed by me that he would return to Monterey as soon as possible. I would add, that when I directed Lieutenant Colonel Frémont, in a conversation with him, to embark his battalion at San Pedro, he told me he was always sick when at sea, and that he never would go there if he could avoid it. I then told him that he could see to the embarkation of his battalion, and then come up himself by land, which order I subsequently sent to him in writing.

Question. Do you know, or believe, that any person came from Los Angeles with him on that occasion, except Don Jesus Pico and one servant?

The judge advocate suggested that the question ought to indicate to the court the bearing and relevancy of the inquiry. If this reveals to the witness the object to which it is desired to lead him, that is unavoidable.

Lieutenant Colonel Frémont replies that the object will be approached with all proper directness, and that the object is *most important*.

Answer. I understood, and I believe, that the two persons mentioned in the question were the only persons who accompanied Lieutenant Colonel Frémont to Monterey.

Question. Did not Lieutenant Colonel Frémont in that interview make known to you that he wished to know whether you, as governor, would assume the government responsibilities, accruing during the time that he was governor, under Governor Stockton's appointment?

Answer. I have no recollection of his having asked me. If he had, I should have answered in the negative.

Question. Did you not *tell* him that you would not assume one cent of those liabilities? and do you not know that his drafts on account of those expenses are now protested to the amount of some twenty thousand dollars, and subject to be doubled, and he to be sued for the whole?

Answer. I do not remember of telling him as stated in the question. I do not know, at this time, that his drafts have been protested.

Question. Did he not immediately offer his resignation of his commission in the army? and did you not refuse it? and, if so, please relate all that passed?

Answer. In the conversation with him at Monterey, I think he did offer to resign his commission, which I refused to accept.

Question. Did you not tell him that his resignation should not lie on your table one moment?

Answer. I have not the remotest recollection of having told him so.

Question. You testified yesterday as follows: "He then told me that, perhaps, I had Colonel Mason there to take advantage of some unguarded expression of his. The reply to me was offensive, and I told him that I could hardly believe that he should come into my quarters, and intentionally insult me. He made no reply," &c., &c. Now, did he not reply that he did not come to insult you?

Answer. I have no recollection of his having told me so.

Question. Was not his offer to resign made after that?

Answer. His offer to resign was made some time during the conversation, and I presume must have been subsequent to the above remark.

Question. Did you not express great satisfaction when Lieutenant Colonel Frémont said he would obey you?

Answer. I did. I think I repeated two or three times to Lieutenant Colonel Frémont that I was greatly satisfied that he had concluded to obey my orders.

Question. Did you not immediately after, to wit, on the 28th of the same month, send Colonel Mason to Los Angeles with the following order, as the first paragraph?—and is that letter and order already set out in the proceedings?

Answer. This is my writing, and this is my letter.

The letter of the 28th of March from General Kearny to Lieutenant Colonel Frémont, sent by Colonel Mason, as hereinbefore recorded in these proceedings, was shown the witness, with this question, and then read to the court:

Question. Did you yourself go to Los Angeles some time after, and if so, when?

Answer. I went to Los Angeles, and arrived there on the 9th of May, 1847.

Question. What state of affairs did you find between Colonel Mason and Lieutenant Colonel Frémont, growing out of the execution of your orders to Colonel Mason? Did you find a duel impending, with double barrelled guns and buckshot cartridges—the weapons selected by Colonel Mason?

The court was ordered to be cleared.   Lieutenant Colonel Frémont stated to the judge advocate that this inquiry had a most important bearing on the charge of mutiny, as grounded on the conduct of Owens and the California battalion.   If the court should object to the inquiry at this time, he requested the decision of the court to be suspended, to permit the defence to resume the cross-examination of the witness on other matters, and that the defence will come to-morrow morning prepared to explain to the court in writing the effect and importance of this inquiry.

After mature deliberation, the court decided as follows: The court see no relevancy of the question, or the subject which it introduces, to the matter under trial, and cannot entertain the question, or the matter to which it relates, in any shape.

The court was then opened; Lieutenant Colonel Frémont in court.   The decision in close session was announced.

General Kearny, a witness.—Cross-examination continued.

Question. Did you not, on the 13th of January, write to Commodore Stockton as governor, and commanding the United States forces, and is this a correct copy of your letter?

Answer. My command at Los Angeles, on the 13th of January, was composed of about 500 sailors and marines, besides about 60 dragoons and a few volunteers which had accompanied us from San Diego; as so very large a proportion of the command consisted of sailors and marines, I made but few movements with them without consulting Commodore Stockton's wishes.   This is a copy of my letter of that date.

The letter here shown the witness, was then read as follows:

HEAD-QUARTERS, ARMY OF THE WEST,
CIUDAD DE LOS ANGELES, U. C.,
January 13, 1847.

SIR: I fear, from the armistice which I this morning saw, signed by Lieutenant Colonel Frémont, and sent to me by you, that our countrymen under Colonel Frémont are entirely ignorant of our eing here; that they are embarrassed in their movements; and, I further fear that, unless something is done *at once* to inform them of the true state of affairs here, that they may capitulate and retire to the upper country.

To avoid so serious an evil, I advise and offer to take one-half of this command, from 250 to 300 men, and march at once to form a junction with Lieutenant Colonel Frémont.

Very respectfully, your obedient servant,

S. W. KEARNY,
Brig. General.

Commodore R. F. STOCKTON,
   Gov. of California, com'd'g. U. S. forces.

A true copy:

E. D. TOWNSEND,
Asst. Adj. General.

Question. In your testimony on Wednesday last, you say: "I never heard of Commodore Stockton's conferring a commission on Lieutenant Colonel Frémont, further than having appointed him military commandant of California." Now, were not copies of these two papers, in which he is described as "Major Frémont," among those which were furnished to you by Commodore Stockton at San Diego, in December last, and were they not filed in the War Department by you since your return from California, and after your arrival in this city in September last?

Answer. I think that copies of these papers were furnished to me by Commodore Stockton.

The papers shown the witness, with this question, then read as follows:

CIUDAD DE LOS ANGELES,
August 24, 1846.

SIR: By the Mexican newspapers, I see that war has been declared both by the United States and Mexico, and the most vigorous measures have been adopted by Congress to carry it to a speedy conclusion. Privateers will, no doubt, be fitted out to prey upon our commerce, and the immense value of that commerce in the Pacific ocean, and the number of valuable men engaged in it, require, immediately, all the protection that can be given to them by the ships under my command. I must therefore withdraw my forces from California as soon as it can be safely done, and, as soon as you can enlist men enough to garrison this city, Monterey, San Francisco, Santa Barbara, and San Diego, and to have a sufficient force besides, to watch the Indians and other enemies. For these purposes, you are authorized and required to increase your present force to 300 men; fifty for San Francisco, fifty for Monterey, twenty-five for Santa Barbara, fifty for this city, and twenty-five for San Diego; and one hundred to be kept together with whom those in the several garrisons can, at short notice, be called upon at any time, in case of necessity, to act.

I purpose, before I leave the territory, to appoint you to be the governor, and Captain Gillespie the secretary thereof; and to appoint, also, the council of state and all the other necessary officers.

You will, therefore, proceed, without delay, to do all you can to further my views and intentions thus frankly manifested.

Supposing that by the 25th of October you will have accomplished your part of these preparations, I will meet you at San Francisco, on that day, to complete the whole arrangement, and to place you as governor over California.

You will dispose of your present force in the following manner, which may be hereafter altered as occasion may require:

Captain Gillespie to be stationed at this city with fifty men and officers in the neighborhood; twenty-five men, with an officer, at Santa Barbara; fifty men and officers at Monterey, and fifty at San Francisco. If this be done at once, I can at any time safely withdraw my forces as I proceed up the coast to San Francisco, and be ready, after our meeting on the 25th of October, to leave the desk and the camp and take to the ship and to the sea.

Faithfully, your obedient servant,
R. F. STOCKTON,
Commander-in-chief and Governor
of the Territory of California.

To Major FREMONT,
California battalion, Angeles.

A true copy of the enclosure in General Kearny's despatches to the department of September 21, 1847.
E. D. TOWNSEND,
Assistant Adjutant General.

Know all men by these presents:

That I, Robert F. Stockton, governor and commander-in-chief of the territory of California, reposing special confidence in the ability and patriotism of Major J. C. Frémont, of the United States army, do hereby appoint him to be the military commandant of the territory of California.

To have and to exercise all the powers and privileges of that office until the governor of the said territory shall otherwise direct.

Therefore, by these presents, I do hereby command all civil and military officers and citizens to obey him accordingly.

Given under my hand on this second day of September, Anno Domini one thousand eight hundred and forty-six.
R. F. STOCKTON.

CIUDAD DE LOS ANGELES, *Sept.* 2, 1848.

A true copy of the enclosure in General Kearny's despatches to the department of September 21, 1846.
E. D. TOWNSEND,
Assistant Adjutant General.

Question. Did you not file those papers in the war office since your return from California, and after your arrival in this city in September last?

Answer. I see on those papers certificates from Captain Townsend that I did so. I think Captain Townsend is mistaken.

Question. In your letter to the adjutant general, of the 17th January, produced in evidence yesterday, the concluding paragraph is as follows: "I have to state that the march of the troops from San Diego to this place was reluctantly consented to by Commodore Stockton, on my urgent advice that he should not leave Lieutenant Colonel Frémont unsupported to fight a battle on which the fate of California might, for a long time, depend. The correspondence to prove which is now with my papers at San Diego, and a copy of which will be furnished to you on my return to that place." Are these three letters copies of the correspondence alluded to in that paragraph?

Answer. They are. To make the subject complete, an order of Commodore Stockton, of the 23d of December, is wanting.

The papers shown to the witness with this question were then read to the court, being—

1st. Letter from General Kearny to Commodore Stockton, dated San Diego, December 22, 1846, already on this record at page —.

2d. A letter from Commodore Stockton to General Kearny, as follows:

HEAD-QUARTERS, SAN DIEGO,
December 23, 1846.

DEAR GENERAL: Your note of yesterday was handed to me last night by Captain Turner of the dragoons.

In reply to that note, permit me to refer you to the conversation held with you yesterday morning at your quarters. I stated to you distinctly that I intended to march upon St. Louis Rey as soon as possible with a part of the forces under my command, that I was very desirous to march on to the Pueblo to co-operate with Lieutenant Colonel Frémont, but my movements, after taking St. Louis Rey, would depend entirely upon the information that I might receive as to the movements of Colonel Frémont and the enemy. It might be necessary for me to stop the pass at San Filipe, or march back to San Diego.

Now, my dear general, if the object of your note is to advise me to do any thing which would enable a larger force of the enemy to get into my rear and cut off my communication with San Diego, and hazard the safety of the garrison and the ships in the harbor, you will excuse me for saying I cannot follow any such advice.

My purpose still is to march for St. Louis Rey as soon as I can get the dragoons and riflemen mounted, which I hope to do in two days.

Faithfully, your obedient servant,

R. F. STOCKTON,
Commander-in-chief and Governor
of the Territory of California.

To Brigadier General S. W. KEARNY,
United States Army.

From true copy:

W. H. EMORY,
Act. Adj. Gen., army of the West.

A true copy:

E. D. TOWNSEND,
Assistant Adjutant General.

3d. Also, a letter from General Kearny to Commodore Stockton, as follows:

SAN DIEGO, *December* 23, 1846.

DEAR COMMODORE: I have received yours of this date, repeating, as you say, what you stated to me yesterday, and in reply, I have only to remark, that if I had so understood you, I certainly would not have written my letter to you of last evening.

You certainly could not for a moment suppose that I would advise or suggest to you any movement which might endanger the safety of the garrison and the ships in this harbor.

My letter of yesterday's date stated that, "If you can take from here," &c., &c., of which you were the judge, and of which I knew nothing.

Yours, truly,

S. W. KEARNY, *Brig. Gen.*

Commodore R. F. STOCKTON,
Commanding U. S. Navy, &c., &c., San Diego.

From true copy:

W. H. EMORY,
Acting Adjutant General, Army of the West.

A true copy:

E. D. TOWNSEND,
Assistant Adjutant General.

Question. Is this a copy of the order you allude to, as necessary to complete the matter?
Answer. It is.

The paper shown to the witness, with this question, was then read to the court, as follows:

[GENERAL ORDERS.]

SAN DIEGO, *December* 23, 1846.

The forces composed of Captain Tilghman's company of artille-ry, a detachment of the 1st regiment of dragoons, companies A and B of the California battalion of mounted riflemen, and a detach-ment of sailors and marines from the frigates Congress and Savan-nah and the ship Portsmouth, will take up the line of march for the Ciudad de los Angeles on Monday morning, the 28th instant, at 10 o'clock, A. M.

By order of the commander-in-chief.

J. ZEILAN,
Brevet Captain and Adjutant.

From true copy:

W. H. EMORY,
Acting Adj. Gen., Army of the West.

A true copy:

E. D. TOWNSEND,
Assistant Adjutant General.

Lieutenant Colonel Frémont presented the following paper:

Lieutenant Colonel Frémont desires to say to the court, that all the papers from the war office exhibited to the court this day, were received from the war office after the adjournment of the court yesterday evening, and that he has many other papers received at the same time, and not yet examined to ascertain their materiality. He has but few questions now to ask, and will termi-nate the cross-examination this evening, reserving the privilege of introducing further papers from the war office, received last eve-ning, if found material when examined to-night.

Question. Did you order Lieutenant Colonel Frémont, with the men of the topographical party lately under his command, to re-pair with his men to Monterey, in order to return with you to the United States?

Answer. In my letter to Lieutenant Colonel Frémont of March 28, 1847, the order was given to him. The letter has been before the court.

Question. Did they accordingly appear (and at a fixed hour) in Monterey, all mounted, and Lieutenant Colonel Frémont at their head, to be viewed and ordered by you?

Answer. They appeared, with Lieutenant Colonel Frémont at their head, about the 29th May, 1847, after I had been to Los Angeles and ordered Lieutenant Colonel Frémont to go from there to Monterey.

Question. Did you leave any of the men of the topographical party behind in California?

Answer. Some of the volunteers asked to be discharged in Cali-fornia, and I directed Lieutenant Colonel Frémont to discharge them accordingly. I will explain. When Lieutenant Colonel Fré-

mont brought his command mounted near to my quarters, I asked
of them if any wished to be discharged in California. Some did
wish it, and I gave the directions to Lieutenant Colonel Frémont
accordingly to discharge them. Those who wished to be discharged separated themselves from the main party, and moved to
one side of the street.

Question. Did you leave Mr. Keen, the artist, and Mr. King, an
assistant, behind? and are they not yet behind?

The judge advocate said he did not see the bearing of the question, though he saw no other material objection to it. General
Kearney said he was willing to answer. Lieutenant Colonel Frémont said, he would withdraw it if any member of the court had
the least objection. No objection being made, it was put.

Answer. Those gentlemen were left behind in California not by
by my orders or directions.

Question. Did you leave behind, and refuse Lieutenant Colonel
Frémont permission to go to Yerba Buena for them, the geological
and botanical specimens which he had been collecting in the two
years of his last expedition?

Answer. Lieutenant Colonel Frémont expressed a wish to go to
Yerba Buena, which I refused to grant him.

Question. Did you not stop the topographical pursuits of Lieutenant Colonel Frémont, by ordering him to turn over his instruments to another officer, and by assuming command over his men?

The judge advocate repeated that he saw no objection to this
question, except its irrelevancy.

Lieutenant Colonel Frémont expressed a wish to have it answered.
No objection being made, it was put.

Answer. Any one can judge and answer that question as well as
myself. I required Lieutenant Colonel Frémont to turn over his
instrument to the senior topographical officer in California. I think
they were received by Lieutenant Halleck, of the engineers, for
Lieutenant Warner, of the topographical engineers, and I also required Lieutenant Colonel Frémont, with his party, to remain with
me, and under my orders, on the march from California to Missouri.

Question. How, and in what manner, was the arrest of Lieutenant Colonel Frémont effected in Fort Leavenworth; by a sealed
letter, or by reading an order to him in presence of a witness? and
in what part of the fort, and how did he get there?

Answer. Lieutenant Colonel Frémont came to near the office of
Lieutenant Colonel Wharton, commanding at Fort Leavenworth;
I asked him to dismount and come into the office; he did so. Upon
his taking a seat, at my request, Lieutenant Colonel Wharton being present, I gave him a copy of the first paragraph of an order
of mine, dated August 22, 1847, which is in my letter book.

The order was then read to the court, as follows:

[Orders.]
FORT LEAVENWORTH,
August 22, 1847.

1. Lieutenant Colonel Frémont, of the regiment of mounted rifle-men, will turn over to the officers of the different departments, at this post, the horses, mules, and other public property in the use of the topographical party now under his charge, for which receipts will be given. He will arrange the accounts of these men, (nineteen in number,) so that they can be paid at the earliest possible date.

Lieutenant Colonel Frémont having performed the above duty, will consider himself under arrest, and will then repair to Washington city, and report himself to the adjutant general of the army.

* * * * * * * * *

The rest of the order was also read to the court, but being found not relevant to this case, is not recorded.

Question. Had an orderly been sent out to Lieutenant Colonel Frémont's camp, about two miles from Fort Leavenworth, to direct him to repair to that place where he was arrested?

The judge advocate said he saw *no* objection to the question, except its irrelevancy.

Lieutenant Colonel Frémont said that he considered it relevant.

Answer. An orderly was sent by me for Lieutenant Colonel Frémont, at Fort Leavenworth, to Lieutenant Colonel Frémont's camp; Lieutenant Colonel Frémont shortly after came to my office. I know not whether the orderly saw him.

The cross-examination was here closed, with the understanding, as heretofore expressed to the court by Lieutenant Colonel Frémont, and acceded to.

The testimony, taken to-day, was read over to the witness, and then, at fifteen minutes before three, the court adjourned to meet to-morrow, at ten o'clock.

WEDNESDAY, *November* 17, 1847.—10 o'clock.

The court met pursuant to adjournment. Present: all the members, the judge advocate, and Lieutenant Colonel Frémont.

The proceedings of yesterday were read over. General Kearny being in court, said: I wish to make an explanation in relation to my testimony of yesterday.

General Kearny then stated: upon reflection, and upon examination, I find that my doubts of yesterday, relating to the two papers of Commodore Stockton, referred to by the accused, as having been filed by me in the War Department, are now dispelled. These papers were sent by me, with many others, to the War Department on the 21st of September. I therefore take great pleasure in stating the fact, and in adding that the certificate of Captain Townsend on those papers is most fully and perfectly correct.

Lieutenant Colonel Frémont presented a paper, as follows:

Lieutenant Colonel Frémont respectfully states to the court that he has a number of papers, most of them recently received from the departments, which he will, probably, at some stage of the trial, require the present witness to identify, and some on which questions may be founded. But he will here stop the present cross-examination, and prevent any delay or trouble to the court.

The court was cleared for deliberation. After some time spent in closed session, the court was opened. Lieutenant Colonel Frémont in court.

At one o'clock the court took a recess of fifteen minutes; the time having elapsed, it was again in session. Present: all the members, the judge advocate and Lieutenant Colonel Frémont.

General Kearny, a witness.—Cross-examination continued.

Question by a member. Was Commodore Stockton regarded by you as governor and commander-in-chief of the land and naval forces in California, on the march from San Diego to Los Angeles, or at any other time after you first communicated with him in California; and if so, to what extent, and under what orders or authority did you so regard or recognize him? and under what orders or authority did Commodore Stockton assume, or attempt to exercise the functions of governor and commander-in-chief in California? and did the exercise of these functions by Commodore Stockton, or any orders to or from him, *interdict* your military authority over the troops in the department, to the command of which you had been assigned; if so, please state how far, and fully?

A member objecting, the court was cleared. After deliberation, the court decided that the question shall be put. The court then opened. Lieutenant Colonel Frémont present. The decision in closed session was announced.

General Kearny, a witness.

Answer. I found Commodore Stockton, on my arrival at San Diego, on the 12th of December, 1846, in command of the Pacific squadron, having several ships in harbor at that place, either two or three; most of his sailors were on shore. He had assumed the title of governor of California in the month of August previous; all at San Diego addressed him as governor; I did the same. After he had determined upon the march from San Diego to Los Angeles, the corps being paraded for it on the 29th of December, he, in the presence of several officers, among whom were myself, Captain Turner, of the dragoons, and Lieutenant Minor, of the navy, and others, whose names I do not recollect, remarked to them, "gentlemen, General Kearny has kindly consented to take command of the troops on this expedition.   *   *   *   *

The judge advocate remarked to the president that this is in evidence before.

No objection being made by the court, the witness continued to answer the question of the court, as follows:

*   * "You will, therefore, consider him as your commander. I will go along as governor and commander-in-chief in California." Under Commodore Stockton's directions, every arrangement for that expedition was made. I had nothing whatever to do with it. We marched from San Diego to Los Angeles; whilst on the march, and a few days before reaching Los Angeles, a commission of two citizens, as I believe, in behalf of Governor Flores, came to Commodore Stockton with communications to him as the governor or commander-in-chief in California. Commodore Stockton replied to that commission without consulting me. On the march, I at no time considered Commodore Stockton under my directions; nor did I at any time consider myself under his. His assimilated rank to officers of the army at that time was, and now is, and will, for upwards of a year, remain with that of colonel. Although I did not consider myself at any time, or under any circumstances, under the orders of Commodore Stockton; yet, as so large a portion of my command was of sailors and marines, I felt it my duty on all important subjects to consult his wishes; and so far as I consistently could do so to comply with them. He was considered by me as the commander-in-chief in California until he had, of his own accord, on the 29th of December, turned over a portion of that command to me. I believe the authority under which Commodore Stockton exercised the functions of governor was claimed by him as the right of conquest, as he considered it, of California, in the month of August.

Commodore Stockton, in his letter to me of the 17*th of January*, 1847, states that I would consider myself suspended from the command of the troops in this place, meaning Angeles; the troops at that place were the sailors and marines, a small detachment of volunteers, and about 60 dragoons; the dragoons under the command of Captain Turner, besides the battalion of California volunteers, under the command of Lieutenant Colonel Frémont. The word "suspend," as used in Commodore Stockton's letter to me, I considered applicable to his sailors and marines, and accordingly gave up the command of them immediately.

Question. Did Commodore Stockton attempt any exercise of authority on land after the arrival of Commodore Shubrick?

Answer. I believe not, further than the command of his own sailors and marines at San Diego.

Question. Did any order to, or from, Commodore Stockton, other than that of the 17th January, just mentioned, prohibit your command over Lieutenant Colonel Frémont?

Answer. Not to my knowledge.

The judge advocate here showed General Kearny an official copy of the letter of Commodore Stockton, in relation to which he was testifying.

General Kearny said: I see that the date of this letter is the 16th, and not the 17th. The letter was then read as follows:

HEAD-QUARTERS, CIUDAD DE LOS ANGELES,
January 16, 1847.

SIR: In answer to your note received this afternoon, I need say but little more than that which I communicated to you in a conversation at San Diego: that California was conquered, and a government put into successful operation; that a copy of the laws made by me for the government of the territory, and the names of the officers selected to see them faithfully executed were transmitted to the President of the United States before your arrival in the territory.

I will only add that I cannot do anything, nor desist from doing anything, or alter anything on your demand, which I will submit to the President, and ask for your recall. In the mean time you will consider yourself suspended from the command of the United States forces in this place.

Faithfully, your obedient servant,

R. F. STOCKTON,
Commander-in-chief.

To Brevet Brig. Gen. S. W. KEARNY.

A true copy.

E. D. TOWNSEND,
Assistant Adjutant General.

The court was then ordered to be cleared. After some time spent in secret session, the court was opened. Lieutenant Colonel Frémont present in court.

Question by a member. When you gave your order of the 16th January, 1847, to Lieutenant Colonel Frémont, and received his answer of the 17th, was he under duress from Commodore Stockton's exercising supreme authority, and having the means and the determination to enforce it?

Answer. I think not. I gave my order to Lieutenant Colonel Frémont, or rather my order to Lieutenant Colonel Frémont was written before my receiving the letter from Commodore Stockton of the 16th of January. I would explain to the court that, though I can remember about the time the letter was written, I cannot state the time of its delivery. Lieutenant Emory, I believe, delivered it, and he is here in the city.

The testimony taken to-day having been read over to the witness, the court, at five minutes before three, adjourned to meet to-morrow at 10 o'clock.

————

THURSDAY, *November* 18, 1847.—10 *o'clock.*

The court met pursuant adjournment.

Present: All the members, the judge advocate, and Lieutenant Colonel Fremont.

The proceedings of yesterday were read over.

General Kearny, being in the court, asked the court leave to make an explanation and said:

My answer to the last question put to me yesterday is not sufficiently explicit. I wish now to state that the word duress, in that question, is a technical one; and, from my understanding of it, I would say, in reply to the question put to me, that I never heard that Commodore Stockton would have——

The judge advocate stated that the court would wish the witness not to give in evidence what *he had heard*.

General Kearney said: I do not believe that Commodore Stockton would have used his force of sailors and marines to compel Lieutenant Colonel Frémont to obedience to his orders; but I believe that Lieutenant Colonel Frémont's obedience to Commodore Stockton's orders was in consequence of his preference between Commodore Stockton and myself.

I would also wish to state my understanding of the raising of the California battalion, under Lieutenant Colonel Frémont. My belief is that he commenced raising it in the month of June, 1846, taking for its basis the topographical party which had accompanied him from Missouri; that, in the month of August, Lieutenant Colonel Frémont and Commodore Stockton, being in Los Angeles, the latter gave to the former officer his instructions of August 24th; that, in consequence of those instructions, Lieutenant Colonel Frémont went to the north and increased his command; that, about the 13th of October, Lieutenant Colonel Frémont, with such men as he had raised, left the bay of San Francisco, in the ship Sterling, to proceed to San Pedro; that, when near Santa Barbara, he turned round and went back to San Francisco and the Sacramento, at his own volition, to increase his command, and, as I believe, without the orders and contrary to the wishes or expectations of Commodore Stockton. He increased his command to about 400 men, and with that battalion, thus increased, marched to Los Angeles, where he arrived on the 14th of January, 1847.

The judge advocate stated to the court as follows: That this statement, just made by General Kearny, showing his belief of the mode and circumstances under which the California battalion was raised and brought into the service of the United States is not evidence as to the facts. Many of the facts happened before he reached California. He speaks of what he understood there and believes now. This witness has testified as to the subject on his cross-examination. Generally he was asked, "Do you know," &c.; and in his replies he generally said, "I do not know," and then proceeds to give his belief and understanding. One of the questions in this matter of the California battalion was in the form—"Did you ever hear or understand," &c.; another inquiry, what "Commodore Stockton informed him" as to the raising of these troops in the Sacramento valley. At length, in regard to the witness speaking of his "understanding," the judge advocate interposed, and the witness replied that he had been interrogated as to many matters of which he knew nothing; but that he had given his impressions and opinions, in order to answer the questions of the accused in good faith, and to give all the information in his possession.

The witness has now come into court and stated, for the purpose of explanation, his belief and opinions on the whole subject. The judge advocate supposes the defence do not object. In regard to his statement now, and his cross-examination before, his belief is not evidence to the facts.

General Kearny's understanding of the facts, rather than the facts themselves, appeared to be what the defence wished to show; many papers, reports, and statements have been placed before the the court; they may all go properly to prove certain points in the case; but they have not come in the form of evidence, to prove what is stated in them; nor were they, it is supposed, offered with that view. The court, it is understood, on both sides, when it comes to decide the case, will distinguish between what is, and what is not evidence.

The statement of General Kearny on another point, to wit, his belief of the motives which led Lieutenant Colonel Frémont to obey Commodore Stockton, and to refuse to obey him, is still further from the rule of evidence. He may state facts to show this, and the court will weigh the facts.

While the judge advocate was preparing this note he received the following note from Lieutenant Colonel Frémont, which he read to the Court, as follows :

Mr. PRESIDENT : Lieutenant Colonel Frémont respectfully intimates to the court, under the advice of his counsel, that what the witness has sworn in relation to his belief of Lieutenant Colonel Frémont's reasons for obeying Governor Stockton in preference to himself, and his other testimony on his own belief, is not evidence, and might be expunged from the record ; but he will not make that request, but will ask the rights of defence, at the proper time, which all this additional and presumptive testimony by General Kearny gives to him.

The Court was cleared for deliberation. After mature deliberation the court decided :

That the explanation of the witness must be admitted on the record.

In a previous part of the proceedings, while this witness was under cross-examination by the accused, he was distinctly questioned as to his understanding and impressions of certain matters collateral to the matter under trial. It was several times intimated to the accused by the judge advocate that the tenor of these questions was irrelevant to the main subject under trial. But, in reply, the accused signified to the court that these matters, however irrelevant they might appear to the court, would in the sequel be found important to his defence. Under this declaration the court acceded to the wishes of the accused by allowing these questions to be put. The witness has distinctly stated, in a previous part of his examination, that he had been repeatedly questioned upon matters about which he had no personal knowledge, but that he had, in a spirit of good faith to the accused, stated all he had heard or understood in regard to the matters upon which he had been questioned.

The explanation of the witness this morning is no more irrelevant than his previous testimony, which he desired to explain; nor is it more so than the questions from the accused, to which that previous testimony was in answer. That question and answer, having been originally introduced on the cross-examination, the witness has as undoubted a right to explain it as though the matters explained were within his own knowledge.

It will be the duty of the court, at the proper time, to decide what portion of the testimony which has been delivered before it is relevant to the case, and what part, if any, is irrelevant, and to dismiss from their minds that which has not been delivered upon a proper knowledge of facts, the more especially so should it bear against the accused.

The court was then opened. Lieutenant Colonel Frémont in court. The decision in closed session was announced.

General Kearny, a witness.—Cross-examination continued.

Question by the court. After the receipt of Commodore Stockton's letter, of the 16th of January, 1847, suspending you from the command of the " *United States forces*" at Ciudad de los Angeles, did you continue in the command of any portion of those *forces,* and what portion?

Answer. I continued in the command of the dragoons, and none others.

Question by judge advocate. You said, in your examination yesterday, that "Commodore Stockton was considered by you as the commander-in-chief in California, until he had, of his own accord, on the 29th of December, turned over a portion of that command to you." What portion, or what command did he turn over to you; and of what forces was he commander-in-chief ?

Answer. The sailors, marines, and a few volunteers were turned over by him to me on the 29th of December. I considered him commander-in-chief over them and over the battalion of California volunteers, until the arrival of the latter at Los Angeles, when they came under my command; or near to Los Angeles.

Question by judge advocate. Did he, at any time from the 12th of December, when you and your dragoons met him at San Diego, to the 18th of January, when you and your dragoons left him at Los Angeles, exercise command over you or your dragoons, or attempt in any way to subject you to his authority?

A member objected. The court was cleared for deliberation:

the objection was sustained. The court was then opened; Lieutenant Colonel Frémont in court. The decision in closed session was announced.

The court having no further questions to ask General Kearny; Lieutenant Colonel Frémont not wishing at this time to ask him any further questions, he was permitted to retire.

Major P. St. G. Cooke, of the 2d dragoons, a witness for the prosecution, being duly sworn by the judge advocate according to law, testified as follows:

Examination in chief by judge advocate.

Question. State what commission, in the service of the United States, you had in California on the 24th of March, 1847?

Answer. I had a commission of a captain in the 1st regiment of dragoons, and had also been commissioned a major of the 2d regiment of dragoons, but without my knowledge at that time. I also commanded the battalion of Mormon volunteers, under an appointment of lieutenant colonel from Brigadier General Kearny.

Question. What command were you exercising, by assignment from Brigadier General Kearny, on the 24th of March, 1847?

Answer. Command of the southern military district of California.

Question. Was your authority in that command resisted by Captain Richard Owens, commanding the California battalion? If so, state the circumstances.

Answer. On the 24th of March I rode out from Los Angeles to the mission of San Gabriel, accompanied by two staff officers, Lieutenant Davidson, of the dragoons, and Assistant Surgeon Sanderson. I called on Captain Owens in his quarters, and, shortly after, asked to look at the artillery. He showed them to me in the court of the mission, and I observed two mountain howitzers, which I believed to have been brought to the country by the dragoons. I had received verbal instructions from General Kearny, by Captain Turner, to have them turned over to company C, of my command, and had, before I left town, ordered mules and drivers to be sent after them; of which I informed Captain Owens. He answered that I could not get them; that he had received orders not to let them go from his hands. I had a good deal of conversation with him, and endeavored, by every argument I could think of, to convince him that he was wrong. He had told me that he had not seen a circular of Commodore Shubrick and General Kearny's, or the department orders, placing me in command of that district. These I read to him. Returning to his quarters, he showed me an order signed by Lieutenant Colonel Frémont on the subject, which I read. He declined giving me a copy of it. As I was about leaving, he expressed a great desire that I would wait the return of Lieutenant Colonel Frémont, who, he said, would return very soon, and nothing could suffer from it in the meantime. Returning to town, I, soon after, sent a written order to Acting Captain Wilson, of a company of artillery, in the battalion, as I understood, to turn over all the artillery and ordnance stores in his charge to an officer I would appoint to receive it, Captain Wilson having previously, in a conversation, informed me that the artillery was under his charge, and given me to understand that he would turn it over to me if ordered. The next day, I think, I received an official letter from Captain Wilson, stating ———

The judge advocate here showed a paper to the witness, and asked if that was the paper he referred to, which he answered in the affirmative.

The papers here shown the witness, then read as follows:

CIUDAD DE LOS ANGELES,
March 25, 1847.

SIR: I have referred your order of the 24th instant to my immediate commanding officer, who declines permitting me to deliver the ordnance stores now at the mission of San Gabriel.

I have the honor to enclose you a copy of his instructions to me.

Very respectfully, your obedient servant,

JOHN K. WILSON,
Capt. Artillery and Ordn. officer, Cal. Bat.

To Lieutenant Colonel P. St. G. COOKE,
Commanding southern military dep't.

MISSION SAN GABRIEL,
March 25, 1847.

SIR: From the nature of the instructions I have received from Lieutenant Colonel J. C. Frémont, it will be impossible for me to permit you to comply with the order you have referred to me, viz., to deliver the ordnance and ordnance stores to any officer whom Lieutenant Colonel Cooke may appoint.

Very respectfully, your obedient servant,

R. OWENS,
Act. commandant Cal. Bat.

To J. K. WILSON,
Capt. Artillery and Ordnance, Cal. Bat.

Major Cooke, a witness, continued:

Question. What department order do you refer to?

Answer. 10th military department order, No. 2, dated, I think, 1st March, 1847.

Question. Read this letter. Is it the order of Lieutenant Colonel Frémont, which you say Captain Owens showed you as his reason for refusing to permit you to take the howitzers?

Answer. Yes; I believe it to be a copy of the order.

The order of Lieutenant Colonel Frémont to Captain Richard Owens, as recited in the 7th specification to the first charge of this record, and admitted in evidence by consent of Lieutenant Colonel Frémont, shown the witness with the foregoing question.

Question. Was the mission of San Gabriel within the limits of the southern military district of California, to the command of which you were assigned in department orders, No. 2, of March, 1st, 1847?

Answer. Yes.

The examination in chief here closed. Witness turned over for cross-examination.

Question. Did you write the letter of which this purports to be a copy, and if so, is this a true copy?

The court was here ordered to be cleared.
After deliberation the court was opened; Lieutenant Colonel Frémont in court.

The judge advocate stated to the court that the paper shown the witness appeared to be an official copy, certified by Assistant Adjutant General Townsend, of a report made by the witness to General Kearny of the circumstances, in relation to which he has just testified.

Answer. It appears to be accurate. I wrote such a report.

The letter then read, as follows:

HEAD-QUARTERS, SOUTHERN MILITARY DISTRICT,
CIUDAD DE LOS ANGELES, *March* 25, 1847.

SIR: I arrived here with company C, 1st dragoons, and four companies of my battalion, early the 23d instant. After marching into town I occupied a house belonging to government, by company C, and encamped the battalion in the edge of the town. Yesterday morning I sent Lieutenant Smith, with his mounted men, against Indians who were complained of as having attacked and occupied a ranche about 35 miles distant. I then, with Lieutenant Davidson and Doctor Sanderson, rode out to the San Gabriel mission, to examine the quarters and see the California battalion. Captain Owens was in command, and they numbered, I was informed, *two hundred and six* without the staff. Whilst examining the ordnance, which is all there, I remarked that I had ordered mules to be brought out that day for the two dragoon howitzers; Captain Owens immediately said he had received positive orders not to let *any* of it go from his charge, and that he could not let me have it. He said he had never seen the printed "circular," or 10th military department order, No. 2. I showed them, and read them to him, and asked him if he did not acknowledge the authority of the United States government? He said he considered Colonel Frémont as chief military authority in the country, with perfect temper. I exhausted every resource of information and argument; touched every motive for obedience and union in this far distant land, amongst enemies; appealed to his patriotism, and painted the disastrous circumstances likely to result to public interests, and to persons, from this treasonable course, in vain. He showed me Lieutenant Colonel Frémont's orders to him on his departure to Monterey. He declined permitting me to take a copy; I read it, as did Dr. Sanderson. It contained a paragraph to this effect: That he (Captain Owens) was to obey the orders of no officer not coming expressly from him, (Colonel Fremont,) and another paragraph forbidding him to deliver the artillery or ordnance to any corps, without express orders from Lieutenant Colonel Frémont. In obedience to those orders, he would refuse to obey General Kearny, or the President of the United States, the same. On my return to town, believing it my duty to use every effort to fulfil my orders, I sent to Major J. K. Wilson, who has been acting captain of artillery and ordnance, and who had told me he had charge, or command, of all the ordnance, a very pointed order to bring in all artillery, &c., which had been entrusted to him, or attached to his particular command, and deliver it to an officer I should designate to receive it and give receipt for it. After leaving it to be inferred that he could and would comply, I have received his refusal, or excuse, as will be seen in his letter and its enclosure, (one from Captain Owens,) copies of which are enclosed, marked 1 and 2. I have every reason to doubt that steps were taken to allow the men of that battalion to decide, knowingly, upon their being mustered into service according to law and orders. One of them (their adjutant, he told me) said he would have been willing, for one, and also, that Lieutenant Colonel Frémont had not gone out to San Gabriel to attend to it. I look upon them generally as good citizens, but cruelly and studiously misguided, and deceived. I would attempt to undeceive them, but that I deem that the public good requires that the matter should be unknown. I shall observe, if this precaution is used by others. If these Americans are taught not to obey the legal authority of the government, what dangerous impression must have unavoidably been imparted to the late enemy, who surround us, who gallop over the country armed to the teeth, and many of them with weapons taken in battle from our troops! I sacrifice all feeling or pride to duty, which I think plainly forbids any attempt to crush this resistance of misguided men. It would be a signal for revolt. The general's orders are not obeyed!

My God! to think of a howitzer brought over the deserts with so much faithful labor by the dragoons; the howitzer with which they have four times fought the enemy, and brought here to the rescue of Lieutenant Colonel Frémont and his volunteers, to be refused to them by this Lieutenant Colonel Frémont, and in defiance of the orders of his general! I denounce this treason, or this mutiny, which jeopardizes the safety of the country, and defies me in my legal command and duties, by men too who report, and say, that they believe that the enemy approaches from without, and are about to rise in arms around us. Mr. Russell left here with an express party for the States a few hours before my arrival. He was sent, I presume, by Lieutenant Colonel Frémont, as Captain Owens told me had taken public animals from San Gabriel; it is said here he went to take a petition, which has been signed here by some of the Californians, in favor of Lieutenant Colonel Frémont.

Lieutenant Gillespie is still here.　　I have deemed it my duty to send this information by express.

I am, very respectfully, your obedient servant,

P. ST. GEO. COOKE,
Lieut. Col. commanding.

Capt. H. S. TURNER,
A. A. A. Gen., Monterey.

P. S.—I was informed by Captain Owens that there was at least 100 horses at San Gabriel; the adjutant said he knew there were 150 a few days ago.

P. ST. GEO. COOKE.

A true copy:

E. D. TOWNSEND,
A. A. General.

The testimony of this witness to-day being then read over to him, he said:

I wish to explain, that Captain Owens refused to turn over to me any of the ordnance—not the *howitzers* only.

The court then, at 5 minutes before three, adjourned to meet to-morrow at 10 o'clock.

———

FRIDAY, *November* 19, 1847.—10 *o'clock.*

The court met pursuant to adjournment.
Present: all the members, except Lieutenant Colonel Craig. Present also, the judge advocate and Lieutenant Colonel Frémont.
A member stated that he was requested to inform the court, on the part of Lieutenant Colonel Craig, that he was sick, and unable to attend the court to-day; but expected to be in his seat to-morrow.
Whereupon, the court adjourned to meet to-morrow, Saturday, November 20, at 10 o'clock.

———

SATURDAY, *November* 20, 1847.—10 *o'clock.*

The court met pursuant to adjournment.
Present: all the members, except Lieutenant Colonel Craig. Present also, the judge advocate and Lieutenant Colonel Frémont.
The president stated that Lieutenant Colonel Craig was still too unwell to attend the court.　Whereupon, in expectation that he would be able to take his seat on Monday, the court adjourned to meet again on Monday, the 22d, at 10 o'clock.

MONDAY, *November 22, 1847—10 o'clock.*

The court met pursuant to adjournment.

Present: All the members except Lieutenant Colonel Craig; present, also, the judge advocate and Lieutenant Colonel Frémont.

The president stated that Lieutenant Colonel Craig being still unable to attend the court at the arsenal, he had applied, through the adjutant general of the army, for an order to remove the place of holding the court to the city, and suspended the proceedings of the court until the answer to the application could be returned to him from the adjutant general.

The court was ordered to be cleared. The president presented a reply from the adjutant general, stating that it was deemed not expedient to remove the court to Washington.

Whereupon, after mature deliberation, and with the expectation that Lieutenant Colonel Craig will be then able to take his seat, the court resolve to adjourn to meet on Wednesday at 10 o'clock.

The court was then opened. Lieutenant Colonel Frémont in court.

The court then adjourned to meet on Wednesday, November 24, at 10 o'clock.

WEDNESDAY, *November 24, 1847.--10 o'clock.*

The court met pursuant to adjournment.

Present: All the members; the judge advocate and Lieutenant Colonel Frémont.

The proceedings of Thursday, Friday, Saturday, and Monday, were read over.

Major Philip St. George Cooke, 2d dragoons, a witness for the prosecution.

Cross-examination continued.

Question. Where did you first hear of General Kearny's intention to arrest Lieutenant Colonel Frémont?

On motion of a member, the court was ordered to be cleared. The court decided that the question, under the rule previously announced, shall not be put; and the court directed the following order to be put on record:

" The court takes occasion to declare, that while it admitted General Kearny's explanations of Thursday last on its record, it did not and cannot admit as evidence the expressions of his belief as to Lieutenant Colonel Frémont's motive in obeying Commodore Stockton, made in continuation of his answer to a question from the court."

The court was then opened. Lieutenant Colonel Frémont in court. The decisions in closed session were announced.

Major Cooke, a witness.—Cross-examination continued.

Question. At what time did you first learn *from General Kearny,* or from any person by his authority, that he intended to arrest Lieutenant Colonel Frémont?

On motion of the judge advocate, the court was ordered to be cleared.

The judge advocate received with this question the following statement, which he submitted to the court in closed session:

" The defence thinks this question material, and if objected to, desire the opportunity to submit an explanation in writing."

The court ordered that they will receive the explanation from the defence before deciding the admissibility of the question.

The court was then opened. Lieutenant Colonel Frémont in court. The order in closed session was announced.

A paper was here received from Lieutenant Colonel Frémont, and read to the court, as follows:

Mr. President: Lieutenant Colonel Frémont is advised by his counsel to say that the question proposed is not with a view to establish the fact of General Kearny's intention to arrest Lieutenant Colonel Frémont, that fact being established by his (General Kearny's) own evidence; but it belongs to a class of questions going to show that General Kearny made known his intention to many of his friends to arrest Lieutenant Colonel Frémont, which persons have been summoned as witnesses; that, at the same time, the intent to arrest was kept a secret from Lieutenant Colonel Frémont and his friends; and if the answers to the questions proposed to be put (for this purpose) should be such as the questions imply, then Lieutenant Colonel Frémont is advised by his counsel that such answers will become material under that branch of defence which goes to impeach the motives and the credit of General Kearny.

J. C. FRÉMONT,
Lieutenant Colonel U. S. Army.

The court was then ordered to be cleared. After mature deliberation, the court decided that the *question shall not be put.*

The court was then opened. Lieutenant Colonel Frémont in court. The decision in closed session was announced.

Major Cooke, a witness.—Cross-examination resumed.

Question. Where was it first made known to you by General Kearny that you were to be a witness on the trial of Lieutenant Colonel Frémont?
Answer. He never made it known to me.
Question. Did any person on his behalf make it known to you?
Answer. No.
Question. Have you made a publication in any newspaper touching the events about which you are now to testify?

On motion of the judge advocate, the court was ordered to be cleared.

The court decided that the question is inadmissable in its present form. "If the defence can produce any paper which they suppose written by the witness, the statements in which may contradict any thing offered by him in his present testimony, or which may go to discredit him as a witness, the court will permit the witness to be interrogated as to whether he wrote such paper."

The court was then opened. Lieutenant Colonel Frémont in court. The decision in closed session was announced.

Major Cooke, a witness.—Cross-examination resumed.

Question. Was this publication (a long printed article from the Missouri Republican of June 14th, 1847) written by you?

The paper was then read to the court, as follows:

Correspondence of the Missouri Republican.

From California, San Diego, Upper California, February, 1847.

About ten months ago, the people of California who had long suffered the want of the protection of a regular government, and utterly disgusted with their neglect and treatment by the remote parent State, Mexico, entertained in their assembly the subject of declaring their severance from Mexico, and applying to some powerful nation for protection. It is well known that the majority not only favored the proposition, but an application for a political connexion with the United States. The most influential and best informed of the citizens, with one voice express the conviction that then, or after the war, the presence in the territory of a single individual of high standing and character, and commissioned by our government, would have insured a peaceful and honorable annexation, highly satisfactory to the mass of the people.

About this time, Lieutenant Gillespie, of the marine corps, arrived in Monterey, and set off in haste to follow Captain Frémont, whom he overtook far on his way to the United States. The captain returned with him.

Immediately after and before the declaration of war was known, if made, a revolution was commenced under a flag with the device of a bear, and acts of war were committed upon a portion of the people. They were not acknowledged by the naval authorities, but supplies were furnished to Captain Frémont. A revolution even *thus* commenced with the assistance of the naval forces, was apparently successful in the course of the summer. An express was sent about the 1st of September to Washington, by the Rio Gila and New Mexico, announcing the peaceable possession of the territory by the United States.

On the 30th of June, 1846, Brigadier General S. W. Kearny (on that very day promoted by selection from the whole army) marched with an army from Fort Leavenworth. He was clothed with the most ample powers to *revolutionize* or *subdue*, and to govern, New Mexico first, and then California. The first task being most successfully accomplished, he marched from Santa Fé, on the 25th of September, in command of the 1st dragoons, the advance of his forces, for California, to fulfil the second of the high but laborious commissions of his government.

Before he left the Rio Grande, the messengers of peace from California were met by him. The general then reduced his force to the mere *escort* of a squadron of 100 men, and pursued his course. After a march of a thousand miles over mountains of rocks, barren prairies, and deserts, without water, he arrived with his men only half mounted, and on broken down mules, at the first ranche, *sixty miles* from San Diego.

Then the following course and condition of affairs were soon learned. The Californians proper, who are a proud race, disgusted at the conduct of the revolution and the government which had been established, and suffering outrages from its irregular military hirelings, had risen in arms. They had re-taken all the towns south of Monterey; Lieutenant Gillespie having surrendered the capital, the Pueblo de los Angeles. An attack on it from its sea-port, San Pedro, under the orders of Commodore Stockton, had signally failed. San Diego, commanded from the sea, was now in our possession, but blockaded by land. Commodore Stockton (styling himself governor) was there with the Congress and Portsmouth, and perhaps other ships of war. Lieutenant Colonel Frémont had *retired two months before to the upper country*, to raise an irregular force, and was reported on his return with 400 men and some Indians. The Californians, *individually*, the most formidable horsemen in America, were under arms to the number of 800, and carried on a guerrilla warfare. About 100 of them were posted at San Pasqual, on the best road from General Kearny's position to San Diego.

Before learning this last item, the general succeeded in giving information of his approach at San Diego, and Captain Gillespie, an officer of the navy, and a small party of mounted volunteers joined him on his march on the 5th of December; that evening he learned of the force at San Pasqual, ten or twelve miles distant; he attempted to surprise them at daybreak the next morning. The night was unfortunately cold and rainy; the enemy had received information of the approach of foes, they knew not whom, and were found fully prepared at dawn of day. They were impetuously charged and driven from their ground, more than half of the squadron being mounted on worthless mules; they were pursued rashly and too far by the others, despite the general's efforts to stop it. The enemy then, in daylight rallied, surrounded and attacked, with every advantage, these foremost pursuers, 38 in number, all of whom but one was killed or wounded. Then the dragoons met with the irreparable loss of these fine officers and some of its best non-commissioned officers and men. The general himself received two severe wounds. The remnant of this heroic band, with bleeding wounds, succeeded in rallying on a mountain howitzer which then approached, and the enemy again retired. They encamped on the ground. The next day, reduced by twenty killed, and encumbered with seventeen wounded, having marched about ten miles, they were threatened with attack on the plain by the enemy in increased numbers. The dragoons charged them, and drove them from a rocky hill which they themselves took possession of; that night a messenger, with written information of their situation, succeeded in passing the enemy's videttes, and carrying it to Commodore Stockton, about 25 miles off San Diego. He sent a written *refusal by three men who were captured.* The general and his party remained besieged on the hill for three days; fortunately water was obtained by digging at its foot, and they subsisted on mule flesh.

The most intelligent persons in San Diego believed them lost; there was time for an overwhelming force to arrive from the Pueblo; large re-inforcements were on their way.

After two days, on the third night, Lieutenant Beal, of the navy, who would not believe that succor could be refused, succeeded in making his way to San Diego. The next night 150 men were sent; they arrived at the close of the *fourth* night thus passed on the hill, and just as the general, determined to cut his way through the enemy at all hazards, had burned all his baggage.

Arrived in San Diego, General Kearny exhibited to Commodore Stockton his commission and powers to command, and to govern in the territory; but badly wounded, and with the command of *so slight* a military force, he with proper delicacy refrained, for the present, to exert his authority, and so he expressed himself. In about two weeks, having recovered his strength, and anxious for the public service and the safety of Lieutenant Colonel Frémont, he spoke and wrote to Commodore Stockton, urging that a force should be marched for the Pueblo for his support, or at least to make a demonstration in his favor. This was roughly refused for two days, and *Frémont was denounced* by Commodore Stockton. He was induced finally to change his mind, and on the 29th of December, General Kearny marched in command of about 700 dismounted dragoons, marines and sailors. Commodore Stockton had by this time, however, *refused to submit to the authority of the government, and to General Kearny's commission and powers from the President of the United States!* He refused to surrender his assumed authority as governor and commander-in-chief of all the forces. Only anxious for the service of his country, General Kearny submitted to serve her as best as he could. Commodore Stockton accompanied the march.

On the route some citizens who had been neutral arrived in camp, commissioned by the Californians to ascertain what terms would be granted to them. Commodore Stockton, in reply, offered such as are generally considered not only extraordinary, but insulting.

On the 8th of January—the memorable and glorious anniversary —about mid-day, the enemy made his appearance on the opposite side of the San Gabriel river. He was about *five hundred* strong in cavalry, and formidable in artillery, which included some 9-pounders. Commodore Stockton rode up to General Kearny and proposed that the army should go into *camp*. General Kearny positively refused, and, under the cover of his artillery fire, crossed the river in presence of the enemy, and by a general charge, which he headed in person, drove him from the field.

The next day, the 9th, there was another engagement, principally of artillery, in which the Californians were driven from a strong position, and at night the army encamped on the river of the Puebla, in the suburbs of the capital. That night it was evacuated by the enemy, and taken possession of next morning by our troops. Then General Kearny urged that a force might be given him to go to the assistance of Lieutenant Colonel Frémont, whom it was reported and believed the enemy had gone to attack. It was refused.

Meanwhile the enemy, insultingly rejected by Commodore Stockton, sought terms of capitulation from Lieutenant Colonel Frémont. This officer, *knowing* that General Kearny and Commodore Stockton were *within five miles*, made with them articles of capitulation and peace, which he signed as "military commandant of California."

On hearing this, Commodore Stockton was *indignant*, and used *threatening language*. As a counter action, *Frémont threatened to report to General Kearny*.

Lieutenant Colonel Frémont visited General Kearny, and *asked him if he would make him governor*. The general, not *then acquainted with some occurrences*, gave him *reason to expect the appointment in a month or two*, when affairs should be so settled as to admit the control of a civil government.

Lieutenant Colonel Frémont *then went to Commodore Stockton*, and HE made him governor on the *spot*.

General Kearny, about this time, had sent Lieutenant Colonel Frémont a copy of his powers, which gave him the command of troops "raised in California," together with an order. Lieutenant Colonel Frémont refused to obey the order, with the excuse, in substance, that he could not obey him, before his difficulty as to command should be settled with Commodore Stockton.

General Kearny, finding himself "one too many" at the Puebla, then immediately marched back with his handfull of dismounted dragoons to San Diego, where he arrived on the 23d of January.

On the 20th, Lieutenant Colonel Cooke arrived there with his battalion of infantry volunteers, with which he brought wagons through from Santa Fé. The general, leaving him in command of all the troops, set sail on the 30th for Monterey and San Francisco.

Information has since been received of the arrival at Monterey of Commodore Shubrick, commander-in-chief of the naval forces in the Pacific, in the ship Independence, and also, of the storeship Lexington, with the company of artillery.

The permanency of the late suspension of arms has generally been doubted, but now the dawn of a better state of affairs may be perceived.

One more incident, which was overlooked. Commodore Stockton issued a flaming order, as commander-in-chief of the battles of San Gabriel and the Plains of Mesa; in them he had no command or control.

On the impulse he wrote, as he has said, despatches, in which he praised General Kearny and Captain Turner, (1st dragoons,) who commanded a third of the troops. Afterwards he said he had no idea of "trumping up" his enemies, and that he would send after the despatches and alter them. Lieutenant Gray, of the navy, had been sent to bear despatches by Panama; he *was* overtaken and stopped at San Diego, and then again sent forward. On learning these facts, General Kearny sent Lieutenant Emory, topographical engineer, to accompany Lieutenant Gray to Washington.

The officers of the navy, with one exception, and those of the army, have been on excellent terms.

The government have no money and *no rations* in this country. The troops live exclusively on fresh beef.

I have given a hasty sketch of prominent transactions and facts in this country. I have neither time nor inclination to comment upon them. *I have not been an actor in any of the scenes, and this is written without the knowledge or even suspicion of any one of those actors.*

JUSTICE.

Letter from California.—A very concise, and apparently impartial narrative of affairs in California, developing some very extraordinary facts, will be found in our columns to-day. It was received by the last arrival from Santa Fé.

On motion of the judge advocate, the court was ordered to be cleared.

The court, after mature deliberation upon the contents of said publication, finding in it nothing contradictory of the evidence of the witness, or going to discredit him, decide that the question shall not be put; but that the publication be entered on the records with the question, as part of it.

The court was then opened, Lieutenant Colonel Frémont in court. The decision in close session was announced.

Major Cooke, a witness.—Cross-examination continued.

Question. Did you ever apply for the lieutenant colonelcy of the rifles? and if so, did you apply in person at Washington City, and where was the then Brevet Captain Frémont at that time?

On motion of the judge advocate, the court was ordered to be cleared.

The court decided that the question shall not be put.

The court was then opened, Lieutenant Colonel Frémont in court. The decision in closed session was announced.

Major Cooke, a witness.—Cross-examination continued.

Question. Is your letter or report of the 25th of March, which was read in your cross-examination last Thursday, your official report to your superior officer? and does it refer to the same events as those you narrated in your testimony in chief? and did you ever make any other official report of those occurrences to General Kearney, or to any other officer for him?

Answer. It was my official report; it refers to the same subject as my evidence in chief; I do not remember having ever made any other report to him, or to any one else.

Question. In that report you say: "I have every reason to doubt that steps were taken to allow the men of that battalion to decide knowingly upon their being mustered into service, according to law and orders. One of them (their adjutant, he told me) said he would have been willing, for one, and also that Lieutenant Colonel Frémont had not gone out to San Gabriel to attend to it." Is Mr. Loker the person you there refer to, who told you he was adjutant? if not, who is the person?

Answer. He is the person.

Question. Did not Mr. Loker tell you that the reason he would have been willing to engage under the orders you refer to, was that, being an officer, it would have made little or no difference in his pay, and that the same reason did not apply to the men? or words to that effect?

Answer. To the best of my recollection, he referred to his being an officer, in the conversation I had with him, as making a difference between him and the battalion; and, if I remember right, to his having no family; but I think he made no reference to the subject of pay.

Question. When he told you, as you say, "that Lieutenant Colonel Frémont had not gone out to San Gabriel to attend to it," did you understand him that *no one* had gone out for that purpose? and that it was not attended to? Did he not tell you that he, (Loker,) as adjutant of the battalion, had gone out and attended to it?

Answer. I understood him that the order had been taken by some one, and that it had been attended to by some one; I forget who.

Question. In your official report, why did you not state this conversation as you now state it?

Answer. I thought that it would be inferred from my official report that some one had attended to it, as I had mentioned Lieutenant Colonel Frémont by name as not having attended to it. I think that was my idea; I do not know, on reflection, what I thought about it then; I do not remember what my thoughts were, it is so long ago.

Question. Had you any other ground than the information which you say Mr. Loker gave you, for saying, "I have every reason to doubt that steps were taken to allow the men of that battalion to decide knowingly upon their being mustered into service, according to law and orders," and if so, what?

On motion of the judge advocate, the court was ordered to be cleared.

The court decided that it is no matter of charge before this court against Lieutenant Colonel Frémont, that proper exertions were not made by him to muster the California battalion in service according to orders; they therefore decline to inquire into that matter by putting this question.

The court was then opened, Lieutenant Colonel Frémont in court. The decision in closed session was announced.

Major Cooke, a witness.—Cross examination continued.

Question. In your testimony in chief you say: " As I was about leaving, he (Owens) expressed a great desire that I should wait the return of Lieutenant Colonel Frémont, who, he said, would return very soon, and that nothing would suffer in the meantime." Now why did you omit to state that particular in your official report?

Answer. I presume I did not think it necessary to do so. In fact, I did not clearly understand at the time what he meant.

Question. In your report you say: " Whilst examining the ordnance, which is all there, I remarked that I had ordered mules to be brought out that day for the two mountain howitzers;" and in a subsequent part you say: " My God! to think of this howitzer, brought over the deserts with so much faithful labor by the dragoons, the howitzer with which they have four times fought the enemy, and brought here to the rescue of Lieutenant Colonel Frémont and his volunteers, to be refused to them by this Lieutenant Colonel Frémont, and in defiance of the orders of his general. I denounce this treason or this mutiny, which jeopardizes the safety of the country and defies me in my legal command and duties; by men, too, who report and say that they believe that the enemy approaches from without, and are about to raise in arms around us." Now, please to state whether, by the " *two dragoon howitzers*" first spoken of, you mean the two howitzers carried into California by the dragoon party under General Kearny, and referred to in the seventh charge against Lieutenant Colonel Frémont; and if so, why, in the paragraph last quoted, do you speak of but *one?*

Answer. I did refer to the two howitzers taken to that country by the dragoons. In the last paragraph quoted, I referred to but one, because the case was so widely different from the other.

Question. State the difference between the two cases?

Answer. One had been lost in battle, and the other, as I believed, General Kearney had marched to the support of Lieutenant Colonel Frémont. I did not mean that I did not consider Captain Owens equally bound to turn over both, in a military point of view.

Question. The one lost in battle, where and how was it recovered?

Answer. I know nothing about it of my own knowledge.

Question. How do you know that was the same one?

Answer. Lieutenant Davidson who was with me had had command of them, and recognized them when I went out.

Question. In your report you say: "I sacrifice all feelings of pride to duty, which I think plainly forbids any attempt to crush this resistance of misguided men. It would be a signal for revolt." *Of whom* did you anticipate a "*revolt*," and what did you mean by the word "*crush?*"

Answer. I meant, to enforce my orders by force, by the word "*crush;*" the revolt I anticipated from the natives of the country.

Question. Do you mean that you did not know of the dragoon howitzers being there, until Lieutenant Davidson recognized and pointed them out to you?

Answer. No, I did not mean so.

Question. Did you have any verbal or special orders in relation to the ordnance, arms, &c., and the "*resistance*" and "*revolt*" of which you testify?

Answer. I had some verbal orders and suggestions in relation to the arms, communicated however in the form of written memoranda. I had no orders in relation to resistance or revolt.

Question. Will you produce those written memoranda?

Answer. I have them not. I lost all my papers by an accident, in returning to the United States.

Question. Will you state the tenor of these orders and instructions, and the words as near as possible, and who they were from?

Answer. They were from General Kearny; I was directed, I believe, to put the howitzers again in charge of the dragoons, and my attention was especially directed to the safety of the other artillery; San Louis Rey was suggested as a position for a part or the whole of it.

Question. Have you stated the whole of these orders and instructions?

Answer. I do not remember any thing else just now contained in the memoranda. I received, at the same time, an official letter from General Kearny.

Question. Could you, in your opinion, obtain a copy of those memoranda containing those orders or instructions from general Kearny, or do you know whether he lost them?

Answer. I believe they were taken down in Captain Turner's handwriting, to aid his memory simply.

Question. Has the official letter, which you mention, been given in evidence?

Answer. I believe not.

Question. Can you produce it to-morrow?

Answer. I do not know whether I left the original in California, or lost it. General Kearny, probably, has a copy of it.

Question. What force had you to "*crush*" the resistance you apprehended, and which you meant to use for that purpose?

Answer. I am not aware I have said I meant to have used force.

Lieutenant Colonel Frémont proposed to alter the question by striking out the word meant, and substituting "might have used."

The witness answered the question in that form.

Answer. About 300 troops, to the best of my recollection, cavalry and infantry.

Question. Were they Mormons?

Answer. Four companies of Mormons, and one of dragoons.

The testimony of to-day was then read over to the witness for explanation, if erroneously recorded. Whereupon, Major Cooke said: "I would explain that I do not know whether the letter from General Kearny to me, called for by the defence, was considered by him an official letter, or semi-official, such as he was in the habit of writing; and I do not know whether he has a copy or not."

Whereupon, at three minutes before three, the court adjourned to meet to-morrow morning at 10 o'clock.

THURSDAY, *November 25, 1847.—10 o'clock.*

The court met pursuant to adjournment.

Present: All the members, the judge advocate, and Lieutenant Colonel Frémont.

The proceedings of yesterday were read over.

Lieutenant Colonel Frémont read a paper to the court as follows:

Mr. PRESIDENT: Under the instructions of his counsel, Lieutenant Colonel Frémont asks leave, most respectfully, to suggest to the court that he has a legal right to have the question answered which was yesterday put to the witness, (Major Cooke,) namely, Whether he was the author of the publication then shown to him? And, if answered in the affirmative, that he had the legal right to use the contents of the said paper either to contradict his testimony on this trial, or to show hostility and ill will to him, (Lieut. Col. F.,) or to use it for both purposes; and, in either case, he is further advised to say, that he would have the legal right, after receiving the affirmative answer, either to use the publication at once, by founding interrogatories upon it, or to reserve it for use in the general defence. This, he is advised by his counsel, is law, and may be seen in the ordinary treatises on evidence, (*Greenleaf, pages* 708, 627; *Phillips, page* 765, *vol.* 3;) and also in the treatises on martial law, (*Hough, page* 917, *and the authorities therein cited.*)

Lieutenant Colonel Frémont is also advised to say, that courts martial, being a derivation from the ancient courts of chivalry, in which *"honor and arms"* was the subject, the honor of arms, in addition to truth and justice, (the object of all courts,) is still an essential part of a court martial's object; and, under that point of view, they are not to be restricted to the rigid rules of a criminal trial at the Old Bailey, or of a civil suit at Nisi Prius, but may take a wider and a higher range to get at the honor of the parties and witnesses before the court, in order to keep bright the honor of arms, as well as to attain the ends of truth and justice. And this view of the court martial's power, he is instructed to say, is clearly shadowed forth in the duty imposed on the court to observe the conduct of the military citizens before them, and to report for superior revision every instance of falsehood, prevarication, or dishonorable behavior in the *military* prosecutor and witnesses, in order that they themselves may be brought to trial, if found dishonoring the profession of arms by any thing they say, or do, or refuse to say, or do, before the court, (*De Hart on courts martial, pages* 182-'3-'4.) From this it results that, in relation to military witnesses, (and that is the case of the witness now before the court,) a course of examination is intended, by the law martial, of a wider and higher character than that which is tolerated in the ordinary criminal or civil tribunals of the country. Honor becomes an object in such an examination; and in that point of view, and in addition to the legal rights to use the contents of the paper either to contradict the witness, or to expose his enmity, or for both purposes, Lieutenant Colonel Frémont is instructed to say that he has a right to have the question *put* to the witness, the witness having the privilege to refuse to answer, if he will say upon oath that the answer may subject him to punishment.

The publication before the court is one of several, believed to have been made by officers of the army, all subsidiary in effect, if not in design, to the accusation preferred against Lieutenant Colonel Frémont by General Kearny, and now on trial before this court; publications not only wrong in themselves, but aggravated by being made anonymously, and against an officer about 3,000 miles from the scene of the publication, and then under a secret intended arrest by General Kearny.

Lieutenant Colonel Frémont is further instructed to say that, this being a cross-examination of a witness, who the testimony already shows to have reported Lieutenant Colonel Frémont to his superior officer for treason and mutiny, and one whom he would have deemed it his duty to have "*crushed*" by the arms of his Mormons and dragoons, if he had not been afraid of "*a revolt*" from the people of California, he, the witness, appears in the category of an inimical witness, and becomes subject to all the modes of examination known to the books in the case of such witnesses. And he is here instructed by his counsel to read a couple of authorities to this point, and to claim the full benefit from the law they lay down:

"The power and opportunity to cross-examine is one of the principal tests which the law has devised for the ascertainment of truth, and this is certainly a most efficacious test. By this means the situation of the witness with respect to the parties and the subject of litigation, his interests, his motives, his inclination and prejudices, his means of obtaining a correct and certain knowledge of the facts to which he bears testimony, the manner in which he has used those means, his powers of discerning facts in the first instance, his capacity for retaining and describing them, are fully investigated and ascertained, and submitted to the consideration of the jury."—(*Starkie, vol.* 1, 185–'6; *Greenleaf, p.* 602–'3.)

"The most effectual method (of cross-examination) is to examine rapidly and minutely, as to a number of subordinate and apparently trivial points in his evidence, concerning which there is little likelihood of his being prepared with falsehoods ready made. * * * It frequently happens that in the course of such a rapid examination, facts most material to the cause are elicited, which wereeither denied, or but partially admitted before."—(*Alison's Practice, quoted in Greenleaf, vol.* 1, *p.* 524.)

Claiming the benefit of this mode of cross-examination in the present instance, and intending to ask no question which he does not believe he has a legal right to *put*, Lieutenant Colonel Frémont, under the instructions of his counsel, most respectfully asks that, before rejecting any question which he may offer, the court will be pleased to hear his reasons for offering it—a privilege which he believes the court will not deny him when asked, and which he only asks now generally, and for the whole trial, to avoid troubling the court with a special request in each case as it arises.

J. C. FRÉMONT,
Lieutenant Colonel, mounted riflemen.

The court was then ordered to be cleared. After mature deliberation, the court decided as follows:

The court adhere to their decision of yesterday, in relation to the question, as to the authorship of a paper signed "Justice," in the St. Louis Republican.

At the same time, the court will admit questions, to the witness, under the usual rules, with a view to show that he has expressed hostility, or did entertain hostile feelings, or expose his enmity, or to contradict the testimony he has given on this trial.

The court was then opened. Lieutenant Colonel Frémont in court. The decision in closed session was announced.

The judge advocate signified to Lieutenant Colonel Frémont that whenever he wished to make explanations to the court, in support of questions objected to, that he should intimate the same to the judge advocate whenever the court should be ordered to be cleared to consider of such question.

Major Cook, a witness.—Cross-examination continued.

Question. Has the witness been able to obtain, from General Kearny, the originals, or copies of the memoranda of orders and instructions, mentioned yesterday, and lost, by accident, by the witness?

Answer. No. The memoranda were on a scrap of paper, taken down by Captain Turner, as I understood him, merely to refresh his memory. I did not know that it was expected of me to speak to General Kearny about them; but merely about the letter alluded to in my testimony of yesterday. The memoranda had no signature, and I never attached any importance to them; I certainly have given their most important contents. I here present the letter, or rather a copy from the letter book of General Kearny, which is in his own handwriting.

Copy of a copy admitted by consent, and read as follows:

HEAD-QUARTERS, 10TH MILITARY DEPARTMENT,
Monterey, U. C., March 1, 1847.

SIR: By department orders, No. 2, of this date, you will see that you are entrusted with the command of the southern military district, and required to look to its protection and defence, for which purpose the California volunteers, (now at the Ciudad de Los Angeles,) the Mormon battalion, and company C, 1st dragoons, are placed under your orders.

The southern district is the most important one in the department, and the one in which (for many reasons) difficulties are most to be apprehended. The route between California and Sonora leads from the frontier of that district, and that is the only one by which Mexican troops can be brought into this country.

With the knowledge of this fact, I advise you to have the pass near Warner's rancho (Agua Caliente) well guarded, and the road from it in the direction of San Felippe and the desert reconnoitred and examined as frequently as circumstances may render necessary. Troops sent for these purposes should be kept much in motion. The friendship and good will of the Indians on that frontier can easily be secured, and it should be done. It is highly important that a very discreet officer should be in command of the troops you may station at "the city of the Angels," which has been for so long a time the capital of the territory, and the head-quarters of the Mexicans and Californians when in arms against us. Great discontent and animosity, on the part of the people there, towards the Americans have existed, and in consequence of complaints made by them of the volunteers engaged in our cause. It is not necessary to inquire if these complaints are well founded or not. The fact that the people have been unfriendly and opposed to us is sufficient to make it our duty to reconcile and make friends of them, and this most desirable object may be effected by a mild, courteous, and just treatment of them in future. I urge this subject upon your attention, and trust that you will impress it upon those officers and troops you may station there.

In my letter to you of the 11th ultimo, (a copy of which is enclosed herewith,) I directed you, under certain circumstances, to send a company of the Mormon battalion to San Diego. I have now only to add that should the circumstances, alluded to occur you will send a company, or more, as you may deem necessary.

The selection of a place for your head-quarters is a matter of some consideration and importance. I suggest that it be the " Ciudad de Los Angeles," but leave that subject for your decision, as I am unwilling to embarrass you, or place any impediments in your way that might prevent you from performing the high duty expected of you.

Very respectfully, your obedient servant,

S. W. KEARNY,
Brigadier General.

Lieut. Col. P. S. G. COOKE,
Commanding Southern Military District, San Luis Rey.

True copy from my letter book:

S. W. KEARNY,
Brigadier General.

NOVEMBER 24, 1847.

Question. Are these the orders under which you would have "*crushed*" the resistance of Captain Owens and his battalion, if you had not been afraid of exciting a revolt among the people?

Answer. Those are the only orders I had at that time; and, under ordinary circumstances, I should have deemed it my duty to have enforced my orders in relation to the artillery, founded on the verbal orders of the general.

Question. Is it the same people who are spoken of by General Kearny as being so badly used by the California battalion, whose revolt you apprehended if you attempted to enforce your orders in relation to the artillery?

On motion of a member, the court was ordered to be cleared.

The court decided that the question shall be put.

The court was then opened, Lieutenant Colonel Frémont in court.

The decision in closed session was announced.

Major Cooke, a witness.—Cross-examination continued.

Answer. The revolt which I apprehended, in case of a collision between different parts of the American forces, was from the inhabitants of my district generally; and I had no thought at the time of any particular class of them.

Question. Can you state those verbal orders with any greater particularity than you have heretofore done?

Answer. I think that among them may have been a suggestion to station a part of my forces at San Louis Rey. I received such a suggestion, and I do not remember any shape in which it came.

Question. In what capacity did you give your order to Midshipman Wilson to turn over the artillery to an officer to be designated by you?

Answer. As the superior military officer in the department.

Question. Was it addressed to him in any other capacity than as midshipman or passed midshipman?

Answer. I do not remember the form of the address.

Question. Was there any contingency resulting from all the orders which you have received, in which you would have used the

Mormons and dragoons to " *crush*" Lieutenant Colonel Frémont, if you had found him instead of Captain Owens at the head of the California battalion? and does that word " *crush*," as used by you, mean *killing*?

At the request of the judge advocate, the court was cleared.

The court decided that the question be not put.

The court was then opened, Lieutenant Colonel Frémont in court.

The decision in closed session was announced.

Major Cooke, a witness, on cross-examination.

Question. Was Lieutenant Colonel Frémont at Los Angeles when you arrived there with the Mormons and dragoons?

Answer. No.

Question. Did you endeavor to get possession of Lieutenant Colonel Frémont's house in Los Angeles in his absence, and were you opposed and prevented by Colonel Russell?

Answer. On my arrival at Los Angeles, I was in want of quarters for the men under my command. I was informed there was a large house in the village occupied by a number of officers of the California battalion. I caused official inquiry to be made whether the building was rented by the United States, or for United States purposes. The assistant quartermaster, Myers by name, I believe, answered the official note, that it was rented for private purposes, and not public. Mr. Russell was not at Los Angeles when I arrived there, as I was told; I did not see him at all.

Question. Did you wait upon Lieutenant Colonel Frémont, or call upon him, in any way, after his return to Los Angeles?

Answer. No.

Question. Did you ever salute him as an officer? and especially at Los Angeles, or on the march from Monterey to Fort Leavenworth?

Answer. I was introduced to Colonel Frémont by Colonel Mason——

The court took a recess of five minutes, at the expiration of which time the court was again in session.

Present: all the members, the judge advocate, and Lieutenant Colonel Frémont.

Major Cooke, a witness,

Continued his answer to the question, as follows:

——and he received me with such extreme coolness and reserve, that I judged my acquaintance was disagreeable to him. I met him in the street once afterwards with ladies, and I saluted the whole party. I was present at two parties with him, in which we held no intercourse. On the return march to Fort Leavenworth, I very seldom saw him, and do not remember having met him face to face, the circumstances under which salutes are generally given.

Question. Was that introduction in your own quarters, and after Lieutenant Colonel Frémont had been a week in Los Angeles without your calling upon him?

Answer. That introduction was in the common room of a boarding house, probably a week after Lieutenant Colonel Frémont's arrival; I understood that the regulations required Lieutenant Colonel Frémont to report his arrival to me, as commanding officer of the post.

Question. Did he (Lieutenant Colonel Frémont) march and encamp in the rear of General Kearny's Mormon escort, from Monterey to Fort Leavenworth?

Answer. Not universally.

Question. How came Lieutenant Colonel Frémont to be in your quarters? Was he sent for by Colonel Mason? and did Colonel Mason ever ask you to be present when he was going to have an interview with Lieutenant Colonel Frémont?

On suggestion of the judge advocate, the court was here ordered to be cleared. The court decided to admit the question.

The court was opened. Lieutenant Colonel Frémont in court. The decision in closed session was announced.

Major Cooke, a witness, on cross-examination.

Answer. As I said before, I did not consider it in my quarters. He was sent for by Colonel Mason; and Colonel Mason required of me to be always present at his interviews with Lieutenant Colonel Frémont. He expressed that wish in a manner which I took to be obligatory.

Question. Did you ever, in any such interview, take a seat at a table, with pen, ink, and paper, or pencil and paper, and take notes of Lieutenant Colonel Frémont's answers to Colonel Mason's interrogatories? and if so, did you give him notice of what you did, or read your notes to him, Lieutenant Colonel Frémont? and what did you do with them?

Answer. I never took a memorandum.

Lieutenant Colonel Frémont said, he wanted an answer upon every clause—whether he took a seat at the table, &c.?

Answer—I never took a seat at a table with pen, ink, or paper, or pencil, or paper, or took notes of Lieutenant Colonel Frémont's answers to Colonel Mason's interrogatories.

Question. Did you ever hold a blank book in your hand, and a pencil in your hand, and appear to be writing anything during such interviews?

Answer. I have no recollection of it; and do not believe I did it.

Question. What reason did Colonel Mason give you for requiring you to be always present when he had interviews with Lieutenant Colonel Frémont?

Answer. I do not recollect that he gave me reasons. He may have done it; but I do not recollect what they were, if he did.

Question. Were you present at the time, if there was any such, when the interview led to a challenge and acceptance to fight a duel the next morning, with double-barrelled guns and buck-shot cartridges, and which duel is still impending?

The court was ordered to be cleared. After mature deliberation, the court decided that: The court rejects the question, and reminds the accused of its decision upon the same matter, when another witness was under examination, that the court could not entertain this subject in any shape.

The court was then opened. Lieutenant Colonel Frémont in court. The decision in closed session was announced.

Major Cooke, a witness.—Cross-examination continued.

Question. Were you present on any occasion when Colonel Mason used such language as this to Lieutenant Colonel Frémont : "None of your insolence, or I will put you in irons?" or words to that effect?

At the suggestion of the judge advocate, the court was ordered to be cleared. The court decided that the question shall not be put. The court was opened. Lieutenant Colonel Frémont in court. The decision in closed session was announced.

Major Cooke, a witness.—Cross-examination continued.

Question. Do you know that, in the month of February, 1847, and in furtherance of the objects of the treaty of Cowenga, safe conducts had been sent by Governor Frémont to the province of Sonora; relying upon the faith of which safe conducts, one Moréno and other Californians, who had been active partisans in the insurrection of September, 1846, returned to their families at Los Angeles, having with them the written safeguards of Governor Frémont. Now, did you not immediately after their arrival at Los Angeles, arrest and imprison Moréno and his companions, thus violating the safeguards of Governor Frémont? and did you not release them from apprehension of an insurrection?

At the suggestion of the judge advocate, the court was ordered to be clearned.

After mature deliberation, the court decided that: The court deems the question irrelevant, and directs that it shall not be put. The court was then opened. Lieutenant Colonel Frémont in court. The decision in closed session was announced.

The testimony of to-day was here read over to the witness. The court then adjourned at six minutes before three, to meet to-morrow at 10 o'clock.

FRIDAY, *November 26, 1847.—10 o'clock.*

The court met pursuant to adjournment.

Present: All the members; the judge advocate, and Lieutenant Colonel Frémont.

The proceedings of yesterday were read over.

Lieutenant Colonel Frémont read a paper to the court, as follows:

MR. PRESIDENT: Lieutenant Colonel Frémont is instructed by his counsel to say, that in offering a question on yesterday in relation to the impending duel with Colonel Mason, with double barrelled guns and buckshot cartridges, after a similar question had once been rejected by the court, they (the counsel) had an object in view which they believe to come within the scope of this trial, and to be both relevant and material. He is also instructed to say that his counsel, as well as himself, have no doubt that the court would now hear an explanation of that object, if the privilege of explanation was asked; but believing that this can be delayed, and properly come in as part of the general defence, no further request will now be made on that subject.

Lieutenant Colonel Frémont also desires to say that, anxious to accelerate the progress of this trial, and unwilling to give the court the least trouble, he will hereafter, in the cross-examination, waive every question to which there is an objection from any member of the court, or from the judge advocate, and thus prevent the trouble and delay of clearing the court and judging the question, hoping to show its relevancy in the general defence, and to supply the place of the answer it implies by direct testimony.

J. C. FRÉMONT,
Lieutenant Colonel mounted riflemen.

The court was then ordered to be cleared. After some time spent in secret session and deliberation, the court was opened. Lieutenant Colonel Frémont in court.

Major Cooke, a witness.—Cross-examination continued.

Question. Did you charge Don José Antonio Carrillo, one of the officers in the California force during the insurrection, with being engaged in a *conspiracy with Lieutenant Colonel Frémont* against the United States, and with having engaged to furnish him 200 California horsemen; and did you not threaten to imprison him for the same?

Answer. No.

Question. In the postscript to your report are the following words: "I was informed by Captain Owens that there were at least one hundred horses at San Gabriel. The adjutant said he knew there were one hundred and fifty a few days ago." Now do you know whether Lieutenant Colonel Frémont was ordered to produce those horses within a brief time; and when produced were they not, or a great part of them, and the pick and choice of them, sold for a trifle, say, some three dollars a head?

Answer. When Lieutenant Colonel Frémont was settling up his affairs at Los Angeles, that is, turning over public property, under the orders of Colonel Mason, quite a large number of horses were turned over. There was considerable delay in getting the whole of them that were turned over; they were not all turned over at one time; the best were assigned to company C, 1st dragoons, and a large number were sold for a mere trifle, being found in a very bad condition. I think many of them were sold for three dollars or less.

Question. Do you not know that those horses, one hundred and twenty in number, were specially prepared by Lieutenant Colonel Frémont to go to Mexico, and failing in that, to bring home his topographical party to the United States; and were not these horses ordered to be produced by Lieutenant Colonel Frémont, and afterwards a large number of them sold, as stated in the last question, for three dollars or less?

The judge advocate said: He did not see the importance and relevancy of this inquiry. Lieutenant Colonel Frémont requested that the question might be answered.

No objection was made.

Answer. In one of Lieutenant Colonel Frémont's interviews with Colonel Mason at Los Angeles, in April last, in answer to inquiries as to public horses, Lieutenant Colonel Frémont said that he had sent about one hundred and fifty or one hundred and sixty horses, I think, to be grazed and fattened at some ranche in the vicinity; that he expected to return from Monterey, and to use these horses in surveying some southern route to the United States, (I think the Gila route;) I do not know what horses they were, or what corps or party they belonged to at that time, if to any. Colonel Mason did not assent to it, or reduced their number to sixty—this to the best of my recollection, and I have not a clear recollection of the last part of it; whether these were the same horses, or some of them that were sold afterwards under my orders, I do not know, and had no opportunity of knowing.

Question. In your report are these words: " The late enemy who surrounded us, who gallop over the country armed to the teeth, and many of them with weapons taken in battle from our troops." When and where were the weapons you speak of " as taken in battle from our troops" so taken, and under what commander were our troops when their weapons were so taken; had there been any arms lost in battle by our troops in California, except by the dragoons under General Kearny at San Pasqual?

The judge advocate said that an official report made by Major Cooke of Captain Owens's resistance of his authority, a subject about which the witness has testified in his examination in chief, had been introduced on his cross-examination, and this was done under the rule which authorizes a party, in cross-examination, to oppose the statements which the witness makes on oath with statements which he has made elsewhere on the same subject. But this report refers to matters not relevant to the charges, and not embraced in his testimony; such subjects, because they appear in the report, are not matters for the court to investigate. The judge advocate, however, has no objection to the witness answering the question.

Answer. My whole answer to the question must be hearsay, founded on report. The weapons which I alluded to were sabres taken in battle at San Pasqual, as I suppose, from men that had been killed; General Kearny commanded in that action; I am not aware that any arms had been lost in battle elsewhere by our troops in California, though there might have been in Captain Mervine's defeat near Los Angeles, which is the only battle that I now remember that our troops in California were engaged in, except under the orders of General Kearny. The siege and capitulation of Los Angeles might be considered by some a battle, and, if I am not mistaken, some arms or artillery were surrendered on that occasion.

Question. In your cross-examination of yesterday you speak of *"verbal orders from General Kearny,"* under which, as well as under your written orders, you say you would have *"crushed"* the resistance of Captain Owens. Now, will you please to state in what manner those *"verbal orders"* were applicable to any such resistance, and if said orders were not given when Lieutenant Colonel Frémont was in the actual command of the California battalion, and before the command of that battalion devolved upon Captain Owens?

Answer. I believe I did not speak of crushing resistance of Captain Owens yesterday. The verbal order alluded to might be considered as giving a higher importance, in my view, to the object to be attained, which was to turn over to company C, 1st dragoons, the two mountain howitzers as a part of their armament. When those verbal orders were given, and when they were received, Lieutenant Colonel Frémont was in the neighborhood, I believe, of the California battalion, but calling himself governor; I do not know whether he was in the actual command of it or not. I received at the same time with those memoranda, or verbal orders, the department order placing me in command of the district. But it did not include the command of that battalion prior to their being mustered into service.

Question. In saying that you were never told by General Kearny, or any one on his behalf, of his intention to have you as a witness against Lieutenant Colonel Frémont, do you make any difference between personal and official knowledge, or between direct and indirect information, or between belief or positive knowledge; or do you mean to say that you had no knowledge of General Kearny' intention to use you as a witness until the subpœna or order was served upon you, say at Vera Cruz?

A member objected. The defence said they would waive the question.

On motion of a member, the court was cleared.

The court decided that the question shall be put. The court was then opened—Lieutenant Colonel Frémont in court. The decision in closed session was announced.

Major Cooke, a witness.—Cross-examination.

Answer. General Kearny refused applications of mine to return with him to the United States, until in a private letter I made a very warm appeal, which I believed that he could not resist, to be allowed to return to join my regiment in the south. He assented a very short time before our departure. In coming down the Missouri, in August, I sought information of him on the point of my being a witness, and the only satisfaction I got was an impression that, if Lieutenant Colonel Frémont was tried shortly at all, it would be exclusively on documentary evidence, owing to the great delay which was anticipated might ensue by the call for witnesses from California. I went to Vera Cruz with no expectation that I would be recalled, and when I received the order from the adjutant general, it was with great surprise.

Cross-examination of this witness here closed.

Question by judge advocate. You have explained, in cross-examination, that part of your report which speaks of the Californians having arms taken from our people in battle; what amount of arms did you mean?

Answer. A few sabres, that is, I saw two or three, no more myself.

This witness then retired.

Captain H. S. Turney, a witness for the prosecution, duly sworn by the judge advocate according to law, testified as follows:

Examination in chief by the judge advocate.

Question. State whether you were sent by General Kearny to convey orders to Lieutenant Colonel Frémont at Los Angeles; if so, what orders, when you delivered them, and what Lieutenant Colonel Frémont said officially to you in reply to said orders?

Answer. I was sent by General Kearny to convey orders to Lieutenant Colonel Frémont, at Los Angeles; I do not recollect the number of the order; I think, however, it was department order, No. 2, but I am not certain; I delivered them about the 11th of March. The day after I delivered the orders, I had an interview with Lieutenant Colonel Frémont. He then informed me that he would proceed the next day to the mission of San Gabriel to execute the order.

Question. Was this order now shown you, the order which you delivered to Lieutenant Colonel Frémont, and which you have referred to?

10th military department, orders No. 2, March 1st, 1847, as recorded in the seventh specification to the first charge, here shown the witness by consent.

Answer. That is an extract from the order, and correct as far as it goes; I think it is all of the order that referred to Lieutenant Colonel Frémont; I think there were other paragraphs in the original order.

Question. Was this circular here shown you delivered to Lieutenant Colonel Frémont at the same time?

Answer. It was.

The circular here shown the witness was the joint circular signed W. Branford Shubrick, commander-in-chief of the naval forces, and S. W. Kearny, brigadier general, U. S. army, and governor of California, of date 1st March, 1847, at Monterey, as recited on this record in the seventh specification to the first charge.

Question. In what capacity, by commission in the army, and by appointment in General Kearny's staff, did you deliver those orders to Lieutenant Colonel Frémont?

Answer. By commission in the army as captain in the first regiment of dragoons, and as acting assistant adjutant general of the 10th military department, commanded by General Kearny.

The direct examination here closed; then cross-examination as follows by Lieutenant Colonel Frémont:

Question. Do you recollect, when the topographical party of Lieutenant Colonel Frémont was brought, himself at their head, in front of General Kearny's quarters in Monterey, that General Kearny called out one of the men, (William Findlay,) and that you whispered to General Kearny, and then he sent Findlay back: now, if you know these circumstances, do you know what was the object of General Kearny in so calling out Findlay, and in so sending him back?

Answer. I recollect when the topographical party of Lieutenant Colonel Frémont was paraded in front of General Kearny's quarters, himself at their head; I recollect that General Kearny called out a man by the name of Findlay. It occurred to me at that moment that General Kearny's object was to question Findlay with respect to some information Findlay had that day given to an officer of the navy, who reported it to me, and I to General Kearny, in relation to certain conduct ascribed to a man by the name of Goday, belonging to Lieutenant Colonel Frémont's party.

On suggestion of the judge advocate, the court was here cleared. The court decided that the witness shall continue his answer to the question. The court was then opened. Lieutenant Colonel Frémont in court. The decision in closed session was announced.

Captain H. S. Turner, a witness.—Cross-examination continued.

Answer continued. I asked General Kearny if such was his object. He answered, it was. I then said to him: perhaps, sir, it would not be agreeable to the officer who gave me the information that you should notice it in this public manner.

Question. Did you know that Lieutenant Colonel Frémont and his men, being encamped in the edge of the town of Monterey, he (Lieutenant Colonel Frémont) was ordered by General Kearny to come into the town, and stay in the town; and if so, was not this written two days before the commencement of the return march of General Kearny, his Mormon escort, and Lieutenant Colonel Frémont's topographical party, to the United States?

Answer. I recollect that a letter was addressed by General Kearny to Lieutenant Colonel Frémont, which letter was left in my hands, to be delivered to Lieutenant Colonel Frémont on his arrival at Monterey, directing him to remain in the town for certain purposes; that is all I recollect about it. I will state further, that at the time this letter was given to me, Lieutenant Colonel Frémont had not arrived at Monterey, and did not arrive for some days; about a week.

Question. Do you recollect a conversation in Monterey at that time, in which General Kearny directed Lieutenant Colonel Frémont to leave his camp and come into the town; and were you not requested by General Kearny to be a witness to that conversation?

Answer. At General Kearny's request I was a witness to a conversation between himself and Lieutenant Colonel Frémont; I think he told Lieutenant Colonel Frémont, on that occasion, that he must come into town and remain there.

Question. When did you first hear of General Kearny's intention to arrest Lieutenant Colonel Frémont?

Answer. I cannot say; I do not recollect the time; I think, though, it was some time in the month of May, on the return of General Kearny from Los Angeles.

Question. When did you first know of General Kearny's intention to have you as a witness on the trial of Lieutenant Colonel Frémont?

Answer. I received a letter in St. Louis, about the 5th of September, from General Kearny, who was in this city; a private letter. I was informed, in that letter, that my name had been given in as a witness for the trial of Lieutenant Colonel Frémont. That was the first intimation that I had that I was to be a witness. *   *   *   After a pause, the witness added: I am mistaken in saying the 5th of September; it was the 5th of October, or about the early part of October, of this year.

Question. Do you know whether it was a calculation of General Kearny that Lieutenant Colonel Frémont would have his trial delayed till he (Lieutenant Colonel Frémont) could get witnesses from California? or that he would be tried wholly on documentary or written testimony?

Answer. I never heard anything on the subject.

The cross-examination here closed; the witness was permitted to retire.

The court was ordered to be cleared. After some time in closed session, the court was opened; Lieutenant Colonel Frémont in court.

The court then, at three minutes before 3, adjourned to meet to-morrow, at 10 o'clock.

SATURDAY, *November* 27, 1847.—10 *o'clock.*

The court met pursuant to adjournment.

Present: All the members, the judge advocate and Lieutenant Colonel Frémont.

The proceedings of yesterday were read over.

Major Philip St. George Cooke came into court and said: I wish, Mr. President, to make an explanation of my testimony of yesterday. Leave being granted, Major Cooke said:

"Will the judge advocate read over my answer of yesterday, relative to Lieutenant Colonel Frémont being in the actual command of the California battalion, and my command over that battalion."

The question and answer were read over to the witness, whereupon he testified as follows:

I do not know that I used the exact words, as recorded, "but it did not include the command of that battalion prior to their being mustered into service;" which do not convey my full meaning. I must have alluded to the fact that the department order evidently contemplated the battalion's being immediately mustered into service. If I had been at Los Angeles when that order was received, I certainly should not have considered the battalion as under my orders until Lieutenant Colonel Frémont had mustered them into the service, if he remained in command of them. But arriving there afterwards, finding the battalion there embodied and stationed, I considered it as certainly subject to my orders as the commander of the military district, and in the absence of Lieutenant Colonel Frémont, their commander, who was senior to me.

The witness then retired, the defence having no further questions to ask.

Mr. Edwin Bryant, a witness summoned on the part of the prosecution, was duly sworn by the judge advocate, according to law.

The judge advocate said he had sworn this witness for the prosecution, according to the agreement with the defence, as appears hereinbefore on this record; and, having no questions to ask him, he was now subject to cross-examination by the defence.

Cross-examination, by Lieutenant Colonel Frémont, as follows:

Question. Did you sell or dispose of lands or lots in California, by order of Governor Kearny? and, if so, are these the orders and advertisements under which you acted?

Answer. I did not sell any lots or lands in California, by order of General Kearny. I advertised lands by his permission; the sale did not take place; this is the decree of Governor Kearny, I suppose.

The following, shown to witness with this question, then read:

Great sale of valuable real estate in the town of Francisco, Upper California.

By the following decree of his excellency, General S. W. Kearny, governor of California, all the right, title and interest of the United States, and of the territory of California, to the beach and water lot on the east front of the town of San Francisco, have been granted, conveyed, and released, to the people, or corporate authorities of said town.

DECREE OF GOVERNOR KEARNY.

I, Brigadier General S. W. Kearny, governor of California, by virtue of authority in me vested by the President of the United States of America, do hereby grant, convey and release unto the town of San Francisco, the people or corporate authorities thereof, all the right, title and interest of the government of the United States, and of the territory of California, in and to the beach and water lot on the east front of the said town of San Francisco, included between the points known as the Rincon and Fort Montgomery, excepting such lot as may be selected for the use of the United States government by the senior officers of the army and navy now there; provided the said grounds hereby ceded shall be divided into lots and sold by public auction to the highest bidder, after three months' notice previously given; the proceeds of said sale to be for the benefit of the town of San Francisco.

Given at Monterey, capital of California, this 10th day of March, 1847, and the 71st year of the independence of the United States.

S. W. KEARNY,
Brigadier General and Governor of California.

A member of the court presented the following note to the president, which was read aloud by the judge advocate:

Mr. President: A member suggests that it would save time to allow the accused to state, quite briefly, the purpose or object of the question.

The judge advocate said that he supposes the object of Lieutenant Colonel Frémont is, to show that General Kearny, as governor of California, exercised authority to sell public land. In the *eighth* specification, under the first charge, it is charged that Lieutenant Colonel Frémont bought land for public use. The object appears to be to justify the exercise of such authority on the part of Lieutenant Colonel Frémont. The judge advocate does not feel called upon to object to this mode of reaching that object.

The witness then rose and stated further in explanation, as follows:

I supposed the question to refer to this decree, under which, as I said, the land was not actually sold. I did, however, as alcalde of San Francisco, by Governor Kearny's appointment, grant and sell lots, belonging to the public, without special orders from Governor Kearny, but under the usages and customary powers of the alcalde.

Question. Did you act as cadi, or alcalde, by appointment of General Kearny, in San Francisco? and, if so, what law was enforced among the people by you after Governor Kearny's proclamation of March 1st, 1847? and is this a true copy of that proclamation?

Answer. I was alcalde in San Francisco; I believe this to be a true copy of the proclamation In administering justice, I endeavored to conform, as near as I could, to the Mexican laws and customs.

The proclamation, shown the witness with this question, was then read to the court, as follows:

TO THE PEOPLE OF CALIFORNIA.

The President of the United States having instructed the undersigned to take charge of the civil government of California, he enters upon his duties with an ardent desire to promote, as far as he is able, the interests of the country and the welfare of its inhabitants.

The undersigned has instructions from the President to respect and protect the religious institutions of California, and to see that the religious rights of the people are, in the amplest manner, preserved to them; the constitution of the United States allowing every man to worship his Creator in such a manner as his own conscience may dictate to him.

The undersigned is also instructed to protect the persons and property of the quiet and peaceable inhabitants of the country against all or any of their enemies, whether from abroad or at home; and when he now assures the Californians that it will be his duty and his pleasure to comply with those instructions, he calls upon them all to exert themselves in preserving order and tranquility, in promoting harmony and concord, and in maintaining the authority and efficiency of the laws.

It is the wish and design of the United States to provide for California, with the least possible delay, a free government similar to those in her other territories, and the people will soon be called upon to exercise their rights as freemen, in electing their own representatives, to make such laws as may be deemed best for their interest and welfare. But until this can be done, the laws now in existence, and not in conflict with the constitution of the United States, will be continued, until changed by competent authority; and those persons who hold office will continue in the same for the present, provided they swear to support that constitution, and to faithfully perform their duty.

The undersigned hereby absolves all the inhabitants of California from any further allegiance to the republic of Mexico, and will consider them as citizens of the United States. Those who remain quiet and peacable will be respected in their rights, and protected in them. Should any take up arms against, or oppose the government of this territory, or instigate others to do so, they will be considered as enemies and treated accordingly.

When Mexico forced a war upon the United States, time did not permit the latter to invite the Californians, as friends, to join her standard, but compelled her to take possession of the country to prevent any European power from seizing upon it; and, in doing so, some excesses and unauthorized acts were, no doubt, committed by persons employed in the service of the United States, by which a few of the inhabitants have met with a loss of property. Such losses will be duly investigated, and those entitled to remuneration will receive it.

California has for many years suffered greatly from domestic trouble. Civil wars have been the poisoned fountains which have sent forth trouble and pestilence over her beautiful land. Now, those fountains are dried up; the star spangled banner floats over California; and as long as the sun continues to shine upon her, so long will it float there, over the natives of the land, as well as others who have found a home in her bosom; and, under it, agriculture must improve, and the arts and sciences flourish, as seed in a rich and fertile soil.

The Americans and Californians are now but one people; let us cherish one wish, one hope, and let that be for the peace and quiet of our country. Let us be a band of brothers, unite and emulate each other in our exertions to benefit and improve this our beautiful, and which soon must be, our happy and prosperous home.

Done at Monterey, capital of California, this first day of March, A. D. 1847, and in the 71st year of independence of the United States.

S. W. KEARNY,
Brig. Gen. U. S. A., and Governor of California.

Lieutenant Colonel Frémont presented a note to the court, which was read by the judge advocate, as follows:

Mr. PRESIDENT: The object of this enquiry is to show that California was left without any known law after the proclamation of Governor Kearny, of March 1st, 1847; and that the alarm of the people, in consequence, was one of the causes of discontent verging towards insurrection, which then existed, and to allay which was one of the causes of the extraordinary ride made by Lieutenant Colonel Frémont, from Los Angeles to Monterey, in March, 1847, and one of the causes of the delay which occurred in executing an order of General Kearny's.

J. C. FRÉMONT,
Lieut. Col. mounted riflemen.

Question. Did you consider that proclamation as extending the constitution of the United States to California, and abrogating all the existing laws of the country repugnant to that Constitution? and, if not, how did you consider the proclamation as affecting the jurisprudence of the country?

Answer. I did not consider that there was any essential change in the laws and jurisprudence of the country in consequence of that proclamation; but that the change mentioned in the proclamation was prospective, and it never took place.

Question. What construction or operation did you give to this clause in that proclamation: "But until this can be done the laws now in force, and not in conflict with the constitution of the United States will be considered in force until changed by competent authority," &c.

Answer. I supposed, when I accepted the office of alcalde, that in a short time there would be a written system of laws for the government of the country, in forming which the people of the country would participate to some extent. And until that change should take place, and was authorized, I administered justice according to the Mexican laws, as far as I could ascertain them.

Question. How did you consider the inhabitants of California, as citizens of the United States or as Mexican citizens, under these words of the proclamation: "The undersigned hereby absolves all the inhabitants of California from any further allegiance to the republic of Mexico, and will consider them as citizens of the United States?"

Answer. I did not consider them as citizens of the United States; I considered the proclamation, as I before said, prospective in many respects.

Question. Did you, in your capacity of cadi, or alcalde, consider the capitulation of Cowenga in force after the date of the said proclamation, or did you consider the capitulation as abrogated by the proclamation?

Answer. I considered that General Kearny exercised the legal authority in the country; and, if there was any conflict, which I now specially notice, between the two documents, I should consider that his abrogated the other.

The cross-examination here closed.

Question by judge advocate. Do you know whether there was any alarm or discontent, verging towards insurrection among the people of California, caused by that proclamation or following it, so as, in your judgment, to be attributed in any degree to that proclamation?

Answer. I do not know of any such alarm; there were rumors of insurrection and invasion below, but from what cause I never understood.

Cross-examination resumed.

Question. Is this article in the California Star, of May 15, 1847, a correct account of any of the rumors of insurrection to which you allude?

Answer. I read this article in California, and it was the current rumor.

The newspaper paragraph shown the witness with this question, then read as follows:

FROM BELOW.

We have just learned, by a recent arrival from Los Angeles, that another outbreak was apprehended. Our informant, on his way hither, met several large cavalcades driven by Californians in arms. And again, on the Cowenga plains, near Los Angeles, three horsemen, bearing the Mexican flag, fled upon being discovered. Another account, which we do not consider credible, announces the commencement of hostilities. It is true that immense bands of horses are almost daily driven to the leeward from the north side of the bay. And although the disturbances may not yet have commenced, we have cause to believe, in the language of our informant, that they are "fixen' for it."—*California Star, May* 15, 1847.

The witness was then permitted to retire.

The court at 12 o'clock took a recess of ten minutes, at expiration of which time the court was again in session. Present: All the members, the judge advocate, and Lieutenant Colonel Frémont.

The judge advocate informed Lieutenant Colonel Frémont that the only witnesses summoned on the part of the prosecution, who had not been sworn and cross-examined, are Doctor Sanderson, Major Swords, of the army, and the Hon. W. P. Hall; the latter was not in attendance to-day. Lieutenant Colonel Frémont said he had no questions to ask of Doctor Sanderson or Major Swords; that he would, at any convenient future occasion, when the prosecution might introduce him, examine Mr. Hall on the few points in regard to which his testimony was required by the defence. And the judge advocate said further: The 9th specification to the 1st charge recites an order from Lieutenant Colonel Frémont to the collector of San Pedro. The original was exhibited to Lieutenant Colonel Frémont during this trial, and was admitted by him to be authentic, and that the same is truly set out in the specification. The latter part of the specification is an averment of the amount received by the collector under the order, and the rate of discount on the paper at San Pedro. In proof of the amount, the judge advocate has received the original certificates which the collector received from Mr. Hutteman, and for which he was allowed credit in the settlement of his custom-house accounts with Lieutenant Davidson, of the quartermaster's department, who was ordered by Governor Kearny to audit the said custom-house accounts. In proof of the discount, the judge advocate has an official report of the said collector to Governor Kearny; also, General Kearny can now testify to the current rate of discount on this paper at the time and place. But the judge advocate thinks it of no importance to establish this point, except in so far as he is required to go through and exhaust the specifications. This statement, in the specification, stands as in the original charges. But it appears that this paper, if good at all, as against the government, was good for par, and, if taken at all, ought to have been taken at par in payment of government dues. Lieutenant Colonel Frémont, however, admits the statement in this 9th specification to the 1st charge, both as to the amount received by the collector, from Hutteman, and the discount at which said paper could be purchased at San Pedro, and is willing that it shall stand as proved, and go to the court for what it is worth.

The judge advocate then said, the evidence for the prosecution is now closed.

Whereupon Lieutenant Colonel Frémont presented a written address to the court, which was read by the judge advocate, as follows:

Mr. President: Lieutenant Colonel Frémont desires respectfully to call the attention of the court to the fact that the accuser and principal prosecuting witness in this case has, on two occasions, vouched Lieutenant W. H. Emory, of the topographical engineers, as able to testify to an important point, to which both the court and the defence have directed questions; also, that Lieutenant Emory, in immediate connexion with the accuser, was a prominent actor in, and witness of, all the events in which the matters of accusation before the court appear to have had their rise, in such manner and under such circumstances as naturally to point him out as the most important witness, after the accuser himself, on the side of the prosecution; and yet that he has not been so summoned, and it is understood the prosecution decline now to call him.

Lieutenant Emory formed a portion of the guard which accompanied General Kearny from New Mexico to California; was with him at San Pasqual and on the hill of San Bernardo, and thence to San Diego, and during his sojourn at the latter place, from the 12th to the 28th December; was present at the organization of the expedition from San Diego to Los Angeles, and is reported by General Kearny as the acting assistant adjutant general on the march of that expedition, and in this capacity, as making the official report of killed and wounded in the actions which occurred during the march. He subsequently acted as adjutant to General Kearny, and it was through him that the order was sent which is introduced as the ground-work of the first specification of "mutiny" against Lieutenant Colonel Frémont, and in relation to the delivery of which General Kearny has twice vouched him as the proper person to testify. He is likewise the officer selected by General Kearny as his confidential messenger to bring into the government his account of the occurrences and state of affairs in California, subsequent to the breaking out of the dispute between Commodore Stockton and General Kearny.

In courts of law, as Lieutenant Colonel Frémont is advised by his counsel, the omission to call a witness under such circumstances would be very unfavorably interpreted, as raising a suspicion that the witness might have testimony in his knowledge that the party whose place it was to call him desired to exclude, or else to force upon the opposite party to call him, and thus cut off their rights of cross-examination. Courts martial will be slow to come to a conclusion that would thus reflect upon any member of the service; but they will not be less willing to prevent the injustice which would be the effect, whatever might be the motives, of such an omission; and, in the present instance, Lieutenant Colonel Frémont feels certain they will not hesitate to make such an order as will secure him in the rights which he has in the premises.

In courts of law, as Lieutenant Colonel Frémont is further advised, a witness, under such circumstances, would be called by the court, or directed by them to be called, for the prosecution.—See case of the Queen vs. Bull, 9 Carrington and Payne, page 22.

The present case would seem to come clearly within the rule here laid down, and the calling of the witness to be more especially within the province of the court, inasmuch as he has been pointed out by the accuser in the case, in reply to a question of the court, as the only person able to testify to the information sought.

Accordingly, Lieutenant Colonel Frémont respectfully makes this request of the court. But, in case the court should not find it proper or expedient to grant it, then Lieutenant Colonel Frémont respectfully asks the privilege of cross-examining Lieutenant Emory, under the rule which gives to a party calling a witness who is of necessity inimical to him, the same rights of cross-examination as if he were called by the other party. The rule is very distinctly laid down in De Hart's Courts Martial, pages 407–'8:

"Where a witness examined in chief, by his conduct in the box shows himself decidedly adverse to the party calling him, it is in the discretion of the court to allow him to be examined as if he were on cross-examination. *But, if he stands in a situation which of necessity makes him adverse to the party calling him, it was held that the party may, as a matter of right, cross-examine him.*"

In addition to the facts already stated, which show Lieutenant Emory, from his connexion with the prosecution to be properly in all respects the witness of that side, and necessarily predisposed in its favor, there are others, which it is thought can leave no doubt in the minds of the court that the rule above quoted applies to the case with great force.

Returning to the United States as the confidential messenger of General Kearny, Lieutenant Emory began a strictly partizan work when he arrived at the isthmus of Panama, writing thence a letter of a partizan character, which was published over his name in newspapers of the United States. As he proceeded on his journey, simultaneous with his arrival at Havana, then at New Orleans, then at Louisville, and, finally, at Washington, most injurious statements concerning Lieutenant Colonel Frémont were made in those cities, in many instances in connexion with his name, and in some instances he vouched as the informant. Finally, since his arrival in Washington, he has avowed himself the author of two injurious charges against Lieutenant Colonel Frémont, and has acknowledged to be at personal enmity with him.

Lieutenant Colonel Frémont respectfully presents these considerations to the court, and will very cheerfully abide their decision upon what he has asked.

J. C. FRÉMONT,
Lieutenant Colonel mounted riflemen.

The court was then ordered to be cleared. The court asked of the judge advocate an explanation of the circumstances under which Lieutenant Emory is brought before the court as a witness.

The judge advocate said: The witnesses for the prosecution, as I understood from the adjutant general's office, were given in by General Kearny, with his charges against Lieutenant Colonel Frémont. The military witnesses of the prosecution were ordered by the adjutant general to attend the court. The citizen witnesses were named to me from the adjutant general's office, and I, as judge advocate, issued summonses to them. I summoned no other witnesses for the prosecution. Lieutenant Emory was not required as a witness by General Kearny. He was under orders for Mexico as a lieutenant colonel of volunteers. He was summoned on the part of the defence. His evidence did not appear to me necessary to support any part of the charges. He delivered to Lieutenant Colonel Frémont the order of General Kearny of the 16th of January; but the fact of the receipt of that order was acknowledged in Lieutenant Colonel Frémont's written reply to General Kearny; and further acknowledged to General Kearny, by Lieut. Colonel Frémont, in a personal interview, as General Kearny was prepared to testify, and has testified before this court.

The prosecution, therefore, has no occasion for Lieutenant Emory as a witness.

After mature deliberation, the court decided as follows: The court is of opinion that it does not appear to have been incumbent on the prosecution to summon Lieutenant Emory as a witness; and that it is not the custom to bring military persons from their duty to be witnesses for the prosecution, when their testimony is not necessary, although the prosecution may know that such persons have knowledge of the matters under trial.

In relation to the second request of the accused, the court recognises the rights of parties calling unwilling or adverse witnesses, as sustained by the leading authorities, and will not fail to secure them when the matter or manner of a witness calls for its action; but cannot decide beforehand the relation of the witness to the accused as inimical or otherwise.

The court was then opened. Lieutenant Colonel Frémont in court. The decision in closed session was announced.

The defence having no further matter at present to submit to the court, the court was ordered to be cleared; and resolved to adjourn. Whereupon the court was opened. Lieutenant Colonel Frémont in court; and the court, at half-past two, adjourned to meet on Monday, at 10 o'clock.

Monday, *November* 29, 1847—10 *o'clock.*

The court met pursuant to adjournment. Present : all the members, the judge advocate, and Lieutenant Colonel Frémont.

The proceedings of yesterday were read over.

Wm. H. Emory, a lieutenant colonel of volunteers, in the service of the United States, a witness, called on the part of the defence, being duly sworn, according to law, by the judge advocate, testified as follows : Examined in chief.

Question by Lieutenant Colonel Frémont. Were you on social and friendly terms with Colonel Benton *before* you went to California, and returning from that place, did you not avoid seeing Colonel Benton at Louisville, Kentucky, and avoid giving him any news from California, even at second hand, or by message; and was not this conduct towards Colonel Benton in consequence of your *animosity* to Lieutenant Colonel Frémont, and of your talk, writings, and publications against him, Lieutenant Colonel Frémont? and of all which Colonel Benton was then ignorant?

The judge advocate said, in presenting the foregoing questions, that it was intimated to him that the defence proposed, under what they took to be the decision of the court on Saturday, to show, at the outset, by the witness, his hostility to the defence; and, after that, to cross-examine him. The judge advocate proposed to clear the court, and take their opinion whether this course was allowable, and in accordance with their opinion of Saturday.

The witness being in court, said : He would, under permission of the court, answer with great pleasure any and every question which the defence may wish to ask of him.

The President said, "the court will be cleared." And a member suggested, "that is a question for the court."

The Court was then cleared. After mature deliberation the court decided that the question shall not be put; and further, that the court recognizes the rule, when a witness appears by his demeanor and testimony in court, or by his necessary relation to the parties, to be hostile to the party calling him, that the court may, in its discretion, allow the examination by the party calling such witness, to take something of the form and character of a cross-examination. In this case the court recognizes nothing in the known official and legal relations of Lieutenant Colonel Emory to either the prosecution, the leading prosecuting witness, or the defence, to justify it in receiving him in court as an adverse or reluctant witness for the defence. If his demeanor and testimony shall show him to be such, the court will allow him to be so interrogated by the defence as may appear necessary to elicit the truth; but the examination so allowed, and assimilated to a cross-examination, cannot confer on the party calling a witness the right to impeach his veracity, or character, or motives. A cross-examination to that extent is not allowable to the party calling a witness, except, perhaps, in the case of a witness necessarily called to the formal proof of an instrument. The court cannot allow the defence to impeach their witness either on their own application, or by his own consent, though they may, by another witness, disprove a particular material fact. Their examination must therefore be directed to the matters properly in issue, and if on those matters the witness exhibits hostility to the defence, or reluctance to testify, the court will allow such examination as may be necessary to elicit the truth.

The court was then opened. Lieutenant Colonel Frémont in court. The decision in closed session was announced.

Lieutenant Colonel Wm. H. Emory, a witness; examination continued by the defence.

Question. Did you write a letter from the Isthmus of Panama for publication in the United States, which related to the military operations in California? and if so, is this a copy of that letter?

The paper shown the witness, with this question, then read as follows:

The following is a true and correct copy of a lettter published in the New York Courier and Enquirer, of April 23, 1847.

To the Editor of the Courier and Enquirer.

PANAMA, *March* 15, 1847.

SIR : By the arrival of the United States ship Dale, this day, I am placed in possesssion of "*the Californian extra*," published at Monterey, January 28, 1847, containing a letter dated Ciudad de los Angeles, January 14, purporting to give an account of the battles of the 8th and 9th of January.

Many copies of this paper are in the mail bag of the Dale, intended for circulation in the United States. The letter in question states, "the skill in management and determined courage and bravery of our commodore (Stockton) gave to all the fullest confidence of a victorious result of this brilliant affair," &c.

It also states, "the success attending the Californians in their fight with Captain Mervine at San Pedro, and afterwards with General Kearny at San Pasqual, *made them very bold and arrogant, and every man of us was determined to retrieve, if possible, the credit of the American arms.*"

Now, sir, the *facts* are as follows: No order of any moment was given, either in the fight of the 8th or 9th, which was not given by General Kearny in person, or through the undersigned, as his acting assistant adjutant general.

General Kearny commanded the troops in both battles. At the battle of San Pasqual, which took place one hour before day on the morning of the 6th December, General Kearney attacked, beat and chased some miles, 160 well mounted Californians, with less than 100 dragoons, emaciated by an unexampled march over the deserts of America of more than 2,000 miles.

The statements and imputations in the "California extra" are therefore false.

Very respectfully, yours,

W. H. EMORY,
Lieut Corps Top. Engineers.

On suggestion of the judge advocate, the court was ordered to be cleared.

The court decided that the question be not put.

The court was opened, Lieutenant Colonel Frémont in court.

The decision in closed session was announced.

Lieutenant Colonel Emory, a witness, on examination by the defence.

Question. Who was the commander-in-chief on the expedition from San Diego to Los Angeles in January, 1847?

Answer. My information in regard to that matter is this: On the 28th of January, General Kearny sent for me, and directed me to leave my party at San Diego, and to act as his assistant adjutant general in an expedition which he contemplated to the City of the Angels. He informed me at the same time, that Commodore Stockton had consented, or had given him, I do not recollect which word it was, the command of the sailors and marines. My information, therefore, is confined very much to the immediate command of the troops. I was, at the same time, aware that Commodore Stockton claimed to be the governor and commander-in-chief of the territory of California. The first act in which this fact was brought to my personal knowledge, and in which I had to act officially, was on the 12th of January, 1847. I received from Commodore Stockton—I presume he sent it to me, it came through one of the gentlemen attached to his personal staff, I do not recollect which one it was at this moment—a general order in which he signed himself governor and commander-in-chief of the territory of California.

The judge advocate inquired: Have you that order?

Witness replied: I have not; it is the order congratulatory of the little affairs of the 8th and 9th; it has been published in the papers. The order was dated on the 11th of January; I think it was brought to me next day.

The witness resumed:

This order I took to General Kearny, and asked if I should have it read to the troops. He answered me, No. On the march Commodore Stockton, I understood, did several acts in that capacity. They did not come under my personal observation; I know of them rather from hearsay. General Kearny never explained to me the official relations existing between himself and Commodore Stockton, until the 17th of January; nor did Commodore Stockton ever explain them to me.

Question. Do you remember of any occasion on the march in which Commodore Stockton ordered an encampment of the forces to be changed from the place ordered by General Kearny? and if so, will you please to state your own official situation at that time, and what passed between yourself and Commodore Stockton in relation to that change of encampment?

Answer. I presume that the date is not material. I have an exact recollection of the circumstance. I was sent forward by General Kearny to select a camp. Commodore Stockton was in the advance at the time. He suggested to me a certain hill as a good place to encamp; he suggested the top of the hill. On examining the ground, I found it was not what I supposed he thought it to be, and I also thought it was too far from water; and I considered that I had discretionary power in regard to that matter, and put the camp at the foot of the hill. Commodore Stockton rode up to me, and asked me by what authority I had changed the ground. I told him that I did it of my own accord. He then ordered me, or directed me to put it on the hill; and I did so. Something else passed in reference to it, I understood, in camp; but of that I have no personal knowledge. In saying I have an exact recollection, I refer entirely to the circumstance, to the fact that there was a difficulty about such a matter; and I do not refer to the words; I will not pretend to say that I have an exact recollection of the words, which, at the time, I considered altogther unimportant.

Question. Did you, as assistant adjutant general to General Kearny, deliver to Lieutenant Colonel Frémont the order of General Kearny, forbidding the reorganization of the California battalion, which reorganization Commodore Stockton had previously ordered, and if so, what was the time, and especially, the time of the day, at which you delivered that order?

Answer. I delivered an order to Lieutenant Colonel Frémont, forbidding the reorganization of the battalion; I cannot recollect the exact hour when that order was delivered, but very near it; it was a little after dark. Lieutenant Colonel Frémont's candles were lit when I was at his house; I recollect that circumstance; and I think, when I started from my own quarters, it was about dusk; but of that I will not be certain. I know that it was somewhere immediately after dark; my impression is it was about 7 o'clock; it was on the 16th of January.

Question. Was the order of General Kearny (forbidding the reorganization) given by him *before* or *after* he (General Kearny) was suspended from command of the forces at Los Angeles by Commodore Stockton?

Answer. Of that I have no information. It was not till the next day that General Kearny showed me Commodore Stockton's letter; of that, therefore, I have no knowledge. It may have been the night of the 16th that General Kearny showed me Commodore Stockton's letter, I will not be certain about that; but I had no knowledge of it when I delivered to Lieutenant Colonel Frémont the order from General Kearny.

Question. At what time was that order *written?* (the order to Lieutenant Colonel Frémont, forbidding the reorganization of the battalion?)

Answer. It was written some time during the day; the precise time I cannot recollect. I was very much occupied all that time, on the hill. My recollection of that order is, that the general sent for me to write it, and that I returned again to the hill, and it was sent to me by an orderly. I think after I wrote it, at the general's dictation, I left it with him to copy, or have copi d; my recollection is not exact as to the precise time; Captain Turner was present, I think, and he can give the necessary information

Question. At what time of the day was the order finally sent to you by General Kearny, to be delivered to Lieutenant Colonel Frémont?

Answer. That I have no recollection of; I am not certain that it was sent to me. Perhaps I went after it. I recollect the time of the delivery of it, from the fact that it was about candle light.

Question. Will you please state what reference was made to the California battalion, if any, through you as assistant adjutant general, in the orders of the day, issued at the Ciudad de los Angeles in the month of January, 1847?

The judge advocate asked the witness if he had the order-book? He replied:

I do not know what the question refers to; I do not recollect any reference to the California battalion, except in the special order; if it is explained to me what it refers to, perhaps I can answer.

Question. What time of the day of 17th of January was it that you were first informed of the suspension of General Kearny—was it before or after the interview between Lieutenant Colonel Frémont and General Kearny, at the quarters of the latter?

Answer. I think it was after, though I do not know exactly at what hour that interview was. I was not present at it, but I think it was after.

Question. Is this a correct copy of a report made by you of the killed and wounded, in the actions of the 8th and 9th of January?

Answer. I think it is.

The report here shown the witness, the same as that copied on this record, being the reports to Governor Stockton of W. H. Emory, acting assistant adjutant general, and surgeon's report of killed and wounded enclosed therein.

Question. Is the address of that report precisely as you wrote, to wit: " His Excellency R. F. Stockton, governor of California, &c., &c. &c.?"

Answer. That I cannot recollect. I have referred to my own copy, and find there but one " &c.," but it is probable I put three in the original.

Question. At what time did you leave San Diego for the United States, and where was General Kearny at that time, and did he at any time before your departure make known his intention to arrest Lieutenant Colonel Frémont, or say anything about the arrest; and if so, what?

The judge advocate said:

Mr. PRESIDENT: The latter part of the question includes an inquiry which the court has refused to allow to be put. I bring this to your notice, in deference to the decision of the court; but say, that I have no objection to its being answered. If you will clear the court, I will ascertain its opinion.

The court was then cleared. After mature deliberation, the court decided:

The court has deemed an inquiry, as to the time General Kearny made known his intention to arrest Lieutenant Colonel Frémont, improper, as a collateral inquiry addressed to persons not of intimate official relations to the commanding general, but makes no objection to these questions to the members of his staff. The question will be put.

The court was opened. Lieutenant Colonel Frémont in court. The decision in closed session was announced.

Lieutenant Colonel Emory a witness on examination by the defence.

Answer. I left San Diego on the 25th of January, 1847. I understand he had arrived at San Diego, but I did not see him. He did not make known to me his intention to arrest Lieutenant Colonel Frémont.

Question. Did you learn from General Kearny that he would punish Lieutenant Colonel Frémont for mutiny when he got the power; and, if so, do you know whether he meant the arrival of the Mormons as the power for which he was waiting?

Answer. I did not learn from General Kearny that he would punish Lieutenant Colonel Frémont for mutiny when he got the power.

Question. Did you learn from him that he would reduce him to obedience when he got the power; and, if so, did he mean by getting the power, the arrival of the Mormons?

Answer. He informed me that he should take affairs into his own hands as soon as he felt himself sufficiently strong. He did not, that I recollect, use the word Mormons, or make any reference to that battalion. He did not mention Lieutenant Colonel Frémont's name.

Question. What did you understand by that, and especially by the words "sufficiently strong?"

Answer. I understood by it numerical strength—physical strength. I understood that, as soon as he got sufficient force—a sufficient body of troops—that he would carry out the orders of the President of the United States.

Question. What did you understand by the words "take affairs into his own hands?" Did you understand by it that he would use force, and that Lieutenant Colonel Frémont was to be one of those on whom the force was to be used?

Answer. I did.

Question Did you hear from General Kearny anything in relation to the coming of the Mormons after the difficulties about the command at Los Angeles?

Answer. Not from General Kearny. I met Mr. Hall a few hours after I had parted from General Kearny. He was the messenger from Colonel Cooke's battalion.

Question. Did you hear General Kearny speak of the convention of Cowenga, and call it illegal, or anything to that effect?

Answer. I did not.

Question. Did you hear General Kearny speaking of that convention as giving immunity to men who ought to be punished for their crimes, or anything to that effect?

Answer. I did not myself hear General Kearny say a word in reference to the convention.

Question. Did you, or any person from your information, and with your knowledge and consent, write a letter from Havana to the editor of the Picayune, in New Orleans; and, if so, is this a true copy of that letter?

The question was read to the court, and with it the following newspaper article:

[From the New Orleans Picayune, of April 27, 1847.]

Corrrespondence of the Picayune.

HAVANA, *April* 8, 1847.

DEAR SIRS: The British steamer Dee, which arrived last evening from Jamaica, brought to this place Captain Emory, of the topographical engineers, who accompanied General Kearny to California, and Lieutenant Gray, both bearers of despatches; the former from General Kearny, and the latter from Commodore Stockton. General Kearny arrived at the frontier settlements of California in December, found the Californians had raised in a body and expelled the Americans from the country, or obliged them to take shelter on shipboard.

General Kearny met the enemy in force at a place called San Pasqual, when an action took place, and where, at the expense of more than one-third of the little band that accompanied him—say one hundred—he defeated the enemy, cut his way through to San Diego.

I am sorry to inform you that disputes, of a serious nature, have taken place between General Kearny and Commodore Stockton. Stockton had refused to obey the instructions of his government, declining to give up the command of the civil government of Calinia to General Kearny.

Into this dispute, it is to be lamented, that Stockton drew Colonel Frémont on his side. It is to be hoped the President will cause the affair to be investigated at once.

The Independence, bearing the broad pendant of Commodore Shubrick, arrived at Monterey, California, on the 27th January.

Commodore Biddle, in the Columbus, was also expected in a few days. The store ship Livingston had arrived. It was supposed that, on the arrival of Commodore Biddle, he would issue an order for the arrest of Commodore Stockton. General Kearny had gone to Monterey with his few remaining men. Commodore Stockton remained at the head of affairs in Los Angeles.

None of the ports on the Pacific had been blockaded, and vessels were entering and discharging at Mazatlan without any molestation.

On the 8th January, near the Pueblo de los Angeles, a battle took place, in which the Californians were defeated, with considerable loss, and the peaceable possession of that territory to the United States restored.

Commodore Stockton accompanied General Kearny on the occasion; in fact, the expedition was composed principally of sailors and marines.

On arrival in front of the enemy, Commodore Stockton proposed to General Kearny to halt, but, it being on the 8th of January, the General very laconically replied, that he would not on that day do so, and the engagement commenced.

The judge advocate, on reading the question and newspaper article to the court, asked the president to order the court to be cleared.

Before the president's order was announced, the witness said: "No. I did not write that article, and know nothing about it."

The president ordered the court to be cleared. The court decided that the question shall not be put; nor will the court consider the answer of the witness.

The court was then opened. Lieutenant Colonel Frémont in court. The decision and record of the court, in closed session, as made by their order, was then announced.

The testimony of to-day was read over to the witness. He said, in explanation, "that the 16th of January I was very much occupied in laying out a fort on the hill, and directing the workmen." Whereupon, at five minutes before three, the court adjourned to meet to-morrow at 10 o'clock.

TUESDAY, *November* 30, 1847.—10 *o'clock.*

The court met pursuant to adjournment.

Present: All the members, the judge advocate, and Lieutenant Colonel Frémont.

The proceedings of yesterday were read over. The witness, Lieutenant Colonel Emory, being in court, asked permission to make an explanation.

Leave being granted, he said: " I spoke yesterday in connection with the expedition from San Diego to Los Angeles of the 28th of January, it is an error of date; I should have said 28th of December, 1846."

Lieutenant Colonel Emory, a witness.—Examination by the defence continued.

Question. Is the paper herewith shown you a copy of the paper referred to as "*false*" in the letter from the Isthmus of Panama to the New York Courier and Enquirer, which letter is under your name, and was yesterday offered in evidence to the court, and the question in relation not allowed to be put?

The paper, submitted with this question, read to the court with the question, and as part of it.

Before reading the paper, the judge advocate made the following note: "This question was offered by the defence in connection with, and explanation of, the inquiry yesterday ruled out by the court. It therefore falls under the decision of yesterday. I shall, therefore, consider it not admitted to be put to the witness, and shall not take the opinion of the court, unless the defence insist."

When the question and paper were read, and the foregoing note of the judge advocate, on motion of a member, the court was cleared.

After mature deliberation, the court decided "that the question, now offered, being based upon the authorship of a newspaper article, which was not permitted by the court to be inquired into yesterday, there is evident impropriety in offering it now."

The court, influenced by a disposition to render the accused every possible courtesy and consideration, has forborne to admonish him, upon its record, of several instances of disregard of its rules, announced in the form of rejections of questions which have been offered.

This question, and the introduction of the paper which accompanies it, are both deemed improper by the court. The paper attempts, by introducing certificates, taken ex parte, and not sworn to, to contradict witnesses before the court, and especially and pointedly to contradict and discredit a witness introduced by the defence; and further to show, by such certificates, matters not relevant to this trial, and which this court cannot inquire into."

The court therefore directs, that while the question may stand on the record to show the character of the inquiry, the paper shall be returned to the accused, and not admitted on its record.

The court was then opened. Lieutenant Colonel Frémont in court. The decision in closed session was announced.

Lieutenant Colonel Emory, a witness.—Examination by defence continued.

Question. Did you, on your arrival at New Orleans, or before, furnish, or did any person, with your knowledge and consent, give to the Picayune newspaper an account of affairs in California? or did you give any such account to any body? and, if so, is this a true copy of what was so given out, or furnished? and was it published while you were in the city of New Orleans? and have you ever avowed or disavowed the reference therein made to you as the person from whom the particulars given in said publication was derived?

The court was ordered to be cleared.

After mature deliberation on the question and paper, the court decided that the question shall not be put to the witness.

The paper, read with the question, is as follows:

[From the New Orleans Picayune of April 22.]

Late from California.

By the barque Catharine, Captain Swift, from Havana, we have very late advices from California. Captain W. H. Emory, of the corps of topographical engineers, came passenger on her. Captain Emory was made acting adjutant general of the army of the west, in place of Captain Turner, who succeeded to the command of the 1st dragoons, after the death of Captain Moore, and in this capacity has been sent home by General Kearny to report the re-conquest of California, and the present condition and resources of that country. From Captain Swift we learn the following particulars, derived by him from Captain Emory:

"General Kearny reached the mouth of the Gila river about the 25th November. Captain Emory, while making a reconnoissance of that river, captured the Mexican mail passing from California to Sonora.

"By this General Kearny learned the Californians, had risen, captured the American garrison at Puebla de los Angeles, driven all the Americans in the interior of the country to the seaboard, and defeated the expedition of Captain Mervine and Colonel Frémont.

"General Kearny reached the first settlement in California, known as the Pass of San Felipe, on the 2d of December. There he found the news all confirmed. On the 5th he met Captain Gillespie, who had slipped out from San Diego, with thirty-five men, to apprise him of his danger. He learned from him that every pass was strongly guarded, and the exact position of the enemy. The general determined, at once, to cut his way into San Diego.

"His force was something short of one hundred dragoons, and five or six mounted men in the employment of the topographical engineers, all emaciated by the long march, (2,500 miles across the desert,) and mostly destitute of clothing. With seventy of this force, the rest being left with the baggage, General Kearny charged into the Mexican camp at the village of San Pasqual, on the morning of the 6th December, one hour before day, and after a desperate fight, in which he lost thirty-five, killed and wounded, routed the enemy, and chased him some miles. The enemy's force engaged was two hundred; his loss considerable. The general was himself severely lanced in two places, and every officer in the charge was killed or wounded, except Captains Turner and Emory, and Dr. Griffin, and these received lances in their clothes.

"The killed were—Captains Moore and Johnson, and Mr. Hammond, of the 1st dragoons; Sergeants Moore, Whiteburst, and Cox, and Corporals Clipper and West, and ten privates, 1st dragoons; one private topographical engineers, and one volunteer.

"The wounded were—General Kearny; Lieutenant Warner, topographical engineers; Captains Gillespie and Gibson, of the volunteers, and Mr. Robedent, interpreter, and ten privates of the 1st dragoons.

"The day after the battle the general moved on slowly towards San Diego, having on the way one or two skirmishes. He arrived at San Diego on the 10th, and finding there more men than were necessary to garrison the town, he proposed to Commodore Stockton (the men being chiefly sailors and marines, and not under the general's orders) to let him have a portion of them, and march on the Puebla de los Angeles, the heart of Mexican power in California.

"To this the commodore assented, and on the 28th December General Kearney marched with about 500 men on the Puebla, accompanied by the commodore. On the 8th of January the enemy showed himself in force, to dispute the passage of the San Gabriel river. After a short exchange of artillery, General Kearny ordered the heights charged, and drove him from his position.

"The next day, January 9th, the enemy again offered battle—was defeated, and sued for peace. Our loss in both affairs was only two killed and fifteen wounded. The enemy's force was 600 men and four pieces of artillery. Their loss is variously estimated at from 40 to 80 in killed and wounded. All is now quiet in California.

"Captain Emory has brought home with him the results of his survey across the continent, made with the advanced guard of the army of the west.

"He reports the sufferings of the little party which accompanied General Kearny before the battle of San Pasqual, where they got some of the enemy's food, as great in the extreme.

"Their clothes were nearly worn out, and for many days previous poor and worn down pack mules were their only food.

"Captain Emory sailed from San Diego on the 25th of January. On that day the gallant Lieutenant Hall, of Missouri, arrived there to report to General Kearny the arrival of the battalion of Mormons, under Lieutenant Colonel Cooke.

"The Independence, Commodore Shubrick, arrived at Monterey 15th January.

"The Livingston arrived on the 27th. The transport ships, with the New York regiment, were daily expected.

"The Dale arrived at Monterey, from Francisco, on the 30th December. She sailed from that place and arrived at Panama on the 16th March.

"Frémont was to have made a junction with General Kearny's forces at the Puebla, but did not do so.

"After the battle of the 9th January, Andreas Pico, the second in command of the Mexican forces, having twice broken his parole, and expecting no quarter from General Kearny, went off with a small portion of the enemy's force and effected a treaty with Colonel Frémont, securing to himself immunity for his crimes. This treaty, though illegal, being executed without the authority of the commanding general, may, it is supposed, be respected by the general from motives of policy."

The court was then opened; Lieutenant Colonel Fremont in court. The decision in closed session was announced.

Lieutenant Colonel Emory, a witness.—Examination by defence continued.

Question. Did you, either directly or indirectly, give any information to the editor of the Louisville Journal, or to any person for that paper, about the first of May last; and, if so, is this a copy ot what was then published as bottomed on your information?

The court was ordered to be cleared. After mature deliberation, the court decided that the question shall not be put, and that the newspaper article appearing to come from the Louisville Journal be not recorded. The court declining to encumber its record further with such publications, after the questions founded on them have been rejected as irrelevant or improper.

The court was then opened—Lieutenant Colonel Fremont in court. The decision in closed session was announced.

Lieutenant Colonel Emory, a witness.—Examination by defence continued.

Question. In your testimony of yesterday you say: "I understood that as soon as he (Kearny) got a sufficient force—a sufficient body of troops—he would carry out the orders of the President of the United States." Now, what orders of the President remained to be executed at that time, and which could, in any contemplation of those orders, require the *"numerical and physical strength"* of the Mormons or other troops to be employed by General Kearny upon Lieutenant Colonel Frémont?

Answer. The orders of the President of the United States were, as I understood them, to put General Kearney in authority as well as to retain possession of the country against the enemy.

The examination of this witness by the defence here conclued.

Cross-examination by judge advocate.

Question. In answer to a question yesterday, you said that your information as to the command during the expedition from San Diego to Los Angeles was confined to the immediate command of the troops. You did not state who had that command, nor who was in immediate command of the troops, and in the battles of the 8th and 9th?

Answer. General Kearny.

Question. You mentioned an instance where orders were given you, as assistant adjutant general, by Commodore Stockton, and obeyed by you. Did you consider Commodore Stockton as commanding the troops? Do you know of other facts and occurrences on that expedition tending to show who was in the actual command, as between Commodore Stockton and General Kearny?

A member objecting, the court was cleared. The court decided that the question shall not be put. The court was then opened; Lieutenant Colonel Frémont in court.

Lieutenant Colonel Emory, a witness, asked permission to make an explanation. Leave being granted, he said: In regard to the immediate command in the battles of the 8th and 9th, I wish to say that I have understood, since I came to this city, that orders were given by Commodore Stockton; but I was in a different part of the field, and know nothing about it.

The following paper was presented to the court by Lieutenant Colonel Emory:

A paper has been read to the court reflecting upon me individually, and in my character as a witness in the case now under consideration; charging me with having avowed personal enmity to the accused; with having made publications or furnished information injurious to him; with being identified with the prosecution; and, under these circumstances, that my evidence has been sought to be withheld. A question put to me for the purpose of corroborating these statements was rejected by the court. I now ask that I may be permitted to answer it, to the end that I may show the statement to be incorrect so far as it charges me with personal hostility to the accused; with being the author of any charge against him; with being a party to the prosecution now pending; or having sought by publication to prejudice him before the public, or forestall its opinion in relation to an official controversy to which circumstances had rendered me to a greater or less extent cognisant.

W. H. EMORY,
Lieutenant Colonel of volunteers.

The court was ordered to be cleared. The court decided that they cannot accede to the application of the witness.

The court was then opened; Lieutenant Colonel Frémont in court. The decision in closed session was announced.

Lieutenant Colonel Frémont presented the following papers:

Mr. PRESIDENT: Lieutenant Colonel Frémont asks for one day (to-morrow) to arrange the documentary part of his evidence, and will be ready at 10 o'clock, on Thursday morning, to proceed with his defence.

C. J. FRÉMONT,
Lieutenant Colonel, mounted riflemen.

Mr. PRESIDENT: Lieutenant Colonel Frémont respectfully states to the court, that in presenting the questions going to ascertain the authorship of the newspaper articles referred to, or of the information on which they were based, he designed to establish, as he believes is the fact, that at the same time that General Kearny held the secret purpose of a future trial and arrest of Lieutenant Colonel Frémont, a confidential member of General Kearny's staff, sent into the United States to bear his reports to the government, made it a part of his business, subsidiary in effect, if not in design, to that intention of General Kearny, to circulate and publish statements calculated to prepare the public mind for that arrest and trial, and to prejudice it against Lieutenant Colonel Frémont. This fact, the counsel of Lieutenant Colonel Frémont believe, would be both relevant and material to show in that branch of the defence which goes to impeach the motives and credit of the prosecutor. Lieutenant Colonel Frémont thinks this explanation due to a right understanding of his object, and also respectful to the court.

> J. C. FRÉMONT,
> *Lieutenant Colonel, mounted riflemen.*

The examination of this witness here concluded.

The testimony of to-day was then read over to him; and then, at four minutes before three, the court adjourned to meet on Thursday, at 10 o'clock,

---

THURSDAY, *December 2, 1847.—10 o'clock.*

The court met pursuant to adjournment.

Present: All the members, except Major Graham, who reported by letter to the president that he was too unwell to attend the court this day, but hoped to be able to attend to-morrow. Present, also, the judge advocate.

Whereupon, the court adjourned to meet to-morrow morning, at 10 o'clock.

FRIDAY, *December 3, 1847.—10 o'clock.*

The court met pursuant to adjournment.

Present: All the members, the judge advocate, and Lieutenant Colonel Frémont.

The proceedings of Tuesday and yesterday were read over.

Various papers, as documentary evidence, were then presented to the judge advocate by the defence, with the remark that, as these papers were, in several instances, extracts, the defence submitted at the same time complete copies, where such had been furnished from the departments, though the defence deem the extracts only to be relevant. In cases where only extracts are submitted, it is because only extracts have been received by the defence.

The judge advocate read to the court the heading of these several papers, as description of them, and then said: as he had never seen these papers before—as some of them did not appear to come in the form of evidence, though others appeared in that form, and might be important to the defence—he proposed, for the purpose of informing both himself and the court of the character of these papers, and their admissibility in evidence, in order to save time and accomplish both these purposes at once, to clear the court and read the papers; and then submit them to the court, with his own views in regard to them, if necessary.

Whereupon, the court was ordered to be cleared; and, after being engaged in hearing the papers read till twenty minutes of three, the court was opened, and then adjourned to meet to-morrow at 10 o'clock.

SATURDAY, *December 4, 1847.—10 o'clock.*

The court met pursuant to adjournment.

Present: All the members, the judge advocate, and Lieutenant Colonel Frémont.

The proceedings of yesterday were read over. Lieutenant Colonel Frémont presented a note, as follows:

MR. PRESIDENT: Lieutenant Colonel Frémont desires to say, the documentary evidence offered by him on yesterday is offered *as a whole*, and as such he is advised by his counsel that it is material to his defence that it be received; and, therefore, if any part of said documentary evidence should seem to be objectionable, he asks to be heard in support of its relevancy and materiality before it is excluded.

J. C. FRÉMONT,
Lieutenant Colonel, mounted riflemen.

Whereupon, the court went into closed session, and remained so till near three o'clock, examining the papers yesterday submitted by the defence as documentary evidence. The court was then opened. Lieutenant Colonel Frémont in court. The president informed him that the court was not yet ready to announce its decision on the document before it; and then, at five minutes before three o'clock, the court adjourned to meet on Monday, 6th instant, at 10 o'clock.

MONDAY, *December 6, 1847.—10 o'clock.*

The court met pursuant to adjournment.

Present: All the members, the judge advocate, and Lieutenant Colonel Frémont.

The proceedings of Saturday were read over. The court was then cleared to resume the consideration of the documents laid before it by the defence on Friday.

After mature deliberation, the court decided: That the reports which are submitted to it from commanders on the coast of California to the Navy Department, and the correspondence among officers and other persons in the Pacific, are not evidence to prove their contents, and cannot be received as such; for the reason, that they are not delivered on oath; that they are not delivered before the court by a witness, placed subject to cross-examination; that they contain many statements which have no relation to this trial, and which this court cannot entertain; that they contain many other statements, which, though they may have been derived from the best information in possession of the writers, do not even appear to have been of their own knowledge. As regards Commodore Stockton's report, the court further remarks, that he is a witness in attendance on the court, and can give his testimony in the usual and legal mode.

If these reports of naval commanders to the Navy Department are offered to prove, not the facts stated in them, but the powers and authority which these commanders asserted and exercised, it will be necessary to show with them the distinct recognition and approval of the government, in order to set them up against the express orders of the government to General Kearny; and, even then, this court cannot doubt that such recognition and approval cannot operate retrospectively, so as to annul previous orders at and for the time when such previous orders were actually in force.

And the court is of opinion, further, that where instructions from the departments of the executive government are produced, to show the authority under which commanders have acted, it is necessary to show also that they were received, to have been in force.

The court deems it necessary to bring back the evidence to the issue.

The court has maturely examined the many papers submitted to it, and directed the following to be admitted on its record.

1st. Lieutenant Colonel Frémont's appointment as major, from Commodore Stockton, as follows:

U. S. Frigate Congress,
Bay of Monterey, July 23, 1846.

Sir: You are hereby appointed to the command of the California battalion of United States troops, with the rank of major.

Respectfully, your obedient servant,

R. F. STOCKTON,
Commander-in-chief, & c.

To Major Frémont,
Commanding California battalion.

—and 2d. Lieutenant Colonel Frémont's commission of governor, from Commodore Stockton, as follows:

To all whom it may concern, greeting:

Having, by authority of the President and Congress of the United States of North America, and by right of conquest, taken possession of that portion of territory heretofore known as upper and lower California; and having declared the same to be a territory of the United States, under the name of the territory of California; and having established laws for the government of the said territory, I, *Robert F. Stockton*, governor and commander-in-chief of the same, do, in virtue of the authority in me vested, and in obedience to the aforementioned laws, appoint *J. C. Frémont, esq.* governor and commander-in-chief of the territory of California, until the President of the United States shall otherwise direct.

Given under my hand and seal, on this sixteenth day of January, Anno Domini, one thousand eight hundred and forty-seven, at the Ciudad de los Angeles.

R. F. STOCKTON,
Governor, &c.

The court does not find among the papers any others which appear proper to go on its record as evidence now as produced. It has classed these papers, according to its present judgment of them, under four heads.

1st. Such as come in form of evidence, but are not relevant in this trial.

2d. Such as are not evidence, and besides contain nothing relevant to this case.

3d. Such as may be useful evidence, if proved.

4th. Such as are already on the record, and therefore need not be repeated on it.

And the court directs all these to be returned to the defence, and that the judge advocate signify to Lieutenant Colonel Frémont the view which the court has taken of them; at the same time to inform him, that the court will receive argument from him to show the admissibility in evidence of these papers, which he may wish again to present to it. In such case, however, the papers will be presented singly, or only such papers in connexion as may be necessary to constitute a single piece of evidence, and the court will decide on each as it is introduced. But the court remains of opinion that complete copies of documents must be offered, and not extracts only. After examination, the extracts indicated may be taken, if found correctly to represent the sense and effect of the original.

The foregoing general opinions of the court, in regard to documents as evidence, are maturely considered. But the court will receive argument from the defence on the admissibility of all evidence, before finally deciding on it.

The court was then opened. Lieutenant Colonel Frémont in court. The decision in closed session was announced.

Whereupon Lieutenant Colonel Frémont presented a note to the court as follows:

Mr. PRESIDENT: Lieutenant Colonel Frémont is advised by his counsel to say, that he will to-morrow morning file a paper in support of his right to use the evidence which he has offered, according to the leave given by the court; at present he is ready to proceed with his testimony.

J. C. FRÉMONT,
Lieut. Colonel mounted rifles.

Commodore Robert F. Stockton, U. S. navy, a witness for the defence.

Being duly sworn by the judge advocate, according to law, testified as follows:

May it please the court, before delivering my evidence, I desire to say: having been subpœnaed as a witness to attend before the court, and supposing that my testimony would be required, as to facts which were spread over a considerable portion of time, and followed each other in such rapid succession, and desiring on the one hand to say nothing that was not pertinent to the matter at issue before the court, and on the other hand to omit nothing that might be important to that issue, I thought it best for my own satisfaction to write out all that I deemed necessary; this manuscript I have now in my hand, and I ask leave of the court to read it as my testimony.

The defence consented that the witness shall deliver his testimony in that form, subject to such questions as they may afterwards deem necessary.

The judge advocate also consented. On motion of a member, the court was ordered be to cleared.

After mature deliberation, the court decided that, in accordance with the established usage of courts martial, the witness be required to deliver his testimony in the ordinary manner.

The court was then opened. Lieutenant Colonel Frémont in court. The decision in closed session was announced.

Commodore Stockton then said: Situated as I am, standing here in a most embarrassing, responsible, and anomalous condition, where it is hardly possible for me to testify, unless I am testifying in my own case in some sort, and may, without design from any quarter, be called upon to implicate myself, I cannot receive the notice of the court of their refusal to grant my request without reserving to myself the right to lay before the court a written statement of my views in regard to the matter, and with this reservation I am ready to testify.

Question by Lieutenant Colonel Frémont. You know the subject matter of inquiry before this court; will you please proceed to give, in a narrative form, the evidence which seems to you to be material and relevant?

On announcing the foregoing question, a member suggested that the judge advocate should read to the witness the charges and specifications. The judge advocate objecting, the court was ordered to be cleared, which was done accordingly; and the court decided that the charges and specifications be not read to the witness. The court ordered further, that, on opening the court, the witness be informed that, in the course of his testimony, it is his legal right to refrain from saying anything that will implicate himself.

The witness cannot be required to testify upon any matters not relevant to the charges and specifications, and while it is the duty of the court to protect witnesses from the requirement to testify upon matters not connected with the charges, or which might go to implicate them, yet a witness can claim no right to any mode of delivering his views or testimony not in accordance with the order of the court.

In proceeding with the testimony, the court does not assent to the reservation made by the witness.

The court was then opened. Lieutenant Colonel Frémont in court. The decision in closed session was announced.

Commodore Stockton, a witness for the defence, in answer to the last recorded question, said: In the latter part of the month of October, 1845, I received authority from the United States Navy Department to hoist my broad pendant on board the United States frigate Congress, then lying in the harbor of Norfolk. I also received instructions to proceed to sea, under sealed orders, which were not to be opened until my arrival off the capes of Virginia. Having arrived at that point, I opened the said sealed orders, by which I was ordered to proceed to the Sandwich Islands, and when I had performed the duty assigned to me at that place, I was directed to proceed to Monterey, on the coast of California, with despatches to the American consul at that place; after which I was directed to report to Commodore Sloat as forming one of his squadron. I arrived at Monterey about the middle of July, 1846, where I found the United States flag flying. I immediately went on board the United States frigate Savannah, then lying off that harbor, and reported myself to Commodore Sloat as forming one of his squadron. The commodore stated to me, that whilst lying off Mazatlan, in the month of June, he had received intelligence that hostilities had commenced between the United States and Mexico; whereupon he had come to Monterey, had sent on shore and hoisted the United States flag without resistance, and that he intended to return to the United States. About one week after this, Brevet Captain Frémont, of the topographical engineers, and Lieutenant Gillespie, of the marine corps, came on board of the Congress to see me. They informed me that they had arrived at Monterey, a day or two previous, with about one hundred and sixty volunteers; that they had had an interview with Commodore Sloat, on board of the Savannah, who told them that he did not intend to move from Monterey; that he had no service for them, and that he would have nothing to do with them. I stated to those gentlemen that I was only second in command, and could not, with propriety, express any opinion in relation to the conduct of Commodore Sloat. Captain Frémont said he would return on shore and determine, in the course of the night, whether he would return to the United States or remain in the territory. I suggested to him that it was possible I would have the command of the forces on shore and afloat within a few days; that on my assuming the command I would immediately communicate to him my intentions as to future operations. I now began to feel somewhat concerned in view of the great responsibility that was likely to be thrown upon me by the sudden and unexpected departure of Commodore Sloat for the United States, and of being left amongst an exasperated people without men, money, or provisions, adequate to the difficulties and dangers which seemed to obstruct my way.

The testimony of the witness was then read over to him; and then, at five minutes before three, the court adjourned to meet to-morrow at 10 o'clock.

TUESDAY, *December 7, 1847.*—10 *o'clock.*

The court met pursuant to adjournment.

Present: All the members, the judge advocate, and Lieutenant Colonel Frémont.

The proceedings of yesterday were read over.

The following note was presented by Lieutenant Colonel Frémont:

MR. PRESIDENT: When it was made known to the court on yesterday that Lieutenant Colonel Frémont would desire to file a paper this morning in support of his right to use the documentary testimony offered to the court, it was supposed that the examination of Commodore Stockton would be over by this time: this not being the case, he does not wish to interrupt the testimony, and defers filing the paper, and will file no general argument, but follow the court's intimation to offer the papers singly, or in pieces, connected with each other.

J. C. FRÉMONT,
Lieutenant Colonel, mounted rifles.

Commodore R. F. Stockton, a witness for the defence, continued his testimony as follows:

According to the best information that we could get, Pio Pico, the governor, and General Castro, the military commandant of the territory, were in the vicinity of the Ciudad de los Angeles, at the head of about 700 cavalry. The governor had issued a proclamation, couched in the most extravagant language, denouncing and threatening vengeance against the foreigners who were in the territory. Two Americans had already been murdered; the others that were in the territory, as well as the emigrants expected in September, might have the same fate, unless prompt and energetic measures were taken to disperse the armed Californians, and to capture and drive out of the country the Mexican officers, who seemed to be gaining confidence by our indecision and inactivity. I now urged on Commodore Sloat that he should give me the command immediately, if he intended to return to the United States, as he had previously suggested. He told me again that, on account of his ill-health, he would return to the United States as soon as possible, but he was not disposed yet to give me the command afloat. I then stated that it was very important that these Mexican officers should be driven out of the country or taken prisoners, and requested him to place under my command the United States ship-of-war Cyane, then laying in the harbor; he did so. Having then the command of all the forces on shore, and the Congress and the Cyane, I immediately sent to Captain Frémont to inform him of what had occurred, and to let him know that, if he and Lieutenant Gillespie, with the men who were with them, would volunteer to serve under my command, as long as I was in possession of the territory and desired their services, that I would form a battalion, and would appoint Captain Frémont the major and Lieutenant Gillespie a captain, and all the other necessary officers. This was all done in the course of the day and the next morning; and they were ordered to embark on board the United States ship Cyane, to be landed at San Diego. In this way was the navy battalion of California mounted riflemen formed, and brought into the service of the United States. I call it navy battalion, because it was not brought into service under the laws of the army.

The president here said: A member wishes the court to be cleared, and it is ordered to be cleared accordingly; which was then done.

After some time in closed session and deliberation, the court was opened, Lieutenant Colonel Frémont in court.

Commodore Stockton, a witness for the defence, continued his testimony as follows:

Captain Frémont, of the topographical engineers, and Lieutenant Gillespie, of the United States marine corps, laid aside for the time being—the one his commission as captain of topographical engineers, and the other as a lieutenant of marines, and volunteered to serve, and the men with them, under the command of a naval officer; they were brought into the service to aid the sailors and marines who were employed on shore. The law authorizing the formation of this battalion was the law of necessity—to reinforce and strengthen a legal force of sailors and mariners; which force was placed under my command; and because that force was not considered alone sufficient to rescue and defend our fellow countrymen from impending peril. This battalion was attached to a force organized by acts of Congress, and authorized, as is always the case with sailors and marines, when necessity requires, to be employed on shore. The motive or object of forming this battalion was not *mere* conquest—the smallness of my force would not have permitted me to entertain such a thought. It was for a higher and nobler motive—it was to rescue and to defend our fellow countrymen whose lives were supposed to be in danger by having hoisted the United States flag at Monterey, as well as other anterior proceedings. This is the reason why the naval force was increased by this battalion.

I could not have exposed such men as formed the battalion, as well as my own gallant troop, to the inclemency of the weather, the fatigues of the march, and the dangers of battle, for any objects of mere conquest. On or about the 29th of July, Commodore Sloat sailed in the United States sloop Levant, and left me in command on shore and afloat. The squadron, at this time, consisted of the Congress and the Savannah, lying in the Bay of Monterey; the Portsmouth, at San Francisco; the Cyane, as before stated, on her way to San Diego; the Warren, off Mazatlan, and the store ship Erie, at Sandwich Islands. Having made necessary arrangements, I left the United States frigate Savannah, Captain Mervine, at Monterey, for the protection of that town, and sailed in the Congress for San Pedro, which was distant from the Ciudad de los Angeles, where the enemy was said to be encamped with seven pieces of artillery, about twenty-eight miles. On our way to San Pedro we stopped at Santa Barbara, which place we took possession of; leaving a small force there for its protection, we went on our way to San Pedro. On our arrival at San Pedro, or during that day, I received information of the arrival of the Cyane at San Diego, and of the safe landing of the battalion, and that Major Frémont had found great difficulty in procuring horses. This was, I think, in the beginning of August. We immediately commenced landing our troops, and forming our camp at San Pedro. I sent on board of a merchant vessel and procured two or three pieces of small ordnance, which, with an eighteen-pounder carronade, which we took from the ship, all mounted on cart wheels, formed our park of artillery. A day or two after our arrival at San Pedro, two commissioners came to me from General Castro's camp, on the Mesa, to enter into negotiations. But before they could enter into any negotiation I was required to stop my forces where they then were. I told the commissioners that I had come there to take the country; that I would not stop my forces; that I would either take the country or be licked out of it. The commissioners left without imparting to me the object of their desired negotiation. A day or two after this, and whilst we were in the midst of our preparations, learning how to form line and to form squares, of which the only man in the whole concern that knew anything, as I am aware, was Lieutenant Zeilin, of the marine corps, and perhaps the men who were with him, another flag of truce was brought by other commissioners. One of these commissioners brought a letter from General Castro, in which he used the most extravagant language, and said he meant to defend the territory. I told him there was no answer to such a letter as that from me. In a day or two after, having previously informed Major Frémont of my movements and intended movements, we started for the camp of the Mesa, expecting to be joined by Major Frémont on the route. The afternoon of the day on which we commenced our march, we received information that the enemy had buried and otherwise concealed their artillery, and had all dispersed and run away, the general and the governor having, as was supposed, fled to Sonora. On our march to the city, we were joined by Major Frémont with about one hundred and twenty volunteers, and we all entered the city together and took quiet possession of the government house. After making arrangements for the security of peace and tranquility within the city, I gave orders for the apprehension of all the Mexican officers that were left in the territory, for which purpose armed parties of the volunteer riflemen were despatched in various directions. We succeeded in taking many of them, and the rest surrendered themselves. They were all given their liberty on their parole. I then turned my attention to the establishment of a civil government in the territory; every part of the territory of Upper California, so far as I know, having then yielded to our arms. I commenced the work of civil government so soon, because I wished that the people throughout the territory should, as soon as possible, feel the benign influences of free government in the protection of their lives, their liberty, and their property. I appointed Major Frémont military commandant of the territory of California, and Captain Gillespie military commandant of the southern department. I ordered or requested Major Frémont, as soon as his other duties would permit him to do so, to go to the Sacramento, and there to get as many volunteers as he could for the purpose, in the first place, of increasing the battalion to three hundred men, and, in the next place, to procure a force which I might take down to the southern coast of Mexico, where I contemplated making an attack. In the beginning of September I left the city of the Angeles, with the sailors and marines, marched to San Pedro, and embarked on board of the Congress, having previously informed Major Frémont of my intention to go south and make an attack on Mazatlan and Acapulco, one or both, and that I would meet him at San Francisco on the 25th day of October, where I would receive the men that he might be able to procure for me, and where I would appoint him governor of the territory. We sailed from San Pedro about the 5th day of September. On our way north we stopped at Santa Barbara, and, having taken on board the small force we left there when we went down, and everything being tranquil there, the American flag flying, and the alcalde and prefect, appointed by myself, continuing in the uninterrupted performance of their duties, I proceeded to Monterey. Before I left the city of the Angels I ordered elections.

The judge advocate said: I request Commodore Stockton to confine his testimony to such matters as concern Lieutenant Colonel Frémont and these charges.

Commodore Stockton replied : He had no desire to say a single word not bearing on the trial, and thought this matter of the civil government the most important of all.

The defence. We think so.

Commodore Stockton resumed his testimony :

Before I left the City of the Angels, I ordered elections to be held for the appointment of civil magistrates throughout the territory. We proceeded from Santa Barbara to Monterey, where we found all peaceful and quiet. At Monterey, I received intelligence that Suter's

Fort, on the Sacramento, was threatened with an attack by one thousand Wallah, Wallah Indians. I sent the Savannah immediately to San Francisco, and having appointed Lieutenant Maddox, of the marine corps, military commandant of the middle department, we sailed with the Congress immediately for San Francisco. On my landing at San Francisco, I was received by the people in mass, down at the water's edge, with every demonstration of joy for the conquest of the country, and every demonstration of respect for myself as governor of the territory and commander-in-chief. About the last of September, or the beginning of October, I received a courier from Captain Gillespie, the military commandant of the City of the Angels, that an insurrection had broken out in the south, and that he was besieged in the government house in the city. I immediately sent to Major Frémont, who, I had been informed, was near Suter's Fort, a message informing him of what had occurred below, and ordering, or requesting him to procure as many saddles and men as he could and come to San Francisco, as soon as possible. Whilst I was waiting for Major Frémont, I sent officers in different directions to raise as many volunteers as they could, for the purpose of marching against the insurgents. In the meantime, I engaged the merchant ship Sterling, to take the battalion down to Santa Barbara, whilst I should go to San Pedro in the Congress. Somewhere about the 12th of October, Major Frémont arrived and immediately embarked on the board the Sterling with his volunteers, to the amount of about one hundred and seventy. The Sterling and the Congress sailed together the day after the embarkation of the battalion, but separated that afternoon in a fog.

Here the court, at one o'clock, took a recess of ten minutes; at the expiration of which time, the court again in session.

Present: all the members, the judge advocate and Lieutenant Colonel Frémont.

Commodore Stockton, a witness, resumed his testimony as follows:

Between Monterey and San Francisco, I spoke a merchant ship, from Monterey, with despatches from the commandant there, containing information that he expected an attack would be made on the town, and requiring immediate aid. I ran into the bay of Monterey with the Congress, and landed two officers and fifty men and some ordnance; and having done all I could besides for its protection, I sailed for San Pedro; on my arrival at San Pedro, I found the Savannah, Captain Mervine, whom I had despatched to San Pedro, on first receiving intelligence of the insurrection in the city. He informed me that about two weeks before he had landed his men, a part of his crew, sailors and marines, and that part of the California battalion under command of Captain Gillespie, who had been besieged in the city, and who had come on board the Savannah by an honorable capitulation entered into with the insurgents; that he had taken no artillery with him; that on his march to the city where he intended to go, he met the insurgents, or a part of them, with one piece of artillery; that he had

had a fight with them; that he had tried to take the insurgents' gun three or four times, by charging upon it, but that he could not overtake it, as they hitched their horses and run off with it every time he approached it; that after having lost several men in killed and wounded, he thought it best to return to his ship. We immediately commenced landing our force at San Pedro; hoisted the American flag there again and formed our camp. The enemy were in great numbers in our neighborhood; they had driven off all the animals from that part of the country, and would not permit man or beast to come near it. We remained several days, expecting to hear from Major Frémont, but having almost worn out officers and men by watching and chasing the enemy, and not having a hoof either for food or transportion, and as the season for the southeast gales of wind, which are very violent on that coast, was approaching, when ships can no longer ride in safety in that exposed anchorage, and having given up all expectation of hearing from Major Frémont, I embarked the troops again; and leaving the Savannah there to look out for Major Frémont, I went in the Congress down south, to see if I could get into the harbor of San Diego, where the ship could lie in safety while we were making preparations to march on the city. We attempted to cross the bar, when the ship got a shore, and we were obliged to return to the anchorage outside.

About this time, the Mexican brig Malek-Adhel, a prize to the United States ship Warren, arrived from Monterey, bringing despatches from Major Frémont, who informed me that on his way to Santa Barbara, he had fallen in with and spoken a merchant ship, who had informed him of all the occurrences that had taken place at the south, and that it would be impossible for him to procure animals, either for food or transportation, at Santa Barbara; and that he thought it best to go into Monterey, where he would be able to obtain animals, and would make the earliest preparation possible to march on the city. I went to San Pedro, in the Congress, and despatched the Savannah to Monterey, to assist Major Frémont in his preparations for the march. I returned again to San Diego, and having buoyed the bar, I was fortunate enough to succeed in getting the ship into that harbor. On our first arrival off that harbor, Lieutenant Minor, who was in command at San Diego, came on board, and stated that the town was besieged by the insurgents, and that he required more men and some provisions. I immediately sent Captain Gillespie, with that part of the battalion which had been on board the Savannah, on shore, and also some provisions; and, at the suggestion of Lieutenant Minor, I ordered him to send the merchant ship Stonington, then lying in the harbor of San Diego, to Ensenada, about ninety miles south of San Diego, to see if they could not procure—

The judge advocate asked the court to be cleared. It was cleared accordingly. The judge advocate submitted to the court the relevancy of the present testimony.

The court directed it to be recorded as its decision, that the details of naval and military operations on the coast, and in the conquest of California, are not the subject of inquiry before the court; that but little of the history and narrative already given in evidence by the witness, has any relation to the charges on trial; that this mode of delivering by each witness, in the narrative form whatever may appear to such witness relevant to the trial, or interesting to be said, renders it impracticable for the court to restrict the evidence to matters which it ought to inquire into. Therefore, the court orders that this form of giving testimony be suspended, and that the examination of witnesses be by question and answer. Then, the court will judge of the materiality and relevancy of each question; giving to the party, offering a question objected to, the opportunity of explaining its propriety.

The court was then opened. Lieutenant Colonel Frémont in court. The decision in closed session was announced.

When the decision was announced, Commodore Stockton requested the question in answer to which he had been testifying to be read over to him, as indicating the character of testimony required of him; which was done accordingly.

Commodore Stockton then wished to make some explanations to the court, when he was informed by the president that the hour of adjournment of the court having nearly arrived, the testimony of to-day must now be read over to him, and the court would receive his explanation to-morrow morning.

The testimony of to-day was read over to the witness, and then, at 3 o'clock, the court adjourned to meet to-morrow at 10 o'clock.

WEDNESDAY, *December 8, 1847.—10 o'clock.*

The court met pursuant to adjournment. Present: All the members, and the judge advocate. Lieutenant Colonel Frémont not yet present. The reading of the proceedings of yesterday, for the verification of the record, was then commenced; during which, and shortly after the commencement of the reading, Lieutenant Colonel Frémont came into court. The reading of the record of yesterday was continued and finished.

Commodore Stockton, a witness, presented to the president a paper, which the president handed to the judge advocate to be read as an explanation offered by the witness. A member made objection. The court was cleared for deliberation. The court decided that the explanation of the witness be received and read in open court, and appended to this record. And the court ordered it to be recorded as their decision, "that the court does not recognize the right claimed or asked by Commodore Stockton to come before it to vindicate, by his testimony in this case, or by any means, his official conduct as a naval commander. But the court will permit the witness to continue his answer to the question already propounded to him, under the authority of the court, and to relate the condition of affairs in California, as regards the civil government and military authority there, when the acts were done which are now the ground of accusation against Lieutenant Colonel Frémont; reminding the witness, however, that the court cannot take cognizance of his official conduct, except as in the exercise of his powers conferring authority on Lieutenant Colonel Frémont, and that his testimony must be confined to matters that affect the conduct of the accused in the facts on which he is arraigned.

The court is not to be understood as assenting to the reasoning in the explanations of the witness submitted this morning in deducing from the facts, should they come in proof as he considers them to be, the conclusions which he draws. This belongs to the judgment of the court.

The court was then opened. Lieutenant Colonel Frémont in court. The explanation of Commodore Stockton was then read in open court; also, the decision in closed session was announced.

Commodore Stockton, a witness, resumed his testimony in answer to the interrogatory on record, as follows :

May it please the court, to show how willing I am to submit to the decision of this court, and to show how desirous I am to conform, as nearly as possible, to their wishes, I will omit in my testimony the incidents that occured, in the interval of time between the date where my testimony of yesterday ceased, and the time when I first received intelligence of General Kearny's arrival.

In the beginning of December, 1846, Mr. Stokes, an English gentleman, brought me a letter, being then at San Diego, from General Kearny, announcing his arrival at Warner's ranche. I present the letter. It was then read by the judge advocate, as follows :

HEAD-QUARTERS, ARMY OF THE WEST,
Camp at Warner's, December 2, 1846.

SIR : I (this afternoon) reached here, escorted by a party of the 1st regiment dragoons, I came by orders from the President of the United States. We left Santa Fé on the 25th September, having taken possession of New Mexico, annexed it to the United States, established a civil government in that territory, and secured order, peace, and quietness there.

If you can send a party to open a communication with us, on the route to this place, and to inform me of the state of affairs in California, I wish you would do so, and as quickly as possible.

The fear of this letter falling into Mexican hands, prevents me from writing more.

Your express by Mr. Carson was met on the Del Norte, and your mail must have reached Washington, at least, ten days since.

Very respectfully, your obedient servant,
S. W. KEARNY,
Brigadier General, U. S. A.

Commodore R. F. STOCKTON,
U. S. N., com'd'g Pacific squadron, San Diego.

You might use the bearer of this (Mr. Stokes) as a guide to conduct your party to this place.

Commodore Stockton resumed his testimony:

The letter was received late in the afternoon; I immediately ordered Captain Gillespie to mount all the volunteers for whom he had horses, and, with a field piece, to proceed without delay to General Kearny's camp. I wrote a letter in reply to General Kearny, which I present. It was then read by the judge advocate, as follows:

HEAD-QUARTERS, SAN DIEGO,
December 3, 1846, half-past 6 o'clock, p. m.

SIR: I have this moment received your note of yesterday, by Mr. Stokes, and have ordered Captain Gillespie, with a detachment of mounted riflemen and a field piece, to your camp without delay.

Captain Gillespie is well informed in relation to the present state of things in California, and will give you all needful information. I need not, therefore, detain him by saying any thing on the subject. I will merely say, that I have this evening received information, by two deserters from the rebel camp, of the arrival of an additional force in this neighborhood of one hundred men, which, in addition to the force previously here, makes their number about one hundred and fifty.

I send with Captain Gillespie, as a guide, one of the deserters, that you may make inquiries of him, and if you see fit, endeavouring to surprise them.

Faithfully, your obedient servant,

R. F. STOCKTON,
Commander-in-chief, and Gov'r of the territory of California.

To Brig. Gen. S. W. KEARNY.

U. S. Army.

Commodore Stockton resumed his testimony, as follows:

About 7 o'clock, Captain Gillespie left San Diego, accompanied by Acting Lieutenant Beale, of the navy, Passed Midshipman Duncan, some of the carbineers belonging to the Congress, Captain Gibson, of the battalion, with some of the volunteers, amounting in all to about thirty-nine persons, and one field piece. Every horse, capable of use in the garrison, having been put into requisition for that purpose. Mr. Stokes returned to General Kearny's camp with Captain Gillespie; and I also sent a Californian as a guide for General Kearny, that he might show the general where the enemy were encamped, if he felt disposed to make an atttack.

A few days after this Mr. Stokes returned to San Diego, and informed me that early in the morning of that day, which I think was the 6th of December, General Kearny had made an attempt to surprise the enemy at San Pasqual; that a battle had ensued; that General Kearny had lost a great many killed and wounded, and one of his guns; that the general had been worsted, but to what extent he could not say, as he left as soon as the firing ceased, without communicating with any person on the field of battle.

The next day, I think it was, Lieutenant Goday, with two other men, came in express from General Kearny's camp, and they brought this letter from Captain Turner to me.

Read as follows, by judge advocate:

HEAD-QUARTERS, CAMP NEAR SAN PASQUAL,
December 6, 1846.

SIR: I have the honor to report to you, that at early dawn this morning General Kearny, with a detachment of United States dragoons, and Captain Gillespie's company of mounted riflemen, had an engagement with a very considerable Mexican force near this camp.

We have about 18 killed, and 14 or 15 wounded; several so severely that it may be impracticable to move them for several days. I have to suggest to you the propriety of despatching, without delay, a considerable force to meet us on the route to San Diego, via the Solidad and San Bernardo, or to find us at this place; also, that you will send up carts or some other means of transporting our wounded to San Diego. We are without provisions, and in our present situation may find it impracticable to obtain cattle from the ranches in the vicinity.

General Kearney is among the wounded, but it is hoped not dangerously; Captains Moore and Johnson, 1st dragoons, killed; Captain Gillespie, badly, but not dangerously wounded; Lieutenant Hammond, 1st dragoons, dangerously wounded.

I am, sir, very respectfully, your obedient servant,
H. S. TURNER,
Captain U. S. A. comd'g.

Commodore R. F. STOCKTON,
U. S. Navy, San Diego.

Commodore Stockton resumed his testimony, as follows:

Mr. Stokes informed me that the general had 350 men. Lieutenant Goday could not accurately inform me in regard to the number of the force on either side; I supposed, however, from what Mr. Stokes had said, that the Californians were much more numerous than I had thought, and that I would be obliged to go with the whole force which I could spare from garrison to the relief of General Kearny

The, necessary preparations were accordingly made as soon as possible; and the advance was ordered to be prepared to leave San Diego at seven o'clock in the evening, with two pieces of artillery —I think this was about the 9th of December—with orders to march to the mission of San Diego, where I intended the next day to join them with the rest of the force. About the time the advance was ready to start, an Indian came in from General Kearny's camp, who stated that he left there in company with Lieutenant Beale and Mr. Carson, and that they were coming in behind him. The intelligence brought by this Indian, as to General Kearny's condition, was such, that I thought it was necessary to send to him immediate aid; and that they might get to him sooner than we could have done in the manner I first proposed, as we had no animals to drag the artillery, I ordered the advance stopped; and having increased it to about 215 men, I placed it under the command of my aid de-camp, Lieutenant Gray, and ordered him to take a field-piece with him, and to proceed immediately to relieve General Kearny. This was about 10 o'clock at night. About this time, Mr. Beale came to San Diego, and he confirmed the worst accounts that I had heard in regard to the situation of General Kearny. Mr. Gray was immediately hurried off; and as I was informed as to the number of Californians, I directed Lieutenant Gray to march until daylight, and then conceal himself and his force from the enemy during the day, and march to General Kearny's camp the night following; forbidding him to engage the enemy, if he could avoid it, until after reporting to General Kearny. On the 12th day of December, I think it was, I had the great happiness of hearing that General Kearny, and his whole force, with Lieutenant Gray, were in sight from our fort on the hill. I had no horse to ride, because I had sent them all with Captain Gillespie to General Kearny, but I walked out to meet him, and bid him welcome. He and his officers and men were received, as I believe, with the greatest degree of cordiality and kindness. I conducted the general to my own quarters, and the others were provided for in the best possible way. At his own request, other quarters were provided for him, for which purpose Lieutenant Minor, who was then acting as governor of the town, was turned out of his quarters. After General Kearny arrived, and in my quarters, and in presence of two of my military family, I offered to make him commander-in-chief over all of us, and I offered to go as his aid-de-camp. He said no; that the force was mine, and that he would go as my aid-de-camp, or accompany me. This was done in seriousness and sincerity.

Commodore Stockton offered a certificate signed by two naval officers, Purser Spieden and Surgeon Moseby, confirming the statement just made by him of this conversation between himself and General Kearny.

It was read to the court. Members of the court suggested that it was unnecessary to offer the paper; and Commodore Stockton resumed his testimony, as follows:

A few days after this, and when General Kearny had removed to other quarters, I made a formal call upon him, with all the officers that could be spared from duty; during that interview I made the same offer to him, pretty much in the same language, and received pretty much the same answer. My motives for making this offer to General Kearny were two; the first was, his high character as a soldier; the second was, that I desired that he should know that I was disposed, on his first arrival, to give all power into his hands, without making a question of rank at all.

There never was a question of rank, that I am aware of, between

General Kearny and myself, until after our arrival at Ciudad de los Angeles. About the time, I think it was, when General Kearny was leaving my quarters, he handed me his instructions from the War Department; and when I read them, I was simple enough to believe, that he had handed them to me that I might be gratified by seeing how fully and thoroughly I had anticipated the wishes of the government. When I returned the papers to him, with a note of thanks for the opportunity to read them, I sent him copies of some of my own despatches to the government, that he, as a friend, might participate in the pleasure I felt, of having in anticipation executed the orders of the government.

I now set to work to make the best preparations I could make to commence our march for the Ciudad de los Angeles. During this time, an expedition that we had sent south for horses returned, and brought with them a number of horses and cattle. Captain Turner was allowed to take his pick of the horses for the dragoons; after he had done so he wrote to me this note:

Read by judge advocate, as follows:

San Diego, December 23, 1846.

Commodore: In compliance with your verbal instructions to examine and report upon the condition of the public horses turned over to me, for the use of "C" company, 1st dragoons, I have the honor to state, that, in my opinion, not one of the horses referred to is fit for dragoon service, being too poor and weak for any such purpose; also that the company of dragoons under my command can do much better service on foot, than if mounted on those horses.

I am, sir, with high respect, your obedient servant,

H. S. TURNER,
Capt. 1st Dragoons, Comd'g company C.

Commodore R. F. Stockton,
U. S. Navy, commanding.

Commodore Stockton resumed his testimony, as follows:

By this note, you will perceive, that the dragoons were placed under my command; a mounted howitzer also, which was brought by the general, was handed over to me. After this, and whilst at San Diego, the general, in a conversation with me, introduced the subject of the governorship, and intimated that he thought he ought to be governor, under his instructions. This, of course, amazed me, because I had more than once voluntarily offered to place him at the head of affairs in California, which offer he had as often refused. We argued the matter, however, he relying upon his instructions from the War Department, to which I replied, in substance, as follows:

Your instructions say that, "should you conquer the country, you will establish a civil government;" that I had conquered the country; that I had established a civil government therein, which government was in successful operation at that time throughout the territory, except at Santa Barbara and the Ciudad de los Angeles, where it had been interrupted, temporarily, by the insurgents; that all that the government had ordered to be done had already been accomplished; that nothing remained to be done; that I had informed the government of these things, and that I had stated to the government, that I intended to appoint Major Frémont governor of the territory, and Captain Gillispie secretary thereof. This conversation passed off, however, without at all interrupting the kind feelings which had commenced with our first acquaintance.

The testimony of to-day was then read over to the witness; and then, at ten minutes before three, the court adjourned to meet tomorrow at ten o'clock.

THURSDAY, *December 9, 1847.—10 o'clock.*

The court met pursuant to adjournment:
Present: all the members, the judge advocate, and Lieutenant Colonel Frémont.
The proceedings of yesterday were read over.
Commodore Stockton, a witness for the defence, continued his testimony in chief, as follows:

I continued our preparations for the march, under the impression that General Kearny was going with me as my aid-de-camp, of his own choice; that he preferred that situation rather than one of greater responsibility. I was confirmed in this belief by a note which I received from General Kearny, in answer to one written by me to him, both of which, I believe, are now on the record of the court, in which he again repeats that he will accompany me, and give me the aid of his head and his hand. It seemed, however, that I was either mistaken in my views, or that General Kearny suddenly altered his mind; because, on the morning of the day in which we left San Diego, and after the forces had been paraded preparatory to march, and I was about mounting my horse, General Kearny came to me and inquired who was to command the troops? I said to him that Lieutenant Rowan, 1st lieutenant of the Cyane, would command the troops. He gave me to understand that he would like to command the troops, and after some further conversation on the subject, I agreed to appoint him to the command. I immediately sent for Lieutenant Rowan, and assembled the officers that were near at hand, and stated to them that General Kearny had volunteered to take command of the troops; that I had appointed him to the command of the troops, but, that I retained my own position as commander-in-chief.

The commodore here offered a letter from Lieutenant Rowan, in regard to this conversation and the appointment of General Kearny to the command of the troops.
The judge advocate said it was not necessary to confirm his testimony in such way; that the letter was not evidence; that the

court had objected to the introduction of correspondence, except between the parties—General Kearny and Commodore Stockton. The judge advocate, however, had no doubt of the authenticity of the paper, and would read it to the court if Commodore Stockton desired.

Commodore Stockton said it would be a satisfaction to him to have it before the court, as Lieutenant Rowan was not here to give his evidence.

Objection being made in the court to reception of papers not evidence, the letter was returned to Commodore Stockton.

Commodore Stockton resumed his testimony, as follows:

I directed my aid-de-camp and the commissary to make a note of what I said on the occasion; the impression made upon my mind was, that General Kearny had, for the time being, laid aside his commission of brigadier general, and had volunteered to serve under my command, and to perform the duties which had been assigned to Lieutenant Rowan as commander of the troops. When the force was paraded, the dragoons were' among the troops. With these impressions and views, and considering that I, and I alone, was responsible for the result of the expedition, we commenced our march for the City of the Angels, during which march I performed all the duties which I supposed devolved upon the commander-in-chief of the forces, and, as I supposed, with the hearty acquiescence of General Kearny. General Kearny had repeatedly said he would aid me; I felt grateful to General Kearny and the officers with him, and endeavored to manifest it in all that I did in relation to them. I endeavored to treat him with the greatest possible consideration and respect; I did not proclaim through the camp that I commanded General Kearny; I did not send my aid-de-camp to General Kearny to say to him that I ordered him to do this, and that I ordered him to do that; but I sent all my messages to him in the most respectful and considerate manner. Besides being prompted to this course by my own feelings of respect for General Kearny, I did not think it at all necessary to send to him anything more than the expression of my wishes. A few days after we commenced the march, I went in advance when the troops arrived at San Bernardo; I made my head-quarters a mile and a half or two miles in advance of the camp, and I sent to General Kearney to send me the marines and a piece of artillery, which was immediately done. I was in the habit of sending my aid-de-camp to General Kearny to inform him what time I wished to move in the morning, and I always decided upon the route we should take, and where we should camp.

When we were approaching a ranche of Señor Juan Avila, I went in advance some distance to look out for the ground to camp; whilst I was on the hill near this ranche, Captain Emory, General Kearny's aid-de-camp, and Captain Gillespie, of the California battalion, rode up. Captain Emory said he thought that was a good place to encamp. I said yes. When the troops came up I observed the camp was being made below the hill, and sent for Captain Emory; I asked him by whose order the camp was making down below the hill? He said by order of General Kearny. I told him to go to General Kearny and tell him that it was my order that the camp should be immediately moved on top of the hill; Captain Emory immediately said that it was not the general's fault; that he had not informed the general that I wished the camp upon the hill. I then told him to go to the general and say to him, that I wished the camp made on the hill; which I presume he did, as the camp was soon after made upon the hill. During our march, and on our approahcing the river San Gabriel, and after the enemy had commenced firing, I observed the guns being unlimbered; I was told that it was done by the order of General Kearny, to return the fire of the enemy. I ordered the guns limbered up, and the forces to cross the river before a shot was fired. I proceeded with the two 9-pounders, and crossed the river, with troops following on. As soon as we got across with the 9-pounders, they were put in battery, and we commenced firing. After the troops got across the river, they began to form in squares. At this time, I observed that the enemy was about to charge our left flank. I ordered the men of the left flank to be kept in line, that we might have a more extended fire. At this time, I observed that the men of the right flank had been formed into a square, and General Kearny at their head. I sent my aid-de-camp, Mr. Gray, to General Kearny with instructions to move the square and the two pieces of artillery immediately up the hill. In the meantime, the enemy made the charge on the left flank, but were received with such a shower of lead that they drew off. We then charged up the hill with the two 9-pounders. I ordered the troops all to lay down, and ran the two 9 pounders in advance, and the battle was continued between the artillery.

On the morning of the day we left our camp to march into the city, General Kearny came to me, bringing with him Mr. Southwick, who was acting as engineer, and inquired by what road I proposed to march into the city. He asked Mr. Southwick to mark the different roads which led into the city upon the sand. He did so, and I selected the broadest and plainest road that led directly into the main street; and when we marched into the city, I led the way at the head of the advanced guard.

After having directed the troops to be formed in the square, I took the marine guard and two pieces of artillery for the purpose of securing possession of the height that overlooked the town. On my arrival there, however, I found the riflemen, belonging to the battalion, in possession. On my return, I gave the orders where the different officers and troops were to be quartered; and ordered the same flag to be hoisted on the government house which was hauled down when Captain Gillespie left there, in September, under an honorable capitulation made with the insurgents.

A few days after our arrival, I received a letter from General Kearny, which, I believe, is on the records of this court now, volunteering to take a portion of the force to go out and meet Lieutenant Colonel Frémont, who, we had heard, was in the neighborhood. This letter was addressed to me as governor of the territory, and commanding the United States forces.

Witness said to the judge advocate, "will you be kind enough to look at the letter."

The judge advocate referred to the record, and found in the proceedings, of November 16th, the letter referred to by the witness, addressed to Commodore Stockton, governor of California and commanding United States forces.

The witness resumed his testimony as follows:

As I have stated, the civil government had been already put into operation; having only been interrupted at San Barbara and the City of the Angels; peace having been restored, the civil government in those places went again into operation, and therefore there was nothing for me to do in relation to the establishment of a civil government, except to hand to Lieutenant Colonel Frémont the commission as governor, which I had pledged my word to do; which I had informed the government I would do, and which would probably have been done, on the 25th day of October, if the insurrection had not broken out. Being desirous to get down on the southern coast of Mexico, I proceeded as rapidly as possible to make the necessary arrangements to leave the Ciudad de los Angeles. In the meantime, Lieutenant Colonel Frémont reported to me his arrival with the other part of the battalion. The position of the parties, and my own position at this time, was, in my judgment and opinion, this: General Kearny had laid aside, for the time being, his commission as brigadier general, and was serving as a volunteer under my command. The troops which were placed, by my orders, under the command of General Kearny, were the dragoons, sailors and marines, and Captain Gillespie's two companies of the California battalion, and no other. On the arrival of Lieutenant Colonel Frémont, he reported to me; and I did not give, nor did I intend to give, General Kearny any control or command over that part of the California battalion. It was under my own immediate command. Lieutenant Colonel Frémont, at this time, was also serving under my command as a volunteer; he having likewise laid aside his commission in the army; and I was recognized in every thing up to this time, as far as I know, as their mutual commander-in-chief. Having appointed Lieutenant Colonel Frémont the governor, I appointed Captain Gillespie to be major of the battalion; and, if I understand the matter before this court, the disobedience of orders charged against the accused, whilst I was the commander-in-chief, is, that he would not obey an order which required him not to recognize my appointment of Captain Gillespie as major of the battalion.

On the 16th of January, I think it was, in the afternoon, I received a letter from General Kearny, which is now, I believe, on the record of this court.

Here the record was examined by the judge advocate, and the letter, which Commodore Stockton stated, to be referred to, found at page 117.

Commodore Stockton resumed his testimony, as follows:

Considering this letter coming from a volunteer officer under my command, not from General Kearny, I immediately suspended him from the command which I had given to him, when he resumed his position as Brigadier General Kearny, over whom I never pretended or desired to have any command or control. In a day or two after this, General Kearny announced to me, in a letter, which I believe is also before the court, that he was going to leave the City of the Angels with the force which came with him into the country. I present, in print, a copy of that letter, which I believe to be correct.

Read by judge advocate as follows:

HEAD-QUARTERS, ARMY OF THE WEST,
Ciudad de los Angeles, January 17, 1847.

SIR: I have to inform you that I intend to withdraw to-morrow from this place, with the small party which escorted me to this country.

Very respectfully, your obedient servant,
S. W. KEARNY,
Brigadier General.

Commodore R. F. STOCKTON,
U. S. Navy, acting Governor of California.

Commodore Stockton resumed his testimony, as follows:

General Kearny having thus withdrawn from my command and camp, I permitted him to take with him all the United States troops belonging to the army, and only retained my sailors and the battalion that had been raised to aid them. I believe I have stated, in a preceding part of my testimony, that I informed the government I intended to appoint Captain Gillespie secretary of state. I will now say that I had a conversation with Lieutenant Colonel Frémont, on the subject of appointing Captain Gillespie major of the battalion, and in relation to the person who should be appointed secretary of state, instead of Captain Gillespie; Captain Gillespie preferring the position of major. It was agreed that Colonel Russell should be appointed secretary of state. I have said also, in a preceding part of my testimony, that I was received at San Francisco, and acknowledged to be the governor of the territory and commander-in-chief. I beg now to offer to the court this letter, merely to show how I was considered at the City of the Angels, and that as I began governor, I left there as such.

The paper, placed in the hands of the judge advocate, appeared to be a letter, dated Ciudad de los Angeles, January 19, 1847, signed by about twelve names, and addressed to Commodore Stockton.

The judge advocate, without reading it, returned it to Commodore Stockton, as not admissible in evidence.

Commodore Stockton, a witness for the defence, resumed his testimony in chief, as follows:

Two or three days after General Kearny withdrew, I left the City of the Angels for San Diego, when I embarked my sailors and marines on board of their respective ships, having transferred the civil government to Lieutenant Colonel Frémont, and having left with him, for the protection of the territory, the whole battalion of volunteers.

I exercised no authority in the territory after the final embarkation of my men, except that which was induced by a letter which I received from Lieutenant Colonel Cooke, a copy of which I have not, as it was sent to Commodore Biddle; I have here my reply to Lieutenant Colonel Cooke, and my letter to Commodore Biddle, which I offer to the court.

The judge advocate examined the letters, and thought them not material to the case.

Commodore Stockton said, it might be a question how far he had exercised any authority in the country, after the appointment of Lieutenant Colonel Frémont as governor.

The judge advocate returned the letters to Commodore Stockton, suggesting to him that he had better relate in his testimony the transaction which he proposed to explain by the introduction of these letters.

Lieutenant Colonel Frémont also thought that the letters ought to be received, to explain the matter and the acts of Commodore Stockton, after his appointment as governor, and for other reasons.

The court was ordered to be cleared; and in close session, the court directed that the papers be not received.

The court was then opened. Lieutenant Colonel Frémont in court. Decision in closed session was then announced.

Commodore Stockton, a witness, added:

I have nothing more, I believe, to say in answer to the first interrogatory.

Question by Lieutenant Colonel Frémont. Did Lieutenant Colonel Frémont call upon you on the night of the 16th of January, 1847; if so, will you please state for what purpose he came, and, as nearly as possible, state what occurred during that conversation?

Answer. I think that Lieutenant Colonel Frémont came to my quarters on the evening of the 16th, and I believe that it was in consequence of my having sent to him to come to receive his commission as governor. During that interview, I think, Lieutenant Colonel Frémont stated that he had received a letter from General Kearny, which he intended to answer the next day. It was during this interview, I think, that I showed to Lieutenant Colonel Frémont the letter which I had received from General Kearny, the letter of the 16th, and I think that I showed him, or read to him, my reply.

Lieutenant Colonel Frémont then stated that he had no further questions to ask the witness.

And Lieutenant Colonel Frémont presented to the court the following note:

Mr. PRESIDENT: Lieutenant Colonel Frémont requests that an order may be made on Major Cooke to produce the original letter, or a copy, if the original is not tó be procured, which is referred to by Commodore Stockton in his testimony this day, and in relation to which he offered the answer which he made to it, and the letter which he wrote in consequence to Commodore Biddle. Lieutenant Colonel Frémont believes that this letter will be important to him in his defence.

J. C. FRÉMONT,
Lieutenant Colonel, mounted riflemen.

The court was ordered to be cleared. The judge advocate stated that Major Cooke, having been examined by both parties before the court and dismissed, and being supposed by the judge advocate to be no longer required, had been discharged from further attendanc on the court, at his earnest solicitude to return to his regiment in Mexico.

The court decided that it will be proper for Lieutenant Colonel Frémont to explain to the court the points involved in the trial, upon which the letter from Major Cooke to Commodore Stockton is thought by him to have a bearing. The court will then be able to decide upon the application in reference to the production of the aforesaid letter, and the recalling of Major Cooke as a witness.

The court was then opened. Lieutenant Colonel Frémont in court. The decision in closed session was announced.

Cross-examination of Commodore Stockton, by the judge advocate.

Question. In your last answer, you speak of a conversation between Lieutenant Colonel Frémont and yourself, which you say you think occurred the 16th January, 1847. Do you know whether this conversation took place on the 16th or 17th of January.

Answer. I believe it was the 16th.

Question. Look at this paper : your commission to Lieutenant Colonel Frémont appointing him governor. Have you any recollection of the day on which that was delivered to Lieutenant Colonel Frémont. If so, please state it ?

Answer. I believe it was on the evening of the 16th that I sent for Lieutenant Colonel Frèmont and gave him his commission of governor, but my recollection of it is not perfect.

Question. Will you say whose hand writing that is in ?

Answer. I think it is in the hand of my clerk, Mr. Simmons; he is not here.

Question. What orders and instructions from the President of the United States or Secretary of the Navy had you in California, on the 16th January, 1847, in regard to the establishment of a civil government in that country ?

Answer. Well, I do not think I had any.

Question. Did you ever receive, and if so, when did you so receive the instructions from Secretary Bancroft to Commodore Sloat, dated July 12, 1846 ?

Answer. I think I received no other instructions, except those Commodore Sloat turned over to me, and some others, received by Mr. McCrae; afterwards the orders went to Commodore Shubrick or Biddle, and if sent to me, were only sent through courtesy. I have no recollection of having received these instructions of the 12th of July. My right to establish the civil government was incident to the conquest, and I formed the government under the law of nations.

Lieutenant Colonel Frémont presents to the court the following note:

Mr. PRESIDENT : Lieutenant Colonel Frémont wishes to know whether the question to Commodore Stockton, in relation to the receipt of the instructions of the 12th July, 1846, is *founded* on the use which Lieutenant Colonel Frémont has heretofore proposed to make of these instructions, and which were rejected by the court when offered by him.

J. C. FRÉMONT,
Lieutenant Colonel, mounted riflemen.

The court was then cleared: and it ordered to be entered on the record that the court perceive that Lieutenant Colonel Frémont's objection to the cross-examination is founded on misapprehension.

The court has not excluded on the part of the defence the instructions of the Navy Department to Commodore Sloat, of the 12th July, 1846. These instructions when offered by the defence, a few days ago, were returned, as then stated, because they are already on the record, and, therefore, need not be repeated on it.

The court directed that the judge advocate take measures, by telegraph, to stop Major Cooke on his way to St. Louis, and direct him to wait further instructions from this court.

The court was then opened. Lieutenant Colonel Frémont in court. The decision in closed session was announced.

The testimony of to-day was read over to the witness; and then, at three minutes before three, the court adjourned to meet to-morrow at 10 o'clock.

———

FRIDAY, *December* 10, 1847.—10 *o'clock.*

The court met pursuant to adjournment.
Present : all the members, the judge advocate, and Lieutenant Colonel Frémont.
The proceedings of yesterday were read over.

Lieutenant Colonel Frémont read to the court the following note:

Mr. PRESIDENT : Under the order of the court of yesterday, "to explain the points involved in the trial, upon which the letter from Major Cooke to Commodore Stockton is thought to have a bearing," Lieutenant Colonel Frémont says, that the part of the letter which he deemed relevant was that which stated the rumored approach of the Mexican General Bustamenta; and, the part of the defence to which he deemed it applicable, was that which grew out of the charge of disobedience, in not repairing to Monterey in the time limited by General Kearny.

Lieutenant Colonel Frémont further says that when he made the request yesterday to have an order upon Major Cooke to produce the original, or a copy, of his letter to Commodore Stockton, he did not know that he had been released from his attendance as a witness, and had left the city; that, knowing this now, he does not ask to have him recalled.

Lieutenant Colonel Frémont further desires to say that, after witnesses have been examined, he will agree to their immediate discharge, (if his consent is deemed material by the court, and his counsel advise him that it is,) in all cases in which he sees or expects no further benefit from their attendance.

J. C. FRÉMONT,
Lieutenant Colonel, mounted rifles.

Commodore Stockton, a witness, being in court, asked leave to make an explanation.

Leave being granted, he said:

Mr. President: In my testimony I disclaimed having any knowledge of military tactics. In consequence of the want of such knowledge, it may be possible that a part of my testimony may not be understood, as I designed it should be; therefore I take this opportunity to say that I stated that General Kearny was at the head of a square formed by the men on the right flank. I intended to convey the fact that General Kearny was at the head of a square on my right; whether it was the right flank of the middle division, or anything else, I do not pretend to know. The position of this square was directly between myself and some other portion of the troops, with the volunteers on my right. I beg leave, sir, also, to add to my testimony of yesterday this note of explanation.

It was read, as follows, by the judge advocate:

Commodore R. F. Stockton begs leave to add to his narrative, in response to the first interrogatory, the general declaration that he wishes to be understood as meaning, distinctly, to convey the idea that General Kearny was fully invested by him with the command of the troops in the battles of the 8th and 9th of January, subject to the orders of him, the witness, as commander-in-chief.

Most and nearly all of the execution of details was confided to General Kearny, as second in command. The witness, in enumerating some of the orders given, and some of the details executed by himself, meant merely to cite instances in which General Kearny recognized and acknowledged him, the witness, as commander-in-chief on the field of battle as well as on the march.

He could not attempt to enumerate and specify the many and important acts of General Kearny, as second in command. The witness was wholly and solely responsible for the success of the expedition; but he takes great pleasure now in saying that he was efficiently sustained by the gallantry and good conduct of General Kearny, and all the officers and men under his command.

The cross-examination here concluded.

Question by Lieutenant Colonel Frémont. Were the instructions of November 5th, 1846, from the Navy Department, in which you were directed to relinquish to General. Kearny the control of the civil administration, and operations on shore, communicated to you? and if so, when, and by whom?

Answer. My impression is that I received them from Commodore Biddle, some time in the month of March.

Question by Lieutenant Colonel Frémont. Did you furnish to Governor Frémont a copy of those instructions?

Answer. I did not.

Lieutenant Colonel Frémont stated that he had no further questions to ask the witness.

The court was then cleared. After some time spent in consideration of interrogatories to be put to the witness by the court, the court was opened; Lieutenant Colonel Frémont in court.

Examination of Commodore Stockton, a witness, by the court.

Question. Was your letter of suspension of General Kearny, dated 16th January, 1847, of any other effect or force than to withdraw from his command the sailors and marines belonging to your squadron?

Answer. The effect that it actually had is one thing; the effect that I designed is another thing; now, which is meant?

The judge advocate inquired of the president whether the court should be cleared to make their answer to the witness's inquiry.

The witness then said:

I will answer it according to what I suppose to be the meaning of the court. I meant to suspend him from the command of all the troops I had placed under him, as I have before testified.

A member suggested that the whole of the question is not answered; and that the object of the question was to inquire whether the suspension referred only to the sailors and marines, as stated in it.

While another question was preparing from the court, Commodore Stockton said:

Perhaps I can save a question by answering, that I meant to suspend General Kearny from the command of all the troops at Los Angeles, except the dragoons of the regular army.

Question. Was that the limit of your object in suspending General Kearny?

Answer. Yes.

Question. To which branch of the service did the 9-pounders

you have referred to in your testimony belong? to the army, or to the navy?

Answer. To the navy. They were taken from the enemy and put to the use of the naval force on shore.

Question. Were those 9-pounders manned by soldiers of the army, or by sailors or marines of the navy?

Answer. By sailors; there may have been some marines with them.

Question. In the conversation with Lieutenant Colonel Frémont, in the evening of January 16, as you think it was, did he tell you he had had a conversation with General Kearny on the subject of the order from the latter to him of that day's date, and in regard to the appointment of governor of California, and if so, what passed between you and Lieutenant Colonel Frémont at that time on those subjects?

Answer. I think not.

Question. You say, " General Kearny came to me and inquired who is to command the troops." Did the word *troops* in that question include the dragoons? and did your answer, that Lieutenant Rowan, of the Cyane, *was to command*, include the dragoons?

Answer. The dragoons, as I supposed, had been transferred to my command when General Kearny agreed to go as my aid-de-camp, as well as the mountain howitzer, as I before testified. In a general order issued by myself, directing the troops to march on a certain day, the dragoons were included. When the troops were paraded, preparatory to the march, and when it was expected that General Kearney was going as my aid, the dragoons occupied the post which had been assigned them in my general order; and I transferred the whole as they stood to the command of General Kearny.

The court had no further question to ask.

Lieutenant Colonel Frémont, being asked by the judge advocate, said he had none.

The judge advocate then announced that unless objection was made by the court or the defence, he should discharge the witness from further attendance on the court.

Lieutenant Colonel Frémont assented.

A member requested that the court be cleared, which was done.

The court assented to the discharge of the witness.

The court was then opened; Lieutenant Colonel Frémont in court.

The decision in closed session was announced.

Archibald H. Gillespie, a captain of the marine corps, a witness for the defence.

Being duly sworn by the judge advocate, according to law, testified as follows:

Examined in chief by Lieutenant Colonel Frémont.

Question. Did you ride out of Los Angeles to meet Major Cooke when he was going into that city in March last? and did you inform him that Lieutenant Colonel Frémont was then gone to Monterey, but would be back in a few days? and if so, please state all that passed?

Answer. I did ride out on Major Cooke entering into the City of the Angels in March last, for the purpose of paying my respects to him and showing him any attentions he might require. Colonel Cooke took me to be Colonel Frémont. I told him that I was Major Gillespie, relieved from duty in the California battalion; that Colonel Frémont had gone to Monterey; would be absent but a few days; and that I believed he had gone to see General Kearny in relation to his late orders; having reference to the order of the 1st March. We continued riding on into the city, and halted in the government house. It had previously been occupied by troops as government quarters; it had been occupied by myself, and also by General Kearny. There were two rooms in the house still occupied by officers who had been ordered to vacate them. From the street I went with Colonel Cooke to one of those rooms; I think it was Mr. Loker's, the adjutant. After making inquiry respecting these two rooms that were still occupied, Colonel Cooke inquired whether the house that was then occupied by Lieutenant Colonel Frémont, and where the flag was still flying, was rented upon public or private account; I informed him that I understood it had been rented by Colonel Frémont on private account,—

The judge advocate suggested to the president whether he should take the opinion of the court on the relevancy of the testimony.

On motion of a member, the court was cleared. After mature deliberation, the court decided that the court does not see the relevancy of the question, and the answer, thus far, but will permit the answer to be continued.

The court was then opened. Lieutenant Colonel Frémont in court. The decision in closed session was announced.

Captain Gillespie, witness, continued his testimony, as follows:

——but that, by inquiring of Major Reading, he would be able to ascertain the fact; and that I would show Lieutenant Davidson round to Major Reading's quarters. Colonel Cooke thanked me, and ordered Lieutenant Davidson to accompany me, at the same time saying to Lieutenant Davidson, that if he found the quarters were on public account, and that Colonel Russell still occupied a room in them, to order him to quit them immediately. I then rode with Lieutenant Davidson to Major Reading's quarters, leaving Colonel Cooke. That is all that passed.

Question. Are you certain of the words used by Colonel Cooke on that occasion, to wit: "*order him to quit them immediately?*"

Answer. Yes; I am very certain.

Question. Do you know whether those quarters were those of Lieutenant Colonel Frémont, and his furniture (such as it was) then in them?

Answer. The quarters were Colonel Frémont's, so far as I know;

I was always under the impression; it was so understood that they were his; and his furniture was in them.

Question. Did you comprehend who were to take these quarters on the turning out of Colonel Russell, and whether the Mormons, or others under the command of Major Cooke, or himself, was to occupy those quarters?

Answer. I suppose that some of Major Cooke's men were to occupy those quarters; but who, I did not know.

Question. Were you an officer of the California battalion at Los Angeles, at the time the order was given by Commodore Stockton to re-organize that battalion; and if so, will you tell what was the nature of the re-organization commanded by Commodore Stockton, and forbid by General Kearny?

Answer. I was an officer of the battalion; I never knew of any order to re-organize the battalion; and the only change that did take place in it was Commodore Stockton appointing me to be the major of the battalion, at the time of Colonel Fremont's receiving his commission as governor.

Question. At what time did you first know or learn that you were to be major of that battalion? and upon what event was your promotion dependent?

Answer. I learned it either upon the 16th or 17th of January, 1847; I am not certain which; it was two or three days before I received the commission; the commission is dated on the 18th; I received it on the 20th; I am not aware of any particular event on which my promotion was dependent, unless it be Colonel Frémont's having received the commission of governor of the territory.

Question. Did you believe at the time of the rumored approach of the Mexican general, Bustamente, that the state of the country was such as to permit of safe travelling from Los Angeles to Monterey? and are you aware of any circumstance, in connexion with the unsettled state of the country, which delayed Lieutenant Colonel Frémont's journey to Monterey, after the arrival of Colonel Mason at the Ciudad de los Angeles?

Answer. The state of the country at the time, was such as would not permit of safe travelling, not only from the Californians, which were supposed to be in arms upon the road, but also from the Indians, who had become very bold and wounded several travellers.

I do not recollect any circumstances that delayed Colonel Frémont at Los Angeles, after the arrival of Colonel Mason, except that Colonel Frémont was very much occupied in making transfers, and settling his public accounts.

Question. Did you at any time communicate to General Kearny your rank and position in the California battalion; and if so, will you state when and where that communication was made?

Answer. I did state to General Kearny my position in the California battalion, on the 5th of December, 1846, at about 1 o'clock in the day, on the mountains between Santa Maria and Santa Isabelle, when I, at the head of a detachment of volunteers and sailors, met him, having been ordered by Commodore Stockton to proceed to Warner's pass to communicate with General Kearny.

Question. What force did you carry out to meet General Kearny, and what proportion of the American force, engaged at the battle of San Pasqual, consisted of the force you carried out?

Answer. The force consisted of 26 men of Captain Gibson's company, Lieutenant Beale and Midshipman Duncan, and 10 carbineers, of the Congress; and a brass 4-pounder field-piece. And, during the action of San Pasqual, Captain Gibson's company, Lieutenant Beale and myself, were all that were engaged; Midshipman Duncan and the carbineers, and the field-piece, having been ordered to the rear with the baggage.

Question. Do you know whether the mules ran off with the cannon, which was lost in that action, or whether the men were first killed or lanced defending it?

On motion of a member the court was ordered to be cleared.

After deliberation, the court decided that this question came under the exclusion, by the rule of the court on collateral facts elicited on cross-examination.

The court was then opened. Lieutenant Colonel Frémont in court. The decision in closed session was announced.

Captain Gillespie, a witness for the defence, examination in chief continued.

Question. After your return to San Diego with General Kearny, and previous to the march of the expedition for Los Angeles, did General Kearny attempt or claim to exercise any command over you?

Answer. No. He did not.

Question. Were you ordered by General Kearny to return to the United States, by orders of the first of March last? and if so, was that order countermanded; and if so, by whom, at what time, and all the circumstances relating to that countermanding?

Answer. By the orders of March first, I was relieved from duty in the Californian battalion, and directed to report to the commanding officer of my corps at Washington city. About the 10th of April, I received an order from Commodore Biddle, dated 31st of March, directing me to report to him at Monterey. Upon the receipt of this order, I addressed a letter to Commodore Biddle stating that I was very much occupied in settling accounts, which occurred during the siege of Los Angeles; and that, as soon as possible, I would obey his order. As it was necessary to see Commodore Stockton in relation to these accounts, I was obliged to await the arrival of the Congress at San Pedro. Previous to his arrival, I received a second order from Commodore Biddle, dated the 4th of May; the first order was handed to me by Colonel Cooke, Colonel Mason having just arrived from Monterey; the second order was handed to me by Lieutenant Sherman, acting aid to General Kearny: it having been requested by Commodore Biddle that these orders should be delivered in that manner.

Question. Do you know of any circumstances which induced you to believe that you were retained in California by the interference of General Kearny? and if so, what were those circumstances?

The judge advocate requested that the court might be cleared; and it was cleared accordingly.

After deliberation, the court decided that, the court consider the question irrelevant and order that it cannot be put.

The court was then opened. Lieutenant Colonel Frémont in court. The decision in closed session was announced.

Lieutenant Colonel Frémont said: He would request to be neard in regard to the relevancy of the question to-morrow.

The judge advocate said: It was the previous order of the court, that a party offering a question could be heard before it was ruled out, if he desired.

The testimony of to-day was read over; and then, at five minutes before three, the court adjourned, to meet to-morrow at 10 o'clock.

SATURDAY, *December* 11, 1847.—*10 o'clock.*

The court met pursuant to adjournment. Present: all the members, the judge advocate, and Lieutenant Colonel Frémont.

The proceedings of yesterday were read over.

Lieutenant Colonel Frémont read a paper to the court, as follows:

Mr. PRESIDENT: Lieutenant Colonel Frémont is instructed by his counsel to say, that they feel great embarrassment from the decision of the court of yesterday evening, in excluding the question which was last offered. That question was in these words: "Do you know of any circumstances which induced you to believe that you were detained in California by the interference of General Kearny? If so, what were those circumstances?" The decision of the court was in these words: "The court consider the question irrelevant and that it cannot be put."

The counsel are of opinion that it is relevant, but will not argue against the opinion of the court. At the same time, they put into the hands of Lieutenant Colonel Frémont, to be offered to the court, a statement from Major Gillespie, showing what the substance of the answer would be, if the question were put. And the counsel further instruct Lieutenant Colonel Frémont to say, that this statement is offered merely to show the *relevancy* of the question offered, and not to show its *effect;* believing that the effect and the sufficiency of the answer to the question, if admitted, belongs to a different stage of the trial, and is to be judged in connexion with any other testimony going to the same point.

J. C. FRÉMONT,
Lieutenant Colonel, mounted rifles.

And with the foregoing paper Lieutenant Colonel Frémont offered to the judge advocate a statement from the witness, in explanation, as suggested in the note of Lieutenant Colonel Frémont.

The judge advocate proposed to read it to the court. Objections appearing in the court, the court was ordered to be cleared. After deliberation, the court decided as follows:

The court having heard the paper just read by Lieutenant Colonel Frémont, ordered that its decision of yesterday be reconsidered, and that Lieutenant Colonel Frémont be invited to explain to the court the relevancy of the question, in his view, to the matter under trial.

The court cannot, however, hear the paper from Captain Gillespie, offered by Lieutenant Colonel Frémont, in explanation of the relevancy of the question of yesterday.

This would be not only to admit on its records the testimony in substance, whether relevant or irrelevant, but to admit an intimation from a witness what would be his testimony on an assumed enquiry.

The court was then opened. Lieutenant Colonel Frémont in court. The decision in closed session was announced. The written statement of Captain Gillespie was returned to Lieutenant Colonel Frémont under the decision.

Lieutenant Colonel Frémont presented to the court a note, as follows:

Mr. PRESIDENT: Lieutenant Colonel Frémont says to the court that he will cheerfully avail himself of the court's permission, to present his views at the next meeting of the court, and at present is ready to go on with the other testimony.

J. C. FRÉMONT,
Lieutenant Colonel, mounted rifles.

Captain Gillespie, of the marine corps, a witness for the defence, continued his testimony.

Question. You spoke of several orders yesterday, and of some letters of your own, in answer or relative to some said orders: will you please produce all such orders and letters, if in your power or possession, to be used as evidence before this court?

Answer. I have the orders at my quarters, and will bring them on Monday.

Lieutenant Colonel Frémont said he had no other question to ask at present.

On suggestion of the judge advocate, the court was cleared. After deliberation the court was opened. Lieutenant Colonel Frémont in court.

The judge advocate read and submitted, for the consideration of the court and the defence, the following paper:

Mr. PRESIDENT: As we have now, on the 31st day of the session of the court, apparently, as yet, only opened the defence, having up to this time examined and cross-examined only three witnesses for the prosecution, and introduced one other, to afford the defence the opportunity to cross-examine him, and having as yet examined and cross-examined for the defence only three witnesses, and as there remain behind, (I believe,) yet to be called for the defence, some fifteen or more witnesses, I propose, hereafter, when a witness is called, to ask the defence to state specifically what is expected to be proved by such witness. Then, in all cases where I am informed that the facts are as the defence supposes them to be, I shall, with consent of the court, admit them as proved; when I am not so informed, and am not at liberty to make such admissions, the defence can proceed to the proof. But in either case, and before either admission or proof, the court will have the opportunity to decide the relevancy of the evidence offered to the case under trial.

The taking of testimony in the way we are pursuing, in a case so involved as this, must be attended with tedious delays, from the number of witnesses yet to call, the necessary objections to testimony, the frequent clearing of the court on isolated points of evidence and single questions, the number of separate discussions and decisions in closed session, one after another. Much less time, it is obvious, will be required to consider evidence in a body than in such detail. To the defence, the mode I propose can only be an advantage, inasmuch as the relevancy and effect of testimony will be more apparent to the court, when its end is reached, than when the object is only aimed at in the opening of the examination. In the present way, it is possible, objections may be raised, and evidence ruled out, because the object of it is not sufficiently disclosed. Minor points, the defence and the court apparently let go by, rather than take time in arguments and decisions.

I think, on the whole, it is manifest that we shall, in the mode proposed, receive the evidence of the defence in a better, more connected, and condensed form; and that we shall proceed more rapidly, and in a clearer order, to the decision of the case; a result which Lieutenant Colonel Frémont and the court, and every one concerned in this protracted trial, are anxious to reach.

J. F. LEE,
Captain United States Army, and Judge Advocate.

The defence said: We will consider and answer on Monday. The judge advocate assented.

The judge advocate then proposed to suspend the cross-examination of Captain Gillespie, and introduced the honorable W. P. Hall, member of Congress, who was in attendance, and requested to be examined and discharged; which was agreed to.

Willard P. Hall, a witness summoned on the part of the prosecution, was then duly sworn by the judge advocate according to law.

The judge advocate said he had no questions to ask Mr. Hall; but he had introduced him, in compliance with the understanding entered into with the defence, to call all the witnesses for the prosecution for the purpose of cross-examination.

Cross-examined by Lieutenant Colonel Frémont.

Question. Did you consider the letter addressed to you by Lieutenant Colonel Frémont, and set forth in specification five, of charge first, as endeavoring to persuade and excite you to aid and abet Governor Frémont in resisting and making mutiny against his superior officer, (General Kearny;) and if so, please to state the words of the letter upon which you rely for such references?

Answer. I did not so consider it.

Question. What was the state of the country at the time you received the letter from Governor Frémont, in point of quiet and tranquility, or otherwise?

Answer. The country, as far as my information extends, was quiet and peaceable.

Question. Did Major Cooke, of the dragoons, ever admit to you that he was the author of the article from California, dated in February last, and published in the Missouri Republican, of June last?

The judge advocate said: The question is not admissible. The court decided the same point in the examination of Major Cooke.

Lieutenant Colonel Frémont said: He did not press the answer, and considered the question ruled out.

A member doubting whether the question ought to remain on the record, the court was cleared.

The court decided that a party cannot, with due respect to the decisions of the court, repeat questions which the court has already deliberately decided to be inadmissible.

The following note was received from Lieutenant Colonel Frémont, while the court was in closed session:

Mr. President: Lieutenant Colonel Frémont having inquired of the witness, since the court was cleared, whether Major Cooke had ever made the admission to *him*, which the question implies, was informed that he had not; and Lieutenant Colonel Frémont desires this statement to go upon the record to prevent an implication, which he *now* knows to be erroneous, to be drawn from his question. And he would further state, for his own justification in offering the question, that it was founded upon information from others, and not from Mr. Hall.

J. C. FRÉMONT,
Lieutenant Colonel, mounted riflemen.

The court was then opened. Lieutenant Colonel Frémont in court. The decision in closed session was announced.

Lieutenant Colonel Frémont said: He had no further questions to ask of the witness.

The witness was then examined by the court, as follows:

Question by the court. What position, civil or military, did you occupy in California on or about the 11th February, 1847?

Answer. I was a private in company C, in the first regiment of Missouri mounted volunteers.

Question by the court. What did you consider the purport and object of the letter of Lieutenant Colonel Fremont to you, dated 11th February, 1847; and particularly the words: "I cannot, without considering myself derelict to my trust, and unworthy the station of an American officer, yield, or permit myself to be interfered with by any other, until directed to do so by the proper authorities at home, predicated on full and ample despatches that I forwarded to Washington as early as August of last year. I require the co-operation, with a view to the important object of preserving the peace and tranquility of California, of every American citizen and soldier in the territory, &c.?" And whom did you consider referred to by the words "any other," in the foregoing extract; and did you consider that your co-operation was so required?

Answer. I considered the object of the letter to be that stated by Colonel Frémont in the letter; and he meant to avow in that letter that he would not permit any one to interfere with him. I have no idea whom he meant by the expression, "any other;" I suppose it to be merely a general expression. I did not suppose that he alluded to any one in particular. The expression, "I require the co-operation, with a view to the important object of preserving the peace and tranquility of California, of every American citizen and soldier in the territory," I have never particularly scanned; I did not attach any particular importance to that expression in the letter at the time.

The court had no further questions.

Lieutenant Colonel Frémont had no questions to ask the witness.

Mr. Hall was accordingly discharged from further attendance as a witness on this court.

Mr. William Broome, a witness on the part of the defence, was then called, and sworn by the judge advocate according to law.

Lieutenant Colonel Frémont presented to the court the following note:

Mr. PRESIDENT: Lieutenant Colonel Frémont informs the court that the testimony of Commodore Stockton is considered so full, upon the points to which the witness now before the court was summoned to testify, that no questions will be put to him on the part of the defence; and he is accordingly turned over for cross-examination.

J. C. FREMONT,
Lieut. Col., mounted rifles.

The judge advocate said he had no questions to ask. The court had no questions to ask.

The witness was then discharged.

Lieutenant Colonel Frémont read to the court the following paper:

Mr. President: In examining the charges and specifications, Lieutenant Colonel Frémont perceives some which do not appear to him to be presented as crimes in themselves, to be prosecuted, but only as evidences of another crime, to wit, the assumption of the title and power of governor of California. If this should be the case, (and of this Lieutenant Colonel Frémont does not undertake to judge,) he suggests that it may shorten the labor of the defence if the judge advocate should so state, and give a memorandum, to be entered of record, of the specifications so intended.

In making this request, Lieutenant Colonel Frémont takes leave to say, that it is not his desire to escape present or future trial, for anything contained in any of the specifications; and, therefore, hereby offers to make matter of record this, his *declaration*, that in the event that the judge advocate should be permitted, or directed, to give the memorandum which this application supposes to be consistent with the facts of the case, that he (the said Lieutenant Colonel Frémont) will never plead in bar, either *autrefois convict*, or *autrefois acquit*, (as the case might be under the issue of this trial,) to any future prosecution upon the matter charged in the specifications which may now be specified and excepted in the memorandum, if given.

J. C. FRÉMONT,
Lieut. Col., mounted rifles.

Andrew F. V. Gray, a lieutenant in the navy, a witness on the part of the defence, being duly sworn by the judge advocate according to law, testified as follows.

Examination in chief by Lieutenant Colonel Frémont.

Question. State the position which you held under Commodore Stockton at San Diego?

Answer. I was his aid, and one of the lieutenants of the Congress.

Question. Did you hear Commodore Stockton offer to go as General Kearny's aid, and did you hear General Kearny offer to go as Commodore Stockton's aid?

Answer. I did.

Question. Did you hear the address of Commodore Stockton to his officers at the time when the position which had been assigned to Lieutenant Rowan was given to General Kearny; and if so, will you state what passed upon that occasion?

Answer. I was present on the occasion referred to; I heard Commodore Stockton confer the command of the forces on General Kearny, reserving to himself the office of commander-in-chief. The words were: "Gentlemen, General Kearny has kindly offered to go with us; public duty requires that I should appoint him to the command of the forces; you will obey him accordingly; reserving to myself the office of commander-in-chief." Those are the words as nearly as I can recollect them.

Question. Did you bear an order from Commodore Stockton, on the 8th of January, 1847, on the field of battle, to General Kearny; if so, state the order and the circumstances?

Answer. I did bear such an order, on the 8th of January, to General Kearny on the field of battle. The enemy had been observed to withdraw their guns from the height; the commodore directed me to go to General Kearny and say to him, to send a square and a field piece immediately upon the height, to prevent the enemy returning with their guns. I went and gave him the order, and on my returning to Commodore Stockton, observed the division, or square, near General Kearny, moving towards the hill.

Question. Did you bear that order in your character of aid-de-camp to Governor Stockton, the commander-in-chief?

Answer. Yes.

Cross-examined by judge advocate.

Question. Do you recollect the words and manner in which you delivered that order? Did you deliver it so that General Kearny must have received it as a peremptory order, or as a suggestion?

Answer. I carried it as an order in the usual respectful way. How general Kearny received it, of course I cannot say. He did not show by his manner that it was disagreeable, according to the best of my recollection.

The defence and judge advocate have no further questions to ask Lieutenant Gray. The court had no question to ask Lieutenant Gray, and he was permitted to retire, but, at the request of the defence, was not discharged.

The president of the court received an application from Lieutenant Colonel Emory, stating the necessity of the public service in regard to the condition of his regiment in the field, and asking for his discharge from further attendance on this court.

The defence and judge advocate were not to-day prepared to answer on the application of Lieutenant Colonel Emory, whether he would or would not be again wanted. They would reply on Monday.

The testimony of to-day was read over, and then, at twenty minutes after two, the court adjourned to meet on Monday, at 10 o'clock.

MONDAY, *December* 13, 1847.—10 *o'clock.*

The court met pursuant to adjournment:

Present: All the members, the judge advocate, and Lieutenant Colonel Frémont.

The proceedings of Saturday were read over.

Hon. Willard P. Hall, a witness for the defence on Saturday, appeared in court and asked leave to make an explanation of his testimony on that day.

Leave being granted, Mr Hall said: On looking over the report of the evidence before the court, as published in the National Intelligencer of this morning, I find that the second question put to me by the court is stated differently from what I understood it at the time. The said report appears to be correct from the record which I hold in my hand.

I understood the question to inquire of me whom I understood to be referred to by the words "any other," in an extract from Colonel Frémont's letter, in which I thought the words "any other" were preceded by the words "General Kearny," so as to read "General Kearny, or any other." In which understanding of it, I replied that I did not know, or consider who was particularly referred to by the words "any other." I now say, as the words stand in the question and the letter, I understood the words "any other" to refer to General Kearny.

Question by Lieutenant Colonel Frémont. Was General Kearny there at the time?

Answer. He was not.

Question by Lieutenant Colonel Frémont. Do you know when he was, and whether Governor Frémont knew where he was?

Answer. I cannot say where he was; at what particular point; I knew he had gone in a vessel up the coast, and I was expecting him down every few days to San Diego. It is impossible for me to say whether Colonel Frémont knew where he was.

Question by Lieutenant Colonel Frémont. Do you know whether Governor Fremont expected him down?

Answer. I do not.

Question by Lieutenant Colonel Frémont. At what time did General Kearny actually come down to San Diego?

Answer. I do not think that he ever returned to San Diego.

The defence had no further questions for this witness. The court had none. Mr. Hall retired.

The following paper was submitted by the judge advocate:

The judge advocates submits, in answer to the note of Lieutenant Colonel Frémont, presented to the court before the close of the session on Saturday, that he does not find in any of the charges or specifications now on trial any ambiguity which can require explanation. Lieutenant Colonel Frémont refers the court and the judge advocate to the charges generally, without distinguishing the specification, which he thinks not sufficiently explicit. The judge advocate, therefore, answers generally, and says: That he thinks all the specifications direct, explicit, and free from any sort of ambiguity; that the legal offence in the acts alleged is in each and every specification carefully expressed, and then again defined by the charge under which the specifications are laid. The judge advocate says, further, that nothing of criminal accusation is conveyed, except what is precisely expressed.

In regard to the assumption of the office and title of governor of California by Lieutenant Colonel Frémont, which is alleged in several of the specifications, from acts done by him in that capacity, the judge advocate thinks, that the legal offence charged in these acts appears, as in all the others, to be distinctly explained, viz: that the said assumption of the said office of governor, was in contempt and resistance of the lawful authority of General Kearny, was a usurpation of his powers, and was mutiny.

On the reading the foregoing paper, the defence said, that they would defend the acts referred to, as if they were criminal in themselves.

The judge advocate said: if that was the import of the paper submitted by the defence on Saturday, he would say, with the permission of the court, he considers that such acts as the purchase of land from Temple, and the order to the collector of San Pedro come no further within the purview of the court than as facts evidencing an assumption of the functions of governor, alleged to be in derogation of the authority of General Kearny in the specifications, when these acts are referred to.

The judge advocate said: he would submit the matter to the court.

The court was then cleared. The court assented to the explanation made by the judge advocate.

The court was then opened. Lieutenant Colonel Frémont in court. The decision in closed session was announced.

The following note was read to the court by Lieutenant Colonel Frémont:

MR. PRESIDENT: Lieutenant Colonel Frémont wishes to make his apology to the court, and that of his counsel, for what appeared to the court to be disrespect to the court's decision, in repeating a question which had been ruled out once before. It was the question to the Hon. Mr. Hall, and in relation to Major Cooke, and the article signed "*Justice*" in the Missouri Republican. Lieutenant Colonel Frémont and his counsel disclaim all intentional disrespect, and give as a reason for repeating the question, and for wishing to press the inquiry to which it relates, that Lieutenant Colonel Frémont differs in his recollection from some part of Major Cooke's testimony, and when he comes to make his own statement in his general defence, may feel it to be due to himself to state that difference, especially if supported by something which may go to weaken the testimony of Major Cooke. Among those things which weaken testimony, Lieutenant Colonel Frémont is advised to say, that *enmity* on the part of the witness is one; and making publications injurious to the accused, is another, especially when relating to the matter of the accusation; and, that in both these points of view, Lieutenant Colonel Frémont and his counsel believe it to be material and relevant to his defence to show, if such is the fact, that Major Cooke, is the author of the article referred to.

J. C. FRÉMONT,
Lieutenant Colonel, mounted riflemen.

Lieutenant Colonel Frémont also read and presented to the court the following paper:

Mr. President: Lieutenant Colonel Frémont is instructed by his counsel to say, that keeping a witness away, or attemping to keep a witness away from a trial, is an offence against the administration of justice in all courts, and may be punished as such; and that, in the case of prosecutions, and when such offence is committed by the prosecutor, it may be given in evidence in impeachment of his motives and credit.

He is advised further to say, that the fact that Major Gillespie was not technically a witness in this case at the time of the alleged attempt to keep him away, makes no difference; that General Kearny knew his own design to arrest Lieutenant Colonel Frémont, and also knew that Major Gillespie, from his intelligence, activity, and long and intimate connexion with Lieutenant Colonel Frémont in California, must necessarily be an important witness for him, and the degree of that importance incapable of being appreciated until the nature of the charges against Lieutenant Colonel Frémont should be known.

Supposing it to be an offence, in any case, and going to the impeachment of motives and credit in any prosecutor in any court, to endeavor to keep away witnesses for the defence, Lieutenant Colonel Frémont is instructed by his counsel to say, that the case now presented, if true, is the strongest which can be imagined. It is the case of a general prosecuting his subordinate, for alleged crimes on the coast of the Pacific ocean, the subordinate brought home for trial without a knowledge of a charge against him, and the prosecutor bringing his own witnesses in his train. This would seem to make the case strong enough, but other features rise up to aggravate it. It is in evidence from Major Cooke, that General Kearny calculated that there would be no trial at present, or for a long time, or a brief trial upon documentary testimony alone; that, for want of evidence from California, Lieutenant Colonel Frémont would probably ask and obtain a long postponement of his trial, or would go into trial upon the written testimony at hand. Thus, for want of that testimony which he had no chance to bring, and to keep away which it is now proposed to submit evidence against General Kearny, it was calculated that the charges would hang a long time over him, during which it might happen that not only newspaper articles, but books such as this, (showing the second volume of Fayette Robinson's account of the war,) might be published to enlighten the public upon his guilt and infamy; or, going to trial at once, to avoid that consequence, he would be subjected to summary conviction on the papers produced against him. In a case thus aggravated, and where the commanding general has appeared himself in the double character of prosecutor and witness, Lieutenant Colonel Frémont is instructed by his counsel to say, that the testimony he now offers as to keeping away Major Gillespie, (for he was actually prevented from attending until after this trial begun,) is both relevant and material testimony, and should be admitted by any court, and above all by a court martial.

Lieutenant Colonel Frémont is further instructed by his counsel to say, that it is no objection to the form of his question, because it asks the witness to state the circumstances which induced him to believe that General Kearny interfered to detain him in California, and prevent him from returning to the United States at the same time with Lieutenant Colonel Frémont. He is advised that testimony is divided into *positive* and *presumptive*, and that the latter, founded upon circumstances, is always as legal and often more convincing than the former. But the question is not now upon the *sufficiency*, but upon the *relevancy* of the testimony offered; and under this aspect of the question, Lieutenant Colonel Frémont is advised that the question is relevant, and applies to that branch of the defence which goes to impeach the motives and the credit of the prosecutor.

Lieutenant Colonel Frémont further says to the court that, if the testimony of Major Gillespie is admitted to prove an interference from General Kearny through Commodore Biddle, to keep him (Major Gillespie) away, he will then, and in the wake of that glaring case, attempt to show to others, that of acting Lieutenant Louis McLane, of the United States navy, a major in the California battalion, and one of the commissioners in negotiating the capitulation of Cowenga; and Midshipman Wilson, a captain in the same battalion; both of them standing in relations to be material witnesses to Lieutenant Colonel Frémont. Both of these officers had the promise of Commodore Stockton to return; both of whom were entitled to that justice from their long absence and hard service; and both of whom were detained and sent to sea by Commodore Biddle; while Lieutenant Radford, the brother-in-law of General Kearny, without equal claims to ask a return, was indulged with that favor. If the testimony of Major Gillespie is admitted, Lieutenant Colonel Frémont will afterwards, with the leave of the court, endeavor to show circumstances which may justify a probable presumption that Messrs. McLane and Wilson were also detained for the same purpose that Major Gillespie was, and more effectually! for, being sent to sea, they have not yet arrived in the United States.

J. C. FREMONT,
Lieutenant Colonel, mounted riflemen.

On the reception of these papers, the court was cleared.

The court was then opened. Lieutenant Colonel Frémont in court.

The judge advocate stated to the court that the counsel for Lieutenant Colonel Frémont was necessarily absent this morning, being unexpectedly called to the Senate of the United States; and he proposed to the president that the court do now adjourn.

Whereupon the court adjourned at one o'clock, to meet to-morrow morning at 10 o'clock.

TUESDAY, *December* 14, 1847.—10 *o'clock.*

The court met pursuant to adjournment.

Present: All the members, and the judge advocate

The proceedings of yesterday were read over for the verification of the record. Lieutenant Colonel Frémont appeared in court during the reading of the record.

The following note was received from Lieutenant Colonel Frémont:

MR. PRESIDENT: Lieutenant Colonel Frémont submits, as an additional circumstance in the case before the court, that of the alleged detention of Major Gillespie and the two naval officers mentioned, that it appears from the testimony of General Kearny, in his cross-examination, on the fifteenth day of the trial, that he (General Kearny) had communicated to Commodore Biddle his intention to arrest Lieutenant Colonel Frémont.

J. C. FRÉMONT,
Lieutenant Colonel, mounted rifles

Whereupon, the court was ordered to be cleared. In answer to the argument of Lieutenant Colonel Frémont to those reasons why the court ought not to reverse its decision on the question which it refused to allow put to Captain Gillespie, the judge advocate respectfully submits the following note:

Lieutenant Colonel Frémont proposes to show facts from which he concludes that certain officers of the navy were detained on duty by Commodore Biddle, at the suggestion of General Kearny, and thence to infer that the motive of General Kearny, in such suggestion, was to keep away witnesses from this trial.

The persons referred to were officers in the public service, and such within the jurisdiction of this court, and liable to the summons of the government, at the suggestion of the accused. It was not within the power of General Kearny or Commodore Biddle to withdraw or withhold them from such summons. The suggestion that the detention of them in this case was with a view to deprive the accused of the benefit of their testimony at this trial, as it could not, by any legal possibility, have such effect, if the accused required them here, as the detention was in the regular course of public duty, and by the act (the withholding of leaves of absence) of a superior officer, an act which was wholly within his discretion, is a suggestion not supported by any legal or moral presumption which the facts carry with them.

If Lieutenant Colonel Frémont should show that Commodore Biddle detained Captain Gillespie in California, it would infer nothing against General Kearny; if he should show reasons to believe—if he should even prove conclusively that he detained him at the suggestion of General Kearny—it would infer nothing as to the motives of General Kearny. Such suggestions, if they influenced Commodore Biddle, must have been good and sufficient reason to his mind; and how shall this court distinguish between the public

and honest reasons which satisfied Commodore Biddle, and the secret and corrupt ones which are ascribed to General Kearny? and
how ascertain if both are applicable to the case which operated
with General Kearny? It is evident, therefore, that the only proof
of corrupt motives in General Kearny must be proof of a conspiracy between him and Commodore Biddle, and of that the proof
must be clear and direct. It cannot be reached in the way Lieutenant Colonel Frémont proposes: by showing such facts as he
suggested, and which he supposes to raise a presumption against
General Kearny. On the contrary all the legal and moral presumptions which such facts carry with them are the direct opposite.
The acts of a public officer, in the common duties of his office—acts
which lie within the proper official discretion—carry presumption
of good motives with them. They are certainly not to be received
in a court of justice as raising presumptions of criminal motives.
As, in this case, the act offered in proof was the act of Commodore
Biddle; to conclude from it any corrupt motive in General Kearny,
if he had any influence in it, the proof must be clear of a conspiracy.

The other circumstances suggested by Lieutenant Colonel Frémont, appear to the judge advocate in the same light. Midshipmen Wilson and McLane may or may not have had such title of
long absence and hard service to return home as Lieutenant Colonel
Frémont supposes; they may or may not have had, in this respect, a
better claim than Lieutenant Radford to the favor of Commodore
Biddle; still, if these facts be granted, and, notwithstanding that
Commodore Biddle did not detain Midshipmen Wilson and McLane
with the squadron, and did allow Lieutenant Radford to come home,
the court ought not to find in any of these circumstances, nor, further,
in the circumstances referred to, that Lieutenant Radford, who has
not been a witness on this trial, is the brother-in-law of General
Kearny, any legal or moral presumption whatsoever, that the official action of Commodore Biddle, in these matters, had any reference to this trial.

Both Commodore Biddle and General Kearny must have known,
as all officers in our service know, that under our government,
trials are not conducted under surprise and fraud; that every opportunity of defence, all necessary time for preparation, every
means to collect testimony, are always allowed. As to the calculation ascribed to General Kearny, that by keeping away those
witnesses, Lieutenant Colonel Frémont must either go to trial unprepared, or must afford him, during the necessary delay of preparation, the means to prejudice the public mind by newspaper publications, the judge advocate thinks the court cannot find, in such a
suggestion, anything sufficiently natural and probable to justify the
court in concluding therefrom any evidence as to the private motives which influenced the official action of Commodore Biddle or
General Kearny.

If Lieutenant Colonel Frémont can impeach General Kearny as
a witness on this trial, by any reasonable legal proof, the court
ought, doubtless, to give to it all due consideration and weight.

But the court cannot receive, in proof to that end, circumstances which carry with them no such inference or conclusion whatever.

Whereupon the court decided to admit the question to be put to Captain Gillespie.

The court was then opened, Lieutenant Colonel Frémont in court.

The proceedings in closed session were announced.

The following note was received from Lieutenant Colonel Frémont:

MR. PRESIDENT: Lieutenant Colonel Frémont takes leave to say that the main point relied upon by the judge advocate in his reply, to wit: that the public service required Major Gillespie to be detained in California, is probably a mistake of the fact, and possibly might be so proved upon the spot by Major Gillespie.

J. C. FRÉMONT,
Lieut. Colonel, mounted rifles.

Captain Gillespie, a witness for the defence.

The judge advocate read to the witness the question just admitted by the court, as follows:

Question by Lieutenant Colonel Frémont. Do you know of any circumstances which induced you to believe that you were retained in California by the interference of General Kearny? and if so, what were those circumstances?

Answer. There were circumstances which induced me to believe that I was detained in California by the interference of General Kearny, in consequence of having been informed by Commodore Biddle, after he, Commodore Biddle, had said to me, that he had nothing to do with me, and that I could return to the United States when I pleased; that he had received a note from General Kearny——

Here a member interposed as to the delivery of hearsay evidence.

The judge advocate said he had no objection to the witness stating what Commodore Biddle told witness of what had been said or written to Commodore Biddle by General Kearny. He admitted, as evidence to the facts in this matter, what Commodore Biddle said to witness.

The witness continued:

Commodore Biddle told me that he had received a note from General Kearny, and that I must remain in Monterey until further orders; that he wished to avoid difficulty between the army and navy. I remained in Monterey, I think, some four days after this time, when I was informed by Commodore Stockton that he had obtained Commodore Biddle's permission for me to leave, and that Commodore Biddle required that I should give my word of honor.

The judge advocate said he had admitted what Commodore Biddle said to witness, because Commodore Biddle-was not here to testify; but he did not admit what Commodore Stockton said, because Commodore Stockton could give his testimony to the point if required.

The witness continued:

I believe that is my answer to the question; and that is all the circumstances I know to induce the belief that I was detained by the influence of General Kearny.

Question by Lieutenant Colonel Frémont. Please to state the cause, and all the particulars, of your going on board the Columbus, and what passed?

Answer. At about half-past 8 o'clock at night, having returned on board of the Congress from shore, I was informed by Commodore Stockton's orderly that Lieutenant Stanley, of the Columbus, wished to see me on deck. Lieutenant Stanley informed me that he had been ordered on board by Commodore Biddle, who said that, having understood I was about leaving Monterey the next morning, I should not quit the town until further orders; and that he (Mr. Stanley) had been ordered to search for me on shore, had he not found me on board of the Congress. Considering this order very harsh and oppressive, after having made all my preparations to leave Monterey, for the purpose of making preparations for the overland journey, I was induced, although the hour was late, to go on board of the Columbus to see Commodore Biddle, and, if possible, to obtain a revocation of this last order.

On arriving alongside of the Columbus, it was 9 o'clock, p. m. Colonel Mason pushed off in one of the Columbus's cutters. I hurried on board, and gave my card to Lieutenant Madison Rush, officer of the deck, who informed me that I might possibly see the commodore, as Colonel Mason had just left him; Commodore Biddle having been aroused from his bed to see him. In a few minutes I was admitted. The substance of the conversation between myself and Commodore Biddle, in this interview, which relates to this question, I have given in my first answer to the question.

Question by Lieutenant Colonel Frémont. Please state when and how long it was after your interview with Commodore Biddle that you set out for Washington city, and when you arrived here? and if you set out after the departure of General Kearny and Lieutenant Colonel Frémont?

Answer. It was some four days after this conversation that I was permitted to leave Monterey. The conversation took place on Saturday night; General Kearny left on Monday morning. I think it was on the 31st May that the conversation took place, and that General Kearny left on the 2d of June.

The judge advocate, supposing the witness did not apprehend the exact import of the question, read it over to him.

Witness answered: It was a month after General Kearny left that I set out for Washington city; that I left the Sacramento valley for Washington city; I arrived here on the 16th November last.

Question by Lieutenant Colonel Frémont. What occasioned the delay of a month in your departure from California?

Answer. Collecting animals, and the outfits necessary for such a journey.

Question by Lieutenant Colonel Frémont. Do you know the respective periods that acting Lieutenant Louis McLane, and Midshipman Wilson, and Lieutenant Radford, had been out on service? and whether Midshipman Wilson had any special reason, connected with his own examination, to induce him to wish to come home? and whether Messrs. McLane and Wilson were not officers in the California battalion? and where are they now?

Answer. My impression is—

The president here announced that a member wished the court cleared; and he ordered the court cleared, which was done.

The court decided that the question shall be put.

The court was then opened; Lieutenant Colonel Frémont in court. The decision in closed session was announced.

Captain Gillespie, a witness, answered as follows:

I cannot answer positively as to the respective periods the gentlemen, named in the question, had been out; but my impression is that Mr. McLane had been out three years; Lieutenant Radford over four years, and Midshipman Wilson had been in the Pacific between six and seven years; I am not certain as to the exact period. Midshipman Wilson was very desirous to return to the United States, in consequence of his being entitled to his examination. Messrs. McLane and Wilson were officers of the California battalion; the former was on board of the Columbus when I left San Francisco, and is now probably on his way home. The latter was ordered on board of the Portsmouth sloop-of-war, and is, no doubt, cruising in the Pacific.

Question by Lieutenant Colonel Frémont. Were you on *special* service in California? and, on learning that fact, did Commodore Biddle take, or decline to take, control over you?

Answer. I was on special service in California; and, on learning that fact, Commodore Biddle said to me: "I have nothing to do with you; you can return to the United States when you please." This occurred when I arrived at Monterey; when I reported to him, in obedience to his orders. I do not recollect the precise day; it was in the last week in May; it was during my interview on the ship. This was at my first interview with him; not the interview afterwards, as referred to in my testimony, when he told me of the note he had received from General Kearny.

Question by Lieutenant Colonel Frémont. Have you any written orders in relation to the matters on which you have testified on this day, or on the last day of your examination? and if so, can you produce them to the court?

Answer. I received this order by the hands of Captain Turner, at the City of the Angels, on the 11th March, 1847.

Order read by the judge-advocate, as follows:

[Extract.]

ORDERS ⟩   HEAD-QUARTERS, 10TH MILITARY DEPARTMENT,
No. 2. ⟨   *Monterey, March 1st, 1847.*

II. Lieutenant Gillespie, of the marines, now serving with the battalion of California volunteers, is relieved from that duty. He will repair to Washington city, and report himself to the commanding officer of his corps.

By order of Brigadier General S. W. Kearny.

H. S. TURNER,
Captain and A. A. A. General.

I also received this order from Commodore Biddle, by the hands of Colonel Cooke, at the City of the Angels, about the 10th April; Colonel Mason having just arrived from Monterey.

Read, as follows:

U. S. SHIP COLUMBUS,
Monterey, March 31, 1847.

SIR: By direction of the Secretary of the Navy, I have assumed the command of the squadron in the Pacific.

Any appointment that you may hold for the performance of any duty on shore is hereby annulled; and you will, without delay, repair to this place and report yourself on board this ship.

Very respectfully, your most obedient servant,

JAMES BIDDLE.

Lieutenant A. H. GILLESPIE,
Marine Corps.

I also received this order from Commodore Biddle, by the hands of Lieutenant Sherman, acting aid to General Kearny, at the City of the Angels, about the 17th of May; I think General Kearny having just arrived from Monterey.

Read, as follows:

U. S. SHIP COLUMBUS,
Monterey, May 4, 1847.

SIR: Upon the receipt hereof, you will forthwith leave the Pueblo de los Angeles, repair to San Pedro, and report yourself to Lieutenant Commanding Bailey, for a passage to this place in the Lexington. On your arrival here report to me on board this ship.

Respectfully, your most obedient servant,

JAMES BIDDLE,
Commanding Pacific squadron.

Lieutenant A. H. GILLESPIE,
United States marine corps.

Question by Lieutenant Colonel Frémont. Do you know whether *La Ciudad de los Angeles* was the seat of government for California at the time that Governor Frémont succeeded Governor Stockton? and if so, how long had it been so?

Answer. It was the seat of government of California at the time referred to in the question; how long it had been so, I cannot say. I do not recollect at this moment; but it had been for a considerable time.

Question by Lieutenant Colonel Frémont. Do you know whether the public horses, in the use of the United States, over the territory of California, during the administration of Governor Frémont, were taken by order of General Kearny, and receipts for them refused; and whether the same did occur with respect to other public property? and what number of public horses might have been so taken? whether they did amount to a thousand?

The court was ordered to be cleared. The court decided that the question shall not be put. The court was then opened; Lieutenant Colonel Frémont in court. The decision in closed session was announced.

Lieutenant Colonel Frémont had no further questions to ask this witness.

Cross-examination by judge advocate.

Question. After your first interview with Commodore Biddle, when you came to Monterey in consequence of Commodore Biddle's orders to you, which you received at the City of the Angels, and when he, hearing from you, that you were in California on special duty, thereupon declined taking any control of you, all of which you have stated, did you then remain at Monterey till your second interview with him?

Answer. Yes. I was on board the Congress with Commodore Stockton.

Question. Where were you then going when you received orders from Commodore Biddle to remain at Monterey?

Answer. I was going to the Sacramento valley to make preparations for our departure for the overland journey.

Question. Did Commodore Biddle inform you, or do you know what was the object of his order to you to remain at Monterey till further orders?

Answer. Commodore Biddle did not inform me what his object was; but, telling me that he had received a note from General Kearny, the inference was that such was General Kearny's wish that I should be detained.

Question. Do you know whether it was intended to keep you from going to the Sacramento valley, or to prevent you from coming home?

Answer. It certainly was intended to prevent me from going to the Sacramento valley at that time; and it was generally understood that the object was to prevent me from going in advance of General Kearny to the Sacramento valley; which detention would delay my early arrival in the United States.

Question. Do you know whether General Kearny or Commodore Biddle had any knowledge of your wish and intention to come home when you received Commodore Biddle's order to remain at Monterey?

Answer. I cannot say positively as to General Kearny's knowing, although I am under the impression that I conversed with him on the subject when I called to pay my respects to him at the Angels. Commodore Biddle did know, as he had been spoken to on the subject by Commodore Stockton, and that I was to make all preparation for the journey home.

Question. Do you know whether General Kearny had any special object in view in wishing to prevent you from going to the Sacramento valley?

Answer. I cannot say positively; it is merely supposition.

Question. Do you know or believe that the intention of General Kearny was to prevent your going at that time to the Sacramento valley, and not to prevent your coming home?

Answer. I do believe that the intention was to prevent my going to the Sacramento valley; and this wish, taken in connexion with the difficulties in California, I have always supposed he desired to delay my preparations for the United States.

Question. Was there any way of your returning to the United States at that time, except in the party of General Kearny?

Answer. I never contemplated returning with General Kearny, but with Commodore Stockton.

Question. Could General Kearny, knowing that you did not mean to return with him, have known of your intentions to return at all at that time?

Answer. I suppose he did, it was a public thing that Commodore Stockton was coming, and it was public that night at Monterey, by my conversation with the officers, that I was coming home, and that I was to leave for the Sacramento next morning, the 1st of June.

The cross-examination was here suspended.

The testimony of to-day was read over to the witness.

Lieutenant Colonel Frémont wished to ask a further question; it was put as follows:

Question. Was the Sacramento valley the place where you made preparations for your return to the United States, and were you to make preparations also for Commodore Stockton in that valley? and did the delay of these preparations delay the departure of Commodore Stockton? and what was the extent of those preparations, in horses, mules, &c.?

Answer. At the time I received the order to remain in Monterey, it was my intention to make preparations for the overland journey of Commodore Stockton's party, which I commanded at Suter's fort, in the Sacramento valley; most certainly the delay of these preparations did delay the departure of Commodore Stockton. The extent of the preparations consisted in collecting animals; upwards of one hundred mules and horses, making pack saddles, and every thing necessary for an overland journey

The reading of the testimony taken to-day was completed, and then, at five minutes before three, the court adjourned to meet to-morrow, at 10 o'clock.

———

WEDNESDAY, *December* 15, 1847.—10 *o'clock.*

The court met pursuant to adjournment.
Present: All the members, the judge advocate, and Lieutenant Colonel Frémont.
Official notification being received from the office of the adjutant general of the promotion of Major E. W. Morgan, major of the 11th infantry, to be Lieutenant Colonel of the 13th infantry, and produced before the court, Lieutenant Colonel Morgan took his seat in the court according to his rank, that is to say, next below Lieutenant Colonel Craig.
The proceedings of yesterday were read over.

The cross-examination of Captain Gillespie resumed.

The judge advocate submitted the following note:
The court having admitted in proof of an attempt, on the part of General Kearny, to keep a witness from this trial, the fact that Commodore Biddle, by suggestion of General Kearny, ordered Captain Gillespie to remain at Monterey, the judge advocate, first objecting that it was impossible to get behind the official and public act, and discover the private and secret motive; and further, that out of all the infinite variety of official reasons which were applicable to such cases, and might have induced the action in this matter, of the commander of the Pacific squadron, and the governor of California, it was impossible by any legal or natural reason to select and infer the particular motive in regard to witnesses for this trial, except on the supposition and proof of a conspiracy between Commodore Biddle and General Kearny; then found himself put to the proof of a negative, to show that the motive suspected was not the motive which operated on Commodore Biddle and General Kearny; that General Kearny had no knowledge or reason to suppose that Captain Gillespie was coming home, and no knowledge that Commodore Stockton was coming home; but that he supposed Captain Gillespie was only going to the Sacramento valley, and that the order, for proper reasons, was intended to prevent him from going there.
These facts, however, appeared, from the cross-examination, not to be within the knowledge of Captain Gillespie. The judge advocate will, therefore, offer hereafter the testimony of General Kearny He will now attempt to show, by Captain Gillespie, that he had rented a house at the city of the Angels, for six

months; and afterwards, by other testimony, to show that General Kearny knew this, and that he supposed (however erroneously) Captain Gillespie was not going home, but was merely going to the Sacramento valley, and meant to return from that place to the City of the Angels.

The judge advocate offers this explanation to show the court the object of his present inquiry of the witness.

Lieutenant Colonel Frémont submitted the following note:

Mr. PRESIDENT: Lieutenant Colonel Frémont, by the advice of his counsel, submits, that the judge advocate is acting irregularly in reading to the court, at this time, anything in the way of reply to Major Gillespie's testimony, and that he should reserve such statements until he is ready to prove them, and the proper time has arrived for him to reintroduce General Kearny.

> J. C. FRÉMONT,
> *Lieutenant Colonel, mounted rifles.*

The judge advocate then said: "He had not replied to Captain Gillespie's testimony, or made any reflections upon it. His object was to explain why he was about to make an inquiry in relation to Captain Gillespie's house at the City of the Angels; which, if unexplained, and its bearing on this particular matter before the court not understood, might appear to be wholly irrelevant, and an improper inquiry into the private affairs of an officer. He submits to the court, whether his proceeding in this matter is irregular."

The court was then ordered to be cleared. Lieutenant Colonel Frémont submitted the following note:

Mr. PRESIDENT: The paper read by the judge advocate is evidently founded upon a conversation last night with General Kearny, and under the advice of his counsel, Lieutenant Colonel Frémont denies the right of the judge advocate to come into court with such statements to interrupt the progress of the testimony, and to weaken or break the force of the testimony which is in the course of delivery. Lieutenant Colonel Frémont is advised by his counsel to say that there will be a stage, in the further progress of this case, when Brigadier General Kearny can be regularly reintroduced as a witness; and until that time arrives, and until he is so introduced, and the right of cross-examination of him in open court again acquired, Lieutenant Colonel Frémont is advised by his counsel that what General Kearny may tell the judge advocate in the recess of this court is not to be repeated here.

> J. C. FRÉMONT,
> *Lieutenant Colonel, mounted rifles.*

The court was then cleared.

The judge advocate said in closed session, that the witness was now under cross-examination by the judge advocate, that if the progress of the testimony was interrupted, it was no interruption of the defence; that the judge advocate has the right, in his judgment, to explain to the court the relevancy of any testimony which he offers to introduce; that in this case it merely unmasks to the witness for the defence, and to the defence, the aim of the prosecution, and explains the bearing of the inquiry to the court.

The defence has ever been invited by the judge advocate, in open court, to pursue such course with their own witnesses when they are brought into court.

After mature deliberation the court decided that the papers be entered on record, and the examination of the witness be continued, as proposed by the judge advocate.

The court was then opened. Lieutenant Colonel Frémont in court. The proceedings in closed session were announced.

Captain Gillespie, a witness, on cross-examination by judge advocate.

Question. Had you, when you left the City of the Angels, hired a house there for some time to come; and if so, how long; and do you know whether such facts was known to General Kearny and Commodore Biddle?

Answer. Previous to my leaving the City of the Angels, the term for which I had rented quarters for myself and for the officers, who lived with me, had expired. To secure them for a longer period, it became necessary for me to rent them for six months. I do not know that such fact was known to General Kearny, but it was certainly known to Commodore Biddle, for he told me that I had a house at the Pueblo, and my impression is that Commodore Biddle received his information from General Kearny and Colonel Cooke.

Question. You have stated, in your examination in chief, that the state of the country made the road from Los Angeles to Monterey unsafe for travelling, and that several passengers had been wounded; at what time did this happen, and during what time was the road unsafe?

Answer. I think the first rumor of the approach of a Mexican force, under General Bustamente, to assist the Californians, was in the middle of February; this rumor created a very great excitement throughout the country. The Californians had already become quite bold. The excitement continued to increase, almost daily, until Commodore Stockton went south of San Diego, in the month of April, to look after the supposed approaching force. During all this time, the roads were unsafe in all parts of the country south of Monterey; and it was necessary for persons to go armed and in parties, not only to protect themselves from the Californians, but from the aggressions of the Indians.

Question. Do you know whether the road was, during the whole time, regularly travelled by the mail carriers, and whether it was travelled by Colonel Frémont and Colonel Mason and Captain Turner at different times, each without any armed escort?

Answer. As regards the mail carriers, they travelled it part of the time; I cannot say they travelled it all the time.

Captain Turner, in this time, also arrived at the Ciudad de los Angeles; I do not know what party he had. Colonel Mason came to the Angeles by sea; that is, to San Pedro, 27 miles from Los Angeles; and on his return, I was informed, took with him an armed escort of men he had hired at the Pueblo for that purpose. Colonel Frémont also travelled the road with a small party of two or three; but performing his journey with extraordinary despatch, could not afford an opportunity for either Californians or Indians to attack him. Colonel Frémont travelled the road twice; the second time, I think, he had a party.

The cross-examination here closed. The judge advocate submitted a note in regard to the cross-examination of Captain Gillespie, about the quarters at San Diego, occupied by Mr. Russell.

Lieutenant Colonel Frémont presented a written objection to the reception of such paper from the judge advocate.

The court was cleared. The court decided that, as the note of the judge advocate has the effect to open discussion on a collateral matter, the court directs that it be not placed on record, nor the reply of the accused thereto.

The court was then opened. Lieutenant Colonel Frémont in court. The decision in closed session was announced.

Captain Gillespie, a witness.—Examination by the court.

Question by the court. Could you have left California for the United States sooner than you did, if General Kearny had not interfered, as you suppose?

Answer. Yes I could.

Question by the court. Do you know any circumstances inducing you to believe that General Kearny endeavored to prevent yourself, or Midshipmen McLane and Wilson, appearing as witnesses before a court that might be ordered for the trial of Lieutenant Colonel Frémont?

Answer. I do not know of any circumstances; but I believe, and have always supposed, that my detention had reference to the difficulties that existed in California. I know of nothing relative to Messrs. Wilson and McLane being detained from attending on this court.

Question by Lieutenant Colonel Frémont. Will you please to explain to the court the course of travelling, to get from Monterey to the United States, by the route on which the parties of Governor Stockton and General Kearny travelled? and whether said route brought the parties through the Sacramento valley?

Answer. To arrive at the Sacramento valley, Commodore Stockton and General Kearny took different roads; the former, by way of Sonoma and *Napa* valley; the latter, as I have been informed, crossed the river San Joaquim; both roads brought the parties to Sacramento valley.

The Sacramento valley is the starting point for all parties leaving the northern part of California for the United States. It is about 350 miles from Monterey.

Question by the court. You speak of the difficulties existing in California; what difficulties do you allude to?

Answer. I had reference to the difficulties existing between Commodore Stockton and General Kearny, as also to matters connected with Colonel Frémont.

The examination of the witness was here concluded, and he retired, but was not discharged.

Lieutenant Colonel Frémont presented the following note:

Mr. President: Lieutenant Colonel Frémont has to ask, that the judge advocate be instructed to inform Commodore Stockton that he will be further wanted as a witness, and that he will be notified hereafter of the *time* at which he will be wanted. Also, that Joseph B. Childs, of California, now at Mrs. Peyton's in this City, be summoned for the defence.

J. C. FRÉMONT,
Lieutenant Colonel, mounted rifles.

Which the court ordered accordingly.

Theodore Talbot, a lieutenant in the first regiment United States artillery, a witness for the defence, was then duly sworn by the judge advocate according to law, and testified, as follows:

Examined by Lieutenant Colonel Frémont.

Question. Did you arrive at Los Angeles, in January last, as an officer in the California battalion? and if so, in what rank?

Answer. I did; I was the adjutant of the battalion; it was about the 13th of January.

Question. Did you copy a certain letter for Lieutenant Colonel Frémont, on the 17th of January last? and if so, can you identify that letter, and tell what you did with it?

Answer. Lieutenant Colonel Frémont handed me a letter in his own hand writing, which he asked me to copy; it was his letter to General Kearny, of January 17, 1847, and is in one of the specifications against Lieutenant Colonel Frémont.

The letter was here shown the witness, in the charges. He said: It is the letter in the first specification to the first charge. The letter was read to the court. The witness continued: Lieutenant Colonel Frémont then left me to go to General Kearny's quarters, desiring me as soon as I had copied the letter to send it to him, by Mr. Carson. I copied the letter, and gave it to Mr. Carson to carry.

Question. Did Mr. Carson go off with the letter? and do you know where he is now?

Answer. Mr. Carson started with the letter from Colonel Frémont's quarters. I believe that he is now on his way to California.

The defence had no further questions to ask the witness. The judge advocate and the court had no questions to ask him.

The testimony of the witness was then read over to him.

Lieutenant Talbott was then discharged from further attendance as a witness on this court.

George W. Hanly, a witness for the defence, was duly sworn by the judge advocate according to law, and then testified as follows:

Examined by Lieutenant Colonel Frémont.

Question. Were you at San Diego, in California, in December, 1846? and, if so, did you accompany Governor Stockton a part of the way on the march to Los Angeles? and what order, if any, did you receive from Governor Stockton with respect to Lieutenant Colonel Frémont? and what did you do in consequence?

Answer. I was in California. I accompanied Governor Stockton as far as San Luis Rey. I was bearer of despatches from Commodore Stockton to Colonel Frémont. I embarked at San Diego on the brig Malek Adhel, and landed at San Buena Ventura; I landed there then on the evening of the 8th of January, and found Colonel Frémont on the morning of the 9th.

Question. Will you tell where you found Lieutenant Colonel Frémont? and how you got to him? and whether you delivered Commodore Stockton's despatches?

Answer. I found him at the camp of the Willows. I had three horses, and hired an Indian as a guide; a gentleman accompanied me, named Pedro Carillo. I did deliver Commodore Stockton's despatches on the morning of the 9th of January.

This was to the north of the pass of San Fernando.

Question. Will you please to tell whether you did not pass through a detachment of the enemy in the night, to deliver your despatches?

Answer. Between twelve and one o'clock at night I passed the enemy's camp of from sixty to one hundred men, supposed to be; I was told so by one who was with me.

Question. Was that in the rear of Lieutenant Colonel Frémont?

Answer. It was.

The defence had no further questions.

The judge advocate had no questions to ask. The court had none?

The testimony was then read over to the witness. The witness was then discharged from further attendance on this court.

The court then adjourned, four minutes before three, to meet to-morrow at 10 o'clock.

THURSDAY, *December* 16, 1847.—10 *o'clock.*

The court met pursuant to adjournment.

Present: All the members, the judge, advocate and Lieutenant Colonel Frémont.

The proceedings of yesterday were read over. The following note was received from Lieutenant Colonel Frémont:

MR. PRESIDENT: In relation to the proposition of the judge advocate to make statements preparatory to the examination of witnesses, Lieutenant Colonel Frémont deems it best to adhere to the rule of law in the admission of testimony. The proposition would work well in some cases, and ill in others; and Lieutenant Colonel Frémont thinks better to go on as heretofore, stating the object of the testimony, and its substance when objected to, and let each case depend upon its own circumstances.

J. C. FRÉMONT,
Lieut. Col., mounted rifles.

On motion of a member, the court was ordered to be cleared.

An article in the Baltimore Sun newspaper, purporting to be a report of proceedings in this court, was brought to the notice of the court by a member.

Whereupon, after deliberation, the court ordered: That the reporter of the Baltimore Sun be excluded from the court room for an improper and false report, purporting to be a part of the proceedings of this court on the 11th instant, published in the Sun of the 13th instant, which report is in these words: " Major Graham. Was the order a written order? (much merriment.) Several members of the court and judge advocate, no, no; a written order on the field of battle, and in the midst of an action!"

The court was then opened. Lieutenant Colonel Frémont in court. The proceedings in closed session were announced.

Major Graham said to the president that he believed the reporter of the paper, alluded to in the order of the court, was seated at the head of a table in the court. The president enquired of the person indicated if he was the reporter of the Sun? He replied in the affirmative, but stated that he was reporter for other papers besides the Sun newspaper.

The president stated the order of the court excluded him, and he retired from the court room accordingly.

Mr. Samuel J. Hensley, a witness for the defence, was then duly sworn by the judge advocate, according to law, and testified as follows:

Examined by Lieutenant Colonel Frémont.

Question. Were you an officer in the California battalion; and if so, of what rank; and are you an inhabitant of California; and if so, how long have you resided there?

Answer. I was an officer in the California battalion, a lieutenant of company C, at the time the battalion was organized at Monterey. I arrived in California on the first of November, 1843, and I was a resident of California, and made it my home till I left with Commodore Stockton.

Question. Were you in the march of the American forces from San Diego to Los Angeles in the latter part of December, 1846, and beginning of January following; and if so, did you observe Governor Stockton exercising the authority of commander-in-chief on that march; and if so, by what acts?

Answer. I was in that march, and recognized Commodore Stockton as the commander-in chief. In his general order for the march, he signed himself commander-in-chief. I met Commodore Stockton in the square at San Diego, and he requested me to select seven or eight riflemen as his body guard, to act as spies during the march, where the face of the country should require it. Mr. Christopher Carson was to have command of it.

Question. What rank did you have in the expedition?

Answer. Captain in the California battalion, company B, mounted riflemen.

Question. Did you see Mr. Christopher Carson at Los Angeles on the 17th of January; and if so, in what part of the town; and what passed between you?

The judge advocate did not see the relevancy of the question.

Lieutenant Colonel Frémont said, to explain would be to point his own witness to the answer.

The judge advocate had no objection that the witness should be directed to the object of the question.

Lieutenant Colonel Frémont said, it was to ascertain from the witness whether he met Mr. Carson coming from General Kearney's quarters.

Answer. My company was stationed on the hill, overlooking the town; and on or about that day (I am not able to say positively the day) Mr. Carson came to my tent; I asked him the news down in town, and if there was any prospect of company B being moved down. He told me he could not say, he had just returned from General Kearny's quarters, from taking a letter from Lieutenant Colonel Frémont, but he did not know if it related to moving the company or not.

The judge advocate said he had no special objection what Mr. Carson said, but the rule of evidence and the rule of this court, expressed on its record, prohibited hearsay evidence.

He requested the court to be cleared. The president, after some remarks, ordered the court cleared.

Lieutenant Colonel Frémont requested to submit a note to the court, which the president assented to:

Lieutenant Colonel Frémont read the following note:

Mr. PRESIDENT: Lieutenant Colonel Frémont is instructed by his counsel to say that the main fact at this point being proved, to wit: that Mr. Carson was sent by Lieutenant Talbott to carry the letter from Lieutenant Colonel Frémont to General Kearny, and the fact of Mr. Carson's present absence in California having been proved, it becomes consistent with the rules of evidence to let in inferior evidence, not good in itself, but corroborative of the main fact, and to justify the inference that the letter sent by Mr. Carson was actually delivered, and at General Kearny's quarters. And that such hearsay as this, thus given in corroboration of the legal proof, and heard at a time when there was no motive to say an untruth, and not even a suspicion of any trial or question, in which it could ever be used, is taken out of the general rule of hearsay evidence. The general rule is to prevent hearsay from being used as evidence to establish or prove a fact, but not to prevent it from being adduced to corroborate what is already sworn to, or to justify an inference fairly inferrable from a fact or circumstance already sworn to.

J. C. FRÉMONT,
Lieutenant Cotonel, mounted rifles.

After mature deliberation, the court decided that, if the object of the testimony is to draw an inference of the actual delivery of the letter to General Kearny, and at his own quarters, as stated in the paper of the accused, it is unnecessary, as the fact is proved by General Kearny, and appears not to be controverted. If the object is to prove the delivery by Mr. Carson, the testimony offered is inadmissible as hearsay, and as going to contradict, on a collateral point, the answer of a witness elicited by their own cross-examination.

The court was then opened; Lieutenant Colonel Frémont in court. The decision in closed session was announced.

Mr. Hensley, a witness.—Examination in chief by the defence continued.

Question. Did Mr. Christopher Carson command the scouts on the way from San Diego to Los Angeles; and did you see him often; and was he often in view of General Kearny, or in communication with him?

Answer. He did command the scouts; he was in advance of me; I presume General Kearny saw him very often, as I did; he often returned with messages from ahead, which brought him before the command.

Question. Do you know the state of the country in point of domestic tranquillity and general safety for travelling, before and after the promulgation of General Kearny's proclamation of March first? and if so, will you please to state it?

Answer. The country appeared perfectly tranquil after we arrived in the Angels, which was about the 11th of January. From that time until the last of March, when there was some excitement in the country, when it was considered unsafe for travelling. There was excitement about the Mormons coming into the country then, and, afterwards, by the reports of the approach of Bustamenta with a large force.

Question. Did Governor Frémont reside without military protection in Los Angeles before the arival of the Mormons?

Answer. His force was at the mission of San Gabriel, about three leagues or nine miles from Los Angeles; none of his force, except some of the officers, lived in the Pueblo.

Question. Do you know at what time the rumor of the approach of General Bustamenta first reached Los Angeles, and what was the effect of that rumor upon the tranquillity of the country?

Answer. That rumor was in the last days of March, as well as I recollect. It created such an excitement that I was told there were several armed parties of Californians seen through the country.

One, I understood, entered the town. But I did not see any of them. There was a rumor arrived from Lower California that they were landing some arms and ammunition. Colonel Cooke came to my quarters, and I explained to him all I had heard in regard to it.

Question. Was any outbreak or insurrection expected?

Answer. There was; we were daily expecting an outbreak.

Question. Do you know of any intention of Governor Frémont to go to Monterey in the month of April; and if so, was yourself or Major Reading to go with him; and what was the opinion of Major Reading as to the safety or danger of that journey?

Answer. He spoke of going up at that time; Major Reading and myself expected to accompany him on account of the report and rumors of an outbreak. Major Reading came to me and was unwilling to go, and asked me to dissuade Colonel Frémont.

Question. Do you know of any persons attacked on the road about that time and driven back; and if so, who?

Answer. There was a Mr. Fisher attacked at Cowenga; he was a member of the California battalion; about 12 miles from Los Angeles, and wounded by the Indians, and had to return. There were several other parties attacked on the road further up the country. I saw men who said they were attacked; I saw one man who was wounded.

Question. Do you know, or have you heard, and believe that any men of the discharged California battalion were attacked on their way to Monterey, or beyond?

Answer. I was not with any party that was attacked. I had the word of Captain Swift and private Harber.

Question. What effect did the approach of the Mormons cause at Los Angeles? and what were the feelings of the people towards the Mormons?

Answer. The native Californians were very much opposed to them; had a great dread of them; and offered, if the volunteers would remain neutral, that they would hoist the American flag, and whip them out of the country; they said the people in the United States were fighting them, and they had a right to do so too.

Question. Did you go to the south to procure horses for Governor Stockton, before the arrival of General Kearny? and if so, do you know what they were for?

Answer. I was sent from San Diego, on the last of November, to Lower California with company B, to procure horses, mules, and working bullocks. I was sent down by water in the ship Stonington, and ordered to get as many as I could for the march on Los Angeles; I returned on the 23d or 24th of December with 140 head of horses and mules, and about 300 head of cattle.

Question. At what time did you leave California for the United States? and in what party?

Answer. I left the valley of the Sacramento on the 19th day of July, 1847, in Commodore Stockton's party.

Question. Did you see on the road any of the officers belonging

to the topographical party under Governor Frémont? If so, who
were they?

Answer. I saw Mr. King and Mr. Kerne, on Bear river, in the
Sacramento valley; they were there waiting for Commodore Stockton's party to cross the mountains.

They followed after Lieutenant Colonel Frémont's party in the
rear, and not overtaking them, waited for Commodore Stockton.

The judge advocate said: He did not see the relevancy of the
testimony, but would record it if not objected to by the court.

The witness continued his testimony:

I went with them to that place, finding they were too late to
overtake Lieutenant Colonel Frémont. Mr. Kerne returned with
me to Napa valley, and obtained permission from Captain Gillespie
to cross the mountains in Commodore Stockton's party. They
travelled with us four days in the mountains and there stopped on
account of sickness; I have not heard from them since.

The testimony of the witness was read over to him. He then
said: The general orders I spoke of were brought to me by Lieutenant Minor, who read them to me as being Commodore Stockton's general orders, issued against the Pueblo, and explained
them to me as from him as commander-in-chief.

Lieutenant Colonel Frémont presented the following note:

Mr. PRESIDENT: Lieutenant Colonel Frémont asks that a copy
of the minutes of this trial, as far as it has gone, may be delivered to him by the judge advocate.

J. C. FRÉMONT,
Lieutenant Colonel, mounted rifles.

The court was then cleared. After some time in closed session,
the court was opened; Lieutenant Colonel Frémont in court.

The court then adjourned, at four minutes before 3, to meet
to-morrow, at 10 o'clock.

FRIDAY, *December* 17, 1847.—10 *o'clock.*

The court met pursuant to adjournment.

Present: all the members and the judge advocate.

The record of yesterday was then read over: Lieutenant Colonel
Frémont appeared in court during the reading.

The court was then cleared, to consider the application made
by Lieutenant Colonel Frémont, before the adjournment of yesterday, to be furnished a copy of "the minutes of this trial;" and
the court decided that the court has no means of making, or procuring to be made, a copy of its voluminous record; nor does the
court deem it proper that its record, by copy or otherwise, go
beyond its own keeping. The court cannot authorize any du-
plication of its minutes. The judge advocate will, as he has here-

tofore done, furnish the accused with copies of all interlocutory decisions.

The court was then opened; Lieutenant Colonel Frémont in court. The decision in closed session was announced.

Mr. Hensley, a witness for the defence :

The judge advocate had no questions to ask the witness; the court had no question to ask him. Mr. Hensley then retired; but, at the request of Lieutenant Colonel Frémont, was not discharged.

Lieutenant Colonel Frémont read the following note to the court:

Mr. PRESIDENT: Lieutenant Colonel Frémont has an application to make, and an argument to read in support of it, in relation to the question offered when Major Gillespie was last before the court, and which was not allowed to be put. It was the question in relation to the public horses, &c., and the application now is to put the substance of what Major Gillespie's answer would have been, as he (Lieutenant Colonel Frémont) is informed and believes, if it had been put. If necessary, this *substance* of his answer can be verified by affidavit.

J. C. FRÉMONT,
Lieutenant Colonel, mounted rifles.

The court was then cleared. On motion the court decided to reconsider its decision rejecting the testimony in question, and to hear the argument which Lieutenant Colonel Frémont wishes to offer in support of the admissibility of the testimony.

The court was then opened. Lieutenant Colonel Frémont in court. The decision in closed session was announced.

Lieutenant Colonel Frémont read a paper to the court; during which he commenced reading what appeared a statement from Captain Gillespie.

A member objecting, the court was cleared.

The court decided that it will hear Lieutenant Colonel Frémont's argument to show the admissibility of the testimony offered, in accordance with its last decision, and that he may state the character and effect of the testimony which he offers; but not offer a written statement or affidavit from the witness, in advance of the decision of the court.

The court was then opened. Lieutenant Colonel Frémont in court. The decision in closed session was announced.

Lieutenant Colonel Frémont finished reading, and submitted to the court the following paper:

Mr. PRESIDENT: Lieutenant Colonel Frémont is instructed by his counsel to say, that the proceedings of a general court martial are analagous to those of courts of law in this, that they are subject to revision and reversal before a superior tribunal, and, therefore, should show upon the face of the record everything which is necessary to enable the superior tribunal to judge correctly of the proceedings. The President of the United States is that superior tribunal; and one of the most material enquiries is to judge whether evidence has been improperly either admitted, or rejected, by the court; and to enable him to form such judgment, Lieutenant Colonel Frémont is advised that the substance of the evidence, when suggested by the party offering it, to have been improperly rejected, should be spread upon the records of the court; and he refers to the opinion of the then Attorney General of the United States, Mr. Wirt, (quoted as law by De Hart, in his treatise on courts martial, p. 206,) in support of the views of his counsel, now presented to the court.

The following is the opinion of Mr. Wirt:

"In the case of Captain Nathan H. Hale, who was tried by a general court martial at Plattsburg, N. Y., on the 5th June, 1818, there was an appeal made by the prisoner to the President, on the ground that the court had refused to receive certain evidence, which was both legal and material to the defence. Upon the question which then arose, as to the power to grant a new trial, the Attorney General (Mr. Wirt) said: 'The President of the United States had the power to order a new trial for the benefit of the prisoner; and such power was derived from the language of the 65th article of war, of the act of Congress of April 10, 1806, which says that, in certain cases, the proceedings are to be laid before him, for his confirmation or disapproval, and *orders in the case;* the last words having no other just interpretation than the acknowledgment of such authority.' In revising a sentence, and ordering a new trial, he is, however, to be governed by the same considerations which would determine a superior court of law, in an appeal from the inferior civil courts.'"

Lieutenant Colonel Frémont is further instructed by his counsel to say, that the rules and articles of war for the army of the United States, being founded on those of Great Britain, and mainly copied from them, the construction of the British rules and articles, and the practice under them, is good evidence of what should be the construction and practice under those of the United States; and that, in the points now presented to the court, the British practice is the same as expressed in Mr. Wirt's opinion; the King of Great Britain being the reviewer and the ultimate judge of the court's proceedings.

Major James, author of so many valuable military works, expressly lays down the law to this effect, in his introduction to his large collection of court martial cases, published in 1820, and comprehending the charges, opinions, and sentences of general courts martial, and the action of the revising authority upon them, from 1795 to that time, being twenty-five years of the most illustrious service of arms, in the most enlightened period of the world. In that introduction he says:

"After each charge has been thoroughly investigated, before a body of honorable men, and the nature and complexion of the offence sifted to the bottom, the matured and well digested result is submitted to the consideration and final approval or disapproval of the KING, as the acknowledged head of the army, the source of its rules and regulations, and its ultimate resort."

That this review by the king is not a matter of form, but of great substance, requiring a full view of all the proceedings of the court, and of the conduct of all parties, (the accused, the prosecutor, and the witnesses,) is shown in the sentence immediately preceding the one quoted: " Even the fate of a prosecutor, or witness, who may have travelled out of the province of fair accusation or candid testimony, into frivolous and vexatious matter, or been actuated by vindictive motives, is brought before the discriminating and just eye of the sovereign, and dealt with accordingly."

And to give a practical illustration of this full examination of the whole case by the sovereign, and especially of the decisions of the court, in rejecting proper evidence, and in not adhering to the rules of evidence, as regarded by courts of law, he (Major James) gives, in the margin of the same introduction, the following letter from Lord Erskine, in the year 1820; then in all the ripeness of his intellect, and in all the fullness of his fame:

No. 4, UPPER BERKLY STREET, *May* 9, 1820.

DEAR SIR: I am favored with your letter. The cases of Colonel Stratford and of one of the mutineers who was tried with others at Portsmouth, many years ago, involve a principle highly important to the security of military men, viz: *That courts martial should respect the rules of evidence as they are regarded by courts of law.*

I do not remember the circumstances of Colonel Stratford's case, further (which is all that is necessary) than that evidence had either been *received* by the court martial which a court of law would have *rejected,* or that the court martial had *rejected* evidence which a court of law would have *received.*

The facts were laid before me soon after the trial; I wrote an opinion that the sentence ought NOT to be carried into execution; and I believe that by his late Majesty it was afterwards annulled.

The case of one of the mutineers at Portsmouth I remember more distinctly. He was tried with others, and as it was likely that against one of them who knew the innocence of the person in question no evidence could be given, I advised the attorney who was employed by him, if that turned out to be so, to apply to the court, on the authority of my opinion, to direct such person to be acquitted, and then permit him to establish by his evidence, the innocence of the man in question. This application being accordingly made, the court declared itself to be satisfied that the course proposed was agreeable to the practice of the courts of criminal law, but not of courts martial; they therefore *refused* to adopt it, and having no other defence, he was sentenced to be executed. Being then on a visit to the Isle of Wight, and the attorney from Spithead having communicated to me this decision, I despatched him immediately to Weymouth, with a representation to the late *king,* in which I humbly suggested to his Majesty, that the court martial ought to have *conformed to the rule established* in the *common law courts*, and implored the *king*, in the name of the unhappy man who had been unfortunately convicted, to respite the execution, and to submit his case to the twelve judges for their decision on it.

His Majesty, with his usual humanity and enlightened attention to the demands of justice, instantly sent back the attorney with the respite prayed; and the judges having decided unanimously that the conviction was *unwarranted*, the man was set at liberty.

There can be no doubt, that neither in this case, nor in any other of a similar description, could there have been an appeal to any of the courts of justice. It belongs to the *king alone* to abrogate or confirm the sentence of courts martial; but the judgment of his late Majesty, so remarkable during his long reign for his faithful and enlightened administration of justice, ought to be received as a *precedent* hereafter; and I feel great pleasure, therefore, in making this communication, being deeply interested in everything which concerns the noble profession of my earliest youth.

I have the honor to be, dear sir, your faithful, humble servant,

ERSKINE.

Major JAMES.

To this high authority of Lord Erskine and the twelve judges in England, is to be added that of Major Hough, in his treatise on the law martial, (edition of 1825, p. 371,) where he expressly lays it down that in court martial trials no material deviation from the rules of proceeding in courts of law is to be permitted, except expressly warranted by the military code.

His words are:

"For it is to be observed, that in *all* matters touching the trial of crimes by courts martial, wherever the *military law is silent*, the rules of the *common* law of the land, to the benefit of which all *British* subjects are entitled for the protection of *life* and *liberty*, must of necessity be resorted to; and every material deviation from these rules, unless *warranted* by some *express* enactment of the military code, is, in fact, a punishable offence in the members of a court martial, who may be indicted for the same in the king's ordinary courts."

Lieutenant Colonel Frémont is instructed by his counsel to claim the benefit of the principle here laid down by Lord Erskine, the twelve judges in England, Major James De Hart, and Major Hough; and to ask that the following statement, showing what answer to the question in relation to some one thousand horses taken from Governor Frémont without receipt, and for which he is accountable, and for the payment of a great part of which he is now responsible, would have been, if the question had been allowed by the court to have been put to Major Gillespie.

Lieutenant Colonel Frémont is further instructed by his counsel to say, that in courts of law the party offering testimony, or making any motion, has a *legal right* to be heard in support of his offer, or motion, and also a *legal right* to be heard in answer to *all* objections to such offer or motion, before it can be decided against him. And this being the rule of proceeding in courts of law, he (Lieutenant Colonel Frémont) is advised to say, upon the authority of Lord Erskine, the twelve judges in England, Mr. Wirt, De Hart, Major Hough, and many other writers on the law martial, that the same rule is of lawful obligation in courts martial, and that he cannot legally be deprived of its benefit without his consent.

In conclusion, Lieutenant Colonel Frémont is instructed to say to the court, that the second section of the act of May 29th, 1830, having been passed twelve years after Mr. Attorney General Wirt had placed his strong construction on the words "*orders in the case*," and which act was specially passed to meet the present case, (that of a commanding general becoming the accuser and prosecutor of an officer under his command,) and still repeating the same words on which the Attorney General had founded his opinion as quoted by De Hart, may be considered as a legislative confirmation of his opinion; and that, consequently, the President of the United States is now the supreme court of error and appeals from the decisions and proceedings of all general courts martial, and will take notice of the said errors as they appear upon the record, without any assignment of errors, or writ of errors, or formality of appeal, and is, therefore, entitled to have a full view of every fact which is necessary to enable him to judge the correctness of the court's decisions and proceedings in every particular.

The question to Major Gillespie in relation to the thousand horses, was the first in a series of questions intended to be put to other witnesses in relation to the facts, and the manner of taking the horses, and other circumstances connected with the taking, or resulting from it, which Lieutenant Colonel Frémont would have been ready to explain to the court, (to show their object and relevancy,) if the main question, on which they depended, had been allowed to be put; and he is advised by his counsel that, all the testimony expected to be obtained by said questions is both material and relevant to his defence, and to that branch of it which impeaches the motives of Brigadier General Kearny as a prosecutor, and his credit as a witness, in the case before the court.

To avoid all room for misconstruction of his motives in submitting this paper to the court, Lieutenant Colonel Frémont now declares that his only object is *to obtain the benefit of full evidence as the trial goes along*, and not with any view to the future action of the revising power; and he hereby pledges himself, in no event, to ask, or to permit any person, with his consent, to ask any action whatsoever from the revising power over the proceedings and decisions of this court

J. C. FRÉMONT,
Lieutenant Colonel, mounted rifles.

The court was then cleared.
After mature deliberation, the court decided that it has recognized the general principles claimed by the accused in his note,

that courts martial are governed by the rules of law; and that the law of evidence, as established in the common law courts, governs courts martial; and the court has recognized further, that the record of a court martial should exhibit to the reviewing authority the character of the testimony rejected, as well as the testimony received. Ordinarily, the testimony rejected is indicated by the question which stands on the record. Where the question is not sufficiently explanatory of the testimony, the court receives explanations from the party offering it, which goes upon the record and shows its character.

The court does not find any different explanation in the paper just submitted by Lieutenant Colonel Frémont to show the admissibility of the testimony about the horses. Lieutenant Colonel Frémont merely states that he considers it material and relevant, and going to impeach the credit and motives of the prosecuting witness. The court will, however, now hear from the accused an explanation of the scope and bearing of the testimony proposed to be elicited by the series of questions to which this is to lead.

The court has admitted the right of the accused to be heard in explanation of proposed questions by entering it on its record as a rule of its proceedings.

The court was then opened. Lieutenant Colonel Frémont in court.

The decision in closed session was announced Lieutenant Colonel Frémont read to the court the following note:

Mr. PRESIDENT: Lieutenant Colonel Frémont will give the substance of what he expects to prove by each witness as each is produced before the court. The first one would be Major Gillespie, and his statement would be more general and comprehensive than that of other witnesses; but a proper introduction to their testimony, which would be more special and pointed than his, and going beyond his testimony in many points deemed material by the counsel of Lieutenant Colonel Frémont. That, by Major Gillespie, he expects to prove the general facts, that a great number of mules and horses, say 1,000, were taken from the possession of Lieutenant Colonel Frémont without receipts, for which Lieutenant Colonel Frémont is accountable, and many unpaid for, for which he is liable to be made responsible; that, after the capitulation of Cowenga, the horses and mules belonging to the government were ordered to be collected at different points and held subject to the orders of a United States officer, it being understood that receipts would be given, in the event of any animals being taken; that horses and mules were so taken from the possession of General Vallego, to whom the custody of them was confided; also, from Lieutenant Kerne, at Suter's fort. That many were taken from other places, and all without receipts or reference to Lieutenant Colonel Frémont, then the governor and commander in California, under the appointment of Governor Stockton, and according to the laws of nations; and Lieutenant Colonel Frémont wishes to prove the taking those horses from him in the manner aforesaid, as evidences and proofs of the *temper* in which General Kearny acted towards him, and of the indignities, outrages, and illegalities practised upon him by General Kearny, and to be used for what they are worth when Lieutenant Colonel Frémont comes to make his general defence.

J. C. FRÉMONT,
Lieutenant Colonel, mounted rifles.

Whereupon, the court was cleared; and the court decided that the question be put.

The court was then opened. Lieutenant Colonel Frémont in court. The decision in closed session was announced.

The court then at ten minutes before three, adjourned to meet tomorrow, at 10 o'clock.

SATURDAY, *December* 18, 1847.—10 *o'clock.*

The court met pursuant to adjournment.

Present: All the members, the judge advocate, and Lieutenant Colonel Frémont.

The proceedings of yesterday were read over. At the request of a member, the court was cleared. After deliberation in close session, the court was opened. Lieutenant Colonel Frémont in court.

Lieutenant Colonel Frémont read the following note:

MR. PRESIDENT: Lieutenant Colonel Frémont asks that Lieutenant Radford, of the United States navy, now in this city, may be summoned as a witness for the defence; also, that Major Swords, of the army, and Captain Turner, of the army, be notified that their further attendance before this court will be required.

J. C. FRÉMONT,
Lieutenant Colonel, mounted rifles.

George Minor, a lieutenant of the navy of the United States, a witness for the defence, being duly sworn according to law, by the judge advocate, testified as follows:

Examination in chief by Lieutenant Colonel Fremont.

Question. Please to state whether you were at San Diego, in California, at the time General Kearny arrived there, and what you know, if any thing, about the command in chief of the troops from that place to Los Angeles?

Answer. At the time General Kearny arrived at San Diego, I was commanding officer of the United States forces at that place. The command was subsequently turned over to Lieutenant Rowan, of the navy, who was my senior officer. On the morning of the 29th of December, 1846, it was given to General Kearny; Commodore Stockton called together the staff officers, and told them that

General Kearny had kindly consented to take command of the expedition then about marching against the Angeles, and that we would obey and respect him as such. But I will accompany the expedition as commander-in-chief, I think were his words.

On the March, I frequently received orders from General Kearny, and also from Commodore Stockton. I believe that covers the question.

Question. Do you know whether General Kearny solicited a place from Governor Stockton in the expedition to Los Angeles?

Answer. I called upon General Kearny, in company with Commodore Stockton and a number of other officers, for the purpose of paying our respects; the Commodore remarked, in the course of conversation, that he had a gallant body of men, which he would be pleased to have the general to command, as he knew more about land fighting than he did; that he (Commodore Stockton) would accompany him (General Kearny) as his aid. General Kearny declined, and said that he would go as aid to the commodore. To the best of my recollection that is the conversation.

On the morning of the 29th of December, I saw General Kearny come from his quarters and go to the commodore; then the commodore called us together as I have stated.

Question. Do you remember whether the words of Commodore Stockton, in relation to reserving the chief command, were delivered in a low or an emphatic tone?

Answer. In an emphatic tone.

Question. Was that a long time or a short time before the march began?

Answer. A short time. To the best of my recollection not more than half an hour.

Question. Was it before or after the offer to serve as aid?

Answer. After; some days after.

Question. Do you know whether the approach of the Mormons excited discontent or disturbance in the country?

Answer. It caused great alarm among the Californians; at least it did in my district. I was governor of San Diego by appointment of Governor Stockton.

Lieutenant Colonel Frémont presented the following note:

MR. PRESIDENT: Lieutenant Colonel Frémont desires to say that Lieutenant Minor, of the United States navy, was summoned as a witness, in this trial, at a time when the arrival of Commodore Stockton was uncertain, and that the full testimony of the commodore has rendered unnecessary the further examination of Lieutenant Minor on his part.

J. C. FRÉMONT,
Lieutenant Colonel, mounted rifles.

The judge advocate had no questions to ask Lieutenant Minor.

The court was cleared to consider whether the court had any question to put to the witness. The court was then opened. Lieutenant Colonel Frémont in court.

Lieutenant Minor, a witness for the defence.

Question, by the court. You say the approach of the Mormons caused a great alarm among the Californians in your district; what was apprehended by the Californians? and why?

Answer. Report had preceded them to California, that they were a lawless and abandoned set, and Californians are easily alarmed at any reports. I allude to the whole tribe of Mormons; not to Colonel Cooke's command. A family that had seceded from that religion threw themselves on my protection, and I assigned them quarters near San Diego. When they heard of the approach of the Mormon battalion, they became alarmed and wished me to put them in greater security; they wished me to put them on board a ship, which I declined doing.

The testimony of the witness was then read over to him.

Lieutenant Minor was then permitted to retire; but, at the request of Lieutenant Colonel Frémont, was not discharged.

William W. Russell, a witness for the defence, was then duly sworn according to law, by the judge advocate, and testified, as follows:

Examination in chief, by Lieutenant Colonel Fremont.

Question. Were you an officer in the California battalion at the time of the capitulation of Cowenga? and if so, what rank?

Answer. I was an officer in the California battalion; and my rank, as appeared by commission, was that of major of ordnance.

Question. Were you sent to Los Angeles from the plains of Cowenga, by Lieutenant Colonel Frémont? and if so, at what time? and for what purpose?

Answer. I was sent by Colonel Frémont, from Cowenga to Los Angeles, on the 13th of January, 1847, for the purpose of ascertaining who was in chief command at Los Angeles; and to make a report of the capitulation made on that day, to whomsoever I might find in chief command.

Question. Will you state how you executed that mission?

Answer. I went to the quarters of General Kearny first, and inquired of him, whether his arrival in the country had superseded Commodore Stockton who had before been recognized as chief commander. From General Kearny I learned that Commodore Stockton was still in chief command, and by him I was directed to make my report to the commodore.

Question. Will you state what passed, if anything, between yourself and General Kearny, in relation to the governorship of California, by Lieutenant Colonel Frémont? and if so, what it was?

Answer. I had but a short interview with General Kearny on my first arrival at Los Angeles, before, by his direction, I went to make my report to Commodore Stockton. After a discussion with Commodore Stockton, about the treaty, of perhaps an hour, I returned to General Kearny's quarters, in pursuance of an invitation from him when first there; and discussed very freely with him, General Kearny, the entire affairs of California, New Mexico, and so forth. In that conversation he expressed great pleasure at Colonel Frémont's being in the country, and spoke of his eminent qualifications for the officer of governor; his knowledge of the Spanish language, the manners of the people, &c., and of its having been his intention to have appointed him governor if the instructions, he told me, brought with him from the Secretary of War had been recognized in California. I believe that answers that question.

Question. Will you please to state all that passed on the subject of the governorship, and the particulars of the conversations as nearly as you can possibly remember and repeat them, with circumstances of time and place?

Answer. It was a subject of very much conversation, protracted to a late hour at night. He told me of his civil appointments in New Mexico, and of his determination to have appointed Colonel Frémont. In that conversation he told me that Commodore Stockton was unfriendly both to Frémont and himself; cautioned me to be particularly guarded in any conversation or discussion with Commodore Stockton, in reference to the treaty of Cowenga, and all other matters connected with California; expressing great pleasure at Lieutenant Colonel Frémont being there, as I understood him, intending to confer upon him the office of governor. I do not exactly understand what further details are called for. It was a long conversation, protracted till late at night. I prefer the questions should be put in shorter interrogatories.

Question. Did he say anything about his own return to the United States? and if so, what?

Answer. He did; so soon as he could organize a civil government, it was his intention to return to the United States; and finding so suitable a person as Colonel Frémont in the country to take the place of governor, his design of returning home need not long be postponed. I do not pretend to quote his words.

Question. Did he (General Kearny) give any opinions of his own about the capitulation of Cowenga? and if so, how far did it coincide, or otherwise, with the opinion he attributed to Commodore Stockton?

Answer. General Kearny coincided with the capitulation. I remember the more distinctly, because previous to my second interview with Commodore Stockton, on the evening of my arrival, 13th of January, he furnished me arguments in support of the capitulation; and, I think, requested Captain Turner to accompany me to Commodore Stockton's quarters and hear, or to be present, at the further discussion between the commodore and myself; and Captain Turner, I think, did go with me. In the second interview with Commodore Stockton, the objections first urged by him to the capitulation seemed to have been removed, and he, Commodore Stockton, then repeated his determination to appoint Colonel Frémont governor, immediately on his arrival at Los Angeles. I will further state, that in my first interview with Commodore Stockton, (when, I think, Captain Turner was also present—I think he went with me on both occasions,) he, the Commodore, made some objections to the capitulation.

Question. Did he, General Kearny, or did he not, exhibit his opinions of the capitulations of Cowenga in *contrast* to those of Commodore Stockton; one as inimical to the capitulation, the other as friendly?

Answer. He did, unquestionably, between my first and second interviews with Commodore Stockton, speak of Commodore Stockton being inimical, and he favorable to the treaty; and, as before stated, furnished me with arguments to combat the Commodore's objections.

Question. Did you sleep at General Kearny's quarters the night of the 13th of January? and if so, by whose invitation?

Answer. I did; and by the invitation of General Kearny.

Question. Will you please to state whether you slept with or near General Kearny, and whether the conversation in relation to Lieutenant Colonel Frémont, and subjects connected with him, was kept up after lying down?

Objection was made to the question by a member.

The judge advocate said: he had no objections to this witness's answering such questions going to contradict General Kearny.

The court was then cleared. And the court decided: that the question is excluded under the rule as to the contradiction of witnesses by a party on collateral matter, elicited by his own cross-examination.

The court further considered the inquiry immaterial and irrelevant.

The court was then opened. Lieutenant Colonel Frémont in court. The decision in closed session was announced.

Lieutenant Colonel Frémont read the following note:

Mr. PRESIDENT: Lieutenant Colonel Frémont is advised by his counsel, respectfully to say to the court, that he wishes to have an opportunity to deliver an argument to show the propriety and materiality of the testimony expected to be obtained by the answer to the question.

Lieutenant Colonel Frémont is further instructed to say, and for the purpose of saving time, and preventing the necessity for future separate decisions on different points, that it is his intention to put questions to the witness in relation to all the points on which General Kearny was cross-examined, and answered negatively in his cross-examination, concerning the events and conversations in which he, General Kearny, was concerned at Los Angeles, from the 13th to the 17th of January, inclusive; and this with the view to contradict General Kearny.

Lieutenant Colonel Frémont gives this notice to the court, that if there is any objection made to this intended examination of Colonel Russel, it may be known now, that the argument on Monday morning may be a response to all objections going to this part of the examination of Colonel Russel.

J. C. FRÉMONT,
Lieutenant Colonel, mounted rifles.

The court was then cleared. After mature deliberation, the court decided that the court will receive the argument of Lieutenant Colonel Frémont on the propriety and materiality of this inquiry.

The court intimates to the accused, in reference to the notice given by him, that the court must be understood as adhering to its rule on collateral matter elicited by cross-examination.

The court was then opened; Lieutenant Colonel Frémont in court. The decision in closed session was announced.

The testimony of to-day was read over to the witness; and then, to afford Lieutenant Colonel Frémont the opportunity to present his argument, the court, at twenty-five minutes past 2, adjourned to meet on Monday, at 10 o'clock.

MONDAY, *December* 20, 1847.—10 *o'clock*.

The court met pursuant to adjournment.

Present: All the members and the judge advocate.

The proceedings of Saturday were read over, during which time Lieutenant Colonel Frémont appeared in court.

Lieutenant Colonel Frémont read to the court the following paper:

MR. PRESIDENT: The question offered, and not allowed to be put, is this: "Will you please state whether you slept with or near General Kearny; and whether the conversation in relation to Lieutenant Colonel Frémont, and subjects connected with him, was kept up after lying down?" and the decision of the court upon it was in these words: "That the question is excluded under the rule, as to the contradiction of witnesses by a party on collateral matter elicited by his own cross-examination. The court further considers the inquiry immaterial and irrelevant."

Lieutenant Colonel Frémont is advised by his counsel that the question, as offered, affirms nothing, implies nothing, and leads to nothing, that it is merely introductory; and that it is not, until the answer is given to it, that any opinion can be formed of its character under any of the aspects mentioned by the court, as the reason for rejecting it; and that he has not been called upon to state what the answer was expected to be. Believing that the decision of the court was premature, and that an argument upon a mere introductory question would lead to no result, and might be followed by other arguments on other questions, Lieutenant Colonel Frémont deemed it due to frankness and conducive to full and fair decision, to lay open at once his whole object to the court, and to make known his intention to offer a series of questions, founded upon General Kearny's negative answers, to questions put to him on cross-examination, with the view now to contradict the answers which he then gave. In this design, Lieutenant Colonel Frémont gave the notice to the court, (at the same time that he asked leave to submit an argument in support of the question ruled out,) which made known his intention to offer further questions, with a view to contradict General Kearny; and in regard to which notice and request the court decided as follows:

The court will receive the argument of Lieutenant Colonel Frémont, on the propriety and materiality of this inquiry, (the question ruled out.)

The court intimates to the accused, in reference to the notice given by him, that the court must be understood as adhering to the rule on collateral matters elicited by cross-examination.

Lieutenant Colonel Frémont does not understand by the word "*rule*" as used in the two decisions of the court, anything else than the rules of evidence, as understood by the court.

In this case, he replied to it, and is advised by his counsel to say that there is no evidence which would exclude the question which he has offered, or any one that he intends to offer; that while he admits the rule he denies its application; and insists, under the advice of counsel, that the question which he had asked, neither in itself nor in connexion with those to which it is introductory, is either irrelevant, or immaterial, or in reference to any previous collateral question; and he is instructed by his counsel to say that, in the whole course of this trial, they have deemed too highly of the dignity of this court, and of the gravity of the case before it, (to say nothing of some self respect,) to occupy its attention intentionally, for a single moment, with questions either immaterial or irrelevant. That, with respect to collateral inquiries, they made up their minds, after due consideration and in an early stage of this proceeding, not to institute a single one. Intentionally, they know they have not, in point of fact, they believe they have not; and it is now the purpose of this argument to show that they have not. This leads to the inquiry: what is immaterial? what irrelevant? what collateral?

First.—*As to immateriality.*

It is perfectly well known to the profession that in a large proportion of the questions put or offered in every trial that occurs, are upon their face, and to those who have not studied the case as counsel, entirely immaterial. And it is also known to them that it is the *right* of counsel, and often the *duty* of counsel, to put preliminary or introductory questions, or even main questions, in a way not to show their object or bearing; and consequently, not to show their materiality. To ascertain the materiality of evidence *beforehand* (and that after the evidence is known) is often difficult, and sometimes impossible; and Lieutenant Colonel Frémont is instructed to say that courts of law, while prompt to reject illegal testimony, are slow to reject for immateriality. And that for several reasons.

1st. Because, like innocent medicines, the immaterial evidence, if admitted, will do no harm, if it does no good.

2d. Though apparently immaterial, it may turn out to be otherwise; and then its rejection may have been wrong.

3d. Because it is really difficult to ascertain before you come to its final application, and the use that is to be made of it, (by the party that wants the use of it, and knows how to use it,) whether particular evidence is material or not.

4th. Because *some* credit is due to the counsel, or who have the conduct of the case ; and who can hardly be presumed to trifle intentionally with the court, with the case, and with themselves, by offering immaterial evidence; that is to say, evidence which can have no influence one way or the other, for that is the test of immateriality.

For this reason and others, the judge will often say, when the objection is to the immateriality, that, although he cannot see the materiality himself, yet it may turn out to be so, and he will not stop it. And so are all the books. To quote one (Phillips, vol. 3, pages 433, 434) will be sufficient. He says : "It is frequently difficult to ascertain, *a priori*, whether proof of a particular fact offered in evidence will or will not become material; and in such cases, it is the usual practice of the court to give credit to the assertion of the counsel who tenders such evidence, that the fact will turn out to be material." Deeming this to be sufficient on the head of immateriality, Lieutenant Colonel Frémont proceeds to the next head of objection to his question.

Second.—Irrelevancy.

This is also admitted by all the books to be a difficult inquiry, and often impossible to be determined *a priori*. It is near akin to immateriality, and, in the practice of the courts, is governed by the same rules. What is relevant in courts of law is often never discovered till near the end of the case; and it may happen that testimony, now upon the minutes of this trial, may appear to all other eyes to be irrelevant; and yet, in the general defence, may be found to be not only relevant but effective. The test of irrelevancy is direct and simple, and comes to the inquiry whether the answer, in any possible shape, or in the slightest degree, can have any influence whatever upon the mind of the court or jury, not merely on the main issues joined, but in any question of fact arising in the whole course of the trial. This is the test, and is so expressly laid down by Phillips, vol. 3, page 736. These are his words:

" To determine whether a question be relevant, on cross-examination, frequently involves a nice and difficult inquiry into the nature of the issue or points in question, and the manner in which the answer may be brought to bear upon it. We are to ask, would the answer, in any possible shape, or in the slightest degree, affect any question of fact which can be raised in the case. If it may, the inquiry is relevant."

Holding this to be the law of the land in relation to the *test* of relevant or irrelevant questions, Lieutenant Colonel Frémont is instructed by his counsel to say that, neither in the question rejected by the court, nor in those to which it was introductory, and which were intended to follow, if the introductory one had been admitted, (and still less in the whole put together,) was there anything irrelevant, that he does expect (in the language of the law) to prove something by those questions, which something, in some "*possible shape*," and in some "*degree*," and that not the "*slightest*," will "*affect*" some question of "*fact*" in some part of this cause.

Third.—As to the collaterality of the question, the answers to which are proposed to be contradicted.

Lieutenant Colonel Frémont is instructed to say that this head of the argument is the most important of the ground for the court's decision, and becomes more so from the expressed intimation from the court, " that it (the court) must be understood as adhering to its rule on collateral matter elicited by cross-examination."

The first inquiry under this head is to know what is a *collateral* question, the answer to which cannot be contradicted. Literally, it is a question by the side (*con* and *latus*) of the cause, and not *in* it; and legally, it is the same. In the first place, the question to be collateral must be wholly irrelevant to the matter in issue. In the second place, it must be put with the *view* to discredit the witness by other testimony, if, by his answer, he denies the fact. And the example usually put is this: " *Have you* (the witness) *stood in the pillory?*" It is to such questions as these, *to wit*: wholly irrelevant, and put for the purpose of discrediting the witness, that his answers must be taken as true, and constituting the case in which no contradiction of his answer will be allowed by other witnesses.

This is the law, as Lieutenant Colonel Frémont is advised; and so say all the books. Thus *Hough*, page 914, copying from Phillips, *says:* " A witness cannot be cross-examined to any fact, which, if admitted, would be *collateral* and *wholly irrelevant* to the matter in issue, for the purpose of contradicting him by other evidence in case he should deny the fact, and, in this manner, to discredit his testimony; and if the witness answer such irrelevant question before it is disallowed or withdrawn, evidence cannot afterwards be admitted to contradict this testimony on this collateral matter." And so says Phillips himself in vol. 3, page 726. Thus: " A witness cannot be asked as to a mere collateral fact having no relevancy to the issue, in order to draw from him an answer which might, by other evidence, be shown incorrect, and thereby discredit him;" (Ibid, page 727;) and case cited, where the evidence was " overruled as irrelevant, not having the remotest influence." And so says Greenleaf, vol. 1, page 526: " But it is a well settled rule that a witness *cannot be cross-examined as to any fact which is collateral and irrelevant to the issue merely* for the purpose of *contradicting him* by other evidence, if he should deny it, thereby to discredit his testimony." And so says Starkie, page 189: " It is to be here observed that a witness is not to be cross-examined as to any distinct collateral fact for the *purpose* of afterwards impeaching his testimony by contradicting him."

This being the legal definition of a collateral question, and this the view with which it must be put, before the answer to it acquires the privilege of non-contradiction, Lieutenant Colonel Frémont is ready to bring his question, ruled out by the court, and those intended to follow it, to the test of this definition, and submits that they do not come within its prohibitions.

The question actually ruled out is, in itself, and kept by itself, insignificant, and even frivolous. It is in these words: "*Please state whether you slept with or near* General Kearny; *and if so, was the conversation in relation to Lieutenant Colonel Frémont and subjects connected with him, kept up after your lying down?*"

This is a pointless question as it stands; and if merely immaterial and irrelevant, it might have been better, and saved much time and trouble, to have suffered it to be answered at once, and be done with it.

But it is evidently a mere introductory question; and if admitted, and the answer had been in the affirmative, would have immediately been followed by others, to learn what was the subject of that night's conversation.

This is so obvious, and also so necessary to comprehend the reason for rejecting the first question, that Lieutenant Colonel Frémont immediately and in all frankness avowed his intention, in a paper read to the court, to contradict General Kearny's testimony generally in what related to the events and conversations at *Los Angeles,* from the 13th to the 17th of January last, inclusively; and particularly the conversation of the night of the 13th, to which the rejected question points. To give a clear view of the testimony expected from the witness now before the court, (Colonel Wm. H. Russell,) it is here declared to the court, that he is expected to contradict General Kearny in his answers on the cross-examination, to most of the questions put to him on the tenth day of the trial, (Friday, November 12th,) counting from the second question put on that day to the end of the answer to the 14th, at the words, "*civil government.*"

For the convenience of the court, and as a sufficient illustration of his intention in the proposed inquiry into the conversation of the night of the 13th of January, Lieutenant Colonel Frémont, herewith, submits the reported account of the cross-examination of General Kearny to the same points, cut from the National Intelligencer, (he having no copy of the journal,) subject, of course, to be corrected by the minutes of the court.

FRIDAY, *November* 12.—*Tenth day.*

The court met pursuant to adjournment; all the members present.

The cross-examination of Brigadier General Kearny, on the part of the defence was resumed.

Question. In your direct examination on a former day, in giving an account of an interview with Lieutenant Colonel Frémont at your quarters, you omitted to state whether any other person was present. Will you now state how that was?

Answer. There was no one present but Lieutenant Colonel Frémont and myself.

Question. In your direct examination, in giving an account of that interview, you stated that Lieutenant Colonel Frémont asked you whether you would appoint him governor of California. Now, had you not volunteered the offer to him of that appointment before, through Colonel Russell, with many encomiums upon Lieutenant Colonel Frémont?

Answer. I had not. I may have spoken to Colonel Russell highly of Lieutenant Colonel Frémont.

Question. Did Colonel Russell, by your invitation, sup with you on the evening of the 13th, being the day previous to the arrival of the California battalion at Los Angeles?

Answer. Captain Turner, of the dragoons, and myself messed together; we occupied at Los Angeles but one room; Colonel Russell supped with us, and slept with Captain Turner on the evening and night of his arrival at that place. He supped with us by our mutual invitation, very probably by my own.

Question. Did he lie in bed with you, by your invitation that night, the whole night or any part of it?

Answer. He did not. He lay with Captain Turner.

Question. Do you recollect whether you made use of any unusual means to keep him awake, and to keep up conversation with him?

Answer. I do not; but I know that I went to sleep before himself and Captain Turner.

Question. Did you in the night, while you were with Colonel Russell in bed, say to him, "Russell, you are drowsy;" and thereupon send out for spirits, in order to keep him awake and in conversation?

Answer. I have no recollection of having done so, and I do not believe that I did so.

Question. Was the praise of Lieutenant Colonel Frémont the theme with you in your conversation that night?

Answer. I think it highly probable. I may have spoken to Lieutenant Colonel Russell that evening very highly of Lieutenant Colonel Frémont.

Question. Was the capitulation of Cowenga a subject of conversation by you with Colonel Russell on that night?

Answer. I think it was.

Question. Did you applaud that capitulation?

Answer. I did not say any thing against it. I understood it had been discussed by others.

Question. Did you inform Colonel Russell that Commodore Stockton was highly opposed to that capitulation?

Answer. I had understood that Commodore Stockton was opposed to it; and I think I told Colonel Russell so.

Question. Did you not inform Colonel Russell that Lieutenant Emory was an enemy to Colonel Frémont, and warn him, as a friend of Lieutenant Colonel Frémont, against that enmity?

Answer. I do not think I did so.

Question. Did you not say these words to Colonel Russell : This, Colonel Russell, is the hot bed of Colonel Frémont's enemies?

Answer. I never said to Colonel Russell any thing of the kind, and never said so to any one.

Question. Did you say to him anything of Lieutenant Emory's enmity to Lieutenant Colonel Frémont, and if so, what was it?

Answer. I have no recollection whatever of having said to Colonel Russell anything relating to the enmity of Lieutenant Emory to Lieutenant Colonel Frémont.

Question. Did you not on the 16th of January, in your personal interview with Lieutenant Colonel Frémont, make to him an offer, of your own head, of the governorship of California, observing that you would very soon return to Missouri, and in four or six weeks would make him governor?

Answer. I did not. But in a conversation with Lieutenant Colonel Frémont, on the 17th of January, I stated that before leaving Santa Fé I had applied for permission to return home; and that, previous to my doing so, I would most probably organize a civil government in California. He asked me if I would appoint him the governor, and when? I told him that at that time I considered that the state of the country required a military government, but that, possibly, in a month or six weeks, the country might be sufficiently quieted to admit of the establishment of a civil government?

From this view of General Kearny's cross-examination on the tenth day of the trial, the object of the questions offered, and those intended to be offered, may be seen; and from this view of the nature and objects of those intended questions, he submits, under the advice of counsel, that not one of them is subject to the rule which protects the answers to collateral questions from contradiction. In the first place, not a question of all those put to General Kearny, at the time referred to, was collateral, that is to say, wholly irrelevant; and not one of them was put with the design to discredit him.

On the contrary, every one was deemed to be relevant, and material, and pre-eminently so; and rendered material and relevant by General Kearny's own direct and narative testimony on the first day of his examination; and so far from wishing to discredit him by those questions, and getting a chance to contradict him, he (Lieutenant Colonel Frémont) fully expected affirmative instead of negative answers in every instance, and desired such affirmative answers as being beneficial to him, while the negative ones were injurious.

To comprehend the whole force of this effect of the answers, (injurious if negative, beneficial if affirmative,) it is necessary to go back to the direct examination of General Kearny on the first day of his examination, and to that part of it, which is in these words:

He (Lieutenant Colonel Frémont) *asked me whether I would appoint him governor, I told him I expected shortly to leave California for Missouri, that I had, previously to leaving Santa Fe, asked permission to do so, and was in hopes of receiving it; that as soon as the country should be quieted, I should most probably organize a civil government; and that I, at that time, knew of no objec-*

tion to appointing him as the governor. He then stated to me that he would see Commodore Stockton, and unless he appointed him as governor at once, he would not obey his orders; and he left me. This is swearing in the direct testimony in the narative form, given of his own motion by General Kearny, and without any question to extract it, and which clearly presents the alleged refusal of General Kearny to appoint him (Lieutenant Colonel Frémont) governor of California at once, as the reason why he (Lieutenant Colonel Frémont) disobeyed him; and further made his obedience of Governor Stockton dependant upon the reason; thus ascribing a base and sordid motive for the crime of mutiny and disobedience of orders, with which he now stands charged before this court.

The question now is to admit testimony to disprove the allegation of that base and sordid motive, and the objection is, that the testimony offered is irrelevant and immaterial; and further more is excluded by the rules of evidence in relation to collateral testimony. Upon the first two points, that of relevancy and materiality, Lieutenant Colonel Frémont takes leave to say to the court that he needs no counsel to inform him how deeply he feels the materiality and relevancy of every thing which goes to overthrow the base and sordid part of the accusation against him, but conforming to the practice of judicial proceedings he has to speak, under the instruction of counsel, to that point, and to declare it to be the opinion of his counsel, as heretofore argued in the beginning of this paper, to be both relevant and material to his defence, and in the highest degree so relevant and material, to prove every circumstance which goes to contradict and discredit General Kearney's testimony in relation to that imputation of base and sordid motives for a crime, sufficiently great in itself without the super-addition of an infamous motive.

With respect to the objection founded on the alleged collaterality of the questions put to General Kearny in his cross-examination, and the answers to which it is now proposed to contradict, for the purpose of discrediting him, Lieutenant Colonel Frémont is instructed by his counsel to repeat that the objection is founded in a total misapprehension of the nature of a collateral question. And further, he is instructed to say that the cross-examination of General Kearny, on the points on which it is now proposed to contradict him, was fair in itself, conformable to all fair practice in courts of law, and such as honor and law requires, and such as this court should now enforce, if the cross-examination had not anticipated their duty. A witness, who is to be discredited by giving his former acts or declarations in evidence, has a right to speak for himself, and to be heard for himself, as to his own declarations; and if the party intending to impeach him does not give him that privilege, the court will, and for that purpose will call back the witness, and examine him themselves; and so are all the books.

Thus: the credit of a witness may be impeached either by cross-examination, subject to the rules already mentioned, or by general evidence affecting his credit, or by the evidence that he has before done or said that which is inconsistent with this evidence as to the trial; or lastly, by contrary evidence as to the facts themselves.—Starkie, v. 1, 210.

In the next place, the witness may be contradicted by others who represent the fact differently, or by proof that he has said or written that which is inconsistent with his present testimony; for this purpose, a letter may be read in which he has given a different account of the matter.—Ibid, 212.

It is a general rule that whenever the credit of a witness is to be impeached by proof of any thing that he has said or declared, or done in relation to the case, he is first to be asked, upon cross-examination, whether he has said or declared, or done that which is intended to be proved. For, in every such case, there are two questions: first, whether the witness ever did the act, or used the expressions alleged; secondly, whether his having done so impeaches his credit, or is capable of explanation.—Ibid, 212,—'13.

If the adverse counsel has omitted to lay such a foundation by previously interrogating the witness on the subject of those declarations, the court will, of its own authority, call back the witness, in order that the requisite questions may be put.—Ibid, 214.

That the witness sought to be impeached, must himself, in the first place, be interrogated as to the proposed contradiction, is now the settled rule of the English *nisi prius*.—Phillips, v. 3, 773.

Tinsdale, C. J.—I understand the rule to be, that before you can contradict a witness, by showing that he has at some other time said something inconsistent with his present evidence, you must ask him as to the time and place, and person involved in the supposed contradiction. It is not enough to ask him the general 'question, whether he has ever said so and so, because it may frequently happen, that, upon the general question, he may not remember having so said, whereas, when his attention is challenged to particular circumstances and occasions, he may recollect and explain what he has formerly said.—Ibid, p. 774.

To the same effect as above, see Greenleaf, vol. 1. pp. 542, 543, 544, 545.

And upon this reading, and without multiplying further authorities upon the point, Lieutenant Colonel Frémont submits, that so far from losing his privilege now to contradict and discredit General Kearny in the particulars referred to, he has done precisely what law and honor require to enable him to do so, and what the court would be now bound to do, if he had not himself done it.

Lieutenant Colonel Frémont, without going beyond the evidence already delivered, takes leave to say to the court, that he has been brought across the continent, from the Pacific ocean to the Atlantic, a virtual prisoner, to be tried for offences of which he had no warning or notice, and charged to have been committed three thousand miles distant; that this was done by his commanding general, combining in his own person the threefold character of accuser, prosecutor, and witness; and by his authority and influence bringing his own witnesses along with him, and not only leaving behind, but procuring to be kept away, witnesses necessary to Lieutenant Colonel Frémont; that while the arrest and consequent trial was a *surprise* upon him, the particular testimony of General Kearny in relation to the governorship was a sudden and total *surprise*, of which Lieutenant Colonel Frémont had not the slightest intimation or suspicion, and which he instantly felt to be of the deepest concern to his honor. The infamous motive attributed to him being, in his estimation, more dishonorable than the crime itself, with which he is charged, great as that crime is, and standing as it does in the military code at the head of all the military crimes. The proof, in contradiction of that imputed infamous motive, seemed to be difficult, and was so, for General Kearny had sworn to the absence of all persons at the time of this alleged conversation between two persons, one of whom has the privilege of swearing against the other, and in which this other, so sworn against, seemed to be without help, except from God. Nothing but circumstances and conversations occurring at other times and at other places, could protect him from the fatal effect of the ruinous testimony then sworn pointedly against him. He (Lieutenant Colonel Frémont) knew there were circumstances to invalidate that testimony, he knew that there were declarations made by General Kearny himself which would invalidate it; he knew, (that while many invalidating circumstances would be proved by others,) the more important fact of General Kearny's own declaration could be proved by a gentleman and an officer of rank and character, (Colonel W. H. Russell,) then occupying a station, and fulfilling a duty, that of bringing the capitulation of Cowengo, in the negotiation of which he was one of the American commissioners to the commander-in-chief at Los Angeles.

A part of these declarations have been already proved by Colonel Russell; he has already testified to a part of his conversation with General Kearny, the whole being voluntary on the part of the general, and upon his own seeking, and with the evident design to have them repeated to Lieutenant Colonel Frémont, and to make him join General Kearny against Governor Stockton, his lawful commander. A part of these declarations, and a most essential part, has already been delivered, and Lieutenant Colonel Frémont now insists, under the advice of counsel, that he has a right to pursue the inquiry into these conversations, and especially into the *bed scene* of the night of the 13th of January last, and to contradict and discredit General Kearny (if he can) upon every point on which he was interrogated, and answered negatively in his cross-examination, in relation to the conversations of the day and night of the 13th of January.

J. C. FRÉMONT,
Lieutenant Colonel, mounted rifles.

The court was then cleared. After mature deliberation, the court make the following decision:

Lieutenant Colonel Frémont offers by the testimony of Mr. Russell, to contradict the negative answers made by General Kearny, on his cross-examination, concerning the events and conversations in which he, General Kearny, was engaged at Los Angeles, from the 13th to the 17th of January.

In deciding on the admissibility of such testimony, the court deems it proper to refer to the previous course of this trial in regard to the evidence.

In the opening of the trial, the defence was notified by the judge advocate that the prosecution would adhere to the charges, and could not accompany the defence into any inquiry whatever out of the charges. The defence, however, at a later stage, urged that a court martial ought not to be restricted to the rigid rules of a criminal trial at the Old Bailey, or of a civil suit at Nisi Prius; and the court, being unwilling to exclude any testimony from which the defence might expect to derive benefit, has relaxed the rules of evidence, and admitted testimony which did not appear material or even relevant.

But this indulgence cannot be carried by the court to the extent of violating those leading principles in the law of evidence, which are essential to the administration of justice and the ascertainment of truth.

One of which leading principles forbids the trial of collateral issues; and this is not merely technical, but is essential to truth and justice; for it is essential that the court should not lose sight of the true issue, and go into the trial of other issues; and it is essential that one party shall not have the privilege of selecting ground, not covered by the cause, on which to try the credit of the witnesses of the other party, and thence try the cause. In view of this essential rule of evidence, the court notified the accused, when it admitted an unusual latitude in the cross-examination of General Kearny, that the defence could not, by such cross-examination, prepare collateral issues for this court to try.

The court cannot perceive that it has any bearing on this trial, whether Mr. Russell slept with General Kearny; whether General Kearny gave him spirits to drink; whether General Kearny warned him of Lieutenant Emory's hostility to Lieutenant Colonel Frémont, which the defence offer to prove by Mr. Russell, and which General Kearny has denied.

Nor further—while the court will admit in evidence any conversations of General Kearny's, or any acts of his, which go to contradict his testimony in regard to what passed between himself and Lieutenant Colonel Frémont, on the subject of the governorship— can it perceive that his conversations with Lieutenant Colonel Frémont's friends, on the 13th of January, respecting his opinions on the capitulation of Cowenga, or respecting the opinion of Commodore Stockton on that subject, or his encomiums to them on Lieutenant Colonel Frémont previous to the 17th of January, meet any point before this court; and this is the course of investigation referred to by the court, when it decided that the *inquiry*, as distinguished from while embracing the question, is immaterial and irrelevant.

In regard to this particular question, the court is of opinion that it was not necessary to wait for the answer, as suggested by Lieutenant Colonel Frémont, before the court could judge of the relevancy of the testimony offered.

The question sufficiently explained itself, and the nature of the evidence it was to elicit. The court adheres to its decision of Saturday.

The court was then opened; Lieutenant Colonel Frémont in court. The decision in closed session was announced.

Mr Wm. H. Russell, a witness for the defence.—Examination in chief by Lieutenant Colonel Frémont continued.

Question. Did you return to Lieutenant Colonel Frémont the next day; and if so, what did you inform him of your interview with General Kearny, exclusive of what may have passed in the night of the 13th of January.

Answer. I procured a horse, mine being exhausted, from a Spanish gentleman, considering it a matter of great importance to Colonel Frémont that I should communicate to him the result of my report and observations in the Angeles previous to his arrival. I rode out and met him at the head of the battalion some five or six miles from the Angeles, and informed him that both General Kearny and Commodore Stockton were anxious to confer upon him the office of governor, and his only difficulty then would be in the choice between them. I informed him that General Kearny admitted to me that he was then, and had been acting under the orders of Commodore Stockton. This much of the conversation, in all probability, occurred at General Kearny's table, and I have no doubt is exclusive of the bed scene.

Question. Did you tell Lieutenant Colonel Frémont, to whom you made your report, of the capitulation of Cowenga?

Answer. I told Colonel Frémont that I had first called on General Kearny on the evening of the 13th, and learned from him (General Kearny) that Commodore Stockton was in chief command, and that I had accordingly, by the direction of General Kearny, made my report to Commodore Stockton, and that he (Commodore Stockton) had finally concluded to ratify the capitulation.

Question. Did you enter Los Angeles with Lieutenant Colonel Frémont, and do you know whether Commodore Stockton assigned him (Lieutenant Colonel Frémont) his quarters?

Answer. I entered Los Angeles, with Lieutenant Colonel Frémont, on the morning of the 14th, and conducted Colonel Frémont to quarters assigned to him by Commodore Stockton through me.

Question. Were you appointed secretary of state in California, and if so by whom, and at what time was the place first offered to you?

Answer. I was appointed secretary of state, in California, by Commodore Stockton; the date of my commission is the 16th of January, 1847. It was tendered to me by Commodore Stockton, on the evening of the 14th of January; I declined accepting until I had a consultation with my friends, and among them was General Kearny and Captain Turner; and either one or both of these gentlemen advised me to accept, and I accordingly did so.

Question. Did you know at that time who was to be governor?

Answer. Perfectly well. Commodore Stockton informed me on the evening of the 13th, my second interview with him, that he intended to confer the office of governor on Colonel Frémont, as I understood, immediately on his arrival in the Angeles; and I think it was a matter of ordinary publicity throughout the city.

Question. Do you know any thing about the delivery of the respective commissions to yourself as secretary, and Lieutenant Colonel Frémont as governor?

Answer. I do. On the morning, I suppose the 16th—I want to qualify that—I was at Commodore Stockton's quarters, and he informed me that the commissions of Colonel Frémont as governor, and my own as secretary of state, were then in the act of being made out by his clerk, and desired me to ask Colonel Frémont to be at his quarters by a given hour, when the commissions would be ready for delivery. I made this communication to Colonel Frémont, and at the appointed hour returned with him to Commodore Stockton's quarters, when he, the commodore, accordingly handed the commissions to each of us.

I want to qualify about the 16th; I am told there is some little discrepancy. I presume it was the 16th, because the commissions bear that date; and for the further reason, that it was within two or three days of the arrival of Colonel Frémont at Los Angeles?

Question. Had you been intimately associated with Lieutenant Colonel Frémont in California? and had you been in public life in Missouri or Kentucky, so as to induce him to wish to have-you for secretary of state under him?

Answer. I was upon terms of intimacy with Lieutenant Colonel Frémont, and was induced, by my respect for him, to tender my services as a voluntary aid, and was admitted a member of his military family; and was shortly thereafter appointed ordnance officer by him, with the rank of major, I believe it was. I was a member of the Kentucky legislature when quite a young man; subsequently, a member of the Missouri legislature two or three times; United States marshal of Missouri, until turned out by President Tyler. I had the honor of serving in the Florida war with a member of this court, Colonel Taylor, and of being sent by Mr. Van Buren to West Point, as a member of the board of visitors, when Colonel De Russy was superintendent of that institution.

The testimony of the witness to-day was then read over to him; and then, at four minutes before three, the court adjourned, to meet to-morrow at ten o'clock.

Tuesday, *December* 21, 1847.—10 *o'clock*.

The court met pursuant to adjournment.

Present: all the members, and the judge advocate.

The record of yesterday was read over, during which Lieutenant Colonel Frémont appeared in court.

Mr. Wm. H. Russell, a witness for the defence.

Examination in chief by Lieutenant Colonel Frémont, continued.

Question. Do you know whether Lieutenant Colonel Frémont proposed your appointment to Commodore Stockton, and for the sake of having the assistance of a secretary versed in civil affairs?

Answer. To a modest man, that is rather a difficult question. Colonel Frémont knew my profession to be that of the law, and I had been for many years connected with politics; and, I have no doubt, charitably or kindly supposed I possessed some civic qualifications. Colonel Frémont did propose my appointment to Commodore Stockton. Captain Gillespie had been first indicated as the person best suited for that station, when Colonel Frémont urged my appointment for the reason above mentioned.

Question. Did Commodore Stockton tell you that Lieutenant Colonel Frémont proposed you to him for the secretary of state, and if so, at what time?

Answer. Commodore Stockton told me that Lieutenant Colonel Frémont had proposed me for the office of secretary of state. He told me so on the night of the 14th of January, the occasion of my first conversation on that subject with him—Commodore Stockton.

Question.—Did you see any symptoms of an attack upon the Mormons? if so, tell all about it.

Answer. From the moment that it was understood that the Mormons were to be marched from the Mission of San Luis Rey to the Angeles, there was great excitement among the Californians, with threats to attack them. I learned from an aged and respectable Californian——

Objection being raised to this testimony by the judge advocate, the court was cleared. And the court made the following decision:

The court considers that the excited and insurrectionary state of the country is relevant, in connection with the execution of General Kearny's orders to Lieutenant Colonel Frémont, of the 1st March and 28th March. But it appears to the court that it would carry this investigation too far, to proceed in an inquiry into the causes which produced this state of the country, so as to seek to ascertain to what extent it was produced by fear of the Mormons, by rumors of an invasion by the enemy, under General Bustamente, by the proclamations of General Kearny, and the system of government which he established in California, or by the unsettled temper and reluctant submission of a recently conquered people.

It therefore appears to the court, that any further inquiry in this connexion should be confined to the actual state of the country, at the time, without involving its causes in the investigation.

The court was then opened. Lieutenant Colonel Frémont in court. The decision in closed session was announced.

Wm. H. Russell, a witness.—Examination in chief continued.

Question. Did you see an armed body of Californians at or near Los Angeles, with the avowed purpose of attacking the Mormons?

Answer. I saw repeatedly armed parties of Californians, that it was generally understood had for their purpose of organizing, the intention of attacking the Mormons. This occurred between the 15th and 22d or 23d of March, when I left the country.

Question. Were you told by respectable and influential Californians that the people were generally exasperated, and would probably rise if the Mormons came among them?

The judge advocate submitted to the court the admissibility of this form of testimony.

Lieutenant Colonel Frémont offered to withdraw it, if objected to. The court not objecting, it was answered, as follows:

Answer. I was told so by several respectable and influential Californians.

Question. Do you know whether Lieutenant Colonel Frémont lived alone, (without troops,) as governor in Los Angeles, after the capitulation of Cowenga? and whether he went alone to see the insurgent chiefs before that capitulation?

Answer. He lived in the government house, unattended by a guard, other than three or four friends, who resided with him. Those gentlemen were Major Reading, paymaster, Captain Owens, part of the time, and myself, up to the time of my leaving. The battalion was at the mission of San Gabriel, about nine miles from the Angeles.

He went alone to the camp of the insurgents on the same day of the capitulation at Cowenga. The insurgents were situated about one and a half miles or two miles from the California battalion; and Colonel Frémont must have remained a space of time exceeding one hour; he remained so long as to excite uneasiness on the part of his troops as to his personal safety.

Question. Did you accompany Lieutenant Colonel Frémont on the march of the California battalion from Monterey to the Ciudad de Los Angeles? and were there any outrages committed by him, or suffered by him to be committed, on the Californians by the troops under his command? or were there any outrages or abuses committed by those troops, that you heard of?

The judge advocate said, "that no such allegation has been brought by him before the court; nor is he aware that any evidence is before the court, to show that any outrages were committed by Colonel Frémont's battalion; and, when this subject was brought before the court, in the cross-examination of General Kearny, the court decided not to inquire into it."

Lieutenant Colonel Frémont said: "Such a charge against him, of having committed and tolerated outrages on the people, was made by General Kearny in an official report to the adjutant general of the army; which report was on the record of this court, and which charge is reiterated in the testimony of General Kearny. Lieutenant Colonel Frémont is anxious to meet the charge."

The court was cleared. And the court decided, as follows:

This matter was brought before the court by the defence, in their cross-examination of General Kearny, by producing before it, and exhibiting to the witness, an official report of his, and by inquiring of him whether Lieutenant Colonel Frémont was alluded to in a passage of that report, wherein his name is not mentioned, nor necessarily implied.

The court, then, twice deliberately refused to receive any testimony in support of the imputation on the California battalion, or Lieutenant Colonel Frémont, as its commander; and it cannot, under its decision at that time, give any force to the imputation as in any degree sustained by evidence on its record, although the imputation found place there by the defence's own action.

The imputation being so unsustained and forbidden by the court to be inquired into on its introduction, the court cannot now admit rebutting testimony, where it finds nothing to rebut.

The court was then opened: Lieutenant Colonel Frémont in court.

The decision in closed session was announced.

Mr. Wm. H. Russell, a witness.—Examination in chief continued.

Question. Did the capitulation of Cowenga, and the pacification of the country, follow the visit of Lieutenant Colonel Frémont to the camp of the insurgents?

Answer. Most certainly. The capitulation took place on the evening of the day that he visited the Californian camp; and I considered the country sufficiently pacific to authorize me, almost alone, to ride from Cowenga to the Angeles on that evening.

Question. Do you know General Kearny's opinion of the Mormons as shedders of blood, and if he said anything on that head in relation to Governor Boggs?

The judge advocate said: The question does not appear to be relevant.

Lieutenant Colonel Frémont submitted the following note:

Mr. President: The object of the question is, to show the character of the people whom General Kearny was sending against Lieutenant Colonel Frémont, and that General Kearny knew of their bad character in the respect supposed by the question.

J. C. FRÉMONT,
Lieut. Col., mounted rifles.

The court was then cleared; and the court then decided that the question be not put.

The court was then opened: Lieutenant Colonel Frémont in court.

The decision in closed session was announced.

Mr. William H. Russell, a witness.

Lieutenant Colonel Frémont said he had no more questions to ask the witness.

Cross-examination by the judge advocate.

Question. Did General Kearny in this conversation with you on the 13th of January, at Los Angeles, say that he did then intend, or he had intended, to appoint Lieutenant Colonel Frémont governor?

Answer. He stated to me that it was his intention, if his instructions from the Secretary of War had been recognized, to appoint Lieutenant Colonel Frémont governor.

Question. Do you recollect that General Kearny told you expressly that he was serving under Commodore Stockton, or, did he say anything more explicit on that point than as stated by you—that Commodore Stockton was in chief command, and, that you would carry the capitulation of Cowenga to him?

Answer. He told me distinctly that he was serving under Commodore Stockton, and had been doing so from San Diego.

Question. Was Captain Turner present at that conversation?

Answer. I am not positive, but I believe that he was.

The judge advocate said he had no further question to ask.

The court was then cleared to consider questions proposed by members of the court.

The court was then opened: Lieutenant Colonel Frémont in court.

The testimony was then read over to the witness; and then, at ten minutes before three, the court adjourned to meet to-morrow at 10 o'clock.

WEDNESDAY, *December 22, 1847.—10 o'clock.*

The court met pursuant to adjournment.

Present: all the members, the judge advocate, and Lieutenant Colonel Frémont.

The proceedings of yesterday were read over.

Wm. H. Russell, a witness.

Question by the court. How often did you see the armed parties of Californians, which it was generally understood had organized with the intention of attacking the Mormons, how large were those armed parties, and what was their organization?

Answer. I saw them repeatedly; their numbers were small, fifteen to twenty, I think. I never saw more than that together: I know nothing special of their organization from my own observation.

Question by the court. At what hour of the day did you go with Lieutenant Colonel Frémont to Commodore Stockton's quarters for the purpose of receiving your commissions?

Answer. Not earlier than noon. It may have been later, but I am confident not later than the middle of the afternoon.

Question by the court. Did you hear or witness any discussion by, or in presence of Commodore Stockton and Lieutenant Colonel Frémont, in relation to the appointment of Lieutenant Colonel Frémont to the governorship of California, and especially in reference to the propriety of Lieutenant Colonel Frémont's accepting such an appointment from Commodore Stockton rather than General Kearny; if so, when did such discussions take place, and what was the nature and import of them? Please state all you know of these matters.

Answer. I did not; I never heard any such discussion.

Question by the court. Did General Kearny, in his conversation with you on the evening of the 14th January, propose to give you the appointment of secretary of state, or say anything to you on this subject at that or any other time?

Answer. General Kearny, I think on the evening of the 13th, both in regard to myself and Colonel Frémont, expressed pleasure at our being in the country, and of his intention, if his instructions had been recognized, of availing himself of our services. I do not remember, in reference to myself, whether he mentioned my name in connection with the office of secretary of state, or a judgeship; I only remember distinctly that he spoke of his intention of appointing Colonel Frémont governor.

Question by the court. When you were sent to Los Angeles by Lieutenant Colonel Frémont, to ascertain who was in chief command, did you receive from Lieutenant Colonel Frémont any instructions for your conduct, in the event of your finding, on arriving at Los Angeles, the chief command to be claimed by both Commodore Stockton and General Kearny?

Answer. My instructions were, from Colonel Frémont, to proceed to the Angeles and carefully inquire as to whom was in chief command, and make my report accordingly. No such contingency was contemplated by Colonel Frémont, when he despatched me on that mission, as that the chief command would be claimed by both.

Question by the court. Why did you first report to General Kearny instead of Commodore Stockton?

Answer. I bore a letter to General Kearny from Colonel Frémont, in acknowledgment of one received by Colonel Frémont whilst on the march, and for the further reason, that we were totally ignorant of the object of General Kearny being in the country; and my orders from Colonel Frémont were, that I should ascertain all about it.

Question by the court. You said in your direct examination, "I informed him (Colonel Frémont) that both General Kearny and Commodore Stockton were anxious to confer upon him the office of governor, and his only difficulty then would be in the choice between them." Please to state the nature of the " *difficulty*" to which you allude in your testimony, and the manner in which that difficulty was removed, if within your knowledge?

Answer. I learned from General Kearny that he brought with him instructions from the Secretary of War, and that he felt himself authorized, in virtue of said instructions, to assume chief command; from Commodore Stockton I learned, on the same evening, that his relations to the territory as chief commander were in no wise changed by the arrival of General Kearny in the country. I apprehended some difficulty from this apparent collision between these gentlemen, and was induced thereby to institute the inquiry that led me to the result that Commodore Stockton was still rightful commander, and so reported the evidence and admission of General Kearny to Colonel Frémont.

Question by the court. State all the conversation that passed between you and Lieutenant Colonel Frémont, on the subject of choice of commanders, after you returned and reported to him the result of your visit to Los Angeles?

Answer. I met Colonel Frémont at the head of his battalion on the morning of the 14th of January, as stated in my chief examination, about five or six miles from the Angeles. I told him that I had had much conversation with both General Kearny and Commodore Stockton, touching their respective positions in the country; that I was satisfied, from what had occurred, that General Kearny was a better friend of his than Stockton; but, from Kearny's own admission, I regretted to have to give it as my opinion that we should have to look to Commodore Stockton still as commander-in-chief; that I found Stockton exercising the functions of commander-in-chief, and submitted to implicitly, as I thought, by Kearny.

This is the substance of my conversation to Colonel Frémont; and he, I think, with equal reluctance at the time, came to the same conclusion.

Question by the court. Please state the *particular* conversation you had with General Kearny in relation to his right to command in California?

Answer. I had a conversation first with General Kearny, based on his instructions, which he seemed to consider full; and I inquired of him why he had not insisted on obedience from Commodore Stockton, and he informed me the reason was that he had but few troops. The second conversation was in reference to the assimilated rank of army and navy officers of his grade and Commodore Stockton's. I distinctly remember that I maintained that his position as brigadier general ranked Stockton's; he thought otherwise, and claimed chief command in virtue of his instructions only.

He thought that Stockton, as a commodore commanding a squadron, ranked him as brigadier general, which I, the next day, communicated to Colonel Frémont as a matter of surprise to me. It was that admission of General Kearny mainly that led me to the conclusion that Stockton was still rightfully in the command; both pretending to rely on instructions received from Washington. General Kearny's I saw; Commodore Stockton's I never saw.

Question by the court. Was any one present at this conversation?

Answer. I do not know. Captain Turner probably was. He occupied the same room with General Kearny, and was in and out throughout the evening.

Question by the court. Did you see an extract from the army regulations on the subject of relative rank of army and navy officers during the conversation with General Kearny, or were such regulations alluded to in that conversation? or what induced you to think and say that Brigadier General Kearny ought to rank Commodore Stockton?

Answer. I did not see the regulations referred to. My opinion was founded upon my own judgment, unassisted by any positive information.

Question by the court. Did General Kearny say anything in regard to there being such a grade in the navy as commodore? and if so, what?

Answer. I do not remember whether the grade of commodore was mentioned or not. His remarks referred to the commandant of a squadron.

Question by the court. Have you stated in your examination in chief all the conversations of General Kearny with you, near the 17th of January, 1847, in relation to the governorship? If not, give any such conversations not before given.

Answer. I think I have substantially stated everything that occured in regard to the governorship.

A member called the attention of the witness to his answers on his examination by the defence, which, after the decision of the court, seemed not to refer to the conversation on the night of the 13th of January—the "bed scene," as the witness styled it.

The object of the court was to know whether, on that occasion or any other, anything had passed between the witness and General Kearny, in regard to the governorship, further than as already stated by him.

Witness answered: I will add that, in all the conversations I held with General Kearny that evening, I understood it to be his wish to appoint Colonel Frémont governor, if he could rightfully do so.

Question by the court. Did General Kearny admit, in any manner, that Commodore Stockton had a right, in consequence of relative rank, to command him (General Kearny) or any troops in the army service?

Answer. I understood General Kearny to claim his right to command in the country, founded on his instructions only. I am positive that, on the mere question of rank, he yielded precedence to Commodore Stockton.

Question by the court. Have you been paid as an officer in the California battalion? If so, how and when?

Answer. I received in this city last July or August, from the army paymaster, Major Van Ness, a sum less than three hundred dollars, in part payment of my services as an officer in the California battalion. I claimed pay up to my arrival in the United States, but it was disallowed by the Secretary of War, to whom it was referred.

I received a certificate of pay from a paymaster in California, appointed by Commodore Stockton, on which I have never received anything.

No further questions to this witness by the court.

Question by Lieutenant Colonel Frémont. On what day did Governor Stockton leave Los Angeles? and when did Lieutenant Colonel Frémont commence the exercise of his duties as governor and commander-in-chief in California, under the appointment of Governor Stockton?

Answer. He left within a few days after the delivery of the commissions, or the dates of the commissions, I do not remember which; and immediately thereupon Colonel Frémont commenced the exercise of the duties of governor.

Question by Lieutenant Colonel Frémont. Was he (Lieutenant Colonel Frémont) recognized, obeyed, and respected as governor and commander-in-chief? and did he reside at the old established seat of government?

Answer. He was as fully recognized as governor and commander-in-chief as any governor ever was; and he resided in the Angeles, the ancient capital of California; and in a house vacated for his use by Commodore Stockton.

Question by Lieutenant Colonel Frémont. Do you know whether he was ever *relieved* in any lawful manner of that office?

Answer. I am positive he was not, up to the moment of my leaving the country, about the 22d or 23d of March last; and the more positive that he was not, because through my office of secretary of state, by a rule established by Governor Frémont, all such communications passed.

Question by Lieutenant Colonel Frémont. Do you know whether the *definite instructions* of the 5th of November, 1846, directing the naval commander to "relinquish to Colonel Mason or General Kearny the direction of operations on land," and the "control over the administrative functions of government" and to "turn over to him all papers necessary to the performance" of these duties, were ever communicated to Governor Frémont, either by the general government of the United States, by Commodores Shubrick or Biddle, by General Kearny, or any other person whatever? and if such instructions had been communicated to him, would you not have been likely, in your capacity of secretary of state, to know it?

Answer. I think they never were, up to the time of my leaving the country, the 22d or 23d of March. If they had been communicated to Governor Frémont, I think, from my position as secretary of state, I would unquestionably have known it.

Question by Lieutenant Colonel Frémont. Do you know anything of the situation, value, and uses, as respects the public service, of the island called White or Bird island, in the bay of San Francisco, which was purchased by Governor Frémont, and which is mentioned in the sixth specification of the first charge, and in the third specification of the third charge against Lieutenant Colonel Frémont?

The judge advocate said: In regard to this question that he had entered on the record, under sanction of the court, that the purchase of the land from Temple was an act not called in question before the court, except as stated in the specifications, as an assumption of the office of governor, and in contempt of the lawful authority of General Kearny. The judge advocate supposed, therefore, that the court could not inquire into the situation, value, and uses of this land.

The court was then cleared; and the court decided: "that the question has no relation to the charges."

The court was then opened. Lieutenant Colonel Frémont in court.

The decision in closed session was announced.

W. H. Russell, a witness.

Question by Lieutenant Colonel Frémont. Was the state of the country so quiet, subsequent to the capitulation of Cowenga, and previous to the middle of March, that an American citizen or officer might ride through it without a guard?

Answer. I consider it entirely settled, so much so, that I rode with a Spanish gentleman, who was one of the chief officers in the insurrection, from the Angeles to San Diego, and back again; stopping at Spanish houses. Colonel Frémont himself, with one of the Picos and a servant, rode from Angeles to Monterey, a distance of over 400 miles, and back again.

Question by Lieutenant Colonel Frémont. Did obedience to the command of Commodore Stockton, in preference to that of General Kearny, when both were claiming the chief authority, present any advantages personal or military to Lieutenant Colonel Frémont?

Answer. I think not; General Kearny was known to have funds, and expected shortly an arrival of troops. He was, besides, known to be a warm friend of Colonel Frémont's family; and I am satisfied that Colonel Frémont elected to obey Stockton alone from a conviction of duty.

Question by the court. Was Lieutenant Colonel Frémont recognized as governor by General Kearny, Colonel Mason, or any other officers of the army?

Answer. I do not know that he ever was.

Question by judge advocate. You did not then refer to the officers of the army with General Kearny in California, when you said that he was as fully recognized as governor and commander-in-chief as any governor ever was?

Answer. No. I did not refer to them—they were 400 or 500 miles from us—with the exception of Cooke, who was at the mission of San Luis Rey, I suppose 100 miles from us. I meant the population, native and foreign.

Question by judge advocate. You have said that Lieutenant Colonel Frémont was never relieved, in any lawful manner, of the office of governor, before you left the country. Had he not, while you were there, received General Kearny's orders, dated 1st March, and styled 10th military department, orders, No. 2; and had he not received the joint circular proclamation of Commodore Shubrick and General Kearny of same date?

Answer. They were received a few days before I left the country; he was not relieved, for, on the receipt of those papers, he went to Monterey to see these gentlemen in person; and before his return from Monterey I left the country. The joint proclamation I saw, the order I never did.

Question by the court. How long had you resided in California, and what other governors had you known there besides governor Frémont?

Answer. I reached California in the month of August, 1846, and understood Commodore Stockton was governor and commander-in-chief. I never knew any other governor but Governor Frémont.

The testimony of to-day was then read over to the witness. On motion, the court was cleared. After some time in deliberation in closed session, the court was opened. Lieutenant Colonel Frémont in court.

Mr. Wm. H. Russell, a witness.

Question by the court. You have spoken of both General Kearny and Commodore Stockton relying on their instructions for the authority they claimed, and that you did not see Commodore Stockton's instructions. How did you know that Commodore Stockton relied on instructions?

Answer. I told Commodore Stockton that I had seen the instructions of General Kearny, and that they seemed to be very full; and I desired to know from him whether he possessed any instructions that would countervail those of General Kearny. He replied to me that he had full and plenary instructions carried out by him sealed, not to be opened until he reached a given point; but he would not exhibit them like slaves did their papers; that he had no fear of his power being impaired by the instructions of General Kearny; and, from his confident manner, I felt fully assured that he had counterpart, or paramount instructions to those of General Kearny, and continued in that opinion up to my arrival in Washington city, in July, or August of the present year. This occurred on or about the 14th of January after my arrival at the Angeles, it may have been the 13th; I think not, however.

Question by the court. Was Lieutenant Colonel Frémont informed by Commodore Stockton, of his having, or claiming to act under instructions?

Answer. I think he was by me. Whether by Commodore Stockton directly, I cannot tell. I reported to Colonel Frémont all those conversations.

Question by Lieutenant Colonel Frémont. What numbers of the Californians were there supposed to be under arms within a short distance, at the time and place of the capitulation of Cowenga.

Answer. They were variously estimated; no one, I presume, accurately knew; they were estimated from 200 to 400, with how near an approximation to the truth I cannot say.

The remainder of the testimony of the witness to-day was then read over to him, and Mr. Russell was permitted to retire; but, at the request of Lieutenant Colonel Frémont, was not discharged.

Edward F. Beale, a passed midshipman in the navy of the United States, a witness for the defence, was then duly sworn by the judge advocate according to law, and testified as follows: Examined in chief by Lieutenant Colonel Frémont.

Question. What position and rank do you hold in the navy of the United States?

Answer. A passed midshipman.

Question. Were you with the squadron at Monterey, in July, 1846, when the British squadron, under Admiral Seymour, arrived there, and within a few days after the American flag had been raised by Commodore Sloat?

Answer. I was.

Question. Did you understand that any apprehension was felt on the approach of the foreign squadron, that an attempt would be made to displace the American flag?

Answer. It was not a squadron. It was a line of battle ship, commanded by Admiral Seymour. We did not know what their instructions might be; we felt insecure; so much so that we sent our men to quarters.

Question. Were the decks of the frigate Congress cleared, and other preparations made for action?

Answer. We prepared for action.

Question. Do you know whether General Kearny is acquainted with Mr. Christopher Carson? Did you ever see them together? If so, when and where?

Answer. I know that General Kearny is very intimately acquainted with Mr. Christopher Carson. When two men are frequently seen together, the fact is not sufficiently singular to fix it in the memory. I know, however, two or three occasions when they were together.

Question. Did General Kearny, to your knowledge, remain some days on a hill of rocks, called San Bernardo? and did you and two other persons undertake to go from there to San Diego, through the enemy's lines, for the purpose of communicating to Governor Stockton the condition of General Kearny's party, and request relief to be sent?

Answer. I did.

Question. Previous to your starting for San Diego, had public property been burned at General Kearny's camp, with a view to cutting through the enemy.

The judge advocate submitted to the court the relevancy of the present testimony.

Lieutenant Colonel Frémont said: That the question belonged to a series of questions, and that he would, to-morrow morning, submit to the court an explanation of the propriety and materiality of the present inquiry.

Thereupon, and it being near the hour of adjournment, the court, at ten minutes before three, adjourned to meet to-morrow at 10 o'clock.

THURSDAY, *December 23, 1847.*—10 *o'clock.*

The court met pursuant to adjournment.

Present: All the members, the judge advocate, and Lieutenant Colonel Frémont.

The proceedings of yesterday were read over. Lieutenant Colonel Frémont read to the court the following note:

Mr. PRESIDENT: As questions proposed for nearly the same objects, as were intended by the one objected to at the close of the session yesterday, and others which were to follow it, were over-ruled by the court in the early part of this trial, on the cross-examination of General Kearny, Lieutenant Colonel Frémont will not now press the inquiry, though still believing it, under the advice of his counsel, to be relevant and material.

J. C. FRÉMONT,
Lieutenant Colonel, mounted rifles.

Midshipman Edward F. Beale, a witness for the defence.—Examination in chief by Lieutenant Colonel Frémont continued.

Question. State who were the persons who accompanied you in going through the enemy's lines from the hill of San Bernardo to San Diego, for the purpose mentioned in your testimony yesterday?

The judge advocate submitted to the court the relevancy of this inquiry.

A member objecting, the court was cleared. And the court decided that the military details of General Kearny's march from Santa Fé to San Diego are not material to this trial, and that the inquiry into them should not be pursued.

The court was then opened; Lieutenant Colonel Frémont in court. The decision in closed session was announced.

Midshipman Edward F. Beale, a witness for the defence.—Examination in chief continued.

Question. You stated in your testimony yesterday that you remembered two or three occasions that you had seen General Kearny with Mr. Christopher Carson; please state those occasions, and whether you know of any instance in which General Kearny called up Carson to consult with him?

Answer. The first occasion that I recollect distinctly, was when we were laying at San Bernardo; General Kearny called for Mr. Carson to consult with him and others, and asked his opinions. The other was to consult with Mr. Carson on the practicability of going in with the force of General Kearny, without waiting for reinforcements. A third occasion was when, at San Diego, Mr. Carson, General Kearny, and myself went down to shoot General Kearny's pistols off; all those occasions in December, 1846.

Question. Did General Kearny, at first, refuse to let Carson go with you to San Diego, saying he could not spare him, or any thing to that effect?

Answer. He did.

Question. At what time did you leave California to return to the United States? and what was the state of the country in regard to tranquillity when you left it?

Answer. About the 25th of February, 1847; the country was quiet.

Question. Had any rumors of the coming of the Mormons into the country then reached there; and, if so, what was the effect of those rumors?

The judge advocate suggested that the question appeared to come under the decision of the court on the 21st instant.

On motion of a member, the court was cleared; and the court ordered it to be entered on its record, that its decision on the 21st, expressly informs Lieutenant Colonel Frémont of the opinion of the court, that while the actual state of the country may be shown, the causes of that state should not be investigated.

The question goes to one of these causes, and that one the same that led to the court's decision.

The court was then opened. Lieutenant Colonel Frémont in court. The decision in closed session was announced.

Midshipman Edward F. Beale, a witness for the defence.

Lieutenant Colonel Frémont said he had no more questions to ask.

The judge advocate had no questions to ask.

Question by a member. Was there anything peculiar which caused the preparation for action on the approach of the line of battle ship, commanded by Admiral Seymour, at Monterey, and what was it? Is it not customary to prepare for action when a strange armed ship appears in sight?

Objection being made by a member, the court was cleared; and the court decided that the question be not put.

The court was then opened. Lieutenant Colonel Frémont in court. The decision in closed session was announced.

Midshipman Edward F. Beale, a witness. The court had no question to ask.

The testimony of to-day was then read to the witness. Midshipman Beale was then, by consent of Lieutenant Colonel Frémont, discharged from further attendance as a witness on this court.

The judge advocate here said that he offered to the court, from Lieutenant Colonel Frémont, the despatch of Commodore Stockton to Lieutenant Colonel Frémont, delivered to him at the camp of the Willows, by Mr. George W. Hawley, as testified to by him in his testimony before the court, on the 15th instant; which despatch was handed to him by the defence, after the testimony of the witness on that day was delivered; but, at the time when the court was about to adjourn, and when the judge advocate had no opportunity to place the despatch before the court.

He now brought it before the court on the application of Lieutenant Colonel Frémont.

The despatch was then read. On inquiry of a member whether the judge advocate admitted the authenticity of the paper, as it had not been proved:

The judge advocate replied that he had no doubt of its authenticity, and admitted its authenticity.

A member objecting to the recording of the despatch, the court was cleared, and the court decided that the despatch be recorded.

The court was then opened. Lieutenant Colonel Frémont in court. The decision in closed session was announced.

The despatch was as follows:

CAMP AT SAN LOUIS REY,
January 3, 1847.

MY DEAR COLONEL: We arrived here last night from San Diego, and leave to-day on our march for the City of the Angels, where I hope to be in five or six days. I learn this morning that you are at Santa Barbara, and send this despatch by the way of San Diego, in the hope that it may reach you in time. If there is one single chance against you, you had better not fight the rebels until I get up to aid you, or you can join me on the road to the Pueblo.

These fellows are well prepared, and *Mervine's* and *Kearny's defeat have given them a deal more confidence and courage.* If you do fight before I see you, keep your forces in close order; do not allow them to be separated, or even unnecessarily extended. They will probably try to deceive you by a sudden retreat, or pretended runaway, and then unexpectedly return to the charge after your men get in disorder in the chase. My advice to you is, to allow them to do all the charging and running, and let your rifles do the rest.

In the art of horsemanship, of dodging, and running, it is in vain to attempt to compete with them.

In haste, very truly, your friend and obedient servant,

R. F. STOCKTON.

To Lieut. Col. FREMONT, &c., &c., &c.

I understand that it is probable they will try to avoid me and fight you separately.

Mr. William N. Loker, a witness for the defence, was then duly sworn by the judge advocate according to law, and testified as follows:

Examined in chief by Lieutenant Colonel Frémont.

Question. Were you an officer of the California battalion in January last, and what position did you hold in it?

Answer. On arriving at Los Angeles, I was first lieutenant of company A, and was shortly thereafter appointed adjutant of the battalion.

Question. Did you in the capacity of adjutant, by direction of Governor Frémont, communicate to the battalion the order of General Kearny, of March 1st, for mustering them into service, according to the terms of the law of May and June, 1846?

Answer. I was sent, not an order from General Kearny, but an act of Congress regulating the enlistment of volunteers; the said act was sent by General Kearny, and it was under this act that he, General Kearny, wanted the battalion mustered into service.

The paper was sent to them—the battalion; and I also let them know that General Kearny wanted them mustered into service according to it.

Question. Did you communicate this fact to Major Cooke?

Answer. I did; I overtook Major Cooke riding out to the mission, and after I had passed him, he called to me to ask if I was going to the mission, or if I knew the way, and to give him directions. We rode on to the mission. He then asked me what objection I had to remaining in the service; he remarked, at the same time, that he thought it very strange that the battalion refused to be mustered into the service, and asked me what objection I had to coming in. I told him that I had none. He then asked me the reason; and I told him that my being an officer, it did not affect my pay at all, while it did the men. He then asked me if the men knew the orders of General Kearny, about their being mustered into service. I told him that such orders had been conveyed to the men. I also told him that most of the men had refused to be mustered in.

Question. Do you remember an instance when Lieutenant Colonel Frémont was refused, by General Kearny, permission to encamp at a certain spot on the march, and on or about the 8th of June, 1847, on the Stanislaus river, and directed to encamp close by the encampment of the Mormons?

The judge advocate said he did not see the relevancy of this inquiry.

A member objecting, the court was ordered to be cleared.

Lieutenant Colonel Frémont offered and read to the court the following paper :

Mr. PRESIDENT: The object of this question, and of inquiries hereafter to follow, is to show that Lieut. Col. Frémont, without being informed that he was then, or would be at any subsequent time placed in arrest, was nevertheless virtually constituted a prisoner, under guard of the Mormons, before leaving California, and so marched across the continent, by General Kearny, under circumstances of indignity not allowed by the service even towards prisoners. The army regulations direct that an officer of a company, in arrest, shall be marched in the rear of his company, and a regimental officer in the rear of his regiment; but in the present case, without any arrest, or any notice of intended arrest, Lieutenant Colonel Frémont, and the party of citizens who had aided him for a number of years in his explorations and surveys in the west, and over whom General Kearny had assumed the command, were marched not in the rear of a company—not in the rear of a regiment—not in the rear of an army; but in the rear and under the surveillance of the Mormon guard and servants of General Kearny: this aggravated by a succession of indignities, commencing with a public exhibition and public insults before the assembled inhabitants and officers of the navy, at Monterey, on the Pacific, and receiving their crowning accumulation of affronts at Fort Leavenworth, on the Missouri. It is not intended to follow this train of indignities *seriatim*, but to produce to the court a few glaring instances, as Lieutenant Colonel Frémont is advised by his counsel he has a right to do, for the purpose first, of showing the vindictive temper of General Kearny towards him, and thence impeaching his motives in instituting this prosecution, and his credit as a witness before this court.

J. C. FRÉMONT,
Lieutenant Colonel, mounted rifles.

The court was then cleared.

After some time in deliberation in closed session, the court was opened. Lieutenant Colonel Frémont in court.

The testimony of to-day was read over to the witness, and then, at three minutes before three, the court adjourned to meet to-morrow at 10 o'clock.

———

FRIDAY, *December 24,* 1847.—10 *o'clock.*

The court met pursuant to adjournment.

Present: All the members, except Colonel Payne. Present, also, the judge advocate.

The president informed the court that Colonel Payne was absent from sickness. Whereupon the court adjourned, to meet on Monday the 27th instant, at 10 o'clock.

MONDAY, *December* 27, 1847.—10 *o'clock.*

The court met pursuant to adjournment.

Present: All the members, the judge advocate, and Lieutenant Colonel Frémont.

The proceedings of Thursday and Friday last were read over.

The court was then cleared to consider the admissibility of the evidence offered by Lieutenant Colonel Frémont on Thursday, and which the court had under consideration previous to adjournment on that day.

And the court made the following decision:

The explanation of the proposed inquiry by the defence avers, that Lieutenant Colonel Frémont was marched across the continent a virtual prisoner, under circumstances of virtual indignity, &c., from his commander, General Kearny, not allowed towards even prisoners; and of these circumstances the defence offer, in general terms, to show in evidence a few glaring instances, without having sufficiently specified the acts.

The court, before deciding on this inquiry, will receive from the accused a statement of those instances of indignity, specifically, which he proposes to present to show a course of oppression.

The court was then opened. Lieutenant Colonel Frémont in court. The decision in closed session was announced.

Lieutenant Colonel Frémont read to the court the following paper:

Mr. PRESIDENT: Lieutenant Colonel Frémont supposed, under advice of his counsel that, stating the general object of the course of inquiries which he proposed to institute, would be a sufficient explanation for the action of the court. If not only the nature of the inquiries, however, but a detailed statement of the facts themselves proposed to be proved, is required, it will take time to consult with the witnesses, to ascertain what each was cognizant of and remembers, and afterwards to draw up a statement of the facts it is proposed to embrace. What is proposed to be proved under the question before the court, is a distinct fact in itself, to wit: that Lieutenant Colonel Frémont having selected a certain convenient place to encamp, was refused permission to encamp there, and without any apparent motive, unless to place him in the neighborhood and under the surveillance of General Kearny's party of Mormons, was ordered to encamp in another place. Other facts, to be brought out in subsequent inquiries, will tend to the same end; and Lieutenant Colonel Frémont, by advice of his counsel, respectfully submits, that to require, before a decision is had upon this point, a circumstantial development of all the testimony that he desires to bring to the notice of the court, can go to no inquiry but to the *sufficiency* of the facts for the point that he proposes, and that the present is not the appropriate time to judge of more than the *relevancy*, without bringing into question the sufficiency of testimony. If the court, however, prefer to know, not only the character and intent, but also the extent and sufficiency of the whole testimony to a certain point, before any part of it is allowed to be introduced, Lieutenant Colonel Frémont will endeavor to meet their wishes, and will request leave to present a paper for that purpose to-morrow morning.

J. C. FRÉMONT,
Lieutenant Colonel, mounted rifles.

The court was then cleared. And the court made the following decision:

The court does not understand, from the explanation made by Lieutenant Colonel Frémont on Thursday, nor from his note of this day, the character of the evidence which he wishes to introduce. The acts which he has referred to, as acts of official oppression and of personal indignity and affront, on the part of General Kearny towards him, appear to the court as acts done in the usual routine of military service. Under this aspect only the court could not inquire into them.

The court will receive from Lieutenant Colonel Frémont, as already suggested to him, an explanatory and specific statement of what he expects to show. The court will then be able to judge whether the testimony offered ought to be received as tending to discredit a prosecuting witness before a court martial.

The court was then opened. Lieutenant Colonel Frémont in court. The decision in closed session was announced.

Mr. W. N. Loker, a witness.—Examination in chief by the defence continued.

Question. Did General Kearny, at the same place, refuse an application made by Lieutenant Colonel Frémont, through you, for leave to go ahead to Suter's fort, for the purpose of making preparations for himself and party, in the journey to the United States And did General Kearny subsequently, when near Suter's fort, refuse an application made by Lieutenant Colonel Frémont through you, to be allowed time to procure dried meat for the subsistence of the party in the journey to the United States? And was the party well or ill provided at the time of that refusal, in respect to provisions and other necessaries for the journey?

On motion of a member, the court was cleared; and the court decided that this question makes part of the inquiry which the court has suspended until Lieutenant Colonel Frémont can offer the necessary explanation.

The court was then opened. Lieutenant Colonel Frémont in court. The decision in closed session was announced.

Mr. W. N. Loker, a witness.—Examination in chief by the defence continued.

Question. Did you, by direction of Lieutenant Colonel Frémont, in June last, and when on the Cosumné river, carry to General Kearny a message in relation to a band of horses? If so, please state what occurred.

The judge advocate suggested that the question made part of the suspended inquiry.

Lieutenant Colonel Frémont said it had been decided by the court that the subject of the horses should be enquired into.

The question was then put to the witness.

Answer. After arriving at the Cosumné river, I started on to Suter's fort, and was ordered by Lieutenant Colonel Frémont, to go by General Kearny's camp, and report our arrival on the river, and to know his orders regarding a band of horses. On arriving at General Kearny's camp, and while in conversation with him, he asked me if the band of horses was on the Cosumné, above his camp. I told him that they were. He then said: Tell Colonel Frémont that I do not wish any of those horses touched until they are turned over to Major Swords, the quartermaster; and then ordered me to turn them over to Major Swords. Those orders were sent back to Colonel Frémont by a man that I took with me for the purpose of carrying back the order. I believe that answers the question.

Question. Who afterwards took possession of those horses, and under what circumstances?

Answer. When the band of horses arrived at the American fork, I went down with the guard that had them in charge; and finding Major Swords at the crossing, I told him I had a band of horses which I was ordered by General Kearny to turn over to him. He said he could not receive them, as General Kearny had given him no such orders, and refused to receive them. I then sent them up to Suter's fort, with the request to the lieutenant in command, to have a guard over the horses till the next morning. In the morning, I was over to General Kearny's camp, and could not get to the fort in time to see the horses divided; that is, to take charge of the horses before Major Swords took them. I had sent to the lieutenant in command, to take charge of the horses till I came. I did not get there in time; and, when I did get there, Major Swords had taken his pick of the horses.

Several of our men came to me complaining that Major Swords had taken his pick out of the horses, and, also, all the mules but two.

I spoke to Major Swords, and told him that I understood from General Kearny that we were to have an equal division. He told me that General Kearny's orders to him was to take what horses he wanted. I also requested of him to let me have half of the mules. He said he had great use of the mules in General Kearny's camp—he could not give them up.

I believe that is all that took place in regard to that matter.

Question. Did Major Swords give you any receipt for the horses and mules which he took, or make inquiry of you to whom he should give receipts?

Answer. He did not. He said nothing to me about receipts, nor I to him. From the conversation I had with General Kearny, I supposed the horses belonged to him, (General Kearny.) I do not mean that they belonged to him personally; but that he had perfect control over them.

Question. What was the number of the band, and when were they left at Cosumné river, and by whom?

Answer. The number, as near as I can recollect, was about one hundred, of which eight or ten were mules. They were left there by Colonel Frémont, about the 7th of October, of the year 1846.

Question. Do you know from whom Lieutenant Colonel Frémont had obtained those horses? Whether he had not obtained them from General Vallejo, and other Californians of Sonoma, to whom Lieutenant Colonel Fremont was responsible?

Answer. I think most of the horses were obtained from the Vallejos, and from other persons on the Sonoma side, and receipts given for them by Colonel Fremont.

A member said: Do you know this fact you are now stating?

Witness answered: I did not see receipts written. I heard several persons say that they held receipts; and I knew several persons to apply for horses.

Question. Was it not customary for Lieutenant Colonel Frémont to give receipts to the Californians for all the animals he took from them, both during the revolution and during the war?

Answer. As far as I can recollect, receipts were always given when horses were taken. I have myself written receipts for horses, when I have been out; which Colonel Fremont has always acknowleged.

Question. Were not the horses, which were taken from the Vallejo, and others in Sonoma, taken by Lieutenant Colonel Frémont during the revolution and before the war?

Answer. All the horses taken from the Vallejos, and other persons on the Sonoma side, were taken during the revolution, and before we heard of the war between the United States and Mexico.

Question. Did you at Suter's fort, in the Sacramento valley, inform General Kearny that Messrs. Kerne and King, of the topographical party, had not come up, and would be kept behind if the party were compelled to start immediately? and what was General Kearny's reply?

A member said: That the question appeared to him to come under the class of questions suspended for explanation.

The judge advocate said: He did not understand the bearing of the question at all.

Lieutenant Colonel Frémont replied that it referred to the keeping away of witnesses.

Answer. On the 15th of June, I went over to General Kearny's camp, near Suter's fort, to take a letter from Colonel Frémont. I then asked General Kearny when he would move camp; he told me to-morrow morning. I then told him it was impossible for us to be ready by that time; and also told him that if we went at that time, we would leave two of our party Mr. King and Mr. Kerne. He told me to tell Colonel Frémont that he expected him and his party to camp with him on that night; that is, on the 16th.

Question. Where did General Kearny encamp the next night? and did he thence continue his journey?

Answer. He encamped on a dry creek, about twenty miles from the American fork, from Suter's, making a march of about twenty miles on that day. That is what I was told. I did not move that day with camp. I did not leave Suter's till next day. I did not see their camp ground of that night. General Kearny continued his journey next day about twenty miles to Johnson's rancho.

Question. Do you know whether General Kearny was again informed at Johnson's rancho, that those gentlemen had not yet got up?

On motion of a member, the court was cleared. The court decided that, as the defence now (although to-day for the first time) inform the court that they charge General Kearny with keeping away Messrs. Kerne and King from attending as witnesses on this trial, the court will receive evidence from Lieutenant Colonel Frémont in proof of it.

The court was then opened. Lieutenant Colonel Frémont in court. The decision in closed session was announced.

The testimony of to-day was read over to the witness, and then, at three minutes before three, the court adjourned to meet to-morrow at 10 o'clock.

TUESDAY, *December 28, 1847.—10 o'clock.*

The court met pursuant to adjournment.

Present: All the members and the judge advocate.

The proceedings of yesterday were read over, during which Lieutenant Colonel Frémont came into court.

Mr. Wm. N. Loker, a witness, wished to make an explanation. Leave being granted, he said: I said yesterday that I waited on General Kearny on the 15th of June, at his camp near Suter's fort, with a letter from Lieutenant Colonel Frémont. It was the 14th. General Kearny said he would march the next day; he did not, however, march till the 16th.

On motion of a member, the court was cleared. The court was then opened. Lieutenant Colonel Frémont in court.

Mr. Wm. N. Locker, a witness for the defence.—Examination in chief continued.

The last question proposed by Lieutenant Colonel Frémont, on yesterday, was then read to the witness, as follows: Do you know whether General Kearny was again informed, at Johnson's rancho, that those gentlemen had not arrived?

Answer. When I arrived in camp at Johnson's rancho, it was late at night. I know nothing of what transpired through the day at the camp, for I was not there. I do not know, except by hearsay, that General Kearny knew that those gentlemen had not got up.

Question. Did General Kearny, from Johnson's rancho, make, for a succession of days, rapid and unusual marches?

A member objecting, on the ground of irrelevancy, the court was cleared. And the court decided that: The court does not perceive, in the circumstances as yet brought in evidence, anything going to prove, or raise a presumption that General Kearny left these persons, Messrs. King and Kerne, in California, with the design of keeping witnesses from this trial. But as the defence have urged this testimony on the court, declaring that they expect to prove against General Kearny the corrupt detention of witnesses from the trial, the court will allow them to continue their testimony to this point, under the expectation that by its continuance the circumstances now in evidence, and apparently irrelevant, will be connected with the impeachment of the witness.

The court was then opened. Lieutenant Colonel Frémont in court. The decision in closed session was announced.

Mr. Loker, a witness, in answer to the last question, said: The first three or four days' travelling, I think, he made thirty or thirty-five miles a day; which, in the state that our horses' feet were then in, would have been hard travelling for them. I was not with General Kearny, as he started early in the morning; we started about twelve o'clock in the day. Nor did we (Colonel Frémont's party) overtake him, until we reached Mountain lake, three or four days' march from Johnson's rancho. Our lowest march on the route, generally, from California to the United States, when we made any day's march at all, was about eighteen miles; on some days we did not go more than ten or twelve miles—which we hardly called a day's march—we merely moved camp in these cases; and we have made as high as forty on good roads; our horses were then shod. I suppose the distance from Johnson's rancho to Mountain lake is about one hundred miles; I only know it from travelling over it.

Lieutenant Colonel Frémont read to the court the following paper:

Mr. President: Lieutenant Colonel Frémont states that he expects to be able to prove that, on the 14th of June last, at New Helvetia, in California, on the return march of Brigadier General Kearny to the United States, he wrote and caused to be delivered to him a letter, of which the following is a copy made at the time, to wit:

NUEVA HELVETIA, UPPER CALIFORNIA,
June 14, 1847.

SIR: In a communication which I received from yourself, in

March of the present year, I am informed that you had been directed by the commander-in-chief not to detain me in this country against my wishes, longer than the absolute necessities of the service might require.

Private letters, in which I have entire confidence, further inform me that the President has been pleased to direct that I should be permitted the choice of joining my regiment in Mexico, or returning directly to the United States. An application which I had the honor to make to you at the Ciudad de los Angeles, for permission to proceed immediately to Mexico, having been rejected, and the duties of the exploring expedition, which had been confided to my direction, having been terminated by yourself, I respectfully request that I may now be relieved of all connexion with the topographical party, which you have taken under your charge, and be permitted to return to the United States. Travelling with a small party by a direct route, my knowledge of the country and freedom from professional business, will enable me to reach the States some forty or fifty days earlier than yourself, which the present condition of affairs and a long absence from my family make an object of great importance to me.

It may not be improper to say to you that my journey will be made with private means, and will not, therefore, occasion any expenditure to the government.

I have the honor to be, with much respect, your obedient servant,

J. C. FRÉMONT,
Lieutenant Colonel, mounted rifles.

Brigadier General S. W. KEARNY,
Commanding western army,
Nueva Helvetia, Upper California.

—And that on the same day he (Lieutenant Colonel Frémont) received an answer, in writing, of which the original is herewith shown to the court, in these words, to wit:

CAMP NEAR NEW HELVETIA, (CALIFORNIA,)
June 14, 1847.

SIR: The request contained in your communication to me of this date, to be relieved from all connection with the topographical party, (nineteen men,) and be permitted to return to the United States with a small party, made up by your private means, cannot be granted.

I shall leave here on Wednesday, the 16th instant, and I require of you to be with your topographical party in my camp (which will probably be 15 miles from here) on the evening of that day, and to continue with me to Missouri.

Very respectfully, your obedient servant,
S. W. KEARNY,
Brigadier General.

Lieutenant Colonel FRÉMONT,
Regiment mounted riflemen, New Helvetia.

—Also, he expects to be able to prove that at Monterey, in California, about the end of the month of May last, he was ordered to appear, with the citizens formerly under his command as his topographical party, and with them was exhibited at a fixed hour and place, and under the view of an assemblage of persons, to wit: Commodore Biddle and many others, in an insulting and degrading manner, felt and seen to be so by all honorable men then present; and, besides the degradation of the exhibition, was insulted twice by him, the said General Kearny.

Also, he expects to be able to prove that, after crossing the great Sierra Nevada, he (Lieutenant Colonel Frémont) applied to General Kearny for leave to come direct through the *Great Basin* to the United States for the purpose of completing and correcting his outward exploration of a new route to California, to the south of the Great Salt lake, and to be able to make a topographical map thereof similar to the Oregon road map, and about four hundred miles shorter between the two points of crossing the Rocky mountains and the Sierra Nevada, than the route on which General Kearny travelled between the same two points, and sent a map, which is herewith shown to the court, to illustrate the difference between the two routes, and to show the advantage it would be to future travellers and emigrants to have said new route established, and topographically mapped; and the said General Kearny refused the application, and ordered Lieutenant Colonel Frémont to follow his (General Kearny's) trail, concealing from him at the same time his design to arrest him. Also, that he expects to be able to prove that, at Fort Laramie, on the north fork of the Great Platte river, Brigadier General Kearny refused permission to Lieutenant Colonel Frémont, and the citizens of the topographical party who were with him, to return to the frontier of Missouri by a shorter route than by Fort Leavenworth, concealing from him all knowledge of his intention to arrest him, and giving, as a reason for it, a different one from that of a design to arrest him at that place.

Also, that he expects to be able to prove that neither himself nor the citizens of the topographical corps who were with him were spoken to by any officer at Fort Leavenworth except Colonel Wharton, and he merely in doing the part of a witness to the arrest and in answering some question to Lieutenant Loker; and this for about the space of five hours, during which time they were standing about the fort waiting upon the leisure of the ordnance sergeant, who was to receive their arms and horses, all which time they were not approached, spoken to, or noticed by any officer of the fort, nor offered the least hospitality, and this under circumstances which induce Lieutenant Colonel Frémont to attribute their conduct to the presence and influence of General Kearny.

And Lieutenant Colonel Frémont is advised by his counsel that the evidence to the foregoing effect would be material to his defence, and that it could only be duly and properly judged of in connexion with all other testimony in the general defence; and that he has a right to use it in such defence, and in *connexion* with all other testimony to the same effect, and to make it available for

what it is worth, in the impeachment of the motives and credit of
General Kearny in this prosecution.

J. C. FRÉMONT,
Lieutenant Colonel mounted rifles.

The court was then cleared; and, after deliberation, the court
made the following decision:

The court cannot inquire into the refusal of General Kearny to
grant Lieutenant Colonel Fremont's application at New Helvetia,
on the 14th June, 1847, to be relieved from connexion with the
topographical party, and to return himself to the United States
by another route than that by which General Kearny was returning.

To grant, or refuse the indulgence asked, was entirely within
the discretion of the commanding general. The court cannot presume either injustice or harshness in the refusal. It is clearly not
a matter to be given in evidence to impeach the motives of the witness, and to discredit him here.

The court has the same opinion in regard to the refusal of
General Kearny to grant Lieutenant Colonel Frémont's subsequent
applications; first, near the Sierra Nevada, and next at Fort
Laramie; to leave General Kearny and return to the United States
with his topographical party.

Another allegation is founded on a parade or inspection of Lieutenant Colonel Fremont's topographical party by General Kearny,
at Monterey, before the march to the United States. The court
cannot regard this inspection by General Kearny of a party in the
military service and then under his command for the purpose of
accompanying his march homeward as a public exhibition for
insult to the head of the party, without having before it the nature
of the alleged insults. It is, in evidence, that General Kearny
paraded the party at Monterey to ascertain who of them wished to
be discharged there, and who of them wished to return to the
United States.

For this purpose, General Kearny's order of the 28th March,
1847, also in evidence, directs Lieutenant Colonel Frémont to
bring his party to Monterey. The act thus appears to have been
in the routine of military duty, and not a matter for investigation
here, while the nature of the alleged accompanying insult is in no
manner specified, conformably to the court's decision of yesterday,
so as to enable the court to judge whether it may go to the point
of discrediting a prosecuting witness before a court martial.

The court cannot inquire into the reception given to Lieutenant
Colonel Frémont and his party by the officers at Fort Leavenworth,
in order to ascertain, as alleged, that he was not approached,
spoken to, nor offered the least hospitality by any officer at the
fort.

The court could not receive in evidence, to discredit General
Kearny as a witness, any testimony that he did not himself offer
civilities or hospitalities to Lieutenant Colonel Frémont. Still less
can it inquire into such matters in regard to the other officers at

Fort Leavenworth, and attribute their conduct to the presence and influence of General Kearny, as supposed, by Lieutenant Colonel Frémont.

The court finds nothing in any, or all of the acts, alleged by Lieutenant Colonel Frémont, which can justify it in admitting them in evidence; and it therefore decides that the inquiry be not allowed.

The court was then opened; Lieutenant Colonel Frémont in court. The decision in closed session was announced.

Lieutenant Colonel Frémont submitted to the court the following letter:

Mr. PRESIDENT: Lieutenant Colonel Frémont, under the present decision of the court, will avail himself of his right to produce to the court, at a future day, the substance of the evidence that would have been given, had the inquiries been allowed, upon the points brought to the notice of the court, to be so entered upon the record.

J. C. FRÉMONT,
Lieutenant Colonel, mounted rifles.

And Lieutenant Colonel Frémont read to the court the following note:

Mr. PRESIDENT: Lieutenant Colonel Frémont, by advice of his counsel, would respectfully inquire of the judge advocate whether the *reason* given by a member for moving that the court be cleared, upon the question concerning the rapid and unusual marches of General Kearny, is entered upon the record; and if not, would respectfully request that it be now done.

J. C. FRÉMONT,
Lieutenant Colonel, mounted rifles.

The court was ordered to be cleared. The judge advocate said the record now stands, "a member objecting on the grounds of irrelevancy, the court was cleared."

The court ordered it to be entered on the record, that the court approves the record as it now stands.

And the court took into consideration the note submitted by Lieutenant Colonel Frémont, informing the court that he will hereafter offer, to go on the record, the substance of the evidence which was to-day ruled out by the court.

And the court decided that the court has now on its record two papers from the accused giving the substance, and some details, of the evidence he proposed to submit in the course of this inquiry, which inquiry the court has disallowed. The court does not recognize the "right," claimed by the accused, to place again on its record the substance of the evidence proposed.

The court was then opened; Lieutenant Colonel Frémont in court. The decisions in closed session were announced.

Mr. Wm. N. Loker, a witness.

Lieutenant Colonel Frémont had no further questions to ask this witness.

Cross-examination by judge advocate.

Question. Do you know of any instance where public horses, for which Lieutenant Colonel Frémont was responsible, were taken by order of General Kearny for the public service, or for any use, and receipts refused by order of General Kearny?

Answer. I know of no instance where horses were taken by General Kearny, and receipts asked for and refused.

Question. Did you march from Monterey with Lieutenant Colonel Frémont's party?

Answer. I did.

Question. Were Mr. King and Mr. Kerne with you?

Answer. They were not.

Question. Can you state why they were not with you at Suter's fort when you informed General Kearny of their absence?

Answer. Mr. King had business at Yerba Buena, and all through the upper Pueblo valley, as commissary of the battalion, getting receipts, &c. Mr. Kerne was down at Monterey on business with Commodore Stockton, relating to accounts which he made while in command at Suter's fort. He had not got through his business when we left Monterey; we left him there.

Question. Do you know that General Kearny gave any orders to obtain them in California?

Answer. I know of no such orders that General Kearny gave in relation to their detention.

The testimony of to-day was here read over to the witness; and then, at five minutes before three, the court adjourned to meet tomorrow at ten o'clock.

———

WEDNESDAY, *December* 29, 1847.—10 *o'clock.*

The court met pursuant to adjournment.

Present: All the members, the judge advocate, and Lieutenant Colonel Frémont.

The proceedings of yesterday were read over.

Mr. Wm. N. Loker, a witness.—Cross-examination by judge advocate continued.

Question. Did you ever turn over to Major Swords, or to any other officer, by order of General Kearny, any other horses than the band you have spoken of on the Cosumné river?

Answer. Those are the only horses I ever turned over to Major Swords, or to any other officer, by order of General Kearny.

Question. What were the number of the topographical party which returned with you to the United States, exclusive of Mr. King and Mr. Kerne, who did not return?

Answer. Nineteen, I think.

The judge advocate had no further questions to ask the witness.
The court was then cleared.

After a short time in closed session, the court was opened. Lieutenant Colonel Frémont in court.

The court had no questions to ask the witness, Mr. Loker.

Lieutenant Colonel Frémont read to the court the following note:

Mr. PRESIDENT: Lieutenant Colonel Frémont, by advice of his counsel, now again offers to the court a portion of the documentary testimony heretofore presented, but not placed upon the record, adopting in the introduction the mode for which the court expressed its preference. Further documentary evidence will hereafter be offered.

Lieutenant Colonel Frémont will also request leave to present to the court, either before the close of the session to-day, or immediately after the reading of the journal to-morrow morning, a paper preliminary to the general defence.

J. C. FRÉMONT,
Lieutenant Colonel, mounted rifles.

And Lieutenant Colonel Frémont then read to the court several papers, in explanation of the bearing and effect of documents which he offered in evidence.

The court was then cleared, to take the same into consideration, and decide on the admissibility of the evidence offered. Pending which, the court adjourned at ten minutes before three, to meet to-morrow at 10 o'clock.

THURSDAY, December 30, 1847.—10 o'clock.

The court met pursuant to adjournment.

Present: All the members, the judge advocate, and Lieutenant Colonel Frémont.

The proceedings of yesterday were read over, and the court was cleared to resume the consideration of the documentary evidence offered on yesterday.

And the court had under consideration the following paper, submitted yesterday by Lieutenant Colonel Frémont:

MR. PRESIDENT: Lieutenant Colonel Frémont offers to the court the paper, marked L, with the three printed extracts wafered upon it. This paper, with the extracts, was heretofore offered to the court, and rejected as irrelevant. It is now offered again, with a request that the extracts be received as evidence, or entered as rejected on the minutes.

Lieutenant Colonel Frémont is advised by his counsel, that these extracts are all material to his defence, and to that part of it which denies the *usurpation* of the office of governor in California.

The *usurpation* he denies; the fact of exercising the governorship he avows and justifies: 1. Under the law of nations, and the appointment of Governor Stockton. 2. Under the approbation of the President of the United States. The appointment by Governor Stockton has been heretofore proved. The approbation of the President is now proposed to be proved, and by the extracts offered, one from the President's annual message of December, 1846, the other two from the Secretaries of War and Navy.

Lieutenant Colonel Frémont is advised by his counsel, that the appointment by Governor Stockton was valid under the law of nations, without any approval by the President; but the present prosecution being ordered by the President, (he alone having the legal right to order it,) it becomes material to show that he has approved the act for which Lieutenant Colonel Frémont is now prosecuted by his order. The *relevancy* of this testimony offered, is the only question now before the court; its sufficiency belongs to the " *defence*," and to the time for the general consideration of all the testimony.

The extracts offered are cut from a copy of the message and documents, printed by order of one of the Houses of Congress, and by the public printer, for the time being, a full copy of which is herewith shown to the court; and this proof of their verity is considered by the counsel of Lieutenant Colonel Frémont, a sufficient authentication to admit them to be read as evidence. The whole message and documents are produced to satisfy the court that the extracts are in them.

J. C. FRÉMONT,
Lieutenant Colonel, mounted rifles.

L.

Extract from the President's annual message, December, 1846.

" Our squadron in the Pacific, with the co-operation of a gallant officer of the army, and a small force hastily collected in that distant country, have acquired bloodless possession of the Californias, and the American flag has been raised at every important point in that province.

" I congratulate you on the success which has thus attended our military and naval operations. In less than seven months after Mexico commenced hostilities, at a time selected by herself, we have taken possession of many of her principal ports; driven back and pursued her invading army, and acquired military possession of the Mexican provinces of New Mexico, New Leon, Coahuila, Tamaulipas, and the Californias, a territory larger in extent than that embraced in the original thirteen States of the Union, inhabited by a considerable population, and much of it more than a thousand miles from the points at which we had to collect our forces and commence our movements. By the blockade, the import and export trade of the enemy has been cut off, *   *   *

" By the laws of nations a conquered territory is subject to be governed by the conqueror during his military possession, and until there is either a treaty of peace, or he shall voluntarily withdraw from it. The old civil government being necessarily superseded, it is the right and duty of the conqueror to secure his conquest, and to provide for the maintenance of civil order and the rights of the inhabitants.

" *This right* has been *exercised*, and this duty *performed* by *our military and naval commanders*, by the establishment of *temporary governments* in some of the conquered provinces in Mexico, assimilating them, as far as practicable, to the free institutions of our own country. In the provinces of New Mexico, *and of the Californias*, little, if any, further resistance is apprehended from the inhabitants to the temporary governments which have thus, from the necessity of the case, and according to the laws of war, been established. It may be proper to provide for the security of those important conquests by making an adequate appropriation for the purpose of erecting fortifications and defraying the expenses necessarily incident to the maintenance of our possession and authority over them."

Extract from the report of the Secretary of War, December, 1846.

" Commodore Stockton took possession of the whole country as a conquest of the United States, and appointed Colonel Frémont governor, under the law of nations, to assume the functions of that office when he should return to the squadron."

Extract from the report of the Secretary of the Navy, December,
1846.

" On the 25th of July, the Cyane, Captain Mervine, sailed from Monterey, with Lieutenant Colonel Frémont and a small volunteer force on board, for San Diego, to intercept the retreat of the Mexican General Castro. A few days after, Commodore Stockton sailed in the Congress frigate for San Pedro, and, with a detachment from his squadron of three hundred and sixty men, marched to the enemy's camp. It was found that the camp was broken up, and the Mexicans, under Governor Pico and General Castro, had retreated so precipitously that Lieutenant Colonel Frémont was disappointed in intercepting him. On the 13th, Commodore Stockton was joined by this gallant officer, and marched a distance of thirty miles from the sea, and entered, without opposition, Ciudad de Los Angeles, the capital of the Californias; and on the 22d of August the flag of the United States was flying at every commanding position, and California was in *the undisputed military possession of the United States.* The conduct of the officers and men of the squadron in these important operations has been characterized by activity, courage, and steady discipline, and entitles them to the thanks of the department. Efficient aid was rendered by Lieutenant Colonel Frémont and the volunteers under his command. *In his hands,* Commodore Stockton informs the department, he will leave the military government when he shall leave California, in the further execution of his orders."

And the court made the following decision:

Lieutenant Colonel Frémont offers to show from the President's message of 8th December, 1846, and the accompanying reports of the Secretaries of War and the Navy, that he held the office of governor of California, under the approbation of the President of the United States, by whose order he is now on trial for usurpation of that office. The extract from the President's message goes only to assert, as a principle of the law of nations, or of war, that a conqueror may establish a temporary civil government in a conquered territory, and to inform Congress that such power had been exercised by our naval and military commanders.

The extract from the report of the Secretary of the Navy states, in closing a narrative of events in California, the intention of Commodore Stockton, as he informs the department, to leave the military government of the territory in the hands of Lieutenant Colonel Frémont.

The report of the Secretary of War relates the conquest of California, according to such unofficial information as had been received at the department prior to December, 1846; and it concludes this narrative by reporting that Commodore Stockton had taken possession of the country for the United States in August, 1846, and had appointed Colonel Frémont governor under the law of nations.

The court has examined the entire documents submitted to it, and finds nothing in them applicable to the case now on trial.

It cannot be a question here, whether, by the law of nations, a conqueror may establish a military or temporary civil government in a conquered country; nor is it a question here, whether, if Commodore Stockton, as supposed by the Secretary of War, had conquered California and appointed Lieutenant Colonel Frémont governor, he would have acted according to the law of nations.

Lieutenant Colonel Frémont is charged on this trial with resisting the lawful authority of General Kearny, sent to California by order of the President of the United States, with instructions and authority to exercise the chief command, military and civil. Neither this alleged resistance to General Kearny by Lieutenant Colonel Frémont, nor the appointment of Lieutenant Colonel Frémont as governor by Commodore Stockton, in January, 1847, when General Kearny was then present, claiming the chief command under special orders of the President, could be contemplated in the President's message of December, 1846, nor by the reports from the War and Navy Departments of the same date.

The court cannot receive these documents as evidence to prove, or in any way tending to prove, the President's approbation of the position or acts of Lieutenant Colonel Frémont in the matter under trial.

The court places the documents on its record for the consideration of the reviewing authority.

And the court had under consideration the following paper, sub-- mitted yesterday by Lieutenant Colonel Frémont:

Mr. PRESIDENT: Lieutenant Colonel Frémont offers to the court the original leter herewith presented, marked Q, and heretofore re- turned by the court as *irrelevant.* He is advised by his counsel that this letter is material to his defence, and to that part of it which rests upon the allegation of his service, as part of the naval forces for the conquest, preservation, and civil government of Cali- fornia; the letter being proof that Governor Stockton, commander- in-chief, caused the battalion commanded by the then Major Fré- mont to be *paid by the purser under his command,* and *out of naval funds.* If rejected as irrelevant, Lieutenant Colonel Frémont asks that the letter (after due proof of its authenticity) may be entered on the minutes of the court.

J. C. FRÉMONT,
Lieutenant Colonel, mounted rifles.

Q.

Letter (original) from General Stockton to Major Frémont, dated

CIUDAD DE LOS ANGELES, *September* 1, 1846.

SIR: The amount of money for which you have made a requisi- tion cannot be furnished you at this time. Mr. Speiden, the pur- ser of the Congress, says he can only spare twenty thousand dol- lars; which I hope will answer your purposes until we hear from home, and receive information from the government how and where (if hostilities continue) we can be furnished with funds.

It is quite probable that we may not be able to get any money at Mazatlan.

Respectfully, your obedient servant,

R. F. STOCKTON,
Commander-in-chief, &c.

Major FRÉMONT, *California battalion.*

And the court made the following decision:

Lieutenant Colonel Frémont offers a letter from Commodore Stockton to himself, as the commander of the California battalion, stating that the purser can only spare twenty thousand dollars, which Commodore Stockton hopes will answer Lieutenant Colonel Frémont's purposes, as evidence going to show that the California battalion was paid out of naval funds.

The court cannot receive the letter as competent evidence to that point. The best evidence is required in every case. The appro- priation laws, or the proper officers of the War, or Navy, or Trea- sury Departments, furnish the best evidence to show the fund or appropriation, to which payments have actually or legally been charged.

The court does not now undertake to decide the effect and bear ing of this point in the case, but the admissibility of this evidence to the point.

And the court had under consideration the following paper, submitted yesterday by Lieutenant Colonel Frémont:

Mr. PRESIDENT: Lieutenant Colonel Frémont offers, as evidence in this case, the despatch from Commodore Stockton to the Secretary of the Navy, dated January 22, 1847, marked X, heretofore offered to this court as evidence, and returned as not being evidence, and irrelevant. Lieutenant Colonel Frémont is advised by his counsel that this despatch is evidence, and is material. It is a despatch to *inform* the President that, on the 22d day of January last, the civil government of California was in successful operation, Lieutenant Colonel Frémont being governor, and Colonel Wm. H. Russell, secretary; and this prosecution being against him for *usurpation* of that office, the counsel of Lieutenant Colonel Frémont hold it to be relevant and material to prove that the President was *officially informed* of his appointment, and of his entrance upon his duties; and that the despatch containing that information was received at the Navy Department in the latter part of April last, long before this trial was ordered, and before the letter of June 11, 1847, was written, (marked C C;) a letter wholly inconsistent with disapprobation of Governor Frémont's appointment.

Deeming all this to be relevant and material in this prosecution, and the official copy of the despatch, herewith offered, to be sufficient evidence that they were received at the Navy Department, the counsel of Lieutenant Colonel Frémont ask that it may now be received as such, or entered upon the minutes as rejected.

This being a case in which the President *only* could order a trial under the act of May 29, 1830, to wit: the case of a commanding general becoming the accuser or prosecutor of an officer under his command, Lieutenant Colonel Frémont is advised that it is *relevant* to his defence to prove (if he can) that the President was *informed* of the *fact*, as well as of the *intention* of Governor Stockton to appoint him (Lieutenant Colonel Frémont) governor and commander-in-chief in California, and that long before this trial was ordered, and never objected to it. Lieutenant Colonel Frémont is advised that he has a right to use this fact, to go with other evidence, to prove that the President approved of his appointment.

J. C. FRÉMONT,
Lieutenant Colonel, mounted rifles.

And the court made the following decision:

Lieutenant Colonel Frémont offers a despatch of Commodore Stockton to the Navy Department, dated January 22, 1847, received at the department in April, 1847, to show that the government was officially informed, as stated in that despatch, that the civil government of the territory of California was in successful operation, and Lieutenant Colonel Frémont was acting as governor.

Lieutenant Colonel Frémont offers this report, in connexion with the fact that instructions from the government to General Kearny, dated June 11, 1847, and issued after the receipt of this despatch, express no objection to Lieutenant Colonel Fremont's appointment as governor by Governor Stockton, as evidence to prove the President's approbation of Lieutenant Colonel Frémont's appointment.

The court repeat here, in application to this special point, the opinion hereinbefore more generally expressed and applied, that, if the reports of officers to the department are offered to show the powers which such officers claimed and exercised by sanction of the government, the distinct approval of the government must also be shown. And the mere report to the department, standing by itself, is no evidence to prove the sanction of the government; the more especially to prove such sanction, and set it up against previous express orders of the government.

The court, therefore, decide that the report of Commodore Stockton is not admissible in evidence, as offered, to prove the President's approval of Lieutenant Colonel Frémont's holding the office of governor of California in resistance of General Kearny, as charged in this prosecution; and is, further, not admissable in evidence as going to any other point in this case.

The court find other matter in this report of Commodore Stockton's making it improper to go on the record of this court. Whether the battle of San Pasqual was a victory or defeat of the United States troops, is a matter not in issue on this trial. If it were, Commodore Stockton's opinions of a battle, when he was not present, is not evidence, and the court cannot receive attacks on the professional conduct and character of officers not on trial here, and in regard to matters not in issue here, and especially by statements which would not be evidence if the subject was properly before the court.

And the court had under consideration the following paper, submitted yesterday by Lieutenant Colonel Frémont:

Mr. PRESIDENT: Lieutenant Colonel Frémont offers to the court the extract, herewith presented, marked C C, being part of a letter of instructions to Brigadier General Kearny, dated Washington, June 11, 1847, having been heretofore presented to the court, and returned as irrelevant; and in offering it he is instructed to say, that his counsel consider it both relevant and material in the following passage, to wit: "*The President is persuaded that when his definite instructions were received (those of November, 1846) all questions of difficulty were settled, and all feelings which had been elicited by the agitation of them have subsided.*" "*And should Lieutenant Colonel Frémont, who has the option to return or remain, adopt the latter alternative, the President has no doubt you will employ him in such a manner as will render his services most available to the public interest,*" &c. The counsel for Lieutenant Colonel Frémont believe the first of these extracts to be material to him in two points of view; first, as showing that the instructions of November, 1846, were definite, which leaves the inference that the previous instructions were *indefinite;* secondly, that the President expected these *definite instructions* to settle all difficulties, and consequently to be seen by the parties to the difficulties, (of whom Governor Frémont was one,) and which instructions were never made known to him. The.second of these extracts is considered material in this, that it shows Lieutenant Colonel Frémont had the option, under the President's orders, to remain or not in California, consequently that it was a violation of his right (under the President's sanction) for General Kearny to refuse him leave to go and join his regiment in Mexico, and afterwards to refuse him leave to return with his exploring party to the United States; and the *relevancy* of all this being now the only question, Lieutenant Colonel Frémont is advised that he has the right to have the said extracts admitted as evidence, or spread upon the record as rejected.

J. C. FRÉMONT,
Lieutenant Colonel, mounted rifles.

CC.

Extract from instructions to Brigadier General Kearny, dated

WAR DEPARTMENT, *June* 11, 1847.

* * * * * * *

When the despatch from this department was sent out in November last, there was reason to believe that Lieutenant Colonel Frémont would desire to return to the United States, and you were then directed to conform to his wishes in that respect. It is not now proposed to change that direction. But since that time it has become known here that he bore a conspicuous part in the conquest of California; that his services have been very valuable in that country, and doubtless will continue to be so should he remain there.

Impressed, as all engaged in the public service must be, with the great importance of harmony and cordial co-operation in carrying on military operations in a country so distant from the seat of authority, *the President is persuaded that, when his definite instructions were received, all questions of difficulty were settled, and all feelings which had been elicited by the agitation of them have subsided.*

Should Lieutenant Colonel Frémont, *who has the option to return or remain,* adopt the latter alternative, the President does not doubt you will employ him in such a manner as will render his services most available to the public interest, having reference to his extensive acquaintance with the inhabitants of California, and his knowledge of their language, qualifications, independent of others, which it is supposed may be very useful in the present and prospective state of our affairs in that country. * * *

Very respectfully, your obedient servant,

W. L. MARCY,
Secretary of War.

And the court made the following decision:

Lieutenant Colonel Frémont offers the President's instructions to General Kearny, issued at Washington, June 11th, 1847, (when, as appears in evidence on this trial, General Kearny was leaving California on his return to the United States,) to show:

1. That the expression in these despatches, "definite," as applied to the instructions of November, 1846, makes an inference that the previous instructions were "indefinite."

2. That, as in this despatch, it is stated that Lieutenant Colonel Frémont had the option to return or remain in California, General Kearny's previous orders to him, (or orders given when General Kearny had not received the despatch in question,) in refusing him permission to join his regiment in Mexico, and in refusing him permission to return to the United States with his exploring party, were violations of his (Lieutenant Colonel Frémont's) rights.

The court decides that this despatch is not admissible as evidence, going to either point; and that, as to the latter point, it is not a matter before the court. As to the former, the instructions issued and in force before November, 1846, could not be rendered indefinite or imperative, or be in any way affected, for the time when they were actually in force, by any such subsequent reference to them by the department, even if such had been intended or could be inferred from the despatch of June, 1847.

And the court had under consideration the following paper, submitted yesterday by Lieutenant Colonel Frémont:

Mr. President: Lieutenant Colonel Frémont offers, as evidence in this case, the extract, as received from the Navy Department, of a despatch from Commodore Shubrick to the Secretary of the Navy, dated harbor of Monterey, February 12, 1847, marked DD, being the same heretofore offered and returned by the court as not being evidence, and irrelevant. Lieutenant Colonel Frémont is advised by his counsel that the said despatch is material and relevant to his defence, as connecting itself directly with the instructions of July 12, 1846, specially charging the naval officers on the California station with the conquest, preservation, and civil government of California, from which they were never relieved till the arrival of the orders of the 5th of November, 1846, which was in the month of February of the next year, and after the difficulties had occurred.

This letter of Commodore Shubrick expressly states those difficulties, and show his own conduct to be in accordance with the instructions of July 12, 1846, and that he considered the appointment of Governor Frémont, (though unacceptable, as he was "led to believe," to the people,) yet not to be disturbed until the President was heard from, to whom the intention to make that appointment had been long before communicated. His words are:

"With regard to the civil government of California, authority for the establishment of which is contained in your instructions to Commodore Sloat, of the 12th of July last, which I received by the Lexington, measures have been, in my opinion, prematurely taken by Commodore Stockton, and an appointment of a governor made of a gentleman who, I am led to believe, is not acceptable to the people of California; *but as the intention to make the appointment was, I understand, communicated to the President as early as August last, and information as to his wishes may be soon expected, I have determined to await such information, and confine myself at present to arrangements for the quiet possession of the territory, and for the blockade of the coast of Mexico.*"

When this was written, General Kearny had been to Monterey, and had made known his difficulties, as shown in a previous part of the same letter, and had been sent by Commodore Shubrick in the Cyane to San Francisco, he (Commodore Shubrick) refusing to disturb Governor Frémont in his governorship of the territory, and General Kearny acquiescing in that refusal and going off to the bay of San Francisco. The arrival of the " *definite instructions* " of the 5th of November, 1846, soon after, induced Commodore Shubrick to relinquish the control of the civil government and the command of the land forces to General Kearny, *neither of them communicating these instructions to Governor Frémont, or relieving him.*

This reference of Commodore Shubrick to the instructions of July 12, 1846, is fully justified by those instructions which were then in his (Commodore Shubrick's) possession, and which contained these words:

" *The object of the United States is, under its rights as a belligerent nation, to possess itself entirely of Upper California.* * *
* * * * *The object of the United States has reference to ultimate peace with Mexico; and if, at that time, the basis of the uti possedetis shall be established,* THE GOVERNMENT EXPECTS, THROUGH YOUR FORCES, TO BE FOUND IN ACTUAL POSSESSION OF CALIFORNIA."

These instructions were directed to Commodore Sloat, whose hands they did not reach, nor did they reach Commodore Stockton; but they are in accordance with all other instructions to the navy in relation to the conquest of California, and show the *intention* of the government to conquer and hold it through the naval *forces;* of which naval forces the California battalion, under Lieutenant Colonel Frémont, was part at the time Brigadier General Kearny attempted to get command of it on the 16th day of January, 1847 Commodore Shubrick's letter with these instructions in his hands. and knowledge of all the difficulties, and his refusal to join General Kearny in opposing Governor Frémont, was a virtual confirmation by him of Governor Stockton's appointment, and is, therefore, material and relevant in this case.

Lieutenant Colonel Frémont therefore requests, that the letter herewith offered, (that of Commodore Shubrick,) be received as relevant, to stand for what it is worth in the general defence; and, if refused, that the same may be entered upon the minutes.

J. C. FRÉMONT,
Lieutenant Colonel, mounted rifles.

DD.

Extract of a letter from Commodore Shubrick to the Secretary of the Navy, dated,

U. S. SHIP INDEPENDENCE,
Harbor of Monterey, February 13, 1847.

SIR: Since my letters of the 26th, 27th, and 28th ultimo, no important change, so far as I can learn, has taken place in the territory. The people seem to be settling down into quiet acquiescence in the change of government; those best acquainted with their temper and disposition do not apprehend further disturbance of the peace of the country.

General Kearny arrived here on the 8th, in the sloop-of-war Cyane, and after the adoption of such measures as we thought necessary here, I sent him to San Francisco in the Cyane, to which place I should have accompanied him, but that I am looking daily for the arrival of Commodore Stockton from St. Diego, and it is important that I should receive his reports before I go farther.

You will have learned ere this, that an unfortunate difference has taken place between Commodore Stockton and General Kearny, and between the general and Colonel Frémont, growing out of the appointment of Colonel Frémont as civil governor of California by the commodore, and the refusal of the colonel to acknowledge the authority of the general.

I have, as enjoined on me by my instructions, exchanged opinions with General Kearny, and shall continue to concert with him, such measures as may seem best for keeping quiet possession of California.

With regard to the civil government of the territory, authority for the establishment of which is contained in your instructions to Commodore Sloat of 12th of July last, which I received by the Lexington, measures have been, in my opinion, prematurely taken by Commodore Stockton, and an appointment of governor made of a gentleman who I am led to believe is not acceptable to the people of California; but, as the intention to make the appointment was, I understand, communicated to the President as early as August last, and information as to his wishes may be soon expected, I have determined to await such information, and confine myself for the present to arrangements for the quiet possession of the territory, and for the blockade of the coast of Mexico.

*   *   *   *   *   *   *   *

I am, very respectfully, sir, your obedient servant,
W. BRANFORD SHUBRICK,
Commander-in-chief, &c., &c.

The Hon. GEORGE BANCROFT,
Secretary of the Navy.

NAVY DEPARTMENT,
November 5, 1847.

A true copy of the original.
Attest:

JOHN APPLETON,
Chief Clerk.

And the court made the following decision:

The court decided that the despatch of Commodore Shubrick to the Navy Department is not evidence; and the court finds in said despatch nothing relevant to this case. But the court submits the despatch, with the argument of Lieutenant Colonel Frémont, for the consideration of the reviewing authority.

The court was then opened. Lieutenant Colonel Frémont in court. The decisions in closed session were announced.

Lieutenant Colonel Frémont read to the court a paper, preliminary to the general defence; upon the reading of the paper, the court was cleared for deliberation.

After some time in closed session, the court was opened. Lieutenant Colonel Frémont in court. And then, at three minutes before three, the court adjourned to meet to-morrow at 10 o'clock.

FRIDAY, *December* 31, 1847.—10 *o'clock.*

The court met pursuant to adjournment.

Present: All the members, except General Brooke, president, who was absent, as a member informed the court, by reason of sickness. The court then went into closed session, and adjourned to meet on Monday morning, at 10 o'clock.

MONDAY, *January* 3, 1848.—10 *o'clock.*

The court met pursuant to adjournment.

Present : all the members, the judge advocate, and Lieutenant Colonel Frémont.

The proceedings of the two last days of the session, to wit, the the 30th and 31st of December, 1847, were then read over.

The judge advocate read to the court a note, in reply to the paper presented by Lieutenant Colonel Frémont on Thursday.

The court was then cleared; and the court made the following order:

The court having heard read a paper "preliminary to the defence" of the accused, upon which no action of the court is asked, and which presents some matters to the court over which it has no jurisdiction; and having, likewise, heard read a reply to the said paper by the judge advocate, directs that the papers be not entered on the record, but be put in the appendix to these proceedings.

The court was then opened. Lieutenant Colonel Frémont in court. The decision in closed session was announced.

Lieutenant Colonel Frémont informed the court that he had no more witnesses to examine; but would submit a list of the remaining witnesses summoned for the defence, that the judge advocate might have the opportunity to cross-examine them.

He would also submit some documentary evidence to-morrow.

The judge advocate said he would recall some witnesses of the prosecution, to examine them as to the matter brought out by the defence. Brigadier General Kearny, the leading witness, was not well enough to attend the court to-day.

Whereupon, the court adjourned at half past 12 o'clock, to meet to-morrow at 10 o'clock.

TUESDAY, *January* 4, 1848.—10 *o'clock.*

The court met pursuant to adjournment.

Present: All the members, the judge advocate, and Lieutenant Colonel Frémont.

The proceedings of yesterday were read over.

Lieutenant Colonel Frémont submitted the following note:

Mr. PRESIDENT: Lieutenant Colonel Frémont, by advice of his counsel, presents herewith, a list of the remaining witnesses, who have been summoned for the defence, in order that they may be called and examined, should the court or the judge advocate have any interrogatories to propound to them. The greater number of these witnesses were summoned before Lieutenant Colonel Frémont was informed upon what charges he was to be arraigned; still more before he could be aware to what limits he would be restricted in his testimony. In some instances they were summoned to supply, in a degree, the place of persons who from their positions and the duties they fulfilled would have been better witnesses, but who were kept away, or whose attendance the concealment from Lieutenant Colonel Frémont of his intended arrest and trial, prevented him from securing. They are all able to testify, however, to points that, Lieutenant Colonel Frémont is instructed by his counsel, are strictly relevant to the case, and material to his defence; but as they are mostly points that the court has over-ruled, or others having the same or similar bearing, Lieutenant Colonel Frémont will not, in the present position of the trial, press his right of inquiry. He desires, however, that the witnesses named may be severally called and sworn, so as to be open to examination by the court or the judge advocate, and also that they be not discharged until the final result of the trial.

J. C. FRÉMONT,
Lieutenant Colonel, mounted rifles.

List of witnesses.—Marion Wise, Risden Moore, —— Brackenridge, R. Owens, Wm. Findlay, J. Ferguson, Eugene Russell, Wm. Brown, Jas. Brown, —— Davis, R. Jacobs, Colonel Childs, —— Vincenthaler, L. Gorday.

The judge advocate said he had no questions to ask these witnesses, and did not think it necessary that he should swear them in the case.

The court had no questions to ask them. While waiting for

some documentary evidence for the defence from the Navy Department, and the defence having no further evidence at present, the prosecution called Major Thomas Swords of the quartermaster's department, United States army.

The court was then cleared. After some time in closed session, the court was opened. Lieutenant Colonel Frémont in court.

Major Thomas Swords, of the quartermaster's department, United States army, a witness for the prosecution, was then duly sworn by the judge advocate according to law, and testified as follows:

Examined in chief by the judge advocate.

Question. What rank did you hold in California on the staff of General Kearny?

Answer. I was a quartermaster in the army with the rank of major; and ranking officer in California of that department.

Question. Did you receive any orders from General Kearny, or were any orders from him communicated through you to the quartermaster's department, in regard to public horses for which Lieutenant Colonel Frémont was responsible?

Answer. My general instructions were, which I think I received from Lieutenant Sherman, whom I relieved at Monterey, as the orders of General Kearny, to take up all public horses that could be found in the country; those for which owners could be found to turn them over to the owners, and to take their receipt or acknowledgement of having received the horses. I mean, horses in public use, claimed by persons as their property, but which had been taken by Colonel Frémont's battalion, or had got in any way into the public service. Horses and mules, both, the answer applies to.

About the time we reached the Sacramento, on our return home, I was told by General Kearny he had learned there was a band of horses at or near that place, and he directed me to select from them such as I might require for the public service for our trip home. I took from that band the horses and mules that were required, and accounted for them on my property return, which was rendered to the treasury. My returns show that I took twenty-one horses and five mules. I made a note on the return (here exhibited to the court) that these "twenty-one horses and five mules were taken from the Californians."

I also took up at Monterey, in conformity to General Kearny's instructions, during the months of April and May, thirty-five horses, which I accounted for, on my return, to the treasury, in these words: "35 horses taken up in the country as belonging to the United States, having been in former possession of Lieutenant Colonel Frémont's battalion of volunteers."

I took up no other horses that I recollect, except such as I turned over to the owners, on their producing satisfactory proof that they have never been paid for them. I do not think these exceeded half a dozen. I will state that I never gave any receipt for the horses and mules I took up in California; I never found any person who was responsible for them, and who required receipts.

The judge advocate said he had no further questions to ask Major Swords.

Cross-examination by Lieutenant Colonel Frémont.

Question. When you say that horses were "taken up," do you mean that you found them going at large, and so took them up?

Answer. There were individuals in the country who were instructed to take up all horses going at large, and which were recognized as having been in the public service. These instructions were given by me as chief of the quartermaster's department.

Question. Do you mean that all the horses you received were found at large by the persons so instructed, and were taken up as estrays?

Answer. I do not know how they found them; they were agents of the quartermaster's department; they reported to me that they found some running at large, and others in possession of individuals who had them without any known authority.

Question. By what test did you determine that they were public horses?

Answer. Some of them, I think, had the public brand on them, U. S., and others with a large letter F, which I was told was the mark of those that had been in Colonel Frémont's battalion.

Question. Did you know by whose authority they were so branded?

Answer. I do not.

Question. Did you know by what means, or under whose authority, they came into the public service, and by whom were you told that the horses so branded were public.

Answer. Well, I do not know by what means or by whose authority they came into the public service. I cannot recollect by whom I was told that the horses were public. It was a matter of notoriety in the country. When these agents that I have spoken of would bring in horses, I would ask them if they knew they were public, and they would designate some brand or mark by which they knew it.

Question. Were they first put into the public service when you received them, or had they previously been in possession of the California battalion, when commanded by Lieutenant Colonel Frémont?

Answer. My instructions to the agents were to take up those that had been in public service, and were considered by me as public property.

At the request of Lieutenant Colonel Frémont the question was again read to the witness, and he was asked if he had further answer to make to it. He replied, I have no further answer to make. I do not know whether they had been in Colonel Frémont's battalion.

Question. How could the agent know what *you* considered public property?

Answer. Their instructions were to take up those that had been in public service. I stated what I considered them.

Question. Do you know whether the horses and mules which had been in possession of Lieutenant Colonel Frémont, throughout the country, were not generally taken by 'the authorized officers or agents of General Kearny?

Answer. I do not.

Question. Were any taken or received by you that had been in the possession of Lieutenant Colonel Frémont, or of the battalion under his command?

Answer. All those taken or received by me, I had understood, had been in possession of Lieutenant Colonel Frémont's command.

Question. In your testimony in chief you say that General Kearny told you he understood there was a band of horses in the neighborhood, and instructed you to select from them such as were wanted for your party. Did he tell you how he got that information, and to whom the band belonged?

Answer. When I first heard him speak of it, I think he said he got the information from Mr. Kerne. He may have mentioned that the horses had been in the service of Colonel Frémont's battalion; but I cannot recollect distinctly; it was a mere casual conversation.

Question. How did you identify the band? Had they the public brand?

Answer. The band at the Sacramento were driven up into a "corral"—an enclosure—and I was told that that was the band; I think by Mr. Loker, the staff officer of Lieutenant Colonel Frémont. I think they had not the public brand; some may have had it; but I do not recollect distinctly of having seen it.

Question. How far was Lieutenant Colonel Frémont's camp from the place where you took the horses on the Sacramento? Did you see Adjutant Loker frequently during the day on which you took them? Did you see Lieutenant Colonel Frémont soon after?

Answer. I was not at his camp; from what I understood I should think his camp was a mile to two miles from us; I saw Mr. Loker frequently during the day. I do not recollect when I first saw Lieutenant Colonel Frémont; afterwards, I recollect seeing him on the day we broke up our camp, which I believe was the first time, and that was a day or two after I took the horses.

Question. Were the horses you have mentioned all that were taken or received by you, or to your knowledge, by any officer or agent of General Kearny, of those which had been previously in the service of the United States or of Lieutenant Colonel Frémont?

Answer. They are all that were taken or received by me. I received from Lieutenant Sherman, and receipted to him for thirty-five horses and six mules, which I believe were taken up under general instructions from General Kearny, similar to my own. I do not know of any others. I would state, that I received from Lieutenant Rowan of the navy, and receipted to him, at San Diego, for five horses, which had been in the public service; whether they had been in the service of Lieutenant Colonel Frémont's party, I do not know.

Question. Was not the number you took (horses and mules together) at the Sacramento, more than twenty-six?

Answer. I think not. My return calls for that number; and my intention was to take up on my return all I received, and I think I did so.

Question. Did you, at the time, take any memorandum of the number?

Answer. I think not. I do not recollect.

Lieutenant Colonel Frémont had no further question.

Question by the court. Did you cause to be demanded of, or taken from, Lieutenant Colonel Frémont, or the California battalion, or any other troops, horses which were then in his or their possession or public use?

Answer. I never mentioned the subject to Lieutenant Colonel Frémont or any of his party, except at the Sacramento. I never did demand, or take from Lieutenant Colonel Frémont, the horses that were in his use or possession, except so far as his general control may be supposed to have extended over the band at the Sacramento. They were not in his use at the time; or if so, I did not know it.

Question by the court. Did you consider all horses and mules which had been captured by, or surrendered by the enemy to, the United States forces, as belonging to the United States government?

Answer. I know of no horses or mules captured or taken, from the enemy, except one band captured by General Kearny, as we first entered California; which I certainly considered as public property.

Question by the court. Were any of the horses or mules, taken up as United States property by your instructions, claimed as private property? and if so, by whom?

Answer. Some of the horses brought in were claimed by different individuals, Californians, as their own private property. Those to which they established a claim, were given up to them; sometimes it was done by order of the alcalde, and sometimes by investigation of myself.

Question by Lieutenant Colonel Frémont. In your returns to the department, you speak of "thirty-five horses taken up in the country, as having belonged to the United States, in former possession of Lieutenant Colonel Frémont's battalion of volunteers;" how did those horses get out of the possession of that battalion?

Answer. They were found in the country, without, as I am aware, anybody being particularly in charge of them; and, as the agent of the government to take charge of such public property, I took charge of them myself.

Question by Lieutenant Colonel Frémont. By whom were they so found? and where?

Answer. They were brought in by different persons; who, I do not know; people would come and say they had found a public horse, and I would take charge of it. The agents had instructions, also, to take up such as they knew to be public property.

Question by the court. Did you refuse to give receipts for any of those horses or mules to the United States agents from whose custody they were taken, when applied for?

Answer. Receipts were never called for, and of course I never refused to give receipts; but I was anxious to give receipts, and made inquiries if any one was responsible for them, with a view of giving receipts.

Question by Lieutenant Colonel Frémont. Did any one prevent you from giving receipts for those you took from adjutant Loker, on the Sacramento?

Answer. No person prevented me from giving receipts for those or any others; receipts were never asked; I did not know who was responsible for those, if any body was.

Question by Lieutenant Colonel Frémont. Did you keep, at the time, any memorandum of the horses you received at Monterey?

Answer. I did not, any more than my general return; my instructions were to the commissioned officer of volunteers, in charge of the horse guard, to keep account of all those brought in and taken out.

The testimony of this witness here closed.
Lieutenant Colonel Frémont presented the following note:

Mr. PRESIDENT: Lieutenant Colonel Frémont submits a series of papers, marked from A to E, inclusively, to be used as presumptive evidence, in addition to positive evidence heretofore adduced, to establish that persons standing in a relation to him to be material witnesses, have been kept away by General Kearny, through Commodore Biddle.

The first of the papers is from Midshipman Wilson to the Secretary of the Navy, dated Monterey, (of California,) June 9, 1847, in which he sets forth his right to return, and asks the secretary to give such an order as will induce the commander on that station to allow him, the said Midshipman Wilson, to return to the United States.

He states that he has been on duty constantly since the year 1841; is the only midshipman of the first part of that date then on that station; refers to Commodore Stockton as *acquainted* with the *circumstances of his detention*, and who had endeavored to induce Commodore Biddle to allow him to return; but without success.

Lieutenant Colonel Frémont states that Midshipman Wilson was an officer in the California battalion; that he is mentioned in the specification, and was present at the scene at Monterey; and, from his situation, must have been a material witness for Lieutenant Colonel Frémont. The paper is a certified copy of the original in the Navy Department.

The paper B is an extract from a despatch from the Secretary of the Navy, dated October 25, 1847, and directed to Commodore Jones, directing him to permit to return to the United States the midshipmen of the classes of 1840 and 1841, of whom Mr. Wilson was one, and expressly stating that it was "*just*" that they should be allowed to return to the United States, to have the opportunity of standing their examination for promotion—the detention of Mr. Wilson being, in the opinion·of the Secretary of the Navy, an act which authorized the interference of the department, and authorizes the presumption that he was detained for some extraordinary and unknown cause.

The paper C is an extract of a despatch addressed to Commodore Shubrick, dated August 21, 1846. It directs Commodore Shubrick to send home for examination the midshipmen whose term of service commenced in the first and second quarters of 1841, by the first public vessel that might return, that they might prepare themselves for their examination.

The paper marked D is an official certificate from the records of the department, showing, *first*, that Lieutenant William Radford sailed from New York, for the Pacific ocean, the 19*th of October*, 1843; *secondly*, that Passed Midshipman Lewis McLane sailed from Norfolk, for the same station, on the 4*th of September*, 1843; and, *thirdly*, that Midshipman John K. Wilson sailed from Norfolk, for the same station, *on the* 1*st of November*, 1841; and that he was, under the regulation of the department, entitled to his examination in July, 1847.

Paper E is the letter of the Secretary of the Navy, dated December 16, 1846, and shows that the wishes of the department, in regard to the midshipmen of the class of 1841, of whom Mr. Wilson was one, and that the justice of his return was fully conceded.

Lieutenant Colonel Frémont asks that the foregoing papers be received as circumstantial and presumptive evidence, to go with it, to establish that Messrs. McLane and Wilson were detained by Commodore Biddle, through the interference of General Kearny, he (General Kearny) having, at that time, the secret intention (known to Commodore Biddle) to arrest Lieutenant Colonel Frémont, in relation to his conduct in California, of which Messrs. McLane and Wilson, from their intimate service with him in the California battalion, must have been known to have been well acquainted, and also friendly to him.

J. C. FRÉMONT,
Lieutenant Colonel, mounted rifles.

The court was then cleared. And the court decided that the papers cannot be received in evidence, as raising any presumption that witnesses were kept from this trial by General Kearny. The court further remark, that Midshipman Wilson's letter refers to Commodore Stockton as acquainted with the circumstances of his detention, which he, Midshipman Wilson, does not indicate. Whatever this letter is offered to prove, presumptively, Commodore Stockton can be called to prove directly, if the defence desire it.

The court was then opened. Lieutenant Colonel Frémont in court. The decision in closed session was announced.

The judge advocate said General Kearny was now in attendance as a witness, recalled by the prosecution.

Lieutenant Colonel Frémont presented the following note:

Mr. PRESIDENT : Lieutenant Colonel Frémont is instructed by his counsel that it is not conformable to practice that any witnesses, on the part of the prosecution, should be introduced, or re-introduced, at this stage of the trial, except upon new matter introduced by the defence. He shall, therefore, by advice of his counsel, object to any witnesses of the prosecution being re-introduced, until he is informed precisely upon what points it is proposed to interrogate them ; and until he shall have had time afterwards to examine whether they have previously been interrogated on the same subjects, and whether the matter is new matter brought in by the defence.

J. C. FRÉMONT,
Lieutenant Colonel, mounted rifles.

The court was then cleared; and the court made the following decision:

The court decides that Lieutenant Colonel Frémont's objection to the course proposed to be pursued cannot now be entertained.

If, in the course of the examination of the witness recalled by the judge advocate, the accused should conceive that any question which may be put is objectionable under the principal he cites, then, and not till then, will be the proper time for objections to be made and decided on by the court.

The court was then opened. Lieutenant Colonel Frémont in court. The decision in closed session was announced.

Whereupon, the court adjourned, at one minute before three, to meet to meet to-morrow at 10 o'clock.

WEDNESDAY, *January 5*, 1848—10 *o'clock.*

The court met pursuant to adjournment.

Present: all the members, and the judge advocate.

The proceedings of yesterday were read over; during which Lieutenant Colonel Frémont came into court.

Lieutenant Colonel Frémont presented the following note :

Mr. PRESIDENT : Lieutenant Colonel Frémont perceives what he deems to be an omission in the minutes of the court. On yesterday evening he received a reprimand from the court, through the President, in about these words :

"Lieutenant Colonel Frémont : I am directed by the court to inform you that they consider the last question offered by you as highly improper."

This reprimand, thus given by the order of the court, becomes the act of the court and a part of its proceedings; and is required, together with the question which gave rise to the reprimand, to be entered on the minutes of the court. Not being there, Lieutenant Colonel Frémont respectfully asks that they may be now entered.

J. C. FRÉMONT,
Lieutenant Colonel, mounted rifles.

The court was then ordered to be cleared. After deliberation, the court made the following decision :

The accused yesterday addressed a question, orally, direct to the judge advocate, inquiring in whose hand writing questions were written which he was preparing for a witness.

The court, through its president, verbally admonished the accused that it considers his question, thus addressed, highly improper. The court considered an informal admonition to the accused sufficient notice of what it trusted was an inadvertance, without making a formal reprimand up its record.

The record of yesterday will stand.

The court was then opened. Lieutenant Colonel Frémont in court. The decision in closed session was announced.

Lieutenant Colonel Frémont offered to the court the following note :

Mr. President : Lieutenant Colonel Frémont is instructed by his counsel to say that there is reason to believe that the questions read on yesterday, by the judge advocate, together with many other questions proposed by him to be put to General Kearny, were brought to this court in the hand writing of General Kearny himself. Lieutenant Colonel Frémont was advised by his counsel that it was proper to bring this circumstance, before further proceedings, to the notice of this court, which he did in as delicate and inoffensive manner as the case allowed of. He is advised that a witness cannot interrogate himself, and shall not be permitted to arrange his own course of interrogations, to make them square with the answers he wishes to give; he is advised that the interrogator, upon either side, cannot put leading or suggestive questions, and this when witnesses are unimpeached and uncontradicted, and with far more reason, in a case like the present, where the witness has repeatedly had the benefit of explanation, after giving testimony as fully as he desired through a long course of examination and cross examination. Under such circumstances, if a witness be allowed to reappear at all, it should be in entire ignorance of the course of examination to which he would be subjected, with the questions framed in the strictest conformity to the rules of evidence, and afterwards be delivered over to the most searching and sifting re-cross-examination.

Lieutenant Colonel Frémont is further advised that it is the legal presumption in courts martial that the witness is ignorant of what is testified by others; and although the fact may be otherwise, yet the legal presumption remains, and this court can act upon nothing but the legal presumption. And under the silence which this legal presumption supposes and makes obligatory, even if other rules were not to the same effect, it would be impossible for one witness to arrange questions and answers with a view to what other witnesses had said.

Lieutenant Colonel Frémont is therefore instructed by his counsel to say that, in their opinion, he has a right to know whether the witness (General Kearny) drew up the questions, or any of them, for himself to answer; and if so, that the fact goes so strongly to his credit, and the credit of what he may swear, and so vitally concerns the pure administration of justice, that not one of the questions so framed by General Kearny for himself shall be allowed to be put to him.

J. C. FRÉMONT,
Lieut. Col., mounted rifles.

The court was ordered to be cleared.

And the court ordered that the examination of the witness be proceeded in.

The court was then opened. Lieutenant Colonel Frémont in court. The decision in closed session was announced.

Brigadier General S. W. Kearny, a witness, re-introduced into court on the part of the prosecution.

Examined in chief by Judge Advocate.

Question. Did you apply to Commodore Biddle to detain Captain Gillespie at Monterey, in California?

Lieutenant Colonel Frémont presented the following note :

Mr. PRESIDENT: Lieutenant Colonel Frémont objects to that question as being a leading one in a case in which, by law, a leading question cannot be put.

J. C. FREMONT,
Lieut. Col., mounted rifles.

The judge advocate said he would change the form of the question.

But the court, on motion of a member, was ordered to be cleared.

The judge advocate proposed to withdraw the question objected to. And then the court, without deciding whether the question was admissible or not, was ordered to be opened.

The court was then opened. Lieutenant Colonel Frémont in court. The proceedings in closed session were announced.

Gen. Kearny, a witness.

Question by judge advocate. State all facts within your knowledge concerning the order of Commodore Biddle to Captain Gillespie, in the latter part of the month of May, 1847, ordering him to be detained at Monterey.

Answer. I left Los Angeles on the 13th of May, 1847; Lieutenant Gillespie left there on the same day. I reached Monterey on the 27th of the same month; Lieutenant Gillespie, I think, reached there on the evening previous. Before leaving Los Angeles I understood that Lieutenant Gillespie had rented the room, or the house, which he then occupied for the' ensuing six months. I left Monterey for the United States on the 31st of May. The evening previous, Colonel Mason, upon whom was to devolve the management of the military and civil affairs in California, or, in other 'words, who was to relieve me in my authority, came to me, and told me that he had understood that Lieutenant Gillespie was making arrangements, or about to leave Monterey for San Francisco, or the Sacramento, or one or both, which I do not remember, and that he feared Lieutenant Gillespie's appearance in that district of country might serve to produce an excitement among the people. I told Colonel Mason of what I had understood at Los Angeles of Lieutenant Gillespie's renting a house there; and if he apprehended any difficulty from Lieutenant Gillespie's moving through the country to the Sacramento, or San Francisco, I forget which, I advised him to go to Commodore Biddle, and to make a statement of it. I wrote to Commodore Biddle an unofficial communication, (I have no copy, and I took no copy of it;) but the purport of it was, as I remember, that, inasmuch as California was then quiet, I thought the quiet could be best preserved by preventing Lieutenant Gillespie from going about the country. I will add, that I arrived at Johnson's, the frontier settlement in California, on the 17th of June, where I met Mr. Bryant, who accompanied me home, and from him I first learned that Lieutenant Gillespie had any wish or expectation of coming home by land at that time.

Question by judge advocate. State all the facts within your knowledge in relation to the detention of Midshipmen Wilson and McLane with the squadron in the Pacific?

Answer. I know nothing whatever in relation to the detention of Midshipman Wilson. In relation to Lieutenant McLane, of the navy, he told me that he was desirous of coming home with me. I have a very high opinion of Lieutenant McLane, and I was extremely desirous of the pleasure of his company. One day, in conversation with Commodore Biddle, I remarked to him that several of his officers, Lieutenant McLane amongst them, were desirous of accompanying me home by land. I added that I would be pleased or-gratified if he would admit it. His reply to me was, that officers of the navy were much better off when serving on their own element, or on ship-board, or something to that purport. I urged the subject no further upon him.

Question by judge advocate. Will you state all the orders and instructions that you gave in California to officers of the quartermaster's department, or to any other officers or agents, in regard to public or other horses which had been in the use of the battalion of California volunteers?

Answer. A few days before leaving Monterey, I was informed by Lieutenant Colonel Frémont that there was a band of public horses at Cosumné river, (which is about twenty-five miles, I believe, from Nueva Helvetia,) and that those horses might be serviceable to us on our expedition homewards. I gave directions that they should be driven up to Nueva Helvetia; and I directed that they should be turned over to Major Swords, the quartermaster, who was with me, that he might select such as were necessary for us. That verbal order, together with two written orders of mine, are the only ones which I remember to have given in California on the subject of horses. The written orders I have copied from the orders I sent to the Adjutant General's office. All officers know that officers in command of departments send to the Adjutant General's office copies of all orders issued by them.

General Kearny then presented the two orders, extracts from which were read, as follows:

ORDERS, ⎱ HEAD-QUARTERS, 10TH MILITARY DEPARTMENT,
No. 3. ⎰   *Monterey, California, March 8,* 1847.

III. A number of horses, saddles, bridles, &c., having been forcibly taken from the Californians by the volunteers raised for the United States service, under instructions of previous commanders, some of which have been turned over to the quartermaster's department, the officers in charge thereof are hereby directed to restore all such property to the owners, upon their identifying the same, and giving an acknowledgment of their having received it.
               S. W. KEARNY,
                     Brigadier General.

ORDERS, ⎱ HEAD-QUARTERS, 10TH MILITARY DEPARTMENT,
No. 5. ⎰   *Monterey, California, March 17,* 1847.

*   *   *   *   *   *   *   *   *

II. It having been reported that there are several horses in the quartermaster's charge at this place, which belong to the inhabitants near the bay of San Francisco, such horses, if any, will be sent to Captain Folsom, (assistant quartermaster,) at San Francisco, who will endeavor to see that they are returned to their owners.
               S. W. KEARNY,
                     Brigadier General.

Question by judge advocate. What conversation did you have with Colonel Russell, at Los Angeles, in May, 1847, in regard to your having served under the orders of Commodore Stockton, and in regard to Commodore Stockton's rank as compared with your own?

Lieutenant Colonel Frémont objected to the question, and submitted the following note:

MR. PRESIDENT: Lieutenant Colonel Frémont is advised by his counsel to object to this question, because it does not refer to new matter introduced by the defence, and because the witness (General Kearny) has had full opportunity, both on his direct and on his cross-examination, to testify to the point of the inquiry as to his having served under Commodore Stockton; and because the question of superior rank between General Kearny and Commodore

Stockton, according to the recollection of Lieutenant Colonel Frémont and his counsel, was introduced by General Kearny himself in his testimony, and, so far as mentioned by Colonel Russell, was in answer to questions from the court. Lieutenant Colonel Frémont and his counsel believe (relying on recollection) that the defence never asked a question upon the point of any witness whatever, or at any time, and desire the minutes to be examined, if any member of the court or the judge advocate thinks differently.

J. C. FREMONT,
Lieutenant Colonel, mounted rifles.

The court was then cleared. And the court decided that the question of the judge advocate be not put.

The court was then opened. Lieutenant Colonel Frémont in court. The decision in closed session was announced.

Genearl Kearny, a witness.

The judge advocate said he had no further question to ask General Kearny, and he was now subject to cross-examination by the defence, on his testimony of to-day.

Cross-examination by Lieutenant Colonel Frémont.

Question. Have you drawn up any questions on the matters to which you have been testifying, and brought or sent them to this court to be answered by yourself?

The court was ordered to be cleared. And the court decided that the question cannot be put.

The court was then opened. Lieutenant Colonel Frémont in court. The decision in closed session was announced.

General Kearny, a witness.

Question by Lieutenant Colonel Frémont. Did you know the points on which you were to be examined by the judge advocate on this day, and did you come with answers ready prepared in your own mind to meet those points?

The court was then cleared. And the court decided that the question cannot be put.

The court was then opened. Lieutenant Colonel Frémont in court. The decision in closed session was announced.

General Kearny, a witness.

Lieutenant Colonel Frémont presented the following note:

Mr. PRESIDENT: Lieutenant Colonel Frémont desires to say to

the court that it is now near the time of adjournment, that he cannot finish his re-cross-examination of General Kearny in the little time that remains, and would prefer to offer his questions to-morrow.

J. C. FRÉMONT,
Lieutenant Colonel, mounted rifles.

The court was then cleared; and when opened, the testimony of to-day was read over to the witness.

And then, at twenty minutes before three, the court adjourned, to meet to-morrow at 10 o'clock.

THURSDAY, *January* 6, 1848.—10 *o'clock.*

The court met pursuant to adjournment.

Present: All the members, the judge advocate, and Lieutenant Colonel Frémont.

The proceedings of yesterday were read over.

Brigadier General S. W. Kearny, a witness, on re-cross-examination by the defence.

Question. In your testimony of yesterday you say that Colonel Mason told you that he understood Captain Gillespie was about to leave Monterey for San Francisco, or the Sacramento, or both, (you not remembering which,) and he feared his (Gillespie's) appearance "*in that district of country*" might serve to produce an excitement among the people: now which district of country do you mean by the use of the definite article "*that*"?

Answer. I meant the district of country to which Lieutenant Gillespie was going.

Question. Did the fear of the excitement extend to both districts?

Answer. It was information which I myself received from Colonel Mason. His fears were, as I understood him, that the excitement might be produced, in the district of country to which Lieutenant Gillespie was going.

Question. What people do you mean, thus expected to be excited by the appearance of Captain Gillespie among them?

Answer. It was Colonel Mason's meaning, not mine.

Question. Did you *act* upon Colonel Mason's meaning, without knowing what it was, and thereupon use your influence with Commodore Biddle to detain Captain Gillespie?

Answer. As I stated in my testimony yesterday, the information I received of Lieutenant Gillespie's intended movements, or expected movements, was entirely from Colonel Mason. I had no information of his intended or expected movements from any other source. I was of the opinion that the quiet of the country would be best preserved by Lieutenant Gillespie's not going into the upper district of country, and I so wrote to Commodore Biddle.

Question. What was the nature of the excitement expected?

Answer. I presume that Colonel Mason, upon whom was to devolve the governorship of the country, the day subsequent to his conversation with me, apprehended that there might be produced some objection to his authority in the country.

Question. What people, Americans or Californians, do you mean us to understand as being thus excited?

Answer. I presume both.

Question. Did you expect Captain Gillespie to excite an insurrection against your successor, Colonel Mason?

Answer. I did not.

Question. Were you at that time on terms of special intercourse with Major Gillespie, and do you know whether Colonel Mason was so also?

Answer. There was at no time any difference between Lieutenant Gillespie and myself. Whenever we met we exchanged salutations as between gentlemen; there was nothing further between us. I know not of the intercourse between Lieutenant Gillespie and Colonel Mason.

Question. You said in your testimony, yesterday, that you thought the quiet (of the country) would be best preserved by preventing Lieutenant Gillespie from going about the country. Now, what did you mean by these words, "*preventing him from going about the country?*"

Answer. I meant that the quiet of the upper district of the country would be best preserved, in my opinion, by Lieutenant Gillespie not going there.

Question. What law prevailed at that time, martial, or civil, in California?

Answer. The civil law, as far as the military authorities would admit of.

Question. What character had Major Gillespie as an orderly, or as a seditious citizen?

On motion of a member, the court was ordered to be cleared.

Lieutenant Colonel Frémont said he wished to prepare and present a paper in regard to the question offered, before the court decided on it, which was assented to under the rule of the court. After a while, Lieutenant Colonel Frémont read to the court the following paper:

Mr. President: The witness now before the court (General Kearny) is introduced by the prosecution to counteract the testimony of Major Gillespie in a most material point in this prosecution, that of keeping away a probable witness for the defence. It is a re-examination, and a re-cross-examination before this court. It is the re-introduction of an impeached witness to overthrow an unimpeached one; it is the production of an interested, against a disinterested witness. Under such circumstances, Lieutenant Colonel Frémont is instructed by his counsel to say that he has a right to re-cross-examine with all the latitude that he would have if standing at the Old Bailey on a trial for insurrection or mutiny, unless where his right should be restricted by some statute of the United States; and he refers to the case of the trial of Governor Wall, for murder, in the year 1802, in chastising to death a soldier for alleged mutiny, to show the extent of those rights. The question before the court on that trial was the same that it is in this— namely, mutiny, or no mutiny; and the counsel was allowed to lay their questions at a distance from the object, so that the object might not be seen, and were allowed to inquire into every minute circumstance that bore upon the issue in its broadest sense, and especially as affecting the credit of witnesses. The judges on that occasion were the Lord Chief Baron, of the Exchequer; Sir Archibald McDonald, with Sir Soulden Lawrence, of the King's Bench; and Sir Giles Rooke, of the Common Pleas. The attorney general was Sir Edward Law, afterwards Lord Ellenborough; and the solicitor general was Mr. Spencer Percival, afterwards prime minister. It must be admitted, Lieutenant Colonel Frémont is instructed by his counsel to say, that these gentlemen and the eminent counsel for the defence knew how to conduct a trial where the question was mutiny, or no mutiny. And he is further instructed to say, that that is the question now before this court, and under the same law under which the question was then tried at the Old Bailey. The mutiny articles of the rules and articles of war in the United States are copied from the British mutiny act of George II; and the rules of testimony must be observed by this court material as observed in common law courts, unless as altered by the law martial. Every question offered, therefore, which would be admitted in a common law court must be admitted in a court martial, unless it can be shown to be forbid by the law martial. This, Lieutenant Colonel Frémont is instructed by his counsel, is the law, and is the extent of his rights before this court; he, therefore, claims the right to have put to the witness the question which he has offered, and many others judged by his counsel to be material.

J. C. FRÉMONT,
Lieutenant Colonel, mounted rifles.

The court was then cleared; and the court made the following decision:

That the court perceives nothing in this testimony of General Kearny, contradicting any fact in the testimony of Captain Gillespie. Captain Gillespie testified to certain facts from which he inferred that he was detained in California by the interference of General Kearny; but stated that he knew no facts from which he inferred that he was detained to keep him from this, or any such trial. The facts, however, having been offered in evidence by the defence, with the avowed purpose of raising an inference in regard to this trial, General Kearny has been recalled to explain the circumstances of his official action in this matter.

This statement, that his official action was induced by the application of Colonel Mason, and his own opinions in regard to the subject which Colonel Mason brought to his attention, whether arising in his own mind, or caused by the representations of Colonel Mason, cannot be controverted by showing that neither his own, nor Colonel Mason's opinions were well founded; nor ought this court to investigate those opinions, or inquire into the character and conduct of Captain Gillespie in California.

The court decides that the question cannot be put.

The court was then opened. Lieutenant Colonel Frémont in court. The decision in closed session was announced.

General Kearny, a witness.—Re-cross-examination by the defence continued.

Question. What did Colonel Mason inform you was the answer of Commodore Biddle, when he returned ?

Answer. I think Colonel Mason informed me that Lieutenant Gillespie would not be permitted at that time to leave there.

Question. At what time did you understand the detention was to cease, and Major Gillespie be allowed to go about the country ?

Answer. I understood nothing on the subject, further than what I have stated.

Question. Why did you write to Commodore Biddle about the hire of the house at Los Angeles ? What connexion had it with the expected excitement at San Francisco, or on the Sacramento ?

Answer. I considered the renting of the house at Los Angeles, by Lieutenant Gillespie, as proving on his part, that it was to be the place of his residence for a short time thereafter.

The question was read again to the witness; he said: It had no connexion, that I am aware of, with the excitement at San Francisco.

Question. How far is it from Los Angeles, where Major Gillespie had rented the house, to the settlements on San Francisco and the Sacramento ?

Answer. From Los Angeles to Monterey is considered about four hundred miles; from Monterey to the settlements on the Sacramento about two hundred; a less distance than that to the settlements on the San Francisco.

Question. Did Colonel Mason tell you that Commodore Biddle spoke of the dissensions between the army and navy as a reason for detaining him ?

Answer. He did not.

Question. Was any thing of the kind contained in your own letter to Commodore Biddle ?

Answer. There was not.

Question. Did you, or Colonel Mason, give any information to Major Gillespie of the design to have him detained, and the reason why ?

Answer. I did not. I cannot answer for Colonel Mason.

Question. Was Major Gillespie in Monterey at the time you wrote to have him detained ?

Answer. I believe he was; that is, he was either in town or in the harbor.

The testimony of to-day was read over to the witness.

On motion of a member, the court was cleared. After deliberation, the court was opened; and then, at three minutes before three, the court adjourned, to meet to-morrow at 10 o'clock.

FRIDAY, *January* 7, 1848—10 *o'clock.*

The court met pursuant to adjournment.

Present: all the members, the judge advocate, and Lieutenant Colonel Frémont.

The proceedings of yesterday were read over.

Brigadier General S. W. Kearny, being in court, said: There is a question put to me yesterday, which says, "Why did you write to Commodore Biddle about the hire of the house at Los Angeles?" I was an invalid during the examination of yesterday, and that expression in the question escaped my attention. I did not say that I had written to Commodore Biddle about that house. I said I informed Colonel Mason of it. If the question had been according to my testimony, "Why did you inform Colonel Mason," &c., my answer to it would be correct.

The court was then cleared. After a short time in closed session the court was opened. Lieutenant Colonel Frémont in court.

Lieutenant Colonel Frémont read to the court a paper in relation to the record.

The court was cleared; and the court decided that: "The paper of the accused will be returned to him, its subject matter having been before disposed of.
The record will stand.

The court was then opened. Lieutenant Colonel Frémont in court. The decision in closed session was announced.

General Kearny, a witness.—Re-cross-examination by the defence continued.

Question. Did Colonel Mason know of your intention, at the time you gave him the letter to Commodore Biddle, to arrest Lieutenant Colonel Frémont?

On motion of a member, the court was cleared. And the court decided that the question be not put.

The court was then opened. Lieutenant Colonel Frémont in court. The decision in closed session was announced.

Lieutenant Colonel Frémont presented the following note:

Mr. PRESIDENT: Lieutenant Colonel Frémont asks a short time

to draw up a paper to be submitted to the court.   It will be ready in less than an hour.

J. C. FREMONT,
Lieutenant Colonel, mounted rifles.

The court was then cleared; and the judge advocate was instructed to ask Lieutenant Colonel Frémont on what subject he wishes to offer a paper.   Lieutenant Colonel Frémont replied that the paper would be on the subject of the court's decisions on this question, and all of the same class.

The court decided to hear the paper prepared by Lieutenant Colonel Frémont.

When Lieutenant Colonel Frémont's paper was prepared, the court was opened; and Lieutenant Colonel Frémont came into court and read the following paper:

Mr. PRESIDENT: Lieutenant Colonel Frémont is instructed by his counsel to say, that he has a right to inquire into every fact and circumstance that may affect the probable truth of the reason assigned by General Kearny for causing the detention of Major Gillespie at Monterey.   The *fact* of the detention, through the instrumentality of General Kearny, is admitted; proved by Major Gillespie, acknowledged by General Kearny.   The *motive* of the act only remains to be ascertained.   The motive alleged by General Kearny, to wit: that it was apprehended that if Major Gillespie was permitted to go about the country its quiet would be disturbed, is different from that supposed in the inquiry, and its truth can only be judged of from circumstances and probabilities.   It is not given to the court to search the heart of the witness, and ascertain there whether he has assigned the true motive.   They must judge from circumstances and probabilities, and these circumstances and probabilities must be brought before them before they can judge.   And, as a pertinent inquiry to this end, Lieutenant Colonel Frémont is instructed by his counsel again to offer the question which was overruled yesterday, viz: "What was Major Gillespie's character as a peaceable, or as a seditious citizen?" and respectfully to request that it be now allowed to be put.

Lieutenant Colonel Frémont is further advised by his counsel that, it having been shown in testimony that a person so situated as to be a material witness for his defence was detained at the other side of the continent, through whatever motive, by Commodore Biddle, at the instance of General Kearny, and at the desire of Colonel Mason, he (Lieutenant Colonel Frémont) has a right to inquire into every fact and circumstance that may go to show a mutual understanding of intent, or an accord of action between Commodore Biddle, General Kearny, and Colonel Mason, and to show evidence of hostility to Lieutenant Colonel Frémont in either or all of them, to stand for what it may be found to be worth in impeaching the testimony of General Kearny, and in going to show that other persons besides Major Gillespie, who might have been, from their positions and the information in their possession, important witnesses before this court, were, by the same or similar means, kept at a great distance. And, as a pertinent introduction to this inquiry, Lieutenant Colonel Frémont is instructed by his counsel again to offer the question, "Was Colonel Mason, at the time you sent the letter by him to Commodore Biddle, informed of your intention to arrest Lieutenant Colonel Frémont?" and respectfully to request that it be now allowed to be put.

And Lieutenant Colonel Frémont is instructed by his counsel to say that all acts of officers, done under the color of their office, is subject to examination before courts martial or courts of law, and may be examined into as fully as the acts of any other persons clothed with authority; all of whom are bound to use their power justly and for the public good, and are liable for any abuse of that power; and that, in this case, (which is the charge of keeping away of a witness by the joint act of three officers, one of them having the secret purpose to bring the officer to trial, who would need the benefit of the testimony so kept away,) the intent of the officer intending to arrest another, and procuring the testimony to be kept away, is examinable, and that *his statement of reasons for his official conduct may be controverted*, and that upon his own cross-examination, or by other testimony.

In this case he is instructed to claim the exercise of the right of controverting General Kearny's act, and to deny his right to claim for it official immunity. If the principle is allowed, a commanding officer has nothing to do to convict any person but to order off all the witnesses, and when his secret purpose is ripe, to bring on the trial, and have a conviction without the means of defence; or to hang up infamous charges over an officer's head, during the pendency of which he is lying under a black cloud of suspicion and accusation.

Lieutenant Colonel Frémont is further instructed by his counsel that the act of Keneral Kearny, in procuring Major Gillespie to be detained, was not official, but extra-official; that being done by an officer does not make it official, except in discharge of his military duties. In this case it has been proved to the court, *first*, that Captain Gillespie was an officer of marines; *secondly*, that he was on *special* service in California; *thirdly*, that General Kearny had previously relieved him from service in the California battalion, and ordered him to repair to the United States, and left him at large to do so.

Lieutenant Colonel Frémont is further instructed by his counsel, respectfully, to bring again to the notice of the court, a brief exposition of some of the purposes, objects, and powers intended to be embraced in the right of cross-examination. For this purpose, he quotes from Greenleaf's Evidence, pp. 522,—'3,—'4, (last edition.)

"The power of cross-examination has been justly said to be one of the principal, as it is certainly one of the most efficacious, tests which the law has devised for the discovery of truth. By means of it, the situation of the witness with respect to the parties and to the subject of litigation, his interest, his motives, his inclinations and prejudices, his means of obtaining a correct and certain knowledge of the facts to which he bears testimony, the manner in which he has used those means, his powers of discernment, memory, and description, are all fully investigated and ascertained, and submitted to the consideration of the jury before whom he has testified, and who have thus had an opportunity of observing his demeanor, and of determining the just weight and value of his testimony. It is not easy for a witness, who is subjected to this test, to impose on a court or jury; for however artful the fabrication of falsehood may be, it cannot embrace all the circumstances to which a cross-examination may be extended.

"The most effectual method is to examine rapidly and minutely as to a number of subordinate and apparently trivial points in his evidence."—*Greenleaf's evidence, pp.* 522–23–24.

J. C. FRÉMONT,
Lieutenant Colonel, mounted rifles.

The court was again cleared; and the court decided that the court will allow any cross-examination which could tend to expose corrupt motives in General Kearny, in his application to Commodore Biddle to detain Captain Gillespie in Monterey, or to prevent him from going to the upper district of California. But the court cannot pursue a course of inquiry for that purpose which cannot have any such tendency.

If Colonel Mason knew of General Kearny's intention to arrest Lieutenant Colonel Frémont, it would raise no presumption against General Kearny of a corrupt design to detain witnesses from the trial of Lieutenant Colonel Frémont, in the order which was given to Captain Gillespie by Commodore Biddle.

Nor can this court go into any inquiry as to the character or conduct of Captain Gillespie in California, as a quiet or seditious citizen, to see how far General Kearny, Colonel Mason, or Commodore Biddle had sufficient reasons for the order which was given to Captain Gillespie by Commodore Biddle.

The attempt to show corrupt motives in General Kearny, Commodore Biddle, and Colonel Mason, by possible inferences from official acts, which raise no such natural or probable inference, is an imputation of conspiracy, and abuse of authority, which this court will not make or investigate, except on the offer of proper legal proof.

The court was then opened; Lieutenant Colonel Frémont in court. The decision in closed session was announced.

Lieutenant Colonel Frémont presented the following note:

Mr. PRESIDENT: Lieutenant Colonel Frémont states to the court that he has no further questions to offer.

J. C. FRÉMONT,
Lieutenant Colonel, mounted rifles.

General Kearny, a witness.

Question by a member. Was the subject, touching the probability of any officer or officers of the navy or marine corps becoming a witness or witnesses, in the event of the trial of Lieutenant Colonel Frémont, ever entertained between Commodore Biddle and yourself; or, to your knowledge, between Commodore Biddle and any other person, either verbally or otherwise, either directly or indirectly? Please state all the facts within your knowledge touching this subject.

The question was objected to by the accused as a leading question.

The court was then cleared. The objection was overruled, and the question ordered to be put as a question by the court.

The court was then opened; Lieutenant Colonel Frémont in court. The decision in closed session was announced.

The court was cleared on objection of a member to the record of the proceedings in closed session. The court decided that the record stand.

The court was then opened; Lieutenant Colonel Frémont in court. The decision in closed session was announced.

And then, at two minutes before three, the court adjourned to meet to-morrow at 10 o'clock.

———

SATURDAY, *January 8,* 1848.—10 *o'clock*

The court met pursuant to adjournment.
Present: All the members, and the judge advocate.

The proceedings of yesterday, for the verification of the record, were then read over; during which, Lieutenant Colonel Frémont came into court.

Brigadier General S. W. Kearny, a witness.

The question yesterday ordered to be put to the witness by the court, but not answered, by reason that the time prescribed by law for the adjournment of the court had come, was here read to the witness, as follows:

Question by the court. Was the subject, touching the probability of any officer or officers of the navy or marine corps becoming a witness or witnesses, in the event of the trial of Lieutenant Colonel Frémont, ever entertained between Commodore Biddle and yourself; or, to your knowledge, between Commodore Biddle and any other person, either verbally or otherwise, either directly or indirectly? Please state all the facts within your knowledge touching this subject.

Answer. Such a subject was never entertained between Commodore Biddle and myself, or any other person, to my knowledge. I never conversed with Commodore Biddle; I never wrote a line to him; I never conversed with Colonel Mason; I never wrote a line to him on that subject, or any subject having the remotest connexion therewith; and I never conversed with any other person; and I never wrote a line to any other person on the subject. The only time I had any control over Lieutenant Gillespie, of the marine corps, I ordered him to repair to Washington city; which was on the first day of March, 1847, and as will be seen in the second paragragh of 10th military department order, No. 2, which has been produced before this court by Lieutenant Gillespie himself.

I issued that order after having conversed with Commodore Shubrick upon the subject of the disposition to be made of Lieutenant Gillespie. It met with Commodore Shubrick's approbation.

The court was then cleared. And the court ordered that Mr. Wm. H. Russell, a witness for the defence, be recalled to answer a question from the court.

The court was then opened. Lieutenant Colonel Frémont in court. The proceedings in closed session were announced.

Mr. William H. Russell, a witness.

Question by the court. To the question by the court, "Did General Kearny admit, in any manner, that Commodore Stockton had a right, in consequence of relative rank, to command him (General Kearny) or any troops in the army service," you answered: "I understood General Kearny to claim his right to command in the country founded on his instructions only. I am positive that, on the mere question of rank, he yielded precedence to Commodore Stockton." State now whether General Kearny *admitted* to you, in any manner, that Commodore Stockton had a right, by virtue of relative rank, to command him (General Kearny) as a brigadier general in the army, or to interfere with his command of the army troops within the 10th military department, to which he had been assigned?

Lieutenant Colonel Frémont presented the following note:

Mr. President: Lieutenant Colonel Frémont desires to say to the court that he apprehends it was not known in California, at that time, that there was any 10th military district or department.

> J. C. FRÉMONT,
> *Lieutenant Colonel, mounted rifles.*

The court was then cleared. On motion of a member, the words, "in the 10th military department, to which he had been assigned," were stricken out; and the question was made, in the latter part, to read, "command of any army troops in California."

The court was then opened. Lieutenant Colonel Frémont in court. The decision in closed session was announced.

Mr. William H. Russell, a witness.

Answer. As before stated in my chief examination, I was despatched by Lieutenant Colonel Frémont, on the evening of the capitulation of General Andreas Pico, commander-in-chief of the Californians, to Los Angeles, where both Commodore Stockton and General Kearny were, and specially instructed by him (Colonel Frémont) to ascertain, by all means possible, who was in chief command, and to make a report accordingly of the capitulation of that day. I called first on General Kearny, and delivered to him a note or letter addressed to him by Colonel Frémont, in acknowledgment of one that he, Colonel Frémont, had received from General Kearny on the march. I told General Kearny my business, and was directed by him to make my report to Commodore Stockton, whom he acknowledged as being in chief command, and admitted to me that he had served under him as such from San Diego to Los Angeles. I accordingly made the report to the commodore. On the same evening, General Kearny showed me his instructions from the Secretary of War, and inquired of me what I thought of them, or whether they did not give him the chief command. That led to the discussion of relative rank; when General Kearny, in terms not to be misunderstood, admitted to me that Stockton, in virtue of his position as commander of a squadron, ranked him as a brigadier general. I thought otherwise. He yielded that question though, and claimed his position in virtue of his instructions only. I am confident that this admission of General Kearny applied to the California battalion, for it was in reference to the battalion alone that I instituted the inquiry. I know of no distinction, in reference to any troops in California, made by General Kearny; but the inquiry was particularly in regard to Colonel Frémont, by whom I was sent.

Brigadier General S. W. Kearny, a witness.—Called by the court.

Question by the court. Did you, in any conversation before or about the middle of January, 1847, admit the superior rank of Commodore Stockton, or in any manner acknowledge or yield military precedence to him? If so, how?

When the question was read, the following paper was presented by Lieutenant Colonel Frémont:

Mr. PRESIDENT: If General Kearny is to be interrogated to the same point, for the purpose of contradiction, Lieutenant Colonel Frémont is advised to say that the rules of evidence require the witnesses to be confronted; he, therefore, asks that the rule be enforced, and that Colonel Russell be called in, and that he and General Kearny stand face to face, and each be subject to further interrogatories.

J. C. FRÉMONT,
Lieutenant Colonel, mounted rifles.

The court was cleared. And the court decided that the mode of examination was correct when objected to by the accused, the matter being within the discretion of the court, and that it proceed accordingly.

The court was then opened. Lieutenant Colônel Frémont in court. The decision in closed session was announced.

Brigadier General Kearny, a witness.

The question was then read to the witness, as follows:

Question by the court. Did you in any conversation, before or about the middle of January, 1847, admit the superior rank of Commodore Stockton, or in any manner acknowledge or yield military precedence to him; if so, how?

Answer. I did not, I never admitted it to any one; in a conversation with Colonel Russell, at Los Angeles, on the 13th of January, 1847, I told Colonel Russell, and I explained to him the relative positions occupied by Commodore Stockton and by myself. I told Colonel Russell that Commodore Stockton I acknowledged as the governor, or as acting as governor and commander-in-chief in California; and that I had from San Diego, on our march to that place, been in command of the troops on the expedition, and that I had been placed in the command of those troops by the act of Commodore Stockton himself ; that was about the purport of my conversation with Colonel Russell, to the best of my recollection— nothing more and nothing less. I will state to the court, if it thinks proper, in full what I considered the positions occupied by Commodore Stockton and myself in California. I found Commodore Stockton acting as governor and commander-in-chief in the territory, on my arrival there at San Diego, on the 12th of December, 1846. Commodore Stockton gave to me the command of his sailors and marines, which he had prepared for an expedition towards Los Angeles. He told his officers to look upon me as their commander; in consequence of which I took pleasure in complying with Commodore Stockton's wishes or suggestions, as far as I could consistently do so, and as far as the public service would, in my opinion, admit of it. He had, at that time, the relative rank with a colonel in the army; if he had been a lieutenant in the navy, with the relative rank of a captain in the army, I would have treated him with the same courtesy. During our march, his authority and command, though it did not extend over me, or over the troops which he had himself given to me, extended far beyond where we were moving. It extended to volunteers stationed at Nueva Helvetia, at Sonora, at Monterey, and, I think, some few at San Francisco, and it extended, also, over the California battalion of mounted riflemen, under Lieutenant Colonel Frémont, the command of which I had not then claimed. Though I had the instructions with me, of the President of the United States, in letters conveyed to me by the Secretary of War, of 3d June and June 18th, 1846; yet I did not, until the 16th January, 1847, attempt to avail myself in full of them. During our march, many messages were brought to me from Commodore Stockton; those messages I looked upon as suggestions and as expressions of his wishes. I have since then learned, that he has considered them in the light of orders. I most assuredly never laid aside my rank or commission, as a brigadier general in the army of the United States.

Question by the court. Did you before the 17th of January, 1847, in any manner avow or express an intention of appointing Lieutenant Colonel Frémont governor of California, if your instructions had been recognized? or the further intention to return to the United States as soon after that time as you could organize a civil government?

Answer. I never did, before the 17th of January, avow or express an intention of appointing Lieutenant Colonel Frémont governor. I conversed with Colonel Russell freely on the subject of Lieutenant Colonel Frémont, and I remember that I spoke highly of him, for I then had a high opinion of him. I never expressed or avowed the intention of returning to the United States, as soon as I could organize a civil government; I might have told Colonel Russell, and I have no doubt did, that I wished to return to the United States, or that I expected to return to the United States, but not that I intended to return to the United States. The subject was not an open one with me; though I expected and though I wished to return, the subject was not under my control, for I had, on the 16th of September, 1846, before leaving Santa Fé for California, written to the adjutant general of the army, informing him of my intention of proceeding to California, and asking, under certain circumstances, for permission to return to Missouri. An answer to that letter I did not receive until brought to me by Colonel Mason, on the 13th of February. To show to the court that the question was not an open one with me, I will read an extract from my letter to the adjutant general of the army, dated Santa Fé, September 16th, 1846, as follows:

" I have now respectfully to ask, that in the event of our getting possession of Upper California, of establishing a civil government there, securing peace, quiet, and order among the inhabitants, and precluding the possibility of the Mexicans again having control there, that I may be permitted to leave there next summer, with the 1st dragoons, and march them back to Fort Leavenworth, on the Missouri."

Question by the court. Did you take any part in the formation of a civil government by Commodore Stockton, or give any advice in relation to appointments to office in such government, or the acceptance of such appointments. If so, how?

Answer. I took no part whatever in such formation. In a conversation with Colonel Russell in my quarters, a few days subsequent to his arrival there, he informed me that Commodore Stockton had offered him the appointment of Secretary of State, and asked my advice as to his acceptance of it, which I declined giving. He told me he would accept of it, and that if the managment of affairs in California fell into my hands, he would resign his appointment to me; I told him I would make no agreement with him; that he might take his course and I would take mine.

The court had no further questions to ask the witness.

The testimony was then directed to be read over to him.

General Kearny said to the court: "I wish, before leaving this court, to make an explanation of part of my testimony given before the court on my cross-examination. I ask of the court permission to do so."

Leave being granted, General Kearny said: "In my cross-examination I stated that I did not know what had brought Colonel Russell to Los Angeles, in advance of Lieutenant Colonel Frémont, and that I did not know whether Lieutenant Colonel Frémont had sent the capitulation of Cowenga to me or to Commodore Stockton; my recollection then did not serve me; when I made that statement, I did not recollect it. Upon reading over in the newspapers Colonel Russell's testimony, I did remember, and I will now state my recollection: That Colonel Russell coming to my quarters on the 13th of January, 1847, at Los Angeles, and speaking to me of the capitulation of Cowenga, he asked me to whom he should deliver it; and I told him to take it to Commodore Stockton, who was the governor, or acting as the governor and commander-in-chief in California. In that light, as I have previously stated in my cross examination, I looked upon Commodore Stockton, and I continued to do so, up to the 16th of January, 1847.

"I would also wish to make an explanation, in relation to my testimony, relating to the number of Californians who had gone, as I supposed, to San Fernando, to meet Lieutenant Colonel Frémont and his battalion.

"In my testimony, I stated that I had never heard the number exceeded fifty or sixty. I wish to be understood by that, that I have no knowledge on the subject whatever; and that I only spoke of what I heard and understood, subsequent to the arrival at Los Angeles of Lieutenant Colonel Frémont and his battalion."

The testimony of to-day was then read over to the witness.

Lieutenant Colonel Frémont presented the following note:

Mr. PRESIDENT: Lieutenant Colonel Frémont does not understand whether the court has decided that the two witnesses (General Kearny and Colonel Russell) shall not be confronted *at all*: if not so decided, he now asks that it may be done, and Colonel Russell be interrogated by the court on all points on which he has been so contradicted.

J. C. FRÉMONT,
Lieutenant Colonel, mounted rifles.

The president replied: "The court have decided not to confront the witnesses."

Whereupon Lieutenant Colonel Frémont presented the following note:

Mr. PRESIDENT: Lieutenant Colonel Frémont asks that Colonel William H. Russell may be called back by the court, to be interrogated by it on all the points on which General Kearny has contradicted him under questions by the court, without confrontation, the court having decided that they will not be confronted.

J. C. FRÉMONT,
Lieutenant Colonel, mounted rifles.

The court was then cleared. And the court decided that—
The court has asked such questions as to it seemed necessary to the distinct understanding of the recollections and meaning of witnesses. The court has not sought to array witnesses against each other in contradictory statements, but rather to elicit whatever might go to reconcile statements apparently such; nor has the court had any purpose to imply a distrust of any witness. The court supposes itself in possession of whatever can be elicited from the witnesses in this view.

If, however, the defence have material omissions to supply, the court will recall any witness and put any questions proposed by them, which it may consider necessary to this investigation.

The court was then opened. Lieutenant Colonel Frémont in court. The decision in closed session was announced.

Brigadier General Kearny, a witness.

Question by the court. You have stated that you did not claim the command in California, under your instructions, until the 16th of January, 1847. Please state the reasons for not doing so until that time; and then, was it by a general order issued by you?

Answer. As I stated in my cross-examination, that in a conversation with Commodore Stockton, on the 28th December, I told him that though I had the instructions from the President of the United States to take charge of the civil and military affairs in the country, yet I would not relieve him in those duties until my command was increased, having then but a few dragoons—a body guard with me.

I did not claim the management of affairs in California by a general order, but in letters to Commodore Stockton of the 16th and 17th of January, 1847, which are on your record.

Lieutenant Colonel Frémont presented the following note:

Mr. PRESIDENT: Lieutenant Colonel Frémont asks that Commodore Stockton may be called back by the court to be re-cross-examined by the court on all the points on which General Kearny has testified differently from him (Commodore Stockton) on this, his re-introduction as a witness.

J. C. FRÉMONT,
Lieutenant Colonel, mounted rifles.

On motion of a member, the court was ordered to be cleared. Brigadier General Kearny said:

Mr. PRESIDENT: Before the court is cleared, I wish to make a statement.

No objection being made, General Kearny said:

I consider it due to the dignity of the court, and the high respect I entertain for it, that I should here state that, on my last appearance before this court, when I was answering the questions propounded to me by the court, the senior counsel of the accused, Thomas H. Benton, of Missouri, sat in his place, making mouths and grimaces at me, which I considered were intended to offend, to insult, and to overawe me.

I ask of this court no action on it, so far as I am concerned. I I am fully capable of taking care of my own honor.

The president of the court said:

He regretted very much to hear it. He had not observed it. He referred to the power of courts martial under the law in regard to violations of order in its presence, and he read the 76th article of the Rules and Articles of War, as follows:

" No person whatsoever shall use any menacing words, signs, or gestures, in presence of a court martial, or shall cause any disorder or riot, or disturb their proceedings, on the penalty of being punished at the discretion of the said court martial."

The honorable Thomas H. Benton, of counsel for Lieutenant Colonel Frémont, then addressed the court as follows:

I desire the judge advocate will take down what I say.

He then continued:

Mr. PRESIDENT: On or about the first day of General Kearny's examination before this court, when he stood in that corner, and when he twice swore that Colonel Frémont had the originals now of certain papers, if he had not destroyed them, he fixed his eyes upon Colonel Frémont, fixedly, and pausingly; and looked insultingly and fiendishly at him. The judge advocate, by leading questions, led General Kearny into a modification of what he had previously sworn——

Here a member of the court rose and said:

Mr. PRESIDENT: I rise to bring the attention of the court to a point of order which ought, I think, to be preserved. Remarks reflecting upon the integrity of our proceedings are not, in my opinion, admissible.

Colonel Benton said: I admit the power of the court to punish, but they must first hear.

The member, above alluded to, again rose and said:

Mr. PRESIDENT: I wish it to be distinctly understood that, in rising, I intended to interpose no impediment to a free and full reply, on the part of the senior member of the counsel for the defence, to the remarks which have been made by General Kearny.

My object in rising was, to call attention to what appeared to me a violation of that respect which is due to the court, in a comment upon the integrity of its proceedings. The gentleman has said that the judge advocate, who is the officer of the court, representing the government, which prosecutes in this case, had put a leading question to the witness for the prosecution, and had thus led him into a modification of that to which he had twice previously sworn. These were the words, said the member, which he had risen to object to, and he hoped they would not be permitted to go upon the record. The member further said:

Mr. PRESIDENT: It is a well known principle of law, that a party cannot be allowed to put a leading question to a witness who testifies on the part of that party, and especially when it could lead the witness to a modification of what he had said. Such a course would have been corrupt in the judge advocate, and the court would have been derelict to its duty to have permitted such a proceeding.

It being now a few minutes of three o'clock, when by law the court must adjourn, the judge advocate requested Colonel Benton to continue his remarks, without waiting for the judge advocate to record them, and he (the judge advocate) would endeavor to remember, and afterwards record them.

Colonel Benton continued his remarks, according to the recollection of the judge advocate, as follows:

When General Kearny fixed his eyes on Colonel Frémont, I determined if he should attempt again to look down a prisoner, I would look at him. I did this day; and the look of to-day was the consequence of the looks in this court before. I did to-day look at General Kearny when he looked at Colonel Frémont, and I looked at him till his eyes fell—till they fell upon the floor.

As to this court, I disclaim any intention to disturb its order, entertaining, as I do, the highest respect for the court.

The president of the court said: He had observed General Kearny look towards Colonel Frémont during the trial, and on the occasion referred to, but not with an insulting expression of countenance; on the contrary, he (the president) thought the expression was one of politeness and kindness.

The hour of three having arrived, the president gave the order for the adjournment of the court.

General Kearny rose and said: I wish, in the presence of the court, to say, that I have never offered the slightest insult to Colonel Frémont, either here as a prisoner on this trial or any where, or under any circumstances whatsoever.

And the court adjourned to meet on Monday at 10 o'clock.

Monday, *January* 10, 1848.—10 *o'clock*.

The court met pursuant to adjournment.

Present: All the members, the judge advocate, and Lieutenant Colonel Frémont.

The proceedings of Saturday were read over.

A member requested that a correction might be made of the record of the last day, in regard to the remarks of a member.

The counsel of Lieutenant Colonel Frémont requested that a correction of the record be made in regard to his remarks.

Brigadier General Kearny asked leave to make a statement to the court.

A member suggested that the statement be made in writing.

The court was then ordered to be cleared. And the court decided that any remarks or statements, other than explanations of testimony which the witness might wish to make to the court, should be presented in writing.

And the court decided that the corrections suggested by a member, and by the counsel of the accused, be made on the record of the last day's proceedings.

And the court directed it to be entered on the record, that the matter referred to by the counsel of the accused in the proceedings of a previous day in this court was not an irregularity; that there was no leading question put to the witness; that the question, as shown by the record, was regular; though the point and subject of the question was not of the smallest importance.

A written statement was received in closed session from General Kearny, in regard to the remarks of the counsel on Saturday.

And the court decided that the subject be not further entertained, and that, accordingly, the statement of the witness be not recorded.

And the court made the following order: the court has before decided that, to supply material omissions, witnesses will be recalled to answer such questions as the court may consider necessary to this investigation.

Under that decision the defence can submit to the court such questions as they desire it to put to Commodore Stockton, and the court will consider whether they are necessary to complete the investigation before it, and decide on recalling him accordingly.

The court was then opened. Lieutenant Colonel Frémont in court. The decisions in closed session were announced by the judge advocate.

And the president read aloud the following order, made by the court in closed session, and which he, the president, was directed to read aloud on the opening of the court:

The recollections and impressions of the members of the court confirm those of its president, as expressed on Saturday, in reference to the looks of the witness on the occasions referred to by the senior counsel. The court considers the act, avowed by the counsel, of attempting to look down a witness before it, as improper and indecorous; but, as it did not come to the notice of the president, and the counsel has disclaimed any intention of disrespect to the court, no further action will be taken.

The president inquired of Lieutenant Colonel Frémont, if he had any questions which he wished the court to put to Commodore Stockton, to which Lieutenant Colonel Frémont replied in the negative.

Lieutenant Colonel Frémont presented the following paper:

Mr. PRESIDENT: Lieutenant Colonel Frémont asks leave to introduce witnesses to testify to the character of one of his witnesses, namely, Colonel Wm. H. Russell, who has been contradicted in a material part of his testimony by General Kearny. He offers, for that purpose, the Hon. Henry Clay, the Hon. Mr. Crittenden, Mr. Justice Catron of the Supreme Court, the Hon. Mr. French, the Hon. Mr. Moorehead, the Hon. Mr. Jamieson, and perhaps others.

J. C. FRÉMONT,
Lieutenant Colonel, mounted rifles.

The court was then cleared. And the court decided that the court does not consider contradictory statements, where fraud is not imputed, as involving a right in a party to sustain the credit of a witness by evidence to his general character.

In the case presented here, apparently in reference to the examination of witnesses by the court itself, which could not be supposed to aim at discrediting any witness, and which has not impeached any witness, the court cannot now admit testimony which would be of doubtful admissibility to rebut an examination by a party.

To grant the request of the accused might imply a doubt on the part of the court as to the integrity and general character of the witness, which the court does not entertain.

The court was then opened. Lieutenant Colonel Frémont in court. The decision in closed session was annnounced.

Lieutenant Colonel Frémont read a paper to the court.

The court was then cleared, and the court made the following order:

The paper of the accused renews before the court a matter twice before disposed of; characterizes the action of the court improperly; and is in substance and in terms a protest against a decision of this court. The court directs the paper to be returned to the accused.

The court was then opened, Lieutenant Colonel Frémont in court.

The decision in closed session was announced.

Lieutenant Colonel Frémont presented the following note:

Mr. PRESIDENT: Lieutenant Colonel Frémont, by advice of his counsel, now requests that the judge advocate be sworn as a witness in this case, for the purpose of ascertaining whether General Kearny did or did not give information to the person who drew up the seventh specification of the first charge in this case, General Kearny having testified that he did not.

J. C. FRÉMONT,
Lieut. Colonel, mounted rifles.

The court was cleared; and the court made the following decision:

The matter is a collateral one introduced on cross-examination, and as such excluded under the court's rule.

It moreover goes into the origin of the charges, which the court has received in the usual form of authentication, and cannot now inquire into.

The court was then opened, Lieutenant Colonel Frémont in court.

The decision in closed session was announced.

Lieutenant Colonel Frémont said he had no more witnesses to bring before the court, but that he had some documentary evidence which he would present to-morrow.

And then, at three minutes before three, the court adjourned to meet to-morrow at 10 o'clock.

TUESDAY, *January* 11, 1848.—10 *o'clock.*

The court met pursuant to adjournment.
Present: all the members and the judge advocate.
The proceedings of yesterday were read over.
Lieutenant Colonel Frémont came into court.
Lieutenant Colonel Frémont read the following note:

Mr. PRESIDENT: Lieutenant Colonel Frémont offers to the court the accompanying paper, being a certified copy of the order issued by Brigadier General Kearny at the time of meeting the express (Mr. C. Carson) from California in October, 1846, for the purpose of proving that he, General Kearny, then had what he himself calls in the order " *positive information*" that the province of Upper California *had been taken possession of by the Americans;*" and that it be entered on the minutes as evidence, to be used in the general defence for what it may be worth.

J. C. FRÉMONT,
Lieut. Colonel, mounted rifles.

Objection being made to the reception of the document in evidence, the court was cleared; and the court decided that the document be admitted on the record.

The court was then opened, Lieutenant Colonel Frémont in court.

The decision in closed session was announced.

On announcing the proceedings in closed session, a member moved that the court be cleared, which was done; and the court directed that the record be amended, which was done accordingly.

The following is the document offered by Lieutenant Colonel Frémont:

ORDERS }   HEAD-QUARTERS, ARMY OF THE WEST,
No. 34. }   *Camp on the Rio del Norte, below Socorro, N. M.,*
                                    October 6, 1846.

1. Positive information having been this day received, per express *en route* to Washington, that the province of Upper California has been taken possession of by the Americans, the necessity no longer exists for taking a considerable force into that country. Companies C and K, 1st dragoons, under Captain Moore, are therefore selected to accompany the general to California. The remaining three companies of dragoons present, B, G and J, under Major Sumner, will remain in this territory, at some point in the Rio Abaja country, to be selected by himself, suitable for obtaining supplies for the winter, and for giving protection to the inhabitants from hostile Indians.

Assistant Surgeon Simpson will remain with Major Sumner's command.

2. Mr. Carson, who arrived to-day express from California to Washington, having been engaged to return with the general, will deliver his letters, despatches, &c., into the hands of Mr. Thomas Fitzpatrick, who will convey them with all despatch to the city of Washington.

By order of Brigadier General S. W. KEARNY.

                                    H. S. TURNER,
                              Captain, A. A. A. General.

The court was then opened, Lieutenant Colonel Frémont in court.

Lieutenant Colonel Frémont read a paper to the court, offering again the paper rejected by the court on Friday last, and offering again the paper rejected on yesterday, and offering an affidavit on the same matter from Wm. Carey Jones, Esq.

The court was ordered to be cleared. And the court decided that "it adheres to its decision, and that the papers be not received."

The court was then opened. Lieutenant Colonel Frémont in court. The decision in closed session was announced.

Lieutenant Colonel Frémont presented the following paper:

Mr. PRESIDENT: Lieutenant Colonel Frémont reads in the reply which the judge advocate made to his (Lieutenant Colonel Frémont's) observations upon what he deemed irregularities in the preliminaries of this trial, the following words:

"7. The seventh objection to the regularity of this trial, is 'the apparent want of a prosecutor on part of the charges.' The charges are officially presented to the court, and are entered on the record as 'charges preferred, by order of the War Department, on information of Brigadier General Kearny,' the department having limited the charges to the matters officially reported by Brigadier General Kearny."

Lieutenant Colonel Frémont here presents to the court the copy of the charges against him, as delivered to him by the judge advocate, to show that the fact of those charges being preferred by order of the War Department, does not appear in that copy, and being advised by his counsel that it is an illegal order, and that, *in this case*, the orders for the preferment of the charges should have been from the President. Lieutenant Colonel Frémont now brings the alleged illegality to the notice of the court, for the purpose of giving his express consent, as he hereby does, to an alteration or correction of the record, by inserting "by order of the President," in place of "by order of the War Department," if such be the facts, (of which he knows nothing,) that the President gave the orders in relation to the charges.

Lieutenant Colonel Frémont is also advised by his counsel that the use of the term "War Department" is subject to objection in *this case*, and to obviate that objection he is willing, and does hereby agree, that the term *Secretary of War* may be substituted in place of War Department. And these corrections, he is advised, are necessary to show the legality of the proceedings, inasmuch as the power of the President over the case is *judicial*, and confided to him for reasons in a case like the present, and cannot be delegated, either expressly or by presumption, either by his own act, or by legal implication.

Anxious that the record should have no legal objections on its face, Lieutenant Colonel Frémont consents to *all* amendments necessary to make it correct.

The present objection is not to a matter of form, but of great substance, and Lieutenant Colonel Frémont desires the action of the court upon it, in order that the correction may be made in whatever way will correspond with the fact.

J. C. FRÉMONT,
Lieutenant Colonel, mounted rifles.

The court was then cleared. And the court made the following decision:

This court has before decided, in another matter involving the same points, that it cannot go behind the admission of the charges before it in the usual form of authentication, to inquire into their origin or authentication.

Nor, if the court had now the power to go behind the due official reception of the charges here, could it assume the power to entertain the question, whether the authority of the War Department is the authority of the President.

Nor, further, is it to be considered by this court, whether the usual style, in documents and acts emanating from the Department of War, be correct in the use of the words "War Department," instead of the official designation of the Secretary of War. Though the law organizing "an executive department, to be denominated the Department of War," directs the "principal officer therein to be called the Secretary for the Department of War, who shall perform and execute such duties as shall, from time to time, be enjoined on, or entrusted 'to, him by the President of the United States," &c., this court could not undertake to decide whether the common designations, "War Department," and "Secretary of War," are sufficient designations, or may be used one for the other in official acts.

The judge advocate may make any correction in the copy of the charges furnished to the accused, which may be needed, to make them conform to the copy on the record of the court.

The court was then opened. Lieutenant Colonel Frémont in court. The decision in closed session was announced.

Lieutenant Colonel Frémont read a paper to the court, offering in evidence, a despatch of the Navy Department, dated June 14, 1847, to the commander of the naval forces in the Pacific ocean.

The court was then cleared. And the court decided: "That the document offered is not relevant to the case under trial. But the court directs that, with the paper of Lieutenant Colonel Frémont, it be placed in the appendix to this record."

The court was then opened. Lieutenant Colonel Frémont in court. The decision in closed session was announced.

Lieutenant Colonel Frémont presented the following paper:

Mr. PRESIDENT: Lieutenant Colonel Frémont, by advice of his counsel, now requests of the court to be allowed time for correcting the published report of the proceedings of the court, by the official record, in order that in analyzing and comparing the testimony given in the case, he may be enabled to use the precise words in which it was taken down. This labor, it is believed, to be carefully and accurately performed, will require four days.

He further requests to be allowed time to prepare his defence. The magnitude of the charges; the length of time over which the alleged offences extend, the variety and importance of the testimony, the great volume of the record which must be gone through with and examined, the multiplicity of the specifications, upon each of which there must be a separate finding, and, of course, a separate defence; all considered, Lieutenant Colonel Frémont is advised by his counsel that he cannot, in justice to the case, ask a less time than one week. Lieutenant Colonel Frémont would, therefore, request, for the purposes above mentioned, to be released from attendance upon the court, until Monday, the 24th instant, at 12 o'clock, noon.

J. C. FRÉMONT,
Lieutenant Colonel, mounted rifles.

And the court decided to grant the request of the accused; and that when the court adjourns this day, it will adjourn till Monday, the 24th instant.

The judge advocate inquired of the court whether he should,

according to the practice in the service, now discharge the witnesses, army officers, and citizens, in attendance on this court.

Which the court decided in the negative. And the court directed that all witnesses who are present under the mandate of the court, and have not been examined, be forthwith discharged.

The court was then opened. Lieutenant Colonel Frémont in court. The decisions in closed session were announced.

And then, at half past two o'clock, the court adjourned to meet on Monday, the 24th instant, at 12 o'clock, noon.

MONDAY, *January* 24, 1848.—12 *o'clock.*

The court met pursuant to adjournment.

Present: All the members, the judge advocate, and Lieutenant Colonel Frémont.

The president announced to Lieutenant Colonel Frémont that the court was prepared to receive his written defence: Whereupon, Lieutenant Colonel Frémont read a paper which is placed in the appendix to this record. On finishing this reading, Lieutenant Colonel Frémont requested permission to continue his defence tomorrow; foɪ which purpose, he requested that the court adjourn till 12 o'clock, to-morrow; which was assented to. The court went into closed session. The record of the last day of the session was verified; and then, at ten minutes of 2 o'clock, the court adjourned to meet to-morrow, the 25th instant, at 12 o'clock.

TUESDAY, *January* 25, 1848.—12 *o'clock.*

The court met pursuant to adjournment.

Present: All the members, the judge advocate, and Lieutenant Colonel Frémont.

The proceedings of yesterday were read over.

Lieutenant Colonel Frémont read, in continuation of his defence, a paper annexed to this record.—See appendix. When the reading was finished, Lieutenant Colonel Frémont requested permission to continue his defence to-morrow.

On motion, the court was cleared; and the court decided to grant the request of the accused; and that, when the court adjourns this day, it will adjourn to meet at 11 o'clock, to-morrow.

The court was then opened. Lieutenant Colonel Frémont in court. The decision in closed session was announced.

The president then adjourned the court to meet to-morrow, at 11 o'clock.

WEDNESDAY, *January* 26, 1848.—11 *o'clock.*

The court met pursuant to adjournment.

Present: All the members, the judge advocate, and Lieutenant Colonel Frémont.

Lieutenant Colonel Frémont read to the court a paper annexed to the record, as the conclusion of his defence.

The court went into closed session. The judge advocate said that, as he was referred to in the defence, in regard to seventh specification of first charge, and the question, whether General Kearny drew the charge in respect to the howitzers there mentioned, or furnished the information to the judge advocate, he would submit to the court a brief note in explanation of that subject, and in reply to that point in the defence.

The court was then opened. Lieutenant Colonel Frémont in court. The decision in closed session was announced; and then the court adjourned to meet to-morrow, at 10 o'clock.

———

THURSDAY, *January* 27, 1848.—10 *o'clock.*

The court met pursuant to adjournment.

Present: All the members, the judge advocate, and Lieutenant Colonel Frémont.

The judge advocate submitted the following note:

The judge advocate submits this note in reply to a point in the paper of Lieutenant Colonel Frémont read to the court yesterday.

Lieutenant Colonel Frémont states that himself and his counsel are informed by the judge advocate that the seventh specification to charge first is copied literally from the charge furnished by General Kearny.

When Lieutenant Colonel Frémont applied to the court to have the testimony of the judge advocate taken on the subject of the authorship of this specification, the court refused the application, and refused to inquire into the subject. As, however, the statement of the judge advocate is brought before the court, it is proper he should explain it, and remark upon the application made of it to the evidence of General Kearny.

The judge advocate said, or meant to be understood, that the part of the specification which refers to the howitzers, is copied from the original charge of General Kearny, and on referring (since the adjournment of the court) to that original, he finds that the copy is made not literally, but without any alteration of the sense. The original says, "did refuse to give up to the 1st dragoons the two howitzers brought by them from Fort Leavenworth." The specification on trial says "surrender" for "give up," and the judge advocate would now explain that the copy is not literal, though the alteration is merely verbal and the sense is the same.

The defence infer from this a contradiction of the evidence of General Kearny.

General Kearny said in his testimony, as referred to by the defence, that he did not *know* that the howitzer at San Gabriel was the one lost at San Pasqual; and, afterwards, that he had no personal knowledge of it, but knew it from the report of Major Cooke. The defence refer to the testimony of Major Cooke, to show that General Kearney gave Major Cooke orders in reference to those howitzers before Major Cooke made a report to him about them, and, therefore, that he could not have got his knowledge from Major Cooke. If, however, General Kearny, at Monterey, had not seen those cannon at San Gabriel; if he heard in any way that such pieces were there, and gave orders in regard to them, and Major Cooke, as he states, went and saw them, and made his official report to General Kearny, at Monterey, then General Kearny would know officially that such cannon were there from such report, and might cite Major Cooke and his report as the evidence to this point, as he did on the original charges, and in his testimony before this court.

In regard to the origin of the charges which the court refused to inquire into, and which is introduced into the defence in connexion with the testimony of General Kearny, and the letter from the War Department to the counsel of Lieutenant Colonel Frémont, which letter the court refused to entertain, the judge advocate has only to say that he understands General Kearny to disown the charges because altered from his, he having preferred only one charge, which the defence understand to be mutiny; and he states further, in regard to these charges, that he gave no information to the person who drew them up. That the charges are drawn by order of the War Department, from the information officially reported by General Kearny to the adjutant general's office, has been officially made known by the department.

In regard to the reference made in the defence to the fact that Captain Turner was not re-introduced by the prosecution, the judge advocate merely replies that he supposes that the rule of law, and the objection of the defence to the re-introduction of witnesses at the stage of the trial referred to, would have applied to Captain Turner. The judge advocate certainly could not, at any time of the trial, have thought it consistent with his duty to have suppressed any testimony, and especially to have failed to take the testimony of the witnesses of the prosecution on points of any importance in the case, where he knew or suspected that their testimony would be favorable to the defence. He would either have examined them himself, or have notified the defence. In the case of this witness, he was equally at the call of either party.

The judge advocate submits the case to the court on the evidence, without argument.

Lieutenant Colonel Frémont presented the following note:

Lieutenant Colonel Frémont would state that, in referring in his defence to the non-production of Captain Turner to certain points of evidence, he had not the remotest intention of intimating that the judge advocate had intended to suppress evidence, but simply to argue that his non-production went to the inference that he could not in any way strengthen the testimony that was impeached.

J. C. FRÉMONT,
Lieutenant Colonel, mounted rifles.

The court then went into closed session, and commenced the reading of the record, which was continued till one minute of three o'clock, when the court adjourned to meet to-morrow at 10 o'clock.

FRIDAY, *January* 28, 1848.—10 *o'clock.*

The court met pursuant to adjournment.
Present : all the members, and the judge advocate.
The court resumed the reading of the testimony on the record, and concluded it.
The court then proceeded to deliberate on the charges.
At 10 minutes of three o'clock, the court adjourned to meet to-morrow at 10 o'clock.

SATURDAY, *January* 29, 1847.—10 *o'clock.*

The court met pursuant to adjournment.
Present: all the members and the judge advocate.
The court resumed its deliberation on the charges, and continued in such deliberation till half after two o'clock, when the court adjourned to meet on Monday at 10 o'clock.

MONDAY, *January* 31, 1848.—10 *o'clock.*

The court met pursuant to adjournment.
Present: all the members and the judge advocate.
The court resumed its deliberation on the case; and then, after full and mature consideration of all the testimony, finds the accused, Lieutenant Colonel John C. Frémont, of the regiment of mounted riflemen, United States army, as follows:

Of the first specification of first charge—guilty.
Of the second specification of first charge—guilty.
Of the third specification of first charge—guilty.
Of the fourth specification of first charge—guilty.
Of the fifth specification of first charge—guilty.
Of the sixth specification of first charge—guilty.

Of the seventh specification of first charge—guilty.
Of tne eighth specification of first charge—guilty.
Of the ninth specification of first charge—guilty.
Of the tenth specification of first charge—guilty.
Of the eleventh specification of first charge—guilty.

Of the first charge—guilty.

Of the first specification, second charge—guilty.
Of the second specification, second charge—guilty.
Of the third specification, second charge—guilty.
Of the fourth secification, second charge—guilty.
Of the fifth specification, second charge—guilty.
Of the sixth specification, second charge—guilty.
Of the seventh specification, second charge—guilty.

Of the second charge—guilty.

Of the first specification, third charge—guilty.
Of the second specification, third charge—guilty.
Of the third specification, third charge—guilty.
Of the fourth specification, third charge—guilty.
Of the fifth specification, third charge—guilty.

Of the third charge—guilty.

And the court does therefore sentence the said Lieutenant Colonel John C. Frémont, of the regiment of mounted riflemen, United States army, to be dismissed the service.

GEO. M. BROOKE,
Brevet Brig. Gen., and Pres. Gen. Court Martial.
J. F. LEE,
Judge Advocate.

—

Remarks by the Court.

The court deems it proper, in view of the mass of evidence on the record, to remark that the court has been unwilling to confine the accused to a strict legal defence, which appeared to lie within narrow limits.

Considering the gravity of the charges, the court has allowed the defence the fullest scope in its power to develope the instructions of the government, and all circumstances relating to the alleged misconduct, as well as to impeach the leading witness for the prosecution. The court has even indulged the accused in a course unusual, and without its approbation, in the final defence, of using indiscriminately, matter which had been rejected or admitted in evidence.

With all this latitude of evidence, and the broader latitude of defence, the court has found nothing conflicting in the orders and instructions of the government; nothing impeaching the testimony on the part of the prosecution; nothing, in fine, to qualify, in a legal sense, the resistance to authority of which the accused is convicted.

The attempt to assail the leading witness for the prosecution has involved points not in issue, and to which the prosecution has brought no evidence. In the judgment of the court, his honor and character are unimpeached.

And then, at half past two o'clock, the court adjourned without day.

GEO. M. BROOKE,
Brevet Brig. Gen., and President.
J. F. LEE,
Judge Advocate.

Under the circumstances in which Lieutenant Colonel Frémont was placed between two officers of superior rank, each claiming to command-in-chief in California—circumstances in their nature calculated to embarrass the mind and excite the doubts of officers of greater experience than the accused—and in consideration of the important professional services rendered by him previous to the occurrence of those acts for which he has been tried, the undersigned, members of the court, respectfully commend Lieutenant Colonel Frémont to the lenient consideration of the President of the United States.

GEO. M. BROOKE,
Brevet Brig. Gen., U. S. A.
THO. F. HUNT,
Lieut. Colonel, and D. Q. General.
J. P. TAYLOR,
Lieut. Colonel, and A. G. S.
R. L. BAKER,
Major Ordnance Department.

Under all the circumstances of this case, and in consideration of the distinguished professional services of the accused, previous to the transactions for which he has now been tried, the undersigned beg leave to recommend him to the clemency of the President of the United States.

S. H. LONG,
Lieutenant Colonel, T. E.
E. W. MORGAN,
Lieutenant Colonel, 13th Infantry.
RICHARD DELAFIELD,
Major of Engineers.

I have carefully examined the record of proceedings of the general court martial, in the case of Lieutenant Colonel John C. Frémont, of the regiment of mounted riflemen, which convened at Washington arsenal in the District of Columbia, on the 2d day of November, 1847, and of which Brevet Brigadier General George M. Brooke was president.

The court find Lieutenant Colonel Frémont *guilty* of the following charges, viz:

1st. " Mutiny. 2d. Disobedience of the lawful commands of his superior officer. 3d. Conduct to the prejudice of good order and military discipline," and sentence him " to be dismissed the service."

Four members of the court append to the record of their proceedings, the following, viz:

Under the circumstances in which Lieutenant Colonel Frémont was placed, between two officers of superior rank, each claiming to command-in-chief in California, circumstances in their nature, calculated to embarrass the mind, and excite the doubts of officers of greater experience than the accused, and in consideration of the important professional services rendered by him, previous to the occurrence of those acts for which he has been tried, the undersigned, members of the court, respectfully recommend Lieutenant Colonel Frémont to the lenient consideration of the President of the United States

GEORGE M. BROOKE,
Brevet Brigadier General, U. S. A.
THOMAS F. HUNT,
Lt. Col. and Deputy Quartermaster Gen.
J. P. TAYLOR,
Lieutenant Colonel and A. C. G. S.
R. L. BAKER,
Major Ordnance Dep't.

Three other members of the court append to the record of their proceedings, the following, viz:

Under all the circumstances of this case, and in consideration of the distinquished professional services of the accused, previous to the transactions for which he has been tried, the undersigned beg leave to recommend him to the clemency of the President of the United States.

S. H. LONG,
Lieut. Col. Topographical Engineers.
RICHARD DELAFIELD,
Major of Engineers.
E. W. MORGAN,
Lieutenant Colonel, 13th Infantry.

Upon an inspection of the record, I am not satisfied that the facts proved in this case constitute the military crime of " mutiny." I am of opinion that the second and third charges are sustained by the proof, and that the conviction upon these charges, warrants the sentence of the court. The sentence of the court is therefore approved, but in consideration of the peculiar circumstances of the case, of the previous meritorious and valuable services of Lieutenant Colonel Frémont, and of the foregoing recommendations of a majority of the members of the court, the penalty of dismissal from the service is remitted.

Lieutenant Colonel Frémont will accordingly be released from arrest, will resume his sword, and report for duty.

JAMES K. POLK.

WASHINGTON, *February* 16, 1848.

APPENDIX, NO. 1.

May it please the court: In the progress of this cause, the undersigned has been called upon as a witness. He cheerfully complied with this requisition of the court, although, as he has already stated, he was fully aware of the anomalous and embarrassing position in which he was thus placed. The views which he then entertained upon this point he frankly disclosed to the court. He had designed to present them more fully before the court, but the form in which the first question propounded to him was couched, relieved him from some of his difficulties.

The question was proposed to him in the following words:

"You know the subject matter of inquiry before this court—will you please proceed to give, in a narrative form, the evidence which seems to you to be material and relevant?"

This form of interrogatory, as the undersigned conceived, left him at full liberty to state, in the narrative which he was asked to give, all those matters which, in the judgment of the witness, bore upon the issue in this trial. In accordance with these impressions, the undersigned occupied the time of the court during a portion of two days in giving a narrative of the incidents which, in his opinion, was pertinent.

At this point of his testimony, the witness was arrested in his narrative by the court, in the following order: " The court directed it to be recorded as its decision, that the details of naval and military operations on the coast, and in the conquest of California, are not subjects of inquiry before the court; that but little of the history and narrative already given in evidence by the witness has any relation to the charges on trial; that this mode of delivering, by each witness, in the narrative form, whatever may appear to such witness relevant to the trial, or interesting to be said, renders it impracticable for the court to restrict the evidence to matters which it ought to inquire into. Therefore, the court orders, that this form of giving testimony be suspended, and that the examination of witnesses be by question and answer. Then the court will judge of the materiality and relevancy of each question, giving to the party offering a question objected to, the opportunity of explaining its propriety."

The question as propounded to him, has, therefore, been but partially answered.

The undersigned, with great and unfeigned respect for this court, begs leave to state, that he has not intentionally trenched upon the discretion apparently reposed in him by the terms in which the question was propounded by the authority of the court. He was, throughout, anxious to confine his testimony strictly to the points in issue. The residue of his testimony would have been equally in exact conformity with his ideas of the liberty allowed him by the language of the question. His design was to testify as to facts going to establish—

1st. That he (the witness) was, and *how* he was placed in chief command of the Upper California province of Mexico; the manner of his appointment, and the extent of his authority.

2d. That the California battalion of volunteers was formed by virtue of such his appointment power and authority; whenever the appointment power and authority of Lieutenant Colonel Frémont were derived.

3d. To show the details of the conquest of California, and of establishing a civil and military government therein, prior to the arrival of General Kearny.

4th. The manner in which the chief authority of that government was devolved upon Lieutenant Colonel Frémont, and the extent to which the orders to General Kearny were anticipated before his arrival at the scene of operations.

5th. To show that General Kearny, whatever his orders were, and however binding, in the first instance, voluntarily waived his rank, authority, and command, whatever they were, and volunteered to serve, and did serve, under the command and authority of the witness; and to show, in the second place, that when he (General Kearny) addressed to the witness his letter of the 16th of January, 1847, in which he " demands" that witness should " cease all further proceedings relating to the formation of a civil government for the territory," his demand was peremptorily repelled by witness, and he (General Kearny) formally and officially, in his letter to witness of 17th of January, 1847, acquiesced in the refusal of witness to recognize his authority.

Witness submits that all these facts are within the discretion allowed to him by the question propounded by the authority of the court; and are not only material to the issue, but essentially necessary to place the conduct of witness in a proper light before the court and country. He submits that the suspension of his answer to the interrogatory will leave the part already recorded in a partial, unintelligible and incomplete form, apparently irrelevant to the case on trial, and injurious to the witness himself.

It must be apparent to all who have perused the charges and specifications against Lieutenant Colonel Frémont, and upon which he is now arraigned for trial, that in some of the transactions in which these charges have their origin, my own official conduct is involved. In regard to such of them as were performed under my order and authority, the responsibility necessarily, to a greater or less extent, rests upon me; and if I had no other authority to exercise the power which I did exercise, my administration, as civil and military governor of California, must be condemned. The evidence which has been laid before the court still more closely connects me with the case.

Under such circumstances, the anomalous character of the position I occupy is striking and obvious. In some sense, and to some extent, the propriety or impropriety of my own conduct is at issue.

It is in such a case that I have been called upon to testify as a witness.

The position is an embarrassing and difficult one; but this embarrassment and this difficulty have their origin, not in the acts themselves, by which I am thus connected with the case, but in the circumstance that as my conduct can, in this cause and before this court, only be incidentally and collaterally involved, it may not be found consistent with these principles by which courts martial are governed, to allow me as wide a latitude in vindicating myself as would be extended were I the party actually arraigned for trial.

It can scarcely happen but that in answering such questions as may be propounded to me as a witness, circumstances may be stated which, taken by themselves, might, at least, leave a doubt as to the legality and propriety of my acts; which, nevertheless, if the accompanying circumstances were shown, the motives which prompted to them displayed, and the objects contemplated and accomplished exhibited, instead of meriting condemnation would command the approbation of every honorable man.

So long as even a shade of a doubt exists as to the propriety of any part of my conduct in California, it is my earnest wish and desire that it should be thoroughly investigated. For such an investigation I am prepared, and shall be ready to meet it whenever and wherever it may be deemed proper and advisable. Nor could any opportunity be afforded more grateful to my feelings of conscious rectitude, than to have this investigation conducted before such a tribunal as that before which I have the honor of now appearing.

While, however, I feel thus solicitous to have any doubts which may rest upon any of my acts dispelled before the country and the world, the same principles and feelings indicate to my apprehension that such result can be accomplished only by a full and thorough investigation. To make the result satisfactory, either to myself or to the country, the examination must be full and thorough. An imperfect or partial investigation, restricted to particular facts segregated from the whole course of my conduct, leaving my motives and designs undeveloped, would, in its results, whatever they might be, prove satisfactory to no one, and least of all to myself.

If, therefore, in my examination as a witness on behalf of the accused, my testimony is to be confined and restricted to special and isolated interrogatories, it will be altogether impracticable for me to lay before the court the entire group of facts and circumstances which is necessary to enable it to place a proper estimate upon either my conduct or my motives. For each and every of the acts of Lieutenant Colonel Frémont, performed under my authority, and in obedience to my orders, I cannot but feel that in some form or other I am responsible, if the acts were in themselves illegal, or the execution of them criminal. While, however, under a sense of imperative duty, I feel bound to assume the responsibility justly attached to whatever I may myself have done, I cannot consent to a judgment of condemnation, either directly or by implication, passing upon me, without the fullest opportunity being afforded of vindicating myself from every species and degree of criminality.

To be required, as a witness, to disclose only such of my acts, and to exhibit only so much of my conduct as might be elicited on this trial, might possibly subject me to the most serious disadvantages. All the facts and circumstances, all the motives and designs which would give color, and impress character upon the transactions, would remain undeveloped.

It is from an application of these peculiar difficulties by which I am surrounded, that I have felt it incumbent upon me to submit these views to the consideration of the honorable court, claiming the fullest latitude allowable to any witness testifying before a court martial.

Animated by no feeling of bravado, claiming no infalibility of judgment, but erect and confident in the correctness of the course I have pursued, I ask for the opportunity of testifying thoroughly and fully.

I therefore most respectfully pray that this honorable court will permit me to conclude the narrative, which I have already more than half completed, in response to the interrogatory propounded.

R. F. STOCKTON.

APPENDIX, No. 2.

---

*Paper " preliminary to the defence," read to the court by Lieuten-
ant Colonel Frémont on Thursday the 30th of December.*

Mr. President: Before entering upon his defence, Lieutenant
Colonel Frémont proposes to bring to the notice of the court, and
to have placed upon its minutes, some instances of what he is instructed to say were *irregularities* of proceeding in the preliminaries of this trial, and before the assembling of this court; and
which he now desires to point out, not with any view to obtain
any action of this court upon them, or to receive any benefit from
their correction, but solely to expose them as *irregularities*, that
they may not be quoted as precedent hereafter.

1st. The first of these suggested *irregularities*, which he proposes
to notice, is the omission to have instituted (in this case) a court
of inquiry previously to ordering a general court martial.

The article in the American rules and articles of war on the
subject of courts of inquiry, is accordant with those in the British
rules and articles of war on the same subject; and the reason and
policy of such courts being the same in both services, it is assumed
that the construction of the articles, and the practice under them
in British courts martial, is a proper guide to what the construction and practice should be in the American service. The practice
and construction in the British service would make an investigation by a court of inquiry, in a case like the present, obligatory
before ordering a court. It is the case of an officer brought home
from a foreign station charged with offences, of the truth or probability of which the officer who is to order the court material
knows nothing, and is bound to know something (enough to justify
the act) before he takes the responsible step of ordering a court.
In all such cases it is the construction of the British rules and articles of war, and the practice under them, that an investigation by
a court of inquiry precedes the order for the general court martial; and that, for wise and obvious reasons, founded both in a
sense of private justice and public convenience. For, to order the
court without a knowledge of the case, would be to act blindly in
the responsible business of putting an officer to the mortifications
and risks of a trial, and the public service to the inconvenience
and interruptions of it. To act upon the story of the accuser
would be to make *him*, and not the *officer* designated by *law*, the
judge of the propriety of ordering the court. And, in the one
case, all the evils of an harrassing and expensive court martial
might be incurred without necessity; in the second case, the pas-
sions of the acccuser would be substituted for that high, disinterested, and responsible judicial discretion which the law attributes

to the few and eminent officers to whom it confides the power of
ordering courts martial. The safe, ready, and cheap resort, is to a
court of inquiry. A few officers (from one to three) may hold it.
Being untrammelled by issues, it inquires fully, and gets at the
facts of the case. Laying the whole before the officer who is to
order the court, he not only sees whether there is probable cause
for trying any one, but who and how many? This is the British
rule and practice; and so say their writers on the law material.
Thus, Hough (edition of 1825, page 23) quoting the general orders
of the commander-in-chief, February 8, 1802, under the head,
" court of inquiry:"

"The frequent assembling of general courts martial being pro-
ductive of much inconvenience to the public service, the commander-in-chief directs that when a charge shall be preferred
against a European or a native, the senior officer on the spot shall
order a full investigation to be made into the grounds of the complaint, the result of which, accompanied by his own report and a
list of the witnesses who have been examined, is to be forwarded
to the general officer commanding in the district."

Again, same paper, (in a note,) citing general orders (horse
guard) February 1, 1804, and quoting McArthur, volume 1, p. 432:

" Several instances having occurred of officers sent home by
commanders-in-chief on foreign stations with articles of accusation against them, *but not duly investigated*, his royal highness
the Duke of York, conceiving the discipline of the army and
the interest of his Majesty's service to be thereby materially
affected, was of opinion that this practice, except in cases of the
most urgent necessity, ought to be avoided; because, though it
might relieve the court martial on the spot from some embarrassments, the measure seldom fails to transfer them to head-quarters
with increased difficulties."

Again, p. 24, citing the case of Lord Bentinck, p. 434:

" They (the court of inquiry,) should be instructed whether they
are to give an opinion as to there being grounds or not for a court
martial; or to state their opinion upon each point separately, that
the commander-in-chief may be able to form his judgment."

Again, p. 27: " As the object of the inquiry is to ascertain how
far there may be grounds for a court martial, it is important that no
fact should be concealed; and, therefore, the witnesses should be
examined as before any other court," &c.

Again p. 30, under the head, preliminaries before a general court
martial:

"If there appear to be grounds, in the opinion of the commander-
in-chief, for the assembling of a general court martial, he will, of
course, direct one to be assembled," &c.

This is sufficient to show the practice and construction of the
British rules and articles of war in relation to courts of inquiry,
and thence to draw the argument that the same practice should be
of obligatory force in the army of the United States, under similar
circumstances, to wit, that of an offence charged on a foreign station,
and where the officer at home ordering the court martial has no op-

portunity, of his own knowledge, to know the circumstances of the case, and thereby to exercise with discretion (judicial discretion) the high judical function of ordering an officer to be tried. Neither the accuser nor the accused can *demand* a court martial of right; the officer ordering the court is to judge the grounds of probable guilt or innocence of the accused, and to act accordingly, either in ordering or refusing the court. In the case before the court the President of the United States is that officer, made so by the act of Congress of May 29, 1830, amendatory of article sixty-five of the rules and articles of war. By that act, whenever a commanding general shall be the accuser or prosecutor of an officer under his command, the general court martial for the trial of such officer shall be appointed by the President; and accordingly the warrant for this court bears upon its face the legal authorization of the President's order. The mere nomination of the members of the court is not the narrow and limited meaning of the act of Congress, or of the article to which it is amendatory, nor of the British article from which it is copied. The ordering of the court, as well as the nomination of its members, is intended; and that is clear from the uniform practice, as well as the reason of the practice, both in Great Britain and the United States.

The order for the court is the great judicial act, and of which the nomination of the members comes. In Great Britain, none but a king or a commanding general can order the court; in the United States, none but the President; a general, commanding an army, or a colonel, commanding a separate department, can order general courts martial.

In neit er country is the Secretary of War known in the transaction. He may lay the case before the King or the President; but the order is theirs, and is an act not of form, but of great substance, equivalent to finding "*a true bill*" by a grand jury. It is the declaration of *probable cause*, without which, no officer or citizen in Great Britain, and no citizen in the United States, can be put criminally on trial. Personal knowledge, in the case of a military offence, may authorize the act which declares the probable cause; where there is no personal knowledge, the investigation by a court of inquiry becomes indispensable.

The trial of an officer before a general court martial (no matter what the event) is the cause of injuries to him, for which there is neither redress nor oblivion. The name of it lives coupled with his name, while history records it, tradition repeats it, or posterity bears it. The daily appearance, as a prisoner, at the bar of the court, is a bitter humiliation. To have one's self sworn against, without the power of reply, is a sickening trial of the human feelings. Expense, loss of time, abstraction from other business, are real injuries. The anxieties and distress of friends and family is a serious aggravation of real evils. Marks of indignity, or degradation, such as deprivation of the sword, real or virtual imprisonment in being confined to quarters, or the place of trial, the rear position in the march; a sort of social excommunication in the interdiction of official visits, or appearance at public places; the daily remarks of the thoughtless or the uncharitable; the exultation of enemies, (of whom every man has some,) all these are humiliating concomitants to the state of arrest and trial. What is common, of evils and mortifications, in all trials, he (Lieutenant Colonel Frémont) has suffered; and also something beyond what is common to other trials, and which will be noticed at the proper place in the general defence. And all this without a previous ascertainment, by a court of inquiry, (the only legal mode of ascertainment in any case,) of probable grounds for a court martial. This is an irregularity which (whomsoever may have been the real author) legally attaches itself to the President of the United States, and which it is the privilege of Lieutenant Colonel Frémont on this trial, as he is to observe upon, before this court, for the future security of others, while disclaiming, as he does, all exception to it in this his own case.

2. The second of the *irregularities* which he brings to the notice of the court is, that of the *ordering* of the charges, and of the authority, or person, by whom they have been admitted, selected, and sent here for trial. General Kearny swears they are not his charges; that he preferred a single charge; that the charges on trial are not his. A letter from the Secretary of War, not admitted upon the minutes of the court, would seem to intimate the contrary, at the same time appearing to assume some power in the War Department over the charges, and a recommendation to the judge advocate to put the specifications under different charges, when there was a doubt as to what offence they would constitute. Now, all this was irregular. Neither the Department of War nor General Kearny have any right to send charges to this court. To the officer ordering the court belongs the right to direct the charges, to order on what acts, and under what heads of accusation, the trial shall be had; and this results from the general power of that officer over the case, and the special knowledge which he is presumed to have acquired over all its facts. The power of ordering the trial would be nugatory, if the same power did not fix the charges. The two acts go together and cannot be separated. The accuser cannot govern the charges. He cannot select what to try and what not. He cannot fix and arrange the accusation to suit himself. If he did, conviction, at all events, and not truth and justice, would be his aim. The name, power, and machinery of the government, cannot be lent to any individual for any such purpose. The Secretary of War, neither in the United States nor in Great Britain, has any power over them. The judge advocate has none, except to put them into form, as an attorney general does of a grand jury presentment. The officer *ordering the court* is the only one that can order the charges, or make alterations in, or additions to, or subtractions from them. Thus, Hough, p. 23, in the note 74, quoting from Tytler, p. 217:

When it is intended that a charge shall be preferred against any person a specific statement should be made thereof, through the staff department, (the adjutant general, the brigade major, or other officer,) to the officer in *command*, in order that *he* may give directions relative to the charge, as well as what other steps he may *think* proper to be taken.

"*The officer in command*" intended by this paragraph is, in the case before the court, the President of the United States; and, therefore, it is he alone (the President) who can give directions relative to the charges, and exercise a judicial discretion in ordering the steps to be taken.

Again, from the same place in Hough:

It is not supposed that a charge, drawn up by those who may prefer it, is to go of course in that state to trial; but it may be formed and altered in such way *as the officer who is to order the trial* may think best, both in regard to the substance as in other respects.

Again, from page 31, of Hough:

If there has been a previous court of inquiry held, the report made in consequence will enable the *commander-in-chief to* give directions relative to *framing* the charges. If there has not been a court of enquiry held, then the judge advocate general would ascertain, from the statement of the party accusing, or by some other means, the nature of the accusation against the accused, and prepare the charges accordingly, for it is not to be supposed that a charge, *drawn up by those who may prefer it*, is to go of course in that state to trial; it may be formed and altered in such way as *the officer who is to order* the trial may *think* best, both in regard to the substance as in other respects.

And with this accords Simmons, page 46, where he says:

The officer ordering the court martial may alter or amend, at any time antecedent to arraignment, except that where the charges are embodied in the warrant for holding the court martial, which sometimes happens when it issues under the sign manual, &c.

From these passages it is clear that none but the officer ordering the trial (in this case, the President himself) can direct or alter charges, or prescribe to the court what it shall try; consequently, it was irregular in the Secretary of War to assume any power over the charges, or to give any recommendation to the judge advocate to multiply the specifications under different heads of charge, when doubtful what offence the alleged acts would constitute if true.

3. The third of these *irregularities*, as they appear to be to Lieutenant Colonel Frémont, is the multiplication of charges upon the same set of facts or specifications.

It is readily admitted that the military charge and its specifications, like the common law indictment and its counts, may lay different degrees of the same genus of offence. Thus, at common law, murder and manslaughter may be joined; and, under the law martial, desertion and absence without leave may be joined. But this is not the case of the irregularity now suggested, which is that of laying the same set of acts or specifications under different charges: in some instances under two different charges; in others, under three. The same act (for example, specification seventh of charge 1, specification fourth of charge 2, and specification fourth of charge 3) is laid under the respective heads of: 1, mutiny; 2, disobedience of orders; and 3, conduct prejudicial to good order and discipline. Now these are different offences in the military code, and each has its degrees; and it is only the different degrees of the same offence which can be laid under the same charge. And the degrees of mutiny are: 1, mutiny; 2, mutinous conduct; 3, riotous conduct. Disobedience of orders is a distinct offence, with its degree, that of neglect or non-observance of orders. The two offences cannot be confounded; for although disobedience of orders is often an ingredient in mutiny, it is a distinct nominated offence in itself; and when a separate offence is always triable before a court martial, before the offender can be punished for it. Mutiny, on the contrary, in all its degrees, may be punished upon the instant, even unto death, by the officer witnessing it; and the extraordinary power of extemporaneous punishment in the case of mutiny, in which the officer becomes both the judge and the executioner of his own judgment upon the spot, without the chance of defence or appeal, is not to be extended to other offences for which the law martial reserves the constitutional right of trial before execution. For disobedience of orders, an officer or soldier is entitled to trial before he is punished, and so for conduct prejudicial to good order and discipline; and in neither of these cases can the officer or soldier be deprived of his right to a trial by confounding his offence with mutiny.

To illustrate these principles by applying them to the case before the court, suppose General Kearny had caused Lieutenant Colonel Frémont to be killed for mutiny without trial; in that case, the killing would have been justifiable homicide, under article 8 of the rules and articles of war, (copied from the British mutiny act of 27 Geo. II.) Suppose he had so put him to death for disobedience of orders, then it would have been murder; for article 9 of the rules and articles of war grants a trial for that offence before punishment; but it might have been murder in a case where the law itself would have inflicted death. Suppose, again, he had been so put to death for conduct prejudicial to good order and discipline, then it would have been not only murder, but murder in a case not punishable with death. These illustrations show the illegality, and the dangerous illegal consequences, of confounding the same act under the different heads of mutiny, disobedience of orders, and conduct prejudicial of good order and discipline; and, as General Kearny could not have confounded them (without illegality) for punishment *without* trial, so cannot this court (without irregularity) confound them for punishment *with* trial.

Besides, there is an objection of a different kind to the regularity of the third charge. That article is, under the 99th article of war, an article only intended, out of abundant caution, to catch the petty offences, not capital, which had escaped legislative attention, and, therefore, not enumerated in the preceding articles. Now, it happens that both mutiny and disobedience of orders are enumerated crimes, and, therefore, not cognizable among the nameless residue intended to be caught by the 99th article; and this for a double reason, that, when the law has named a crime, and fixed its penalty and mode of trial, no discretion is left to the court in these particulars.

And, again, when the law has affixed as great a punishment as death or cashiering to an offence, (as in both mutiny and disobedience of orders,) it should not be in the power of the officer ordering the court and directing the charges to screen the offender, by classing his crimes with the little police offences which involve no serious punishment. And such is the construction of the British courts martial, the articles of war in relation to these non-enumerated offences being the same, both in Great Britain and the United States. Thus Hough, in section xxi. of his work on the practice of courts martial, and at page 630, second London edition:

"The offences within the meaning of this article must not only be of the quality described, '*to the prejudice of good order and military discipline*,' but must have been wholly unspecified in any of the preceding sections of the articles of war. For when an offence is of that specific quality as to be reducible to *a particular* article of war, to which a *known* and *distinct* penalty is attached, it must be prosecuted under *such* article, that the plain *intent* of the *law* and the *purposes* of *justice* may be fully answered. This is as much to be demanded for the safety of the individual, as for the benefit of the public; lest in *one* instance the presumed offender may be deprived of the advantages of having the body of his supposed fault alleged with *certainty*, for the purpose of his more complete *defence*, and for possible ulterior consequences; or may not have a *knowledge* of the punishment to which he may be liable, and so rendered amenable to penalties of an arbitrary character, where the legislature or the crown had determined the kind and degree of punishment. And, in the *second*, lest the general article might be resorted to in a *partiality* to individuals, when the known penalty declared by a particular article might be considered more severe than the *discretionary* punishment which a court martial might be ordinarily disposed to award. In either of which cases the policy of the existing article might be defeated, which is to provide a general remedy for a wrong which had not elsewhere been provided for, and not to *screen* a particular and well known crime by confounding it, in description, with a general, uncertain, and unspecified offence."

The article holds not out a *substitute*, but a *substansive* course of prosecution for offences "not otherwise declared than through its own medium."

A further practical evil of these three-fold charges upon the same set of specifications is, that they involve three trials for the same act, which is two more than the constitution of the United States allows of.

Lieutenant Colonel Frémont concludes this head of *irregularity* with referring to the volume of about five hundred cases of court martial charges, collected and published by Major James, embracing a quarter of a century of time, (from 1795 to 1820,) and covering the period of the wars of the French revolution, the Augustan age of arms, for the negative confirmation of his opinion of *this* irregularity, there not being an instance, it is believed, in the five hundred cases cited by that author, of double or treble charges upon one set of specifications.

4. The fourth *irregularity* in the preliminary proceedings which presents itself to Lieut. Col. Frémont, is in the double specification occurring several times under the charges, as in all those which charge the fact of assuming the governorship of California, as well as the acts done as governor. This duplicity of specifications was brought to the notice of the court and of the judge advocate on a former day of this trial, that he (the judge advocate) might make his election, where no criminality was intended, in one part of the double specifications to except that part from prosecution, and thereby save the defence some trouble. He did so in two instances, leaving others still remaining. That the fact is so, may be seen from the specifications themselves. That such duplicity of specification is irregular, may be seen in any manual upon the practice of courts martial. Thus, De Hart, pp. 298 and 299:

" It (the specification) must not be double; that is, the defendant must not be charged with having committed two or more offences in any one count or specification of the charge. Each specification can set forth but one offence."

This positive rule is suggested to be infringed in specification two, of charge one, and in specification two, of charge two, and in others; and more especially in specification ten, of charge one, where there seems to be four distinct offences laid in one single specification, and three of those doubled.

5. The fifth of these *irregularities*, as they appear to Lieutenant Colonel Frémont, is, that eight out of eleven (from the second to the ninth, inclusive) of the specifications of charge one, are for specific acts, *"and"* for usurpation of office, in *"assuming"* to be governor and commander-in-chief in California—the fact of being so governor and commander-in-chief being a fact which Lieutenant Colonel Frémont put himself to some trouble to prove, leaving open for consideration the single allegation of the *"assumption,"* a single charge of this alleged *"assumption"* would be an intelligible and triable accusation. No specific charge, and eight specifications, each consisting of a piece of testimony to prove the fact, and presenting the *"assumption"* as resulting from the act, instead of the act resulting from the assumption, is to present an unintelligible and untriable set of issues. It is requiring the court to pronounce eight times upon the question of usurping the office of governor and commander-in-chief, (for the court must pronounce upon every specification,) and instead of eight, there might, on tne same principle, have been as many as Governor Frémont did acts in California, thereby converting pieces of testimony into specifications, and involving the solecism of deriving the usurpation from the act, instead of the act from the usurpation. Besides the incongruity and inconsequentiality of this mode of proceeding, to prove the assumption of the governorship, it would seem to impose on the court the necessity of finding the whole eight specifications (as they are called) the same way; for the *"assumption"* being the *gist* in each

case, contrary findings would annul each other. The obvious way of trying the legality of the assumption of the office of governor, legality being the only point in question, would be to make it a single and direct specification, charging it continuously from such a day to such a day, and then the finding would be single and conclusive, and would decide the character of all the acts done during the whole period, as to legality or illegality. As they now stand, even if all the specifications shall be found true, it will only amount to eight acts of usurpation, on so many days, leaving all the rest of the acts of Governor Frémont, during all the rest of his administration, standing unimpeached, and admitted to be legal, or left open for future prosecution, act by act.

6. The sixth *irregularity* which Lieutenant Colonel Frémont presents is near akin to the former, but of more pervading application, being the general mode of presenting what is called "*specifications*," and which is, in many instances, a mere spreading of evidence upon the record in advance of the trial, and without oath, and without cross-examination. Of this character, Lieutenant Colonel Frémont is advised to say, are various letters, orders, instructions, &c., set out at length under different charges; for example, in specification 1, charge 1, and in others not necessary to be specified, as the only object of this notice is to suggest irregularities and give examples, and not to ask their correction.

In this sense is pointed out as a piece of testimony, illegally and injuriously inserted in specification 1, charge 1, the letter from Lieutenant Colonel Frémont to Brigadier General Kearny, dated "*On the march, January* 13, 1847," quoted and presented as an official, voluntary, written, reporting of his battalion and himself to Brigadier General Kearny, and thereby giving to the subsequent refusal to obey General Kearny's order the character of willful mutiny; for which purpose it is quoted, and continued to have its full effect until invalidated on the cross-examination, when it came to light that the said letter was nothing but a familiar note of information, extracted from Lieutenant Colonel Frémont by four importunate notes written by General Kearny to him, requesting information of his situation, and concealing from him the fact of Governor Stockton's presence with General Kearny, and the further fact that he was in chief command. The letter to Mr. W. P. Hall and others are included in the specifications, with a criminal meaning attached to them, to operate illegally and unjustly against the accused, until, in the course of the trial, the time came (upon cross-examination and oath) to show the unjust and injurious application which had been made of them.

Lieutenant Colonel Frémont is instructed to say that the rule is clear that a military charge, and its specifications, must have the precision, without the verbosity of an indictment at common law, and its counts; that both must set forth the accusation in a brief, intelligible, and triable form; that neither can embody the evidence of the case; and that a paper writing can only be set out when it *constitutes the offence* prosecuted, and not the *evidence* of the offence.

7. The seventh and last of the *irregularities* which Lieutenant Colonel Frémont would suggest to the court is, the apparent want of a prosecutor on part of the charges against him. The honorable Secretary of War, (Mr. Marcy,) in his letter of the 27th of October last to the counsel of Lieutenant Colonel Frémont, and in answer to the application that he might be tried on other charges of misconduct, contained in certain newspaper publications, refused such trial for want of a prosecutor, deeming such a personage indispensable to the prosecution of any charge. The following is an extract from his letter:

"It [the War Department] cannot consent to occupy the position of preferring charges which it has no reason to believe can be sustained by proof, *nor would deem it proper, in order, as is suggested, to comply with the forms of proceeding, to direct an officer to act as prosecutor on them.*"

Now, it so happens that General Kearny, in his cross-examination, on the sixth day of this trial, swore as follows:

"*The charges on which Lieutenant Colonel Frémont is now arraigned are not my charges. I preferred a single charge against Lieutenant Colonel Frémont. The charges on which he is now arraigned have been changed from mine.*"

Consequently, so far as *his* charge has been changed, Brigadier General Kearny cannot be presumed to be the prosecutor. A substantive and not a nominal prosecutor, according to the Secretary's letter, was required before any additional charges to those of General Kearny could be instituted, at the request of Lieutenant Colonel Frémont himself; and, for want of such substantive prosecutor, Lieutenant Colonel Frémont was denied a trial upon publications deemed injurious to him, and in direct relation to the matter of this prosecution. Upon the same principle, he presumes a substantive prosecutor would be required upon so much of the present charges as are not the work of General Kearny, and that he (Lieutenant Colonel Frémont) would have a right to know who he was. By the act of May 29, 1830, none but the President of the United States, in a case like the present, (that of a general officer becoming the accuser or prosecutor of an officer under his command,) could order this court; and none but the officer ordering the court (as shown in number two of these suggested irregularities) could order or alter the charges sent here for trial.

The act of May 29, 1830, was founded upon wise reasons, not to be disregarded in practice. Before that act a commanding general might be the accuser, prosecutor and witness against an officer under his command; might arrest him; order a court; appoint the members; direct the charges; revise the proceedings of the court, and confirm or disapprove them. All this from the old British mutiny act of George II., from which the United States rules and articles of war are mainly copied. For the safety of subordinate officers, this is now altered by the act referred to. The President is now to order the court, appoint the members, direct the charges, revise the proceedings, and confirm or disapprove the sentence *when* a commanding general prosecutes or accuses a subordinate. The

President is now to do it, because he is the head of the army, above the commanding general, and is the proper person, and the only proper person, to judge the probable justice of the accusation; the necessity for a court; the fitness of the members; the number and nature of the charges which the *public good* requires to be investigated; to revise the proceedings of the court, and to confirm or disapprove them in *a case* in which the commanding general becomes the accuser and prosecutor of an officer under his command. The President is now to do it. The act of 1830, and the reason of the act, requires this from him; and if any other person has directed, or changed, or added to the charges sent to this court to be tried, it is a disregard of the act, and of the reason of the act, of 1830; and so Lieutenant Colonel Frémont is advised by his counsel to say to this court.

In conclusion, Lieutenant Colonel Frémont states that all irregularities in the preliminaries of trial were waived, and intended to be waived, by the general plea of not guilty, which he put in to all the charges and specifications at the time of his arraignment. He objected to none of these irregularities then; he objects to none of them now, intending to have nothing but a trial on the merits. He now suggests them, not for any action of the court, nor for any advantage to himself, but through respect to the law, and to prevent evil example becoming precedent, and to vindicate his own intellect from the suspicion of admitting the correctness of such proceedings.

JOHN CHARLES FRÉMONT,
Lieutenant Colonel, mounted riflemen.

APPENDIX No. 3.

Note submitted to the court on Monday, January 3, 1848, in reply to the paper of Lieutenant Colonel Frémont, presented on the 30th of December.

The judge advocate submits the following note in reply to the paper of Lieutenant Colonel Frémont, presented just before the adjournment of the court, on the last day of the session, and alleging a series of irregularities in the preliminaries of this trial, which irregularities he treats under seven distinct heads.

1. Lieutenant Colonel Frémont alleges, as an irregularity, that a court of inquiry was not instituted to investigate the matter now under trial, but that, without such preliminary proceeding, it was sent at once to a court martial; and he refers to the practice in the British service as suggesting a rule which ought to be followed in ours.

The judge advocate supposes from Hough's book, (which is cited by Lieutenant Colonel Frémont,) that when charges are brought before the commander-in-chief, in the British service, it is by their practice, as it is clearly by their law, in his discretion whether to send them to a court martial, or to order a court of inquiry. Following the citations made by Lieutenant Colonel Frémont, in which charges are directed to be properly investigated by officers commanding on the spot, before they are transmitted to the court, it is said as follows:

"In the case of an officer, on report of the circumstances of the nature of the complaint, &c., to the commander-in-chief, his excellency would order a court of inquiry to be assembled, or adopt such other measures, by directing the party to be placed in arrest, and charges to be preferred against him, as he might deem proper." Hough, p. 24, (edition of 1825,) note 78.

But whatever be the British rule, it has never been the practice in our service to resort to courts of inquiry where specific charges are preferred with all the necessary specifications of fact, and time, and place, with a tender of the necessary proof, and on the proper official responsibility of an officer preferring the charges.

In such cases, a preliminary court of inquiry has always been considered useless, either to collect the proof, or ascertain the precise ground of charge; and, in general, the official responsibility of the officer preferring the charges has been thought a sufficient security against mere unfounded and vexatious and malicious accusations.

If, however, it were thought expedient to employ courts of inquiry in our service, according to the practice supposed by Lieutenant Colonel Frémont to prevail in the British army, it would not be allowable under our laws. The greater number of our general courts martial (all, indeed, except the courts ordered by the President) are convened under article 65, of the rules and articles of war, by generals commanding armies, or colonels commanding separate departments; and such officers are not permitted to order courts of inquiry. On the contrary, as courts of inquiry are in their nature inquisitorial, and in practice dangerous, our service has been carefully protected against them by our military law, and they are prohibited by the strong language of the 92d article of the rules and articles of war, unless ordered by the President of the United States, or demanded by the accused.

In this case, the demand of the accused was for a speedy trial by a court martial; though, subsequently, the limiting the investigation to the charges of General Kearny was objected to. The court martial, however, had then been ordered. And though it was legally within the power of the President to order a court of inquiry, the general practice of the service was conformed to in cases of specific charges, and a court martial was convened.

But whether the case be one in which the President might have employed the discretion specially confided to him by law, and have ordered a court of inquiry, is a question not to be entertained by this court. And while a conformity to general practice (a departure from which is only permitted by law as a matter of special discretion) cannot be an irregularity, it is clear that the whole subject is out of the jurisdiction of any court martial.

2. The second irregularity complained of is, that the charge preferred by General Kearny was altered by the authority of the War Department without the direct and personal order of the President, who alone, Lieutenant Colonel Frémont supposes, had authority to order any alteration in the charges.

Not to consider whether the rule, which governs on this point of amending charges, being given to our service in the form of a regulation published from the War Department, may be generally or specially abrogated by the department, it would appear conclusive of this objection to cite the decision of the Supreme Court of the United States in the case United States *vs.* Eliason, captain of engineers, where it is declared that the acts of the War Department, in what relates to the army, are the acts of the President, the Department being the official organ by which his acts are promulgated to the army. It has never been supposed, except as the organ of the President, that the Secretary of War exercises command or government over the army.

3. The third irregularity alleged, is the repeating of the same specifications under different charges. This mode of drawing charges the court is aware is according to the long and well established rule of our service, which has been followed and practiced so far back as we have any military records to appeal to; and the judge advocate is not aware that it has been before questioned.

This book of court martial orders, here exhibited to the court, shows such cases from 1815 to 1844, to which time the collection is made up. The first set of charges in this book bears date April 22, 1815, in the case of General Wilkinson, for conduct in the war on the northern frontier. They are signed by Martin Van Buren as judge advocate; appear drawn with care and precision, for the trial was an important one; the officer on trial was a major general in the army, and the case was interesting both to the public and the government. The second charge in this case is "drunkenness on duty," with two specifications, are repeated under the charge third of "conduct unbecoming an officer and a gentleman."

Another case, not in this book, but concerning the same general, may be seen in his memoirs, in the charges sent to a court of inquiry for his supposed connexion with the Spanish government of Louisiana. These charges are drawn in a very elaborate form by Walter Jones, esq , as judge advocate, and there the same practice is followed of laying the same facts under different charges.

The 4th case in this book is of August 14, 1820, Major Chum, 3d infantry; where the same acts are laid under three charges. 1. Disobedience of orders. 2. Fraud. 3. Neglect of duty; which case was revised by the President of the United States.

Not to multiply instances to prove a rule with which all the courts are familiar, the judge advocate cites one other, which, from certain principles involved in it, was interesting to the army, and received special notice at the time from the War Department and the President. It is the case of Mackay, quartermaster, for denying the lawful authority of Major Worth, or any officer not of the engineer corps, to take command at West Point. This was the important principle involved.

In the charges, the same acts are laid under two charges. 1. Disobedience of orders. 2. Unofficer like and insubordinate conduct.

The case was elaborately examined by the Secretary of War, and his report, with the case, laid before the President, Mr. J. Q. Adams.

The order of Major Worth was pronounced illegal; but neither on the trial before the court, nor in the careful revisal of the proceedings by the President, was any error alleged or found in the charges. And so the practice in this matter has continued in our army to this day.

As regards the British service, to which Lieutenant Colonel Frémont refers, a (case) can hardly be drawn from their service to ours. The form of drawing charges, observed in the two services, is wholly different. It appears not to be customary with them, as it (is) with us, to lay a general charge, which defines the legal offence, and under which the acts alleged are recited as specifications. They do not make, as we always do, any distinction between charges and specifications; they set out the acts in the narrative form, giving all necessary particulars, as also time and place. These allegations they call charges; but they do not allege the specific legal offence involved as we do, and which we style the charge. They sometimes put a general averment at the end of the whole, charging that "all which conduct, or any part of it, to be prejudicial to good order and military discipline, and in breach of the articles of war;" or "scandalous," "infamous," "derogatory to character," "betraying professional incapacity," &c., &c.; making, in some cases, what would seem an indiscriminate application of epithets.

The judge advocate refers the court to Hough, pp. 44, 160, 348, and throughout the volume generally, to show the mode in which charges are framed in the British service. With them it seems sufficient to a good charge, that the acts charged be clearly related.

Our own mode, it is obvious, is much more exact in all the requirements of a legal charge. We declare the legal offence which the acts are supposed to constitute, where the same acts under different charges, the court determine to which charge the acts amount.

It is obvious also, why, in British charges, where the legal offence is not declared, the same facts are not repeated, as with us, where the same specification is laid under more than one charge.

In effect, we charge the acts to violate such and such an article of war, indicating the articles; they charge a breach of all the articles—one and all.

In regard to the general principles of criminal law, appealed to by Lieutenant Colonel Frémont, as condemning the mode of framing charges which has been followed here:

The judge advocate supposes the practise of our military courts to be in accordance with all the analogies of the common law. The common law and the military law agree in principle, and the difference is only in the form of the trial.

At common law, the same act may constitute very different offences; the man who applies a torch to a dwelling house and burns down the house, and burns people in it, commits murder as well as arson, and may be indicted for both crimes; and the same facts, and the same evidence, would establish both. At common law he is tried for the same act at different times and on different indictments, and escaping one, may be convicted of the other.

Our military law (and this is the only difference between the two) joins the two indictments, for the same act, in the one trial, for the public convenience, to save separate trials for the one act; to avoid special pleading and technical acquitals, or new trials; and because, otherwise, after each trial, reference must be had to the officer ordering the court, to order a new trial and new charges. A less convenient machinery than the grand jury and the new indictments, of which as many may be at hand as the facts can warrant, or the prosecuting attorney ask for.

The objections which Lieutenant Colonel Frémont urges against joining two offences in the same indictment, would seem in natural reason to apply equally to offences of the same genus, as to offences wholly differing in kind.

The classification of offences in this respect, in regard to the administration of criminal justice, would seem to be a purely arbitrary distinction of law.

Murder and manslaughter are, in their criminal essence, as distinct as murder and theft; and murder and justifiable homicide,

though the same act may constitute either, are, in the criminal disposition and intent, which constitutes the crime, further separated
than larceny is from burglary.

The injustice of confounding crimes, which Lieutenant Colonel
Frémont illustrates in his argument, is certainly equal, whether they
be.of the same genus, or wholly different in kind.

There is another difference in the form of trials, at common law
and the military law, not referred to by Lieutenant Colonel Frémont, but which raises no inference that the military rule is illegal.

In common law courts, different indictments for different crimes
are not tried all at once—as larceny, highway robbery, and murder.
But, in military courts, we try all at once, any number of charges
against the same person; and this never has been questioned, and
the judge advocate supposes is not now questioned, where different
acts, as constituting different offences, are charged.

So that if the strict practice of the common law courts is to sub-
vert our practise in the one case, it will in the other. If we cannot
put the same acts under different charges, we cannot try, at the same
time, different charges for different acts; and every court martial
that ever sat, in Great Britain or the United States, has been
irregular and illegal.

4. The fourth irregularity complained of, is an alleged duplicity
in the specifications which charge certain acts as done in usurpation of the office of governor, &c. The judge advocate does not
recognize any legal duplicity in any of these specifications. The
act is specified, and then the legal offence is pointed out in the act;
without which ingredient in the act, it would be innocent. For
example, the general charge is mutiny; under this are several specifications—each specification sets out one overt act, such as the
order to Wilson, which is recited at length; then the specification
declares wherein the order is an act of mutiny; because therein he
declares himself commander or governor, and raises troops in defiance of General Kearny.

In this is no duplicity, it is a single charge and a single act. It
is merely like the conclusion of an indictment. It adds nothing to
the specification; and the specification would, in ordinary cases, be
good without it, where the offence is evident in the act itself; as
some writers have said (Hough, p. 42, note 1,681) that an indictment would be good without the formal conclusion, "against the
peace and dignity, &c.," though the better opinion and invariable
practice is otherwise. Duplicity is where there are two or more
offences in any one count. For example, says Hough, "one count
cannot charge a murder and a robbery."—Hough, p. 40.

The judge advocate proposes here to the court to take the second
specification to the first charge, (which Lieutenant Colonel Frémont
objects to,) and compare it with a charge in Hough, at p. 348.
This second specification, after reciting the order to Wilson, concludes thus: "thereby raising and attempting to raise troops in
violation and contempt of the lawful command aforesaid of his superior officer, Brigadier General Kearny, dated January 16, 1847,
thereby acting openly in defiance of, and in mutiny against, his

superior officer aforesaid, by raising and attempting to raise troops, and by proclaiming himself to be, and assuming to act as commander of the United States forces in California."

The following will be found in Hough, as a charge or specification, at p. 348 : "5. That the said Major General P. did not on the said 5th day of October, either prior to, or subsequent to, the attack by the enemy on the said division on the day, make the military dispositions best adapted to resist the said attack; and that during the action and after the troops had given way, he did not make any effectual attempt in his own person, or otherwise, to rally or encourage them, or to co-operate with and support the Indians, who were engaged with the enemy who were on the right, *the said Major General P., having quitted the field soon after the action commenced. Such conduct on the part of Major General P., betraying great professional incapacity; tending to the defeat and dishonor of his Majesty's arms, to the sacrifice of the division of the army committed to his charge; being in violation of his duty, and unbecoming and disgraceful to his character as an officer, prejudicial to good order and military discipline, and contrary to the acts of war.*"

This is a case which may be quoted as authority in the British army for the form of military charges. It was the trial of an officer of high rank. The proceedings went to the crown; were received by the prince regent, and his opinion returned through the adjutant general of the British army to the general commanding in Canada.

Now, if this be a good military charge, how can the 2d specification of this 1st charge on this trial be bad? and in which is the duplicity? The one (the specification here) alleges a single act, and two, ingredients of that act, as amounting to mutiny. The British authority alleges four distinct acts or omission; among them, the general undefined allegations of "*not making the best dispositions,*" from which follows, as defining the legal offence constituted by the acts, six general allegations, such as we call charges; and, in addition to these, alleging a breach of all the articles of war.

Lieutenant Colonel Frémont thinks the 10th specification to the 1st charge more obnoxious than the rest to this objection of duplicity. The judge advocate thinks the charge is single, (viz:) usurping the functions and setting aside the lawful authority of his superior officer; of which four distinct acts of the same kind are given, calling and approving general courts martial and discharging officers.

These acts are recited separately and distinctly as several counts.

It would only have varied the form, and not the substance, to have put the legal inference from the acts after, instead of before them. But look at the British practice, as given just before in the case of Major General P., and this is conformable to the general principle and rule, as Hough lays it down in the commencement of his treatise, at page 40. He says: "Laying several overt acts in a count for high treason is not duplicity, because the charge consists of compassing, &c., and the overt acts are merely evidences of it; and the same as to conspiracy;" and he adds in the note, (158,) "thus in mutiny."

5. The fifth irregularity Lieutenant Colonel Frémont attributes to a form of expression used in the specifications, which he considers as charging an act, and presenting the usurpation as resulting from the act, instead of the act as resulting from the usurpation. The judge advocate replies that the charge is mutiny, and the specifications are acts, in which Lieutenant Colonel Frémont assumed the office of governor, &c.; and it appears to the judge advocate to present the same meaning to any legal and grammatical construction, whether it be said that the office was usurped in doing the act, or that he did the act and thereby usurped the office. In either mode of expression, the meaning seems to be free from ambiguity.

6. The sixth alleged irregularity is attributed to the recital in the specification of the letters and documents on which the charges are founded. The judge advocate supposes this to be so far from an irregularity as to be strictly conformable to the best and most exact practice in framing charges for a military court, and to be essential to proper and precise specifications.

The objection is that the documents are evidence, and ought not therefore to be in the indictment; and the principle is supposed, by Lieutenant Colonel Frémont, to be that, when a paper writing is the gist, constitutes the offence prosecuted, then, and not otherwise, can it be put in the indictment.

The judge advocate cannot speak with confidence of the practice in common law courts. He supposes, however, that, in an indictment for forgery, though the act of forgery be only the false signature, yet the whole instrument must be set out.

So, too, for a written challenge to fight a duel. The writing is not the act, nor the crime which is attempting to take life; yet the challenge must go in the indictment. A stronger case is the passing a counterfeit bank note, knowing it to be the counterfeit.

The crime is in passing it. Yet the whole note must be described and recited in the indictment, even to the ornamental parts, the capitals and numerals in the margin.

But these letters and orders, in these specifications, come within the rule, as Lieutenant Colonel Frémont defines it. They constitute the act of offence charged. Take the letter to Mr. Hall. The letter is the act of usurpation, resistance, or mutiny alleged.

It has always been held before a court martial that, in charging a disobedience of a written order, the order must be exhibited in the specification. The accused has the right to require it, to know what order he is charged with disobeying. So, too, in regard to letters, where the offence is writing, or sending the letter.

All this particularity and detail only tends to greater precision. It cannot aggravate charges as by the use of general and descriptive language; and is favorable to the accused, by imposing on the prosecution the necessity of a stricter proof in establishing every averment. So in the case of Lieutenant Colonel Frémont's alleged report of his battalion to General Kearny. The allegation was weakened by exhibiting the letter and its apparent informal character in the specifications.

Charges sent to courts martial for trial are rarely drawn by professional persons. They are not usually subjected to a skilful, technical criticism.

It has been considered that military charges are good and sufficient when they are clear and free from ambiguity, and give the accused exact information of what is charged against him. Such is considered the test of a good charge before a court martial.

7. The seventh objection to the irregularity of this trial, is the alleged "apparent want of a prosecutor on part of the charges."

The charges are officially reported to the court, and are entered on the record as charges preferred by "order of the War Department, on information of Brigadier General Kearny." The department having limited the charges to the matters officially reported by General Kearny.

APPENDIX No. 4.

Argument from Lieutenant Colonel Frémont, offering a despatch from the Navy Department.

Mr. PRESIDENT: Lieutenant Colonel Frémont offers to the court, as evidence to be used in this case, a certified copy of the despatch herewith presented, being an official instruction from the President of the United States, dated June 14, 1847, to the naval commander on the coast of California and in the Pacific ocean. Lieutenant Colonel Frémont deems this paper material to him, as being an authentic declaration from the President, that the conquest of California was *"exclusively"* devolved upon the navy at the commencement of the war; and that the conquest brought with it the necessity of a civil government; and that Commodore Sloat was informed, on·the 12th of July, 1846, that such a government should be established under *his* protection. And such a government having been actually established by Commodore Stockton, successor to Commodore Sloat, in the month of August of that year, this instruction of the President becomes a ratification of what he did, being in exact conformity to the President's intentions, as well as in exact conformity to the laws of nations.

He also offers this paper for the purpose of showing the President's *intention*, that the naval commander, on the California station, should be informed of General Kearny's instructions, before he himself arrived there; and that, *"contrary to all expectation, this despatch did not reach California until after the arrival there of General Kearny,"* (page 3 of the paper offered.)

It is also offered for the purpose of showing the stress laid by the President on the instructions of the 5th of November, 1846, being the first explicit instructions to the naval commanders to relinquish to General Kearny, or Colonel Mason, the entire control over the military operations and the administrative functions of government, and to *"turn over"* to him all papers necessary to the performance of his duties; and that it was *believed* that this explicit despatch of the 5th of November, 1846, might *"anticipate the arrival in California of General Kearny,"* which it is in proof that it did not; and, in fact, all the difficulties had occurred between Commodore Stockton and General Kearny before this despatch arrived.

He also offers it for the purpose of showing that similar instructions, as stated at page four of the paper offered, were despatched to Commodore Stockton on the 14th day of January, 1847, which happened to be the very day that he and General Kearny were contending for the supreme command at Los Angeles, and consequently that all these instructions were too late to prevent collision between the naval and military commanders.

He also offers it for the purpose of showing, as it does at the bottom of page one, that the "*misapprehensions*" between the naval and military officers must have been removed by the very explicit instructions "*which have since been received* in that country" from the Departments of War and Navy; thereby admitting that the explicit orders had arrived *after* the evils had happened which they were intended to-prevent.

He also offers them for the purpose of showing that the instructions to General Kearny of the 3d and 18th of June, 1846, in regard to the conquest and government of California, (unless intended as contingent and subordinate,) conflicting with those of July 12, 1846, directing a civil government to be formed under the protection of the navy, and the country to be held as a conquest by the naval forces and to be so found, though said forces at the conclusion of peace with Mexico, which orders being posterior in date to those of General Kearny, superseded and annulled them, until the subsequent orders of November 5, 1846, (called the "definite" instructions in the despatch of June 11, 1847,) arrived in California, which (as before stated) it has been proved did not arrive until all the difficulties had occurred.

As Lieutenant Colonel Frémont considered this trial of himself to be that of Commodore Stockton in his person, and that the decision of it must involve an examination of all the powers and instructions given to naval officers on the California station, in relation to the conquest and government of California, he, (Lieutenant Colonel Frémont,) while protesting against such a trial, claimed the use of all the naval and military instructions applicable to the case, as fully as if he was actually Commodore Stockton on trial before a naval court martial. The President gave order to have him furnished accordingly, and among the papers so furnished is the despatch now offered, dated as above stated, and signed by the Hon. Mr. Mason, Secretary of the Navy. His counsel deem this paper material to his defence; he therefore asks that it be viewed as evidence, and entered on the minutes of the court.

J. C. FRÉMONT,
Lieutenant Colonel, mounted rifles.

NAVY DEPARTMENT,
June 14, 1847.

SIR: By the arrival of Passed Midshipman Beale, despatches have been received from Commodore Stockton, bearing date February 5, 1847, and by the arrival of Mr. Talbot, a communication has been received from Commodore Shubrick, bearing date February 13, 1847. Mr. Beale reported at the department on the 31st of May, and Mr. Talbot on the 3d of June.

These despatches have all been submitted to the President, and

I am instructed by him to express the great satisfaction with which he has heard of the continued tranquillity of California since the restoration over it of our military authority, and his confident expectation that it will now be maintained without serious disturbance from any source whatever.

The " *misapprehension* " between the commanding officers of the army and navy in California, which is mentioned in the letter of Commodore Shubrick, above referred to, must long since have been removed, *by the very explicit instructions which have since been received* in that country from this department and the Department of War.

At the commencement of the war with Mexico, the United States had no military force in California of any description whatever, and the conquest of that country was, from necessity, therefore devolved exclusively upon the navy.

The conquest brought with it the necessity of a temporary civil government, and on the 12th of July, 1846, Commodore Sloat was informed that such a government should be established under your (his) protection. There was still no military officer in California, but Commodore Sloat was advised, by the same communication of July 12, that Brigadier General Kearny had been ordered overland to that territory, and a copy of the general's confidential instructions from the department was enclosed to him. He was also informed that a regiment of volunteers was expected to sail from New York in the early part of August, which would, in the first instance, report to the naval commander on his station, but would ultimately be under the command of General Kearny, who, it was added, "is appointed to conduct the expedition by land." Contrary to all expectation, this despatch did not reach California until after the arrival there of General Kearny.

On the 13th of August the commanding officer of the Pacific squadron was informed that a company of artillery, under Captain Tompkins, had sailed in the United States ship Lexington; that a regiment of volunteers, under Colonel Stevenson, would soon sail from New York, and that a body of troops, under General Kearny, might soon reach the *coast*, via Santa Fé. Copies were enclosed of so much of the instructions to Captain Tompkins and General Kearny as related to objects requiring co-operation, and of article sixth of the army regulations, in reference to military and naval rank. On this latter subject the general principle was repeated that "no officer of the army or navy, whatever may be his rank, can assume any direct command, independent of consent, over an officer of the other service, excepting only when land forces are specially embarked in vessels of war to do the duty of marines.

On the 5th of November, 1846, Commodore Stockton was informed that "the President has deemed it best for the public interest, to invest the military officers commanding with the direction of the operations on land, and with the administrative functions of government over the people and territory occupied by us."

He was also directed to relinquish to Colonel Mason or to General Kearny, if the latter should arrive before he had done so, the entire control over these matters, and turn over to him all the papers necessary to the performance of his duties. It was believed that even this despatch might anticipate the arrival in California of General Kearny.

Similar instructions were communicated to Commodore Stockton, under date of January 11, 1847, and were renewed to Commodore Shubrick, under date of May 10, 1847. A copy of these last instructions, which on this subject are very full and distinct, is herewith enclosed. I also enclose a copy of document No. 19, which has been already transmitted to you, but which is of so much interest that I send it again.

Possessing the views of the government, as they are given in the despatches above enumerated, and particularly in the letter of May 10, you will have, it is believed, no difficulty in adjusting with entire harmony any differences which may previously have arisen between the army and navy, on the subject of directing the temporary civil government in California.

The experience which we have had, as well in the eastern portion of Mexico as on the Pacific side, has confirmed the President in his purpose of devolving on the senior military officer the duty of civil government in the conquered territory. It is more consistent with the relative duties of the two branches of the service.

The attempt to exercise it by a naval officer necessarily withdraws him from the appropriate sphere of his professional duties. He instructs me, therefore, to impress on the naval officers, that this duty will be required of the military officer of highest rank in the country, who may be on duty; and with this clear repetition of his wishes, it is not apprehended that any collisions will again occur between those whose services are always most efficient when they act in harmony and concert.

Your purpose, in sending home the Savannah and Warren, is approved.

Transmitted herewith is a copy of the printed regulations, respecting the collection of duties in such of the ports of Mexico as may be in our military possession by conquest, together with the modifications subsequently adopted, as indicated in my letter of the 20th of April, and the order of the President of this date.

Commander Rudd and Purser Christian will proceed to join your squadron, via Jamaica, in a vessel which will sail from Baltimore on the 15th instant. Other officers will be added, from time to time, as the service will permit.

I am, very respectfully, your obedient servant,

J. Y. MASON.

COMMANDING OFFICER
    of the U. S. naval forces, Pacific squadron.

—

Mr. PRESIDENT : The crimes with which I stand charged **are,** 1. MUTINY. 2. DISOBEDIENCE OF ORDERS. 3. CONDUCT PREJUDICIAL TO GOOD ORDER AND DISCIPLINE. Either of these would be sufficiently grave in itself; united they become an assemblage of crimes probably never before presented against an American officer.

They descend from the top to the bottom of the military gradation of crime; from that which is capital and infamous, to what involves but little of disgrace or punishment; but from the whole of which it becomes me to defend myself, and from each, in its order, according to the degree of its enormity.

The crime of mutiny stands at the head of military offences, and, in this case, is presented with all the aggravations of which it is susceptible; rank in the offender—time of war—in a foreign country—base and sordid motive—wilful persistance.

It is the most dangerous of military crimes, and, therefore, the most summarily and severely punished. Any officer present at a mutiny becomes the judge and punisher of the offence upon the instant, and may kill the mutineer upon the spot, without trial or warning

More than that, he becomes a great offender himself if he does not do his utmost to suppress the mutiny which he witnesses, and may be punished with death, or such other punishment as a court martial may award.

It is the only case in which death may be inflicted without trial; in all other cases, the supposed offender is presumed to be innocent until he is convicted, and cannot be punished until he has been tried.

Of this great crime, with all the aggravations of which it is susceptible, I am charged to have been guilty, and continuously so from the 17th day of January, 1847, to the 9th day of May following, both days inclusive; during all which time I was liable to have been killed by any officer present who believed me guilty. I was not killed; but am now here to be tried, and with the presumption of guilt against me from the fact of being ordered to be tried.

The order to put an officer upon trial is a declaration, virtually so, on the part of the high authority giving the order, of probable guilt. It is equivalent to the *"true bill"* endorsed by the grand jury on the bill of indictment; and, in this case, is equivalent to three such endorsements on three separate bills, for three several crimes; for the order for my trial extends to the three different charges upon which I am arraigned, and with the trial of the whole of which this court is charged.

Mutiny is not defined in the United States rules and articles of war, or in the British mutiny act from which they are copied, and the decisions as to what will constitute the crime, are very various in both countries. I only refer to this want of definition of the offence, and to these various decisions to say that I have no objection, in my own case, to have my conduct judged by any case that was ever decided to be mutiny, either in this country or in Great Britain, strange and extraordinary as some of these cases may appear.

The first act of this crime, alleged against me, is found in this letter, set out as the basis of specification first in charge first.

Ciudad de los Angeles,
January 17, 1847.

Sir : I have the honor to be in receipt of your favor of last night, in which I am directed to suspend the execution of orders, which, in my capacity of military commandant of this territory, I had received from Commodore Stockton, governor and commander-in-chief in California. I avail myself of an early hour this morning to make such a reply as the brief time allowed for reflection will enable me.

I found Commodore Stockton in possession of the country, exercising the functions of military commandant and civil governor, as early as July of last year; and shortly thereafter I received from him the commission of military commandant, the duties of which I immediately entered upon, and have continued to exercise to the present moment.

I found also, on my arrival at this place some three or four days since, Commodore Stockton still exercising the functions of civil and military governor, with the same apparent deference to his rank on the part of all officers (including yourself) as he maintained and required when he assumed in July last.

I learned also, in conversation with you, that on the march from San Diego, recently, to this place, you entered upon and discharged duties, implying an acknowledgement on your part of supremacy to Commodore Stockton.

I feel, therefore, with great deference to your professional and personal character, constrained to say that, until you and Commodore Stockton adjust between yourselves the question of rank, where I respectfully think the difficulty belongs, I shall have to report and receive orders, as heretofore, from the commodore.

With considerations of high regard, I am, sir, your obedient servant,

J. C. FRÉMONT,
Lieutenant Colonel U. S. Army, and Military
Commandant of the Territory of California.

Brig. Gen. S. W. Kearny,
United States army.

If this letter is mutiny, Mr. President, I shall now add another aggravation to the five aggravations already attending it; I shall justify it before this court! and now most respectfully declare that I would write the same letter over again under the same circumstances. But being prosecuted for it, I am bound to defend myself, and proceed to do it.

In making this defence, I have some RIGHTS, which I propose to use, and my authority for which will be found in *Hough*, *p*. 952, and which I now read, that the court may see the nature and extent of the *rights* which I suppose to belong to me.

Major Hough says:

The prisoner's defence ought to be confined to any statement of his own case which he may think proper to offer to the court, in contradiction to what has been stated by the prosecutor in his opening address, and to observations upon evidence which has been given against him, and to the offering any remarks upon any written evidence which may have been introduced in the course of that evidence. He is likewise at full liberty to remark upon the nature of the evidence given on the part of the prosecution, and to show, if he can, where there is any contradictory evidence, and to impugn the credit of the witnesses that have been examined; to observe upon the non-production of witnesses, who could have better informed the court; to urge the improbability that he should have acted in the manner imputed to him; and to urge all these circumstances to the kind consideration of the court; and if there have been any hostile feelings expressed by the prosecutor towards him, in remarking upon such a circumstance, or as to the motives of the prosecutor, it shall be done in a manner that shall not be disrespectful to the court.

These are my *rights* before this court, and all of which I shall have occasion to exercise, except in one single particular, that of recommending my defence to the *kind* consideration of the court. I will substitute *just* for *kind*, as being more suitable to the character of a judicial tribunal, impersonated with bandaged eyes, to imply a disregard of persons—as more suitable to my own case, which requires justice and not kindness, and more agreeable to my self-respect, which will be best satisfied with a defence on the basis of rigid right. With this exception, and with that reserve of decorum which it needed no book injunction to impose upon me, I shall proceed to state my defence, and to do it with the care and precision which the gravity of the accusation demands.

And first, my own statement:

The two superior officers in California with whom the difficulties began, (Commodore Stockton and General Kearny,) have each had the benefit of stating his own case before this court, showing under what authority they went and acted, what they did, and how they became involved with one another, and how I became involved in their contest.

An incident, and a subordinate in this contest where it originated, and turned up as principal figure in it here for criminal prosecution, I am happy to find that my rights, in one respect, are at least equal to theirs—that of stating my own case as fully as they stated theirs, and showing how I became principal in a contest which was theirs before I heard of it, or came near them; and which, as suggested heretofore, ought to have been settled between themselves, or by the government, whose authority they both bore. A subordinate in rank, as in the contest, long and secretly marked out for prosecution by the commanding general, assailed in newspaper publications when three thousand miles distant, and standing for more than two months before this court to hear all that could be sworn against my private honor as well as against my official conduct, I come at last to the right to speak for myself.

In using this privilege, I have to ask of this court to believe that the preservation of a commission is no object of my defence. It came to me, as did those which preceded it, without asking, either by myself, or by any friend in my behalf. I endeavored to resign it in California, through General Kearny, in March last, (not knowing of his design to arrest me,) when it was less injurious to me than it is at present. Such as it now is, it would not be worth one moment's defence before this court. But I have a name which was without a blemish before I received that commission; and that name it is my intention to defend.

In the winter of 1845–6, I approached the settled parts of Upper California with a party of sixty-two men and about two hundred horses, in my third expedition of discovery and topographical survey in the remote regions of the great west.

I was then brevet captain in the corps of topographical engineers, and had no rank in the army, nor did an officer or soldier of the United States army accompany me.

The object of the expedition, like that of the two previous ones, was wholly of a scientific character, without the least view to military operations, and with the determination to avoid them as being, not only unauthorized by the government, but detrimental or fatal to the pursuit in which I was engaged. The men with me were citizens, and some Delaware Indians, all employed by myself on wages, and solely intended for protection against savages, and to procure subsistence in the wilderness, and often desert country, through which I had to pass.

I had left the United States in May, 1845—a year before the war with Mexico broke out; but I was aware of the actual state of affairs between the two countries, and being determined to give no cause of offence to the Mexican authorities in California, I left my command at the distance of about two hundred miles from Monterey, and proceeded almost alone to the nearest military station, that of New Helvetia, (or. Suter's fort,) and obtained a passport (which I now have) for myself and attendants to proceed to Monterey, the residence of the commandant general or deputy governor, General Castro.

Arrived at Monterey, I called upon the commandant, and other authorities, in company with the United States consul, and with all the formalities usual on such occasions, and was civilly received. I explained to General Castro the object of my coming into California, and my desire to obtain permission to winter in the valley of the San Joaquim, for refreshment and repose, where there was plenty of game for the men and grass for the horses, and no inhabitants to be molested by our presence. Leave was granted, and also leave to continue my explorations south to the region of the Rio Colorado, and of the Rio Gila.

In the last days of February, I commenced the march south, crossing into the valley of the Salinas, or Buenaventura, and soon received a notification to depart, with information that General Castro was assembling troops with a view to attack us, under the pretext that I had come to California to excite the American settlers to revolt. The information of this design was authentic, and with a view to be in a condition to repel a superior force, provided with cannon, I took a position on the Sierra, called the Hawk's Peak, entrenched it, raised the flag of the United States, and awaited the approach of the assailants.

At the distance of four miles we could see them, from the *Sierra*, assembling men and hauling out cannon; but they did not approach nearer; and after remaining in the position from the 7th to the 10th of March, and seeing that we were not to be attacked in it, and determined not to compromise the government of the United States, or the American settlers, who were ready to join me at all hazards, I quit the position, gave up all thoughts of prosecuting my researches in that direction, and turned north towards Oregon.

Disappointed in the favorite design, of examining the southern parts of the *Alta California*, and the valley of Rio Colorado and Gila, I formed another design which I hoped would be of some service to my country, that of exploring a route to the Wah-lah-math settlements in Oregon, by the Hamath lakes; and thence to return to the United States by a high northern route, exploring the country in that direction. In pursuance of this plan, and before the middle of May, we had reached the northern shore of the Great Hamath lake, within the limits of Oregon, when we found our further progress in that direction obstructed by impassable snowy mountains and hostile Indians, of the formidable Hamath tribes, who had killed or wounded four of our men, and left us no repose either upon the march or in the camp.

We were now at the north end of the Greater Hamath lake, in the territory of Oregon, when on the morning of the 9th I was surprised to find ride up to our camp two men—one turned out to be Samuel Neal, formerly of my topographical party, and his companion, who quickly informed me that a United States officer was on my trail, with despatches for me, but he doubted whether he would ever reach me; that he and his companion had only escaped the Indians by the goodness of their horses; and that he had left the officer, with three men, two days behind.

Upon the spot I took nine men, four of them Delaware Indians, coasted the western shore of the lake for sixty miles, and met the party.

The officer was Lieutenant Gillespie. He brought me a letter of introduction from the Secretary of State, (Mr. Buchanan,) and letters and papers from Senator Benton and his family. The letter from the Secretary imported nothing beyond the introduction, and was directed to me in my private or citizen capacity. The outside envelope of a packet from Senator Benton was directed in the same way, and one of the letters from him, while apparently of mere friendship and family details, contained passages enigmatical and obscure, but which I studied out, and made the meaning to be that I was required by the government to find out any foreign schemes in relation to the Californias, and to counteract them. Lieutenant Gillespie was bearer of despatches to the United States consul at Monterey, and was directed to find me wherever I might be; and he had, in fact, travelled above six hundred miles from Monterey, and through great dangers, to reach me.

He had crossed the continent through the heart of Mexico, from Vera Cruz to Mazatlan, and the danger of his letters falling into the hands of the Mexican government had induced the precautions to conceal their meaning. The arrival of this officer, his letter of introduction, some things which he told me, and the letter from Senator Benton, had a decided influence on my next movement.

Three men were killed in our camp by the Indians the night Lieutenant Gillespie delivered his letters. We returned to the camp at the north end of the lake, pursued and waylaid, but killing two of the assailants without loss.

I determined to return to the unsettled parts of the Sacramento, and did so. Soon the state of things in California was made known to me; General Castro approaching with troops; the Indians of California excited against us; the settlers in danger as well as ourselves, and all looking to me for help.

We made common cause, and I determined to seek safety, both for them and ourselves; not merely in the defeat of Castro, but in the total overthrow of Mexican authority in California, and the establishment of an independent government in that extensive province. In concert, and in co-operation with the American settlers, and in the brief space of about thirty days, all was accomplished north of the Bay of San Francisco, and independence declared on the 5th day of July. This was done at *Sonoma*, where the American settlers had assembled. I was called, by my position, and by the general voice, to the chief direction of affairs, and on the next day, at the head of 160 mounted riflemen, set out to find General Castro. He was then at Santa Clara, on the south side of the bay, in an entrenched camp, with 400 men and some pieces of artillery. We had to make a circuit round the head of the bay, and on the 10th day of July, when near Suter's fort, we received the joyful intelligence that Commodore Sloat was at Monterey; had taken it on the 7th, and that war existed between the United States and Mexico. Instantly we pulled down the flag of independence, and ran up that of the United States.

A despatch from Commodore Sloat requested my co-operation, and I repaired with my command (160 mounted rifles) to Monterey. I was ready to co-operate with him, but his health requiring him to return to the United States, he relinquished the command to Commodore Stockton. He (Commodore Stockton) determined to prosecute hostilities to the full conquest of the country, and asked not co-operation, but service under him. He made this proposal in writing to Lieutenant Gillespie and myself. We agreed to it, and so did our men, the latter, as Commodore Stockton so emphatically testified before this court, refusing to stickle about terms and pay, giving their services first, and trusting their government, far distant as it was, to do them justice.

Commodore Stockton has proved the terms of our engagement with him, and that we became a part of the naval forces under his command. I went under him with pleasure. I was glad to be relieved from the responsibilities of my position. At the same time I had no doubt but that the riflemen with me would have chased Castro, with his troops, out of the country, and that the Californian population might be conciliated. If Commodore Stockton had not taken the command and lead in the war, I should have continued the work as I had began it, with the men of my topographical party, and the American settlers, and had not, and have not, a doubt of our success.

We (Lieutenant Gillispie and myself) joined Commodore Stockton for the public good, and with some sacrifice of our independent positions. Neither of us could have been commanded by him, except upon our own agreement. I belonged to the army, and was at the head of the popular movement in California. The common voice of the people called me to the head of affairs, and I was obeyed with zeal and alacrity. Lieutenant Gillespie was of the marines, and was, besides, on *special* duty, by orders of the President, and no officer of any rank could interfere with him. We might have continued our independent position, and carried on the war by land. We judged it best for the United States to relinquish that independence, take service under Commodore Stockton, obey him; and we did so. His testimony is complete on this point. We became part of the naval forces. We went under the command of the naval commander on that station; and it was to the naval commanders there that the President had specially assigned the conquest of California. The California battalion of mounted riflemen was then organized, Commodore Stockton appointing all the officers, myself being appointed major, and Lieutenant Gillespie captain. From that time we were part of the naval forces for the conquest of the country.

I omit details of naval or military events, in order to come to the point which concerns me.

On the 13th of August, 1846, Commodore Stockton, as conqueror, took possession of the City of the Angels, the seat of the governors general of California. On the 17th he issued a proclamation, or decree, as such, for the notification and government of the inhabitants, followed by many others in the same character, and for the better government of the conquered country.

On the 28th of August, he communicated all these acts to the government at home, stating in the communication that, when he should leave California, he should appoint Major Frémont governor, and Captain Gillespie secretary. Four days before that time, namely, on the 24th of August, and in anticipation of his own speedy return to the sea, for the protection of American commerce and other objects, he appointed me military commandant of the territory, and charged me with enlisting a sufficient force to garrison the country, and to watch the Indians and other enemies. In that letter is this paragraph: " *I propose, before I leave the territory, to appoint you to be governor, and Captain Gillespie to be secretary; and to appoint also the council of state, and all the necessary officers. You will, therefore, proceed to do all you can to further my views and intentions thus frankly manifested. Supposing that by the 25th of October you will have accomplished your part of these preparations, I will meet you at San Francisco on that day, and place you as governor of California.*"

A copy of this letter, with a copy of all the rest of the acts of Commodore Stockton, as governor and commander-in-chief in California, was sent to the Navy Department, at the time, (August, 1846,) by Mr. Christopher Carson, who was met by General Kearny, below Santa Fé, on the Rio Grande, and turned back, the despatches being sent on Mr. Fitzpatrick, and were communicated to Congress with the annual message of the President of December, 1846, and are printed in the documents attending the message, from page 668 to 675, inclusively. The Presidential message itself, and the reports of the Secretaries of War and Navy, thus referred to these acts of Commodore Stockton:

Extract from the President's annual message, December, 1846.

Our squadron in the Pacific, with the co-operation of a gallant officer of the army, and a small force hastily collected in that distant country, have acquired bloodless possession of the Californias, and the American flag has been raised at every important point in that province. I congratulate you on the success which has thus attended our military and naval operations. In less than seven months after Mexico commenced hostilities, at a time selected by herself, we have taken possession of many of her principal ports, driven back and pursued her invading army, and acquired military possession of the Mexican provinces of New Mexico, New Leon, Coahuila, Tamaulipas, and the Californias, a territory larger in extent than that embraced in the original thirteen States of the Union, inhabited by a considerable population, and much of it more than a thousand miles from the points at which we had to collect our forces and commence our movements. By the blockade, the import and the export trade of the enemy has been cut off. By the laws of nations a conquered territory is subject to be goverened by the conqueror during his military possession, and until there is either a treaty of peace, or he shall voluntarily withdraw from it. The old civil government being necessarily superseded, it is the right and duty of the conqueror to secure his conquest, and to provide for the maintenance of civil order and the rights of the inhabitants. This right has been exercised, and this duty performed by our military and naval commanders, by the establishment of temporary governments in some of the conquered provinces in Mexico, assimilating them, as far as practicable, to the free institutions of our own country. In the provinces of New Mexico, and of the Californias, little, if any, further resistance is apprehended from the inhabitants to the temporary governments which have thus, from the necessity of the case, and according to the laws of war, been established.

It may be proper to provide for the security of these important conquests, by making an adequate appropriation for the purpose of erecting fortifications and defraying the expenses necessarily incident to the maintenance of our possession and authority over them.

Extract from the report of the Secretary of War, December, 1846.

Commodore Stockton took possession of the whole country as a conquest of the United States, and appointed Colonel Frémont governor, under the law of nations; to assume the functions of that office when he should return to the squadron.

Extract from the report of the Secretary of the Navy, December,
1846.

On the 25th of July, the Cyane, Captain Mervine, sailed from Monterey, with Lieutenant Colonel Frémont and a small volunteer force on board, for San Diego, to intercept the retreat of the Mexican General Castro. A few days after, Commodore Stockton sailed in the Congress frigate for San Pedro, and, with a detachment from his squadron of three hundred and sixty men, marched to the enemy's camp. It was found that the camp was broken up, and that the Mexicans, under Governor Pico and General Castro, had retreated so precipitately that Lieutenant Colonel Frémont was disappointed in intercepting him. On the 13th, Commodore Stockton was joined by this gallant officer, and marched a distance of thirty miles from the sea, and entered without opposition Ciudad de-los Angeles, the capital of the Californias; and on the 22d of August, the flag of the United States was flying at every commanding position, and California was in the undisputed military possession of the United States. The conduct of the officers and men of the squadron in these important operations has been characterized by activity, courage, and steady discipline, and entitles them to the thanks of the department. Efficient aid was rendered by Lieutenant Colonel Frémont and the volunteers under his command. In his hands, Commodore Stockton informs the department, he will leave the military government when he shall leave California, in the further execution of his orders.

It is then certain that, in November, 1846, the President had full knowledge of Commodore Stockton's intention to appoint me governor, when he should return to his ship, to wit, by the 25th of October; and in his message spoke of all his acts in organizing a civil government in a way to imply entire approbation. At the same time that Commodore Stockton sent his despatches, I also wrote to Senator Benton, giving a brief account, for his own information, of what had taken place in California, and especially on the great point of having joined the American settlers in raising the flag of Independence, and overturning the Mexican government in California. It was done before we had knowledge of the war. I felt all its responsibilities, moral and political, personal and official. It was a resolve made by me, not merely upon serious but upon long and painful reflection. I wrote to Senator Benton, if my conduct was not approved, to give in my resignation, and sent a blank for him to fill up to that effect. Happy had it been for me had the government *then* disapproved my conduct!

And here it becomes me to state something, which justice to myself and others, and regard for history, requires to be known. A few facts and dates will establish a great point.

Commodore Sloat arrived at Monterey on the 2d day of July; he did not take it; he hesitated. On the 7th, he did. He had by that time heard of my operations, and supposed I had positive instructions. On the 15th of July, Commodore Stockton arrived; on the 16th, Admiral Seymour, in the Collingwood, of 80 guns; on the 19th, the mounted force, under Lieutenant Gillespie and myself. Upon priority of time in some of these events probably depended the fate of California. Commodore Sloat's action was determined by mine. His action, on the 7th, anticipated the arrival of Admiral Seymour, who found the American flag flying where it is probable he came prepared to be invited to raise the British.

California was saved, and also the grant of the three thousand square leagues of land to the Irish priest, McNamara, (all the original papers of which I have to deliver up to the government,) was left incomplete, and the land saved, as well as the scheme of colonization defeated. History may some day verify these events, and show that the preservation of California, and the defeat of the three thousand square leagues grant, covering the valley of the San Joaquin, was owing to the action which determined the action of Commodore Sloat.

I left Los Angeles early in September. The insurrection broke out there in the same month, and soon spread over all the southern half of California. It extended to near Monterey. It delayed Commodore Stockton's return to the sea, and deferred my own appointment as governor. Instead of being occupied in arrangements to be at San Francisco, on the 25th of October, to be placed "*as governor over California*," I was engaged, with little other means than personal influence, in raising men from the American settlements, on the Sacramento, to go south to suppress the insurrection.

With a small body of men, hastily raised for the emergency, I embarked, according to Commodore Stockton's orders, first, in boats to descend the bay of San Francisco, and then, in the ship Sterling, to go down the coast to Santa Barbara. We had left our horses, and expected to obtain remounts when we landed. Two days after our departure from San Francisco, we fell in with the merchant ship Vandalia, from which I learned, and truly, that no horses could be had below; that, to keep it out of our hands, the Californians had driven all their stock into the interior, and that San Diego was the only point left in possession of the Americans. I therefore determined to return to Monterey, and make the march overland. I did so, and there I learned, on the 27th of October, that I had been appointed lieutenant colonel in the army of the United States. It was now the month of December, the beginning of winter, and the cold distressing rains had commenced. Everything had to be done, and done quickly, and with inadequate means. In a few weeks all was ready; 400 men mounted; three pieces of artillery on carriages; beef cattle procured; the march commenced. I omits its details to mention the leading events, a knowledge of which is essential to my defence. We made a secret march of 150 miles to San Louis Obispo, the seat of a district commandant; took it by surprise, without firing a gun; captured the commandant, Don Jesus Pico, the head of the insurrection in that quarter, with 35 others, among them the wounded captain who had commanded at La Natividad. Don Jesus was put before a court martial for breaking his parole, sentenced to be shot, but pardoned. That pardon had its influence on all the subsequent events; Don Jesus was the cousin of Don Andreas Pico, against whom I was going, and was married to a lady of the Cavillo family; many hearts were conquered the day he was pardoned, and his own above all. Among the papers seized was the original despatch of General Flores, which informed us of the action of San Pasqual, but without knowing who commanded on the American side. Don Jesus Pico attached himself to my person, and remained devoted and faithful under trying circumstances. We pursued our march, passing all the towns on the way without collision with the people, but with great labor from the state of the roads and rains. On Christmas day, 1846, we struggled on the Santa Barbara mountain in a tempest of chilling rains and winds, in which a hundred horses perished, but the men stood to it, and I mention it to their honor. They deserve that mention, for they are not paid yet.

We passed the maritime defile of the Rincon, or Punta Gorda, without resistance, flanked by a small vessel which Commodore Stockton had sent to us, under Lieutenant Selden of the navy. A corps of observation, of some 50 or 100 horsemen, galloped about us, without doing or receiving harm; for it did not come within my policy to have any of them killed. It was the camp of this corps which Captain Hamlyn passed, to give me Commodore Stockton's orders, which he found at the "camp of the willows," as said in his testimony. The defile of San Fernando was also passed, a corps which occupied it falling back as the rifles advanced. We entered the plain of Cowenga, occupied by the enemy in considerable force, and I sent a summons to them to lay down their arms, or fight at once. The chiefs desired a parley with me in person. I went alone to see them, (Don Jesus Pico only being with me.) They were willing to capitulate to me; the terms were agreed upon. Commissioners were sent out on both sides to put it into form. It received the sanction of the governor and commander-in-chief, Commodore Stockton, and was reported to the government of the United States. It was the capitulation of *Cowenga*. It put an end to the war and to the feelings of war. It tranquilized the country, and gave safety to every American from the day of its conclusion.

My march from Monterey to Los Angeles, which we entered on the 14th of January, was a subject for gratulation. A march of 400 miles through an insurgent country, without spilling a drop of blood—conquering by clemency and justice—and so gaining the hearts of all, that, until troubles came on from a new source, I could have gone back, alone and unarmed, upon the trail of my march, trusting for life and bread to those alone among whom I had marched as conqueror, and whom I have been represented as plundering and oppressing! I anticipate the order of time, but preserve the connexion of events by copying here from on original private letter to Senator Benton, written at Los Angeles, the 3d of February, 1847, received by him in May at St. Louis, and sent to the President for his reading, whose endorsement is on the back, in his own hand writing, stating it to have been received from Mr. Christopher Carson on the 8th of June.

Had it not been for the treatment I have received, the secret purpose to arrest, the accumulated charges, the publications against me, and other circumstances of the prosecution, I should have been willing to have read that paper to the court as my sole defence against this charge of mutiny; as things are, I copy from it merely some passages, which illustrate what I have said of the effects of that march from Monterey, and the capitulation of Cowenga.

" Knowing well the views of the cabinet, and satisfied that it was a great national measure to unite California to us as a sister State, by a voluntary expression of the popular will, I had in all my marches through the country, and in all my intercourse with the people, acted invariably in strict accordance with this impression, to which I was naturally farther led by my own feelings. I had kept my troops under steady restraint and discipline, and never permitted to them a wanton outrage, or any avoidable destruction of property or life. The result has clearly shown the wisdom of the course I have pursued.   *   *   *   *   *   *   *
Throughout the Californian population, there is only one feeling of satisfaction and gratitude to myself. The men of the country, most forward and able in the revolution against us, now put themselves at my disposition, and say to me, ' *Viva usted seguro, duerme usted seguro,*' (live safe, sleep safe,) ' we ourselves will watch over the tranquility of the country, and nothing can happen which shall not be known to you.' The unavailing dissatisfaction on the part of (——) own people, was easily repressed, the treaty was ratified."

I terminate my narrative at the capitulation of Cowenga, because at that point I got into communication with my two superiors, became involved in their difficulties, and the events began for which I am prosecuted.

From this point the evidence begins. My narrative, intended to be brief and rapid, was necessary to the understanding of my position in California, and brings me to the point of the particular offences charged against me.

Mutiny is first in the order of the charges, and the first specification under it is, for disobeying the negative order of General Kearny, in relation to the re-organization of the California battalion.

Governor Stockton gave me an order to re-organize it; General Kearny sent me an order not to re-organize it; this on the 16th of January, in the night. The next morning I informed General Kearny, by letter, that I thought he and Governor Stockton ought to adjust the question of rank between themselves; and, until that was done, I should have to obey Commodore Stockton as theretofore; and gave some statement of facts and reasons for my justification.

This letter constitutes the alleged act of mutiny; the ingredient of a corrupt motive, in trying to trade for a governorship, has been since added; and now, let the accuser and prosecuting witness speak for himself.

On the first day of his examination, General Kearny testifies thus:

"On the day subsequent, viz., on the 17th of January, Lieutenant Colonel Frémont *came* to my quarters, and in conversation, I asked him whether he had received my communication of the day previous; he acknowledged the receipt of it, and stated that he had written a reply and left it with his *clerk* to be copied.

"About this time, a *person* entered the room with a paper in his hand, which Lieutenant Colonel Frémont took, overlooked, and then used the pen upon my table to sign it; his *clerk* having told him that the signature was wanting to it. *He* then handed it to me. At my request, Lieutenant Colonel Frémont took a chair by my table while I read the letter.

" Having finished the reading of it, I told him I was an older man than himself; that I was a much older soldier than himself; that I had a great respect and regard for his wife, and great friendship for his father-in-law, Colonel Benton, from whom I had received many acts of kindness; that these considerations induced me to volunteer advice to him; and the advice was, that he should take the letter *back* and *destroy it; that I was willing to forget it.* Lieutenant Colonel Frémont *declined* taking it back, and told me that Commodore Stockton would support him in the position taken in that letter. I told him that Commodore Stockton *could not* support him in disobeying the orders of his *senior officer,* and that if he *persisted* in it he would *unquestionably ruin himself.* He told me that Commodore Stockton was *about* to *organize* a civil government, and *intended* to appoint him *governor* of the territory. I told him Commodore Stockton had no such authority, that authority having been conferred on me by the President of the United States. *He asked me whether I would appoint him governor?* I told him I expected shortly to leave California for Missouri; that I had, previously to leaving Santa Fé, asked permission to do so, and was in hopes of receiving it; that, as soon as the country should be quieted, I should, most probably, organize a civil government, and *that I at that time knew of no objection to appointing him as the governor.* He then stated to me that he would *see* Commodore Stockton, and that unless he appointed him governor *at once,* he would *not obey his orders;* and he left me."

This is the evidence on which the prosecution rests the conviction, both for the fact, and its imputed base motive; and at this point the defence begins, and will be directed at once to both motive and fact, and with the belief of shewing each to be untrue.

First, as to the probability of this testimony in all that imputes the dishonorable conduct to me, which is presented as the motive of the meeting.

I hold it to be improbable on its face, and self-evidently unworthy of credit. It represents me as coming to General Kearny's quarters without invitation, signing a letter in his presence which I had directed to be brought after me, giving it to him to read, and refusing to take it back and accept his pardon and oblivion for having written it. The writing of the letter was avowed at the outset of the trial; the question now is upon what passed at the time of its delivery. The letter contained reasons which placed my refusal to obey his order on high grounds of fact and law; the testimony presents me as descending at once from all those high reasons to the low and base proposal of virtually selling myself to the best bidder, himself or Commodore Stockton, for a governorship. According to the testimony, the proposal was abrupt.

"He asked me whether I would appoint him governor?" and this sudden offer to sell myself, in a case in which the purchaser would be about as censurable as the seller, far from exciting indignation, seems to have been courteously entertained; and far from being instantly rejected, seemed to be accepted, provided a little time was given for payment. "I (General K.) then told him that I expected shortly to leave California for Missouri, &c., &c., and that I, at that time, knew of no objections to appointing him as governor." Thus, he had no objection to the transaction—only wanted a little time for performance. I, on the contrary, was for prompt work; for the testimony immediately says: "He then stated to me that he would see Commodore Stockton, and unless he appointed him governor at once, he would not obey his orders; and he left me."

This is the spirit of trade, with its very language and action, with the clear implication that I immediately went to Commodore Stockton, and not coming back, had received the appointment at once. Now, all this is too cool and quick.

It is improbable on its face, especially coupled with the fact that I left the letter in his hands, after his warning of unquestionable ruin, which now constitutes the alleged act of mutiny, and so put myself completely in his power, both for the fact and the alleged motive. The testimony is improbable.

Secondly. I hold it to be invalidated on the cross-examination.

This is the next point of view in which I propose to examine this part of the testimony. After his examination came his cross-examination; and by means of that probe and sharp searcher after truth, came out many circumstances to invalidate the first swearing. Thus, the testimony opens with saying: "Lieutenant Colonel Frémont came to my quarters," &c., the inference being, that I came of my own head; and, from the sudden manner in which I opened the subject, the further inference being, that I came for the governorship; and third inference being, from my sudden exit and eagerness to see Commodore Stockton, that my whole business was to see from which I could get the governship the soonest. Now, if I did not come of my own head—if General K. himself actually sent for me, and desired to see me on business—then all these inferences, so injurious to me, fall to the ground; and the very first words spoken by the witness, though literally true, become untrue testimony, and impart a character to the interview which the truth requires to be reversed. Now let us see how the fact is.

On the eighth day of the trial, this question was put to General Kearny: "Did he (Lieutenant Colonel Frémont) come of his own head, (as your statement implies,) or did you invite him?"

The answer to that question was this: " I have no recollection of having invited him to come." On hearing this answer, a small slip of paper with a few words written upon it was exhibited to the witness, and this question addressed to him: " Is this paper an original ?" The word original was used on purpose to remind the witness of what had occurred on the first day of the trial, and to show the court that the implication then gratuitously raised against me as a person who would destroy originals, was about to receive a retributive rebuke. To this question and slip of paper, the witness answered: " That is my writing, and that is my note." The note was then read, and was in these words:

" January 17

" Dear Colonel: I wish to see you on business.
"S. W. KEARNY,
" *Brigadier General.*"

This settled the question of the coming, and not only showed that it was upon General Kearney's invitation that I came to his quarters on that day, but that it was an invitation in writing and to a business interview that I was invited, and consequently that it was his seeking and not mine that brought us together, and his business, not mine, that was the object of the interview. The production of this little original worked this great change in the character and effect of the evidence; it reversed the character of the coming, and destroyed all the implications arising from a voluntary coming of my own head, and for a purpose of my own.

But suppose this little original had been actually lost or destroyed, then the first answer of General Kearny, that he had no recollection of having invited me to come, would have stood with the effect of an affirmation that he had not invited me, and would have left in full force all the injurious implications resulting from a gratuitous visit on such an occasion, and with such a conversation sworn against me.

As I would have suffered from implications in the first state of his evidence, I claim the benefit of them in its corrected form; and, further, I present it as an instance of the infirmity of his memory.

The want of recollection in the witness in this important particular, I am instructed by counsel to say, goes to the invalidation of his testimony with respect to the whole interview. The circumstance was an important one. It was a key to the character of the interview; it decided the character of the interview as being at his instance or mine. It decided it to be a business interview, and that business his, and not mine. It precludes the idea of my coming to him for any purpose whatever; it fixes the fact that he sent to me for a purpose, and that not a common one, as he invited me to an interview, which was a private one, at his own quarters. General Kearny was then in the crisis of his difficulties with Governor Stockton; he was making a last effort to get me to join him.

The next circumstance of invalidation which I mention, arising from his own testimony, is in this statement: " He told me that Commodore Stockton was *about* to organize a civil government, and *intended* to appoint him governor of the territory." Now, it appears by his own letter to Commodore Stockton of the 16th of January, that he knew that Governor Stockton was then engaged in appointing civil officers for the territory; that, as to *intending* to appoint me, I could not have said so, because I had been virtually appointed since September of 1846, and actually commissioned the day before; and finally, that Governor Stockton had made known to General Kearny at San Diego, in December, that he intended to appoint me, and had so informed the government at Washington.

Ninth day's testimony.

The next circumstance, to invalidate the witness upon his own swearing, is, what he says he stated in reply to the request to be appointed governor, namely, "that he (General Kearny) at that time knew of no objection to appointing him governor, when he left the country," &c., &c. Time is the material point in this statement, and this point the witness has fortunately made clear, both by collocation and cross-examination. It is placed near the end of the interview, and after the act of meeting, with all its aggravations, had been consummated in his presence; and the cross-examination shews it to be in the right place. This cross-examination took place on the ninth day of the trial, and shews that it was after the supposed crime, for which I am now prosecuted, was consummated in his presence, that he was able to see no objection to appointing me governor of California.

From this it results that my conduct that day did not appear to be mutiny, or, that mutiny was no objection to his appointing me governor of California. In either event, I present the circumstance as invalidating his testimony, as it is impossible to reconcile the opposite opinions of my conduct which the declaration of that day, and the prosecution of this day present.

The next invalidating circumstance which I draw from the cross-examination, is, in the difference which it exhibits to the first day's testimony in relation to this alleged application for the governorship, and the answer to it. The first day's testimony professes to give the interview full and complete, and in the exact words of each speaker; the cross-examination on the 10th day makes material variations. The first day's testimony says: "He asked me whether I would appoint him governor?" That is a single question as to the fact. The cross-examination adds another, as to time, by adding, "and when?"—and that led to a corresponding difference in the answer, by substituting "a month or six weeks," for "shortly." The cross-examination of the same day, and of the 9th also, brought the fact of two material omissions in that report of the conversation of the 17th. One related to the fact of Lieutenant Colonel Frémont's urging him (General Kearny) to have a personal interview with Governor Stockton, and expressing the belief that all difficulties between them could be settled in such an interview; the other, in bringing out the fact that I appeared to be greatly distressed at the differences between the two superior officers. Neither of these important facts are mentioned in the direct testimony, purporting to be verbally exact, and precisely full, neither more or less; but, not only are these points omitt , but, as told, there is no part of the conversation to which they could be applicable—no place where they would fit in; from which the conclusion is inevitable, that some whole topics, and of a very different kind from those related, were forgotten in that report of a conversation.

To be distressed at the state of things between the two superiors, was a different thing from making dissensions between them; to endeavor to get them together for the purpose of reconciliation, was very different from committing mutiny against one of them. Yet these circumstances, so important to the fair and just understanding of my conduct and feelings, are wholly omitted in the direct testimony, and only imperfectly got out in the cross-examination, without the topics to which they belong, and without showing a place in the reported conversation to which they could be applicable, or made to fit; thereby implying greater omissions than have been discovered. As if to deprive me of the merit which these disclosures implied, the witness added, " Lieutenant Colonel Frémont might have effected an interview between Commodore Stockton and myself; perhaps there were but few others at Los Angeles who could have done it."

I certainly believed I could have effected the interview. Governor Stockton had no objection to it, but General Kearny's sudden departure the next morning, without notice to me, frustrated any such attempt at reconciliation.

Tenth day's testimony, near the close.

The next invalidating circumstance, drawn from the cross-examination in relation to the same point, is, in not suppressing, or endeavoring to suppress, the alleged mutiny at the time it is charged to have been committed.

The eighth article of war, copied from the British mutiny act, is imperative that, " any officer, non-commissioned officer, or soldier, who, being present at any mutiny or sedition, does not use his utmost endeavor to suppress the same, or, coming to the knowledge of any intended mutiny, does not, without delay, give information thereof to his commanding officer, shall be punished, by the sentence of a general court martial, with *death*, or otherwise, according to the nature of his offence." As a further test to ascertain General Kearny's opinion of my conduct on that day, the following question was put to him: " Did you do your utmost to supress the mutiny of which Lieutenant Colonel Frémont is charged with being guilty in your quarters, and in your presence?" The judge advocate reminded the witness of his privilege to refuse to answer where he might subject himself to a penalty, but the witness did not claim his privilege, and answered: " Nothing further passed between Lieutenant Colonel Frémont and myself in the interview, than what I have stated;" (adding, the next day, " to the best of my recollection.")

This is clear that General Kearny did nothing to suppress the supposed mutiny, and equally clear that he gives no reason for not doing so. He was in his own quarters—in the house where his troops were quartered—and he testified that he does not think Commodore Stockton would have used force. The inference is, that either he did not consider it mutiny then, or that he had some reason, not yet told, for not doing his duty. The former is the probable one, because it corresponds with the cotemporary declaration of knowing no objections to appointing me governor, and for the further reason that it appears, from his own evidence, that he gave me, in the month of March, several orders to execute, implying trust and confidence, and wholly inconsistent with his duty, under the eighth article of war, and wholly inconsistent with military usage, if he then believed me to be guilty of mutiny.

For these reasons, I consider his testimony further invalidated upon his own evidence, drawn out upon his own examination.

The next circumstance to invalidate the testimony of this witness, arising out of his own cross-examination, is what relates to the bearer of my letter of the 17th of January.

In his direct testimony, General Kearny spoke of him as being my clerk. As I kept no clerk, and knowing that Lieutenant Talcott had copied the letter, and that Mr. Christopher Carson had brought it to me, (for in my anxiety at the state of things, and hope for some better understanding, I went in such haste to General Kearny's quarters, on receiving his invitation, as to leave my own letter in the hands of a copyist, to be sent after me,) I undertook to turn his mind towards the right person, by asking who the person was who brought that letter. To that question he answered: " I do not know. I had never seen him before; nor do I know that I have ever seen him since." I then put the question direct: " Was not that person Mr. Christopher Carson?" To which the answer was: " I think not." This answer terminated the interrogatories upon that point; and, according to the evidence, the fact was established that not only it was not Mr. Carson who brought the letter, but that it was some strange person whom General Kearny had never seen before or since. The defect of memory became so glaring in this instance, that it was deemed essential by my counsel to expose it; and something, like a providence, enabled me to do so.

Mr. Carson, the best witness, had returned to California; Lieutenant Talcott, who copied the letter, and sent him with it, was the next best witness; and he had been ordered to Mexico by sea. In passing some of the Florida reefs, the vessel he was in was wrecked, but the lives of the passengers were saved; and Lieutenant Talcott, with his command, had returned to Charleston. Hearing all this, an order and summons was despatched for him; he came; and, being examined before this court, he testified to the facts that he had copied the letter at my request, and sent it after me by Mr. Carson to General Kearny's quarters. Captain Hensley gave corroborating testimony; and thus the fact established by General Kearny's testimony, that it was not Mr. Carson who brought the letter, nor any person that General Kearny had ever seen before or since, was entirely disproved. Certainly the fact in itself, as to who brought the letter, was not very material; but it became eminently so from the answers of the witness. For General Kearny not to know Kit Carson; not to remember him when he brought the letter on which this prosecution is based; to swear that he had never seen the man before or since, who brought that letter, when that man was the same express from Commodore Stockton and myself, from whom he got the despatches; whom he turned back from the confines of New Mexico, and made his guide to California; the man who showed him the way, step by step, in that long and dreary march; who was with him in the fight of San Pasqual; with him on the besieged and desolate hill of San Bernardo; who volunteered, with Lieutenant Beale and the Indians, to go to San Diego for relief, and whose application to go was at first refused, "because he could not spare him;" who was afterwards the commander of the scouts on the march from San Diego to Los Angeles; not to know this man who had been his guide for so many months, and whom but few see once without remembering; and not only not to know him, but to swear that he had never seen him before or since. This, indeed, was exhibiting an infirmity of memory almost amounting to no memory at all.

In that point of view I present it to the court, and to invalidate all the testimony of General Kearny, with respect to my words, or his words in that alleged conversation of the 17th of January. Acts and facts are more easily remembered than words; persons and things seen are more easily remembered than expressions heard; and after forgetting his own act, in writing to me to come to see him on business; after forgetting the fact of seeing the famous Kit Carson bring the letter which he has so long saved for this prosecution, I am instructed, by counsel, to say that the law discredits him as a witness.

Thirdly. Discredited by his own conduct.

I hold that the charge is discredited by General Kearny's own conduct at the time, in not reporting it to Governor Stockton, or to the government of the United States. In neither of the two letters written by him to Governor Stockton, on the same day with my alleged offer to sell the California battalion to him for a governorship, accompanied by a menace of revolt against Governor Stockton, is testified to have taken place, is the remotest hint or allusion to any such transaction. Now, whatever may have been General Kearny's opinion of his own rights, and of the refusal of Governor Stockton to recognize his claims, considerations of public duty ought to have prompted him, before going away and leaving the interests of the country entirely in the hands of Governor Stockton, with a known intention of presently committing them to me, ought to have induced him to warn that officer of my conduct, and threat of sedition, if any such had taken place.

On the other hand, if considerations of public duty are not the motive that had influence with him, but, instead, his private resentments, these also, whether against Commodore Stockton, myself, or both, would equally have prompted him to the disclosure, had there been any to make; for, if after being informed of such insubordination, Governor Stockton had still persisted in his intentions towards me, (continuing my command, and leaving me in the governorship,) the witness would have fastened upon both a corrupt intrigue and collusion; or, if Governor Stockton had acted upon the information, as would have been proper to act, and as he probably would have acted, namely, taken away my command, and possibly seized my person, then that " UNQUESTIONABLE RUIN," intimated in reserve for me, would have been sooner accomplished.

Had that which is now charged upon me actually taken place, the suppression of the fact, at that time, when fresh and working in the mind of the witness, as it must have done, cannot, with the reasons and inducements which existed for its disclosure, be accounted for on any known principle of human conduct. Besides these two letters to Governor Stockton of that day, both silent on this charge, the witness also wrote to the War Department on the same day, and reporting both Governor Stockton and myself as refusing to obey him, or the instructions of the President; and neither in that letter is there the slightest hint or allusion to any such transaction as General Kearny has now testified to. There is a case at the Old Bailey where a person was convicted and executed, mainly on the presumption which a very similar omission to this raised. It was the case of Governor Wall, tried at the Old Bailey, in 1802, on a charge of murder, committed, under color of official duty, in the punishment of a soldier at Goree, off the coast of Africa, twenty years before.

The soldier was punished with eight hundred lashes, in consequence of which he died two days after. The defence set up, was, that a part of the troops of the garrison were in a state of MUTINY, of which the soldier punished was the ringleader; and that the punishment was inflicted under the article of war which requires an officer present at a mutiny to do his utmost to suppress it.

The prosecution proved *that Governor Wall went away from the place on the day following the alleged acts of mutiny, and with him two officers; and that, arriving in England, he repeated, in writing, to the government concerning the affairs of the garrison,* BUT MADE NO MENTION OF THE ALLEGED MUTINY.

The lord chief baron, McDonald, dwelt upon that omission, and pointed it out to the jury. There was other evidence on the point of MUTINY or no mutiny; but it was nearly balanced, and this omission became the great point in the case. The governor was convicted; and notwithstanding the most powerful efforts to obtain his pardon, the king (George III.) refused to grant it; and he was hung at Tyburn, according to his sentence, and his body given up to the surgeons to be dissected and anatomized.

The presumption raised in the present instance is stronger than in the one I have quoted. There the report referred only to the affairs of the garrison generally; here it relates exclusively to the subject now in issue.

There, if there had been a *mutiny* there was no occasion for the action of the government; for the mutiny, such as it was, had been suppressed and the mutineers punished; here the report was specially for the action of the government on the case stated.

There, the omission was merely a matter left out, not affecting, in any way, what was put in; here, the omission is of the material part, and without which not only an imperfect but a false view is given to the whole. There, the letter was written six weeks after the occurrence, and at a great distance from the scene of it; here, it was written on the spot—the same day. All the reasons for General Kearny to have *reported* my alleged mutiny, and the base motive for it in the imputed attempted bargaining about the governorship, are infinitely stronger than in the case of Governor Wall. The omission was a heavy circumstance against him in his case; it must be more so in the present one; and authorizes me to say that his testimony here is discredited by his own conduct, at the time of these imputed offences.

Fourthly.—I now take a more decided view of this testimony in relation to governorship, and say that besides being improbable on its face, invalidated on the cross-examination, and discredited by his own conduct, it is disproved by facts and witnesses. The imputed bargaining for the governorship is the point of the mutiny and the base and sordid cause of it. Now, if there was no bargaining, or attempt at it, for the governorship, then there was no mutiny; and the whole charge, with its imputed motive and inferences, falls to the ground. And, now, how was the fact? That as early as August, 1846, Governor Stockton, of his own head, selected me for his successor as governor and commander-in-chief in California. That he informed me of it at the time by letter, and also informed the government of the United States of it, and had actually fixed the 25th day of October last for his own return to his squadron, and for my installation as governor, and was only delayed in that intention by the breaking out of the insurrection. That he informed General Kearny of all this at San Diego, by giving him a copy of his official dispatch to the government to read; that, arriving at Los Angeles in January, he immediately proceeded to consummate his delayed intention, making all preparations for his own departure and for my installation, appointing me governor in form, appointing a secretary of my choice, appointing the council, immediately filling up my place in the California battalion by promoting Captain Gillespie to be major; and all these things done and completed by the 16th, and so known generally at the time, and actually known to General Kearny himself, as appears by his own letter, of that date, to "acting Governor Stockton," forbidding the appointments; and also by his cross-examination before this court.

The following are passages from the letter:

"I am informed that you are now engaged in organizing a civil government, and appointing officers for it in this territory." "If you have not such authority, (from the President,) I then demand

that you cease all further proceedings relating to the formation of
a civil government for this territory, as I cannot recognize in you
any right in assuming to perform duties confided to me by
the President." (Tenth day.)

The cross-examination of the same day fully sustains the assertion that, on the 16th, General Kearny knew that Governor Stockton was appointing the governor and secretary for California, and
his letter to the department, of the same date, (16th,) shows that
he not only knew it, but reported it. These facts disprove the
assertion that, on the 17th, I asked General Kearny for the governorship of California; disprove the assertion that I would see
Commodore Stockton, and, unless he gave it at once, I would not
obey his orders. The facts disprove it, for all the forms of be-
stowing the appointment had been completed the day before, while
the appointment itself had been virtually and actually made for
near six months before.

I will now proceed to the positive testimony of an unimpeached and unimpeachable witness, to disprove the testimony of
General Kearny in relation to this governorship.

Colonel Wm. H. Russell, a witness introduced on the thirty-
sixth day of the trial, testified that he was sent by Lieutenant
Colonel Frémont from the plains of Cowengo, about the 13th of
January, to Los Angeles, to ascertain who was in chief command,
and to make report of the capitulation of Cowengo. I leave out,
at this time, all notice of his testimony, except what relates to the
governorship. He says he went first to General Kearny's quarters;
afterwards to Commodore Stockton's; returned, by invitation of
General Kearny, and supped and slept at his quarters. On this return the chief conversation took place, and now the very words of
the witness shall be given. Colonel Russell says: "In that conversation he (General Kearny) expressed great pleasure at Colonel
Frémont's being in the country; spoke of his eminent qualifications
for the office of governor, from his knowledge of the Spanish language, of the manners of the people, &c.; and of his (General
Kearny's) intention to have appointed him governor, if the instructions he brought from the Secretary of War had been recognized
in California." "It (the conversation about the governorship) was
a subject of very much conversation, protracted to a late hour in
the night. He told me of his civil appointments in New Mexico,
and of his determination to have appointed Colonel Frémont governor." "He said that so soon as he could organize a civil government, it was his intention to return to the United States, and
finding so suitable a person as Colonel Frémont in the country to
take the place of governor, his design need not be long postponed.
I do not pretend to quote his exact words."

On the thirty-eighth day of the trial, and after objections to certain questions to Colonel Russell had been sustained by the court,
his direct examination was resumed, and he testified, (after stating
that he rode out the next morning and met Lieut. Colonel Frémont,
then entering Los Angeles, at head of his battalion,) "I informed him
(Lieutenant Colonel Frémont) that both General Kearny and Com-

modore Stockton were anxious to confer upon him the office of governor, and his only difficulty would be in the choice between them." "Commodore Stockton informed me, on the evening of the 13th, on my second interview with him, that he intended to confer the office of governor on Lieutenant Colonel Frémont, as I understood, immediately on his arrival at Los Angeles. I think it was a matter of ordinary publicity throughout the city." "On the morning, as I suppose, of the 16th, I was at Commodore Stockton's quarters, and he informed me that the commission for Lieutenant Colonel Frémont as governor, and my own as secretary of state, were then in the act of being made out by his clerk, and desired me to ask Lieutenant Colonel Frémont to be at his quarters by a given hour, when the commissions would be ready for delivery. I made this communication to Lieutenant Colonel Frémont, and at the appointed time returned with him to Commodore Stockton's quarters, when he (the commodore) accordingly handed the commissions to each of us.

"I want to qualify here, as I am told there is some discrepancy about dates. I presume it was the 16th, because the commissions bear that date, and for the further reason that it was within two or three days of the arrival of Lieutenant Colonel Frémont at Los Angeles." This was on the direct examination.

On the cross-examination, on the fortieth day of the trial, the witness (Colonel Russell) in reply to questions, confirmed all that he had said, and added: "That in all the conversations I had with Gen. Kearny on that evening, (13th January,) I understood it to be his wish to appoint Lieutenant Colonel Frémont as governor, if he could rightfully do so."

On his re-introduction, on the fifty-first day of the trial, General K. was allowed to testify, *not to new matter introduced by the defence*, but to re-testify to the points on which he had before been fully examined, and in so swearing contradicted Colonel Russell. I asked to have the witnesses confronted before the court; it was refused. I asked to introduce gentlemen of the highest standing in the United States, namely, Mr. Clay, and Mr. Crittenden, Mr. Justice Catron, of the Supreme Court, Hon. Mr. French, of the House of Representatives, from Kentucky, Hon. Mr Jamison, of the same House of Representatives, from Missouri, to sustain the general character of Colonel Russell for truth and veracity; it was refused by the court, and this reason assigned:

"The court does not consider contradictory statements, where fraud is not imputed, as involving a right in a party to sustain the credit of a witness by evidence to his general character.

"In the case presented here, apparently in reference to the examination of witnesses by the court itself, which could not be supposed to aim at discrediting any witness, and which has not impeached any witness, the court cannot now admit testimony, which would be of doubtful admissibility, to rebut any examination by a party. To grant the request of the accused, might imply a doubt on the part of the court as to the integrity and general character of the witness, which the court does not entertain."

This reason, and the refusal to confront General Kearny and Colonel Russell at a point of the testimony so vital to my honor, I am instructed by counsel to say, could only have been given upon the admission of full faith and credit being given to Colonel Russell on all the points of his testimony contradicted by General Kearny.

Upon this supposition nothing further would need to be said in support of Colonel Russell's credit, but it is impossible to overlook the glaring fact, on the part of the prosecution, of the non-production of Captain Turner, at the time of the re-introduction of General Kearny. All the testimony, on both sides, shows the general or frequent presence of Captain Turner at the day, the night, the table and the bed conversations on the 13th January, at General Kearny's quarters, which were also the quarters of Captain Turner, and he frequently referred to in the course of the testimony. If he could contradict Colonel Russell, it would be weighty; if he could merely say that he heard no such thing, it would be something; if he could say that General Kearny told him differently at the time, it would be some corroboration of what he now says; but, instead of this, not to re-introduce him at all, when he is the witness of the prosecution, and actually present, as he then was in the ante-room of the court, is to admit the presumption of the law that his non-production under such circumstances, is a circumstance in favor of Colonel Russell's testimony.

The attempt to weaken Colonel Russell's testimony at this point, by taking exception to the word "INTENDED" to return to Missouri, ends in the corroboration of it. At best, it is only the difference between *expected* and *intended*, (and Colonel R., in his direct testimony, said he was not certain of the exact word,) for General Kearny, in his direct testimony, testified that he expected SHORTLY to leave California for Missouri, in consequence of the leave he had asked before he left Santa Fe; and on his cross-examination he substituted "a month or six weeks" for the term SHORTLY, either of which corresponds with Colonel Russell's statement, and nullifies the argument against the "OPEN QUESTION" on which General Kearney so much relied.

And thus, I say that the testimony of General Kearny is disproved by the positive testimony of an unimpeached, an unimpeachable witness, as well as by established facts.

Fifthly. I say that this statement, that I asked General Kearny for the governorship is disavowed by the entire tenor of my life. I have neither begged nor bargained for offices. My first appointment, as second lieutenant of topographical engineers, was given me by President Jackson, Mr. Poinsett being Secretary at War, when I was far distant on the upper Mississippi, assisting Mr. Nicollet in his great survey of that region. My brevet of captain was given by President Tyler, Mr. Wilkins being Secretary at War, without solicitation from myself or friends. The appointment of lieutenant colonel came to me in California, when I was not even thinking of it; and, I am assured by Senator Benton, that it was President Polk's own act, not only unasked by him, but that he refused to consent that any friend should name such a thing to the President.

The three appointments given to me by Commodore Stockton, (those of major of the California battalion, military commandant of California, and governor and commander-in-chief in California,) were all given of his own head, without solicitation or hint from me. Such has been the uniform tenor of my life in respect to office, and General Kearny is no exception to it.

The uniform conduct of my life disavows the application which he says I made to him; and I claim the benefit of that disavowal in a case where a request would be infamous, which I never made, when it might have been done with honor.

Sixthly. Having shown that this testimony of General Kearny is improbable on its face, invalidated on his own cross-examination, discredited by his own conduct, disproved by positive testimony, and disavowed by the tenor of my life, I now come to the last, and only remaining species of the testimony—that of my own declaration. Happily, I have no new declaration to make; I have only to show the statement which I made for the eye of private friendship, in the mere course of narrative, and as a circumstance in the history of the transaction, near twelve months ago, when the event was fresh, no question about it, and none of any kind ever expected. In that private letter to Senator Benton, already referred to, written at Los Angeles, and dated the 3d day of February, 1847, are these words:

"Both offered me the commission and post of governor; Commodore Stockton, to redeem his pledge to that effect, immediately, and General Kearny offering to give the commission in four or six weeks."

This is what I then wrote for the eye of private friendship, and what I now produce to this court as my own testimony in this case. IT IS TRUE. And I now owe it to myself, to my friends, and to good men, whose esteem I desire to possess, to declare, and to make the declaration upon responsibilities infinitely higher than those of military honor and commission, that Brigadier General Kearny, in all that he has testified in relation to this governorship, has borne false witness against me.

I dismiss this topic, the only one in the multiplied charges against me which concerns my honor, with the reflection which springs of itself from the case and finds a response in every generous mind, that General Kearny himself undertook to seduce me with this governorship, and failing to do so, has raised against me the false accusation of applying to him for it, and has sworn to it.

And I here close my defence, both as to the fact and the motive, of specification first, in charge first, for the crime of mutiny.

I proceed now to defend the same act under a different charge; for it so happens in this trial that the same set of acts are placed under different charges, some under two charges, namely, mutiny and disobedience of orders; and some under three, the same act, in some instances, being carried out under the charge of conduct prejudicial to good order and discipline, as well as under the heads of mutiny and disobedience of orders.

I refer to a paper, heretofore filed, for the opinion which my counsel entertain of these multiplied charges upon the same set of acts. They consider them as so many different trials for the same thing, and wholly unjustified by the practice which admits less degrees of the same offence to be found, according to the proof produced on the trial. Here the charges are on the same acts for different kinds of offences, and the same evidence adduced under each, and the same that was adduced before the trial, when the charges were framed, as before this court, when they are tried. My counsel instruct me to say it is a clear case of two trials and three trials for the same matter; but I take no legal objection to it.

To save the labor of re-stating questions, and of re-producing proofs as many times as the same specifications are repeated under different charges, I prefer to pursue each one, when I begin it, through all the charges; and thus finish with it complete, and have all my trials over upon it, before I begin with another. This method will be convenient to me, and probably no disadvantage to the prosecution, as it will get all the chances of conviction, which the multiplied charges require, though, perhaps, not in the order they would regularly imply.

I begin with my letter to General Kearny, of the 17th of January, which he produces, under the charge of disobedience of orders, as well as under that of mutiny, and as evidence to prove both, and which I produce as containing the facts and the law which disprove each. That letter is in words:

CIUDAD DE LOS ANGELES,
January 17, 1847.

SIR: I have the honor to be in receipt of your favor of last night, in which I am directed to suspend the execution of orders which, in my capacity as military commandant of this territory, I had received from Commodore Stockton, governor and commander-in-chief in California.

I avail myself of an early hour this morning to make such a reply as the brief time allowed for reflection will enable me.

I found Commodore Stockton in possession of the country, exercising the functions of military commandant and civil governor, as early as July of last year; and shortly thereafter I received from him the commission of military commandant, the duties of which I immediately entered upon, and have continued to exercise to the present moment.

I found also, on my arrival at this place, some three or four days since, Commodore Stockton still exercising the functions of civil and military governor, with the same apparent deference to his rank on the part of all officers (including yourself) as he maintained and required when he assumed in July last.

I learned also, in conversation with you, that, on the march from San Diego, recently, to this place, you entered upon and discharged duties implying an acknowledgment, on your part, of supremacy to Commodore Stockton.

I feel, therefore, with great deference to your professional and personal character, constrained to say that, until you and Commodore Stockton adjust between yourselves the question of rank, where I respectfully think the difficulty belongs, I shall have to report and receive orders, as heretofore, from the commodore.

With considerations of high regard, I am, sir, your obedient servant,

J. C. FRÉMONT,
Lieutenant Colonel, United States Army, and
Military Commandant of the territory of California.

To Brigadier General S. W. KEARNY,
United States Army.

This letter was signed in the quarters of General Kearny, and in his presence, and delivered to him by myself. He read it in my presence, and has produced it here as evidence against me, and, in so doing, has made it evidence against himself. What he did not then deny, he admitted; and I will show, from his own testimony, that that is the case with the whole letter. He contradicted no part of it; therefore he admitted every part of it; and this results from his own swearing, in which he professes to give an exact verbal account, no more, no less, of all that passed at that interview, of the letter, from my *entrance*, at the beginning, to my *exit* at the end; and not one word of my letter contradicted in the whole account. I will now analyze its statements of law and fact, so far as they apply to this charge of disobedience of orders, and show it to be a complete refutation of the charge founded upon it. The letter is the text of my defence, and the developement of its positions will make its leading argument. I am advised by counsel that it is complete in itself, and, such as it was written that morning, needs no aid from subsequent reflection or legal advice; and on that letter, as it is, both for the law and the fact, I stand all the multiplied trials which are founded upon it.

First. It fixes the *time* of sending the countermanding order to me—a most material point which could not be fixed by any examination, or cross-examination of General Kearny. All the multiplied questions put to him, and by all parties, the judge advocate, myself, and the court, left the *time* of the day uncertain, and led to a wrong time, as being at some period of the day, and even the fore part of the day, of the 16th of January. (See 8th and 9th days of the testimony.) My letter fixes the time; it opens with fixing it. It fixes it to the *night*. The first line acknowledges the receipt of your favor *(i. e.* the countermanding order) *of last night.* No denial was made of having sent this order at night; and thus that period was confessed.

Second. It fixes the character in which I myself was then acting, and a knowledge of which was so material to the case, and so difficult to be obtained from the prosecuting witness. It shows that

I was military commandant of the territory; and that the order I was required to cease from executing was an order in relation to the battalion under my command as military commandant. It fixes the fact that the order came to me in that capacity; for so my letter asserts, and it was not contradicted by General Kearny when read by him.

Third. It fixes the character of Commodore Stockton in giving me the order to reorganize the battalion; for it names him as giving the order, and describes him as governor and commander-in-chief in California.

Fourth. It fixes the fact that on my arrival at Los Angeles, (14th January,) Commodore Stockton was exercising the functions of civil and military governor with apparent deference to his rank by General Kearny, for that is asserted in the letter, and was not contradicted by him.

Fifth. It also fixes the fact that, on the march from San Diego to Los Angeles, General Kearny discharged duties implying the supremacy of Commodore Stockton; for that is asserted to have been learnt by me, from conversations with General Kearny himself, and was not denied by him.

These important facts, five in number, are fixed and established by the letter; for they were not denied when the letter was read. I am advised by counsel that the law takes for confessed whatever is said to a man in his presence, and not contradicted, at the time, by him. General Kearny's testimony, professing to give a full account of all that was said, on both sides, during the whole interview at the reception of the letter, is silent upon all these points; and it is too late now to think of contradicting what was then, by all the rules of evidence, irrevocably admitted. That letter and its delivery in his presence, and being read in my presence, besides containing the facts of the case, and the law of the case, becomes also the evidence of the case. If that order had not been written or sent in the *night*, that was the time for General Kearny to have said so. If the order had not been intended for me, in my capacity of *military commandant of the territory*, that was the time for him to have corrected my error. If Commodore Stockton was not then *governor and commander-in-chief in California*, then was the time for him to have told me so. If Commodore Stockton had not been exercising the functions of *military commander and civil governor*, from the month of July preceding, then was the time for him to have contradicted the assertion of it in my letter. If I had not found the commodore exercising the *same functions* on my arrival at Los Angeles, three days before, with apparent deference on the part of all officers, General Kearny inclusive, that was the time for him to have denied the assertion, or, at all events, to have protested against the inclusion of himself in that obedient and deferential class of officers. If I had not learnt in conversation with himself that, in the march from San Diego, and also there, at Los Angeles, he had not entered upon and discharged duties implying, *on his part*, an acknowledgement of Commodore Stockton's *supre-*

macy, then was the time for him to have told me that I labored under a total mistake in my misunderstanding of his conversations.

If there was no question of *rank* then (on the 17th) depending between himself and Governor Stockton, he ought to have said so. If it had not been right for me to remain as I was *until they adjusted that question,* then was the time for him to say so to me. If the *difficulty* was not between the two superiors alone, then was the time for him to have cast it upon me. If I had ever *reported* to him, or *received orders* from him, surely it was the time to tell me so when he was reading that last paragraph of my letter, in which the contrary is asserted in the declaration, that I should have to *report* and to *receive orders,* " *as heretofore,*" from Commodore Stockton. If all, or any of these points were not true, *then* was the *time,* and *there* was the *place,* and that was *the occasion,* to have denied them. Denial, omitted then, cannot be supplied now. And both law, reason and justice, require my uncontradicted letter of that day to remain as established truth in this question between General Kearny and myself.

Clear and strong in its facts, the letter is equally just and legal in its conclusions. It does not refuse obedience to General Kearny, but defers it until he and Commodore Stockton adjust the question of rank between themselves; it respectfully suggests to him that the settlement of the difficulty belongs to himself and Commodore Stockton; and concludes with stating that until this rank is so adjusted I would have to report, and receive orders, as theretofore, from Commodore Stockton. Now all this, I am advised by counsel, is both law and reason; and to prove this law, and this reason, is now my duty before this court.

I proceed to do it:

First. It shows that there was a question of rank admitted by General Kearny to be depending between himself and Commodore Stockton. He wished to settle it by giving me a contradictory order. I declined the responsibility, and I think rightfully. For, in the first place, it is not for the subordinate to decide between his superiors. He has no legal power to do so; no legal power to require submission from the one decided against; and if he used physical force, it might indeed be a case of mutiny, and that in its proper sense of a military rebellion. Besides, decide which way he might, his danger would be the same. Having no right or power to decide between them—my duty being passive and not active—the only safe or legal course open to me was to remain as I was, reporting to, and receiving orders from, Commodore Stockton. I considered the question to lie between the two superiors, and that seems to be their own opinion of it, from their correspondence at the time, (16th and 17th of January.) The concluding words of General Kearny's letter to Commodore Stockton, of the 17th of January (eighth day of the trial) are express to that point. Those words are too material to paraphrase or put off with a reference; they are these:

" *And as I am prepared to carry out the President's instructions to me, which you oppose, I must, for the purpose of preventing a*

collision between US, *and possibly to prevent a civil war* IN CONSE-
QUENCE *of it, remain* SILENT *for the* PRESENT, *leaving with* YOU *the
great* RESPONSIBILITY *of doing* THAT *for which you have no authority, and* PREVENTING ME *from complying with the President's* OR-
DERS."

This extract and the whole cotemporaneous correspondence between the two superior officers, beginning at San Diego when I was
on the march from Monterey, shows that the contest was between
them; and it shows also the serious point at which it had arrived.
The time of writing the letter, from which this extract is taken, is
now the material point, and that was sufficiently ascertained on
the cross-examination of General Kearny on the eighth day. It
was ascertained to have been written after my refusal to obey him
against Commodore Stockton. The conclusion is inevitable. That
refusal prevented the *collision* and *the civil war* which the letter
mentioned, as being for the present prevented. I prevented it.
My reward has been to have the war directed against myself and
to be tried for capital and infamous crimes, with base and sordid
motives attributed to me.

The question now is disobedience of orders—the order not to re-
organize the California battalion being the specification.

In the British service, from whose rules and articles of war our
own are copied, and where there is a judge advocate general to
direct court martial proceedings with uniformity, the character or
qualities of the order, disobedience to which is criminal, are already
defined. At page 89 of Hough, (edition of 1825,) is found this definition of such an order:

" In the absolute resistance of, or refusal of obedience to, a present and *urgent* command, conveyed either orally or in *writing*,
and directed to be obeyed with promptitude, by the non-compliance with which some immediate act necessary to be done, might
be impeded or defeated, as high an offence is discoverable as can
well be contemplated by the military mind; inasmuch as the principle which it holds out, would, if encouraged, or not suppressed by
some heavy penalty, forbid or preclude a reliance on the execution
of any military measure. It is this positive disobedience, therefore, evincing a *refractory* spirit in the INFEROIR, an active opposition to the commands of a SUPERIOR, against which it must be
supposed the severe penalty of the article is principally directed."

From this definition of the kind of order which the rules and articles of war contemplate, it is clear that it is not *every* order, and
merely because it is an order, given by a superior to an inferior,
that entitles itself to implicit obedience. On the contrary, it must
have certain indispensable requisites to entitle itself to that obedience; and among these are: 1st, legality; 2d, necessary for the
public service; 3d, urgent; by the non-compliance with which
some immediate act necessary to be done is defeated or impeded;
and that the disobedience must be of a kind to evince a refractory
spirit.

I have to answer that the order given by General K. possessed
none of these requisites, and that disobedience drew after it no in-

jury to the public service, and that my refusal to obey it was not in a refractory spirit.

1. It was not a legal order, and this for reasons which I shall fully show in the proper place.

2. It was a mere experimental order of contradiction, to try a question of rank, and against the public service, as the state of the battalion required it to be re-organized, the time for which many of the men and officers were engaged having expired, and to give it a major in place of myself, made governor.

3. So far from being for the public service, it would seem from the sentence in General Kearny's letter to Commodore Stockton of the 17th of January, (already quoted,) in relation to a collision between them, and possibly a civil war, that the battalion was wanted for forcibly asserting his right to the governorship against Commodore Stockton. The letter can have no other meaning, and this interpretation of it is moreover borne out by his letter of the same date to the department, by his testimony before the court, and by the testimony of Lieutenant Emory.

4. The battalion was not, and never had been, under the orders of General Kearny; was not such troops as his instructions contemplated, and several of its officers were from the navy, over whom he could have no control.

5. General Kearny was, at the time of giving the order, suspended from the command of the forces at that place by order of Governor Stockton.

6. If not suspended at the time he wrote and sent the order, then he was himself in mutiny against his own commander, and endeavoring to induce me " to join " in it, and thus was in the commission of the double offence of mutiny himself, and endeavoring to make another join him in it.

7. General Kearny has not shown for what purpose he gave the order against re-organization, but it appears evident it was for an unlawful purpose, *to wit*, for the purpose of keeping the battalion together in his own hands to be used against Governor Stockton. On his cross-examination (eighth day) he *seems* to have known nothing about what he was doing in giving this order, on which I am now doubly prosecuted. To the question: " Did you know what was the nature of the re-organization commanded by Governor Stockton, of the battalion under Lieutenant Colonel Frémont, and forbid by you?" he answered, " I do not. I learned that Commodore Stockton was about to re-organize that battalion, and I forbid it." Thus, a battalion raised, officered, commanded, and organized by Governor Stockton, and being a part of his forces for the conquest, preservation, and government of California, was forbid to be *re*-organized by General Kearny, without knowing what the actual organization was, or what the re-organization would be. He heard something was to be done—he knew not what—and he forbid it. Surely, he should tell what purpose he had in view.

8. It was an order that I could not obey without rebelling against the authority by which the battalion was raised and from which I held my commission as its commander.

From all this it appears that the order not to re-organize the battalion has none of the requisites of an order entitled to obedience; that it was not a lawful order; that it was not intended for the public service; that there was no necessity for it; that no injury to the public service accrued from non-obedience to it; that the refusal to obey it, so far from being in a refractory spirit, was a mere determination to remain as I was, and as I had been, under Commodore Stockton's command, until my superiors settled their own dispute. And I am now advised by counsel to say that that decision was legally right.

In opposition to all this, General Kearny urges, in support of his right to command me, *first*, his rank as brigadier general; *secondly*, his instructions to take command of the troops organized in California; *thirdly*, that I had put myself under his command by reporting to him on the 13th of January. I deny all three of his positions:

1. As brigadier general he had no right to give me any order in relation to Commodore Stockton's forces. He admits this with respect to the sailors and marines; also, with respect to that part of the battalion which was detached, and under the command of Captain Gillespie; it was equally illegal to interfere with that part of the commodore's forces which was under my command.

2. His instructions to take command of the troops organized in California did not apply to those raised by the navy; they did not apply to such forces as I commanded, and of which nothing was known at Washington when the instructions were given.

3. His pretension that I put myself under his command by reporting to him, and on which he mainly relies, is as unfounded as all the rest, but requires a more detailed and precise examination. He lays great stress upon this alleged reporting, and shall have the full benefit of his own testimony in support of his pretension. In his direct examination, he said: " About the 14th of January, 1847, I received from Lieutenant Colonel Frémont a communication dated the day previous, upon the march, and dated January 13, 1846, (presumed to be written by mistake for 1847,) and which I furnished, together with the charges, to the adjutant general."

The paper was read, as follows:

ON THE MARCH, *January* 13, 1846.

DEAR SIR: I have the honor to report to you my arrival at this place with 400 mounted riflemen and six pieces of artillery, including among the latter two pieces lately in the possession of the Californians. Their entire force, under the command of Don Andre Pico, have this day laid down their arms and surrendered to my command.

Very respectfully, your obedient servant,
                    J. C. FRÉMONT,
        Lieutenant Colonel U. S. army and military
                commandant of the territory of California.
Brigadier General S. W. KEARNY.

On the day of the receipt of that report, (viz: of the 13th January,) Lieutenant Colonel Frémont, at the head of a battalion of volunteers, entered the city of Los Angeles. On the 16th January an order was sent to him, relating to this battalion, by my direction, and signed by Lieutenant Emory, a copy of which I have furnished, and which I can identify if shown to me.

This is a copy of the order furnished to him by Lieutenant Emory.

The paper was read, as follows:

HEAD-QUARTERS, ARMY UNITED STATES,
Ciudad de los Angeles, January 16, 1847.

By direction of Brigadier General Kearny, I send you a copy of a communication to him from the Secretary of War, dated June 18, 1846, in which is the following: " These troops, and such as may be organized in California, will be under your command." The general directs that no change will be made in the organization of your battalion of volunteers or officers appointed in it without his sanction or approval being first obtained.

Very respectfully,

WM. H. EMORY,
Lieutenant and Acting Assistant Adjutant General.
Lieutenant Colonel J. C. FREMONT,
Mounted riflemen, commanding
battalion California volunteers.

On his cross-examination, General Kearny thus testifies in relation to that battalion, and the brief note which he treated as a military report for duty: " *The California battalion was under my command from the time of Lieutenant Colonel Frémont's reporting to me on the* 13*th of January.*" He, therefore, swears to the fact of my *reporting* to him, and also being *under* his command; and this double swearing becomes the corner stone of his accusation. Twice afterwards he swears to the same effect, thus: " *I was a brigadier general in the army, and the accused was a lieutenant colonel in it. I was in command of the battalion at the time,*" (to wit: 16th and 17th.) And again: " *I made no attempt to get the command; the battalion was already under me.*"

In this way, and by dint of his own swearing, he gets me, as he swears, under his command, and thereby acquires the right to give me orders, with the resulting consequences of mutiny and disobedience if I did not obey them; and all these rights and consequences flowing from the word *report*, as found in my note of the 13th January to him.

Now let us see with how much truth and justice this is done. From the testimony in chief, at the opening of the trial, quoted above, it would seem that, of my own head, on the 13th day of January, I reported myself and battalion, in the military sense of the word, to General Kearny for duty; that after this reporting, and without any thing else passing upon the subject, and after I had voluntarily put myself and my battalion under the command of General Kearny, I did, on the 17th, refuse to obey the order of General Kearny in relation to said battalion, and thus became guilty of two crimes—mutiny, for which I might have been lawfully killed on the spot; and disobedience of orders, for which I may be sentenced to be shot or cashiered, or otherwise punished by this court.

The first words of the testimony imply voluntary communication. The words are: "about the 14th of January, 1847, I received from Lieutenant Colonel Frémont a communication, dated tne day previous, upon the march, &c., which I furnished, together with the charges to the adjutant general." This testimony presents a voluntary act on my part, a movement of my own head, uninfluenced by any previous act of General Kearny; and so stood the case on the direct examination, on the first day of the trial.

On the seventh day the cross-examination reached this point, and the recorded testimony shows as follows:

Question. Did you, at Los Angeles, from the 10th to the 13th of January inclusive, address notes to Lieutenant Colonel Frémont, and if so, how many, and for what object?

Answer. Between those dates I addressed, I think, three communications to Lieutenant Colonel Frémont. * * * The object of my communication was to inform Lieutenant Colonel Frémont of our being in possession of Los Angeles, and having a strong force, &c.

Question. Were they official orders, or familiar notes of information in regard to impending military events, and desiring information of Lieutenant Colonel Frémont's movements in return?

Answer. They were what are termed semi-official, written in a familiar manner, and of which I have no copies. I keep a copy of all my official communications.

Question. Did either of those notes give the information that Governor Stockton was at Angeles?

Answer. I have no recollection of it.

Question. Did either of those notes, dated at 6 o'clock in the evening of the 6th of January, contain these words: "Dear Frémont: I am here in possession of this place, with sailors and marines. We met and defeated the whole force of the Californians the 8th and 9th. They have not now to exceed 300 men concentrated. Avoid charging them, and come to me at this place. Acknowledge the hour of receipt of this, and when I may expect you. Regards to Russell?"

Answer. I cannot answer, but I think it highly probable it did. As I stated before, I kept no copies of those semi-official papers.

Question. Did you address the accompanying letter to Lieutenant Colonel Frémont, and at the time of its date?

Answer. That is my writing and that is my note.

The letter was read, as follows:

PUEBLA DE LOS ANGELES,
Sunday, January 10, 1847—4, p. m.

DEAR FRÉMONT: We are in possession of this place, with a force of marines and sailors, having marched into it this morning. Join us as soon as you can, or let me know if you want us to march to your assistance. Avoid charging the enemy; their force does not exceed four hundred, perhaps not more than three hundred. Please acknowledge the receipt of this, and despatch the bearer at once.
Yours,

S. W. KEARNY,
Brigadier General U. S. army.

Lieut. Colonel J. C. FRÉMONT,
Mounted rifles, com., &c.

Question. Did you also address this one to him, and at the time of its date?

The witness, having examined the paper, said: That is my writing, and that is my note.

It was read, as follows:

CIUDAD DE LOS ANGELES,
January 13, 1847—12 o'çlock, noon.

DEAR FRÉMONT: We are in force in this place—sailors and marines. Join us *as soon as possible.*

We are ignorant of your movements, and know nothing of you further than your armistice of yesterday.
Yours,

S. W. KEARNY,
Brigadier General.

Lieutenant Colonel FRÉMONT.

Question. Did you also address this to him, and at the time it bears date?

Answer. That is my writing, and that is my note?

It was read, as follows:

PUEBLA DE LOS ANGELES,
January 12, 1847—Tuesday, 6, p. m.

DEAR FRÉMONT: I am here in possession of this place, with sailors and marines. We met and defeated the whole force of the Californians, the 8th and 9th. They have not now to exceed 300 men concentrated. Avoid charging them, and come to me at this place.

Acknowledge the hour of receipt of this, and when I may expect you. Regards to Russell.
Yours,

S. W. KEARNY,
Brigadier General.

Lieutenant Colonel FRÉMONT.

Question. Did you also write this one to him, and were the first two of the five words (*do not* charge the enemy) underscored by you, as they now appear?

Answer. That is my writing, and that is my note, and though I have no recollection of underscoring these words, I have no doubt but I did so.

The note was read, as follows:

CIUDAD DE LOS ANGELES,
January 13, 1847—2, *p. m.*

DEAR FREMONT: We have been here since the 10th. I have plenty of marines and sailors. We know nothing of you, except your armistice of yesterday, signed by yourself. I have sent several letters to you, and fear they have been intercepted, as I have received no answer. Come here *at once,* with your whole force, and join us; or if you cannot, let me know it, and I will go to you. The enemy can not *possibly* have near you more than 300, most probably not more than 150 men. Acknowlege the *hour* of receiving this, and send back the bearer *at once,* and write but little, as it may get into the hands of the enemy, instead of mine.

We defeated the enemy on the 8th and on the 9th, during our march. Since then they have been much scattered, and several, no doubt, gone home.

I repeat, we are ignorant of every thing relating to your command, except what we conjecture from your armistice, signed by yourself. Success to you!

Yours,

S. W. KEARNY,
Brigadier General.

Do not charge the enemy.

Lieutenant Colonel J. C. FRÉMONT,
Mounted rifles, &c.

This is what is shown by the cross-examination!

The note of the 13th, so far from being voluntary, that it was actually pulled and dragged out of me by General Kearny, by dint of repeated, urgent, solicitous, and affectionate notes, all requiring information of my position and movements, and all concealing the fact that Commodore Stockton was with him at Los Angeles, and his commander-in-chief. " Dear Frémont," four times repeated, and four applications for informations of him, show the character of the notes sent and the object of sending them; that they were familiar notes of information, such as are written in all services and between officers of all ranks, and which are used for no purpose in the world except for the sake of the information they contain. But, while the notes show this, the cross-examination was impotent to gain the same knowledge, either of their number, object, or contents. To the question, how many of these notes? he answer three, he " thinks." Not being in the habit of destroying originals, I produce him four. To the question, with what object? he replies that it was to give him (myself) information of

his (General Kearny's) being in possession of Los Angeles, &c.,
&c. The notes being read show that, in addition to that information to me, they desired information from me also. To the inquiry
whether either of these notes gave information that Governor
Stockton was at Los Angeles? the answer is, " I have no recollection of it."

The notes themselves being read, each one shows that the presence of Governor Stockton was not even hinted The same four
notes tell something else very incompatible with the testimony of
a previous day; they tell Lieutenant Colonel Frémont the force
gone against him may be 300 or 400 men. In the previous swearing are these words: " And a small party under Don Andres Pico—
*which party I have never understood to have exceeded fifty or sixty
men*—went to Cowenga, and entered into capitulation with Lieutenant Colonel Frémont."

From these notes, then, the great fact was brought out that the
communication, presented as a voluntary act, was extracted from
Lieutenant Colonel Frémont by General Kearny himself; that, instead of being a military reporting for duty, it was a reporting for
information only; that, instead of being an official communication,
it was a familiar private note, in answer to familiar, private, and apparently, most affectionate notes.

Upon their face they contradict the swearing of General Kearny,
and it is further contradicted by facts and circumstances drawn
from himself, or from authentic sources. The direct testimony at
the opening of the trial, says: " On the day of the *receipt* of that
letter, &c., &c., Lieutenant Colonel Frémont, at the head of a battalion of volunteers, entered the city of Los Angeles." Now, all
the testimony agrees (and such is the fact) that, on my entrance
into Los Angeles with my battalion, I went direct to the quarters
assigned it by Governor Stockton through Colonel Russell; then reported in person to Governor Stockton, and afterwards called on
General Kearny.

That note, so extracted from me, and so perverted, did not fetch
itself to Los Angeles. Some person must have brought it, and did;
and that person was Colonel W. H. Russell; and he has given an
account of his mission, and of his conversation with General
Kearny, wholly incompatible with the present imputed intention of
that note. On the 37th day of that trial that witness (Colonel
Russell) was introduced, and the second question put to him (the
first being only to show his rank in the California battalion) was
this: "Were you sent to Los Angeles, from the plains of Cowenga,
by Lieutenant Colonel Frémont? If so, at what time, and for what
purpose?" And the answer was: " I was sent by Lieutenant Colonel Frémont from the plains of Cowenga, about the 13th of January, 1847, for the purpose of ascertaining who was in chief command, and to make report of the capitulation made on that day to
whomsoever I should find in the chief command of Los Angeles."
The next question: " Will you state how you executed that mission?" Answer. " I went to the quarters of General Kearny first,
and inquired of him whether his arrival in the country had super-

seded Commodore Stockton, who, before, had been recognized as
chief commander. From General Kearny I learned that Commodore Stockton was still in chief command, and by him I was directed to make my report to the commodore." This was the testimony of Colonel R. on that point on his examination in chief. On
the cross-examination (39th day) the following questions were put
by the judge advocate:

" Do you recollect General Kearny told you expressly that he
was serving under Commodore Stockton, or did he say anything
more explicit than, as was said by you, that Commodore Stockton
was in chief command, and you would carry your report of the
capitulation to him?"

Answer. He told me distinctly that he was serving under Commodore Stockton, and had been doing so from San Diego.

Question by judge advocate. Was Captain Turner present at that
interview?

Answer. I am not positive, but believe he was.

On the fortieth day of the trial, the court took up the cross-examination; and, on this point, with the following results:

Question. When you were sent to Los Angeles, to ascertain who
was in command, had you any orders what to do if you found the
chief command claimed by both Commodore Stockton and General
Kearny?

Answer. My instructions from Lieutenant Colonel Frémont were
to proceed to Los Angeles, and carefully to inquire as to who was
in chief command, and to make my report accordingly. No such
contingency was contemplated, I think, by Lieutenant Colonel Frémont, when he dispatched me on that mission, as the command being claimed by them both.

Question by a member. Why did you first report to General
Kearny rather than to Commodore Stockton?

Answer. *I bore a letter* to General Kearny from Lieutenant Colonel Frémont, *in acknowledgment* of one received by Lieutenant
Colonel Frémont *from* General Kearny, and for the further reason
that we were totally ignorant of the object of General Kearny's
being in the country, and my orders from Lieutenant Colonel Frémont were that I should ascertain all about it.

Question by the court. State all the conversation which passed
between you and Lieutenant Colonel Frémont on the subject of
choice of commanders, after you returned and reported to him the
result of your visit to Los Angeles?

Answer. I met Lieutenant Colonel Frémont at the head of his
battalion, on the morning of the 14th of January, (as I stated in
my chief examination,) about five or six miles from Los Angeles,
and told him I had had much conversation with both General Kearny
and Commodore Stockton, touching their respective positions in
the country. That I was satisfied, from what had occurred, that
General Kearny was a better friend of his than Commodore Stockton; but, from General Kearny's own admissions, I regretted to
have to give it as my opinion that we should have to look to Commodore Stockton still as commander-in-chief. That I found Com-

modore Stockton exercising the functions of commander-in-chief, and submitted to implicitly, as I thought, by General Kearny. This was the substance of my communication to Lieutenant Colonel Frémont; and he, I think, with equal reluctance, at the time, came to the same conclusion.

This is the testimony of the witness who bore the note which is represented here, (and made the foundation of the prosecution against me,) as a military report, to put myself and my battalion under the orders of General Kearny, and actually so placing myself and battalion under his orders.

From all the testimony of Colonel Russell it seems clear that General Kearny undertook to gain me over to his side by flatteries, by offering the governorship of California, and by exciting resentment against Commodore Stockton; and failing by all of these means to accomplish that purpose, he tried the experiment of an order upon me, with the menace of "unquestionable ruin," which ruin, it would seem, he has been laboring ever since to effect.

That this construction was not put upon my note at the time it was received, seems clear from official cotemporaneous acts of General Kearny himself. Thus, on the 14th day of January, he writes to the War Department, from Los Angeles, that "this morning Lieutenant Colonel Frémont, of the regiment of mounted riflemen, *reached here* with 400 volunteers," &c., &c. No word of reporting to him, or placing myself and battalion under his command. Surely that was the time to have communicated to the War Department such an essential piece of intelligence. In the concluding part of the same letter he says: "On their arrival (troops from New York and New Mexico) I shall, agreeably to the instructions of the President of the United States, have the management of affairs in this country, and will endeavor to carry out his views in relation to it," words which necessarily mean that he did not consider himself entitled to command until the arrival of those troops, or else that he intended to avail himself of those troops to obtain command.

The letters of the 16th and 17th of January, from General Kearny to Commodore Stockton, are significant at this point. 1. They are totally silent on the subject of my having placed myself and the battalion under his command. 2. They show the whole contest, up to the 17th, to be between the two superiors. 3. The letter of the 17th shows a shifting of the grounds of his claim to command in California, basing it on *his* victories of the 8th and 9th, and the capitulation of the enemy to me on the 13th. The words of the letter, significant of this change, are: "As in consequence of the defeat of the enemy on the 8th and 9th instant by the troops under my command, and the capitulation entered into on the 13th instant, by Lieutenant Colonel Frémont with the leaders of the Californians, in which the people under arms and in the field agree to disperse and to remain quiet and peaceable, the country may now, for the first time, be considered as conquered and taken possession of by us, and as I am prepared to carry out the President's instructions to me, which you oppose, I must, for the purpose of preventing a collision between us, and possibly a civil war in consequence of it, remain silent for the present, leaving with you the great responsibility of doing that for which you have no authority, and preventing me from complying with the President's orders."

The value of this testimony, which would make me to have reported to General Kearny, and placed myself and battalion under his command, must now be understood. I undertake to say there is no authentic modern instance of a note, so innocent in itself and extracted from the writer under such circumstances, so totally perverted from its meaning, and made the foundation of such a prosecution as I have endured.

If men are to be capitally and infamously tried for such a note, no one is safe in writing.

I am charged here with a great military crime. I should have been guilty, not only of it, but of an inexcusable breach of faith, if I *had* made a report of myself and battalion to General Kearny, and so placed under the command of that officer the troops raised by the means and authority of Commodore Stockton, and by him entrusted to me.

I now close this defence to specification first, of charge two, for disobedience of lawful orders.

The second specification, under the head of mutiny, is for raising and attempting to raise troops, on the 25th of January, 1847; and. is in these words:

Specification 2. In this, that he, Lieutenant Colonel John C. Frémont, of the regiment of mounted riflemen, United States army, being in command of a battalion of volunteers organized in California, which were placed by the aforesaid orders of the Secretary of War, of June 18, 1846, under the command of Brigadier General Kearny, did issue an order to Captain J. K. Wilson, at Angeles, January 25, 1847, in the following words, to wit:

ANGELES, *January* 25, 1847.

SIR: You are hereby authorized and directed to raise a company of men to constitute the second company of artillery in the California service, and for that purpose are detached from your present command.

You will please report the number you may be able to enlist with as little delay as possible. You are authorized to enlist the men for three months, and to promise them as compensation $25 per month.

Respectfully,

J. C. FRÉMONT,

Lieut. Col. commanding California force in U. S. service.
To Captain S. K. WILSON,
        Light Artillery.

Thereby raising and attempting to raise troops, in violation and contempt of the lawful command aforesaid of his superior officer, Brigadier General Kearny, of date, January 16, 1847, and thereby acting openly in defiance of and in mutiny against the authority of his superior officer aforesaid, by raising and attempting to raise troops, and by proclaiming himself to be, and assuming to act as the commander of the United States forces in California.

The same act is specification No. 2, in charge, for disobedience of orders—the orders charged to have been disobeyed being the order of January 16, 1847, against the reorganization of the California battalion.

I will consider both of these specifications together, and arrange the matter of defence under three general heads: 1. That I was, at that time, governor and commander-in-chief in California. 2. That General Kearny had no right to command the battalion at that time. 3. That the order of the 16th of January, 1847, besides being illegal in itself, had no relation to any other change in the battalion than the one intended at the time it was given.

1. That I was then governor and commander-in-chief in California is proved by the testimony of Commodore Stockton, and the production of the original commission; and his right to bestow that commission upon me resulted from his own right to constitute himself governor. Both acts were done under the law of nations, and by virtue of the right of conquest; by virtue of the orders and instructions of the President of the United States, charging the naval commanders in the Pacific ocean, exclusively, with the conquest and civil government of California, until relieved under the instructions of the 5th of November, 1846 These instructions did not arrive until after the alleged commission of the act of mutiny and disobedience now under examination; and, when they did arrive, were never communicated to me at all.

I am advised by counsel, that the appointment of himself as governor, by Commodore Stockton, was a valid appointment under the law of nations; and that upon the same principle, his appointment of myself as his successor was equally valid; and that in neither case was the approval of the President of the United States necessary to the validity of the appointment, though each revocable by him at his pleasure; and therefore proper to be made known to him. This I am advised is the law; but being now prosecuted for mutiny and for disobedience of orders, in assuming and usurping the governorship of California, and it being the President alone who could order my trial in this case, (accused as I am by my commanding general,) it becomes material to show that this appointment, and the intention to make it long before it was made, was duly communicated to him, and, while not disapproved, was impliedly sanctioned and never revoked. For the fact of the communication of the intention to appoint me his successor, I refer to Governor Stockton's official despatch of August 28, 1846, from Los Angeles, sent in by Mr. Carson; and for the fact of his communicating the fact of his having appointed me, I refer to his official despatch of January 22, 1847, from San Diego. The first of these despatches arrived by the hands of Mr. Fitzpatrick early in November, 1846, and their general contents were noticed by the President in his annual message of December following, and in the reports of the Secretaries of War and Navy, and all in terms of general approval. Passages from this message and these reports, have been already quoted, and require no repetition; and from them and from the communication of Gov. Stockton's acts as governor, to Congress, at the same by the administration, I assume it to be proved that the intent to appoint me governor was known to the government in November, 1846, and not disapproved by it. The despatch of the 22d January, 1847, was received from Lieutenant Gray, of the navy, in the month of April following; and, so far I can learn, his act was not disavowed in appointing me governor. Even if it was, the disavowal could only operate from the time it would be known to me, which it never was.

The commission from Governor Stockton was in these words: To all whom it may concern, greeting: Having, by authority of the President and Congress of the United States of North America, and by right of conquest, taken possession of that portion of territory heretofore known as Upper and Lower California, and having declared the same to be a territory of the United States, under the name of the territory of California, and having established laws for the government of the same territory, I, Robert F. Stockton, governor and commander-in-chief of the same, do, in virtue of the authority in me vested, and in obedience to the aforementioned laws, appoint J. C. Frémont, esq., governor and commander-in-chief of the territory of California, until the President of the United States shall otherwise direct.

Given under my hand and seal on this sixteenth day of January,
[SEAL.] Anno Domini one thousand eight hundred and forty-seven, at the Ciudad de los Angeles.

R. F. STOCKTON, *Governor, &c.*

On this state of facts, I maintain that I was duly and legally governor and commander-in-chief in California at the time of the act done which is charged as mutiny and as disobedience of orders, in the two specifications, under the two charges referred to.

2. That General Kearny had no right to command the battalion at that time.

The facts and the arguments in support of this proposition are the same which have been already used in answer to specifications first in both the first charges, with the addition of arguments to show that General Kearny had no more right, at that time, to command me, in my governorship of California, than he had to command Governor Stockton while in the same office; and that, in fact this prosecution, in the specifications under consideration, is nothing but a continuation of the contest which began at San Diego with Governor Stockton, and which ought to have been finished with him.

General Kearny claimed authority to command the battalion, first, by virtue of his instructions, and next, by the assumption that I had put myself under his command. I presume this latter ground has been effectually disposed of heretofore. The first one has received some answers, and has others to receive. It has been argued from the beginning—from San Diego to this place, and from December, 1846, to this time—that the instructions to General Kearny were conditional: *"Should you conquer and take possession of New Mexico and California, or considerable places in either, you will establish temporary civil governments therein."* These instructions are evidently conditional, and only applicable to a country unconquered, and without a civil government. On the contrary, before General Kearney left New Mexico he had *"positive"* (using the word of his order) information that all this was already done, and immediately acted upon that *"positive"* intelligence, by diminishing the force with which he had set out. He met Mr. Christopher Carson, bearer of official despatches from Governor Stockton, and of private letters from myself, learned the true state of things from him, turned him back as his guide, reduced *"the army of the West,"* with which he was to conquer California, to an escort for his personal safety in travelling through the country, and went on, as the sequel showed, not to execute government orders, already executed by others, but (what is rarely seen in any military service) to take from others the fruits of their toils, hardships, dangers, and victories. He took the bearer of despatches, sent by the real conquerors, to guide him—show him the way—to the conquered country, before he arrived there, sent for aid from the conqueror, and received it in a handsome detachment, nearly equal to half his force, and after fighting an action with that aid, was four days upon a hill in a state of siege, from which he was relieved by 215 men sent out by Commodore Stockton to conduct him in to San Diego, where he was safe. This was not the conquest of California, nor was the plain of San Pasqual, or the hill of San Bernardo, the conquest of *"considerable places"* in that province, so as to give a right to govern it. The subsequent operations were under the command of Commodore Stockton; and it is because he should appear as conqueror, in order to get a right under his instructions to the governorship, that the claim has been set up by General Kearny to have commanded the troops to Los Angeles, and gained the victories of the 8th and 9th of January, and, thereupon, in conjunction with the capitulation of Cowenga, started a new claim to the governorship, on the assumption that he had just conquered the country. This new claim is started in the letter of 17th January, 1847, from General Kearny to Governor Stockton, and clearly shows his own views, at that time, of the conditional nature of his instructions. The letter has been quoted. Its effective and applicable words at this point are, "As, in consequence of the defeat of the enemy on the 8th and 9th instant, by the troops under *my* command, and the capitulation entered into on the 13th instant by Lieutenant Colonel Frémont with the leaders of the Californias, &c., the country may *now*, for the *first* time, be considered as *conquered*, and taken *possession* of by us; and as I am prepared to carry out the President's instructions to *me*, which *you* oppose," &c. &c

This extract shows General Kearny's own opinions of his instructions at the time he wrote that letter, and that they were conditional upon the fact of conquering and taking possession of the country. It shows his opinion; but, if the facts were not as he supposed, to wit : that *he* was commander-in-chief in the actions of the 8th and 9th, and that the country was then, for the *first* time, conquered and taken possession of. If these facts fail him, as they do, then his new claim to command in California fails also; and Commodore Stockton, as the commander-in-chief, on the 8th and 9th, becomes a second time the conqueror. That the instructions to General Kearny were intended to be conditional, may well be conceived, from the circumstances under which they were issued, as well as from their terms.

The navy had been charged, from the beginning of the war, (and before it in anticipation,) with the exclusive conquest, preservation, and government, in California. In giving a military officer orders to go into California to conquer, &c., &c., the contingency that everything required to be done might have been already done, was too obvious to be overloooked, and would naturally be provided for in making the military instructions conditional.

The naval instructions say: "Previous instructions have informed you of the intentions of this government, pending the war with Mexico, to take and hold possession of California. * * * The object of the United States is, under its right as a belligerent nation, to possess itself entirely of Upper California. * * * The object of the United States has reference to ultimate peace with Mexico; and if, at that peace, the basis of the *uti possidetis* shall be established, the government expects, *through your forces,* to be found in actual possession of Upper California. * * * This will bring with it the necessity of a civil administration. Such a government should be established under your protection. * * * For your further instruction, I enclose to you a copy of confidential instructions from the War Department to Brigadier General Kearny, who is ordered overland to California. You will also communicate your instructions to him, and inform him that they have the sanction of the President."

These instructions were not received by Commodore Stockton, but were anticipated by him, and this anticipation obtained for him the express approbation of the President. The despatch of the 5th November, from the Secretary of the Navy to the commodore, contained this clause in reference to his operations in California: "And it is highly gratifying that so much has been done in anticipation of the orders which have been transmitted."

This was written near four months after the transmission of the orders of July 12, and is a full ratification of all that had been done in anticipation of them.

But a higher view remains to be taken of the conditional character of the instructions to General Kearny, a view which involves their absolute repeal and nullity, unless understood conditionally; and I am advised by counsel that even that understanding of them cannot save them from the fate of total abrogation until subsequently revived by the instructions of the 5th of November, 1846. A few dates and facts establish this view. The instructions to General Kearny, on which he relies for his authority, are dated the 3d and 18th of June, 1846. Now, it so happens that, on the 12th day of July, in the month following, instructions of the most peremptory character were despatched to Commodore Sloat to conquer, hold, and govern California, and to let General Kearny know of these instructions and that they had the sanction of the President. Here are extracts from the orders to Commodore Sloat; and, although they did not reach his hands, nor those of his successor, Commodore Stockton, until after the country was conquered, yet, I am advised to say, their effect is the same upon this prosecution. This is not the case of an officer prosecuted for not obeying instructions, in which case, it must be shown they came to his hands; but, it is a prosecution against me, as successor to Governor Stockton, for doing what the instructions commanded. In this case, the anticipation of the orders is an additional merit in complying with them; and such is the case with the orders in question.

These instructions are near a month later than those to General Kearny, and not only specially confide the conquest, preservation, and civil government of California to the naval commanders, but require the naval forces to hold the country till the peace, and direct General Kearny to be informed accordingly; and further informed that all this instruction to the naval commanders had the sanction of the President.

I, with the battalion I commanded, was part of the naval force to which this duty was confided. (Commodore Stockton's testimony, 37th day.) This order remained in force until the instructions of the 5th of November arrived in California, which was not until the 13th day of February, 1847, AND WHICH WERE NEVER COMMUNICATED TO ME, AND OF WHICH I REMAINED TOTALLY IGNORANT TILL SINCE THE COMMENCEMENT OF THIS TRIAL. Neither General Kearny, Commodore Shubrick, or Commodore Biddle, communicated them to me, although I was then governor and commander-in-chief in California, under the commission of Commodore Stockton, to whom the instructions of the 5th of November were addressed; nor were they communicated to Commodore Stockton himself until more than a month after they had been received. They were evidently concealed from me, for a purpose not yet explained. By these instructions the military and civil duties, confided to the navy, were transferred to the commanding officer on land; another proof that the land officer did not then possess them, and that officer was specially named as General Kearny or Colonel Mason.

The instruction says: "The President has deemed it best, for the public interests, to invest the *military* officer commanding with the direction of the operations on *land*, and with the *administrative* functions of government over the people and territory occupied by us. You will *relinquish* to Colonel Mason, or to General Kearny, if the latter shall arrive before you have done so, the entire control over these matters, and 'turn over' to him all papers necessary to the performance of his duties. If officers of the navy are employed in the performance of civil or military duties, you will withdraw or continue them, at your discretion, taking care to put them to their appropriate duty in the squadron, if the army officer commanding does not wish their services on land."

Until this despatch was received by the naval commanders, those of July the 12th, abrogating those to General Kearny, remained in full force; and it was only by virtue of these orders, of the 5th of November, that he acquired the command, militarily or civilly, in California. And it is in evidence that Commodore Shubrick had received these instructions, of the 12th of July, at the time that General Kearny visited him at Monterey, and had consultations with him, and was sent by him in a ship to Yerba Buena, and did make known to General Kearny, at that time, that the naval commanders were charged with the whole conquest, defence and government of California; and that they (General Kearny and Commodore Shubrick) mutually agreed not to disturb the existing state of affairs until the government had further been heard from.

It is clear that the instructions to the different branches of the service were not properly consistent, and that concurrences might have arisen under them that would have necessarily produced a conflict of authority; but it is also clear that it was the intent of the government that the right and duty of the navy to conquer, preserve and govern California should remain complete and entire until the arrival of the instructions of November 5th, and that no concurrence did arise that, under the plain interpretation of the army instructions, could justify a collision. All this is fairly stated by the Secretary of the Navy, Mr. Mason, under the express orders of the President, in a despatch of the 14th of June, 1847, directed to the naval commanding officer on the California station.

That despatch contains these passages:

"The *misapprehension* between the commanding officers of the army and navy in California, which is mentioned in the letter of Commodore Shubrick, above referred to, must long since have been removed by *the very explicit instructions which have since been received in that country.* * * * * At the commencement of the war with Mexico the United States had no military force in California of any description whatever, *and the conquest of that country was from necessity, therefore, devolved exclusively upon the navy.* * * The conquest brought with it the necessity of a temporary civil government, and, on the 12th of July, 1846, Commodore Sloat was informed that *such a government should be established under his protection.* Contrary to all expectation this despatch did not reach California *until the arrival there of General Kearny.*"

On the 5th November, 1846, Commodore Stockton was informed that the President has deemed it best for the public interests to invest the military officer commanding *with the direction of the operations on land, and with the administrative functions over the people and territory occupied by us.* He was also directed to relinquish to Colonel Mason, or to General Kearny, if the latter should arrive before he had done so, the entire control over these matters, and to turn over to him all papers necessary to the per formance of his duties. *It was believed that even this despatch might anticipate the arrival in California of General Kearny.*

"SIMILAR instructions were communicated to Commodore Stockton under date of *January* 14, 1847, and were renewed to Shubrick under date of *May* 10, 1847. A copy of these last instructions, which on this subject are very full and distinct, are herewith enclosed."

All these despatches were too late. The mischief was all done before they arrived, and they leave the naval officers completely justified, and General Kearny wholly without excuse for attempting to make himself governor in California in a case not contemplated by his instructions, and in which he would have to commence with disorganizing an established civil government before he could begin to organize one. His whole conduct, from the day he met Mr. Carson, was contrary to the intent and meaning of his instructions. He was to conquer California: it was already conquered. He was to establish a civil government: it was already done. He was to lead an army to California: he took only a personal escort. He turned back two-thirds of his dragoons; he should have turned back the whole, and himself with them. He should not have applied to Governor Stockton to send him aid to San Pasqual, and to the hill of San Bernardo, if he intended to contend with him for supremacy after he got there. He should not have attempted to found a claim to the governorship on the victories of the 8th and 9th of January, after the refutation of his claim by Commodore Stockton at San Diego. He should not have pretended to have been commander-in-chief on the march to Los Angeles, in order to found upon it a claim to the governorship in right of conquest. He should not, even if the letter of his instructions had borne him out, (which they did not,) have attempted to take the fruits of conquest from those who had conquered the country before he came to it, and without whose helping hand he could not have got to it.

I have now made clear the right of Governor Stockton, under whom I held the governorship of California at the time of the act done, which is charged in the specifications under examination to be governor himself, upon his own assumption of the office, and afterwards to appoint me his successor; and that these governorships were valid under the law of nations, until disapproved by the President, or the incumbents in some way lawfully relieved or discharged. Having done this, I am instructed by counsel to resume my original position, as in the letter of the 17th January, in declaring that all this difficulty in California was a question between my two superiors, which should have been settled by the government between them, and not settled in my person by trying me for mutiny and disobedience against one of them—charges to which I might have been well exposed in disobeying the other. And I am further instructed by counsel to renew, and to repeat, in the most solemn manner, the PROTEST heretofore filed in the War Office by them, in my name, against the ILLEGALITY and INJUSTICE of thus trying me for the acts of Commodore Stockton and General

Kearny, or for declining the responsibility of settling their disputes of authority.

2. The second head of my defence, in answer to these two specifications is, that General Kearny at that time had no right to command the battalion to which the order of the 16th of January was
applicable. The argument heretofore made on this point, is referred to without repeating it, to show that this battalion was part of
the naval forces under Commodore Stockton, and that it was my
duty, as stated in my letter of the 17th of January, to continue to
receive orders from him in relation to it.

3. The third head of my defence to these two specifications, is,
that the order of the 16th of January, 1847, besides being illegal
in itself, had no relation to any other change in the battalion than
the changes intended at the time it was given. This illegality has
been heretofore shown, both as being issued without authority by
General Kearny, but also, because it was in positive violation of the
rights of the men, most of whom had engaged for the expedition
alone, and that being over, were entitled by their contract, and by
law, to their discharge. Many were accordingly discharged, and
others engaged, and all for the necessary service of the country,
and under my authority as governor and commander-in-chief. The
nullity of the order, as being founded on the familiar note of information *extracted from me* by General Kearny, and perverted into
a military official report, placing myself and the battalion under
his command, has heretofore been shown; and the facts and arguments adduced on that point are now referred to, without being
repeated, as applicable to this order of the 16th of January, at its
present reproduction, and as often as it shall be produced hereafter.
Illegal and null as it was for the purpose of its issue, it is clear
this order had no relation, at the time it issued, but anything but
the re-organization then intended, and which resulted from dis-
charges proper to be made, and promoting Captain Gillespie into
my place, I being that day commissioned as governor and commander-in-chief, to take effect on Commodore Stockton's departure.
The circumstances of the order, delivered in the night, limited it
to that immediate impending operation. The charges, as preferred
by General Kearny, so limited it, he having testified before this
court that he preferred but a single charge; (understood to be mutiny;) that these were not his charges; that they had been changed.
This can only mean that *he* has not extended the order of the 16th
of January to subsequent acts—to changes subsequently made in
the battalion. With this corresponds his testimony before this
court, (9th day, near the close,) that he left no orders for me
when he left Los Angeles. The question then put to General
Kearny on this point was, " *Did you leave any orders for Lieutenant Colonel Frémont, or take leave of him, or give notice to
him of your going away, or let him know where you were
going?*" The answer is, " I did not;" this answer applying
categorically and negatively to all four points of the interrogatory, and establishing the fact that General Kearny left Los
Angeles without leaving any orders for me, without taking leave
of me, without giving me notice that he was going away, and with-

out letting me know where he was going; and I am instructed by counsel to say, that it is carrying the doctrine of constructive criminality rather too far, (even if General Kearny had been my lawful and acknowledged commander,) to construe into the crimes of mutiny, and disobedience of orders, and of conduct prejudicial to good order and discipline, any act done after he was gone, when I had no possible guide but my own discretion. *Specification* 3, under the charge of mutiny, and also for disobedience of orders, is, for the order to Louis McLane, esq., of the United States navy, in his character of major of artillery in the California service, to make further enlistments, and to examine into the defences of the country. The answer to this specification is the same as heretofore, both with respect to General Kearny's authority, and my own rights and duties as governor and commander-in-chief in California, and the nullity and inapplicability of the order of January 16th, 1847. *Specification* 4, under the charge of mutiny, is based on the letter of February 7th, 1847, to Commodore Shubrick—a letter which is set out in full in the specification.

The offence imputed is twofold; first, mutiny, in assuming to be governor, and second, mutiny, in endeavoring to entice Commodore Shubrick to countenance and abet me.

The letter was written in answer to one from Commodore Shubrick to me, and I received another in reply; that in reply I will now introduce, to show that Commodore Shubrick did not look upon what I had written in the light in which the ingenuity of this prosecution has contrived to represent it.

U. S. Ship Independence,
Harbor of Monterey, February 13, 1847.

Sir: I have the honor to acknowledge the receipt of your letter of the 7th instant, and shall detain your courier as short a time as possible for my answer, and will also avail myself of your kind offer to forward despatches to the United States.

When I wrote to you on the 25th ultimo, I was not informed of the arrival of Brigadier General Kearny in California, and addressed you as the senior officer of the army in the terrritory; on the 28th, however, having understood that the general was at Los Angeles, I addressed a similar letter to him.

On the 8th instant, General Kearny arrived in this harbor, in the sloop-of-war Cyane, and left by the same conveyance on the 11th for San Francisco. While the general was here, we consulted fully, as enjoined on me by my instructions, and on him by his, on the measures necessary to be taken by us for the security of the territory of California.

I am looking daily for the arrival of Commodore Stockton in this harbor, when I shall, of course, receive from him a full account of the measures taken by him while in command of the squadron.

It is to be hoped that the pleasure of the President of the United States on the subject of the organization of a civil government, and of the measures taken by Commodore Stockton and yourself, may be soon known, and it will give me pleasure at all times to co-operate with the civil government, as well as with the military commander-in-chief, for the peace and security of the territory.

I regret to say that, not anticipating any unusual draft on them, the funds brought by me are barely sufficient, with the most economical expenditure, to meet the wants of the squadron.

I am, very respectfully, sir, your most obedient servant.

W. BRANFORD SHUBRICK,
Commander-in-chief U. S. naval forces.

Lieutenant Colonel FREMONT, &c., &c., &c.

The plain deductions of this letter are, that Commodore Shubrick and General Kearny, having met at Monterey, had consulted together, compared their several instructions, agreed upon their respective powers, and arranged the course of action they judged proper. All this appears in the third paragraph. What the course of action agreed upon was, is to be drawn from the fifth paragraph; and the necessary inference is that it had been found either not competent or not proper to disturb the existing state of affairs, before "the pleasure of the President" should be further ascertained. The letter does not bear any further interpretation; so that, whatever the tenure of my office as governor may have been previously, this amounts, in the legal phrase, to *quieting me in possession*, by common consent, till such time as the government at home should direct differently or definitively. This is the plain import of the letter, and if anything contrary to it was intended I never heard of it, nor was anything contrary done, till more than two weeks after the contingency reserved (farther instructions from the government) had happened. That I did not misconstrue this letter, as I received it then, and as circumstances justified my construction of it, is rendered certain by the additional light which I have upon it now. This additional light is found in the despatch of Commodore Shubrick to the government, of even date with the above letter to me. In this despatch is the following :

SIR : Since my letters of the 26th, 27th, and 28th ultimo, no important change, so far as I can learn, has taken place in the territory. The people seem to be settling down into quiet acquiescence *in the change of government*. Those best acquainted with their temper and disposition do not apprehend further disturbance of the peace of the country.

General Kearny arrived here on the 8th, in the sloop-of-war Cyane; and, after the adoption of such measures as *we* thought necessary here, *I sent him to San Francisco*, in the Cyane, to which place I should have accompanied him, but that I am looking daily for the arrival of Commodore Stockton from San Diego, and it is important that I should receive his reports before I go further.

You will have learned ere this that an unfortunate difference has taken place between Commodore Stockton and General Kearny, and between the General and Colonel Frémont, growing out of the *appointment* of Colonel Frémont as civil governor of California by the Commodore, and the refusal of the Colonel to acknowledge the authority of the general.

I have, as enjoined on me by my instructions, exchanged opinions with General Kearny, and shall *continue* to *concert* with him *such measures as may seem best* for keeping quiet possession of California.

"With regard to the civil government of territory, *authority* for the establishment of which is contained in your instructions to Commodore Sloat of 12th July last, which I received by the Lexington, measures have been, in my opinion, *prematurely taken* by Commodore Stockton, and *an appointment of governor made*, of a gentleman who, I am led to believe, is not acceptable to the people of California; *but,* as the intention to make the appointment was, I understand, communicated to the President as early as August last, and information as to his wishes may be soon expected, *I have determined to await such information,* and confine myself, for the present. to arrangements for *the quiet possession of the territory,* and for the blockade of the coast of Mexico."

Now, this is conclusive of Commodore Shubrick's intentions and opinions, his views of his authority, and of the manner he determined to exercise it. It is conclusive, that though he was pleased to impute *precipitancy* to the action of Commodore Stockton, and had been "led to believe" that the appointment made by him was not of the right sort of a person, yet that he did not question its legality, nor the authority for making it. It is also conclusive, that whatever doubts he had as to the *propriety* of the appointment made by Commodore Stockton, he did not feel authorized, even under the powers which he held, to disturb it; or at least that he declined to do so, not to disturb, was to continue; "*to await*" information from the government, concerning the appointment, was to recognize the appointment in the meantime, and, in effect, (if that had been necessary,) to confirm it.

Such was the action of Commodore Shubrick after a comparison of his instructions with those of General Kearny, after consultation with that officer; and such was the effect of that action upon my appointment.

I now proceed to show that in determining on this course of action, Commodore Shubrick had the agreement and acquiescence of General Kearny. This appears in the official despatch of the latter, of 15th March, which after relating his meeting with Commodore Shubrick at Monterey, on the 8th of February, proceeds as follows:

"On my showing to Commodore Shubrick my instructions from the War Department of June 3d and 18th, 1846, he was at once prepared to pay *all proper respect* to them; and, being at that time the commander-in-chief of the naval forces on this station, he acknowledged me as *the head and commander of the troops* in California, which Commodore Stockton and Lieutenant Colonel Frémont had hitherto refused. He then showed me the instructions to Commodore Sloat, of July 12th, from the Navy Department, received by the Lexington, at Valparaiso, on the 2d December, and which he had brought with him from there; and, as they contained *directions for Commodore Sloat to take* charge of the civil *affairs in California*, I immediately told Commodore Shubrick that *I cheerfully acquiesced*, and was ready to afford him any assistance in my power. We *agreed* upon our separate *duties;* and *I* then went to the bay of San Francisco, taking with me Lieutenant Halleck, of the engineers, besides Captain Turner and Lieutenant Warner, when was made a reconnoissance of the bay, with a view to the selection of sites for fortifications, for the protection of shipping in the harbor and security of the land forces."

This establishes, that General Kearny acknowledged the *authority* of Commodore Shubrick over the civil affairs of the territory, and *acquiesced* in the determination of that officer not to disturb Commodore Stockton's appointment until further information from the government; and that the two *agreed* upon their separate duties in the premises. This letter also establishes another important circumstance, viz: the true weight and value attached by General Kearny himself to his instructions. "*On showing to Commodore Shubrick my instructions, he was at once prepared to pay all proper respect to them, and being at that time commander-in-chief of the naval forces, he acknowledged me* AS THE HEAD AND COMMANDER OF THE TROOPS," &c. The latter part of the sentence rests entirely upon General Kearny; the letter of Commodore Shubrick containing nothing of the sort, and the phrase used in it toward General K., viz: "*I sent him* in the Cyane," &c., would seem to imply the contrary. But grant General Kearny's position, and it results that in his own estimation, a "*proper respect*" to his instructions only required him to be acknowledged as "the head and commander *of the troops*," and that he did not consider himself entitled under them to interfere with the civil affairs. General Kearny adds, after stating that "he acknowledged me as the head and commander of the troops," the words: "*which Commodore Stockton and Lieutenant Colonel Frémont had hitherto refused.*" Now, what is the testimony to this point? Commodore Stockton testifies: "After General Kearny arrived, and in my quarters and in presence of two of my military family, *I offered* to make him *commander-in-chief over all of us.* He said no; that the *force was mine.*"

The agreement as to their respective powers, between Commodore Shubrick and General Kearny, and the determination of the former, with the acquiescence of the latter, that the state of affairs then existing should await further information from home, was, no doubt, the legal and proper course, and, had it been continued in, every thing would have proceeded harmoniously. It was continued in, so far as appears, until after the receipt of the instructions, which they had determined to await. The wrong consisted in not obeying these instructions. I put out of view, entirely, in this connection, my right to be lawfully and regularly *relieved*, and plant myself on the express letter of the instructions of the 5th November. These are mandatory to the naval commanders to *relinquish* the control of the civil administration," and to "*turn over*" the papers connected with it. The only way in which they could be *obeyed* was, for that commander to inform me of the order he had received, and take from my hands the office, and the archives connected with it, that he might, as directed, "relinquish" and "turn them over" to General Kearny. For some purpose yet unexplained—unless its object is seen in this prosecution—they were not obeyed. I was kept in ignorance of the wishes of the government, and General Kearny undertook by wrongful orders to get possession from me of what he could only lawfully receive from Commodore Shubrick.

And on this I leave the defence of this act, both where it is charged as mutiny, and where as an offence against discipline.

Specification 5, under the charge of mutiny, is based upon the letter to Mr. Willard Hall, and charged a design to persuade him (Mr. Hall) to aid me in my mutiny against General Kearny. The first answer of Mr. Hall to the first question put to him (31st day) entirely negatived that charge. On the day after Mr. Hall came into court, and desired to explain his testimony. The explanation went to show that, by the expression in the letter, "cannot suffer myself to be interfered with by any other," that General Kearny was meant. The answer to the next question, however, was, that General Kearny was not there at the time, and that Mr. Hall did not know where he was, and so negatived the "explanation." Moreover, as I was not in mutiny myself, I could not have been inciting others to mutiny. The letter itself is all the defence which I make to this specification.

Specification 6, under the charge of mutiny, is based on the purchase of an island near the mouth of the San Francisco bay, for the United States, taking the title to the United States, and promising the payment of $5,000.

My answer appears upon the face of the papers, that it was done as governor, and for the benefit of the United States; a fact which, if I understand the prosecution, and the decision of the court, refusing to receive any evidence to the point, is admitted.

Specification 7, under the charge of mutiny, and specification 4, under the charge of disobedience of orders, are for the same act or acts, and will be considered together. Not mustering the men of the California battalion for payment is one of the points of the charge: the evidence shows that the men, without exception, refused to be mustered. The officers, whose pay would not be materially affected, were willing to be mustered. Not marching the battalion to Yerba Buena, and ordering it to remain at San Gabriel, and ordering Captain Owens not to deliver up the cannon of the battalion, are the essential points of the rest of the specification, with the aggravation of not obeying the orders brought by Captain Turner, after promising to do so, and disregarding the proclamation of General Kearny and Commodore Shubrick.

The order by Captain Turner was delivered on the 11th of March: on the 15th I gave my orders to Captain Owens, based upon my intended visit to Monterey, and on their face intended to keep the troops in a condition to sustain themselves, or to repel actual invasion.

No notice of the President's instructions of the 5th of November was sent to me, nor did the joint proclamation, or any other paper that I ever saw, refer to them. I was then governor and commander-in-chief in California, and had a right to be regularly relieved, if any instructions had terminated my power, and no one had a right to depose me by force and violence.

The statement which I shall now make, is based upon the evidence given by different witnesses, who testified to the points I shall mention, of whom Major Gillespie, Colonel Russell, Lieutenant Minor, of the navy, Captain Cooke, Lieutenant Loker, were the principal.

After the capitulation of Cowenga, the country immediately subsided into profound tranquillity, and security of life, person, and property became as complete as in any part of the United States. Travelling or at home, single or in company, armed or defenceless, all were safe. Harmony and good will prevailed, and no trace of the suppressed insurrection, or of resentment for what was passed, was anywhere seen. I lived alone, after a short time, in the ancient capital of the governors general of Los Angeles, without guards or military protection; the battalion having been sent off nine miles to the mission of San Gabriel. I lived in the midst of the people in their ancient capital, administering the government, as a governor lives in the capital of any of our States.

Suddenly, and in the beginning of the month of March, all this was changed. "Men, armed to the teeth, were galloping about the country." Groups of armed men were constantly seen. The whole population was in commotion, and every thing verged towards violence and bloodshed. For what cause? The approach of the Mormons, the proclamations incompatible with the capitulation of Cowenga, the prospect that I was to be deposed by violence, the anticipated non-payment of government liabilities, and the general insecurity which such events inspired. Such was the cause. I determined to go to Monterey to lay the state of things before General Kearny, and gave all the orders necessary to preserve tranquillity while I was gone. I then made that extraordinary ride of which testimony has been given. General Kearny is the only witness before the court, of what took place at Monterey. He seems to know but of two events in my interview with him: that I insulted him, and offered to resign my commission. It can hardly be supposed that I rode 400 miles to Monterey, in less than four days, and back in the same time, for such purposes; yet these are the only things done in that visit, as established by the testimony before the court. To the question, whether I did not mention the government liabilities, the answer was that he did not recollect it, but would have refused if the application had been made. That I was interrogated in presence of a witness, and admonished of the importance of my answers, is proved by himself. It was at that time already resolved, as has since appeared, to arrest and try me for mutiny, so that something of more importance to me still seemed to be impending. A little time was allowed for me to consider. No communication was made to me of the instructions of November 5th. Supposing that I was to be deposed by force and violence,

I submitted, in order to prevent that consequence, and the injurious results to the public service that would follow such a contest, and returned to Los Angeles.

These are the meagre facts which the evidence discloses, and on which I rely for my defence to all the allegations of this specification.

But I think proper to add, that the orders embraced in the specification, though they were all complied with, as far as the state of the country would allow, were, with a single exception—that of re-mustering the battalion—illegal. The instructions of the 5th of November direct that the *naval commander* shall "relinquish" to General Kearny, or Colonel Mason, the control of the civil administration, and "turn over" all papers connected with it. Simple obedience to the instructions themselves, therefore, made their communication to me, and my consequent regular and lawful relief from the governorship, necessary, and all orders of General Kearny, or any other person, inconsistent with that, were unlawful, while the one concerning the archives were contrary to the express letter of the instructions.

Specification 8, under the charge of mutiny, and 5, under that of disobedience of orders, are based on the same act, and receive the same answer with the last mentioned specification.

Specification 9, of mutiny, is based upon the act of ordering the collector at San Pedro, on the 21st of March, to receive government paper in discharge of public dues, &c.; and the answer to it is that the order, in writing, of that day was to cover a verbal order previously given, the officer wishing the written order for his justification; that neither Commodore Shubrick nor any other person gave me any notice of the President's instructions of November 5, 1846, and that I had not then, nor until a week afterwards at Monterey, yielded to what I believed to be a design to depose me, by force and violence, from the governorship of California.

Specification 10, of the charge mutiny, and 6 of disobedience of orders, all refer to acts done when I was governor and commander-in-chief in California, and are in alleged violation of the order of January 16, 1847. I refer to my previous answers to show that I was governor at that time, and to show the nullity and inapplicability of the orders of January 16, 1847.

Specification 11, of mutiny, and 7 of disobedience of orders, are based on the same act; that of not obeying the order to repair to Monterey, given to me on the 26th and 28th days of March. This failure to obey that order is sufficiently accounted for in the testimony, which shows the danger of travelling at that time; and there was nothing on its face, or in the testimony in relation to it, which showed it to be urgent, or that the public service required risks of person or life in attempting to comply with it. The words, "I desire to see you in this place," &c., &c., as used in the order, seems not to come within the meaning of an order to be obeyed at all hazards; and the first clause of the order, written on the 28th day of March, directing me to consider all instructions coming from him (Colonel Mason) as if they had come from General

Kearny himself, seemed to encourage the same idea of the want of urgency in the desire to see me at Monterey.

The following is the clause of that order:

> " HEAD-QUARTERS, 10TH MILITARY DEPARTMENT,
> " *Monterey, California, March* 28, 1847.

"SIR: This will be handed to you by Colonel Mason, 1st dragoons, who goes to the southern district, clothed by me with full authority to give such orders and instructions upon all matters, both civil and military, in that section of country, as he may deem proper and necessary. Any instructions he may give to you will be considered as coming from myself."

The execution of his own order, and of consequent additional orders given to me by Colonel Mason, occupied so much time that it became impossible to reach Monterey within the period fixed by him, and delayed my departure until it was further interfered with by the condition of the country.

As a further answer to all the orders given to me on and after the 1st of March, 1847, I am advised by counsel to say that they are in violation of the orders of General Scott, of November 3, 1846, to General Kearny:

"It is known that Lieutenant Colonel Frémont, of the United States rifle regiment, was, in July last, with a party of men, in the service of the United States topographical engineers, in the neighborhood of San Francisco, or Monterey bay, engaged in joint operations against Mexico with the United States squadron on that coast. Should you find him there, it is desired that you do not detain him against his wishes a moment longer than the necessities of the service may require."

This order was carried out by Colonel Mason, and came to the hands of General Kearny before any orders issued by him with respect to me on the 1st March, on which day he addressed an official letter to me, reciting that he had the directions of the general-in-chief not to detain me, against my wishes, a moment longer than the necessities of the service required, and leaving me at *"liberty"* to leave the country, after I had complied with the instructions in the letter and with the orders referred to. I rely upon the concluding paragraph of this official letter to prove that General Kearny, *at that time,* could not have considered criminal, and worthy of the prosecution now carried on, any act of mine previous to the writing of that letter.

The following is the letter:

> HEAD-QUARTERS, 10th MILITARY DEPARTMENT,
> *Monterey, U. C, March* 1, 1847.

SIR: By department orders No. 2 of this date, which will be handed to you by Captain Turner, 1st dragoons, A. A. A. G. for my command, you will see that certain duties are there required of you as commander of the battalion of California volunteers.

In addition to the duties above referred to, I have now to direct that you will bring with you, and with as little delay as possible, all the archives and public documents and papers which may be subject to your control, and which appertain to the government of California, that I may receive them from your hands at this place, the capital of the territory. I have directions from the general-in-chief not to detain you in this country against your wishes a moment longer than the necessities of the service may require, and you will be at liberty to leave here after you have complied with these instructions, and those in the " orders" referred to.

Very respectfully, your obedient servant,
S. W. KEARNY,
Brigadier General and Governor· of California.

To Lieut. Col. J. C. FREMONT,
Regiment of Mounted Riflemen, commanding
Battalion of California vols., Ciudad de Los Angeles.

Having now answered all the specifications under the charges of mutiny and disobedience of orders, I have to say that five of the same acts, on which these specifications are founded, are also laid under the charge of conduct prejudicial to good order and dis cipline. I am advised by counsel that offences enumerated in the rules and articles of war cannot be prosecuted among the non-enumerated offences of the 99th article of war, (Hough, page 630,) but I take no exception to any illegality or irregularity, if such there be in the charges, and make the same answer to these five specifications, under the charge under which they are last found, as was made under the two preceding charges.

I have deemed it my duty to reply to each specification, because it is the duty of the court to find upon each, and because it is right to show my conduct consistent and proper at all points. I obeyed orders, after the first of March, to avoid bloodshed and violence. Not relieved, as governor, and deeming them illegal, I obeyed. Now, being put upon my trial according to law, I claim the benefit of law, and to be considered governor until I was relieved. In themselves, most of the specifications, after the first leading ones, are either cumulative or insignificant in the presence of the grave ones which precede them, and which would hardly of themselves have been considered worthy of such a prosecution, and while replying separately to each of these minor and cumulative accusations, I refer to the main leading agreement at the opening of the charges of mutiny, in usurping the office of governor, and disobedience to the order of January 16, 1847, as presenting the general and sustained defence which the gravity of the charges required.

I now come to a different part of my defence—but of which I fairly gave notice to the court, and through it to the prosecution at an early stage of this trial—that of impeaching *the motives* and *the credit* of the prosecuting witness. To do this is both legal and fair, where there is just ground for it; and that is abundantly the case in this instance. A prosecutor should have none but public motives; his testimony should be scrupulously fair towards the accused. If he contradicts other witnesses, which General Kearny has so much done, it becomes necessary to weigh their respective credit; and in doing this I have a right, and moreover it is my duty to myself and to others, to produce instances of erroneous testimony he may have exhibited, either from defect of memory or from evil extent; and for that purpose to contrast his own testimony with itself where it varies, or with that of other witnesses where they contradict him. To this part of my defence I now proceed, and speak first of the acts which go to the motives of the prosecutor:

1. Giving me no notice of his intended arrest. He admits that this arrest was resolved upon in January, 1847, and that I had no notice of it until I was actually arrested on the frontiers in the latter part of August following. Others were informed of it, but not myself, the one above all others the most interested to know. I was brought across the continent in a state of virtual imprisonment, to be tried for a multitude of offences, charged to have been committed on the shores of the Pacific, without the warning which would enable me to bring evidence to meet a single charge; while my accuser, and general, brought with him all that he deemed necessary either of written evidence or of witnesses to insure my conviction. It is impossible, in my opinion, to reconcile this conduct with any fair and honorable motive. It laid me under the necessity of choosing between a trial, brought on me by surprise, and almost without the means of defence, or of suffering ruinous charges, enforced by newspaper publications, to hang over my head. The latter, according to Major Cooke's testimony, seems to have been General Kearny's calculations; and as I deemed the effect of such impending charges and publications would be worse than any conviction, I was forced into a trial, unprepared for it, to take the chance of any testimony that might be found.

2. Denying me the privilege of going to Mexico to join my regiment when I had made preparation of 60 men and 120 horses to do so, and had not the least doubt of reaching General Taylor's camp, and thence going to the regiment, expected (according to information received from Washington) to be on the road from Vera Cruz to Mexico. I expected to reach it in July, which would have been in time for the great operations impending, and since so grandly executed.

The refusal to let me go did me many injuries which a soldier can feel; and, besides, left me involved in debts for my preparations, and was, further, in violation of General Scott's directions, not to detain me in the country, against my wishes, a moment longer than the necessities of the service required; and, also, in violation of his own official letter to me of March 1, 1847, leaving me at liberty to quit the country when I pleased, after complying with a few small orders, not amounting to "*necessities*" of the service, but which were complied with.

3. Taking away from me the command of my topographical party; taking away the scientific instruments which I had so long used;

leaving behind my geological and botanical specimens of near two years collection; leaving behind the artist of the expedition (Mr. Kern,) with his sketches and drawings; leaving behind my assistant, (Mr. King;) he and Mr. Kern both standing in a relation to be material witnesses to me in any inquiry into my conduct; denying me the privilege of returning to the United States by any new route which would enable me to correct previous explorations, or ,add to geographical and scientific knowledge; making me follow on his trail in the rear of his Mormon escort. All this after he had, in conformity to General Scott's instructions, previously left me at " *liberty*" to quit California when I pleased, after executing the few small orders above referred to.

4. Interfering with Commodore Biddle to detain Major Gillespie in California, an officer known to have been intimately associated with me in California, and who, arriving here a fortnight after this trial had commenced, has shown himself to be a material witness for me. The fact of interference is admitted; the circumstances attending it are most suspicious; the reasons given for it most inadequate, and, besides, contradicted by the fact that Major Gillespie was soon after allowed " *to go about the country,*" and did not do the mischief which had been apprehended from his being at large. The detention of Major Gillespie was the detention of Commodore Stockton and his party; so that this interference delayed the arrival not only of Major Gillespie, but of Commodore Stockton, Captain Henley, and other material witnesses who came with him.

5. Not communicating to me his knowledge of the instructions of the 5th of November and 12th of July, 1846, when a knowledge of those instructions were so necessary for the safe guidance of my conduct. The excuse, in relation to that of the 5th of November, that he was not in the habit of communicating instructions to juniors, is invalidated by the fact of the previous communication of those of June, 1846, when I was equally junior militarily, and before I had become governor and commander-in-chief.

6. Making injurious representations to the War Department against me and against the battalion under my command, without giving me any knowledge of such representations, and which I have only found out in the progress of this trial, in searching for testimony in the department.

7. My reception at Monterey on March 26th, for the nature of which I *now* refer entirely to General Kearny's testimony. I made a most extraordinary ride to give information to prevent an insurrection. I asked an interview on business, and had it granted, and found Colonel Mason with him. The only thing, it would seem, that I came for in that interview, was to insult General Kearny and to offer my resignation; and he does not even know what I went for. Certainly the public service, to say nothing of myself as an officer, required a different kind of reception from the one I received.

8. The order given to Colonel Mason on the 28th of March, (after what had happened in his presence on the 26th,) to proceed to Los Angeles, where I was with the power and authority over

me, of which I was officially advised by letter of that date. I now only mention the order, in connexion with my reception at Monterey, as represented by General Kearny, and add nothing to it. I do not go beyond the evidence.

9. The fact of not *relieving* me in some legal form from the duties of governor of California, after the President's instructions of the 5th of November arrived, and concealing from me all knowledge of those instructions while putting the interrogatories, the answers to which he has sworn he warned me might be of so much importance.

10. The march of the Mormons upon Los Angeles, when I was expected to be there, and would have been, except for the urgent business which carried me to Monterey—the "*crushing*" that might have taken place, if a "*revolt*" of the people had not been apprehended—and all the circumstances of that movement I leave where the evidence placed it.

11. The conduct of Colonel Mason to me at Los Angeles, (so far as the evidence discloses it,) is by me referred to the full authority over me, with which he was clothed by General Kearny, and of which I was notified in this clause of General Kearny's official letter to me:

HEAD-QUARTERS, 10TH MILITARY DEPARTMENT,
Monterey, California, March 28, 1847.

SIR: This will be handed to you by Colonel Mason, 1st dragoons, who goes to the southern district, clothed by me with full authority to give such orders and instructions in that section of the country as he may deem proper and necessary. Any instructions he may give to you will be considered as coming from myself.

12. The exhibition of myself and the citizens of my topographical party at Monterey, on the 30th May—the circumstances of the march from that place to Fort Leavenworth, and the manner of the arrest there—I leave in like manner where the evidence placed it; giving it as my opinion, in the twelve instances enumerated, besides in many others to be seen in the testimony, that no presumption of acting from a sense of public duty can outweigh the facts and appearances to the contrary, and that all these twelve instances, and others to be seen in the testimony, go to impeach his motives in this prosecution.

I now proceed to the last point of my defence—the impeachment of the credit of General Kearny as a witness before this court. The law gives me the right to do so. Morality condemns the exercise of that right, unless sternly justified by credible evidence. I feel so justified. I also feel that this case, above all others, admits of the exercise of all the rights against this witness which the law and the evidence allow to the accused.

It is a case in which this witness comprises, in his own person, the character of accuser, prosecutor, leading witness, commanding general, arresting officer—and bringing me, by virtue of his superior rank, three thousand miles across the continent, to be tried without warning upon unknown charges, or to be ruined by infamous accusations hanging over me and urged in the newspapers. This is the case, and I claim in it the right of impeaching the credit of the witness, both upon his own swearing and that of others.

Referring then to the points on which the credit of the witness is already impeached in other parts of the defence, I will first call attention, under this head, to what relates to the expedition of December and January, 1846 and 1847, from San Diego to Los Angeles, and especially with reference to the testimony concerning *the command of the troops* in that expedition. This is a matter on which General Kearny lays great stress throughout, bottoming, at one time, his claim to chief authority in the province, mainly on the results of that expedition, and his alleged command of it. I shall, consequently, examine and test what he says in relation to it, with some minuteness.

1. And first, as to the point, *at whose instance was the expedition raised and marched?* There is great discrepancy here. In General Kearny's letter of 17th January, to the department he says:

"I have to state that *the march of the troops from San Diego to this place was reluctantly consented to by Commodore Stockton, on my urgent advice* that he should not leave Lieutenant Colonel Frémont unsupported to fight a battle on which the fate of California might, for a long time, depend; *the correspondence to prove which is now with my papers at San Diego*," &c., &c.

In his cross-examination on the fourth day of the trial, he says:

"In the latter end of December, an expedition was organized at San Diego to march to Los Angeles, to assist Lieutenant Colonel Frémont; *and it was organized, in consequence, as I believe, of this paper, which is a copy of a letter from me to Commodore Stockton,*" (referring to his letter of December 22, hereafter quoted.)

Let us contrast this first positive assertion, and second more reserved declaration of belief, with facts, with other testimony, and finally with the "proof" which General Kearny tenders.

Commodore Stockton testifies:

"After General Kearny arrived, (on the 12th December,) and in my quarters, and in presence of two of my military family, I offered to make him commander-in-chief over all of us, and I offered *to go* as his aid-de-camp. He said no; that the force was mine; and he *would go* as my aid-de-camp, or accompany me."

Now, "*to go*" where? to "*accompany*" where?

This, if not sufficiently explicit, is made entirely so by the certificate of Messrs. Spieden and Mosely, of the navy, offered by Commodore Stockton, in corroboration, under the sanction of his oath, and, of course, forming a proper interpretation of his words. This certificate is as follows:

We, the undersigned, were present at a conversation held between Commodore Stockton and General Kearny, at San Diego, shortly after the arrival of the general, in which conversation the Commodore offered to give General Kearny the " command-in-chief" *of the forces he was preparing to march with to the Ciudad de los Angeles, and to act as aid-de-camp. This offer the general declined,* but *said he would be most happy to go with the commodore as his aid-de-camp,* and assist him with his head and hand.

> WILLIAM SPIEDEN, *U. S. N.*
> SAMUEL MOSELEY, *U. S. N.*

San Diego, *February* 5, 1847.

Again, Commodore Stockton testifies that, at a subsequent interview, a few days afterwards, he made to General Kearny "the same offer, in pretty much the same language, and received pretty much the same answer."

It is certain, then, that General Kearny's letter of the 22d December, was *not* the inducing cause of the expedition, as "*believed,*" in General Kearny's testimony, and that "the march of the troops" was *not* a matter that Commodore Stockton "reluctantly assented to," as *asserted* in General Kearny's official letter; and is also certain that General Kearny could not have supposed either to be the case, for he had been informed ten days before of the design to send the expedition; that it was " preparing to march;" and he had been twice offered, and had twice declined, the command of it.

Commodore Stockton further testifies:

I now set to work to make the best preparations I could to commence our march for the Ciudad de los Angeles.

During this time an expedition that had been sent to the south for horses returned, and brought with it a number of horses and cattle. Captain Turner was allowed to take his pick of the horses for the dragoons. After he had done so he wrote to me this note:

San Diego, *December* 23, 1846.

Commodore: In compliance with your verbal instruction to examine and report upon the condition of the public horses turned over to me for the use of C company, 1st dragoons, I have the honor to state that, in my opinion, not one of the horses referred to is fit for dragoon service, being too poor and weak for any such purpose; also, that the company of dragoons, under my command, can do much better service on foot than if mounted on those horses.

I am, sir, with high respect, your obedient servant,

> H. S. TURNER,
> *Captain 1st dragoons, commanding company C.*

Commodore R. F. Stockton,
United States Navy, commanding, &c.

The exact day of the return of this expedition for horses and cattle does not appear. But, as there had been time for Captain

Turner to be allowed to "take his pick" from the horses, examine them, and make a report upon them by the 23d of December, it is nearly certain that it must have returned by the 22d; and hence it would seem that General Kearny's letter, sent to Commodore Stockton in the night of the last mentioned day, in which he "recommends" the expedition, and in which he claims the whole merit of the march, and to have induced Commodore Stockton reluctantly to consent to it, was not written till he had not only been repeatedly informed that the expedition was in preparation, and he had been twice offered the command of it, but not till the horses and cattle for its use had actually arrived, and probably a part of them turned over to his own company of dragoons. This, indeed, is rendered nearly certain by the fact that the preparations for the expedition were so far advanced that Commodore Stockton's general orders for the march were issued on the day next following General Kearny's letter, which he pretends, under oath, to have been the inducing cause of the expedition.

But General Kearny is entitled to the benefit of the "*proof*" which he vouches to the department in this passage of his letter:

" I have to state that the march of the troops from San Diego to this place was reluctantly consented to by Commodore Stockton, on my urgent advice that he should not leave Colonel Frémont unsupported to fight a battle on which the fate of California might for a long time depend; *the correspondence to prove which is now with my papers at San Diego*, and a copy of which will be furnished to you on my return to that place."

This "correspondence," as he certifies it on the twelfth day of the trial, consists of three letters and Commodore Stockton's general orders for the march. I will set out all of them:

SAN DIEGO, December 22, 1846.

DEAR COMMODORE: If you can take from here a sufficient force to oppose the Californians, now supposed to be near the Pueblo, and waiting for the approach of Lieutenant Colonel Frémont, I advise that you do so, and that you march with that force as early as possible in the direction of the Pueblo, by which you will either be able to form a junction with Lieutenant Colonel Frémont, or make a diversion very much in his favor.

I do not think that Lieutenant Colonel Frémont should be left unsupported to fight a battle upon which the fate of California may, for a long time, depend, if there are troops here to act in concert with him. Your force as it advances might surprise the enemy at the St. Louis mission, and make prisoners of them.

I shall be happy, in such an expedition, to accompany you, and to give you any aid, either of head or hand, of which I may be capable.

Yours, truly,

S. W. KEARNY,
Brigadier General.

To Commodore STOCKTON,
   Commanding United States forces, San Diego.

HEAD-QUARTERS, SAN DIEGO,
December 23, 1846.

DEAR GENERAL: Your note of yesterday was handed to me *last night* by Captain Turner, of the dragoons.

In reply to that note, *permit me to refer you to the conversation held with you yesterday morning at your quarters.* I stated to you *distinctly* that I *intended* to march upon St. Louis Rey *as soon as possible*, with a part of the force under my command, and that I was *very desirous* to march on to the Pueblo *to co-operate with Lieutenant Colonel Frémont;* but my movements after, to St. Louis Rey, would depend entirely upon the information that I might receive as to the movements of Colonel Frémont and the enemy. It might be necessary for me to stop the pass of San Felipe, or march back to San Diego.

Now, my dear general, if the object of your note is to advise me to do anything which would enable a large force of the enemy to get into my rear and cut off my communication with San Diego, and hazard the safety of the garrison and the ships in the harbor, you will excuse me for saying I cannot follow any such advice.

My PURPOSE *still is* to march for St. Louis Rey *as soon as I can get the* DRAGOONS *and riflemen mounted*, which I hope to do in two days.

Faithfully, your obedient servant,
R. F. STOCKTON,
*Commander-in-chief and governor
of the territory of California.*

To Brigadier General S. W. KEARNY,
United States Army.

SAN DIEGO, *December 23, 1846.*

DEAR COMMODORE: I have received yours of this date, repeating, as you say, what you stated to me yesterday; and in reply I have only to remark that, *if I had so understood you*, I certainly *would not have written* my letter to you of last evening.

You certainly could not for a moment suppose that I would advise or suggest to you any movement which might endanger the safety of the garrison and the ships in the harbor.

My letter of yesterday's date stated that "if you can take from here," &c., of which you were the judge, and of which I knew nothing.

Truly yours,
S. W. KEARNY,
Brigadier General.

Commodore R. F. STOCKTON,
Commanding U. S. Navy, &c., San Diego.

GENERAL ORDERS:

The forces composed of Captain Tilghman's company of artillery, a detachment of the 1st regiment of dragoons, companies A and B of the California battalion of mounted riflemen, and a detachment of sailors and marines, from the frigates Congress and Savannah and the ship Portsmouth, will take up the line of march *for the Ciudad de los Angeles* on Monday morning, the 28th instant, at 10 o'clock, a. m.

By order of the commander-in-chief.

J. ZIELAN,
Brevet Captain and Adjutant.

San Diego, *December* 23, 1846.

The character of this correspondence entirely destroys General Kearny's asseverations; both the one in his report that Commodore Stockton "reluctantly consented" to the march of the troops, and the one before the court that he "believed" that the expedition was organized in consequence of his letter of advice.

Commodore Stockton's letter is explicit both of his present and previous "*intention*," "*desire*," and "*purpose*" to march "*as soon as possible;*" while the reference to the dragoons, which were General Kearny's especial corps, shows that the subject of the expedition must have been previously entertained between the two correspondents. Allow General Kearny, however, the benefit of any misunderstanding, touching Commodore Stockton's disposition and intentions, that he may have been under when he wrote his letter, the commodore's reply corrects all such mistakes, and leaves General Kearny's subsequent assertions on this head direct contradictions of the declarations of Commodore Stockton.

The next question in connexion with this expedition is, *who was its commander?* General Kearny says *he* was; Commodore Stockton, sustained by the testimony of many others, says *he* was. As it could not have had *two commanders*, at the same time, I will compare the testimony. General Kearny's claim first comes to attention in a letter to the department, of which the following is the first paragraph:

"Head-quarters, Army of the West,
"*Ciudad de los Angeles, January* 12, 1847.

"Sir: I have the honor to report that, at the request of Commodore R. F. Stockton, United States navy, (who in September last assumed the title of governor of California,) I consented to take command of an expedition to this place, (the capital of the country,) and that on the 29th December, *I left San Diego* with about 500 men, consisting of 60 dismounted dragoons, under Captain Turner, 50 California volunteers, and the remainder of marines and sailors, with a battery of artillery; Lieutenant Emory (topographical engineers) acting as assistant adjutant general. *Commodore Stockton accompanied us.*"

Here the claim to have been the commander is plain, unequivocal, and unconditional. In his letter to me, however, of the same date, (January 12th,) he expresses it perhaps even more strongly; since Commodore Stockton is not mentioned at all, and the pronoun "I" and "me" exclude the idea of any participant in the " possession" or command:

PUEBLA DE LOS ANGELES,
January 12, 1847.—Tuesday, 6, p. m.

DEAR FREMONT: *I am here in possession of this place, with sailors and marines.* We met and defeated the whole force of the Californians the 8th and 9th. They have not now to exceed 300 men concentrated. Avoid charging them, and come to *me* at this place.

Acknowledge the hour of receipt of this, and when *I* may expect you. Regards to Russell.

Yours,
S. W. KEARNY,
Brigadier General.

Lieutenant Colonel FREMONT.

At the next step, General Kearny slightly varies his claim, and admits some qualification to the completeness of his command. This is on his cross-examination.

Fourth day of the trial.

"In the latter end of December, an expedition was organized at San Diego to march to Los Angeles, to assist Lieutenant Colonel Frémont, and it was organized in consequence, as I believe, of this paper, which is a copy of a letter from me to Commodore Stockton, (referring to his letter to Commodore Stockton of December 22.) Commodore Stockton, at that time was acting as governor of California, so styling himself. * * * * He determined on the expedition, and on the morning of the 29th December the troops were paraded at San Diego for the march. The troops consisted of about five hundred sailors and marines, about sixty dragoons, and about forty or fifty volunteers. While they were on parade, Commodore Stockton called several officers together; Captain Turner, of the dragoons, and Lieutenant Minor, of the navy, I know were there, and several others. He then remarked to them to the following purport:

" Gentlemen, General Kearny has kindly consented to take the command of the troops on the expedition; you will, therefore, look upon him as your commander. *I shall go along as* GOVERNOR *and commander-in-chief in* CALIFORNIA." "We marched toward Los Angeles," &c. * * * * "The troops, *under my command*, marched into Los Angeles on the 10th of January," &c.

At the next stage, in reply to a question of the judge advocate, he returns to the positive and unconditional assertion of command:

" By the act of Commodore Stockton, who styled himself governor of California, the sailors and marines were placed UNDER MY COMMAND, on the 29th December, 1846, for the march to Los Angeles. I COMMANDED THEM ON THE EXPEDITION; Commodore Stockton accompanied us. I exercised no command whatever over Commodore Stockton, *nor did he exert any whatever over me.*"

Afterward (fourteenth day) under examination by the court, and when information had been received here of the arrival of Commodore Stockton in the country, the witness greatly modified his position on this point, and admits several acts of authority done on the march by Commodore Stockton, and that he "felt it his duty" to "consult the wishes" of the commodore.

"I found Commodore Stockton, on my arrival at San Diego, on the 12th December, 1846, in command of the Pacific squadron, having several ships, either two or three, in the harbor at that place. Most of his sailors were on shore. He had assumed the title of governor of California in the month of August previous. *All at San Diego addressed him as 'governor.'* I DID THE SAME.

"After he had determined on the march from San Diego to Los Angeles, the troops being paraded for it on the 29th December, he, in the presence of several officers, among whom were myself, Captain Turner of the dragoons, and Lieutenant Minor, of the navy, and others, whose names I do not recollect, remarked to them: 'Gentlemen, General Kearny has kindly consented to take command of the troops in this expedition; you will therefore consider him as your commander. *I will go along as* GOVERNOR *and commander-in-chief in* CALIFORNIA.' *Under Commodore Stockton's directions every arrangement for the expedition was made. I had nothing whatever to do with it.* We marched from San Diego to Los Angeles. Whilst on the march, a few days before reaching Los Angeles, a commission of two citizens, as I believe, on behalf of Governor Flores, came to Commodore Stockton with a communication to him as the governor, or commander-in-chief in California. *Commodore Stockton replied to that communication without consulting me.* On the march I at no time considered Commodore Stockton under my direction; nor did I at any time consider myself under his. His assimilated rank to officers of the army at that time was, and now is, and will for upwards of a year remain, that of a colonel.

"Although I did not consider myself *at any time, or under any circumstances, as under the orders of Commodore Stockton,* yet, as so large a portion of my command was of sailors and marines, I felt it my duty on all important subjects *to consult his wishes, and, as far as I consistently could do so, to comply with them.*"

But it was not till the fifty-first day of this trial, when he had had the benefit of several weeks reflection, added to information of the character of the testimony delivered by Commodore Stockton and others, and when he came into court fortified with his own questions, drawn up by himself to square with pre-arranged answers, that he could be brought to the point of admitting that, during the march, the commodore had exercised the prerogative of sending him what he calls "messages," but the commodore calls "orders," and had directed many movements of the expedition. But even this day's admissions are so reluctant, and with so many reservations, that for the plain fact other testimony must necessarily be brought in.

General Kearny recites twice, and with much particularity in his testimony to this point, *his* version of what Commodore Stockton said to the troops before marching from San Diego on the subject of the command; laboring, by an ingenious turn of the last clause, to draw a distinction between the commander-in-chief *in the territory*, and the commander-in-chief *of the troops.* This is his precise version of Governor Stockton's remarks: "Gentlemen, General Kearny has kindly consented to take command of the troops in this expedition; you will therefore look upon him as your commander. *I shall go along as* GOVERNOR *and commander-in-chief* IN CALIFORNIA.

This fine-spun distinction seems, in fact, the corner stone of General Kearny's claim to have been the commander of the expedition, for while he constantly persists in that pretension, he as constantly admits that Commodore Stockton was the governor and commander in the territory.

I do not refer to this because I attach any value to the point in itself. For any argument that I desire, the version given by General Kearny would answer as well as any other: for if Commodore Stockton was governor and commander in-chief *of California*, his authority was sufficient for my case, since Los Angeles, where I believe the charges are all laid, is certainly within that province. But the distinction drawn in the version given by the witness was considered important by him, and that version is contradicted; and this is the point of view in which I present it. It is contradicted by Commodore Stockton, Lieutenant Gray, Lieutenant Minor, and the certificate of Lieutenant Rowan, all whose concurrent testimony affirms that Commodore Stockton's reservation of authority related to the commander-in-chief of the *expedition*, without the words of qualification to which General Kearny testifies; and it is worthy of note that, though a witness of the prosecution, Captain Turner, was present at the address, the prosecution have not thought proper to bring him to sustain General Kearny thus contradicted.

A few detached passages from the testimony will show how materially General Kearny is contradicted, in other respects, upon this point of the command:

General Kearny: "By the act of Commodore Stockton, the sailors and marines were placed under *my command. I commanded them* on the expedition."

Commodore Stockton: "During which march I performed *all the duties* which I supposed devolved on the *commander-in-chief.*

General Kearny: "I exercised no command whatever over Commodore Stockton, *nor did he exert any whatever over me.*"

Commodore Stockton: "I was *in the habit* of sending my aid-de-camp *to* General Kearny to inform *him* what time *I wished* to move in the morning; and I *always* decided on the *route* we should take, and *when* and *where* we should *encamp.*"

General Kearny: "The troops *under my command* marched into Los Angeles on the 10th of January."

Commodore Stockton: "And when we marched into the city, *I led the way, at the head of the advanced guard.*"

General Kearny: "On the march, I at no time considered Commodore Stockton under my direction, *nor did I, at any time, consider myself under his.*"

Commodore Stockton: "I observed the guns being unlimbered; I was told it was done *by order of General Kearny* to return the fire of the enemy; *I ordered the guns limbered up,* and the forces to cross the river before a shot was fired." "I observed that the men of the right flank had been formed into a square, *and General Kearny at their head.* I sent my aid-de-camp, Mr. Gray, *to General Kearny, with* INSTRUCTIONS *to move that square,* and two pieces of artillery, immediately up the hill."

General Kearny: "During our march many messages were brought to me from Commodore Stockton; those messages I looked upon as *suggestions* and *expressions of his wishes.* I have *since then* learned that he considered them in the light of orders."

Commodore Stockton: "I sent for Captain Emory; I asked him by whose order the camp was making below the hill. He said *by General Kearny's order.* I told him to go to General Kearny and tell him that it was *my order* that the camp should be immediately moved to the top of the hill." "I sent my aid-de-camp, Mr. Gray, to General Kearny, *with instructions* to move," &c. "The witness (Commodore Stockton) in enumerating *some* of the *orders given* and *some* of the details, executed by himself, meant merely to cite instances in which *General Kearny recognized and acknowledged* his (the witness's) *command-in-chief on the field of battle,* as well as *in the march.*"

General Kearny: "During our march, his (Commodore Stockton's) authority and command, *though it did not extend over me, or over the troops which he had himself given me,* extended far beyond," &c.

Commodore Stockton: "Commodore R. F. Stockton begs leave to add, &c., that he wishes to be understood as meaning distinctly to convey the idea that General Kearny was fully invested with the command of the troops in the battles of the 8th and 9th of January, SUBJECT *to the orders of him, the witness, as* COMMANDER-IN-CHIEF. Most and nearly all the execution of details was confided to General Kearny as SECOND in command." "He could not attempt to enumerate and specify the many and important acts of General Kearny *as* SECOND *in command.*" "When the troops arrived at San Bernardo, I made my head quarters a mile, or two miles, in advance of the camp; and *I* SENT *to General Kearny to send me the marines and a piece of artillery, which was immediately done.*" "*I* ORDERED *the troops all to lie down,*" &c. "*After having* DIRECTED *the troops* to be formed, &c., *I took* the marine guard and two pieces of *artillery,*" &c. "On my return, *I* gave ORDERS where the different *officers* and *troops* were to be quartered, and ORDERED the same *flag,*" &c.

General Kearny: "I exerted no command whatever over Commodore Stockton, *nor did he exert any whatever over me.*"

Lieutenant Gray:—"Question. Did you bear an *order* from Commodore Stockton on the 8th of January, in the field, to General Kearny?—if so, state the order and all the circumstances.

"Answer. I did bear *an order* from Commodore Stockton to General Kearny on the 8th of January, on the field of battle. The enemy had been observed to withdraw his guns from the height. The commodore directed me to go to General Kearny, and say to him, to send a square and a field-piece immediately up on the height, to prevent the enemy's returning with their guns. I went and gave him *the order*, and on my return to Commodore Stockton, observed the division, or square, of General Kearny moving toward the hill.

"Question. Did you bear that order to General Kearny in your character of aid-de-camp to Commodore Stockton, the commander-in-chief?

"Answer. Yes.

"Question by the judge advocate. Do you recollect the words and manner in which you delivered that order; did you deliver it so that General Kearny must have received it as an order, or merely as a suggestion?

"Answer. I carried it *as an order*, in the usual respectful way. How General Kearny received it, I, of course, cannot say. He did not show, by his manner, that it was disagreeable to him, according to the best of my recollection."

Finally, I shall conclude this point by showing that General Kearny did not, and could not, at any time, have considered himself the commander of the expedition, or of the troops composing it, and was not so considered by the army officers who had accompanied him into California, and were there. Because,

1. The place which General Kearny held in the expedition was that which had been before assigned to a lieutenant of the navy, serving under Commodore Stockton, and this General Kearny knew. This is the testimony of Commodore Stockton:

"After the forces had been paraded preparatory to the march, and I was about mounting my horse, General Kearny came to me and inquired, 'who was to command the troops?' I said to him, *Lieutenant Rowan, first lieutenant of the Cyane, would command them.* He gave me to understand that *he* would like to command the troops, and after some further conversation on the subject, *I agreed to appoint him to the command,* and immediately sent for Lieutenant Rowan," &c.

2. Because, at the moment of receiving the appointment, he was informed that the command-in-chief was reserved by Commodore Stockton. This is Commodore Stockson's testimony to this point:

" I immediately sent for Lieutenant Rowan, and, assembling the officers that were near at hand, stated to them that General Kearny had *volunteered* to take command of the troops, but that I *retained my own position as commander-in-chief.* I directed my aid-de-camp, and the commissary who was with me, to *take a note* of what I said on the occasion."

And to the same effect is the testimony of Lieutenant Gray and Lieutenant Minor, and the certificate of Lieutenant Rowan.

3. Because both General Kearny, and the officers under him, received and obeyed the orders of Commodore Stockton, in scme instances in opposition to those first given by General Kearny, both on the march and in the battles. The evidence on this point need not be recapitulated. Commodore Stockton testifies to it, Lieutenant Gray testifies to it, Lieutenant Minor testifies to it, and Lieutenant Emory testifies to have received and obeyed orders from Commodore Stockton.

4. Because Lieutenant Emory, attached to General Kearny's dragoon escort, and acting as assistant adjutant general, did not make his official report of losses in action in the expedition to General Kearny, but to Commodore Stockton. True, General Kearny says this was done "without his knowledge or consent;" but that is only the stronger proof that he was not regarded or respected as the commander-in-chief, even by his confidential supporters and military family.

5. Because he admitted to Colonel Russell, as appears repeatedly in Colonel Russell's testimony, that he was serving *under* Commodore Stockton, and had been serving under him from San Diego.

6. Because, when I delivered to him, and he read in my presence, my letter to him of 17th January, in which is this passage:

"*I learned also in conversation with you that, on the march from San Diego, recently, to this place, you entered upon, and discharged duties implying an acknowledgement on your part* OF SUPREMACY *to Commodore Stockton*," he made no denial of it, or objection to it.

7. Because, on the 16th of January, he applied, in writing, to Commodore Stockton, " advising" and " offering" " to take one half" of the command, and march to form a junction," &c., addressing Commodore Stockton in that letter as " governor of California, *commanding United States forces.*"

On the eighth day of the trial General Kearny testified as follows:

" Question. Do you know whether the officers of the battalion raised it and marched it under commission from Commodore Stockton?

"Answer. I have always understood that Lieutenant Colonel Frémont had raised that battalion under the direction of Commodore Stockton.

" Question. With what commission?

"Answer. *I never heard of Commodore Stockton conferring a commission on Lieutenant Colonel Frémont, further than having appointed him military commandant of California.*"

The object of this inquiry was not, by any means, to get an opportunity to discredit the witness. The object was to ascertain before the court that the battalion was enlisted, organized, and officered exclusively under naval authority, and so, of course, subject to the orders of the naval commander; and also to ascertain if these facts were not within the knowledge of the witness when he attempted to get command of the battalion, in opposition to Commodore Stockton; both being inquiries pertinent to the issues of the trial, and the facts being what was desired. But the nature of the last answer was such as to leave the original inquiries unsettled, and to open a *new one.*

The answer was this. *"I never heard* of Commodore Stockton's conferring a commission on Lieutenant Colonel Frémont, further than having appointed him *military commandant* of California."

And the new question raised was whether, in fact, the witness had *"never heard"* of a matter so notorious in that country. Accordingly, on the next day, General Kearny having mentioned the receipt on the 16th December, 1846, of a certain communication from Commodore Stockton, this question was put:

Question. Did not Commodore Stockton, in that communication, *inform you* that Captain Frémont had been appointed by him MAJOR, and Lieutenant Gillespie, of the marines, captain in the California battalion?

And a copy of the paper having been shown to the witness, he answered:

Answer. Among the papers sent to me by Commodore Stockton, on the 16th December, *was* a copy of his letter to the Navy Department, dated August 28, 1846, the second paragraph of which states that he had organized a California battalion of mounted riflemen, by the appointment of all the necessary officers, and received them as volunteers in the service of the United States; *that Captain Frémont was appointed major, and Lieutenant Gillespie, captain of the battalion.*

Again, on the 13th day of the trial, two other papers were shown to the witness, with this question:

"Were not copies of these two papers, describing him (Frémont) as Major Frémont, among those furnished to you by Commodore Stockton at San Diego? And were not copies of them filed in the War Department by you since your return from California, and after your arrival in this city in September last?

"Answer. (After reading over the papers,) I think that copies of these papers *were furnished to me by Commodore Stockton.*"

To the latter part of the question, "were they not filed by you in the War Department since your return from California, and after your arrival in this city in September last." "I see on the papers the certificate of Captain Townsend that I did so; *I think Captain Townsend is mistaken.*"

But on the following day he admitted that Captain Townsend was *not* mistaken; that the papers had been put into his hands by Commodore Stockton in December, 1846, and had been filed by him in the war office as late as the 21st September last. From all this, however, it only resulted that he had *seen* of the appointment of Frémont as major; that he had *"never heard"* of it, was not yet disproved.

This was accomplished in his testimony on the ninth day, when he admitted as follows:

"Commodore Stockton *did* inform me, in the conversation alluded to between us, that California had been conquered in July and

August of the same year, (this conversation was held in December,) and that *Major Frémont* had gone to the north to raise men," &c.

In the same connexion, and for the same purpose, the question arose, whether Lieutenant Gillespie, of the marine corps, was not also an officer of the battalion; and the answer of the witness was again such as not only to leave the original question open, but to raise the new one, which brings the subject within this branch of my defence. The witness's answer was as follows:

"Captain Gillespie had marched with me from San Diego to Los Angeles, and was serving under me. *If his company was with the California battalion* I DID NOT KNOW IT."

It appeared, however, on examination, that the same communication (of 28th August, 1846) that informed the witness that Frémont had been appointed major of the battalion, also informed him that Gillespie had been appointed captain in it. It further appeared, that in the surgeon's list of killed and wounded in the actions of 8th and 9th January, furnished by Lieutenant Emory to General Kearny, and by him sent to the department, Captain Gillespie is reported as an officer of the California battalion; and Captain Gillespie himself gave the following emphatic testimony:

Question. Did you at any time communicate to General Kearny your rank and position in the California battalion? If so, when and where was that communication made?

Answer. *I did communicate to General Kearny my position in the battalion* on the 5th of December, 1846, about one o'clock in the day, in the mountains about half-way between Santa Maria and Santa Isabel. When I met him I was at the head of a detachment of volunteers and sailors, I having been ordered by Commodore Stockton to proceed to Warner's Pass, to communicate with General Kearny.

These inquiries concerning the raising and officering of the battalion were to matters connected intimately with the issues of the trial, and the answers of the witness seemed to indicate a consciousness of it. But I do not desire to present them in any other light than as instances of defective and equivocating memory, and in that view affecting the general credit of his testimony.

Under the same infirmity of memory I am willing to class the extraordinary facility of *omission* betrayed by the witness, in his manner, which seems to be habitual, of *half-telling*, where *whole-telling* is essential. Thus: On the third day of the trial he commences an answer in these words: "About the 14th January, 1847, *I received* from Lieutenant Colonel Frémont a communication, dated," &c.—the inference being, of course, that my communication was voluntary; the fact (and most important one, too) being, that it was drawn out by no less than *four* importunate letters that I had before received. Again, in continuation of the same narration: "On the day subsequent, viz., on the 17th January, Lieutenant Colonel Frémont *came to my quarters*, and in conversation," &c.—the inference being, of course, that I went at my own instance, whereas the fact (most material and relevant, and deciding the character of the interview) turned out, that I went in compliance with the written request of the witness to see me "on business." Again, same day: "I was first *met* by a detachment from Commodore Stockton," &c. . . . . "It *came* from Commodore Stockton, *to give* me information," &c. . . . . ; the inference being, that it went voluntarily, or was sent by Commodore Stockton of his own motion: the important fact appearing, however, when Commodore Stockton came on the stand, three weeks after, that it was sent out at the written request of General Kearny, for a party "to open communication with him," &c. So in the same letter, making this application, he writes to Commodore Stockton as follows: "*Your express, by Mr. Carson, was met on the Del Norte, and your mail must have reached Washington at least ten days since*"—omitting the material fact, that Mr. Carson, in addition to being *met*, was likewise *turned back;* and leaving the inference that he had gone on. Again, in his testimony on the sixth day of the trial, speaking of his position on the hill of San Bernardo, the witness says: "I stated to the doctor and others, that we would leave next morning, which we accordingly did; *Lieutenant Gray, of the navy, with a gallant command of sailors and marines, having come into our camp the night previous*"—the inference being, that Lieutenant Gray and his command came voluntarily, or by chance, into the camp, the fact being, that it was a detachment of 215 men, sent from San Diego expressly for the relief of General Kearny's camp, and in pursuance of his repeated urgent calls for succor—one of them (that by Lieutenant Beale, Mr. Carson, and the Indian) conveyed through the enemy's lines and an insurgent population, under circumstances of devotion and courage unsurpassed, but no mention of which is found in the official report, or in any part of the testimony of General Kearny.

I give these as examples, taken only from two days' proceedings, of a vast deal of the same sort of testimony, running through General Kearny's examination.

The testimony of General Kearny, *in relation to the charges*, is the next point to which I advert under this head of my defence. On the sixth day of the trial General Kearny testifies as follows:

The charges on which Lieutenant Colonel Frémont is now arraigned are not my charges. I preferred a single charge against Lieutenant Colonel Frémont. The charges on which he is now arraigned have been changed from mine.	*	*	*	*	*	*

Question (by Lieutenant Colonel Frémont.) Did you give any information to the person who drew up the seventh specification under the first charge, in relation to the cannon?

Answer. I DID NOT.

This testimony was promptly communicated to the War Office, by my counsel, for the purpose of ascertaining upon *whose* (if not General Kearny's) information the charge had been drawn up, as matter necessary to be known, unless I would proceed in my defence against unknown and secret prosecutors; the Adjutant General, by direction of the Secretary of War, returned for answer the emphatic assurance, that the charges and specifications produced to the court "*were based upon facts alleged and officially re-*

ported to the department by General Kearny; and it is not known or understood that any charge or specification has been introduced, based on facts derived from any other source whatever."

In addition to this positive contradiction by the department, the charges come to the court certified upon their face as being preferred *"upon information of Brigadier General S. W. Kearny;"* and myself and counsel are further informed, by the judge advocate, that the seventh specification of the first charge *is copied literally from the charge furnished by General Kearny in his own handwriting.*

The inquiry into the charges, leads me naturally to the subject upon which that inquiry arose, viz: a certain *mountain howitzer,* lost by General Kearny at the battle of San Pasqual, and recovered by me at the capitulation of Cowenga. The inquiry was not originally made, with any view or expectation that an untrue answer would be given to it, and hence an opportunity arises for contradicting the testimony of the witness. On the contrary, the object of the inquiry was truth. It was to ascertain whether the recovery by me, of a cannon so lost by General Kearny, had been reported by him to the department; and, if not, the argument would be to the impeachment of his temper and motives towards me; for the loss of cannon is always a source of mortification, and its recovery a subject of gratulation and honorable report. It turned out that the recovery had *not* been reported, but to escape the inference thus raised, the witness pleaded want of sufficient knowledge of the fact. This, then, became the point at issue; and to say that this is an incidental question, upon which the answer of the witness must suffice, whether true or false, is to say that he may escape from the consequences of one wrong, by committing a greater; that a fact cannot be proved going to impeach his motives if he chooses to deny it with a falsehood. But it is the rule of law and justice that "a man shall not profit by his own wrong;" and, therefore, I did not consider myself concluded by the answer of the witness; but, finding by inspection of the charges, that the witness (who I had understood was the sole accuser against me) had been sufficient knowledge concerning the cannon, to impute the *having* of it to me *as a crime,* I inferred that he ought to have had sufficient knowledge of it, to report the *gaining* of it *to my credit.* Hence, I continued the inquiry with the following question :

"In the seventh specification, under the first charge, you charge Lieutenant Colonel Frémont with refusing to give up two cannon which had been brought from Fort Leavenworth, and which were then at San Gabriel. Will you state what cannon they were, how they were brought from Fort Leavenworth, and how they got to San Gabriel?"

And hence arose the sweeping declarations already examined, that these charges "were not his;" that they "had been changed from his;" and that he "did not" furnish the information concerning the cannon on which the seventh specification of charge first was drawn up. After which, he continued his answer in these words:

The two howitzers, however, referred to, *are* the two howitzers brought by the first dragoons from Fort Leavenworth to California; one of them, as was previously stated, was lost at the San Pasqual; the other, we took with us.

Question. Do you know that one of those cannon was the one lost by you at San Pasqual?
Answer. I do not.

Two days after, he comes into court with this "explanation:" In reading over, in the papers this morning, the proceedings of Monday, I find the following question put to me by the accused, and my answer thereto, as follows:

Question. Do you know that one of those cannon was the one lost by you at San Pasqual?
Answer. I do not.

I have now to explain, that *I had no personal knowledge of it; I had a knowledge of it* from an official report made to my staff officer by Lieutenant Colonel Cooke.

Now, on this point, General Kearny is contradicted by his own witness; for Lieutenant Colonel Cooke testifies to having received *from* General Kearny orders in relation to the cannon *before* he ever made any report on the subject.

This is from Major Cooke's testimony in chief, delivered on the fourteenth day of the trial:

On *the 24th of March*, I rode out from Los Angeles to the mission of San Gabriel, accompanied　*　　*　　*　　*　　*

I called on Captain Owens at his quarters, and shortly after asked to look at the artillery. He showed them to me in the court of the mission, and I observed *two mountain howitzers*, which I believed had been brought to that country by the dragoons. *I had received verbal instructions from General Kearny*, by Captain Turner, *to have them turned over to company C, under my command;* and had, *before I left town*, ordered mules and drivers to be sent after them.

This relates to occurrences of *the 24th of March*, whilst the "verbal instructions" referred to, afterward ascertained to be written memoranda, were issued from Monterey about the *1st of March*, and the only report made upon the subject by Major Cooke was of *March* 25.

This is Major Cooke's testimony to these points, (eighteenth day of the trial:)

Question. Is your letter or report, of the 25th March, which was read in your cross-examination on Thursday, your official report to your superior officer? and does it refer to the same events as those warranted in your testimony? and did you ever make any other official report of those occurrences to General Kearny, or to any other officer for him?

Answer. *It was my official report. It refers to the same subject as my evidence in chief.* I do not remember having made *any* OTHER *report to him or to any one else.* * * * *

Question. Did you have any verbal or special order in relation to ordnance, arms, &c?.

Answer. I had some verbal orders in relation to arms, communicated, however, in the form of *written memoranda.* * * * I have them not here. I lost all my papers by an accident, &c.

Question. Will you state the tenor of those orders and instructions, giving the words as far as possible, and whom they came from?

Answer. THEY WERE FROM GENERAL KEARNY. I was directed, I believe, *to put the* HOWITZERS in charge of the dragoons. * * * * * I received, *at the same time,* an *official letter* from General Kearny.

A copy of this official letter was produced the next day, and found to be dated at Monterey, March 1, which fixes the time· of those "verbal orders" or "written memoranda." Finally, on the nineteenth and twentieth days of the trial, Major Cooke again testifies concerning the same verbal instructions, as follows:

Under ordinary circumstances, I should have deemed it my duty to have enforced my orders in relation to the artillery, founded on the verbal orders *of the general.*

The verbal orders alluded to might be considered as giving higher importance, in my view, to the *object to be attained,* which was to turn over to company C, 1st dragoons, *the two mountain howitzers.*

From all which, it results that General Kearny's first information concerning the cannon was *not* received through Major Cooke's report, but that the report resulted, in fact, from orders about the cannon, given by General Kearny several weeks before the report was made.

The first great allegations, then, made by General Kearny to escape from the original simple and comparatively innocent fact supposed by the inquiry concerning the cannon, are contradicted, in their whole essence, by the official assurance of the Secretary of War, by the charges as they are certified by the judge advocate to the court, and by the original draft of accusations against me in General Kearny's own hand, while his subsequent "explanation" to escape from *this* labyrinth, by attempting to draw a distinction between *personal knowledge* and *official knowledge,* involves him in the repudiation of his own orders, and in a double contradiction with himself and with Major Cooke, his own witness.

I think it proper, I think it my duty, to introduce here some maxims of the law, which, I am advised, are recognized in all courts.

" Where it turns out that a witness's testimony is corruptly false in any paticular, it should be entirely disregarded by the jury."

" A witness's credibility, being seriously impeached by written, or other plain, deliberate contradictory statement by him, and not supported, ought, it would seem, to be entirely rejected."

" But where a party speaks to a fact, in reference to which he cannot be presumed liable to mistake, if the fact turn out otherwise, it is extremely difficult to exempt him from the charge of deliberate falsehood; and courts of justice, under such circumstances, are bound, upon principles of law, morality and justice, to apply the maxim, *falsus in uno, falsus in omnibus.*"

(See Phillipps on Evidence, v. 3, pp. 397 and 772.)

Mr. PRESIDENT: The length of this defence precludes the necessity of recapitulation. I omit it, and go to the conclusion with a few brief reflections, as pertinent, I trust, as they are true.

I consider these difficulties in California to be a comedy—(very near being a tragedy)—of three errors: *first*, in the faulty orders sent out from this place; *next*, in the unjustifiable pretensions of General Kearny; *thirdly*, in the conduct of the government in sustaining these pretensions. And the last of these errors I consider the greatest of the three.

Certainly the difficulties in California ought to be inquired into; but how? Not by prosecuting the subordinate, but the principals, not by prosecuting him who prevented, but him who would have made civil war. If it was a crime in me to accept the governorship from Commodore Stockton; it was a crime in him to have bestowed it; and, in either event, crime or not, the government which knew of his intention to appoint me, and did not forbid it, has lost the right of prosecuting either of us.

My acts in California have all been with high motives, and a desire for the public service. My scientific labors did something to open California to the knowledge of my countrymen; its geography had been a sealed book. My military operations were conquests without bloodshed; my civil administration was for the public good. I offer California, during my administration, for comparison with the most tranquil portions of the United States; I offer it in contrast to the condition of New Mexico during the same time. I prevented civil war against Governor Stockton, by refusing to join General Kearny against him; I arrested civil war against myself, by consenting to be deposed—offering at the same time to resign my place of lieutenant colonel in the army.

I have been brought as a prisoner and a criminal from that country. I could return to, after this trial is over, without rank or guards, and without molestation from the people, except to be importuned for the money which the government owes them.

I am now ready to receive the sentence of the court.

DOOUMENTS

Relating to the proceedings of the court martial in the case of Liuetenant Colonel Frémont.

APRIL 7, 1848.

Submitted by Mr. BENTON, and ordered to be printed in connexion with the message of the President on the subject.

WASHINGTON CITY,
C street, February 19, 1848.

SIR: I have this moment received the general order, No. 7, (dated the 17th instant,) making known to me the final decision in the proceedings of the general court martial, before which I have been tried; and hereby send in my resignation of lieutenant colonel in the army of the United States.

In doing this, I take the occasion to say that my reason for resigning is, that I do not feel conscious of having done anything to merit the finding of the court; and, this being the case, I cannot, by accepting the clemency of the President, admit the justice of the decision against me.

Very respectfully, your obedient servant,

J. C. FRÉMONT.

To the ADJUTANT GENERAL.

C STREET, *March* 14, 1848.

SIR: I have not yet had the honor to receive any reply to my letter of resignation, of the 17th ultimo; and, as the President's acceptance is necessary to give legal effect to that act, I have to request that, at some convenient opportunity, you will take the trouble to obtain the reply, and make it known to me.

Respectfully, sir, your obedient servant,

J. C. FRÉMONT.

To the ADJUTANT GENERAL.

ADJUTANT GENERAL'S OFFICE,
Washington, March 15, 1848.

SIR: Your resignation has been accepted by the President of the United States, to take effect this day.

I am, sir, very respectfully, your obedient servant,

W. G. FREEMAN,
Ass't Adjutant General.

Lieutenant Colonel JOHN C. FRÉMONT,
Regiment of Mounted Riflemen, C street, Washington, D. C.

NOTES

p. 2, ln. 14   Col. Ichabod B. Crane

ln. 18   Col. René Edward DeRussy

ln. 20   Col. Henry K. Craig

p. 3, ln. 33   George Archibald McCall (1802–68), twice breveted for gallant and meritorious conduct in the Mexican War, attributed his poor health to the many years he had spent in malarial climates. On 5 April 1847 he was granted a four-month leave of absence. Actually, almost two years passed before he returned to military duty—and then he was sent to New Mexico to encourage statehood and to inspect military installations (MC CALL, 64–78).

p. 4, ln. 20   "any" in place of "nay"

p. 17, ln. 9   Lieut. James Rock had settled in San Jose after deserting from Charles Wilkes's exploring expedition in 1841. A few months after his cashiering, he was killed by Indians in the San Joaquin Valley (PIONEER REGISTER).

ln. 15   Capt. Henry L. Ford

lns. 15–17   All these American officers had arrived in California in 1843 or thereafter. Among those not identified earlier is Samuel Gibson (d. 1849), who had come from Oregon. One of Gillespie's men, he had been wounded at San Pasqual. William Findlay and John Scott had been members of JCF's 1845 expedition, and Findlay was in Washington as a witness at the court-martial. Tennessee millwright William Baldridge had been a member of the Walker-Chiles party in 1843. After the war he settled in the Napa Valley and in 1877 wrote *Days of '46*. Hiram Rheusaw, who had gone south with JCF's battalion in July 1846, had come in the Swasey-Todd party; James M. Hudspeth, a native of Alabama, in Lansford W. Hastings's party from Oregon in 1843. In the spring of 1846 Hudspeth had gone east to Fort Bridger and guided the mounted Russell-Bryant party as far west as Skull Valley. For additional biographical details on Baldridge, see GIFFEN, 35, 39, 42–43, 54–58, 75–76; on Hudspeth, see KORNS, 26–27, 44–45, 51–55, 64–65, 84, 131.

p. 40, ln. 40   JCF is quoting from the 25 Oct. 1847 letter of Benton and William C. Jones to Roger Jones, Doc. No. 242, Vol. 2.

p. 42, ln. 5   A lawyer and former member of the Missouri legislature, Capt. Thomas B. Hudson (1814–67) of St. Louis gave to his lieutenant the command of the Laclede Rangers. Acting by permission of General Kearny, he began raising a new company of volunteers from the several corps at Santa Fe for service in California. The company was dissolved by

Col. Alexander W. Doniphan as soon as he learned that California was in the hands of the Americans (HUGHES, 141). Philip St. George Cooke, however, wrote that the troop was never actually raised because of lack of specie and mounts (COOKE, 67).

ln. 7 Capt. James Allen of the 1st Dragoons, with the cooperation of Mormon Church officials, succeeded in mustering into service at Council Bluffs, Iowa, on 16 July 1846, four companies of 400 Mormon volunteers and part of a fifth company, which was filled a bit later. Allen was popular with his men and commanded as lieutenant colonel until his death at Fort Leavenworth on 23 Aug. 1846. Lieut. Andrew Jackson Smith then took command until they reached Santa Fe, when he was relieved by Philip St. George Cooke. For the experience of the Mormon Battalion and its work in opening a wagon road to California, see TYLER.

p. 43, ln. 17 "Rheusaw" in place of "Rousseau"

p. 45, ln. 6 The judge advocate's reply to JCF prompted Benton and William C. Jones to provide for publication in the *National Intelligencer*, 6 Nov. 1847, their letter of 25 Oct. 1847 to Roger Jones, his reply of 27 Oct., and their rejoinder of the same date (Doc. Nos. 242, 248, and 249, Vol. 2).

p. 46, ln. 49 Capt. Benjamin D. Moore, "who displayed great courage & chivalry in the fight," was killed at San Pasqual. Later, in Los Angeles, his comrades gave the name Fort Moore to the earthwork defenses (with six embrasures for cannon) which they constructed on a hill in back of the old Spanish church, Our Lady of the Angels (S. W. Kearny to Mary Kearny, 19 Dec. 1846, in CLARKE, 220; LAYNE, 43).

p. 47, ln. 44 Lieut. George Minor had served aboard Commodore Sloat's flagship, the *Savannah,* and at the time of Kearny's arrival in San Diego was commanding the garrison there.

p. 48, ln. 49 Lieut. Henry Wager Halleck

p. 49, ln. 1 The *Lexington,* with Capt. Christopher Quarles Tompkins (d. 1877) aboard, anchored in Monterey harbor on 28 Jan. 1847. Tompkins went east in May on a sailing vessel and resigned from the service in September. During the Civil War he served the Confederacy as a colonel in the 22nd Virginia Infantry.

p. 50, ln. 32 Twenty-eight-year-old William H. Churchill died 19 Oct. 1847 at Point Isabel, Tex.

p. 53, ln. 34 "Colonel Mason" in place of "Colonel Morgan"

p. 54, ln. 38 Sterling Price (1809–67) commanded the 2nd Missouri Volunteers in the war with Mexico. He was to serve as governor of Missouri from 1853 to 1857 and later as a general in the Confederate Army.

p. 56, ln. 38 On 19 Sept. 1846 Commodore Stockton had ordered his secretary, J. Parker Norris, to carry dispatches from Monterey to Washington (Norris to J. Y. Mason, New York, 29 Dec. 1846, DNA-45, Misc. Letters, Dec. 1846, entry 57, Letters from the Fourth Auditor). Norris returned to California on the *Preble* in April 1847.

ln. 41 On the *Erie,* the same vessel that carried Mason to San Francisco with new instructions for Kearny, Lieut. J. M. Watson (d. 1873) had reached California about 19 Feb. 1847 with dispatches for the commander of the Pacific Squadron. Watson later commanded the *Erie*.

p. 62, ln. 17   The first ten general orders are routine in nature and have not been printed in Vol. 2 as separate documents. They were issued during the march of the battalion from the Mission San Juan Bautista to the Mission San Fernando, and consequently before Kearny's claim to control the battalion. All were issued by order of JCF and signed by Lieut. Theodore Talbot, the adjutant of the battalion. The first, dated 3 Dec. 1846, gave instructions for the care of the camp baggage and animals and forbade any person to pass "the lines of the encampment" or to discharge firearms without permission of the colonel. The second instructed officers who had been making purchases for the United States to render their accounts to paymaster Pierson B. Reading. The third called for "occasional inspections of arms at Evening parade" by William H. Russell, the captain of ordnance. General orders nos. 4, 5, and 6 dealt with Second Lieut. Adam Hewitt's alleged neglect of duty. When that officer was permitted to resign, general orders no. 7 appointed James M. Hudspeth to fill the vacancy. At the Mission San Luis Obispo the eighth ordered a general court-martial of fourteen members to try persons brought before it. The ninth, issued at the Rincon on 4 Jan. 1847, was concerned with the care of the packs. And the tenth, dated eight days later at the Mission San Fernando, constituted a court-martial board of thirteen members to try persons brought before it (DNA-94, General Orders Issued to the California Battalion, LR, K-217 1847).

p. 63, ln. 15   Insert at left: "General Orders, No. 14."

ln. 21   "Rheusaw" in place of "Rheusani"

ln. 32   Two other general orders issued to the battalion by JCF are known to exist. General orders no. 15 constituted a regimental court-martial for the trial of Paul Sweet. General orders no. 16, dated 10 March 1847, instructed Capt. Richard Owens to remain in command of the troops at Mission San Gabriel and Capt. Granville P. Swift to take command of the troops stationed at Los Angeles (DNA-94, General Orders Issued to the California Battalion, LR, K-217 1847).

ln. 33   "Wm. N. Loker" in place of "Wm. N. Loke"

p. 64, ln. 14   This testimony caused JCF's counsel to inquire of the Adjutant General if any charges or specifications had been preferred or incorporated by any person other than Kearny (see Benton and William C. Jones to Roger Jones, 9 Nov. 1847 and the reply of Roger Jones, 11 Nov. 1847, Doc. Nos. 255 and 258, Vol. 2).

p. 64, ln. 7   The San Bernardo is now the San Dieguito River.

ln. 18   Born in the West Indies and appointed to the Navy from Louisiana, Lieut. Andrew F. V. Gray (d. 1860) was serving as aide-de-camp to Stockton when he was sent to Kearny's relief. He had left San Diego on the evening of 9 Dec., hours after Beale and Chemuctah, an Indian, staggered into Stockton's headquarters with a second urgent appeal for aid for the men encamped on the San Dieguito River. Soon after the Treaty of Cahuenga was signed, Stockton sent Gray east with dispatches.

From 1848 to 1851 he saw duty aboard the frigate *Constitution,* flagship of the Mediterranean and African Squadron (DNA-45, entry 464, Subject File ZB).

p. 66, ln. 4   Alexander Godey, Thomas H. Burgess, and a companion had been dispatched by Capt. Henry S. Turner on 5 Dec. with a message to Stockton, asking for aid. They arrived at San Diego safely and were on their way back when they were captured by the Californians. JCF is seeking to show here that the capture was made within full view of the dragoons, thus driving home Kearny's feeble condition and his inability to save the envoys.

p. 85, ln. 22   "Captain Hamley" in place of "Captain Hamlin"

p. 88, ln. 47   "Cahuenga" in place of "Cowengo"

p. 94, ln. 2   See Benton and William C. Jones to Roger Jones, 9 Nov. 1847, and Roger Jones to Benton and William C. Jones, 11 Nov. 1847, Doc. Nos. 255 and 258, Vol. 2.

p. 99, ln. 19   The journal of Capt. Abraham R. Johnston and the reports of Lieut. Col. Philip St. George Cooke and Lieut. William H. Emory are printed in House Exec. Doc. 41, 30th Cong., 1st sess., Serial 517. Cooke's official journal of the march of the Mormon Battalion, presented to the Senate on 17 March 1849, is Senate Doc. 2, 31st Cong., spec. sess., Serial 547.

p. 106, ln. 43 The servant was Jacob Dodson.

p. 110, ln. 43 The correct date is 2 Sept. 1846.

p. 111, ln. 23 Add "47" so as to read "page 47."

p. 114, ln. 7   "Mr. Kern" in place of "Mr. Keen"

p. 133, ln. 39 Cooke was on furlough in the East during the spring of 1846 (YOUNG, 173) and possibly made an application "in person" for the lieutenant colonelcy of the Mounted Rifles (3rd Cavalry) or tried to obtain the appointment through the influence of a friend. However, the only letter in DNA relative to his promotion during this period is one dated 21 June 1846 from Fort Crawford, Wis., in which he protests being the second captain to a squadron in the 1st Dragoons (DNA, AGO, LR, C-203 1846). The Adjutant General interpreted his letter as an expression of hope that Capt. E. V. Sumner would be promoted and Cooke made senior officer of the squadron. But Benton was convinced that Cooke's enmity stemmed from jealousy over JCF's receiving the coveted lieutenant colonelcy.

p. 136, ln. 20 On 11 June, while crossing the Mokelumne River near Sutter's Fort, Cooke lost all of his possessions, including $100 in gold and his 500-page journal of the Mormon Battalion's march from Santa Fe to Los Angeles. The saddlebags were recovered in August by Indians, but it was not until 20 Jan. 1848 that part of Cooke's journal was retrieved. Sutter recorded, "And the Nemutchumny Chief has brought me a part of Col. Cooks Journal, which he have brought from another Indian for a Shirt, and fortunately has not been smoked up" (NEW HELVETIA DIARY, 68, 110).

p. 142, ln. 20   JCF's headquarters in Los Angeles was the home of Alexander Bell at the corner of Los Angeles and Aliso streets (LAYNE, 44).

ln. 22   John J. Myers served as sergeant major of the California Battalion and was later lieutenant.

p. 144, ln. 27   Juan Bautista Moréno

p. 148, ln. 29   "Captain H. S. Turner" in place of "Captain H. S. Turney"

p. 149, ln. 40   "Godey" in place of "Goday"

p. 156, ln. 42   "Mr. Hüttmann" in place of "Mr. Hutteman"

p. 162, ln. 3   Perhaps because the letter was signed, Emory here makes no hurried attempt to deny authorship (before the court can rule on the legality of the question), as he does later regarding an unsigned article in the New Orleans *Picayune,* 27 April 1847 (see p. 167).

ln. 11   "28th of December" in place of "28th of January"

p. 167, ln. 2   "ship *Lexington*" in place of "ship Livingston"

ln. 28   Benton later charged that Emory's answer was fraudulently received and entered in the record by the court. Refusing to permit the question protected Emory from cross-examination and at the same time gave him the benefit of an answer as if the question had been legally put. Furthermore, it shielded him from confrontation on this point by Andrew F. V. Gray, Stockton's former aide, and Richard T. Jacob, an officer in JCF's California Battalion. Both men had been Emory's traveling companions from San Diego to the eastern United States and might be presumed to know something of his expressions and activities. Emory continued to deny that he was the writer of the Havanna letter printed in the New Orleans *Picayune,* 27 April 1847, and intimated that the author of it and other publications with which his name was associated was a naval officer. Benton, however, remained skeptical, pointing out that the only naval officer who returned from the Pacific at the same time as Gray, Jacob, and Emory was a naval surgeon, J. F. Sickles. He came home in poor health, soon died, and was therefore unable to deny Emory's imputations. No naval man, Benton contended, would make a mistake in the name of the supply ship (Benton's speech opposing the nomination of Kearny for the brevet of major general, *Congressional Globe,* July 1848, 30th Cong., 1st sess., Appendix, p. 1020).

p. 170, ln. 3   "Antoine Robidoux" in place of "Mr. Robedent"

ln. 39   "The *Lexington*" in place of "The Livingston"

p. 186, ln. 24   Edward Stokes, grantee of Santa Ysabel rancho fifteen miles southeast of Jonathan T. Warner's rancho, had come to California in 1840 as a sailor on the *Fly.* After his death his widow married Agustín Olvera, one of the Mexican commissioners who signed the Treaty of Cahuenga (PIONEER REGISTER).

ln. 26   Except for a two-year absence, Jonathan Trumbull Warner (1807–95), known in California as Juan José or John J., had been in California since 1831. In 1844 he became a Mexican citizen and was granted Agua Caliente (thereafter known as Warner's rancho) in the San Diego area. At the time of Kearny's arrival, Warner was a prisoner of the Americans in San Diego because Gillespie thought he was too friendly to the Californians (WOODWARD, 25:303, 26:23). During the Gold Rush the rancho became a famous provisioning point.

p. 189, ln. 35 Samuel Mosely was a surgeon on the *Congress*. After he returned east, he served as a member of the Board of Examiners, but he resigned from the Navy in April 1852 after being ordered aboard the *Cumberland* as fleet surgeon of the Mediterranean Squadron (DNA-24, Naval Personnel, Records of Officers, J-1, 1846–58).

p. 192, ln. 44 Rancho Niguel belonged to Juan Avila. Avila was one of three who had come into Stockton's camp on 10 Jan. under a flag of truce to intercede in behalf of the Angeleños, who, they said, would not resist if promised kind treatment and protection (ABELOE, 263; BANCROFT, 5:396–97).

p. 193, ln. 30 John Southwick, carpenter on the *Congress,* was acting as chief engineer in Stockton's battalion.

p. 194, ln. 50 Add "of the manuscript record, page 90 of the printed proceedings."

p. 195, ln. 46 The letter is in the *National Intelligencer,* 10 Dec. 1847.

p. 197, ln. 39 William Simmons was also acting lieutenant in Stockton's battalion (see Stockton to George Bancroft, 5 Feb. 1847, in STOCKTON, Appendix A, p. 13).

p. 198, ln. 3 After the declaration of war with Mexico in May 1846, the Navy Department wrote new orders for Commodore Sloat and entrusted them to Archibald McRae, a passed midshipman from North Carolina, who crossed the Isthmus of Panama and delivered them to Stockton in Santa Barbara in September. McRae was later attached to the Naval Observatory, traveled with Gillis's astronomical expedition (1853–55), and was commanding the U.S. Coast Survey schooner *Ewing* at his death on 17 Nov. 1855.

p. 206, ln. 9 Gillespie's paper on his detention in California appeared in the *National Intelligencer,* 13 Dec. 1847, and embodied the substance of his testimony given the next day. Gillespie wrote that after three days' delay he was permitted to leave Monterey, but only after "pledging my word of honor not to say any thing about General Kearny, for the performance of which, Commodore Stockton went my security."

p. 209, ln. 33 William Broome not identified.

p. 212, ln. 19 "where" in place of "when"

p. 214, ln. 41 A former officer under Kearny and one of his "obsequious followers," according to Benton, Fayette Robinson had just published in Philadelphia *An Account of the Organization of the Army of the United States; with Biographies of Distinguished Officers of All Grades.* His account of Kearny's role in the conquest of California was filled with alleged misstatements and was extremely objectionable to JCF.

p. 219, ln. 15 Lieut. Fabius Stanly (1815–82), son of a North Carolina politician, ultimately became a rear admiral (DNA-45, entry 464, Subject File ZB).

p. 221, ln. 35 The supply ship *Lexington,* under the command of Lieut.

Theodorus Bailey (1805–77), had brought an artillery company to California. During the Civil War Bailey helped take New Orleans and became commander of the Eastern Gulf blockading squadron. He retired in 1866 as a rear admiral.

p. 222, ln. 15 Although the question was not put to Gillespie, Benton saw that the public was informed of what his answer would have been. Gillespie's letter of 14 Dec. to Benton, giving information on the taking of horses, appeared in the *National Intelligencer,* 15 Dec. 1847. He noted that after peace was restored to California, stray horses and mules belonging to the American forces were ordered to be collected at different points "and held subject to the orders of a United States officer, it being understood that receipts would be given in the event of any animals being taken." Participating in the collection, but not exclusively so, were Mariano G. Vallejo, William G. Dana, and Edward M. Kern, who made collections at Soscol, Nipomo, and Sutter's Fort. Gillespie charged that Kearny's officers took horses from all three places and refused to give receipts, thus continuing JCF's fiscal responsibility. And while Gillespie could not tell the precise number of horses so taken, he was under the impression that it exceeded a thousand.

p. 228, ln. 15 "Joseph B. Chiles" in place of "Joseph B. Childs"

p. 229, ln. 4 "George W. Hamley" in place of "George W. Hanly"

p. 233, ln. 18 "Mr. Fisher" was probably Daniel or Ishmael Fisher.

ln. 28 Private Harber does not appear on ROGERS's rosters of the California volunteers or in the SNYDER CALENDAR. Hensley may be referring to either James M. or Joshua Harbin.

p. 236, ln. 8 William Wirt

ln. 9 William Chetwood De Hart

ln. 40 Maj. Charles James

p. 238, ln. 23 Maj. William Hough

ln. 40 There should be a comma after "Major James."

ln. 46 Gillespie's letter of 14 Dec. 1847 to Thomas H. Benton was printed again in the *National Intelligencer* on 18 Dec. with an answer from Henry S. Turner. Turner denied he had taken horses without giving receipts and said he regretted that "Capt. Gillespie should give circulation to such statements when he does not know them to be true."

p. 240, ln. 44 "Vallejo" in place of "Vallego"

p. 243, ln. 17 "William H. Russell" in place of "William W. Russell"

p. 248, ln. 15 *A Treatise on the Law of Evidence,* by Englishman Samuel March Phillipps (1780–1862), went through many British and American editions. The edition JCF was using is not known.

p. 249, ln. 41 In 1846 Simon Greenleaf (1783–1853) added a second volume to his *Treatise on the Law of Evidence,* first published in 1842. Greenleaf was Royall Professor of Law at Harvard.

ln. 45 The most important work of British professor of law Thomas Starkie (1782–1849) was *Practical Treatise on the Law of Evidence,* in three volumes. It was published in London in 1824, went through several revised editions, and was often reprinted in America.

p. 261, ln. 34   As governor of Missouri, Lilburn W. Boggs (1792–1861) had taken a prominent part in the expulsion of the Mormons. He emigrated to California in 1846, wintered at Petaluma, became alcalde at Sonoma in 1847, and ultimately settled in Napa (PIONEER REGISTER).

p. 272, ln. 13   "George W. Hamley" in place of "George W. Hawley"

p. 285, ln. 22   "detain" in place of "obtain"

p. 298, lns. 38–41   If given names were supplied and corrections made in the spelling of proper names, the list of witnesses would read: Marion Wise, Risdon Moore, Thomas E. Breckenridge, Richard Owens, William Findlay, Josiah C. Ferguson, R. Eugene Russell, William Brown, James Brown, Jerome C. Davis, Richard T. Jacob, Col. Joseph B. Chiles, Lorenzo D. Vinsonhaler, and Alexander Godey.

p. 306, ln. 17   JCF's inquiry about the handwriting of the questions proposed for General Kearny was recorded in the *National Intelligencer,* as was his verbal admonishment by the court (*National Intelligencer,* 5 Jan. 1848).

p. 309, ln. 34   "January" in place of "May"

p. 315, ln. 24   The *National Intelligencer,* 12 Jan. 1848, printed the paper offered by JCF:

Mr. President: Lieut. Col. Fremont is instructed by his counsel to say that the decision of the Court of yesterday, in relation to his application for an amendment of the record, appears to him to contain an error of fact. The decision commences with this statement:

"The accused yesterday addressed a question orally, direct to the Judge Advocate, inquiring in whose handwriting questions were written which he was preparing for a witness."

Now, it is not understood that these questions were *"preparing."* They were already *prepared,* written out, wafered upon the minutes, and from these minutes read by the Judge Advocate in open Court, in response to the paper of Lieut. Col. Fremont, objecting to the reintroduction of witnesses of the prosecution until he should be informed of the matters to which they were to testify. It was not, therefore, in reference to questions that the Judge Advocate was "preparing" for a witness that Lieut. Col. Fremont made the inquiry, which he did, but in reference to questions prepared, placed upon the minutes of the Court, and read in response to a paper of his own.

Lieut. Col. Fremont would respectfully request that this correction be made; and would also inquire whether the questions so prepared, placed upon the *minutes* of the Court, and so read before the Court and the defense by the Judge Advocate, are entered upon the record in the proper place; and, if not, he requests that they may be entered, *nunc pro tunc.*

J. C. Fremont
Lieut. Col. Mounted Riflemen

p. 328, ln. 27   Kearny wrote that he was prepared to prove false Benton's

455

statement that "I looked him [Kearny] down; I looked him till his eyes fell—till they fell upon the floor" (*National Intelligencer,* 11 Jan. 1848).

p. 329, ln. 40   The *National Intelligencer,* 12 Jan. 1848, printed the paper offered by JCF on Monday, 11 Jan. JCF desired to have one of his lawyers, William C. Jones, sworn as a witness to prove that Kearny had brought into the court a series of questions drawn by himself for his own interrogation. The establishment of that fact would help to impeach the general credit of Kearny, the chief witness for the prosecution.

p. 347, ln. 21   John McArthur's *Principles and Practice of Naval and Military Courts-Martial* (London, 1805)

p. 349, ln. 47   Alexander Fraser Tytler's *An Essay on Military Law, and the Practice of Courts Martial* (Edinburgh, 1800)

p. 368, ln. 45   JCF's long defense is not a part of the manuscript record of the court-martial in DNA-153, EE-575.

p. 373, lns. 13 and 19   "Klamath" in place of "Hamath"

ln. 23   "9th of May"

p. 374, ln. 19   Note that JCF makes no mention of the work of William B. Ide and others in establishing the independent Bear Flag Republic on 14–15 June 1846.

p. 378, ln. 9   For a discussion of Eugene McNamara's scheme, see Doc. No. 265, n. 1, Vol. 2.

p. 379, ln. 4   "Carrillo" in place of "Cavillo"

ln. 23   "Captain Hamley" in place of "Captain Hamlyn"

ln. 27   "Cahuenga" in place of "Cowenga"

ln. 39   Add prefix "con" for "congratulation."

p. 386, ln. 25   "Talbot" in place of "Talcott"

p. 402, ln. 36   "12th of January" in place of "6th of January"

p. 427 ln. 25   "Captain Hensley" in place of "Captain Henley"

BIBLIOGRAPHY

ABELOE Hoover, Mildred B., and Hero E. and Ethel Grace Rensch. *Historic Spots in California*. Revised by William N. Abeloe. 3rd ed. Stanford, Calif., 1966.

BANCROFT Bancroft, Hubert H. *History of California*. 7 vols. San Francisco, 1884–90.

BENTON Benton, Thomas H. *Thirty Years' View. . . .* 2 vols. New York, 1854–57.

CLARKE Clarke, Dwight L. *Stephen Watts Kearny, Soldier of the West*. Norman, Okla., 1961.

COOKE Cooke, Philip St. George. *The Conquest of New Mexico and California: An Historical and Personal Narrative*. New York, 1878. Reprinted, Chicago, 1964.

CULLUM Cullum, George W. *Biographical Register of the Officers and Graduates of the U.S. Military Academy . . . 1802 to 1890*. 3rd ed. 3 vols. Boston, 1891. Supplementary vols. under various editors to 1950.

DU PONT DuPont, Samuel Francis. *Extracts from Private Journal-Letters of Captain S. F. DuPont, While in Command of the "Cyane," during the War with Mexico, 1846–1848*. Prepared by S. M. DuPont. Wilmington, Del., 1885.

GIFFEN Giffen, Helen S. *Trail-Blazing Pioneer: Colonel Joseph Ballinger Chiles*. San Francisco, 1969.

HEITMAN Heitman, Francis B. *Historical Register and Dictionary of the United States Army*. 2 vols. Washington, D.C., 1903. Reprinted, Urbana, Ill., 1965.

HUGHES Hughes, John T. *Doniphan's Expedition; Containing an Account of the Conquest of New Mexico. . . .* Cincinnati, 1848. Reprinted, Chicago, 1962.

JOHNSON Johnson, Kenneth M. *The Frémont Court Martial*. Los Angeles, 1968.

KORNS Korns, J. Roderic, ed. "West from Fort Bridger: The Pioneering of the Immigrant Trails across Utah, 1846–1850," *Utah Historical Quarterly*, 19 (1951):1–297.

LAYNE Layne, J. Gregg. *Annals of Los Angeles . . . 1769–1861*. San Francisco, 1935.

MC CALL McCall, Col. George Archibald. *New Mexico in 1850: A Military View*. Ed. and with an introduction by Robert W. Frazer. Norman, Okla., 1968.

NEW HELVETIA DIARY *New Helvetia Diary: A Record of Events Kept by John A. Sutter and His Clerks at New Helvetia, California, from September 9, 1845 to May 25, 1848*. San Francisco, 1939.

PIONEER REGISTER Bancroft, Hubert Howe. *Register of Pioneer Inhabitants of California, 1542–1848*. Reprinted from vols. 2–5 of *History of California*, published in 1885 and 1886. Los Angeles, 1964.

ROBINSON Robinson, Fayette. *An Account of the Organization of the Army of the United States; with Biographies of Distinguished Officers of All Grades*. 2 vols. Philadelphia, 1848.

ROGERS Rogers, Fred B. "Rosters of California Volunteers in the Service of the United States, 1846–1847," *Publication* of the Society of California Pioneers (1950) :17–28; (1951) :25.

SNYDER CALENDAR Works Projects Administration, Northern California Historical Records Survey. *Calendar of the Major Jacob Rink Snyder Collection of the Society of California Pioneers*. San Francisco, 1940.

STOCKTON [Bayard, Samuel J.] *A Sketch of the Life of Com. Robert F. Stockton; with an Appendix, Comprising His Correspondence with the Navy Department respecting His Conquest of California; and Extracts from the Defence of Col. J. C. Fremont. . . .* New York, 1856.

TURNER Clarke, Dwight L., ed. *The Original Journal of Henry Smith Turner with Stephen Watts Kearny to New Mexico and California, 1846–1847*. Norman, Okla., 1967.

TYLER Tyler, Sergeant Daniel. *A Concise History of the Mormon Battalion in the Mexican War, 1846–1847*. N.p., 1881. Reprinted, Chicago, 1964.

WOODWARD Woodward, Arthur. "Lances at San Pascual," *California Historical Society Quarterly*, 25 (Dec. 1946) :289–308; 26 (March 1947) :21–62.

YOUNG Young, Otis E. *The West of Philip St. George Cooke, 1809–1895*. Glendale, Calif., 1955.

INDEX

The following abbreviations are used: JBF for Jessie Benton Frémont; JCF for John Charles Frémont; K for Stephen Watts Kearny; and S for Robert Field Stockton.

Cooke, 201–3; as a defense witness, 201–6, 218–22; on tranquillity of California, 203, 226–27; ordered to Washington, 204, 221; detention of in California, 204–6, 214–15, 218–19, 307–8, 311–15, 316, 317; and question of K's taking public horses, 222, 235–41, 455n; arrival in Washington, 219; cross-examined by judge advocate, 222–23, 226–27; and preparations for S's overland party, 223–24; questioned by court, 227–28

Godey, Alexander: captured by *Californios,* 66; mentioned, 149; carries Turner's letter to S, 188; 452n; defense witness, 298

Graham, James D.: member of court, xiv, 2; illness of, 173; unhappiness with reporter, 230

Gray, Andrew F. V.: aids K after San Pasqual, 65, 189; with Emory to Washington, 133; aide-de-camp to S, 193, 451n, 453n; as defense witness, 210; testimony on command of troops, 210–11

Greenleaf, Simon, 249, 317–18, 455n

Griffin, John S.: reports American casualties to Emory, 71; at San Pasqual, 169

Haight (Hait), Jacob, 71

Hall, Willard P.: letter from JCF, 10–11; mentioned, 156; with Mormon Battalion, 170; as prosecution witness, 207; cross-examined by JCF, 208; rank in California, 208–9; explains testimony, 211–12

Halleck, Henry Wager, 48, 96, 114

Hamley, George, 85, 272; testimony on delivery of S's dispatches to JCF, 229

Hammond, Thomas C.: mortally wounded, 169, 188

Harber (Harbin), Pvt., 233

Hendry, James, 71

Hensley, Samuel J.: as defense witness, 230; on S-K command, 230–31; on tranquillity of California, 232–33; at San Diego, 233; in S's party, 233

Hough, William, 238, 249, 349, 350, 352, 357, 360, 361, 362, 370–71, 398, 425, 455n

Howitzers, 43, 46–47, 63–64, 75, 135, 136

Hudson, Thomas B., 42, 449n

Hudspeth, James M., 17, 25, 63, 449n

Hunt, Thomas F., xiii, 3

Hüttmann, Francis, 16

Jacob, Richard Taylor, 298, 453n

James, Charles, 236, 238, 455n

Johnson, Kenneth M., viii

Johnston, Abraham R.: journal of, 99, 452n; killed at San Pasqual, 169, 188

Jones, Roger, 2, 3

Jones, William Carey: counsel for JCF, viii, 4; court rejects affidavit of, 329, 331, 457n

Kearny, Stephen Watts, vii–xv *passim;* 16 Jan. 1847 orders to JCF, 5, 18, 37–38, 401; 1 March 1847 orders, 13, 22–23, 33, 424–25; 28 March 1847 letter to JCF, 17–18, 25, 34; as prosecution witness, 28–39, 48–50, 51–61, 307–10; implies JCF destroyed documents, 32; 1 March 1847 letter to JCF, 32–33, 102–3; retracts implication, 35; implies JCF bargained for governorship, 38–39, 89–93; writes Benton, 41; cross-examined by JCF, 41–43, 46–48, 63–66, 70–115, 310–18; on San Pasqual, 46–48, 63–66, 75; on command, 47–48, 61, 78–79, 116–22, 322–23, 324, 325; 22 Dec. 1846 letter to S, 47; 10–13 Jan. 1847 letters to JCF, 72–74, 403–4; 17 Jan. 1847 note to JCF, 76, 383; 17 Jan. 1847 letters to S, 79–80, 195; 14 Jan. 1847 letter to R. Jones, 80; on S and governorship, 81–85, 323, 324; on Russell's mission to Los Angeles, 87, 324; 16 Jan. 1847 letter to S, 90; 17 Jan. 1847 letter to R. Jones, 94–95; 15 March 1847 letter to R. Jones, 96–99; on removal of JCF as governor, 102; required JCF to surrender instruments, 104, 114; on Monterey interview with JCF, 104, 106–7; and Mason-JCF quarrel, 108; 13 Jan. 1847 letter to S, 108–9; 23 Dec. 1846 letter to S, 112, 432; on arrest of JCF, 114–15; questioned by court, 116–22, 319–20, 321, 322–24; 1 March 1847 letter to Cooke, 140–41;

461

Kearny, Stephen Watts (*cont.*)
orders JCF to remain in Monterey, 150; decree on sale of lands, 152; 1 March 1847 proclamation, 153–54; wounded at San Pasqual, 170, 188; 2 Dec. 1846 letter to Stockton, 186; and the taking of public horses, 222, 235–41, 277–78, 308–9; 14 June 1847 letter to JCF, 281; War Department's 11 June 1847 instructions to, 293; recalled as witness, 305, 307–20, 322–24, 325; on detention of officers in California, 307–8, 311–15, 319–20; on Benton's grimaces, 326; 6 Oct. 1846 order reducing forces, 331; 12 Jan. 1847 letter to War Department, 433

Kern, Edward M.: left in California, 114, 234, 278–79, 280, 285; custodian of public horses, 240, 455n

Larkin, Thomas Oliver: and K, 100; accompanies JCF to K's quarters, 104, 106

Lee, John Fitzgerald: judge advocate, xiii, 2; objects to relevancy of questions or documents, 43–45, 75–76, 86, 101, 108, 142, 144, 146, 202, 205, 259, 260, 261, 270, 271, 274; on detention of officers in California, 216–18; replies to JCF's paper on irregularities, 297, 357–64; JCF's desire to call as witness, 329–30; on K's testimony on howitzers, 335–36

Lexington (supply ship), 167, 221, 454n

Loker, William N.: 13 Feb. 1847 letter to JCF, 63; and Cooke, 134, 273; on refusal of California volunteers to be mustered, 273; as defense witness, 273–74, 276–80; on K's taking public horses, 278, 285; cross-examined by judge advocate, 285–86

Long, Stephen H., xiii-xiv, 2

McArthur, John, 347, 457n

McCall, George A.: member of court, xiii, 2; absence of, 3, 449n; replaced, 3

McLane, Louis: letter from JCF, 8, 21; mentioned, 77; and detention in California, 215, 220, 303–4, 308

McRae, Archibald, 198, 454n

Marcy, William Learned: transmits proceedings to president, 1; 18 June 1846 instructions to K, 5, 18, 31–32, 38; 3 June 1846 instructions to K, 28–31; 12 Sept. 1846 letter to K, 54–55; 11 Jan. 1847 letter to K, 55–56; extract of Dec. 1846 report, 288, 376

Mason, John Young: 5 Nov. 1846 letter to S, 51–53; 11 Jan. 1847 letter to S, 56–58; extract of Dec. 1846 report, 288–89, 377; 14 June 1847 dispatch, 366–68

Mason, Richard B.: sent south to order JCF, 17, 25; mentioned, 49; brings dispatches to K, 53, 96; present at JCF-K interview, 104, 106; and quarrel with JCF, 108, 144; and Gillespie, 308, 311–12

Minor, George, 47, 234; as defense witness, 241–43; on S-K command, 241–42

Moore, Benjamin D.: with K, 46, 331; killed at San Pasqual, 169, 188, 450n

Moore, Sgt., 169

Moore, Risdon, 298

Moreno, Juan Bautista, 144

Morgan, Edwin W., xiv, 2

Mormon Battalion: arrival of in San Diego, 80; question of in trial, 136–37, 141–42, 165–66; and alleged effects of its presence, 233, 242, 243, 259, 260, 261

Mormons, 274

Mosely, Samuel, 189, 454n; certificate of on S-K command, 430

Myers, John J., 142

Newspapers: reporters admitted to trial, 27–28; "Justice" letter of the Missouri *Republican,* 129–33; California *Star* on rumors of insurrection, 156; Emory's letter to New York *Courier and Enquirer,* 161; 8 April 1847 letter in *Picayune,* 166–67; 22 April 1847 *Picayune* article on affairs in California, 169–71; exclusion of Baltimore *Sun* reporter, 230

New York Volunteers, 80, 97

Norris, J. Parker, 56, 450n

Owens, Richard: orders to from JCF, 13–14, 15; and Cooke, 14, 122–26; with JCF in Los Angeles, 260; as defense witness, 298

462

463